Broken Promise

The Subversion of U.S. Labor Relations Policy, 1947–1994

In the series Labor and Social Change

edited by Paula Rayman and Carmen Sirianni

Broken Promise

The Subversion of U.S. Labor Relations Policy, 1947–1994

JAMES A. GROSS

Temple University Press
Philadelphia

Temple University Press, Philadelphia 19122
Copyright © 1995 by Temple University. All rights reserved
Published 1995
Printed in the United States of America

☺ The paper used in this book meets the requirements
of the American National Standard for Information Sciences—Permanence
of Paper for Printed Library Materials, ANSI Z39.48-1984

Text design by Nighthawk Design

Library of Congress Cataloging-in-Publication Data
Gross, James A., 1933–
    Broken promise : the subversion of U.S. labor relations policy,
  1947–1994 / James A. Gross.
        p.   cm. — (Labor and social change)
    Includes bibliographical references and index.
    ISBN 1-56639-325-6 (alk. paper)
    1. Labor policy—United States—History—20th century.
  2. Industrial relations—United States—History—20th century.
  3. Labor laws and legislation—United States—History—20th century.
  I. Title. II. Series.
  HD8072.5.G76   1995
  331′.0973—dc20   94-42510

For Linda, Jim, John, Justin, and Caitlin

Contents

Preface

In 1935 Congress passed the Wagner Act, intended to democratize vast numbers of American workplaces so that workers could participate in the employment decisions that most directly affected their lives. Under the Wagner Act the right of workers to participate in these decisions was considered essential for social justice, and worker organization and collective bargaining were considered essential for a free and democratic society. The Wagner Act also committed the federal government to the encouragement of the practice and procedure of collective bargaining. Industrial democracy was to replace employers' unilateral determination of matters affecting wages, hours, and working conditions. The Wagner Act, therefore, enabled a major redistribution of power from the powerful to the powerless at U.S. workplaces covered by the statute.

Although the Wagner Act's statement of purpose was carried over to the Taft-Hartley Act of 1947, labor never came close to achieving the system of industrial democracy that was envisioned by Senator Robert Wagner and was promoted by the act that bears his name. This book explains why the expectations of the Wagner-Taft-Hartley labor policy were never fulfilled. It shows how a policy that encouraged the replacement of industrial autocracy with a democratic system of power sharing was turned into government protection of employers' unilateral decision-making authority over decisions that greatly affected wages, hours, and working conditions. It discusses the destructive consequences of the contradiction that has been inherent in U.S. labor policy at least since the passage of the Taft-Hartley Act: Congress, by statute, promotes and protects employees' self-organization "for the purpose of negotiating the terms and conditions of their employment or other mutual aid or protection"; at the same time, by statute and National Labor Relations Board (NLRB) case law, it legitimizes employer opposition to the organization of employees, collective bargaining, and industrial democracy. Although the NLRB greatly facilitated the growth of organized labor in the United States in its early Wagner Act years, this study demonstrates how the NLRB has contributed to the decline of organized labor, particularly since about 1970.

This study of the events leading to the current state of national labor policy focuses on the NLRB. However, the research approach used differs from that of the conventional labor law and labor relations literature. The latter tends toward an exclusive concentration on the procedures and doctrines of such administrative agencies as the NLRB and on judicial review of their decisions. This book analyzes how the NLRB's making of labor policy and labor policy making in general have been influenced since 1947 by the president, the Congress, and the Supreme Court, the manipulation of public opinion, resistance by organized employers, the political and economic strategies of organized labor, and the ideological dispositions of NLRB appointees. This approach provides a unique inside look at the process of government regulation of this most important aspect of workplace labor-management relations. And it demonstrates how labor policy can be made without legislative changes through presidential appointments to the NLRB.

The NLRB engages in lawmaking by giving specific meaning to broad statutory language and by filling in gaps in the legislation. In the years since Taft-Hartley, different NLRBs appointed by successive administrations have interpreted the law in sharply contrasting ways. This lack of consistency has resulted not only in conflicting and confusing case law that flip-flops over the meaning of many important provisions of the act but also in complete disagreement between Republican- and Democratic-appointed Boards over the fundamental purpose of the law.

This study examines how the roles of Congress and the Supreme Court in making labor policy have become blurred as a result of Congress's abdication of its legislative responsibility and the Court's propensity (particularly in the 1980s) to substitute its own labor policy preferences for those of the legislative branch. It discusses the failure of the White House, through all its occupants since 1947, to provide the politically risky leadership needed to recommit the country to a labor policy with a precise set of objectives. It includes a thorough discussion of the long-standing and determined opposition of U.S. employers to unionization and collective bargaining, which discloses a coordinated, secret, nationwide effort by the country's most powerful employers to end threats to their management prerogatives posed by what they saw as the Kennedy-Johnson Board's codetermination concept of collective bargaining. To U.S. employers, industrial democracy and free enterprise are fundamentally incompatible. The Kennedy-Johnson Board marked the last time an NLRB was committed to the encouragement of organization and collective bargaining for any sustained period of time.

Even the advocates of organization and collective bargaining, however, prevented the realization of industrial democracy in some ways. Organized labor, for example, often pursued unwise legislative objectives and strategies and was too willing to accept, and even espouse, a limited role in management decision making, thereby voluntarily restricting the scope of collective bargaining far short of the potential that Senator Wagner had envisioned.

The research for this volume was based on records at the NLRB and the National Archives in Washington, D.C.; records at the Truman, Eisenhower, Kennedy, and Johnson presidential libraries; the personal papers of former NLRB chairmen and members and of other influential people inside and outside the Board; records in the National Association of Manufacturers Archives at the Hagley Museum and Library; papers from the George Meany Memorial Archives; and oral history interviews of approximately seventy-five people prominent in the making of post–Taft-Hartley Act labor policy. The interviews with people who influenced the making and reshaping of national labor policy afforded an invaluable and otherwise unattainable sense of the climate of the times, disclosing historical connections that often could not be discerned from documents alone.

This study of post–Taft-Hartley Act NLRBs and U.S. labor policy provides the historical perspective and empirical basis necessary for the reevaluation of national labor policy, which is currently being conducted by the Clinton administration. In 1993 President Clinton asked the secretaries of labor and commerce to form the Commission on the Future of Worker-Management Relations to investigate and respond to the following three questions:

What (if any) new methods or institutions should be encouraged or required to enhance work-place productivity through labor-management cooperation and employee participation?

What (if any) changes should be made in the present legal framework and practice of collective bargaining to enhance cooperative behavior, improve productivity, and reduce conflict and delay?

What (if anything) should be done to increase the extent to which work-place problems are directly resolved by the parties themselves, rather than through recourse to state and federal courts and government regulatory bodies?[1]

The commission, chaired by former Secretary of Labor John Dunlop, issued a fact-finding report in June 1994 and its final *Report and Recommendations* in January 1995.[2] The commission unanimously endorsed "employee participation" and "labor-management partnerships" as "good for workers, firms, and the national economy" and encouraged their expansion and growth.[3] The report favors workers' having "a say," having "a voice," and "being heard" at the workplace, but it does not define precisely what those ideas mean in terms of management prerogatives and power sharing.

The commission concluded that "the current labor law is not achieving its stated intent of encouraging collective bargaining," but a majority of its members recommended legislative changes and interpretations that would "promote expansion of employee participation in a *variety of forms*" and provide workers with the opportunity "to choose, or not to choose, union representation and to engage in collective bargaining."[4] In order to promote a "variety of forms" of worker participation, the commission proposed "clarifying" Section 8(a)(2) of the National Labor Relations Act and its interpretation by the NLRB so that "nonunion employee participation programs should not be unlawful simply because they involve discussion of terms and conditions of work or compensation where such discussion is incidental to the broad purposes of these programs." At the same time, the commission, "concerned that in encouraging employee participation in nonunion settings, it does not adversely affect employees' ability to select union representation, if they so desire," reaffirmed "the basic principle that employer-sponsored programs should not substitute for independent unions."[5]

Commission member Douglas Fraser, former president of the United Automobile Workers, argued that a statutorily created exception to Section 8(a)(2) "would be an invitation to abuse." "The kind of participation and cooperation that should be encouraged," Fraser maintained, "is *democratic* participation and cooperation *between equals*."[6]

The commission recommended steps to improve the representation election process, to improve employee access to employer and union views on independent representation, to increase the use of injunctions to remedy violations of the Taft-Hartley Act, and to facilitate contractual agreement once a majority of workers choose union representation for collective bargaining.[7] There is nothing in the commission's report, however, recommending that the federal government encourage collective bargaining and unionization or stating that unions and collective bargaining are necessary for legitimate, mutual labor-management decision making—that is, industrial democracy.

The issues of labor law reform and the future of U.S. collective bargaining have become subjects of national concern and discussion. The Taft-Hartley Act and its overall administration have been ineffective in encouraging the practice and procedure of collective bargaining and in protecting workers' rights to choose unionism and collective bargaining.

This book is not intended as a detailed blueprint for legislative changes, an in-depth analysis of the current political scene, or an assessment of the political prospects for any current labor reform proposals.[8] The study aims to provide the historical perspective necessary for the reevaluation of national labor policy, highlighting the underlying principles of democracy that constitute the most appropriate standard for assessing not only the current state of labor policy but also proposed changes. It offers a practical and useful basis for policy makers, showing them where we are, how we got here, and what fundamental questions must be addressed if changes are to be made.

At its core any national labor policy involves questions more moral and ethical than legal, economic, or political. In that sense, this book is about an even more important issue: how to reconcile the theory of democracy with practice.

Acknowledgments

In addition to the many capable and generous people whose assistance was acknowledged in my two previously published books covering earlier periods of the National Labor Relations Board and U.S. labor policy, I thank my colleague Cletus Daniel. He was not only a patient sounding board and a constant source of excellent ideas but also a true friend in all seasons.

Special thanks are due Barbara Stoyell-Mulholland, who conducted most of the oral history interviews for this volume and spent many fruitful but lonely hours away from her family doing research in archives and presidential libraries. Patricia Greenfield, Shelley Coppock, and Mairead Connor, all graduate students at the time, also conducted excellent oral history interviews. Ms. Coppock wrote an outstanding master's thesis as well, which provided valuable information on the Kennedy-Johnson Board.

I am pleased to acknowledge my debt of gratitude to the staffs of the National Archives and Records Service in Washington, D.C.; the Harry S Truman Library in Independence, Missouri; the Dwight D. Eisenhower Library in Abilene, Kansas; the Lyndon Baines Johnson Library in Austin, Texas; the John Fitzgerald Kennedy Library in Boston, Massachusetts; the George Meany Memorial Archives in Washington, D.C.; the Hagley Museum and Library in Wilmington, Delaware; and the Cornell University School of Industrial and Labor Relations Labor-Management Documentation Center (LMDC). Richard Strassberg, Director of the LMDC, and staff member Connie Bulkley were particularly helpful. I am very grateful to Frank McCulloch, former Chairman of the NLRB; Douglas Soutar, former Vice-President of Labor Relations for the American Smelting and Refining Company; and Francis O'Connell, former Vice-President of Labor Relations for the Olin Corporation, for donating their useful and informative papers to the LMDC. John Truesdale, NLRB Executive Secretary, greatly facilitated my research.

Special gratitude is due those who helped finance the project, particularly the National Endowment for the Humanities; the American Philosophical Society; the Harry S Truman Library Institute; the Cornell and ILR School Research Grants Committees; the late Shirley Harper, Director of the Martin Catherwood

Library; and David Lipsky, Dean of the School of Industrial and Labor Relations, Cornell University.

I am deeply grateful to Mrs. Nancy Van Camp, long-time secretary and friend, for her patience and skill in transforming my handwritten yellow sheets into impressive-looking word-processed pages. Gratitude is due those men and women who shared their recollections with us in the vital oral history phase of the study. Finally, my thanks and apologies go to all those who made the mistake of asking me how the book was going and were then subjected to more than they really wanted or needed to know about it.

Broken Promise

The Subversion of U.S. Labor Relations Policy, 1947–1994

1

Taft-Hartley
A Fundamental Change in Labor Policy or Merely Adjustments to Eliminate Abuses?

Legislative Compromise Creates Statutory Confusion

In 1935 the Wagner Act established the most democratic procedure in U.S. labor history for the participation of workers in the determination of their wages, hours, and working conditions. The act was not neutral as between individual and collective bargaining; it intentionally favored collective bargaining.

For Senator Robert Wagner, collective bargaining was actually more than a method of negotiating wages, hours, and working conditions or a system of checks and balances based on countervailing power. Wagner believed that "the struggle for a voice in industry through the process of collective bargaining is at the heart of the struggle for the preservation of political as well as economic democracy in America" and that if people "know the dignity of freedom and self-expression in their daily lives . . . they will never bow to tyranny in any quarter of their national life."[1] He wanted management and labor to resolve their mutual problems through a system of self-government. He best expressed his beliefs in a speech delivered in 1937 shortly after the Supreme Court ruled that the Wagner Act was constitutional:

> The development of a partnership between industry and labor in the solution of national problems is the indispensable complement of political democracy. And that leads us to this all-important truth: there can be no more democratic self-government in industry without workers participating therein, than there could be democratic government in politics without workers having the right to vote. . . . That is why the right to bargain collectively is at the bottom of social justice for the worker, as well as the sensible conduct of business affairs. The denial or observance of this right means the difference between despotism and democracy.[2]

1

When Congress passed the Labor-Management Relations Act in 1947 (the Taft-Hartley Act), it was not immediately clear precisely how, if at all, lawmakers had changed the collective bargaining core of the Wagner Act national labor policy. Congressional intent, as expressed in the language of the new labor law, was ambiguous: some provisions of the new law were carried over intact from the Wagner Act, some new statutory language amended that act, and many new provisions were the result of legislative compromise and bargaining between the House and Senate.

The Taft-Hartley Act, for example, actually has two policy statements. First, Congress retained but added to the Findings and Policy section of the Wagner Act. It left intact the Wagner Act declaration that it was the policy of the United States to encourage the practice of collective bargaining:

> It is hereby declared to be the policy of the United States to eliminate the causes of certain substantial obstructions to the free flow of commerce and to mitigate and eliminate these obstructions when they have occurred by encouraging the practice and procedure of collective bargaining and by protecting the exercise by workers of full freedom of association, self-organization, and designation of representatives of their own choosing, for the purpose of negotiating the terms and conditions of their employment or other mutual aid or protection.

But Congress added a paragraph to this section asserting that some practices engaged in by unions were obstructing commerce:

> Experience has further demonstrated that certain practices by some labor organizations, their officers, and members have the intent or the necessary effect of burdening or obstructing commerce . . . through strikes and other forms of industrial unrest or through concerted activities which impair the interest of the public in the free flow of such commerce. The elimination of such practices is a necessary condition to the assurance of the rights herein guaranteed.

That insertion, as well as the addition of several union unfair labor practices (Section 8b) and a provision asserting employers' right of "free speech" (Section 8c), could be interpreted as reflecting a congressional intention to treat employers and labor alike; that is, the amended act (according to this construction) was meant to be a neutral guarantor of equal rights or, at least, of reasonably balanced rights—"reasonably balanced" to be defined by the National Labor Relations Board (NLRB).

Second, Congress placed a new Declaration of Policy immediately before the Findings and Policies section described above. Whereas the Findings and Policies section reaffirms that it is the policy of the United States to encourage collective bargaining, the Declaration of Policy does not even mention collective bargaining but states that it is the purpose of the act to protect (among other things) the rights of individual employees. This declaration reads, in part:

> It is the purpose and policy of this Act . . . to prescribe the legitimate rights of both employees and employers in their relations affecting commerce, to provide orderly and peaceful procedures for preventing the interference by either with the legitimate rights of the other, to protect the rights of individual employees in their relations with labor organizations . . . , to define and proscribe practices on the part of labor and management which . . . are inimical to the general welfare, and to protect the rights of the public in connection with labor disputes affecting commerce.

The amended version of the Wagner Act Findings and Policies section originated in the Senate. The provisions contained in Senator Robert Taft's bill (S. 1126) were generally less harsh than those in Congressman Fred Hartley's House bill (H.R. 3020), which was a direct product of the hostile 1939–40 investigation of the NLRB led by anti–New Deal congressman Howard Smith. The Hartley bill was actually written in Smith's office using his unsuccessful 1940 labor bill as a model.[3]

Smith's bill, among other things, would have eliminated from the Wagner Act's preamble the statement that it was the declared policy of the United States to encourage the practice of collective bargaining.[4] The attempt to delete that statement was revived in the Hartley bill's "Short Title and Declaration of Policy" (which became the new Declaration of Policy section in the Taft-Hartley Act) as well as in Hartley's efforts to strike any favorable reference to collective bargaining from the Wagner Act's Findings and Policies section. The decision to compromise by including in Taft-Hartley both the Hartley Policy Declaration and the Senate-amended Findings and Policies section from the Wagner Act was made during closed-door conference committee bargaining between representatives of the House and Senate. No one debated or formally discussed the reasons for this decision on the House or Senate floor before the adoption of the act.

Taft had printed in the *Congressional Record* a summary of the principal differences between the conference agreement and the bill that the Senate had previously passed.[5] The summary, which Taft did not read or discuss in the Senate, simply stated that the House bill "contained an over-all declaration of policy covering all of the various matters dealt with in the bill," acknowledged that "there was no corresponding over-all declaration of policy" in the Senate bill, and informed the Senate that the conference committee agreement "contains the declaration of policy of the House bill."[6]

Taft and his supporters in the Senate argued that the conference committee bill left undisturbed the act's essential theory that (in Taft's words) "the solution of the labor problem in the United States is free, collective bargaining."[7] Whatever the merits of Taft's claim, Smith, Hartley, and the majority of the House certainly did not intend to promote collective bargaining as the solution to labor problems. Their statement of policy, not only in its omission of any reference to collective bargaining but also in its historical context, was intended at least to weaken, and possibly to eliminate, collective bargaining.[8] The 1947 Declaration of Policy, coupled with a passage added in 1947 to Section 7 that affirms workers' right to refrain from engaging in collective bargaining, could be interpreted to mean that free choice and individual rights are at least as important as the right to collective bargaining.

In addition to changes in the policy and purposes sections of the Wagner Act, the Taft-Hartley Act, passed on June 23, 1947, over President Harry Truman's veto (331–83 in the House and 68–25 in the Senate), contained other provisions that, at least on their face, weakened organized labor's control over its members and reduced its bargaining power. There was, for example, a new section of prohibited union unfair labor practices, an expansion of employer "free speech" rights, prohibition of the closed shop, a denial of bargaining rights and all access to the NLRB to unions that refused to file noncommunist affidavits with the Board, and provisions requiring the Board to petition for an injunction in secondary boycott cases (10[l]), as well as other provisions for the use of injunctions against strikes that imperiled the national health or safety. Other provisions permitted employers as well as employees to file petitions for representation elections and employees to file for decertification elections, allowed union shop provisions in collective bargaining agreements only if a majority of employees eligible to vote authorized such inclusions in NLRB-conducted elections, eliminated the NLRB's Review Section and Economic Analysis function (4[a]), and separated the NLRB's judicial and prosecutory functions by the creation of an independent office of General Counsel (3[d]).[9] Proponents of Taft-Hartley maintained, however, that these provisions did not alter the essential collective bargaining theme of the Wagner Act labor policy but were merely adjustments needed to eliminate certain abuses of union power and to rebalance, or "equalize," the labor-management relationship.

Truman, Organized Labor, and Taft-Hartley: Perspective and Strategy

Harry Truman had become president only weeks before the end of World War II (Franklin Roosevelt had died on April 12, 1945). He was plunged almost immediately into the turmoil of the reconversion period and confronted with the growing problem of how to deal with the Soviet Union in postwar Eastern Europe as well as the threat of depression, shortages of housing and consumer goods, and inflation on the home front.[10]

After V-J Day in August 1945 the Truman administration had tried to modify its wartime wage and price controls without causing unemployment or inflation by encouraging wage increases that did not require compensating price increases and asking labor and management to renew their wartime no-strike and no-lockout pledges.[11] Union leaders, however, refused to renew their no-strike pledge and maintained that wage increases could readily be absorbed out of profits without the need for subsequent price increases.

As a consequence, 1946 set a record for number of strikes, number of workers involved in strikes, and man-days idle as a percentage of working time.[12] Fearing mass unemployment, inflation, and lower real wages, unions conducted a series of major strikes in basic industries such as coal, steel, automobiles, and railroads, causing public opinion, ironically, to place the blame for higher prices on organized labor's demand for higher wages. No longer considered the underdog in the public's mind, "too powerful" became the most used adjective for labor unions, which were criticized for irresponsible strikes, bad-faith bargaining, undemocratic internal practices, excessive initiation fees, apparently irrational jurisdictional disputes, race discrimination, secondary boycotts, corruption, violence, and, in some cases, communist domination.[13]

Truman himself, addressing a joint session of Congress on May 24, 1946, threatened to draft railroad workers who struck government-seized plants (a penalty far more drastic than anything the Taft-Hartley Act would impose) and warned the country that a handful of men now had the power "to cripple the entire economy of the Nation."[14] Only a few hours after Truman's address the Senate passed the Case bill, which among other things authorized stringent penalties for violent or extortionate interference with interstate commerce, damage suits against unions for breach of contract, a prohibition of secondary boycotts, and deprivation of Wagner Act rights for employees involved in wildcat strikes.[15]

Although Truman vetoed the Case bill on June 11, 1946 (a veto that survived override by only five votes), its passage by the Senate, which had been the bulwark against antilabor legislation since the Wagner Act was passed in 1935, demonstrated the strength of anti-union feeling around the country. In great part because of that feeling the 1946 congressional campaign was the most successful for the Republicans since the 1920s. Republicans swept governorships and Senate and House contests. In the House the Republican delegation rose from 190 to 245 and Democratic representation dropped from 248 to 188. In the Senate the Republicans gained thirteen seats (from 38 to 51) and the

Democrats lost twelve (from 57 to 45). For the first time since 1935, the opponents of the Wagner Act had sufficient congressional and public support to change the nation's labor policy.

Truman had reason not to be sympathetic to those labor leaders who beseeched him to veto the Taft-Hartley bill. Although pressed repeatedly to make some proposals to deal with what many considered the evils of jurisdictional disputes, secondary boycotts, and nationwide strikes, the American Federation of Labor (AFL) and the Congress of Industrial Organizations (CIO) took a defensive stand against amendments to the Wagner Act and offered no reasonable alternatives around which friends of labor, particularly in Congress, could rally.[16] Even after the House passed the Hartley bill, the AFL, for example, chose not to try to soften Taft's Senate bill by amendments but merely to oppose the bill in letters to all senators (the same tactic that had already failed to defeat the Hartley bill), motorcades to Washington, D.C., and an intensive radio campaign.[17]

Liberal Republican senator Irving Ives of New York, who with Senator Wayne Morse of Oregon introduced much more temperate labor legislation but was attacked by the AFL as a traitor to labor for finally voting for the Taft-Hartley bill, blamed union inaction in great part for the ultimate outcome:

> I, for one, had hoped that no legislation would be required. But the course of the hearings of the Senate Labor Committee indicated that there is abuse, and there is inequity, and that these abuses must be corrected and these inequities eliminated. No one could have listened to the hearings without knowing that something was wrong. But those immediately connected with the labor unions refused to agree to any type of legislation. We received no help whatever from the representatives of organized labor. Even the legislation that I myself proposed, mild as it was, met with vigorous objection.[18]

After the enactment of Taft-Hartley, AFL president William Green, apparently not appreciating the irony, lamented the ineffectiveness of the Federation's appeals to members of Congress: "I can truthfully say that we never met with men who were so adamant, so uncompromising, evidently determined that they were going to pass this legislation in spite of our protests, and they did." Green maintained that the Taft-Hartley Act "sabotaged" the entire Wagner Act labor policy.[19] The Federation promised to challenge the constitutionality of certain provisions of the new law, to concentrate its efforts to prevent the reelection of every member of Congress who voted for it, and to work unrelentingly for its repeal.[20]

The AFL's most memorable and most criticized overview of Taft-Hartley was that it was a "slave labor law."[21] Underlying this defensive strategy was the conviction that the White House was labor's only hope of defeating this legislation, particularly by a presidential veto that might be sustained in the Senate but not the House.[22] President Truman was not as friendly to labor, however, as many labor leaders would have liked him to be.[23] Truman expressed his opinion frankly in a confidential letter to Senator Joseph Ball of Minnesota, a strong proponent of Taft-Hartley:

> The only thing I am interested in is to get a program which will keep our industrial plants operating and which will in the long run cause a better understanding between industrial management and these all too powerful labor organizations.
>
> My experience since I have been in this Executive position has not been a happy one so far as either management or labor is concerned. Neither one of them has shown an honest effort to cooperate and to reach agreements.
>
> You are familiar with the difficulties I had with the railroads due entirely to the contrariness of two railroad labor leaders, who were hunting publicity and of course, you are familiar with the long history of John L. Lewis—a play actor and a demagogue of the worst type.[24]

Truman definitely had not taken a stand-pat position on the issue of revisions in the Wagner Act. In his State of the Union address on January 6, 1947, for example, he proposed a four-point program to reduce industrial conflict, including enactment of legislative changes to "prevent certain unjustifiable practices." Truman referred specifically to "indefensible" jurisdictional strikes (especially where "minority unions strike to compel employers to deal with them despite a legal duty to bargain with the majority union"), secondary boycotts used in pursuance of "unjust objectives" such as to further jurisdictional disputes or to compel employers to violate the National Labor Relations Act (NLRA), and the use of economic force by labor or management to decide issues arising out of the interpretation or application of an existing collective bargaining agreement. Truman also proposed increasing Department of Labor efforts to assist collective bargaining, broadening social legislation—social security, housing, a national health program, minimum wage—and the appointment of a temporary joint congressional committee to study labor-management relations, particularly "nation-wide strikes in vital industries affecting the public interest" and the causes of labor-management disputes.[25]

Truman vetoed the Taft-Hartley bill, but that decision was so immersed in politics that it is difficult to be certain about his opinion of its specific provisions. Although Truman knew that the bill would be passed over his veto,[26] he also understood that signing the bill into law would have seriously jeopardized organized labor's support of the Democratic Party in the 1948 presidential election and risked driving much of that support into a growing third-party movement led by Henry Wallace. Powerful Democratic leaders such as David Lawrence of Pennsylvania and Frank Hague of New Jersey, for example, warned Truman that "a vote against labor will alienate thousands of them who . . . will then augment Wallace's drive, which up to now has only attracted the most radical."[27] This third party had no serious chance of winning a presidential election but could siphon off enough votes to cost the Democratic Party such states as California, New York, Pennsylvania, and New Jersey, which most observers believed had to be carried to win the election.[28]

Foreign relations were also an important consideration in Truman's decision to veto the bill. NLRB member James Reynolds recalled a private conversation with Truman in which the president asserted that the Marshall Plan and the containment of communism in Europe meant much more to him than the Taft-Hartley Act issue and that the Marshall Plan would be defeated if he was not reelected. Truman also told Reynolds that, although he was pro-labor, "they've gone too far in many ways." According to Reynolds, Truman said that his strategy was to veto the Taft-Hartley bill in order to hold labor's support in the upcoming election but still end up with a "pretty good" labor law (because he knew the bill would be passed over his veto), reelection as president, and the Marshall Plan operating in Europe.[29] Because Truman also wanted some solution to the problem of major strikes, Interior Secretary Julius Krug's opinion that the bill's provisions dealing with national emergency strikes could not halt and might even precipitate an impending major coal strike, leaving the president "just about as powerless to settle a major strike as he would be in the absence of any legislation,"[30] was considered by some political analysts the "real clincher" in the president's decision to veto the bill.[31] It was with mixed motivations, therefore, that Truman asserted in his veto message that the Taft-Hartley bill "taken as a whole would reverse the basic direction of our national labor policy," particularly by unduly weakening unions and converting the NLRA "from an instrument with the major purpose of protecting the right of workers to organize and bargain collectively into a maze of pitfalls and complex procedures [and] costly, time-consuming litigation inevitably embittering both parties."[32]

The Taft-Hartley Labor Policy: Some Expert Analyses

In the days immediately preceding the veto several respected professors and labor relations practitioners gave Truman their perceptive and, in certain important respects, prophetic analyses of the Taft-Hartley bill. They unanimously rejected both the charge that it was a slave labor law and the claim that the bill merely restored equality or balance between unions and employers at the bargaining table and under the law. Moreover, they agreed, as Sumner Slichter of Harvard University put it, that the "bill attempts to deal with many matters which cry for action." Such action had to be taken because, although many union leaders had been outspoken in deploring various abuses—jurisdictional strikes; strikes, picketing, and boycotting to compel violations of the NLRA; raiding to force workers to leave one union and join another; the combination of closed unions with closed shops; the exclusion of black workers from union membership; high initiation fees; and arbitrary denial of good standing to union members—unions had done little to prevent these abuses.[33]

Douglas Brown of Princeton found the bill on balance favorable to wage earners but unfavorable to union organization, "pro-employer," and, "far more important, 'pro-public.'"[34] He feared that, if the federal government did not intervene to prevent the spread of "paralyzing strikes in public service industries," public acceptance of collective bargaining would be seriously undermined and the labor movement would face an antagonism far more dangerous to its interests than the legislative restrictions proposed.[35] (Ironically, former NLRB member William Leiserson opposed the bill primarily because of the way it dealt with strikes, emphasizing the futility of prohibiting concerted action of employees while ignoring the problems that incited that action.)[36]

George Taylor of the University of Pennsylvania found some provisions desirable but most undesirable. He objected to Taft-Hartley mainly because it made a "fundamental change in our national labor policy" by replacing the Wagner Act system of collective bargaining without government interference with a "system of government-managed collective bargaining." Taylor predicted accurately that this approach would force "labor relations questions more and more into the political area and into the hands of lawyers and the courts" in an unwise extension of government control over private affairs.[37]

Despite their diverse reasons for supporting or opposing the bill, all these experts anticipated, with varying degrees of apprehension, the likelihood that employers would use the law to weaken unionization and avoid collective bargaining. Brown was concerned that "short-sighted" managements might take advantage of weaker and less secure unions but mistakenly dismissed such possible attempts as "foolish," because, in his opinion, workers were more likely to support a union that management was trying to undermine.[38]

Slichter feared the growing and "dangerous bitterness" in industrial relations that would be aggravated if the problems covered by the bill were not resolved.[39] Leiserson was convinced that the Taft-Hartley bill was designed to promote individual bargaining and to undermine collective bargaining "while the country is led to believe that collective bargaining [remained] the primary policy of the

Government." Leiserson believed that this deception could lead only to increased work stoppages and other labor-management conflict.[40]

Although the bill respected individual employee rights, Taylor pointed out that its provisions for union decertification elections and employer petitions for representation elections meant that a union would never have more than a tenuous status. He warned that the "interests of neither management nor the public would be served by a positive program to develop union insecurity." A conscious legislative effort to weaken unions and promote their insecurity would widen and intensify industrial conflict and encourage employers to reject unionism and collective bargaining:

> No one outside of certain union ranks wants to prevent employees from having the union they desire. The provisions under discussion, however, are not devoted to protection of the free choice of employees. They are a "natural" for tactical maneuvers by employers or rival unions designed to weaken the union previously selected by a majority of the employees. This part of the Act foments union jurisdictional disputes *and encourages employers to take up battle again over the question of whether or not their employees should be represented by unions.*[41]

As Harry Millis and Emily Brown put it in their comprehensive and contemporary study of the Taft-Hartley Act, *From the Wagner Act to Taft-Hartley,* "in spite of the impressive over-all figures indicating union strength, the disparities are very great, with the balance on this side here, and the other side there. No indiscriminate weakening of the power of unions could be expected to do justice or promote equality."[42] In their opinion much of the "equalize the Wagner Act" theme had little basis in fact and was merely an appealing and effective sales pitch. The legislative revisions that resulted, therefore, went far beyond those changes needed to eliminate abuses and maintain collective bargaining as essential to a democratic society.[43] Millis and Brown concluded:

> On the assumption that unions and collective bargaining are essential for a free and democratic society, and that their contribution to democratic and responsible government in industry must be strengthened, not weakened by law, we conclude that the 1947 amendments to the Wagner Act failed to meet the problems posed. Taft-Hartley, with its confusion and division of purposes, its weakening of all unions rather than carefully directed restraint of specific abuses, its weakening of restraints upon employers who still seek to avoid a democratic system of labor relations, its interference with collective bargaining, its encouragement of litigation rather than of solving problems at the bargaining table, its administrative hodgepodge, was a bungling attempt to deal with difficult problems.[44]

If the calls for equality and balance merely masked an attack on the Wagner Act intended to reduce the bargaining power of unions, then the process leading to Taft-Hartley was, as Millis and Brown claimed, predominantly a struggle over industrial and political power.[45] But even if the insistence on equality and balance by Taft-Hartley's proponents is taken at face value (and in view of the twelve-million-member increase in organized labor from the depression to 1947 and the development over those years of powerful unions such as the Teamsters, Steelworkers, Automobile Workers, Mine Workers—and the always powerful building trades and railway workers), labor had not achieved anything remotely constituting equality of power with regard to the distribution of the nation's income or business profits and had not come close to reaching Senator Wagner's goal of full participation by workers in a system of industrial self-government.[46]

The National Labor Relations Board's Analysis of Taft-Hartley

The administrative agency that would have the responsibility of interpreting and applying this new labor law, the NLRB, had taken an active role in opposing its passage during White House and congressional deliberations.[47] The Board did not share the labor leaders' position that Taft-Hartley was unqualifiedly bad or a slave labor bill. Although NLRB chairman Paul Herzog acknowledged the need for some legislative changes,[48] he told Truman that the cumulative impact of the Taft-Hartley bill's provisions not only weakened the Wagner Act "as a shield for workingmen but converted it into a sword to be used to combat their collective action"—and also made it difficult for the NLRB to administer the law.[49]

Senator James Murray of Montana, a strong opponent of Taft-Hartley, managed to get the NLRB's detailed analysis of the bill into the congressional debates without identifying the Board as the author of the document.[50] In private memoranda to President Truman, moreover, Chairman Herzog, on behalf of the Board, gave fuller explanations of the Board's objections to certain provisions.[51]

The Board strongly objected to the creation of a separate general counsel, who would be "virtually a 'labor czar.'" Policy differences between the Board and its general counsel, Herzog warned, could prevent effective enforcement of the act.[52] As William Leiserson put it prophetically, "the possibilities of conflict of authority between them are many, and these will be conducive neither to good labor relations nor good administration of the law."[53]

The Board also complained that the bill would prohibit it from hiring "economic analysts" just when such experts were most needed: the bill required the

NLRB to deal with difficult matters such as jurisdictional disputes, feather-bedding practices, boycotts, and the appropriateness of union fees.[54] As the NLRB argued, moreover, such expert knowledge was one of the main reasons for establishing an administrative agency.[55] George Taylor saw this aspect of Taft-Hartley as part of a deliberate transfer of authority from the NLRB to lawyers and judges, which he called "a sweeping change in the prevailing concept that the industrial relations experts on the Board are better equipped than a judge to decide questions of fact. A tremendous shift in power is implicit in such provisions."[56]

Given the agency's tremendous backlog of unfair labor practice and representation cases, the NLRB warned that the additional responsibility of conducting probably thousands of union shop authorization elections would be a serious administrative burden likely to interfere with the Board's implementation of the law.[57] The Board also argued that the prohibited boycott activities in Section 8(b)(4) were not defined precisely and that the language of that section was "so broad as to represent an indiscriminate attack on forms of peaceful action by labor unions without regard to whether the objective of the action is the promoting of legitimate interests in wages, hours, and working conditions or the furtherance of such illegitimate objectives as jurisdictional disputes."[58] In a related complaint the Board objected to the differential treatment that favored employers: for example, the requirements that the Board give secondary boycott charges priority over all other cases, including "flagrant cases of unfair labor practices by employers or elections that require expedition," and seek temporary injunctions from district courts whenever there was reason to believe a secondary boycott was in operation.[59] The Board also protested the disparate penalties in the bill. Employees were subject to discharge and unions to damage suits, injunctions, or complete denial of access to NLRB procedures, whereas employers, even those who violated the law repeatedly, were not denied any rights under the act and were subject to only mild remedial provisions such as cease-and-desist orders and the reinstatement of unjustly discharged employees with back pay.[60]

Other provisions, the Board told Truman, undermined employee rights and collective bargaining, particularly the one concerning employer free speech. This provision went beyond the protection of an admitted constitutional right and seriously circumscribed the NLRB's prevention of employer unfair labor practices by granting that such employer statements were not to be considered evidence of an unfair labor practice.[61] Herzog also cited the section forbidding the Board to use the extent to which employees had already organized as the controlling factor in determining an appropriate unit for collective bargaining, because in many industries "organization can proceed only piecemeal and to deny collective bargaining in those areas in which organization has been achieved is to deny it entirely."[62]

Conflicting Statutory Purposes: NLRB Power and Political Consequences

Chairman Herzog made a most important and perceptive observation comparing the Wagner Act and the Taft-Hartley bill, especially those Taft-Hartley provisions allegedly equalizing the law. In enumerating the "little things" throughout the bill "all calculated to destroy the philosophy of the Wagner Act that collective bargaining should be encouraged," Herzog emphasized that Section 7 of the bill "treats protection of the right to 'refrain from' joining a union as one just as worthy of the attention of Congress as the right to join one free from employer interference." He reasoned, "Such [equalizing] provisions do not belong in an Act [the Wagner Act] which was intended to equalize bargaining *power* by encouraging the self-organization of workers, and not to equalize all *rights* as between members of the community."[63]

Interweaving assumptions of employee free choice (the right to refrain) and equality of rights between labor and management, for example, can lead to conclusions that are unfavorable to the encouragement of collective bargaining, as a contemporary scholar has pointed out with respect to the assumption "that the employer is legitimately entitled to play the same role in a representation campaign against the union as the Republican Party plays against the Democrats."[64] As law professor and future secretary of labor Willard Wirtz wrote in the mid-1950s:

> The cliche thinking about "equality" has caused perhaps the greatest difficulty here. The tongue is quicker than the mind, and the phrase than the thought. There is so much appeal in the warm language about treating employers and employees alike, letting them both say whatever they want to in their own promises, serving up a common sauce for goose and gander. It is hard, on the other hand, to persuade by the more intricate logic that the equal treatment of unequals produces only inequality. Denial that the rich and the poor take equal advantage either from the right to beg or from tax exemptions on oil wells invariably invites more suspicion than understanding.[65]

In August 1947, when the Taft-Hartley Act went into effect, the question was whether the new law would leave undisturbed the Wagner Act's encouragement of collective bargaining as the core of the national labor policy (as Senator Taft claimed) or whether it would become, in the name of concern for the individual worker, a justification and a mechanism for the rejection of collective bargaining.[66] Certainly, the concept of government as a *neutral* guarantor of some equal or reasonably balanced rights of labor and management and as a *neutral* guarantor of employee free choice between individual and collective action is inconsistent with the Wagner Act's concept of a government *partial* to the practice of collective bargaining; yet the Taft-Hartley Act contained language supporting both conceptions of government.

In applying this new law, the NLRB would have to give specific meaning to the general designs of the statute, interpret where neither statutory language nor congressional intent was clear, and even fill gaps in the legislation, gaps ranging from small intervals to large expanses. As Clyde Summers put it years later, "the Board, in exercising its functions of interpreting and elaborating the skeletal words of the statute, is compelled to mold and develop a body of law. It cannot act as a mechanical brain but must choose between competing considerations."[67]

Because there were potentially conflicting statutory purposes in the Taft-Hartley Act, the new five-member NLRB was in the unique position of choosing between different labor policies and, over time and political administrations, of swinging labor policy from one purpose to its direct opposite. These swings would directly determine whether the scope of bargaining would expand or contract, would alter the relative bargaining power of the parties, and would affect the ability of unions to organize and managements to resist organization.

The NLRB always had influence over the vital interests of labor and management. After Taft-Hartley it had the authority to determine the underlying direction of U.S. labor policy. It was a power guaranteed to subject the Board to attack and manipulation.

2

Political Maneuvering to Control a New Law, a New Board, and a New Labor Czar

Pressure from the AFL and CIO

Even before the Taft-Hartley Act went into effect on August 22, 1947, supporters and opponents of the new law began maneuvering to influence the NLRB. By early August many of the most powerful CIO unions, in steel, automobiles, electrical, rubber, meat packing, farm equipment, lithography, food and tobacco, and longshore, had announced their intention to boycott the NLRB.[1]

Although only one AFL affiliate, the International Typographical Union, had publicly advocated an NLRB boycott, the Federation deliberately left open the possibility, saying only that a final decision would not be made until the September meeting of its Executive Council.[2] At a conference of two hundred officers of national and international unions summoned to Washington, D.C., on July 9 to discuss the implications of the new law, however, AFL counsel Joseph Padway asserted that "if unions can by-pass the law and do without it, I am here to state that they would be better off."[3]

The AFL and CIO also announced plans to challenge the constitutionality of certain provisions of the act, and AFL lawyers advised their unions to violate those "clearly unconstitutional" provisions requiring union officers to file noncommunist affidavits.[4] The CIO, in addition, publicized its intent to strengthen its political efforts, while the AFL talked openly about abandoning its traditional nonpartisan approach to politics and forming a political action organization that would work in "parallel" with the CIO's political action committee for the defeat of the Republicans in the 1948 presidential election and repeal of the Taft-Hartley Act.[5]

Pressure from Congressional Proponents of Strict Enforcement

Congressional members who favored rigorous enforcement of the Taft-Hartley Act used more direct methods to influence the NLRB. They sought to oust members carried over from the Wagner Act period (Chairman Paul Herzog and members John Houston and James Reynolds), to win the nomination of new members who would strictly carry out the act, and to have the Board and the new general counsel consult with a statutorily established Joint Congressional Committee on Labor-Management Relations chaired by Taft-Hartley advocate Senator Joseph Ball and co-chaired by Congressman Fred Hartley.[6]

The act's proponents had reason to doubt that the NLRB would vigorously enforce the new law. One week after Senator Murray introduced an anonymous analysis of the Taft-Hartley bill into the *Congressional Record*,[7] Hartley, chairman of the House Labor Committee, and Ball, chairman of the Senate Labor Committee, discovered that the Board's staff had prepared the document. Chairman Herzog gathered that there was "considerable irritation" among the Republican members of the two committees.[8]

In a June 16 memorandum to President Truman, Ball charged the Board with circulating to cabinet members and senators an analysis of the Taft-Hartley bill that was a "tissue of distortions" inspired by Lee Pressman, general counsel of the CIO. Ball also accused the Board and Senator Murray of deception in concealing the Board's authorship of the document that Murray put into the *Record*. Ball drew the first battle line when he warned Truman that "very few Senators who are familiar with the administration of the Wagner Act by the Board believe that the Board would interpret the provisions of the new legislation in a way which would be hostile to employees."[9]

Herzog feared that a "great unpleasantness" lay ahead. He noted in his diary that Hartley had blasted the Board publicly, "saying he doubted whether we were fit to administer the new law." Herzog worried that an investigation of "our methods and motives" would occur as early as the following week: "The sort of thing I'd succeeded in avoiding for the past six months."[10] He had good reason to be worried, for in the previous six months he, NLRB General Counsel Gerhard Van Arkel, and other agency personnel had actively but secretly aided the defenders of the Wagner Act. Herzog and Van Arkel had met with Senators Wayne Morse and Irving Ives from early January through May to draft a liberal Republican bill, on the "theory that if we (very secretly) can help such liberal Republicans as Ives and Wayne Morse it may stop reactionary bills by Ball."[11] When Morse and Ives submitted "very reasonable" bills in March, Herzog noted in his diary, "Van Arkel and I had our hands in both, but no one is supposed to know it."[12]

Van Arkel and his assistant, Herman Lazarus, drafted the minority reports on the Hartley and Taft bills for both the House and Senate labor committees, wrote pro–Wagner Act speeches for Democratic members of those committees[13] (Herzog and Van Arkel and Assistant Secretary of Labor David Morse also prepared Secretary of Labor L. B. Schwellenbach's congressional testimony),[14] and participated in a secret meeting with representatives of the Railway Brotherhoods, the CIO, and the AFL to identify the worst features of the legislation, so that President Truman could stress them in his veto message.[15] Herzog also met regularly during this time as part of a special committee set up by Truman to advise him on labor legislation.[16] Herzog coordinated strategy with this group, even conforming his testimony before the Senate Labor Committee in February to the Truman administration "line":

> [Presidential adviser Clark] Clifford and [Assistant Secretary of Labor David] Morse pressed me hard not to make any real affirmative suggestions, lest we let the Republicans "off the hook" of drafting their own legislation. Clifford seems to hope that they put through something drastic, so Truman can veto it and be in a good political situation in 1948. The result is that I shall have to act much less "cooperative" before the Senate Committee (and even Ives) than I want. It will make things much less pleasant, but I guess I have to be a good soldier and follow the Administration line as Schwellenbach is doing.[17]

During this time Herzog did what he could to mollify NLRB and Wagner Act opponents and avoid damaging controversy. In January he began a program of congressional visits intended "without bootlicking" to give them the impression that the NLRB was "not too wild." He also tried to persuade William Green "to testify that the NLRB is no longer pro-CIO" in order to "help with Taft, who still remembers the 1939 hearings."[18] The chairman even maneuvered the Board's case agenda to prevent untimely criticism; he arranged to postpone decisions in two cases in which Reynolds was writing sharp dissents that could have led to serious congressional repercussions.[19]

Opposition to having the incumbent Board members administer Taft-Hartley increased after its passage.[20] Herzog wondered if he could "conscientiously administer an anti-labor bill" and asked himself if he should remain at the NLRB.[21] Van Arkel (and many others at the agency) resigned immediately,[22] saying that Congress was entitled to have the important new post of general counsel "filled by someone who would not start, as I should, with grave doubts concerning both the workability and the fairness of this Act."[23]

Many people urged Herzog to resign, and he was greatly tempted to do so.[24] The Senate, House, and press knew he was hostile to the enactment of the Taft-Hartley bill, and he believed continuing as chairman posed a dilemma: if the act was a failure, Herzog and the Board would be charged with sabotage, and if the act was successful, Herzog and the Board would have helped prove Truman wrong.[25]

Herzog, however, was skilled at bureaucratic maneuvering and appreciated the nuances, including the realization of his own ambitions. Being "very reputation conscious," he worried about how he would look to his liberal friends if he stayed on as chairman after Van Arkel had quit "on principle."[26] On the other hand, Herzog was unsure how to resign "without destroying [his] public usefulness for many years," because many considered Taft-Hartley "a 'moderate' bill" and would not learn otherwise for a long time.[27]

Herzog discussed his situation with Truman. Although the NLRB chairman had developed a close personal relationship with the president,[28] as a notation in Herzog's diary concerning his conferences at the White House indicated—"It's still quite a thrill to sit right next to the *President of the U.S.* and be called 'Paul' by him"[29]—Herzog was in awe of Truman and the presidency. On the same day that Truman delivered his veto message the president told Herzog not to resign.[30] At Herzog's request, his friend Republican senator Ives talked to Taft, who, to Herzog's "total amazement," told Ives he trusted the Board chairman and would not attack him or Truman over the chairmanship issue.[31]

The New Labor Czar: Powerful Enforcer of Taft-Hartley or Unwitting Saboteur?

On June 23, 1947, Truman called Herzog, Reynolds, and Houston to the White House and requested that they remain at their posts.[32] The three issued a public statement that same day indicating that the debate was over as far as the Board was concerned and pledging that they would give the new act the fairest and most efficient administration.[33] Truman added his own commitment to that objective.[34]

One of the most radical changes in the Taft-Hartley Act was the creation of an independent office of general counsel intended to separate the NLRB's prosecuting and judging functions.[35] Congress gave the general counsel "final authority on behalf of the Board" to investigate charges of unfair labor practices, to issue complaints, and to prosecute those complaints of unfair labor practices before the Board. The Board could not direct, control, or review the general counsel's actions in this area, and in the performance of its judicial function the

Board, obviously, could decide only those cases brought to it by the general counsel. The general counsel and not the Board, therefore, had complete control over what unfair labor practice cases would be brought to trial before the Board. The Board retained statutory control over representation case matters.[36]

Given the concentration of power in one person (dubbed the "labor czar" in the press);[37] the statute's failure to define the precise relationship between the general counsel and the Board with regard to the supervision of NLRB officers and employees, enforcement of Board orders, and other important matters; and the potential for internal conflict that could damage the agency, it was most important that the person appointed general counsel be experienced, responsible, and temperamentally able to work closely with Board members in the resolution of problems. Truman, therefore, caused surprise, disappointment, anger, and much speculation when he nominated for general counsel a nationally unknown, sixty-two-year-old NLRB trial examiner, Robert Denham, considered within the agency controversial, an aggressive conservative, and a man of "enormous ego" who was definitely no diplomat.[38]

Board member James Reynolds was most responsible for Denham's becoming general counsel. Reynolds, who knew Denham was "tenacious," was convinced that the first general counsel "had to be a very direct, tough guy, with a deep conviction that Taft-Hartley was the greatest thing since the Magna Charta." When Reynolds asked Denham if he would like to be general counsel, Denham said, "I'd give my right arm for it." Reynolds recalled that when he broached the idea to Herzog and Houston, however, their first reaction was, "My God, that's appalling."[39] According to Herzog, Reynolds made the recommendation because "he wanted a more pro-employer administration of the Act"; Houston approved "because he was a crafty old politician and knew that Denham was the sort of man he was [and] would go to extremes and, in the long run, come a cropper."[40] Herzog agreed to go along.

Magazine sketches at the time described Denham as a gray-haired six-footer with "narrow shoulders which combine strangely with a middle-age waistline and a pair of the largest feet ever to grace official Washington"; a man of "bustling vigor," jovial but "mule stubborn," who always wore a small flower in his lapel and spoke in a "rich bass voice" using "picturesque language" and football and baseball terms while constantly jingling three silver dollars in his hand.[41] NLRB Executive Secretary Frank Kleiler recalled how Denham clicked those silver dollars in his pocket, then played with them, and then put them back and rattled them: "My God, he'd drive me nuts."[42]

Denham had a long and colorful career before becoming general counsel. He was born and raised in St. Louis, Missouri, where his father was a machinist. "An 'undistinguished scholar," he graduated from the University of Missouri

Law School, where he became close friends with Forrest Donnell, a member of the Senate Labor Committee at the time of Denham's nomination. He worked as a cowhand in Texas while serving as a county attorney, joined the army during World War I and commanded a squadron of lumberjacks cutting spruce in the Northwest for the manufacture of airplanes, worked for a series of banks in the 1920s and 1930s in the East and South directing reorganizations and liquidations, and in 1938, when land title problems kept him from returning to central Florida to raise cattle, he became a per diem trial examiner at the NLRB.[43] Along the way, "he lost a good deal of his own fortune in 1929, and what remained went in 1937."[44]

Denham was no less colorful or controversial during his nine years as an NLRB trial examiner. His superiors in the Trial Examiners Division, for example, deleted from one of his decisions an explanation of why he credited the testimony of a white man rather than the contrary statements of several black witnesses, an explanation that drew strong protests from the National Association for the Advancement of Colored People: "The reluctance of the Southern Negro to discuss his affairs with his white bosses, particularly where such matters might tend to prejudice him, and his tendency to concoct almost any fabrication as an answer in such circumstances, is well recognized among the white men of the South. Close and intimate contact with the Negro has taught the white overseers to recognize when a Negro is lying." In another case, involving the Henry Kaiser Shipbuilding Company, Denham "pulled a soft felt hat down over his eyes and spent some hours around the saloons on the Portland, Oregon, waterfront, eavesdropping on the conversations of union men." When the union complained, another trial examiner was assigned to the case.[45]

Personalities have a powerful effect on any organization's operations. Personality clashes, particularly between Denham and Herzog, as well as their conflicting views of the Taft-Hartley Act, would lead the NLRB almost immediately into serious internecine conflict. While Herzog and the Board were working in opposition to the Taft-Hartley bill, Denham was writing his long-time friend Senator Donnell of the Labor Committee recommending changes in the Wagner Act. At his confirmation hearing he told the Senate Labor Committee that he strongly favored the new law, promised to enforce it without reservation, and pledged to replace any NLRB staff member who did not subscribe to the act to the same extent he did.[46] Denham also revealed that during the Wagner Act period he had been one of a small group of conservatives (including Board member Gerard Reilly) fighting a "rear-guard action against the 'radicals' in the NLRB."[47]

Those who knew Denham at the NLRB, moreover, considered him a man of "enormous ego" who "loved the designation of czar."[48] He was also very stubborn, sticking to a position he considered correct "even if he brought the house down, and he almost did."[49]

To Herzog, Denham was a "real reactionary" who "joined the right-wing forces of the trial examiners group," an "S.O.B.," a "neurotic man" with "delusions of grandeur," and a "passion for power," who after years of failure "suddenly sees his name in the headlines all over the United States as the czar of labor, as the most powerful man in the country, as the man who is going to be more important than the five members of the Board put together; it would go to anybody's head [and], of course, it did."[50]

These perceptions of Denham were particularly important, because Herzog was a chairman who took charge of his Board—one who was at the "helm and steered the Board along," as his confidential secretary put it—rather than act merely as one of the five members.[51] Herzog was jealous of his power, but Denham did not want anyone to doubt that the general counsel was the equal of the Board.[52] Although Herzog was more intellectual and politically astute and Denham was rougher and tougher but less sophisticated in dealing with the bureaucracy, each man was powerful in his own way, and they were about to do battle to decide who would run the agency.[53] There was speculation at the time and later that Truman deliberately chose Denham not only to avoid Republican charges that he was trying to put implementation of the act in unsympathetic hands but primarily to subvert the new law by having it vigorously overenforced by an inflexible, conservative zealot, thereby making the act unpopular and strengthening the administration's moves for repeal.[54]

The Joint Labor-Management Committee: Consultation or Dictation?

On July 23, 1947, the Senate Labor Committee, chaired by Robert Taft, conducted confirmation hearings on Denham and Truman's nominees to fill the two additional Board member positions created by Taft-Hartley: Copeland Gray, for a two-year term, and Abe Murdock, for a five-year term.[55] In these hearings and afterward Taft-Hartley advocates maneuvered to establish control over the general counsel and the new Board. They concentrated on Denham during the confirmation hearings, where nothing was subtle about their efforts and objective.

Senator Ball, who only the day before had been appointed chairman of the Joint Committee on Labor-Management Relations established by Taft-Hartley,[56] asked Denham at the outset of the confirmation hearings if he considered it consistent with his responsibilities as general counsel to consult with the Joint

Committee about the interpretation of various provisions of the act before, as general counsel, he took a final position on them. Denham replied that "it would be a privilege to do it." When Denham told Senator Ives, also a member of the Joint Committee, that he was "perfectly willing to cooperate" with the committee and expected to get "a great deal of help" from it, Ives said that was fine because the Joint Committee had "very definite ideas as to the way we would like to see the new labor relations set-up function."[57]

Under questioning from Taft-Hartley opponent Senator Murray, Denham reaffirmed his intention to seek advice from the Joint Committee concerning the meaning and intent of the law. Democratic senator Claude Pepper told Denham that his approach would violate the separation-of-powers concept of government and got Denham to agree that he would be "shocked" if the Supreme Court asked Congress to help it construe a law.[58]

Subsequent attempts to clarify Denham's position only verified that Senator Pepper's original impression was correct. Ives, for example, offered the politically unreal notion that, after consulting with the Joint Committee to get "our ideas as to the meaning of certain provisions of the act," Denham would be free to "pay no attention whatever" to the committee's interpretations, a role Republican senator George Aiken called being "guided without being controlled."[59]

Ball's final clarification confirmed that his Joint Committee on Labor-Management Relations wanted to influence the general counsel in ways Denham welcomed:

> *Senator Ball.* When you are confronted with possible conflicting interpretations, before you make your final decision you would merely consult with this joint commission which . . . contains all the members of the conference committee [House-Senate Conference Committee on the Taft-Hartley bills] and men who are probably in the best position to know what the intent of Congress was, whether it is clearly expressed in the legislative history or not, before you made your decision?
>
> *Mr. Denham.* Yes, sir. I don't think there is any misunderstanding, Senator, between you and me as to what the program should be.[60]

Louis Stark, labor correspondent for the *New York Times,* reported in early August 1947 that after the confirmation hearings the Joint Committee summoned the prospective NLRB members and asked them to respond to questions Denham had formulated. According to Stark, Truman subsequently called the Board members to the White House and told them "point blank" never to forget that they were part of the executive branch responsible to him and "that they were to do their own interpreting of the law . . . and not seek answers to questions from anyone else." Stark also reported that Truman assured the Board "he would not tell [them] what to do and he did not want anyone else to tell the Board its duty."[61]

Confirmation Withheld: Another Attempt at Political Manipulation

The Senate Labor Committee did not question the two Board member nominees about their consultations with the Joint Labor-Management Committee. Copeland Gray, one of Truman's nominees, had never acted in a judicial capacity, had no prior dealings of any sort with the NLRB, and had no business experience outside New York State.[62] The fifty-five-year-old Republican had worked as an office manager, assistant secretary, accountant, and treasurer for Houde Engineering in Buffalo (a subsidiary of Houdaille-Hershey Corporation) before becoming director of industrial relations, a position created at his request in 1937. Gray remained in that job until 1940, when he was put in charge of recruiting personnel for a newly organized subsidiary of Houdaille that manufactured machine guns for the British.

When he returned to Houdaille after the war and found that "they had more labor relations men than they knew what to do with," Gray left the company and set himself up as an industrial relations counselor to New York employers.[63] He also served during the war as a substitute industry panel member on the Regional War Labor Board in New York and, after the war, as an industry member of the National Wage Stabilization Board in Washington, D.C.[64]

The most startling aspect of Gray's testimony was his almost total ignorance of the new law. The nominee said that he had read the act twice "from beginning to end" but did not yet understand it. When Senator Ball asked him if he could recall any of the union unfair labor practices in Taft-Hartley, Gray replied, "I have made no attempt to remember them. It is obvious that if this confirmation comes through, I must make myself completely informed on the requirements of the law." Gray explained that his clients' attorneys handled NLRB matters; he was more interested in bringing about better understanding and closer working relationships between employers and their employees "so that they might work better together, so that the employees might make more wages, so that the business might operate efficiently and profitably."[65] That was not a reassuring answer from someone who would be responsible for interpreting and applying the new national labor law, but only Senator Ball expressed any concern.

The other nominee, Abe Murdock, drew heated questioning from Senator Ball. The fifty-four-year-old former Democratic city and county attorney from

Utah had served four terms in the House of Representatives (1932–40) and one term in the Senate (1940–46). After Murdock stated that his basic philosophy concerning labor legislation had not changed since he had served in Congress, Ball hammered at the fact that, in the Senate, Murdock had voted against the Case bill and had opposed several amendments that were now incorporated into the Taft-Hartley Act. Ball further criticized Murdock for being a staunch New Dealer on the Smith committee in 1939 (House Special Committee to Investigate the NLRB) and for signing a minority report that opposed several provisions of the Smith bill that were also included in the new law.[66] Ball then questioned how an individual who throughout his public life opposed every legislative change now appearing in Taft-Hartley could possibly give the new law "sympathetic administration."[67] Murdock said that the law needed honest and impartial administration, not sympathy, and maintained that he would administer the Taft-Hartley Act and not some position he had taken or report he had issued in the past.[68]

The Senate Labor Committee voted unanimously (12–0) to report Denham's nomination favorably but only nine to three (Taft, Ball, and William Jenner of Indiana dissenting) in support of Gray and Murdock.[69] There was vigorous objection to Murdock's "pro-labor" record in Congress and "passive resistance" to Gray by committee members unimpressed with his experience.[70]

The committee reported the nominations only two days before the Senate was to adjourn. Ball and other Taft-Hartley advocates anticipated that, although Gray would join Reynolds as a conservative minority on the Board, Murdock and Houston would constitute an offsetting liberal pair, leaving Herzog, who had actively opposed Taft-Hartley, as the key swing vote.[71] Truman was accused of using a clever court-packing device to thwart the congressional majorities that passed Taft-Hartley by nominating as Board members "one man who is not rated as big enough for the job and another man who is the known champion of the labor union bosses."[72] The Senate adjourned without acting on any of the nominations.[73] Truman then gave recess appointments to his three nominees, subject to their confirmation at the next Senate session (January 1948),[74] and they were sworn in on August 1, 1947.[75]

Ball's strategy left the unconfirmed general counsel and Board members insecure and vulnerable to political pressure. Deferring action on the nominees, conservative columnist David Lawrence wrote delicately, would give the Senate "more time to give full consideration to the qualifications of the new members." The *New York Times* described the consequences of the delay more pointedly as enabling congressional Republicans to "maintain vigilance" over the administration of Taft-Hartley and to "act on the appointees in the light of their record in office."[76] John L. Lewis put it even more bluntly, charging that confirmation had been blocked so that the Taft-Ball forces could "keep a whip hand" over the nominees. International Association of Machinists president Harvey Brown claimed that the nominees were "being subjected to coercion, with the very real threat that if they fail to play ball with this clique [the Ball-Hartley–led Joint Committee on Labor-Management Relations], they will be fired."[77]

Concluding Observations

The NLRB was subjected to conflicting political pressures even before the act became effective on August 22, 1947. Organized labor was threatening to boycott the NLRB and was publicly complaining about the "Taft-Ball" forces' attempt to intimidate Denham and the Board in a way that let the NLRB know that organized labor was watching it. The senator who would chair the Joint Labor-Management Committee, on the other hand, had openly and directly expressed the committee's intent to control the new general counsel, who in turn had the power to influence the Board's implementation of labor policy. The strategy of withholding confirmation to Denham and new Board members Gray and Murdock, moreover, was intended to convey the message to the three that their careers with the Board depended on their pleasing the most powerful proponents of strict enforcement of the Taft-Hartley Act.

The Board itself, particularly Chairman Herzog (now the key swing vote), was under pressure to prove that its active opposition to the Taft-Hartley bill would not affect its implementation of the Taft-Hartley Act. Charges that Truman was deliberately trying to sabotage the act by appointing Denham as general counsel and Murdock and Gray as Board members also put pressure on the NLRB to handle and decide cases in a way that would disprove those charges rather than let the political chips fall where they may while deciding all cases on their merits. All these forces were brought to bear on an NLRB now divided between Board and general counsel, in such a way that conflicting ambitions, ideologies, and personalities could plunge the agency into a politically damaging internecine struggle.

3

Improper Influences

The Delegation Agreement: The Enough-Rope Approach

The NLRB devoted most of July and August 1947 to preparing and carrying out changes in organization and procedure required by Taft-Hartley; developing new rules, forms, and instructions to personnel; and assembling all regional directors and attorneys at a conference to discuss new and anticipated problems. The Board also designed a new staff structure to administer the act.[1]

Although Congress clearly intended to separate the new general counsel's functions of investigation and prosecution from the adjudication function of the five-member Board, it did so in very general and often imprecise statutory language. The major procedural problem confronting the general counsel and the Board, therefore, was to find a practical and efficient way to make this separation of functions work without encroaching on the fundamental statutory authority of either the Board or general counsel.[2]

The Board, for example, retained full control over all aspects of representation case proceedings and had the authority to appoint all agency personnel, including attorneys. The general counsel, however, was statutorily obliged to "exercise general supervision over all attorneys employed by the Board."[3] Because almost all the operations involved in representation matters and in investigating and prosecuting unfair labor practice cases occurred in the field, the regional personnel who performed these functions could end up receiving directives from and being supervised by two bosses. An alternative, the maintenance of two field organizations, one for representation matters and the other for unfair labor practice matters, made no financial or administrative sense.[4] Herzog called this portion of the statute an "administrative monstrosity."[5]

Denham, at his confirmation hearing, frankly asserted an expansive view of his power.[6] He brought this attitude to his negotiations with the Board over administrative implementation of the separation of functions. Newly appointed executive secretary Frank Kleiler, who participated in these discussions, recalled that the "problems were so impossible" that thought was given to obtaining an opinion from the attorney general to "resolve the questions once and for all."[7] Instead, Denham persuaded the Board to solve the problem by preparing a memorandum of understanding detailing the statutory and delegated responsibilities of the general counsel.[8] According to Herzog, the Board "simply had to surrender that power" to the general counsel, but "there was a bit of Machiavelli in it [because] people realized that if you gave this fellow enough rope he'd hang himself, which he certainly succeeded in doing."[9]

The Board agreed to delegate many of its most important functions to the general counsel, including almost complete authority over personnel.[10] In addition to the statutory duties of investigation and prosecution of unfair labor practice matters, the general counsel, pursuant to what became known as the Delegation Agreement, assumed responsibility in such cases for obtaining compliance with Board orders or, if necessary, seeking enforcement of those orders. The general counsel was also granted the authority to initiate and prosecute all mandatory (Section 10[l]) and discretionary (Section 10[j]) injunctions. In representation cases, the general counsel was given authority to take over the regional office phases of representation proceedings, including receiving and processing all petitions for certification, decertification, union shop authorization and deauthorization elections; conducting representation elections; determining the validity of challenges and objections to the conduct of these elections; and certifying the results of these elections. The Board retained authority to decide appeals from regional board representation case decisions.[11] Although the Delegation Agreement eliminated some of the confusion caused by the separation of functions, serious issues remained unresolved, including the question whether Denham, in the exercise of these functions, would be bound by Board policy and case decisions even if they conflicted with his own views.[12]

The Noncommunist Affidavit

The Delegation Agreement did not repair the fundamental defect in the two-headed agency approach: the possibility that each head, the general counsel and the Board, would contradict the other. Possibility became reality when, before a representation petition was filed or an unfair labor practice complaint issued under the new law, the Board and the general counsel disagreed publicly over the meaning of Section 9(h). The dispute arose over language in that provision requiring each officer of a petitioning or charging union *"and the officers of any national or international labor organization of which it is an affiliate or constituent unit"* to file affidavits with the Board that they were not members of or affiliated with the Communist Party and that they did not believe in and were not members or supporters of any organization that advocated the overthrow of the United States government by force or by illegal or unconstitutional methods.[13] The NLRB could not conduct any investigation concerning representation, entertain any representation petition, or issue any unfair labor practice complaint unless the labor organization requesting such action had filed this noncommunist affidavit with the Board.

The legislative history and statutory language remained unclear, however, as to whether the phrase "officers of any national or international labor organization of which it is an affiliate or constituent unit" meant only unions such as the International Ladies' Garment Workers Union (AFL) or the National Federation of Telephone Workers (Independent) or included the officers of the AFL and the CIO. Denham's interpretation was based mainly on what the general counsel considered the obvious intent of Congress to bar communists from all organized labor.[14] Characteristically, Denham chose to read the law the hard way, announcing a week before Taft-Hartley became effective that he "had no choice" but to deny access to the NLRB to every international union of the AFL and CIO and all their local unions "if a single one of the fifty-two members of the executive board of the CIO [or any member of the AFL executive board] failed to sign" the noncommunist affidavit.[15]

Denham stood firm in his decision, unaffected by pressures exerted on him to change his position by even Thomas Shroyer, general counsel of the Joint Labor-Management Committee, and Secretary of Labor Lewis Schwellenbach.[16] He was also unmoved by the enormous implications of AFL and CIO noncompliance.[17] Most presidents of unions affiliated with the CIO had refused to sign the affidavits, as had CIO president Philip Murray and the organization's secretary-treasurer, James Carey.[18] Although AFL president William Green and most of the members of the Federation's Executive Council were in favor of signing, John L. Lewis almost single-handedly forced the AFL into a boycott of the NLRB as long as Denham's ruling stood. With Lewis the sole dissenter, the council had voted twelve to one on September 8 in favor of compliance, but given Denham's ruling, Lewis's refusal to sign meant that every national and international union affiliated with the AFL and all their local unions were barred from access to the NLRB.[19]

In an extraordinary meeting held at the special request of President Green and Teamsters' president Daniel Tobin, AFL general counsel Joseph Padway appeared before Herzog and the other members of the Board on September 16 and, with Denham present, denounced the general counsel's ruling as unfair and arbitrary.[20] The Federation was attempting to force the Board to choose between it and Denham. Although Board members made no promises, they asked the

AFL and the CIO to present specific cases to the Board for hearing and decision.[21] The first test case to reach the Board, *Northern Virginia Broadcasters, Inc.,* was filed by a local union of the AFL's International Brotherhood of Electrical Workers (IBEW). Because the Board had retained authority to decide appeals from regional board representation case decisions, the local union was able to challenge Denham's interpretation of Section 9(h) before the Board.[22]

Interested parties unabashedly put pressure on the Board while it deliberated this case. The AFL's Executive Council engaged in protracted and widely publicized discussions of the noncommunist affidavit issue on the eve of the Federation's convention in October but postponed action, on the "probability" that the Board's decision was imminent.[23] The press predicted openly that the Board would reverse Denham, and even speculated on how each Board member would vote on the issue and who had switched positions or could switch before the final decision. Attention was focused on interim appointees Murdock and Gray, who were "hoping for Senate confirmation when Congress reconvened."[24]

The White House expressed "extreme interest" in the outcome because it would demonstrate how much statutory authority the Board had retained after delegating a "large segment" of that authority to Denham.[25] Denham, in turn, was applying his own pressure on the Board to uphold his ruling. The general counsel threatened, if his ruling was overturned, to make a public statement charging that Reynolds and Houston had agreed to support his position—implying that Herzog had pressed them to change their minds. Meanwhile, Herzog, characteristically, was trying to delay the Board's decision so that a disagreement between the Board and Denham would not be interpreted as a "split."[26]

Perhaps the greatest pressure came from the Joint Labor-Management Committee, which, before the Board issued its decision, "invited" the members of the Board to appear before it on October 8, to be questioned about their opinion of the Denham ruling.[27] The Board was moved to issue its decision on October 7, although Murdock had wanted to confer with the Joint Committee before the ruling was announced.[28] (The Board and general counsel met with the Joint Committee on October 8 anyway and reached an agreement with it concerning an interpretation of another provision of the act.)[29]

In *Northern Virginia Broadcasters, Inc.,* the Board voted four to one to override Denham's interpretation and require only officers of local, national, and international unions to sign the noncommunist affidavits.[30] Herzog, Reynolds, and Houston signed a majority opinion, Murdock wrote a concurring opinion, and Gray was the lone dissenter. Acknowledging in deference to Denham that there was no "categorical answer" to the question, the majority presumed that Congress used the words "national and international unions" as they were commonly understood in labor relations: "We are familiar with no use of the term 'national or international labor organization' which includes parent federations such as the AFL or the CIO within its meaning."[31] According to the majority, moreover, "nothing could play more readily into the hands of dissension-seeking Communist leadership" than allowing a single noncomplying officer of the AFL or CIO to deny an otherwise complying local or international union access to NLRB machinery for the peaceful resolution of labor disputes.[32]

According to the *New York Times,* Denham "bowed promptly to the NLRB's edict."[33] Senator Ball, chairman of the Joint Labor-Management Committee and strong advocate of the separation of functions, walked a somewhat metaphysical fine line in trying to deemphasize the disagreement between the Board and general counsel. He said that Denham and the Board were both correct but that the Board's position was "probably more in line with what we intended."[34] The act's coauthor, Senator Taft, chairman of the Senate Labor Committee and member of the Joint Labor-Management Committee, told the press that the Board's interpretation was "certainly not in conflict with the intention of Congress."[35] Supporters of John L. Lewis claimed that "he succeeded in having Denham's ears pinned back"[36] and in dividing the administrators of the new law.[37]

The Board's decision removed a major barrier to the operation of the Taft-Hartley Act. Several powerful unions, however, such as the United Electrical Workers of America (CIO), the United Steelworkers of America (CIO), and the United Mine Workers of America (AFL), had announced and persisted in a policy of noncompliance.[38]

The NLRB and the Taft-Hartley Act: The First Seven Months

Because of what Herzog called the "tremendous, perhaps inordinate" amount of time and energy devoted by the Board to the noncommunist affidavit issue,[39] no case involving the new union unfair labor practices, among the most controversial provisions of the act, had reached the Board by mid-March 1948, almost seven months after Taft-Hartley became effective.[40] In speeches delivered as late as the end of April 1948, therefore, Chairman Herzog was saying that the only honest answer to questions about the effectiveness of the new law was that "it is too early to tell."[41]

Nevertheless, the Joint Committee on Labor-Management Relations was required by statute to submit an interim report to the Senate and the House no later than March 15, 1948.[42] Since there was little evidence, including case decisions, on which to base assessments, conclusions, or recommendations, the committee's majority and minority reports were essentially predicated on un-substantiated impressions and political and ideological orientations.

Both sides made several unfounded assertions. The majority claimed, for example, that the number of secondary boycotts had been steadily decreasing under the act; implied a connection between Taft-Hartley and a decrease in strikes, an increase in wages, and gains in union membership; and declared that the rights of individual workers in job security, resolution of grievances, and relations with employers had "in no wise suffered" under the act. According to the majority, moreover, the committee's case studies of labor relations in various plants demonstrated that friction between labor and management was minimized by effective two-way communication when management sincerely accepted collective bargaining and the union understood "that its own well-being is dependent upon that of the company."[43]

The minority, in turn, blamed Taft-Hartley for creating "an atmosphere and a psychology" that encouraged employers to resist union organizing and legitimate union demands. It criticized the majority's plant study reports for adopting the management approach to labor relations and for having all the earmarks of scientific management, emphasizing only "production incentives, management personnel problems, and management prerogatives."[44]

After seven months the reports of this congressional watchdog committee merely continued the debates over Taft-Hartley at the same political and ideological level as before. It was still unclear precisely how, if at all, Taft-Hartley had changed the collective bargaining core of the Wagner Act labor policy. Serious questions had arisen during these first months of Taft-Hartley, however, about congressional interference with the NLRB's administration of the act and the effect of the separation of functions on the work of the agency.

Despite the majority's denial that the Joint Committee had "sought to interfere with the independence or judgment of any agency,"[45] the minority recognized that the performance of the committee's statutory duties necessarily involved a close relationship between the committee and the NLRB with a great risk of "an unwarranted and unconstitutional intrusion in the fields preserved by our Constitution for the executive and judicial power."[46] The minority warned that "close and frequent contact with officials in the other two branches of the Government lends itself to such improper intrusion" and noted that the Joint Committee had held numerous conferences and had many informal contacts with officials of the National Labor Relations Board.[47] The minority limited itself, however, to pointing out the danger rather than charging that an improper intrusion had occurred.[48] Interference with the work of the NLRB meant that Congress or some other politically and economically powerful group would try to control the interpretation of the Taft-Hartley Act and the direction of the national labor policy rather than the administrative agency given that statutory responsibility. Such intrusions had occurred during the time of the Wagner Act and would pose a continuing danger to the NLRB under Taft-Hartley.

Neither the majority nor the minority chose to address the conflict that had occurred between the general counsel and the Board. While the minority remained silent on the subject, the majority provided only political pap: "Board members, the general counsel, and various employees on the staff of each, have expressed to the committee considerable satisfaction in the way the separation of the Board and increase in its membership has worked out in operation."[49]

Internal Conflict and External Pressure: The NLRB's Jurisdiction

Throughout the remainder of Taft-Hartley's first year the NLRB was plagued by internal conflict between the general counsel and the Board and improper interference by congressional committees (and Senator Taft) that seriously threatened the independence and impartiality of the agency's decision making. In that first year, with one minor exception, all the unfair labor practices decided by the Board were based on charges filed and complaints issued before the act became effective. The Board had decided no case that involved an alleged violation of Section 8(b), Taft-Hartley's list of union unfair labor practices.[50]

General Counsel Denham and Chairman Herzog challenged each other's power over the exercise of the NLRB's jurisdiction and, later, the enforcement of Board orders in the courts. Although Congress in the Wagner and Taft-Hartley acts had given the NLRB a jurisdiction coterminous with that of the federal government under the commerce clause of the Constitution,[51] the Board, from early in its history, had refused to hear certain cases within its jurisdiction if the enterprise involved had such a "remote" relationship to interstate commerce or was so predominantly local in character that to assert jurisdiction "would not effectuate the policies of the Act."[52] The Board made it clear that its refusal to act in these cases was an exercise of administrative discretion and was not due to a lack of authority.

Denham challenged the Board not only over its exercise of the agency's jurisdiction but also, more fundamentally, over which of them had the statutory authority to assert or reject jurisdiction. Denham claimed sole authority to decide whether a case affected interstate commerce and which complaints to process,[53] saying that his authority under the law covered every case affecting interstate commerce, no matter how small the effect.

While cases involving this issue were pending before the Board, the combined subcommittees of the House Committee on Expenditures in the Executive Departments and the House Labor Committee, in an extraordinary maneuver, called a hearing to consider a complaint made to the Committee on Expenditures that General Counsel Denham was about to issue an interpretation of the statutory term "affecting commerce"; for the first time since the Wagner Act, the term would include hotels, restaurants, taverns, and laundries.[54] Republican Clare Hoffman, chairman of the Expenditures Committee and long-time foe of the Wagner Act and the NLRB,[55] ran the hearing with five other congressmen, two appointed by him and three appointed by Fred Hartley, chairman of the House Labor Committee.[56]

At the outset of the hearing a representative of the American Hotel Association told the committee that members of the association had attended an informal conference in Denham's office during which they were told that the general counsel would assert jurisdiction over their industry.[57] What the representative of the association did not tell the committee publicly was that Herbert Brownell, former chairman of the Republican National Committee, attended that meeting to plead the hotel industry's case.[58] Brownell, who at the time of the meeting was general counsel of the American Hotel Association, had directed Thomas Dewey's successful 1942 gubernatorial campaign in New York and was one of Dewey's key patronage dispensers. He also managed Dewey's campaigns for president in 1944 and 1948 and would become attorney general of the United States in 1953 after serving as top adviser in Dwight Eisenhower's victorious presidential campaign in 1952.[59] It is reasonable to conclude that this powerful Republican was influential in getting the combined subcommittees of the House Labor and Expenditures committees to take up the matter. Denham appeared before the combined committee on May 7 and took the unwavering position that it was a "rare case in which business does not affect commerce in some degree, and when commerce is affected the Board has jurisdiction."[60] Those committee members who were the staunchest supporters of Taft-Hartley as a balanced law that promoted individual rights and industrial peace vigorously opposed Denham's plan to extend the law to its maximum reach. As one Republican congressman put it, "we did not want to expand this thing."[61]

Their target, ironically, was not Herzog's Board, with its majority of Democratic administration–appointed members (who advocated restraint in extending their jurisdiction), but Denham, their own labor "czar," who was supposed to be sympathetic to their political views. The committee lambasted Denham in its final report for acting contrary to the intent of Congress and Board precedent. In a unanimous and emotional conclusion the committee warned that under Denham's interpretation, the NLRB would have every business establishment in the United States within its power.[62] Possibly, the committee feared only the holdover Truman Board; more likely, it feared unionization and collective bargaining.

On May 17, 1949, ten days after the combined subcommittee's hearing and nine days before the Committee on Expenditures's report, the Board decided, in *A-1 Photo Service* and *Pereira Studio*,[63] that it, not the general counsel, had the final authority to decide whether or not to assert jurisdiction in unfair labor practice cases. Since Section 10(a) of Taft-Hartley empowered the Board to prevent any person from engaging in statutory unfair labor practices affecting commerce but did not direct the Board to exercise that power in *all* such cases, the Board inferred that Congress intended it to continue to have the discretionary power it exercised under the Wagner Act, a discretionary power that, after the separation of functions, could be exercised only by dismissing a complaint.[64] The Board's decision included a caustic dig at the general counsel:

Nothing in the Act or the legislative history indicates that Congress concluded that only the General Counsel had the wisdom to determine what would and what would not effectuate the statutory policy. It is clear that the General Counsel alone was to exercise discretion as to the issuance of complaints, but it is equally clear that the General Counsel's judgment was not to control the Board at the decisional stage of any proceeding. Separation of functions was evidently intended to bar judges from being 'prosecutors'; surely Congress was not seeking, by the same provision, to convert prosecutors into judges.[65]

Pressure from the Joint Committee on Labor-Management Relations

The Joint Committee on Labor-Management Relations reopened hearings on May 24, 1948. The committee considered various matters, including proposed amendments to eliminate union shop authorization elections (Section 9[e][1]).[66] Herzog and Denham united in favor of eliminating these elections,[67] which were needlessly consuming the NLRB's time. Not only had they grown to 70 percent of all types of cases filed with the agency's regional offices, but in over 98 percent of the elections in plants of fewer than one thousand employees (which was over 98 percent of the elections conducted), employees authorized their union representatives to negotiate union shop agreements.[68] Denham told the committee that if emancipation of individual union members from control by their union bosses "was the purpose of the Act, and obviously it was, it was based on a premise that did not exist."[69]

The primary purpose of the hearings, however, was to criticize the Board's first major case decisions interpreting Taft-Hartley. On April 12, 1948, the Board, with Gray dissenting, ruled that Inland Steel's refusal to bargain with the

United Steelworkers of America (CIO) concerning the company's retirement and pension policy was a violation of its statutory obligation to bargain in good faith with the representative of its employees concerning wages, hours, or working conditions.[70] The Board defined wages to include all "remuneration" or "emoluments of value, like pension and insurance benefits" that "accrue to employees out of their employment relationship." It defined "conditions of employment"—a broader phrase than "working conditions"—to include such matters as seniority, union security, discharge, and, in this case, the age at which workers were to be retired.[71]

Three days later Senator Ball, as chairman of the Joint Committee on Labor-Management Relations, announced that his committee would open hearings on May 24 to investigate, among other things (as Ball's stated agenda implied), the inadvisability of making pensions and insurance statutorily approved subjects of collective bargaining.[72] During the hearing an impressive array of management representatives whose companies had pension plans (including the president of Standard Oil of California and the chairman of the board of Quaker Oats, as well as the counsel for the National Association of Manufacturers) condemned the Board's decision for many reasons and called for an amendment to relieve employers of the legal obligation to bargain about employee benefit programs.[73]

Faced with this powerful opposition,[74] Herzog, rather than commit himself to the Board's decision, evaded the issue and tried to mollify the Joint Committee by emphasizing the Board's efforts to obtain early court review of the decision and conceding the possibility that it might not be sustained: "If Congress' intent has been incorrectly construed by the Board, I have no doubt that either the courts or Congress or both will not hesitate to tell us so."[75]

Another of the Board's most important early decisions received no attention from the Joint Committee, possibly because it was announced only two weeks before the hearings began or because it was one of the first major expansions of employers' rights under the free-speech provisions of the act. Before Taft-Hartley the Board held in *Clark Brothers Co., Inc.*[76] that compulsory attendance at company-sponsored anti-union meetings ("captive audience" speeches) was by itself, independent of the content of the speech delivered at such a meeting, an unfair labor practice.[77] Compulsory attendance, the Board reasoned, created a setting conducive to subtle coercion and the imposition of an employer's views on employees. On May 13, 1948, however, a unanimous Board in *Babcock & Wilcox Co.* rejected the *Clark Brothers* doctrine by asserting that the language of Section 8(c) of Taft-Hartley and its legislative history "made it clear that the doctrine of the Clark Brothers case no longer exists as a basis for finding unfair labor practices."[78]

The Board was severely criticized, however, for its ruling in *General Shoe*

Corp.,[79] another employer speech case, decided on April 16, 1948. Based in part on its conclusion that the new Section 8(c) applied only to unfair labor practice cases,[80] a Board majority (Herzog, Houston, and Murdock) rejected the proposition that only conduct declared unlawful by the act could be valid grounds for setting aside an NLRB representation election. The majority concluded, "Conduct that creates an atmosphere which renders improbable a free choice will sometimes warrant invalidating an election, even though that conduct may not constitute an unfair labor practice." This was particularly true, the majority said, in representation election proceedings, where it was the Board's duty "to provide a laboratory in which an experiment may be conducted, under conditions as nearly ideal as possible, to determine the uninhibited desires of the employees."[81] Although not constituting an unfair labor practice in the opinion of the majority, the employer's conduct in *General Shoe*—for two months before the scheduled representation election, vigorously disparaging the union in letters, pamphlets, leaflets, speeches in the plant, and visits to employees' homes—warranted setting aside the election because the employer's actions "created an atmosphere calculated to prevent a free and untrammeled choice by the employees."[82]

Joint Committee chairman Ball told Herzog he found it difficult to follow the majority's reasoning, because free speech applied primarily in election cases, and Congress intended to give employers the same freedom to say what they thought about unionization as unions always had with regard to management. Again, Herzog apologized and tried to placate the committee. He said he was "sorry the General Shoe decision came up in the context of Section 8(c)," because the "offensive thing in the General Shoe case was not what the employer said but what he did."[83] Herzog then took the extraordinary step of discussing the outcome of a pending case to reassure the Joint Committee that the reach of *General Shoe* would be limited.[84] Despite Herzog's downplaying of the significance of this decision, *General Shoe* has become Board doctrine in the more than forty years it has remained in effect.

Joint Committee criticism of certain decisions almost immediately after the Board issued them was clearly intended to influence the Board to abandon, reverse, or at least modify substantially interpretations of the act unacceptable to those who controlled the committee. Certainly a congressional oversight committee is entitled, even obligated, to review and evaluate the work of an administrative agency after a reasonable period of time and after substantial evidence about the agency's work and its effect becomes available. Here, however, the Joint Committee was stepping in almost concurrently with Board decisions on a case-by-case basis; that intrusion was more manipulation than informed review, analysis, and evaluation.

A Flagrant Abuse of Congressional Power:
The Meeting with Taft

The most egregious abuse of power by the Joint Committee occurred after the hearings ended in June 1948. The committee's most politically powerful member, Senator Taft, and its chief counsel, Thomas Shroyer, attempted personally to push Denham and his staff into a course of action desired by certain influential employers.

It began with another of Denham's informal conferences with an interested party. This time, according to Denham, shortly after August 22, 1947, when Taft-Hartley became law, "a group of men in the newspaper and printing industry called upon me" and reported that the International Typographical Union (ITU) would demand a continuation of the parties' closed-shop agreement, now unlawful under Taft-Hartley.[85] On September 22 Joint Committee chief counsel Shroyer addressed the Printing Industry of America convention, congratulated the participants because so many of their suggestions had been incorporated into the act, and assured them that the ITU would not "escape responsibility under the new law."[86] The next day, the general counsel filed the first complaint against a union under Taft-Hartley, accusing ITU No. 12 in Baltimore of refusing to bargain.[87]

One week before the NLRB's hearing in the Baltimore case began, Senator Ball, chairman of the Joint Committee, charged publicly that the ITU's proposals in its Baltimore negotiations were only "a very thinly veiled camouflage for the closed shop." He said that the Joint Committee would meet the next day with Denham and the Board members to discuss the ITU case.[88] Between August 22, 1947, and February 29, 1948, the NLRB brought eighteen separate suits against the ITU and its locals around the country.[89]

The ITU was popularly portrayed—in the words of Denham's old schoolfriend on the Senate Labor Committee, Forrest Donnell—as engaging "in defiance of Taft-Hartley on a national scale,"[90] whereas the ITU claimed that it was a victim of "union destroying" harassment and persecution by Denham.[91] Whatever the merits of these charges and countercharges, the dispute was widely discussed and subject to public scrutiny.

In response to charges filed by the American Newspaper Publishers Association, the general counsel's office on January 8, 1948, opened hearings in Chicago, where the ITU local had been on strike for almost seven weeks. A complaint was subsequently issued, and in late March a district court granted the general counsel's petition for a 10(j) injunction prohibiting the ITU, in part, from seeking to maintain closed-shop conditions.[92]

Senator Taft then intervened on behalf of certain powerful newspaper employers in a way that evoked a stinging rebuke from Truman, an admonition to the NLRB from the president, and thorough and pointed criticism from the press. In response to a request from Truman for a report about the incident, Associate General Counsel David Findling explained that he and Winthrop Johns, who was chief of the general counsel's District Court Injunction Section, went to Taft's office on July 28 "at the request of Senator Taft."[93] John Knight (publisher of the Knight chain of newspapers), the business manager of the *Chicago Tribune,* the editor of the *Chicago Sun,* and the counsel for the Hearst newspaper chain attended this meeting in the senator's office, along with Taft, Shroyer, Johns, and Findling. (Denham, who did not attend, was absent from his office from late June through late August because of illness.)[94]

Taft told the group that the ITU case was the Board's most important case because "it stood as a symbol to many members of the Congress and he believed, to the public, of the effectiveness of the enforcement machinery of the statute." He was "greatly disturbed," therefore, by reports that the injunction was being disobeyed by the ITU. He said that it was the government's responsibility to see to it that the injunction was obeyed. According to a subsequent newspaper account, Taft and Shroyer "suggested" to the NLRB representatives that the solution might be to amend the law to permit private organizations or individuals to obtain injunctions.[95]

Findling and Johns emphasized their responsibility to the public and to the court and promised to bring any violations of the injunction by the ITU to the court's attention. They explained that staff investigators had been sent "into various cities all over the country during the previous several weeks" to find out what was happening in negotiations between publishers and the union but had not completed their written reports.

Taft then reaffirmed his "keen interest" in the matter and added that the Joint Committee considered the ITU case "the most important proceeding that had arisen under the new Act." Taft left for another appointment, but the meeting continued "with the publishers discussing in great detail the present status of the negotiations in Chicago." The publishers told Findling and Johns that if the injunction decree did not prohibit all the conduct the employers considered unlawful, they wanted the general counsel "to enlarge the decree or institute another injunction proceeding."[96] Joint Committee chief counsel Shroyer was present throughout the meeting and repeated the committee's "interest in the situation in the newspaper industry." The meeting ended with the understanding on the part of Findling and Johns that after the NLRB investigators' reports were received, "we might wish to discuss the situation with the publishers' attorneys in Washington."

Truman, without mentioning Taft by name, found it "entirely improper" for any senator, regardless of "what his politics or his rank in the Senate may be," to try "to put the heat on one of the Executive Departments." The president also recalled telling the Board, after Taft-Hartley was passed, that it was part of the executive branch and that since he would not interfere in the agency's internal affairs, he expected it "to be immune to pressure from the Legislative Branch." Truman added, "I sincerely hope that the Counselors of the National Labor Relations Board will bear this admonition in mind in the transaction of public business."[97]

Truman and the press became aware of the meeting when the ITU passed a resolution at its August 1948 convention calling on the president to investigate charges that Taft had "summoned attorneys for Mr. Denham" to his office "to urge them to press contempt action against the ITU for alleged violation of an injunction." On August 23 Denham dismissed the ITU's accusations as "artificial smoke and no fire"; Taft, Denham said, was merely doing what many members of Congress do—inquiring about how the law was working.[98]

In September, Taft characterized Truman's statement as "merely an attempt to curry favor with the labor bosses who control the labor publicity to which he is looking for help in the election."[99] Several months later, in remarks made during a Senate Labor Committee hearing, Taft claimed that he had acted as any senator would in response to a constituent's complaint. In this explanation, newspaper chain owner Knight became merely John Knight of the *Akron Journal*. Taft said he did no more on this single constituent's behalf than ask the NLRB to look into Knight's complaint and take prompt action, in whatever way the NLRB decided was right. In the same hearing, Findling denied that the meeting with Taft in any way affected the general counsel's decision to initiate contempt proceedings against the ITU and to ask the court to prohibit the payment of strike benefits to ITU strikers in Chicago.[100]

Concluding Observations

The 1948 presidential elections were a little over two months away when the press learned of this incident, so some political exploitation by the Democrats and their supporters was inevitable. Truman, for example, quickly promised the ITU convention an immediate and thorough investigation of the union's "shocking charge," and the ITU called on the Republican nominee for president, Thomas E. Dewey, to "disavow the high-handed methods of Senator Taft."[101] But the defenses on Taft's behalf—that the act's opponents were "playing politics," that this was merely a routine inquiry on behalf of a constituent, or that protestations of innocence or imperviousness to pressure from even the most politically powerful should be accepted at face value—were inadequate in the face of uncontroverted facts and their unavoidable implications.

Taft was no ordinary senator; he was the leader of the Republican Party ("Mr. Republican"). He was also the major force behind the new labor law that bore his name and chairman of the Senate Labor Committee. As Republican senator Wayne Morse put it, an "inquiry" by Senator Taft did "not stand on the same footing as an inquiry by other Senators."[102] Taft's deprecating portrayal of himself as a mere servant of his constituents, obliged to assist them regardless of the merit of their claims, does not jibe with the reality of his power. These constituents, moreover, were not just some voters from Ohio but some of the most powerful and influential newspaper publishers in the country, only one of whom (although an important one) could claim an Ohio connection.

The setting for this meeting was not a neutral site or even an NLRB office but the offices of a powerful senator with powerful employers present. The *Washington Post* considered it at least an indiscretion to have held the meeting in Taft's office and "an obvious impropriety, the more gross" if Taft supported the publishers' complaint and tried to influence the general counsel's representatives to do the same in the presence of the publishers.[103] Despite the claim Taft made months after the meeting that he took no position on the merits of the publishers' request, Findling's written recollection of the event is more credible. It was made shortly after the meeting occurred, was detailed as to actions and statements, did not attempt to fix or shift blame or invent plausible explanations to excuse the NLRB participants, and was never directly contradicted or refuted by any of the participants. In fact, the candor of Findling's report to Truman was self-incriminating to the extent that it admitted at least a lack of prudence or sound judgment on the part of the general counsel's representatives for attending and participating in such a meeting.

The appearance of undue influence was increased by the presence of Shroyer, chief counsel of the congressional committee (of which Taft was a member) that had too intimately involved itself with the NLRB's administration of the act. Shroyer's emphasis during the meeting on the importance of this case to the Joint Committee only added to the pressure on the general counsel's representatives to act as directed.

Taft and Shroyer's attempt to influence the general counsel's handling of the ITU case was a direct and improper interference with the NLRB's decision-making process and seriously threatened the impartiality and independence that are essential if a quasi-judicial agency's judgments are to be respected. When, less than one month after the meeting with Taft, the general counsel initiated contempt procedures against the ITU and asked a court to stop the union's payment of strike benefits to its striking members in Chicago, it was inevitable, regardless of the merits of the NLRB's case, that the general counsel's decision would be attributed to Taft's improper political influence.

The meeting with Taft was the most flagrant example of the continuing efforts by politically powerful proponents of Taft-Hartley to ensure that the new law was administered in ways consistent with their objectives. The statutorily created Joint Committee on Labor-Management Relations became the most convenient means of asserting that political power in seemingly respectable ways. Closer examination revealed, however, that the Joint Committee was used to try to manipulate the NLRB to obtain certain preferred outcomes or to discourage the extension or encourage the abandonment of policies and case decisions unacceptable to those who controlled the committee.

Critics of the NLRB's administration of the Wagner Act had charged that organized labor, left-leaning liberals, and leftists improperly influenced the work of the Board. The passage of the new law did nothing to relieve the NLRB from such outside pressures. The shift in national political power simply meant that the pressure on the Board came from different political and ideological directions. The question after November 1948 was what would happen to Taft-Hartley and the NLRB's administration of the national labor policy after Truman's election victory, in which the Democrats not only retained the White House but also regained control of the House and Senate.

4

Repeal Taft-Hartley
A Tale of Missed Opportunities

The Great Political Upset

Public opinion polls taken before the 1948 Democratic convention showed that Truman's approval rating among the American people had dropped from approximately 70 percent immediately after Roosevelt's death to an all-time low of 32 percent.[1] In 1946, for the first time since 1930, the nation had voted the Republican Party into control of both houses of Congress: 51 Republicans and 45 Democrats in the Senate, and 246 Republicans and 188 Democrats in the House. Jubilant Republicans had interpreted the election as a repudiation of New Deal liberalism.[2] While the Republican Party appeared to be growing in strength, unity, and popularity, the Democratic Party was threatened with a disastrously divisive three-way split over civil rights, Henry Wallace's Progressive Party, and an Eisenhower-for-president boom within Democratic ranks.

Truman was the first twentieth-century U.S. president to commit his administration to a program to eliminate racial discrimination. Every Democratic party platform since 1932 had expressed dedication to the constitutional ideal of civil rights, but as Truman noted in his memoirs, "what aroused many Southerners now was that I meant to put this pledge into practice." Truman's position on civil rights led to the formation of the States' Rights Democrats, or Dixiecrats, who selected South Carolina governor Strom Thurmond as their presidential candidate.[3]

Although Truman's progressive stance on civil rights ensured the Democrats the black vote in the 1948 presidential election, the loss of the former "Solid South" appeared to be the difference between victory and defeat in November. Defeat appeared certain when Henry Wallace, former secretary of agriculture and commerce and vice-president during Roosevelt's third term, led a second defection of normally Democratic voters. Wallace's Progressive Party called for a more conciliatory approach to relations with the Soviet Union and appealed to leftists and many liberals in the Democratic Party who disapproved of Truman's cold-war pronouncements and position.[4]

Alarmed by Truman's dismal prospects for reelection, a third defection developed into a movement to draft Eisenhower and dump Truman. The press characterized Truman as mediocre and ineffective with almost no chance of success in the campaign. Eisenhower, a hero to Americans because of his accomplishments in World War II, eventually declined to be a candidate.[5]

Truman found the Democratic Party "dispirited and dejected" when he appeared on July 15, 1948, to accept the nomination at the party's national convention in Philadelphia. He decided, however, to make a fight for it and fashioned a strategy of attacking the Republican-controlled 80th Congress and taking his message "directly to the people in all parts of the country."[6] Truman electrified the convention by summoning the "do-nothing" Republican Congress back to Washington in a special session to give the Republicans an opportunity to enact much of what their own convention platform claimed they advocated. As Truman predicted, the special session produced nothing, adjourning after two fruitless weeks.[7]

Truman opened his presidential campaign with a Labor Day speech in Cadillac Square in Detroit, where, among other things, he called for repeal of the Taft-Hartley Act.[8] The president subsequently traveled about 31,700 miles and made exactly 356 speeches to "big crowds and small groups along the railroad junctions and stops from one end of the country to the other." The crowds, with shouts of "Give 'em hell, Harry," grew larger and larger and increased in enthusiasm, but the polls showed Republican candidate Thomas Dewey far ahead up to election day.[9] The final tally, however, gave Truman 24,105,695 votes to Dewey's 21,969,170. Truman carried twenty-eight states and Dewey sixteen; Strom Thurmond, candidate of the States' Rights Democrats, took four southern states from Truman. As Truman recalled, "On arriving at the White House [after the election], I had a Cabinet meeting and a series of conferences to plan immediate repeal of the Taft-Hartley Act, as promised in the campaign."[10]

A Mandate to Repeal Taft-Hartley: Political Rhetoric and Political Reality

Leaders of organized labor asserted immediately that Truman's election was a mandate to repeal the Taft-Hartley Act. Repeal had priority over other matters, they claimed, because Truman's victory was due in great part to labor's political strength.[11] Labor's contention appeared to receive the affirmation of the Truman administration when Secretary of Labor Maurice Tobin told a cheering

AFL convention that the election result was "a mandate for the positive and unequivocal repeal" of Taft-Hartley and promised that within thirty days after the new Congress convened, the administration would fulfill its campaign pledges to labor.[12]

The AFL and the CIO (without formal joint action) moved ahead quickly with a so-called two-package plan, the first package being an immediate repeal of the Taft-Hartley Act and simultaneous restoration of the 1935 Wagner Act without amendments, and the second package, possible amendments to the Wagner Act, to be offered at some undetermined future date.[13] William Green predicted confidently that the Taft-Hartley law could be "past history" by March 1, 1949.[14]

Political rhetoric aside, political reality did not justify such optimism. Although Truman carried the nation's largest thirteen cities, mostly in industrial states, Dewey took Michigan and all the industrial Northeast except Massachusetts and Rhode Island. It was the midwestern farm vote as well as ethnic and black voters who gave Truman the presidency. Many of the southern states that supported Truman also supported Taft-Hartley, and conservative coalitions, particularly of Republicans and southern Democrats, increased their power in Congress even after Truman's victory. Growing numbers of middle-class Americans, moreover, were content with the status quo.[15] They were unsympathetic to labor unions, whose strikes could disrupt a system in which they were prospering.

There was only a remote chance that the new Democrat-controlled Congress could produce enough votes to repeal Taft-Hartley. Two months before the election the director of the Democratic National Committee's Research Division reported to Truman counsel Clark Clifford that even under the most favorable assumptions there would be at least forty-nine votes (a majority) against repeal in the next Senate.[16] After the 1948 presidential election the Senate had 55 members who had voted for Taft-Hartley, and the House had 226 members who had voted for or favored the law in 1947 (8 more than the 218 needed for a majority).[17]

The Political Maneuvering Begins

Union leaders wanted prompt action to exploit the election euphoria and momentum while it lasted and to avoid drawn-out congressional hearings that would reduce their chances of success. Truman's White House advisers, however, had to decide whether the administration had the votes to put across labor's plan and whether it was wise political strategy to take the chance.[18] Taft and other supporters of Taft-Hartley expressed a determination to fight any attempt to repeal the act but a willingness to agree to "two or three" changes in the law.[19]

Truman began hedging on the question. He reconfirmed his desire to repeal Taft-Hartley but allowed "that in the legislative process some rewriting of the Wagner Act might be necessary since both statutes had got tangled."[20] The president favored what became known as the "one-package" approach: amending the Wagner Act *before* reenactment. In his meetings with leaders of the AFL and the CIO, however, he made no commitment on the Taft-Hartley issue.[21] Into late December Truman continued to meet with a group of advisers on labor problems, including NLRB chairman Herzog.[22]

Republican members of the Joint Committee on Labor-Management Relations moved quickly to counterattack the growing pro-repeal movement by issuing their final report (finding "the law to be working well") on December 31, 1948, eight weeks ahead of schedule.[23] Apparently, Truman's election shortened the time the committee needed for research.

Political maneuvering began in earnest in January 1949. The Truman administration, trying to avoid commitments to organized labor without alienating it, remained flexible on approaches to the Taft-Hartley repeal issue. Truman's State of the Union address on January 5, 1949, was sufficiently vague—calling for repeal of Taft-Hartley and reenactment of the Wagner Act with "certain improvements"—to allow for many interpretations. The AFL and the CIO, of course, saw Truman's comment as a pledge to amend the Wagner Act only after Taft-Hartley was repealed and the Wagner Act reenacted.[24] Other than Secretary of Labor Tobin, however, no one in the administration supported this approach.[25]

Union leaders eventually claimed that they were getting the "run-around" instead of repeal and demanded a record vote on Taft-Hartley to force members of Congress "to stand up and say where they stand."[26] What the unions feared was a prolonged debate on battlegrounds chosen by Senator Taft.[27] An AFL delegation led by William Hushing, the Federation's chief legislative agent, met with Elbert Thomas, new chairman of the Senate Labor Committee, and John Lesinski, House Labor Committee chairman, in a stormy closed-door session. According to reporters nearby, voices were raised, with one louder than the others protesting, "We went all over the country during the campaign ballyhooing repeal of the Taft-Hartley Law and that's what we want."[28]

The Administration's Senate Bill to Repeal Taft-Hartley

The Senate Labor Committee, reportedly under heavy pressure from organized labor for quick action, resolved (eight Democrats to five Republicans) to repeal

Taft-Hartley, restore the Wagner Act intact, and open hearings immediately on amendments to the Wagner Act.[29] When the administration's bill, which Herzog helped draft, turned out to be an already-amended Wagner Act, the Republican members of the Senate Labor Committee, especially Taft, justifiably derided the Democratic majority for trying to hide the fact that they had adopted the "one-package" approach so strongly opposed by the AFL and CIO.[30]

In an important departure from the Wagner Act, the Thomas bill[31] included union unfair labor practices such as engaging in certain types of "unjustifiable" secondary boycotts. In some ways the bill gave unions greater advantages, for example, by providing that no federal or state law could preclude an employer who was covered by the act from entering into a closed-shop agreement with a union. The bill authorized a Labor-Management Advisory Committee but substituted a panel of representatives of labor, management, and the public for Taft-Hartley's more politically manipulative Joint Committee on Labor-Management Relations, made up of Republican and Democratic senators. It also eliminated not only the noncommunist affidavit provision of Taft-Hartley but also the separate office of general counsel.[32]

Liberal Republicans constituted an especially important group of votes that could compensate for the conservative southern Democratic votes likely to be lost to the Republicans. Although Truman was conciliatory to those southern Democrats who fought his nomination, their conservatism remained undiminished, and most of the president's program, particularly civil rights, continued to be fundamentally unacceptable to them. With fifty-four Democrats and forty-two Republicans in the Senate, a defection of fourteen southern Democrats meant that the administration would need nine Republican votes to maintain a bare majority. In mid-February 1949, however, thirty-eight Republicans and fourteen southern Democrats were expected to vote for retention of at least the major provisions of Taft-Hartley—three more than a majority.[33]

Organized labor had no choice but to retreat from its position of demanding absolute repeal of Taft-Hartley and reinstatement of the Wagner Act.[34] Not only did the AFL Executive Council, for example, endorse the administration's bill with its amendments to the Wagner Act, but William Green suggested other amendments the Federation could support, such as the filing of noncommunist affidavits and financial reports, according employers the right of noncoercive speech, and guaranteeing to craft workers a separate unit in an industrial plant. The Federation was adamant, however, in its opposition to the injunction and made elimination of an injunction provision the indispensable condition for its support of the administration's bill.[35] At the same time, in an act of self-defeating stubbornness, the AFL Executive Council rejected CIO president Murray's offer to have the AFL and CIO coordinate their work on legislative matters.[36]

Organized labor had lost whatever strategic advantage it had gained immediately after Truman's great upset victory.

The Senate Labor Committee: An Opportunity Missed

Although Herzog told the Senate Labor Committee that it had "the greatest opportunity in American history to enact fair, rational and sensible [labor] legislation,"[37] the committee hearings failed as a means of providing lawmakers with evidence on which to base their decisions. In fairness to the committee, it should be noted that the NLRB's experience with actions arising under the Taft-Hartley Act was still very limited. At the time of Herzog's testimony on February 2, 1949, for example, the Board had issued only five decisions in cases involving the new union unfair labor practices; six other decisions had been made but not yet drafted.[38]

Much of the committee's time was spent in sometimes entertaining but legislatively useless high jinx such as bantering about whether Truman's election was a mandate to repeal Taft-Hartley;[39] Taft's pointed needling of William Green about how he and the AFL backed the Smith committee's attempt to amend the Wagner Act in 1940 and how many of those AFL-backed amendments were eventually incorporated into Taft-Hartley;[40] Senator Pepper's calling the National Association of Manufacturers (NAM) "a greater enemy to democracy than American labor will ever be" and pointing out the irony of having unions sign noncommunist affidavits while employers "convicted" by the LaFollette Committee of "the most heinous forms of brutality and atrocity . . . akin to fascism" were not required to sign any such affidavit;[41] Democratic Senator Matthew Neely's denouncement of Denham as a "little" Hitler;[42] Senator Murray's castigation of ex–Board member Reilly (who helped draft Taft-Hartley and was now a lobbyist-consultant to General Electric, General Motors, a coal company, and the printing industry) as an ex-liberal who had double-crossed labor;[43] and, after Herzog reported that no featherbedding case had reached the Board, Senators Humphrey and Murray's twitting of an NAM official about management featherbedding: "fancy dinners and parties," "exorbitant expense accounts," "cost-plus contracts," and "lush salaries" for boards of directors who rarely show up for meetings.[44]

Despite abundant political rhetoric about rights, moreover, the low point of the hearings occurred in the committee's treatment of representatives of various civil rights organizations who asked to testify. The committee decided to allot only five minutes to each of these men. Although Senator Wayne Morse said that he was on the board of trustees of the National Association for the Advancement of Colored People (NAACP) and wanted these civil rights leaders to testify, he astonishingly blamed "colored people" for "frequently making the mistake of being entirely too sensitive about these matters, seeing discrimination frequently when discrimination is not intended."[45]

Rather than plead guilty to oversensitivity, particularly after twenty-five futile years of asking Congress to pass even an antilynching law, the black leaders accused lawmakers of giving them the "run-around" on civil rights issues and claimed that African Americans were entitled to "more than a scrap thrown from the table at a Senate Committee hearing." They demanded that an "uncompromising civil rights plank" be written into the labor law and that the NLRB deny certification to any labor organization that denied full membership rights and privileges or segregated or otherwise discriminated against any employee because of race, religion, color, national origin, or ancestry—and not require any employer to bargain with such a labor organization. No one on the committee gave these proposals any significant consideration.[46]

Other matters were discussed seriously. Morse was very concerned, for example, that the NLRB might be subjected to political pressure from a congressional "watchdog committee" such as Taft-Hartley's Joint Committee on Labor-Management Relations, and wished to avoid even the appearance of such influence. When Herzog acknowledged some off-the-record discussion with the Joint Committee concerning the Board's case decisions, Morse warned that the danger was much greater in off-the-record meetings and claimed that, if he were in Herzog's position, he would quit rather than discuss a Board case decision with a watchdog committee.[47]

From the standpoint of potential legislative importance, however, the high point of the hearings occurred when Taft acknowledged defects in Taft-Hartley and expressed a willingness to rectify them by eliminating or modifying several important provisions in ways that made the law less onerous to organized labor. In response to Denham's comment that the mandatory Section 10(l) injunction was often embarrassingly like "hunting a field mouse with a 16 inch gun," Taft admitted that invoking mandatory injunctions only against certain union unfair labor practices was improperly "one-sided." He also volunteered that Section 10(l) injunctions should either be dropped from the statute or be expanded to apply to employer actions—for example, to maintain the status quo while certain employer unfair labor practices were being litigated—such as requiring the reinstatement of employees discharged allegedly for union activity. Taft insisted on retaining the discretionary injunction process in the law, however, and objected to the administration's bill because it eliminated all preliminary injunctions.[48]

Although Taft also rejected the administration's bill because it permitted secondary boycotts except for a few "unjustified" types, he was willing to allow secondary boycotts where struck employers farmed out work to other employers to perform and deliver to customers.[49] He also proposed to eliminate the union shop authorization election[50] and to repeal the Taft-Hartley provision denying economic strikers the opportunity to vote in subsequent representation elections whenever their employer hired permanent replacements while they were out on strike.[51] Although Taft said that he did not foresee the danger at the time Taft-Hartley was passed, he admitted that the provision could be used to break strikes and destroy unions.[52] Finally, he objected to the absence of any prohibition of featherbeddding in the administration bill but acknowledged the need to revise the ambiguous anti-featherbedding language in Taft-Hartley.[53]

Morse and Ives, encouraged by Taft's willingness to make concessions, began to fashion a compromise substitute to eliminate the "unfair features" of both Taft-Hartley and the administration's bill.[54] Taft told reporters, moreover, that he and his two Republican colleagues could agree "on perhaps all but two or three points."[55]

The Senate Labor Committee hearings ended on February 23, however, without any agreement on the contents of the bill the committee would send to the Senate. Without further amendment, prospects for the administration's bill were dismal.[56] In a major speech Truman threatened to stump the country to force Congress to enact his program, but AFL president William Green, recognizing the political realities, retreated even further from labor's original position by intimating a willingness to consider favorably the compromise measure being prepared by Morse and Ives.[57]

Despite these setbacks, Secretary of Labor Tobin persuaded the Democrats on the committee to report the administration's bill to the Senate on March 4 without any changes.[58] During the committee's acrimonious last session Taft and Morse proposed amendments but Chairman Thomas ruled them out of order. Although the Democratic majority defended its decision as necessary to fulfill the party's campaign pledge to organized labor, their refusal to amend the administration's bill in the committee actually guaranteed its defeat on the Senate floor.

Hearings and Debates In the House: Making Labor Policy without Evidence

On the House side a House labor subcommittee, headed by Democrat Augustine Kelley, on February 3, 1949, voted seven to five (along party lines) to report to the full House Labor Committee organized labor's "two-package" proposal to reenact the Wagner Act immediately without hearings and consider amendments later.[59] After Secretary of Labor Tobin (originally a "two-package" advocate) moved quickly to meet with Democratic members of the subcommittee, however, he told Truman that they would support the administration's bill and that a majority of the full House Labor Committee would report it with only minor amendments.[60] A combination of northern and southern Democrats and Republicans on the full committee rejected labor's "two-package" approach, sixteen to nine, and decided to begin committee hearings on March 8 on an administration bill sponsored by House Labor Committee chairman John Lesinski.[61]

Like the Senate hearings, the House Labor Committee hearings, from March 7 to 21, were useless as a source of evidence on which to base legislative proposals. The highlight of the hearings was the revelation by attorney Gerald Morgan, who as legislative counsel for the House had drafted the Smith committee amendments to the Wagner Act in 1940, that he had been paid by the Republican National Committee to draft the Hartley bill in 1947 and assist in the drafting of the final Taft-Hartley bill. He made this statement while denying charges that the NAM had dictated Taft-Hartley. Morgan, who was in the private practice of law at the time, said that he had the expert technical assistance of ex-Board member Gerard Reilly and Theodore Iserman, general counsel of the Chrysler Corporation.[62] As for the low point, once again civil rights leaders complained futilely of too little time to be heard and of being told "you are rocking the boat; don't raise these questions because they will destroy the legislation."[63]

On March 24, amid charges of "railroading" by the Republican minority, the full House Labor Committee voted thirteen to twelve to send an unchanged Lesinski bill to the House. Committee chairman Lesinski rejected all Republican attempts to amend the bill in committee, declaring, "I am taking my orders from the Administration."[64]

Their opponents were active. Labor Committee member Richard Nixon of California revealed that a coalition of Republicans and southern Democrats would submit its own bill on the House floor as a substitute for the Lesinski bill.[65] As originally drafted, the Wood bill (Democrat John Wood of Georgia was a Labor Committee member) incorporated the legislative recommendations made in the final report of the Joint Committee on Labor-Management Relations, including extending the reach of the noncommunist oath requirement within union organizations, adding a seventh union unfair labor practice (forcing an employer to violate Taft-Hartley or some other U.S. law), and applying Taft-Hartley's free-speech provision to representation as well as unfair labor practice cases to eliminate the NLRB's *General Shoe* doctrine.[66]

Conservative proponents of the Wood bill realized, however, what everyone involved in these legislative maneuverings had to know by then: neither a slightly revised Wagner Act nor a more severe Taft-Hartley bill had a chance at passage. Compromise was essential; the crucial question for the antagonists was how much. The Republican–southern Democrat coalition pursued a clever strategy on the House floor of diluting its own Wood bill to make it more palatable to "moderates" and less vulnerable to charges that it was merely the Taft-Hartley Act in disguise.[67] After meeting with Taft and Ives, the coalition softened its bill, which retained the use of the injunction in national emergency disputes, by making the 10(l) injunction discretionary rather than mandatory, narrowing the scope of the noncommunist affidavit requirement, preserving for ninety days the right of strikers to vote in representation elections even if they had been permanently replaced, and abolishing the union shop authorization election.[68]

The AFL's legislative program, moreover, was in a state of disarray. At an angry session of the Federation's National Legislative Council, some protested the failure of the Executive Council's special steering committee to give them guidance on AFL legislative policy on Capitol Hill. Speakers told the conference of eighty legislative agents that without guidance they did not know if any further amendments to the administration bill would be acceptable to the AFL. It was not clear, in fact, whether the Federation had a definite policy concerning amendments. Green, who chaired the steering committee, said that he would convene it in a few days and explained lamely that he had not called it up to then because a previous motion to do so was not "definite."[69]

Shortly after the House hearings opened on April 26, 1949, the AFL's steering committee met with Speaker of the House Sam Rayburn and Secretary Tobin to discuss legislative strategy. The AFL also arranged to have three hundred leaders of state federations of labor and central bodies "observe every vote of every House member from the visitors galleries and keep a tally 'for future use.' "[70]

AFL president Green and CIO general counsel Arthur Goldberg met with Secretary of Labor Tobin on April 27 in an effort to make the Thompson-Lesinski bills more acceptable to voters holding the middle ground. Later that same day, according to press reports, the administration and organized labor agreed to support five amendments to the Lesinski bill strengthening the national emergency strike section by permitting governmental seizure of plants while an emergency board studied the dispute, providing more explicit free-speech guarantees for employers, requiring a loyalty pledge by unions and employers renouncing all forms of totalitarianism and overthrow of the government, and making it an unfair labor practice for unions to refuse to bargain in good faith.[71]

The AFL, however, continued to demonstrate ineptness in coordinating its own legislative efforts. Only one day before the April 27 conference attended by Green, Goldberg, Tobin, and others, W. C. Hushing, chief legislative lobbyist for the Federation, spoke to Rayburn to verify rumors that the Speaker had asked Tobin to prepare amendments "applying the anti-commy affidavits to both labor and management, the free speech and a strengthened national emergency amendment." According to Hushing, he told Rayburn "that under no circumstances would we agree to accept the injunction."[72] That same day, Hushing asked Majority Leader John McCormack if he knew anything about the amendments Tobin was rumored to be preparing. It was only then that Hushing, the Federation's chief legislative lobbyist, learned from McCormack that the important conference involving the AFL and CIO and the Labor Department would be held the next day.[73] Bumbling of this sort helped lose the day for organized labor and the administration.

On April 29 the House overwhelmingly rejected (275–37) Congressman Vito Marcantonio's bill for straight repeal of Taft-Hartley and restoration of the Wagner Act.[74] At this point, support for the administration began to splinter. On May 2 Rayburn made it plain to Truman that the Lesinski bill had no chance unless it included Taft-Hartley's eighty-day national emergency dispute injunction so abhorrent to organized labor. After a subsequent conference with several Democratic leaders in the House, Rayburn announced the contents of a new bill, which he emphasized was not an administration bill and had "not been cleared with the White House." He added, "This is what I thought it should have been in the first place."[75] The new proposal, bearing the name of South Carolinian Hugo Sims, adopted the Taft-Hartley injunction provision for dealing with national emergency disputes and other changes, most of which had been agreed to in Tobin's meeting with Green, Goldberg, Harrison, and others on April 27 when possible amendments to the Lesinski bill were considered.[76]

The insistence on the Taft-Hartley injunction provision by Rayburn and some House Democrats pitted the president against the top House leadership.[77] It also split the Democrats on the House Labor Committee and cost the new bill the support of many of organized labor's most loyal supporters. When the Sims bill was introduced as a substitute for the Wood bill on May 3, however, Labor Committee chairman Lesinski unenthusiastically asked his committee "to stand by loyally and pass the Sims amendment. There is nothing else left to do."[78]

The Sims bill strategy also split organized labor. During the debate representatives of the United Mine Workers, Brotherhood of Railway Trainmen, and several leftist unions, such as the United Electrical Workers; Mine, Mill and Smelter Workers; Food, Tobacco and Agricultural Workers; and the International Longshoremen's and Warehousemen's Union, were calling congressmen off the floor and urging them to vote against the Sims bill. At the same time, representatives of the CIO, United Steelworkers, Textile Workers, and Auto

Workers were telling congressmen to vote for the Sims bill, as were the Teamsters. Several CIO union representatives, including those from the Rubber and Maritime unions, took no position. AFL representatives were divided.[79]

According to one report, Lew Hines, AFL legislative representative, "sat the fight out in the gallery because the AFL position was unclear."[80] When John L. Lewis criticized legislative agents of the AFL "for passing the word at the last minute to House members to put through the Sims bill," William Green claimed that some of the AFL lobbyists had "acted against orders" in backing the Sims measure.[81] Apparently, there was still no coordination between Green and his legislative lobbyists. Some Democrats, such as Kennedy, voted for the Sims substitute only because they were convinced that the Lesinski bill would be defeated by the Wood bill, which looked too much like Taft-Hartley; they believed that the Sims bill was the best compromise that could pass the House.[82]

Despite Rayburn's pleas, the House on May 3 rejected the Sims bill, 211 to 183. Then Republican and southern Democratic proponents of the Wood bill succeeded in voting in eight more amendments that "softened" their bill even further. Administration Democrats, demoralized, offered only dispirited opposition.[83] They realized that a majority in the House wanted a statutory injunction power in labor disputes affecting the national health and safety, as also evidenced by the House's rejection, 238 to 132, of an amendment to strike the Sims bill's injunction provision.[84]

The House then dealt a stunning blow to the administration by passing the amended Wood bill, 217 to 203. Voting for the bill were 146 Republicans and 71 Democrats; 180 Democrats, 22 Republicans, and 1 American Labor Party member voted against it.[85] Only a clever parliamentary maneuver by Congressman Marcantonio prevented final action on the Wood bill and gave the administration seventeen hours to obtain enough votes to recommit the bill. In a hairline 212 to 209 vote the House returned both the Wood and the Lesinski bills to the Labor Committee.[86] Ten southern Democrats who had voted for the Wood bill switched and supported the administration's efforts to recommit the bill.[87]

Although administration Democrats and the labor union supporters in the gallery were jubilant, congratulating themselves for killing the Wood bill, the result of the vote and of all the intricate political maneuvering since Truman was elected was that Taft-Hartley was still the law of the land.

Taft's Concessions: Another Opportunity Missed

On May 4, the same day the House voted for the Wood bill, Taft submitted to the Senate fifty amendments to the Thomas bill. Twenty-two of them were intended to retain the "best features" of Taft-Hartley in the new bill, and twenty-eight were meant to correct "some mistakes" in Taft-Hartley and respond to "reasonable criticisms" of the act by organized labor.[88] Many of Taft's proposed changes in Taft-Hartley were major concessions to organized labor and to Herzog and the Board.[89]

In general, these concessions were made by striking from Taft-Hartley some of the more severe Hartley bill provisions that had been added to Taft's original Senate bill as compromises during the 1947 conference committee negotiations.[90] Among other things, Taft proposed abolishing the office of independent general counsel, making the general counsel once again subject to the Board; permitting the Board to cede jurisdiction to state boards even when state law was not entirely consistent with federal law; eliminating the union shop authorization election; retaining the closed-shop prohibition but allowing employers to notify their unions of job vacancies and giving the unions an opportunity to refer qualified applicants; dropping the anti-featherbedding provision and the provisions requiring a separate union for plant guards and prohibiting the Board from reinstating an individual suspended or discharged for just cause; permitting employees on strike to vote in representation elections even if they were not entitled to reinstatement; increasing the statute of limitations on filing charges with the NLRB from six months to one year; repealing Section 10(l), which made it mandatory for the NLRB to seek temporary injunctions in certain cases (but retaining the NLRB's discretionary power to seek such injunctions against employer as well as union unfair labor practices); continuing the guarantee of free speech but eliminating the prohibition against the use of statements as evidence (and extending the new free-speech provision to representation elections); applying the noncommunist oath to employers and their officers and adding a nonfascist oath; and making major changes in the national emergency dispute provision.[91]

Even potentially more important from an overall labor policy perspective, Taft proposed to delete Taft-Hartley's addition to Section 7 making employees' right to refrain from unionization and collective bargaining as important as the right to join a labor organization and bargain collectively.[92] As already pointed out, the concept of government as a neutral guarantor of employee free choice between individual and collective action is inconsistent with the concept of government as partial to the practice of collective bargaining. Senator Elbert Thomas, speaking against Taft-Hartley during the Senate debates, asserted, for example, that the inclusion of the right-to-refrain provision in Taft-Hartley "can have no other effect than to give specific encouragement to individual bargaining, weaken unions, and discourage collective bargaining."[93] Since the right to refrain was one of the basic philosophical principles of Taft-Hartley, its removal from Section 7 could also have removed doubts about the law's intent to encourage collective bargaining.[94]

The CIO and AFL branded Taft's proposals unacceptable.[95] CIO general counsel Goldberg released to the press a sharply critical letter he had written to the chairmen of the Senate and House labor committees calling Taft's proposals "minor corrections" and "thin sugar coating" that "substantially reenacted the Taft-Hartley Act." Denying that the CIO was "maintaining an unrealistic attitude of utopian perfectionism," Goldberg reasserted the CIO's supposedly unalterable stance: Any amendment providing for injunctions in national emergency or other labor disputes was unacceptable.[96]

Debate began in the Senate on June 6, 1949. On the floor the arguments became so focused on the use of injunctions in national emergency disputes that the outcome of the entire labor legislation issue turned on the acceptance or rejection of the injunction. Democratic majority leader Scott Lucas surprised the Republicans by offering an amendment paralleling Taft's national emergency proposal, retaining the seizure provision but eliminating the injunction. After Lucas and other congressional leaders met with Truman, Lucas told reporters that Truman did not object to his amendment.[97] Senator Spessard Holland of Florida then proposed, as an amendment to the Thomas bill, Taft's national emergency injunction provision minus its seizure section. Consequently, the Senate was presented with a clear-cut choice on the injunction issue.

Four votes taken on June 28 resulted in a crushing defeat for the administration. Although Holland's pro-injunction, no-seizure amendment was defeated 54 to 37, so was Lucas's pro-seizure, no-injunction amendment—by a narrow margin of 46 to 44.[98] (If two senators who had favored the amendment had been present and voted, however, the stunning defeat would have been a major victory. In bitter irony, Senator Wagner, who was seriously ill, was one of the senators who did not vote, "though there were suggestions that his doctor be asked if he could not safely appear for this one tremendous moment so vital to the organized group he has always championed.")[99] The Senate also rejected, 51 to 40, Ives's amendment opposing both seizures and injunctions. In the decisive fourth vote, the Senate adopted, 50 to 40, Taft's amendment to the Thomas bill, giving the president both seizure and injunction power in dealing with national emergency disputes.[100]

Majority Leader Lucas then scheduled a vote on Taft's "omnibus bill," one part being the national emergency section just adopted and the other his proposed twenty-eight changes in Taft-Hartley. Organized labor threw in the towel as Green and CIO president Murray angrily denounced the Senate for approving Taft's injunction proposal and warned that they would campaign in the 1950 congressional elections "with all our energies" to defeat the "reactionaries" of both parties who kept the "threat of court injunctions hanging over labor's head."[101]

Taft ridiculed organized labor for taking an extraordinary position: "We do not want any improvements in the Taft-Hartley. We want everything or we want nothing." He observed sarcastically, "They apparently welcome the retention of every provision which they have criticized and propose to keep them in place for the next two years apparently in order that they may make an issue of that law two years from now in the election."[102]

All the labor bills subsequently died in the Senate and House labor committees, and Taft-Hartley remained in place. The administration abandoned its efforts, preferring to wait until after the 1950 congressional elections.[103] Calls were heard to "get" Taft at the polls in 1950; Truman made a Labor Day pledge to continue the fight until Taft-Hartley was repealed; the AFL continued to refuse to collaborate with the CIO; Tobin lamented the difficulties of working with a divided labor movement; and the press reported that former senator Ball (also former chairman of Taft-Hartley's Joint Committee on Labor Management Relations) was paid by General Motors and General Electric via ex-Board member Gerald Reilly as a lobbyist to help defeat administration efforts to repeal Taft-Hartley[104]—but these were only echoes of past legislative battles.

Concluding Observations

Although Taft's concessions and the other softening amendments to Taft-Hartley offered during the six-month debate on labor legislation fell short of restoring the Wagner Act, they constituted considerable movement in that direction.[105] Organized labor in 1949 rejected changes in the act that it would still be pleading for thirty years later. In the unsuccessful labor reform bills of 1978, for example, organized labor wanted (but did not get) Section 10(l) amended to add discriminatory discharges to those charges for which the general counsel was required to seek temporary injunctive relief. Other changes offered and rejected in 1949, such as permitting the Board to cede jurisdiction to states (elimination of the no-man's land) and giving economic strikers voting rights under certain circumstances even when they had been permanently replaced, were not obtained until the passage of the Taft-Hartley amendments in the Labor-Management Reporting and Disclosure Act of 1959.

From the perspective of long-term U.S. labor policy, however, the political obtuseness of organized labor and its supporters in the administration after Truman's election in 1948 is not the most regrettable aspect of the futile legislative maneuvering in the first six months of 1949. Most damaging was the missed opportunity to fashion a long-range national labor policy and practical statutory measures to deal with basic labor relations problems.

Congress, in dealing with the practical problems of labor relations in 1949, was never able to get beyond short-term manipulation for political advantage and support. The beauty of the Wagner Act was that almost every one of its provisions was rooted in the experience of two pre–Wagner Act labor boards whose personnel played major roles in writing the law. Congress made significant changes in the law in 1947, however, without conducting any thorough nonpolitical study of the experience of the NLRB or the workings of the country's labor relations; important new departures in labor policy were ratified in ignorance or emotion or simply as part of a political bargain. The legislative process in 1949 was no more informed by expertise and in-depth understanding of labor problems than was Taft-Hartley in 1947.

This point was made best (but fruitlessly) by Nathan Feinsinger of the University of Wisconsin before the Senate Labor Committee in 1949:

> If Congress is of the opinion that the claimed abuses at which the act is aimed, or other abuses, must be dealt with by legislation, I respectfully suggest that we must dig deeper than has been done to date.
>
> In legislating against boycotts, featherbedding, the closed shop and the like, we have dealt only with externals. Scratch the surface of some of these practices and you will find they reflect basic social and economic problems, as well as the problems of every day human relations, which, up to now, have been almost totally ignored or bypassed. For example, beneath the issue of featherbedding may lie problems of job security, including the sector of technological unemployment. . . . Beneath the issue of secondary boycotts may be the need for protection against unfair wage competition. And so on.[106]

Congress also missed the opportunity to remove the ambiguity from the national labor policy. That would have required a commitment to or rejection of unionization, collective bargaining, and a system of industrial self-government for workers and employers. Taft-Hartley's emphasis on an individual's right not to participate in that process raised serious doubts about just what the national labor policy was. Nevertheless, that fundamental question remained unanswered.

5

Taft-Hartley Was Here to Stay

One Agency—Two Labor Policies

Beginning in the earliest days of Taft-Hartley, evidence had been accumulating that the separation of powers between the Board and the general counsel was not working. From the hostile negotiations over the delegation agreement in 1947, the dispute over the scope of the noncommunist affidavit provision, and Denham's role in the ITU episode, to the ongoing power struggle over who had the authority to determine the NLRB's jurisdiction, the clashing of two powerful egos—Herzog and Denham—often obscured, or was used to obscure, the fundamental structural defects in the two-headed agency. It was easy to be distracted from deeper causes when, for example, the competition to be what Herzog termed "top fellow" degenerated into the "battle of the bathroom,"[1] with Herzog and Denham vying for the one office with a private bathroom, and the loser, Denham, spending taxpayers' money to regain equal status by adding a bathroom to his office.[2]

Conflicting personalities and flawed organizational structure interacted in the worst ways. The extreme separation of functions triggered a contest between Herzog and Denham for control of the agency, and their rivalry highlighted the most serious negative consequences of Taft-Hartley's unique scheme for segregating powers in the administration of the national labor policy. Labor and management, which were entitled to consistency and clarity in policy and in its interpretation and application, were confronted instead with contradictory policies within the same agency. This situation caused employers and unions to be confused about the rules by which they were to conduct their labor relations and led to otherwise unnecessary litigation to challenge or clarify conflicting policies and interpretations.[3]

The enforcement of policy as well as the making of policy was seriously impeded by Taft-Hartley's separation of powers. Despite his delegated role as enforcer of Board orders in the courts, the general counsel balked at seeking enforcement of Board decisions that were contrary to the position he had taken in his role as prosecutor of those cases before the Board: he considered it a personal embarrassment and an indignity for his staff to make any arguments before the courts that were contrary to the views he had advocated before the Board as prosecutor.[4] Thus the general counsel encouraged and even helped losing parties to appeal to the courts Board decisions with which he disagreed; one part of the agency, therefore, was encouraging a regulated party to litigate against another part of the same agency. On those and other occasions the general counsel proposed either to file his own separate briefs disagreeing with the Board's position or to express such disagreements in the briefs he filed on behalf of the Board.

The NLRB's own field staff, moreover, often received contradictory directions from the Board and general counsel, inevitably damaging efficiency and morale. The NLRB itself was subjected to public ridicule, thereby diminishing the public's respect for its authority and the public confidence any agency needs for effective law enforcement. Although Truman renewed his call for repeal of Taft-Hartley in his January 1950 State of the Union address,[5] in December 1949 his advisers tested organized labor's reactions to a much more limited legislative proposal: a governmental reorganization plan to abolish the independent office of NLRB general counsel and return the functions of that office to the Board. In their meeting with Charles Murphy, administrative assistant to the president, AFL legislative representatives H. C. Hushing and George Reilly acknowledged the importance of eliminating the office of general counsel, particularly because Denham so "closely represented the letter and the spirit of the Taft-Hartley Act." Nevertheless, as they reported to President Green, they told Murphy that the AFL was committed to repeal of Taft-Hartley "at one stroke" and would not accept "piecemeal legislation."[6] As usual, AFL officialdom seemed to be running in different directions, since Green was simultaneously admitting publicly that labor could not even hope for repeal of Taft-Hartley until after the 1950 congressional elections.[7]

The AFL's all-or-nothing approach to the repeal of Taft-Hartley had already caused the Federation to reject Senator Robert Taft's proposal to eliminate the office of independent general counsel, a proposal Taft called "perhaps the most important" in the series of amendments he offered several months after the conclusion of the Senate Labor Committee hearings in 1949.[8] That proposal, of course, was lost along with all the other changes advanced in the failed attempt to repeal Taft-Hartley. The inability of Congress to provide some legislative solution to the separation-of-powers problem allowed the internal battling to continue in the agency to the point where Denham, increasingly frustrated and desperate, began making public accusations against the Board, an action in the ritual of bureaucratic combat guaranteed to force a final resolution of some sort.

Denham Publicly Attacks the Board

Denham and the Board reached another impasse when the general counsel issued an unfair labor practice complaint in *Haleston Drug Stores* (involving a company over which the Board had previously refused to assert jurisdiction)[9] and the Board subsequently dismissed the complaint because the company "would have only a remote and insubstantial effect on interstate commerce."[10]

On December 8 Denham told the Board that it would be impossible for him to participate in the defense of the Board's order when Haleston Drug appealed the Board's decision to the Ninth Circuit Court of Appeals. Not only did Denham decline to be the Board's advocate in the court; he also chose to assist the company in its challenge to the Board's order.[11] As Herzog expressed it, Denham's support of the party attacking the Board's order put the "Government of the United States—indeed one agency of the United States—on both sides of the same case."[12] Denham told the Board that he did not care what it thought or did about the situation.[13]

Shortly thereafter, on January 12, 1950, Denham openly assailed the Board in a bitter and blunt speech to an association of employers. He charged that the Taft-Hartley Act had been sabotaged by most NLRB personnel, from Board members on down, "who were raised in the philosophy and I think I might say the religion" of the Wagner Act:

> When you have spent ten years or so saturated with the statutory and administrative theory that one segment of our economic society must be protected, no matter what, and that the offsetting segment of that society must be saddled with the blame for everything that happens, even though the actual offender may frequently be found in the protected group, that scheme of thinking and reacting is very hard to eradicate. Such eradication can only be accomplished by a firm determination to abandon it when the principle of the theory has been repudiated, as the Wagner Act and its administration was repudiated by the passage of the Taft-Hartley Act.[14]

Some of this reluctance to do a fair job of enforcing Taft-Hartley, Denham told the employer group, stemmed from an expectation in the "present political climate" that Taft-Hartley would be repealed and his own office abolished.[15] Denham also made it seem as if the Board's repudiations of his interpretations of the act were deliberately intended to restrict the application to unions of the law's unfair labor practices.[16] As he was doing himself in *Haleston Drug* and other cases, Denham urged employers to challenge adverse NLRB decisions in the courts.[17]

Throughout his speech Denham never tried to conceal his devotion to Taft-Hartley or his disdain for the Wagner Act. In his opinion the Wagner Act put employers "constantly on the defensive" but left them powerless against many injustices, such as boycotts by "racketeers and unconscionable labor leaders" and economic penalties for refusing to agree with or make concessions to a union; at the same time, employers were prohibited from even expressing an opinion about the "qualifications or character" of the unions seeking employee support.[18] After eighteen months of administering the law Denham could still attest to the Senate Labor Committee, "I believe in the Taft-Hartley Act." Senator Wayne Morse was "simply aghast" when Denham testified that he could not identify a single provision of the law that had "injured labor unjustly" or "had done something to labor which labor did not have coming to it."[19]

Denham's own dealings with the NLRB Union revealed an authoritarian attitude intolerant of collective bargaining. When representatives of the agency's union first approached the new general counsel to complain that he had violated a long-standing procedure negotiated with the Wagner Act Board for posting vacant positions, Denham railed: "Let's get this straight; I'll agree to nothing; there is no place for agreements in the Federal service; it's not in the cards. Promotion and appointment are management's prerogatives, and I don't propose, nor will I permit any of my subordinates to agree to anything. I want the best people in the jobs; that's my responsibility. . . . I am the best judge of who is qualified. When I make a decision, I am not going to change it; I haven't made any mistakes. I shall not hear grievances on it."[20] When the NLRB Union representative reminded Denham that for many years the Board had considered employer bargaining positions such as Denham's an unfair labor practice, the general counsel replied, "That was under the Wagner Act; this is under Taft-Hartley." He later stated with pride that he had abolished that "extraordinary" contract with the NLRB Union.[21]

Reorganization Plan No. 12: Politics and Administration

After more than two years of intra-agency strife and Denham's public attack, the Board, on February 24, 1950—without Denham's concurrence—amended the 1947 Delegation Agreement to require the general counsel to act in full accordance with the directions of the Board in petitioning for the enforcement of its orders and prosecuting appeals and to return to the Board final authority over many important regional personnel matters, including appointments.[22] Around the same time, Herzog initiated closer contact with the White House. On March 1, 1950, for example, he sent a copy of the Board's revised Delegation Agreement to the president's confidential secretary, Matthew Connelly, because it was "quite possible that this action will precipitate further issues." Herzog attached a copy of a *Washington Post* editorial supporting the Board's action and asked Connelly "to call these documents to the personal attention of the President."[23]

In fact, months before Denham's open break with the Board, the administration was discussing strategies to force his resignation or fire him. Stephen J. Spingarn, special assistant to the president, complained to Truman's counsel, Clark Clifford, that while it was one thing for Denham to favor Taft-Hartley, it was intolerable "for him to go out on the stump and propagandize for the continuation of the Act in direct opposition to the President's and the Administration's oft-enunciated position." Spingarn speculated that Denham's departure might help offset the failure to repeal Taft-Hartley, although CIO president Murray's public demands that Truman remove Denham for helping employers destroy free unions made such a step politically costly. Spingarn recommended another course of action: "Issuance of a Reorganization Plan next session abolishing the office of NLRB General Counsel and transferring its functions back to the Board where they were under the Wagner Act."[24]

On March 13, 1950, Truman sent Congress twenty-one reorganization plans affecting the Departments of Agriculture, Commerce, Interior, Justice, Labor, and the Treasury, as well as administrative agencies such as the Interstate Commerce Commission, Federal Trade Commission, Securities and Exchange Commission, and the NLRB.[25] Reorganization Plan No. 12, which concerned the NLRB, abolished the office of general counsel and transferred all its functions to the Board.[26] Truman's reorganization program, designed to achieve greater efficiency and economy in the federal government, was based in great part on the work of the Commission on Organization of the Executive Branch of the Government, chaired by former president Herbert Hoover. The Hoover Commission's Task Force on Regulatory Commissions completed its report on the NLRB in January 1949.[27]

Although indefinite concerning the changes it said were needed in the Board–general counsel arrangement, the task force's report was a thoughtful and useful analysis of the relationship between the NLRB's administrative structure and the performance of its functions, particularly the making of labor policy. Because of the natural and inevitable connection between organizational structure and policy making, however, the task force felt itself hamstrung in fashioning specific administrative recommendations by the "wide divergence of opinion" about what the underlying labor relations policy should be. The report made specific proposals to help resolve the serious problem of delay in NLRB case processing, but unfortunately, Reorganization Plan No. 12 did not even mention the problem.[28]

Most important, the task force recognized that the general counsel was not only a prosecutor and administrator but also a policy maker who could formulate authoritative interpretations of the act or even engage in a form of rule making by refusing to issue complaints in unfair labor practice cases.[29] The general counsel, moreover, made policy independent of both the federal government's departmental structure and the Board—a power unique among administrative agencies. The arrangement displeased the task force because it could lead to "diffusion of responsibility" if applied to other government agencies.[30]

This concentration of wide powers in one official inevitably subjected the general counsel "to heavy pressure from all sides," and his "lack of protection [from] either a multiheaded agency or an executive department" left him, in the task force's opinion, "particularly exposed" and vulnerable to that pressure. Using the general counsel's relationship with the Joint Committee on Labor-Management Relations as an example, the task force observed in diplomatic language, "To the extent this has involved advice and suggestions with respect to interpretation of the Act and its application to specific situations, the practice seems doubtful and likely to blur the desirable separation between the legislature and administration."[31]

It was clear when the House and Senate committees on expenditures began their hearings on Reorganization Plan No. 12 in March and April 1950 that Congress, by approving the hastily negotiated separation-of-functions compromise in 1947, had unwittingly given the general counsel the power to make policy, thereby allowing the NLRB to pursue conflicting labor policies. It was also obvious from the testimony of Herzog and Denham during these hearings that the worst was happening; yet, once again, political considerations dominated.[32] After the resounding defeat of the repeal–Taft-Hartley forces in the previous session, Congress was no longer seriously interested in changing the labor relations law.

Taft's negative attitude and reaction to Reorganization Plan No. 12—a rearrangement fundamentally identical to his own 1949 amendment abolishing the office of general counsel and returning its functions to the Board—characterized the frivolous and evasive nature of the hearings and subsequent congressional debates on the reorganization proposal. Pressed to explain how he could now oppose Reorganization Plan No. 12, Taft said that he had offered his amendment with a "great deal of reluctance" and had "agreed to some things I did not particularly care to agree to" only to gain the support of Republican moderates for the rest of his proposed amendments.[33] His 1949 amendment was imperfect, he added, because "we did not have time last year to work the matter out properly." Now free of any political pressure to offer compromises, Taft twitted the "labor people" who had killed his bill: "If they are willing to take the whole bill with all the other things in it, I think I might be willing even to make the compromise I made last year."[34]

On the counterattack, Taft created unjustified apprehension by claiming, erroneously, that by placing the decision to prosecute entirely in the jurisdiction of the chairman, Reorganization Plan No. 12 made Herzog "an infinitely more powerful figure than the general counsel has ever been."[35] Herzog called this a "misconception," but his and other protests that the Board chairman would be assigned only the general counsel's administrative control over personnel, whereas all investigatory, prosecutory, and policy making would be transferred to the full Board, although correct, were to no avail.[36]

Taft also demeaned Reorganization Plan No. 12 as an administration device to oust Denham because he was "friendly to management."[37] Management attorney Theodore Iserman charged, for example, that the supporters of Plan No. 12 wanted to replace Denham with someone who was "prejudiced against employers in favor of unions."[38] The representatives of organized labor who testified in support of the president's plan, such as Arthur Goldberg, actually reinforced the opposition's charges by emphasizing Denham's "vicious anti-labor administration" and how much they wanted to remove the general counsel from office.[39] Although the administration and the Board wanted Denham out and Herzog's and Denham's intense mutual dislike exacerbated some problems and caused others, shifting the focus of discussion to personalities and ideologies left unresolved the fundamental policy-making and administrative problems caused by the separation of powers.

Similarly, opponents of the reorganization plan maintained that it was designed for political purposes as part of what Taft called a general scheme to nullify Taft-Hartley. Taft claimed that Herzog and the Board had "no sympathy" with the act—while admitting that he had not kept abreast of Board decisions since Taft-Hartley was passed. He also lamented Truman's decision not to reappoint Copeland Gray, "a Board member who recognized the problems of management," and to make CIO and AFL approval a condition of employment for Gray's successor.[40]

The administration, in choosing a replacement for Gray, the "strongest pro-management member of the Board," knew that any plan to return the general counsel's functions to the Board would be jeopardized by an appointment vulnerable to the charge that the Board was "being set up with a stronger labor bias."[41] Truman's choice, Paul L. Styles, NLRB regional director in Atlanta,[42] was considered a "middle-roader" in the business press, and although he had strong backing from organized labor ("more AFL than CIO"),[43] even Taft considered it a fair appointment.[44] (At least in part, Gray was not reappointed because he was in poor health and was losing his eyesight. Herzog remembered Gray as a "terribly sweet, nice man, strongly pro-employer; a saintly creature [but] the job was too much for him.")[45]

Congress gave no serious consideration to the Hoover Task Force's extensive indictments of the NLRB's divided administrative structure,[46] even though Taft admitted that Taft-Hartley's separation-of-powers provision, adopted as a legislative compromise with the House, was "somewhat ambiguous," "a little vague," and "ought to be revised."[47] Reorganization Plan No. 12 was ill-fated even before Republican congressman Ralph Church of Illinois died while attacking it as the House Expenditures Committee's first witness.[48] Despite a direct appeal by Truman to terminate the "two-headed freak,"[49] the Senate on May 11, 1950, voted fifty-three to thirty to reject the administration's plan to reorganize the NLRB.[50] Eighteen Democrats, all but one from southern or border states, voted with thirty-five Republicans to defeat reorganization. Once again, Congress chose to leave a flawed statutory policy in place.

Bureaucratic In-Fighting and White House Politics

The same week the Senate defeated Truman's NLRB reorganization plan, the Fifth Circuit Court of Appeals, in *Postex Cotton Mills*,[51] reversed the NLRB and upheld Denham's contention that officers of the AFL and the CIO had to sign Taft-Hartley's noncommunist affidavit in order for their affiliated national and international unions to have access to the NLRB. Denham considered the Senate reorganization vote and the *Postex* decision personal victories and vindication of his—not the Board's—interpretation and administration of the act.[52]

Denham may have felt sufficiently confident to move quickly to force a showdown with Herzog, but it was inevitable that one or both would have to leave the NLRB. Denham had survived the legislative battles, but he was outmatched when pitted against Herzog in bureaucratic in-fighting. As a special assistant in the White House put it, Herzog waged his battle with "extraordinary subtlety," "watching and waiting for bigger and better errors by Denham," using "restraint," "proper erudition," "protective camouflage," "the public handshake, the smile, and the knife so fast you are never aware of it until the severed head rolls."[53]

During this period Denham and Herzog were engaging in a memorandum war, sending copies of their written exchanges to the White House with neither telling the other that it was being done.[54] On May 22 the Board agreed to meet with Denham without any written statement of his position.[55] That same day, Denham walked from his office to the other end of a long corridor for a two-hour meeting with Herzog and the Board, prompting one Board member to quip: "He met us more than halfway."[56] It was not a meeting of open minds. Before seeing Denham, Herzog informed the Board members of his meeting earlier that same day with Truman and of the "President's plans concerning Mr. Denham." Herzog reported Truman's instruction to him: "that while we should endeavor to cooperate with the General Counsel for the good of the Agency, we should not 'recede an inch' under any circumstances on any matter upon which the Board had already taken a position."[57] An instruction from the president to stand fast was not likely to encourage concessions in negotiations.

According to Herzog's notes of the Board's meeting with the general counsel, Denham asked the Board to rescind its February 1950 amendments to the 1947 Delegation Agreement. He recommended a joint study of Board policies "for the purpose of bringing Board policy more in conformity with the statute," a statement Herzog interpreted as meaning that the Board should reexamine and modify those decisions with which Denham disagreed. The exchanges became heated when the general counsel accused the Board of "pro-labor" interpretations of the act and of being unduly influenced by the 1948 presidential election. In turn, the Board members strongly objected to the general counsel's public attacks on their integrity and objectivity as well as their decisions.[58] In the May 1950 issue of *Factory Management and Maintenance,* for example, Denham had disparaged Reorganization Plan No. 12 as a "flank attack" in a plan to abolish his office and charged that the Board had deliberately nullified Taft-Hartley's intent by applying a liberal philosophy that had serious implications for the integrity of the national labor policy.[59] The meeting degenerated into an exchange of "vituperative criticism."[60]

While the Board waited for Denham's next move, Herzog told Truman that he wanted to leave the Board: "Five years on this job are enough."[61] A year earlier Herzog had lobbied for an appointment to the Court of Appeals for the District of Columbia but withdrew when a district court judgeship was proposed instead.[62] Herzog met again with Truman. When Truman asked him to stay on for another five-year term as chairman, Herzog said he would "only do it, if he [Truman] fired Denham. And he did."[63] On July 24, 1950, Truman, citing the need for his help during the Korean crisis, made Herzog's reappointment official.[64] When the reappointed Herzog was asked about Denham's term, the Board chairman replied disingenuously, "It runs another year and a half, but that's got nothing to with this."[65] All that remained was the formal and public firing of Denham when a justifiable nonpolitical reason arose.

The Confrontation over Enforcement of Board Orders

Denham provided the Board and the White House with the opportunity they needed. In mid-July the Board learned that the general counsel had instructed Associate General Counsel David Findling, over Findling's protests, to make "drastic changes" in an appeal brief in the *Vulcan Forging* case[66] and not to inform the Board or its solicitor, Ida Klaus. Klaus had approved the original brief on behalf of the Board, but Denham told Findling that "it would be time enough for the Board to learn about it when the brief was submitted to the court." (Findling had prepared a memorandum to the Board explaining the general counsel's reasons for altering the brief, but Denham ordered him not to send it.) After the Board told Findling to withhold Denham's brief until it was "rewritten in conformity with the original draft," Denham instructed him to file the brief "regardless of the Board's direction."[67]

Denham gave the Board a choice: Do it his way or end the enforcement proceedings in *Vulcan Forging*.[68] Meanwhile, Herzog was relaying the associated exchanges of memoranda to presidential assistant Charles Murphy. On July 21 Herzog alerted Murphy "that the gauntlet has definitely been thrown down" and asked him to "keep me [Herzog] advised how things are developing on this problem at your end."[69]

On July 31, 1950, Denham filed the *Vulcan Forging* brief with the Sixth Circuit Court of Appeals exactly as he had amended it over Board objections.[70] This action forced the Board into the embarrassing position of bringing its argument with the general counsel to the court and charging publicly, through a motion filed by Solicitor Klaus, that the brief filed by the general counsel was "in fact not the brief of the National Labor Relations Board" and was filed "in contravention of the Board's specific instructions not to file such document as the brief of the Board." The Board asked the Sixth Circuit to reject Denham's document and accept the Board's brief.[71]

Herzog and Denham Play the White House against Each Other

Denham, who did not yet know his fate had been sealed, matched Herzog's efforts to lobby the White House. In an August 8 memorandum to presidential adviser John Steelman, the general counsel offered to make the Enforcement Division an "arm of the Board" rather than part of his staff. This move would allow the Board to make whatever presentation it wanted to the courts, freeing the general counsel to assert his own position before the courts in cases in which he had been reversed by the Board.[72] Denham told Steelman that only White House intervention could end the conflict.[73]

White House advisers suspected a "booby trap" that would make the administration a party to a deal that would further embarrass the Board and favor Denham.[74] They had already concluded, moreover, that there was no solution short of Denham's removal: Denham had to go because of his public attacks on the Board and the administration, his private and public encouragement of litigants to appeal Board decisions, and his appearances in court to contest Board decisions with which he did not agree.[75] Steelman's staff considered Denham's proposal a diversionary tactic "masterminded" by Taft-Hartley proponents, "in order to provide a base for claims later that Mr. Denham made 'constructive' proposals for ameliorating the situation, but they were ignored by the White House."[76] The advisers concluded that Denham's "concern over whether he will be fired has led him to make appearances of friendly, reasonable overtures. No one ought to be deluded by this maneuver."[77]

Herzog, concerned about White House inaction, pressed the matter with Murphy, who in an earlier conversation with Herzog had suggested "sicking" the Senate Labor Committee on Denham. Herzog told Murphy that his plan, not discussed with his Board colleagues, would give Denham "a soap box of official character from which to vent his spleen" so that his "later removal would appear to flow from evidence of his pro-Act and pro-employer bias, rather than from his impossible administrative attitudes."[78] Herzog also forwarded to Murphy a copy of former Republican senator Joseph Ball's *Washington Letter* of August 12, 1950, as an example of the "stuff" Denham was "feeding Joe Ball." According to Ball, the present intrigue in the campaign to get Denham fired was the work of Herzog and Solicitor Ida Klaus, "a niece of ILGWU [International Ladies' Garment Workers Union] President, David Dubinsky." Concerned that the president was about to move, Ball cleverly raised the possibility that Denham "might fight a dismissal in court and the precedents as to presidential powers in such an instance are not completely clear." In an effort to generate support for Denham, Ball disparaged the general counsel's rumored successor, Ivar Peterson, "a former CIO employee now on the staff of pro-union Senator Wayne Morse of Oregon." Ball said that Peterson would "sabotage completely" congressional intent in enacting Taft-Hartley.[79]

In a September 15 letter the five Board members told Truman, "We can wait no longer to bring the matter to your attention."[80] That same day, Denham was called to the White House and given an opportunity to resign. Denham claimed that he was "summarily fired." He recalled that there was "comic haste" about his removal: "The President accepted it [his September 15, 1950, resignation] within a few hours, to take effect two days later. As my successor was not appointed for ten days after I left, it was obvious that the hurry was not to get somebody else in, but to get me out."[81]

Denham did not go gracefully. Within days of his resignation he claimed in a radio interview that he had been asked to resign for administering Taft-Hartley as it was written and Congress intended. He called Herzog a "Wagner Act man," accused Houston and Reynolds of succumbing to the pressures of labor organizations, called Styles "labor's representative on the Board," charged the Board with engaging in a "process of repeal by decisional attrition," and warned that his departure left the NLRB in control of those completely sympathetic to the Truman administration's attitude toward organized labor. He also cautioned that "the country ought to look out" if the "sweeping and exclusive" powers of the general counsel's office were used in a "lop-sided fashion."[82]

The *Washington Post* considered Denham's firing, just before the November 1950 congressional election, "an obvious pay-off to Philip Murray, William Green, and other union leaders for their political support"—although only a "partial payment," since Truman was unable to deliver on his promise to repeal Taft-Hartley.[83] In a bitter and accusatory article in the widely read *Saturday Evening Post,* Denham maintained that there was a connection between Truman's meeting with some fifty officials of the AFL and CIO at a dinner "behind closed doors" and Denham's dismissal one week later. Like Taft, Denham saw his removal as a payoff and "another surrender" to the CIO Political Action Committee. He told all in great detail: his abuse by a "Wagnerian" Board and an anti–Taft-Hartley administration, his confrontation with the NLRB union, the noncommunist affidavit issue, the ITU incident, the "Battle of the Bathroom," the campaigns to repeal Taft-Hartley and institute Reorganization Plan No. 12, his futile attempts to establish "peace" with the Board, and his unfair dismissal ("nothing less than my head would satisfy him [Herzog]").[84]

After recounting his personal travails, Denham turned selfless and, portraying himself as "Horatius at the Bridge," feared for the country now that the NLRB had been "captured by a crew who apparently intended to operate it without heed to the orders of Congress—to substitute government by men for government by laws." He called for a general counsel and an entire Board that believed in Taft-Hartley.[85]

Concluding Observations

After three years U.S. labor policy as expressed in Taft-Hartley was still unclear, in great part because of public disagreement between the general counsel and the members of the Board over the meaning and intent of the statute. Their conflicting interpretations of the law and congressional intent caused confusion and uncertainty and additional litigation for employers and union officials, who did not know which policy would prevail—whether the general counsel would be overruled by the Board, which side the courts would uphold, or even if the provisions of the law would be applied to them. Increasingly, NLRB employees were put in the administrative predicament of receiving contradictory instructions from the general counsel, who supervised them, and the Board, which claimed ultimate authority to direct them.

The separation of functions at the NLRB was neither successful nor worthwhile. It was a fundamental flaw in policy established in the first place as a political compromise with no empirical evidence to justify it. Neither the House proponents of total separation nor the senators who supported the compromise that became part of Taft-Hartley presented a single incident of unfairness, bias, or prejudice caused by the NLRB's internal separation of functions developed under the Wagner Act.[86] The separation of functions was inspired not by evidence but by distrust of the Wagner Act NLRB, a desire to check its alleged one-sidedness and strip it of much of its power, and an antipathy to the entire administrative process.

As Ida Klaus pointed out many years ago, the price paid for the hasty reconciliation in 1947 between the House and Senate conferees was "vague language and difficult and impractical operating and structural machinery." Although Klaus was not a disinterested observer, even Senator Taft, in rejecting Reorganization Plan No. 12, acknowledged the inherent defect in the statutory separation. Because the potential for conflict was built into this statutory scheme, its workability would always be dependent on the spirit of cooperation between the general counsel and the Board. As Klaus put it, "When and where conflict may erupt will depend upon the personnel and policies of the future."[87]

In 1947 the flawed separation-of-functions provision was written into law for unsubstantiated ideological reasons as part of a political deal. In 1950, despite conclusive evidence that the statutory separation was seriously undermining the definition and implementation of labor policy, Congress, for political reasons, chose not to remedy that defect. Congress's record in dealing with labor policy was unimpressive, raising serious doubts about its ability to make and change labor laws on the basis of expertise, evidence, and observation of real-world labor relations experience rather than ideologically inspired emotion, uninformed and unsubstantiated beliefs, and political maneuverings.

The two years after Truman's stunning election upset also demonstrated the weaknesses in organized labor's political power (and political astuteness). Labor's postelection political offensive, which began with the repeal of Taft-Hartley as its objective, ended with nothing but the firing of Robert Denham. The political power of labor unions had been overstated. Taft-Hartley was here to stay.

6

Bargaining National Labor Policy
A Misguided Process

The New General Counsel

Truman appointed George Bott to replace Robert Denham as general counsel of the NLRB. In sharp contrast to the flamboyant and combative Denham, Bott was a quiet, humorous, unpretentious man who got along with everyone and maintained such a low profile that when his appointment was announced, neither Washington reporters nor NLRB publicists could find pictures of him, newspaper clippings about him, or speeches to indicate his views on the act.[1] Before becoming associate general counsel, the forty-year-old agency career man had worked up through the ranks as an attorney in the Detroit regional office, a litigation attorney in Washington, and regional director in Kansas City and Chicago. This experience made him exceptionally well qualified to supervise the NLRB's regional offices, where charges filed, complaints are issued, election petitions processed, and cases tried.[2]

Some employers, echoing Denham, feared that Bott, who began with the Wagner Act NLRB in 1937, was "indoctrinated in the pro-labor philosophy of the Wagner Act" and would give unions the "benefit of the doubt whenever there is one."[3] Organized labor had favored the appointment of Ivar Peterson, an aide to Senator Wayne Morse, but welcomed Bott as one who would end the "harassment" of Denham's antilabor interpretation of Taft-Hartley.[4] Publicly, Bott said only that Taft-Hartley was the law of the land and that he would administer it to the best of his ability.[5]

Bott and the Board moved quickly to reunify NLRB policy where there had been conflict between Denham and the Board over appeals, regional personnel, and jurisdiction. The reconciliation, although amiable, occurred mainly on Board terms. Under a new Delegation Agreement between the general counsel and the Board, for example, Bott agreed that, before filing with an appellate court, the general counsel would submit the written brief to the Board for its approval. The general counsel also agreed to obtain Board approval for the appointment, transfer, demotion, or discharge of any regional director.[6] Finally, three years of conflict between the Board and general counsel ended when, for the first time in its history, the Board, in a series of unanimous decisions, established jurisdictional standards or "yardsticks" to determine the kinds of cases it would and would not take.[7] When Bott agreed to adopt the same standards in issuing unfair labor practice complaints,[8] he was renouncing, without saying so explicitly, Denham's assertion that the Board had to exercise all the jurisdiction it possessed under the statute and yielding to the Board's position in its bitter feud with the former general counsel.

It was clear that the new general counsel and the Board had buried the hatchet, but *Business Week* asked, "Was the hatchet being buried in the Taft-Hartley law?"[9] It was a reasonable, if somewhat flippantly put, question. Bott would be in office barely a month, however, before the Republican Party won major gains in the November 1950 congressional elections, finally snuffing any remaining flicker of hope that Taft-Hartley would be repealed or even amended in any way favorable to organized labor.

Although Truman would have the opportunity to make one more appointment to the Board before Eisenhower and the Republicans won the White House in 1952, Bott's appointment in late September 1950 was the last gasp of a Democratic administration attempting to continue its influence over the making of labor policy through the NLRB. The conclusion of the transition from a Democratic to a Republican administration in 1952 would bring major changes in labor policy, not by legislative enactment (although Republican-inspired amendments to Taft-Hartley were considered) but through reinterpretations of the existing Taft-Hartley law by a Republican-controlled NLRB.

Presidential Politics and Taft-Hartley

After the battles over the general counsel, Reorganization Plan No. 12, and Bott's appointment, no one on either side wanted to renew the fight over the Taft-Hartley Act labor policy. It was now politically impossible to repeal Taft-Hartley and restore the Wagner Act even if an amended Wagner Act was not much different than Taft-Hartley.

Despite organized labor's 1950 congressional election campaign to defeat every senator and representative, regardless of party, who had voted for Taft-Hartley—particularly Senator Robert Taft, whom labor made a symbol of everything wrong with labor policy and the Congress[10]—Democratic majorities were sharply reduced in both the Senate (from 12 to 2) and the House (from 92 to 36).[11] Taft's reelection, moreover, was so overwhelming that the senator became the frontrunning Republican presidential nominee for 1952. Taft captured every major industrial stronghold in Ohio in what the *New York Times* called organized labor's worst political defeat since the Roosevelt era began in 1932.[12] In the euphoria of Truman's 1948 upset victory, organized labor had pushed for repeal of Taft-Hartley; only two years later labor faced a Congress capable of passing labor laws even more restrictive than Taft-Hartley. The AFL understood that it would be dangerous to reopen the subject and risk amendments that could worsen the present law.[13]

There was a definite lull around Taft-Hartley issues for all of 1951 and most of 1952, until the presidential campaigns intensified. The NLRB succeeded in obtaining bipartisan support in October 1951 for an amendment, sponsored by Taft and Hubert Humphrey (the first amendment of the act since 1947), that eliminated the union shop authorization poll as a requirement for a lawful union shop agreement. The outcome of these polls had become a foregone conclusion, and conducting them was a waste of the NLRB's time and the government's money and served no useful purpose. Now, except in right-to-work states, unions and employers could negotiate a union security clause without an authorization election.[14]

On the national political scene the fear of communism gripped the country. That fear, along with an increasingly conservative public mood, would put Eisenhower and the Republicans in the White House. It culminated in the sweeping accusations made by Republican senator Joseph McCarthy of Wisconsin, who never exposed a single communist not already known to the FBI but who "from 1950 to 1954 . . . became a powerful force of intimidation and terror in American political life."[15] The communist enemy was believed to be everywhere—in the State Department, the press, labor unions, Hollywood studios, college campuses, nuclear physics labs, the Unitarian Church, even the U.S. Army. The cry was that the Truman liberals were "soft on communism" or were communist dupes, if not communists themselves.

By 1952 the United States was bogged down in a stalemated war in Korea and the Democratic Party had become identified with a war it could neither win nor end. The war was a source of other troubles for Truman when his dismissal of General Douglas MacArthur as commander in Korea triggered massive, if short-lived, public support for the deposed general. In the spring of 1952, moreover, Truman, ignoring Taft-Hartley's emergency dispute provisions, decided to seize the nation's steel mills in order to maintain production for the Korean war effort and uphold the integrity of the administration's wage and price controls in the face of unauthorized price increases by the industry and a threatened strike by the United Steelworkers of America. Within weeks the Supreme Court ruled the seizure unconstitutional, and Truman was denounced for his action as few presidents ever had been. Corruption sufficient to send nine Democrats to prison also plagued the Truman administration in its last years. Korea, communism, corruption, and Truman's failure to achieve any of his major 1948 platform planks—a new farm policy, national health insurance, repeal of Taft-Hartley, civil rights, and federal aid to education—combined to kill the Democratic Party's chances of holding on to the White House in 1952.[16]

While Truman's approval rating at the polls dropped below 30 percent, General Dwight Eisenhower became the first choice for president among voters not only of every background but also in both the Republican and Democratic parties.[17] Truman met privately with Eisenhower in November 1951 and "guaranteed" him the Democratic nomination and Truman's full support. Eisenhower reportedly declined, saying that he and his family had always been Republicans and "his differences with the Democrats over domestic issues especially labor legislation were too vast for him to even consider accepting."[18] Shortly thereafter, Truman announced that he would not be a candidate for reelection. He supported Adlai Stevenson, Democratic governor of Illinois, and a spontaneous draft-Stevenson movement overcame the governor's genuine reluctance to accept the Democratic nomination.

Eisenhower defeated Taft for the Republican nomination and Stevenson for the presidency with a campaign that one historian called "a masterpiece of evasion."[19] Entrusting the necessary political maneuvering to the Republican Party professionals, Eisenhower proved to the Old Guard Republicans that his domestic views were safe by saying what they wanted to hear: professing reliance on the free market, leaving responsibility for civil rights and racial matters to individual states, and condemning in bland generalizations inflation, taxation, centralized government, dishonesty in government, and "socialized medicine." On the other hand, Eisenhower's defeat of the isolationist Taft was a victory for the eastern internationalist wing of the Republican Party, represented by Dewey and Henry Cabot Lodge. Eisenhowever appeased the defeated Taft and his supporters, however, by selecting Richard Nixon as his running mate.[20]

Although Eisenhower's dramatic announcement, only two weeks before the election, that he would go to Korea to seek peace clinched the outcome, the decisive defeat of Stevenson was due most to Eisenhower's personal popularity as a victorious general, "a hero who could be trusted to lead the nation to peace and prosperity."[21] Image easily dominated issues and ideology as Eisenhower "exuded a genial moral authority that won the hearts of Americans."[22]

A Republican Administration Appeals for Conservative Labor Support

After five consecutive presidential election victories for the Democrats, the Republican Eisenhower's victory was complete, lacking only West Virginia and eight states in the Deep South. Republicans also gained control of the House and Senate, although by narrow margins—48 to 47 in the Senate and 221 to 212 in the House.[23]

Unlike the case in the 1948 presidential campaign, Taft-Hartley was not a central issue in 1952. Eisenhower made only a few vague references to the act, saying that he was for the "idea" of Taft-Hartley but not necessarily everything in the act and would support no amendment that weakened the rights of working men and women.[24] While addressing the AFL convention less than two months before the election, however, Eisenhower said that he knew Taft-Hartley "might be used to break unions." He affirmed, "That must be changed. America wants no law licensing union-busting. And neither do I."[25]

Eisenhower's comment angered Taft, who called it a mistake that would be "used as a general condemnation of the law as a whole."[26] It was Taft, not Eisenhower, who was in control of the Republicans' labor policy. Anticipating that the general would be asked what specific provisions of the law could be used for union busting, Taft advised Eisenhower's campaign chief of staff, New Hampshire governor Sherman Adams, that Eisenhower should say only Section 9(c)(3), which prohibited permanently replaced strikers from voting in subsequent representation elections—a provision that Taft had been willing to change in 1949.[27] Eisenhower did as Taft suggested.

The AFL did not endorse Stevenson until he pledged at the Federation's convention on September 23, 1952, to seek repeal of Taft-Hartley.[28] Even then the somewhat aloof Stevenson and organized labor were not of one mind. Organized labor itself was badly divided on the Taft-Hartley question, with certain unions independently seeking piecemeal revisions to the act for their own advantage at the expense of other unions.[29] Many of the craft affiliates that comprised the Building and Construction Trades Department, such as William Hutcheson's Brotherhood of Carpenters, were among the most powerful unions in the AFL and constituted the core of support in organized labor for the Republican Party, particularly for Eisenhower.[30] Eisenhower and several of his key advisers were convinced that the Republicans would never attain more than minority party status as long as they were identified as the captive of business interests. Achieving a compromise with conservative unionists on Taft-Hartley amendments would seriously undermine charges that the party was antilabor.[31]

The Eisenhower administration, therefore, sought not only to repay its political supporters in the AFL but also to forge a political alliance with the conservative wing of organized labor. At the same time, the craft-dominated AFL began a campaign of special interest lobbying with its friends in the new Republican administration,[32] ultimately getting one of its own appointed secretary of labor: Martin Durkin, president of the AFL's Plumbers union. The *New Republic* remarked, "Ike had picked a cabinet of eight millionaires and one plumber."[33]

Durkin was a close friend of AFL president George Meany and had succeeded Meany as president of the Plumbers union in 1943. Meany denied that he had recommended Durkin (whom he described as a "solid Irishman") in his postelection meetings with Eisenhower but acknowledged urging the president to appoint a union leader as secretary of labor.[34] Durkin was surprised that he had been chosen.[35] Taft called the choice of Durkin an "incredible appointment," claiming bewilderment because Durkin was a "partisan Truman Democrat who fought General Eisenhower's election and advocated repeal of Taft-Hartley."[36]

Undeterred, Durkin said that he hoped to set up a conference with Taft and leaders of organized labor, industry, and Congress to discuss amendments to Taft-Hartley.[37] For the sake of party loyalty, Taft subsequently joined a unanimous Senate Labor Committee in approving Durkin's nomination. In a pointed and prescient question, however, Taft asked Durkin to affirm that he would conduct himself as a "representative of the public and not a representative of a particular organization."[38] The "incredible appointment" made the incredible pledge to keep politics out of the performance of his new job.[39]

Ill-Fated Bargaining over National Labor Policy

Once ensconced in Washington in January 1953, the Republican administration launched a two-pronged approach to changes in the Taft-Hartley labor policy: one, the usual public hearings conducted by the House and Senate labor committees; the other, a high-level, behind-the-scenes attempt to bargain changes in the act. As discussed in the next chapter, the congressional hearings that ran from February to late spring, rather than informing Congress about needed legislative changes, were used by the Republicans to prepare an agenda of doctrinal changes for the NLRB to implement once Eisenhower appointees controlled the Board. The high-level bargaining, on the other hand, made no pretense at empirical fact gathering to fashion more effective legislation but proceeded to a dead end solely on the basis of political maneuvering and intrigue.

On the organized labor side the CIO expected no support for labor from the Republicans and justifiably feared a Republican attempt to split the AFL from the CIO by offering Taft-Hartley amendments favoring only the building trades to the possible detriment of competing industrial unions.[40] The AFL not only refused to cooperate with the CIO in planning a unified amendment policy but also chose to pursue an independent strategy of cooperation with the Eisenhower administration. The Federation put together a craft-dominated advisory committee on Taft-Hartley amendments that conducted a campaign of pure special-interest lobbying.[41] AFL president Meany and these craft union leaders entered into negotiations with the administration by tacitly using Secretary of Labor Durkin to represent their interests at the White House bargaining table.[42]

From the beginning White House advisers emphasized how extremely important it was for members of the administration to avoid public disagreements and confrontations over proposals to amend Taft-Hartley.[43] At the cabinet meeting of February 20, 1953, Durkin was given the authority to coordinate the development of administration policy on labor amendments, but the president's chief of staff, Sherman Adams, cautioned that it was imperative to avoid "conflicting testimony" from within the administration. United Nations ambassador Henry Cabot Lodge urged those present, including Durkin and Secretary of Commerce Sinclair Weeks, to make an extra effort to deny outsiders any opportunity for "wedge driving."[44]

At Adams's suggestion, the Labor and Commerce departments engaged in a series of conferences, but neither would agree to what the other proposed. Although later on Durkin participated in some of these meetings, Undersecretary of Labor Lloyd Mashburn initially represented the Labor Department. Weeks did not attend any of the conferences but was represented by Steven Dunn, the Commerce Department's general counsel.[45] In May, Adams informed the Republican legislative leadership that Weeks and Durkin were "poles apart" and that the White House was trying to get them together to shape an administration policy. In June, Eisenhower told the legislative leadership that Weeks and Durkin "would be forced into some agreement, though he would prefer not to press them."[46]

It was most unlikely, if not impossible, that conservative businessman Weeks and Durkin could have agreed voluntarily on any important changes in Taft-Hartley. Weeks and Dunn's recommendation that the administration adopt no comprehensive policy on labor legislation was based on ideological and philosophical grounds fundamentally inconsistent with the concept of government encouragement and protection of unionism and collective bargaining. Denouncing federal intervention in labor-management relations during the Roosevelt and Truman administrations as a great failure based on "class hatred, government partiality, and the creation of crises," and the NLRB as a "discredited" and "punitive" agency that had deliberately misinterpreted Taft-Hartley, they advocated turning labor relations "back to the states to the fullest possible extent" and limiting federal involvement to those strikes affecting the health, safety, and security of the nation. Weeks and Dunn even objected to Eisenhower and Taft's willingness to grant voting rights to permanently replaced economic strikers, because the risks to a union of losing a strike or even bargaining rights were "constructive deterrents" to strikes.[47]

While these fruitless conferences were taking place, four lawyers, two representing labor and two representing management, met at an American Bar Association conference and decided, apparently spontaneously, to try to fashion amendments to Taft-Hartley that they could recommend to both the Labor and Commerce departments. The management lawyers, Gerard Reilly, a former Board member then representing General Electric, and Theodore Iserman, representing the Chrysler Corporation, had helped write the Taft-Hartley Act; the union attorneys were Herbert Thatcher and Albert Wald, lawyers for the AFL. Durkin knew, through constant contact with Meany and Thatcher, about these four and what they were doing, but Weeks, White House special counsel Bernard Shanley, and White House counsel Gerry Morgan did not.[48]

After the conferences between the Labor and Commerce departments broke down, Shanley and Morgan initiated a series of meetings with Durkin and Dunn separately. As Shanley recalled, "We got along very well with Durkin, except that he kept coming back for more, and it turned out that he was playing off what we were willing to 'give' him against what the two industry lawyers were willing to give the two labor union lawyers."[49]

Although Shanley and Morgan and Durkin reached an accord on some items, Commerce's general counsel Dunn would agree to nothing unless Durkin accepted what Shanley called an "extreme" states' rights provision and an "extreme" substitution of a court system for the Board, as well as "correction of numerous decisions of the Board under secondary boycotts."[50] Shanley, who discovered that Weeks was going around him to plead his case directly to Eisenhower, told the president Weeks's position was "pretty reactionary on the whole."[51]

At this point Shanley and Morgan, with the approval of Eisenhower and Taft, convened an informal committee to see if a larger group of influential legislative leaders could help resolve the Durkin-Weeks impasse. In addition to Durkin, Mashburn and Donahue of the Labor Department, Dunn of the Commerce Department, and Shanley and Morgan, the informal committee included Taft, Senate Labor Committee chairman Alexander Smith (and committee staff Mike Bernstein and Philip Ray Rogers; Rogers was soon to be a member of the

NLRB), and House Labor Committee chairman Sam McConnell.[52] Secretary Weeks attended only one of the informal committee's meetings. During the committee's deliberations Shanley noted that Taft was on crutches, "looking very pale and wan, although he seemed to be his usual self at the table."[53] (Some of the meetings were held in Taft's office to save "wear and tear" on the senator, who was not well.)[54]

Meanwhile, the four lawyers had drafted a series of amendments, which AFL counsel Thatcher took to Durkin after clearing them with Meany. At the same time, Reilly and Iserman discussed the same draft with Dunn. Durkin, according to Thatcher, made some minor changes and then agreed to the lawyers' draft; Dunn said he would consider it only as a possible basis for agreement between Labor and Commerce, provided both sides were free to propose further amendments.[55] The lawyers' draft was printed as a Senate Labor Committee confidential print, and the committee used it as a working paper during its deliberations.[56]

On June 19 Eisenhower sat in on a meeting of Shanley's informal committee in an attempt to encourage Durkin and Weeks to resolve their differences, using the lawyers' draft as a starting point for compromise.[57] Eisenhower's intervention may have moved the Commerce Department, because six days later Dunn said that he would agree to the lawyer's draft if Durkin would—and indicated that "it was his understanding that Durkin had already agreed to it."[58] The confusion was compounded, however, when Durkin amazed everyone present by denying that he had ever agreed to the lawyers' draft and claiming that he had never even seen it until it was printed by the Senate Labor Committee.[59] At that point Shanley was sure Taft "was going to blow up."[60] Eventually, however, the group went through the draft section by section and, according to Shanley, "finally came to substantive agreement on everything but the provision dealing with secondary boycotts."[61] (There was no states' rights provision.) After this meeting Taft left for a New York hospital, where he died a few weeks later.

Despite his protestations of neutrality, Durkin never removed his AFL hat, and as Shanley noted, he made no serious decision without first discussing it with George Meany. Concerned about Durkin's frequent reversals after specific agreement had been reached in the informal committee's negotiations, Shanley had Durkin's movements "checked." Immediately after a negotiation session, Durkin "would walk across the street to see Meany and the decision would go out the window." In Shanley's opinion Durkin was "completely under the control of George Meany."[62]

On July 30 Shanley completed a draft of a message for Eisenhower to send to Congress on Friday, August 7, its tentative adjournment date.[63] The draft message contained a nineteen-point revision of Taft-Hartley that was purportedly the consequence of six months of study by the secretaries of labor and commerce, the chairmen of the Senate and House labor committees and their staffs, and the majority leader of the Senate (Taft).[64] The draft message contained a mild states' rights provision that left control over small employers to the states. Almost every other recommendation, however, favored organized labor. Although the closed shop would still be prohibited, for example, the message called for an amendment to preclude states from enforcing restrictions on union security more severe than the federal law.[65]

Several of the amendments sought by the building trades unions were included in the draft message. Construction and building firms and unions would have been permitted to sign contracts recognizing a union as the employees' bargaining representative before hiring even began on a project. Those contracts, moreover, could require any worker employed to join the union within seven days of being hired, instead of the thirty days specified by Taft-Hartley. Eisenhower also would have legalized a boycott against a subcontractor on a construction project by a union engaged in a labor dispute with another contractor on the same construction project. He would have advocated, in addition, elimination of the mandatory injunction in secondary boycott cases (all injunctions in these and other unfair labor practice cases would be discretionary) and prohibition of any injunction without an opportunity for a hearing before the NLRB.[66]

In a compromise twist on the issue of the voting rights of permanently replaced economic strikers, the message called for an amendment prohibiting such an election for a period of four months after the commencement of an economic strike. In regard to the other Taft-Hartley issue raised by Eisenhower in his election campaign, the draft message recommended elimination of the act's noncommunist affidavit provision and promised "general legislation on a broad front" to deal with the problem of communists in the United States.[67]

The only reference in the message to the NLRB noted the virtually unanimous dissatisfaction with the Board's administration of the act, particularly delays in case handling, and asked the secretaries of commerce and labor and the Board chairman in consultation with the chairmen of the Senate and House labor committees to review the testimony presented to those committees and submit their recommendations to the president before the next session of Congress. The main revision considered favorable to employers would have relieved both parties of any statutory obligation to bargain during the term of a contract over any subject not covered by the agreement.[68]

Since Taft had been so deeply involved in the Eisenhower administration's consideration of amendments to Taft-Hartley, White House advisers agreed that it would not be possible to send a Taft-Hartley message to Congress if the senator died, because "it would look as though we were trying to take advantage of the fact that he was dead."[69] Taft died on July 31, 1953,[70] the day after Shanley sent the draft message to Durkin, Weeks, McConnell, and Smith.

After a cabinet meeting that day during which tribute was paid to Taft, Shanley sounded out Durkin and Weeks separately about their reaction to the draft message. Not surprisingly, Durkin was "quite elated about it," whereas Weeks was obviously unhappy. Later that day a very upset Dunn came into Shanley's office asking sarcastically, "Who had won the election?" Sherman Adams replied caustically, "Commerce is living in the dark ages." Shanley recalled, "It was not a pleasant session."[71]

Dunn reiterated the Commerce Department's willingness to agree to the lawyer group's draft (now a Senate Labor Committee confidential print) and offered to incorporate the Senate committee print in any presidential message to Congress, provided the Department of Labor concurred. Dunn objected, however, to the draft message: "While the committee print made a number of concessions to the AFL's point of view, it did not go nearly so far in weakening the protection provided by the Act to the public, industry, and individual workers, as the proposed message would do." The draft message was unacceptable to the Department of Commerce not only for what it proposed but also for what it omitted, particularly those amendments, Dunn complained, that even the AFL lawyers had approved and those that plugged some loopholes the NLRB "had discovered or created in the Act."[72]

On August 1 Senate Labor Committee chairman Smith, in a memorandum to Shanley, also raised objections to the draft message, particularly the secondary boycott recommendation for building trades unions, which was "likely to arouse the greatest criticism."[73] Smith also invoked Taft's commitment to Section 14(b) in opposing the proposed elimination of that section, adding that "Senators from the south and midwestern states would strenuously object to removal of this provision."[74]

Smith enclosed a memorandum he had requested from Tom Shroyer, who as Taft's counsel knew "more than anybody else, Bob Taft's thinking on this legislation."[75] Shroyer went further than Smith in using the deceased Taft to reject the draft message by professing to know what Taft's position would have been on the recommendations.[76] He advised Smith to delete the statement attributing the message in part to the work of Senator Taft. He granted that some of the draft's nineteen points were in Taft's bill that had passed the Senate in 1949 but reminded Smith "that in 1949 both you and Senator Taft agreed to a number of things solely on the ground it was necessary to prevent complete repeal of the law. This was later demonstrated to have been good strategy."[77]

Most disturbing to Shroyer were the suggested changes in the secondary boycott provision. He advised Smith, "I don't see why anything would be given away on this provision." He wrote: "If the suggestions in the message are carried through, you have put the Main streets and small businesses of America at the mercy of these indefensible tactics. Senator Taft told me the day before he went to New York [to enter the hospital where he died] that he could conceive of no situation wherein he would permit any weakening of the secondary boycott provisions and would insist to the extent of his ability that the loopholes be closed."[78]

Another proposed change that Shroyer claimed Taft "would have condemned as only he could do" were the "inroads upon the closed shop bans": "While it is true that Senator Taft supported the building trades pre-hire contract bill, he always insisted that a means be provided for the employees to de-authorize the union shop at the earliest possible moment." Finally, Shroyer considered the elimination of Section 14(b) "a bad political error," because there were "now at least a dozen states having right to work statutes and their people feel very strongly about them. I think a check will disclose almost all of these states were in the Eisenhower column last Fall."[79] Shroyer warned that if the message were delivered, there would not be much left of the 1952 support for Eisenhower.

According to Shanley, Sherman Adams decided on August 1 to "deep-freeze the message." Shanley agreed that it "was the only thing we could possibly do" after Taft's death; otherwise it would look as if the administration was trying "to pass something over his dead body."[80] Even after his death Taft was controlling labor policy. There was another important reason not to go forward: Senator Smith had asked Shanley for a meeting about the message before it went any further, and Dunn, on behalf of the Commerce Department, repeated his "urgent recommendation that no message be sent at this time."[81]

Although Dunn said that he had heard that the message was being held up, he decided to take no chances. On Saturday, August 1, House Labor Committee chairman McConnell, who also objected to several recommendations in the draft message, told Shanley "confidentially" that Dunn had taken the message to the general counsel of the National Association of Manufacturers.[82] On Monday, August 3, the *Wall Street Journal* printed the full text of the draft message on Taft-Hartley.[83] Whoever informed the *Journal* emphasized the lack of unanimity among the presidential advisers who had worked on the message ("some . . . are violently opposed"), pointedly put responsibility for the message on Shanley, and underscored the similarity between the message and Secretary of Labor Durkin's proposals.[84] Shanley called this "the fatal day."[85]

Shanley confronted the only people who had received copies: Durkin "swore it had never left his brief case," and McConnell and Smith denied giving their copies to anyone.[86] Dunn, according to Shanley, admitted going directly from the White House to the NAM offices after he received his copy of the message but "flatly denied giving it to the NAM." Shanley commented in his diary: "We did, however, have additional proof that the NAM had a copy of the message before it was printed." He added that the *Wall Street Journal* "sent back word that they were pressured through Sinclair Weeks and that is where they had received it."[87]

Leaking the draft message to the press scuttled not only the message but the Eisenhower administration's attempts to forge an alliance with the AFL. Once the proposed message became public, employers who had looked to Taft for leadership in labor legislation were shaken by what they considered the pro-labor slant of the White House message. They were careful, however, to direct their fire not at Eisenhower but at certain allegedly misguided White House staff people—particularly Shanley—who reflected "too much the thinking of New York Governor Dewey." As one Republication conservative put it, "the whole attitude of trying to make a deal with the AFL stems from the New York crowd."[88]

Former senator Joseph Ball made a disparaging reference to the "palace guard" who wanted to sell out to the AFL. When Taft died, Ball said, the "bulwark against such a sellout was gone." Ball found the Eisenhower administration's drift toward a labor policy "dominated by the moguls of the AFL far more frightening" than the Democratic Party's alliance with the CIO.[89] Conservative legislators such as Barry Goldwater told Eisenhower that the recommendations in the message "would go a long way toward destroying the Taft-Hartley Act and toward granting monopolistic powers to labor leaders beyond the fondest dreams of the Roosevelt and Truman Administration."[90]

Under fire, Shanley retreated. He claimed that the draft everybody was trying to pin on the administration was only an "initial," not a final, draft.[91] The administration decided to continue working on the Taft-Hartley message and to delay delivering it until after Congress returned in January 1954. Shanley and Morgan then drafted an innocuous, watered-down statement to be presented at the AFL convention in September.[92] Durkin found it an entirely unsatisfactory "pulling away" from changes in Taft-Hartley he believed the administration had already approved.[93]

Durkin had hoped to appear before the AFL convention with a commitment from the White House to support several important union-advocated changes in Taft-Hartley, particularly in Section 14(b) and the secondary boycott provisions. When he realized that no such commitment would come from the White House,[94] he quit on September 10, 1953. Durkin told friends he had to resign once it became clear that "Weeks would prevail on labor legislation."[95]

When Durkin addressed the AFL convention in St. Louis on September 22, he claimed that when agreement was reached between the president's advisers and representatives of the Department of Labor, "we were told that all nineteen amendments had the approval of the President" and that the secretary of commerce could not exercise any veto power over the agreed-on amendments. After the draft message was leaked to the press, Durkin told the AFL delegates, he met alone with Eisenhower in New York City, where, according to Durkin, the president "agreed that the leak in no way lessened the need for releasing the agreed to nineteen points" and "fully agreed to my position." Durkin claimed that when Eisenhower called him to the White House on September 10 to discuss his letter of resignation, the president said that "he had changed his position since the New York meeting and that he could no longer go along with the nineteen amendments." At that point, Durkin said, he insisted that Eisenhower accept his resignation.[96]

Eisenhower denied emphatically that he had ever broken an agreement with Durkin.[97] In an attempt to relieve the bitterness in AFL ranks caused by Durkin's resignation and to offset Meany's accusation that the administration was dominated by big business, Eisenhower sent Nixon to address the AFL convention. The choice was puzzling to AFL officials, who believed that Nixon and Weeks were mainly responsible for blocking the nineteen amendments.[98]

Nixon brought only a general pledge from the president to recommend changes in Taft-Hartley in 1954 and drew "mocking laughter" that drowned out his voice when he referred to Durkin's charges as a "misunderstanding."[99] Despite Nixon's denials, the AFL convention unanimously adopted a resolution commending Durkin for resigning when the president failed "to keep his agreement" to send "agreed upon amendments" to Congress.[100]

Durkin never fit into Eisenhower's millionaire cabinet. As one press report put it, the rest of the cabinet looked on Durkin "much as an Ivy League team might regard a fellow from Youngstown on a football scholarship."[101] Durkin told a friend that when he walked into a room "everybody stopped talking."[102] Shanley considered Durkin a "very simple" man of "limited capacity" who was "completely under Meany's control."[103] In reflecting on his first year as president, Eisenhower said that Durkin was the only one of his cabinet choices "who proved to be a disappointment," because "he could never free himself of the feeling that he was placed in the Cabinet to be a 'trade unionist.'"[104]

The Aftermath of a Botched Negotiation and a New Secretary of Labor

In the White House negotiations over labor policy Weeks and his conservative colleagues had out-maneuvered more moderate Republicans in the Eisenhower administration as well as Durkin. After the premature publication of the nineteen-point Taft-Hartley revision but before Durkin resigned, for example, Weeks and Dunn, with Nixon's support, devised a strategy to persuade Eisenhower to support a toughening of Taft-Hartley, or at least revisions that favored business while eliminating the more important concessions made to unions in the nineteen points.

The plan was for key cabinet members such as Secretary of the Treasury George M. Humphrey, Secretary of Defense Charles E. Wilson, Secretary of Agriculture Ezra Taft Benson and Postmaster General Arthur Summerfield (all presumed sympathetic because of their backgrounds in business and agriculture) to support Weeks whenever the Taft-Hartley labor policy was debated in cabinet meetings. Weeks and Dunn thoroughly briefed these secretaries before the meetings and even encouraged their business friends to contact them to reaffirm the importance of preserving and strengthening Taft-Hartley.[105] The split in Republican ranks between moderates and conservatives on labor matters made Eisenhower's choice of a new secretary of labor difficult. The Taft wing of the party was unalterably opposed to the appointment of another labor leader, and the moderates vigorously resisted any choice that would further antagonize organized labor—such as Clarence Manion, former dean of the Notre Dame Law School, who had been Taft's choice when Durkin was given the job.[106]

On October 8, 1953, Eisenhower chose James Mitchell, a fifty-two-year-old management-labor relations expert with a reputation as a moderate who was shrewd but fair in his dealings with organized labor.[107] Taft Republicans were unenthusiastic and suspicious, since Mitchell's strongest supporters came from the more liberal eastern Republican bloc that had sought to establish an alliance with the AFL. A disappointed Meany told the press that Mitchell was a "very fine gentleman" and "I think he'll be as good a Secretary of Labor as Brother Weeks allows him to be."[108] CIO president Walter Reuther issued a friendly statement, possibly anticipating that Mitchell would pay more attention to CIO positions than had the AFL's Durkin.[109] Mitchell gave his first major address to the CIO convention, where he said that some provisions of Taft-Hartley were "really dangerous to labor, really loaded, and really unfair."[110]

Because of the hostile reaction from business and political conservatives to the premature publication of the nineteen points and Weeks's increased influence after Durkin's departure, the administration adopted Taft's views on the revision of Taft-Hartley as its guideline to acceptable legislative recommendations. After Eisenhower inquired about the extent to which Taft had agreed with the various amendments considered by Shanley and Morgan's informal committee, Shanley asked Michael Bernstein, counsel to the Senate Labor Committee and close associate of Taft, what "Taft thought about all the different items so that we would be able to have some basis for saying that Senator Taft approved or disapproved."[111]

In early November 1953 Bernstein reported a conversation he had had with Taft only days before the senator's death in which Taft purportedly said he preferred to see Taft-Hartley remain as it was except for "a wholesale change" in the NLRB's personnel and organization. He was particularly concerned to separate "the judicial from the investigating and prosecuting functions, leaving to the Board itself nothing but judicial functions, all other duties to be in the hands of a completely separate and independent administrator."[112] Shortly after Bernstein made his report, there was substantial agreement in the informal committee to adopt Taft's proposed reorganization of the NLRB. The committee's mood shift was illustrated by Shanley's comment that "industry very vitally needed" the reorganization of the NLRB "in order to do away with the regional offices where all the ADAers [Americans for Democratic Action] were sitting waiting for an appropriate time to hit industry over the head."[113]

In drafting a new Taft-Hartley message for Eisenhower to deliver to Congress on January 11, 1954, the informal committee deviated from the Taft guidelines only to add a controversial strike ballot proposal that had "tremendous appeal" for Secretary of Commerce Weeks. Overall, Shanley concluded, "by the time we finished, it was a plan which Senator Taft would have fully approved which was important to be able to say to the leadership."[114] (The draft was the work of Shanley, Morgan, Smith, Bernstein, McConnell, House Labor Committee general counsel Edward McCabe, Sherman Adams, and Jack Martin, administrative assistant to the president. Mitchell also participated "for a time.")[115]

On January 11 Eisenhower delivered a Taft-Hartley message to Congress quite different from the earlier nineteen-point draft message, although it did contain some of the first message's proposals favorable to organized labor. Eisenhower proposed, for example, to ease the ban on secondary boycotts by permitting union action against employers working on materials "farmed out" by a struck employer as well as against secondary employers working jointly on a construction project with a struck primary employer, to permit employers in the construction industry to enter into contracts with unions before any employees were hired as well as agreements requiring employees to become union members within seven days after beginning employment, and to eliminate the mandatory 10(l) injunction in secondary boycott cases.[116]

The press, however, featured Eisenhower's "surprise" strike poll proposal to give workers called out on strike by their unions an opportunity "to express [their] free choice by secret ballot held under Government auspices."[117] (The Weeks-backed strike ballot proposal was rumored to be traceable to the long and bitter steel strike of 1952, when steel executives believed that if their employees had had an opportunity to vote on the company's last wage offer, they would have forced the union leadership to accept it.)[118]

The insertion of Weeks's strike poll guaranteed the failure of Eisenhower's recommendations. Liberal Republican senator Irving Ives immediately stated his opposition to the strike proposal because it was unworkable and its cost of implementation would be prohibitive.[119] The AFL and the CIO called the poll strike breaking and the very union-busting that Eisenhower had promised to eliminate from the act.[120] In his inimitable style, John L. Lewis rejected the entire message: "A few piddling amendments won't make a slave law palatable to free-born citizens."[121]

The strike ballot, never a serious political or moral issue and never on Eisenhower's list of "must" legislation, ironically became divisive and embarrassing to the administration. Labor Secretary Mitchell later admitted to the Senate Labor Committee that he did not know how much such balloting might cost, how the polling might be administered, or what the employees would vote on. He also revealed his own opposition to such a policy, which he said had caused misunderstanding and confusion.[122] By the end of January, Charles Halleck, whom Eisenhower considered "smart, capable, and courageous" and a loyal "team player," urged elimination of the strike vote proposal because of the controversy it was causing.[123]

The Republican majority on the House Labor Committee, along with a small group of conservative southern Democratic members, then broke with the administration's program by voting for a series of amendments making Taft-Hartley more restrictive, thereby ensuring that its revision was even more unlikely. In March and April the committee, chaired by Congressman McConnell, voted to transfer the NLRB's jurisdiction over unfair labor practices to federal district courts,[124] to give employers a right to lockout equivalent to employees' right to strike,[125] to tighten the ban on secondary boycotts,[126] to broaden the definition of a national emergency dispute,[127] and to permit employers to discharge and otherwise discipline strikers without union or employee recourse to the NLRB unless, within ten days before a strike began, a majority of employees eligible to vote chose in a secret ballot election to continue the strike.[128] At the same time, the House Labor Committee supported a stringent strike ballot plan.

Senator Barry Goldwater, who six months earlier had urged Eisenhower to leave Taft-Hartley alone because changes could seriously threaten Republican Party unity, could not be dissuaded from introducing a states' rights amendment that by his own admission would have permitted a state to enact a law forbidding collective bargaining;[129] asserting exclusive jurisdiction over strikes, secondary boycotts, and picketing; or even requiring the consent of 95 percent of the employees in a bargaining unit, rather than a majority of those voting, to certify a labor organization as their representative.[130] For Goldwater, the power to regulate labor relations rested with the states, not the federal government, even if that meant the nation would have forty-eight different labor laws.[131] This move caused the very divisiveness among Republicans that Goldwater had asked Eisenhower to avoid.[132] During a May 6 news conference an uncomfortable Eisenhower, when asked to state his position on the Goldwater amendment, said only that he would not like to see his own Taft-Hartley recommendation altered.[133]

At that point the AFL's legislative representatives concluded that the best they could hope for was "that nothing is done on Taft-Hartley in this session."[134] Democratic senators, opposed to the administration's Taft-Hartley program, maneuvered to have the bill recommitted by offering an antidiscrimination amendment making it an unfair labor practice for an employer or a union to discriminate against an employee in hiring or in employment conditions because of race, creed, color, ancestry, or national origin.[135] Herbert Lehman and Ives, who sponsored the amendment, threatened to press it unless the Senate returned the bill to committee. This strategy finally persuaded many southern Democrats, who already considered the proposed changes in the act too weak and did not want a fight over discrimination when farm bills and other legislation important to them were coming up, to vote for recommittal. Many Republican senators also wanted to avoid being put in the position of voting for or against the amendment, thereby guaranteeing defeat for the administration's Taft-Hartley revision bill.

On May 7, 1954, knowing that a motion to recommit was a motion to kill the administration's bill, the Senate voted fifty to forty-two to send the proposed legislation back to the Senate Labor Committee. The administration's program was also dead in the House Labor Committee, which had been deferring action on a bill until the Senate acted.[136] Now that the ill-fated attempt by the Eisenhower administration to negotiate national labor policy had ended, the attitude of all involved was probably best expressed by Senator Alexander Smith, whose bill had just been defeated: "I feel a sense of relief. I'm just as cheerful as a dickey bird."[137]

Concluding Observations

The Eisenhower administration matched Congress's unimpressive record in dealing with national labor policy. The White House set out to make changes in Taft-Hartley, not as a consequence of experience and persuasive evidence about how the law was affecting real-world labor relations but as an inducement to some unions within the AFL to give their political support to the administration—in order to change the image of the Republican Party as the party of business.

At the White House a few staff technicians attempted to bargain changes in the national labor policy as if the Taft-Hartley issue was just another labor-management dispute that could be resolved by skillful negotiation and mediation. Moreover, the White House demonstrated no sophisticated understanding that the labor policy problem ran as deep as the fundamental determination of whether the federal government should encourage and protect workers' right to organize or should act only as a neutral guarantor of the right to workers to choose to join or refrain from joining a labor organization. In the isolation of the White House the administration's labor policy negotiators seemed oblivious to political and ideological realities as they tinkered with politically charged Taft-Hartley provisions such as those dealing with union security, states' rights, free speech, and secondary boycotts. They seemed particularly naive about power relations within their own party and with Congress.

At the end, the posthumous approval of Senator Taft dictated the administration's legislative proposals. These final proposals were designed primarily not to deal with national labor policy in a serious, comprehensive, and objective way but to maintain Republican Party unity and to reassure American business that the administration had not gone soft on unionism.

In his reflections on his first year in office Eisenhower noted the tendency of legislative leaders to exercise an independence of thought, especially in implementing their own "theories of government," weakening the "ties of party allegiance." Differences with members of his own party, Eisenhower remarked, were often "even more pronounced and deep-seated than with some of the others."[138] Although he anticipated "incessant differences" with Taft and found Taft's attitude toward politics "far more personal . . . than I could ever be," Eisenhower came to consider Taft his ablest associate on Capitol Hill and "one of the stalwarts of the Administration." When differences developed between the White House and some Republican senators, the president said he "could count on Senator Taft to assert his great influence to bring them into line." Eisenhower lamented the loss of the senator: "After his death, no one of real strength has shown up on the senate side."[139]

Ironically, in light of his administration's approach to the national labor policy, Eisenhower criticized certain Republican senators for espousing a theory of legislating by "trading" and, therefore, "modifying and placating." The president complained: "They do not seem to realize when there arrives that moment at which soft speaking should be abandoned and a fight to the end undertaken. Any man who hopes to exercise leadership must be ready to meet this requirement face to face when it arises; unless he is ready to fight when necessary, people will finally begin to ignore him."[140]

There was no leadership of the sort described by Eisenhower in his administration's fruitless reconsideration of Taft-Hartley. For Congress and the administration, the Taft-Hartley Act had become mainly an ideological matter to be manipulated for political advantage, rather than an issue of rights and duties and practical statutory solutions to serious labor relations problems.

Since the passage of Taft-Hartley there had been no consensus on the rights and duties of workers, organized and unorganized. No courageous leadership existed in Congress or the White House willing to take the political risk of facing that fact and "fighting to the end," as Eisenhower put it, to develop and implement a clear and definite statement of those rights in a national labor policy. Instead, there was only the spectacle of the White House first offering changes in Taft-Hartley to gain political support from a segment of organized labor and then renouncing many of those changes and offering to make others unfavorable to organized labor to maintain Republican Party unity. In a forlorn and hypocritical finale, Congress ended the entire misguided process in order to avoid considering a civil rights amendment that would have made racial discrimination an unfair labor practice.

7

The Eisenhower Board Remakes Labor Policy

Changing the Law by Administrative Decision

Despite its failure to amend Taft-Hartley in Congress, the Eisenhower administration was still able to bring about major changes in the meaning of the act: a Republican-controlled NLRB reversed many of the Truman Board's interpretations. By March 1954 the NLRB, for the first time in its history, had a Republican-appointed majority, and by March 1955, a Republican-appointed general counsel.

Until then, Taft-Hartley had been enforced under what critics called "the shadow of a hostile administration" by a Board that had supported the act's repeal in 1949. Taft-Hartley advocates accused the Truman-appointed Herzog Board of sabotaging the act.[1] Actually, Herzog's Board, as was Herzog's style, attempted a middle-of-the-road approach to Taft-Hartley, often resulting in decisions objectionable to organized labor as well as to management.[2] The Herzog Board, however, certainly did interpret several key provisions of the act in ways counter to the interpretations advocated or at least anticipated by management and other supporters of Taft-Hartley.

Criticisms of the Truman Board reached their peak during the 1953 Senate and House hearings on the Eisenhower administration's proposed amendments to the act. Taft-Hartley advocates accused the Herzog Board of giving the broadest construction to the sections of the statute defining employer misconduct, while taking the narrowest possible view of those sections defining union misconduct and creating loopholes enabling unions to circumvent the intent of Congress in passing Taft-Hartley.[3] Almost all these witnesses cited particular Board decisions in support of their charges of pro-union bias and disregard of congressional intent. Most complaints centered on the Herzog Board's decisions concerning employer "free speech," secondary boycotts and picketing, lockouts, federal-state jurisdiction, bargaining during the term of a collective bargaining agreement, and the appropriate subjects of bargaining.[4]

In particular, management witnesses claimed that the Herzog Board had denied them the right of free speech guaranteed by Section 8(c) of the act to discuss unions with their employees, to appeal to strikers to return to work, to publicize improvements in wages and working conditions, and to speak against union organizers during representation campaigns.[5] They wanted the free-speech clause applied to representation cases as well as to unfair labor practice cases, contrary to the Herzog Board's ruling in *General Shoe Corporation*.[6]

They also vigorously protested the Herzog Board's 1951 *Bonwit Teller*[7] doctrine requiring an employer who made a preelection captive audience speech to a massed assembly of employees on company time and property, in violation of the employer's own rule against solicitation on the premises, to provide the union an equal opportunity to reply under the same circumstances. Employer witnesses charged that this was a return to Wagner Act doctrines, forced employers to subsidize union organizing drives and propaganda, and violated an employer's property rights.[8]

Every one of the ninety-two management witnesses who appeared before the House and Senate labor committees in 1953 condemned the Herzog Board for exploiting and creating loopholes in Taft-Hartley's prohibitions against secondary boycotts and other secondary activity by unions. Management representatives found the following decisions particularly objectionable: the Herzog Board's ruling that a "hot cargo" clause in a collective bargaining agreement between a union and a secondary or "neutral" employer removed a boycott or refusal to handle a primary employer's goods from the reach of the act's secondary boycott provisions (*Conway's Express*);[9] the Board's "roving situs" doctrine (*Schultz Refrigerated Service*),[10] which permitted a union to picket the trucks of a primary employer with whom it had a dispute while the trucks were on the premises of a secondary "neutral" employer; its decision in *Grauman Co.*[11] that the secondary boycott ban did not prohibit a union from listing an employer with whom it had a dispute on an "unfair" or "do not patronize" list that included allegedly unfair secondary employers with whom the union had no direct dispute; the Board's conclusion in *Arkansas Express Inc.*[12] that Section 8(b)(4) did not prohibit a union from inducing *employers* to cease doing business with one another since the explicit language of that provision applied only to inducement directed at employees and, therefore, that it was lawful to picket a "neutral" employer's place of business for the sole purpose of inducing customers not to buy the primary employer's product (*Crowley's Milk Co.* and *Joliet Contractors Association*);[13] and similarly, the Herzog Board's ruling in *International Rice Milling*[14] that the secondary boycott provisions applied only to illegal actions that were concerted and not to the actions of an individual employee who refused to cross a picket line at another employer's place of business.[15]

Management witnesses, equating an employer's right to lockout with the union's right to strike, also denounced the Herzog Board for holding that an employer's use of a lockout as a weapon in collective bargaining was prohibited by Taft-Hartley's ban against discrimination for union activity and employer interference with employees' exercise of their right to engage in lawful collective bargaining activities (*Morand Bros. Beverage Co.* and *Davis Furniture Co.*).[16] In addition, employer representatives criticized the Board's decision in *Jacobs Mfgs.*[17] requiring employers during the term of a collective bargaining contract to bargain over any mandatory subject not specifically covered by the existing contract.[18] They also opposed the Herzog Board's expansion of the appropriate subjects of bargaining and sought to exclude "traditional management rights" from collective bargaining.[19]

These witnesses reproached the Truman Board for requiring an employer who doubted a union's majority status to bargain with that union on the basis of authorization or membership cards rather than a representation election (*Dependable Wholesale Co.*)[20] and for defining an employer's duty to bargain to include the obligation to furnish the employees' bargaining representative with sufficient information, financial and otherwise, to substantiate the employer's bargaining position and to enable the union to bargain intelligently (*Southern Saddlery*).[21] Finally, management witnesses wanted to narrow the NLRB's jurisdiction by excluding from coverage insurance agents, farm equipment retailers, hotels, hospitals, public utilities, transit lines, construction businesses, government employees, and all "essentially local business." They also wanted to give the states more power to regulate labor-management relations, particularly strikes and picketing.[22]

The new Republican-appointed Board reversed almost every one of these Herzog Board decisions within the first eighteen months of its control of the NLRB. The testimony of management witnesses before the House and Senate labor committees and, to some extent, the final report of the House Labor Committee[23] constituted an agenda for action by the new Board. The policy changes made by the Eisenhower NLRB were far more comprehensive and drastic than the amendments proposed by the Republican administration in 1954.

The First Eisenhower Appointees: The Importance of Personality and Ideology

The Eisenhower administration was given an opportunity to appoint a majority of the Board earlier than expected when, in addition to the expiration of member John Houston's term in August 1953, Chairman Paul Herzog and member Paul Styles decided to resign during that same summer.[24] At the time these vacancies occurred, the Republican National Committee was complaining to the White House about an imbalance in presidential appointments.[25] In response to these complaints, Eisenhower instructed his cabinet to "appreciate the mandate given to this Administration [in November 1952] to clean out the mess in Washington." Quality was to be the primary consideration in any appointment, Eisenhower said, but second in importance was "that the person's political philosophy should be in line with the Administration's." Eisenhower strongly recommended that all appointments be coordinated not only with members of his staff but also with the Republican National Committee.[26]

Michael Bernstein, who had worked closely with Senator Taft as counsel to the Senate Labor Committee, pressed Eisenhower's special counsel, Bernard Shanley, to "free the Board from the undesirable attributes so frequently described" in the testimony before the Senate and House labor committees. Bernstein told Shanley that criticism of the Herzog Board's administration of the act—criticisms that Bernstein said he could confirm from his almost five years with the NLRB—had persuaded many members of both committees that sweeping changes had to be made in the membership of the Board. Bernstein again invoked Taft's memory: "Senator Taft, himself, before his death had come to feel that a great many problems in connection with Taft-Hartley would be remedied with fundamental changes in the structure and personnel of the Labor Board."[27]

Eisenhower's staff moved quickly to replace Herzog, whose resignation was effective at the end of June 1953, with Guy Farmer, confirmed as NLRB chairman by the Senate on July 10.[28] Philip Ray Rodgers, whom the Senate confirmed on August 28, took the place of Houston one day after his term expired.[29] The third Republican appointee, Albert Beeson, did not take office until March 1954, after extended Senate Labor Committee hearings[30] and internal White House disagreements.

Guy Farmer

Although nominally a political independent, Guy Farmer, a Rhodes scholar, was a political conservative and a strong supporter of Eisenhower in the 1952 campaign. Forty years old at the time of his appointment, Farmer had been an attorney with the NLRB for seven years, beginning as a review attorney in 1938[31] and serving as a regional attorney in the Minneapolis and Los Angeles offices before returning to Washington as associate general counsel from 1943 to 1945. In 1945 Farmer left the NLRB to represent employers with Steptoe & Johnson, a Washington, D.C., law firm headed by Louis A. Johnson, secretary of defense in the Truman administration.[32]

Eisenhower believed there was "too much centralization in Washington at the expense of local self-government." He told his cabinet to "keep the governmental power as far from Washington" as possible.[33] Farmer also subscribed to the Jeffersonian principle that the least government is the best government and, from the outset of his chairmanship, applied that philosophy to the NLRB's assertion of jurisdiction: "The one thing this nation needs more than anything else to maintain its vigor and strength is a revival of interest by local government in taking and solving the problems of their local people. That is why I strongly advocate a gradual but nevertheless marked withdrawal of the hand of the NLRB from strictly local disputes." At his swearing-in ceremony Farmer told reporters that philosophically he favored as much decentralization as possible and that the Board should use its discretionary power to cede authority over labor relations disputes to the states. Because "Uncle Sam's long arm had reached out to assert itself over too many labor relations situations" more suitably resolved closer to their origin, Farmer wanted his Board to follow a rule of administrative self-restraint.[34]

Farmer's vigorous opposition to communism also increased his acceptability to the business community. He spoke of the "menace of Communism" and pledged that the NLRB would do all it could "to dislodge the Communist leech which has sought to imbed itself in the body of labor and drain off its vigor and strength."[35] Early in his chairmanship Farmer said that communism in labor unions was one of the most troublesome problems facing the Board.[36] Years later he recalled how, during the Wagner Act days, the communists were deliberately placed at the NLRB, some in very high places, in an attempt "to mold the Board in the image of communism" and how he became president of the NLRB Union to take it away from the communists. He also recalled many loyalty investigations at the NLRB during his chairmanship, involving not only communists but also homosexuals.[37]

Farmer was also sympathetic to employers' complaints about NLRB bias. Although he considered the Herzog Board "rather reasonable," it was still in his mind a Wagner Act Board committed to helping unions organize and gain collective bargaining rights, even after the passage of Taft-Hartley. In Farmer's opinion the Wagner Act served a good purpose when employees and unions were weak, but Taft-Hartley was needed to protect employers and employees from abuses by now powerful labor unions. Consequently, Farmer did not hesitate to reject Herzog Board and other prior Democratic Board precedents.[38] In one of his first speeches as chairman, for example, he said, "No precedent is good if it is wrong and we do not propose to treat a prior decision as a straight jacket, binding our discretion and unduly restricting us in the exercise of independent judgment as to Congressional intent."[39]

In his public comments Farmer, in thinly veiled criticisms of the Herzog Board, repeatedly emphasized the importance of nonpartisan, impartial, and balanced administration of Taft-Hartley: "We have no license to abuse our position by lending the power and prestige of our Government to help industry or labor. Our job is to administer the law as written and as intended by Congress, and to do this with meticulous impartiality, for impartiality and fairness are synonyms for the public interest."[40] As the new chairman put it on another occasion, "the middle position is not always a comfortable one, but there the Board must stand."[41] Farmer also warned against interpreting the law to achieve some desired result "in accordance with the social, economic or political views of a majority of [the Board's] members." In another swipe at the Herzog Board he promised that his Board would "strive to read the book which Congress wrote and not sneak off to bed with a copy of Grimm's Fairy Tales."[42]

According to Farmer, moreover, it was not the Board's place to legislate labor law or to formulate labor policy: that was for Congress and the president. He warned that the NLRB should never be thought of by its own personnel or by the public as a political organization. He claimed, "Politics play a proper part in the enactment of laws but politics have no place in their administration."[43] Despite Farmer's public protestations, however, the White House intended the new NLRB to interpret Taft-Hartley in ways consistent with the labor policy and philosophy of the Republican administration. Privately, Farmer understood that. In a letter to Eisenhower in November 1953, when the administration's third appointment to the Board was still undecided, for example, Farmer wrote: "It is readily apparent that the person appointed by you to fill the remaining Board vacancy will be in a position to determine in large measure the extent to which the policies of your administration will be effectuated by this agency."[44]

In later years Farmer acknowledged that the Board was a "political animal" and had been "since its inception."[45] It was not that someone in the White House would tell a Board how to decide specific cases, Farmer said, but a member appointed to the Board felt pressure to implement the "philosophy that he thought his administration wanted him to project on the Board."[46] (The Republican National Committee was not above urging the Eisenhower White House to have the NLRB "get rid of every New Dealer or Fair Dealer holding an appointive office at the local [regional] level,"[47] although there is no evidence that Farmer succumbed to such specific pressures.)[48] The pressure is great, Farmer explained, because "this is not pinochle we're playing here. It's not penny-anty. This battle is over control of one of the most powerful agencies that ever existed in Washington—the NLRB." He added, "This is no tea party."[49]

Philip Ray Rodgers

On August 28, only six weeks after Farmer became chairman, Philip Ray Rodgers was sworn in as a member of the Board for a five-year term, replacing John Houston. Rodgers was thirty-seven years old when Eisenhower nominated him on July 29, 1953. He was a Mormon, as was Truman carryover Abe Murdock, with impressive academic credentials: a magna cum laude graduate of the University of Utah in 1939 with master of science and doctor of philosophy degrees in public administration as well as a bachelor of laws from George Washington University. He began his career as secretary to Senator James Davis of Pennsylvania in 1942 and from 1945 to 1947 was an assistant professor of political science and public administration at American University. In 1947 he became chief clerk and then staff director of the Senate Labor Committee.[50]

Those who worked with Rodgers at the Board remembered him as a brilliant, "way to the right" conservative who was "politically oriented" and "thought of himself as the employers' representative on the Board." He was a physically big and handsome man with a large bald head (somewhat "like Ike") who looked formidable and swore a lot but who was actually "one of the boys," pleasant and outgoing, generous and compassionate, and close to and popular with his staff.[51]

Rodgers had worked closely with Taft on the Senate Labor Committee yet was known to have advocated in 1947 the much more restrictive Hartley bill rather than Taft's Senate bill or the House-Senate compromise that became Taft-Hartley. In part, then, his appointment, supported by Taft and Chairman Smith of the Senate Labor Committee, was intended to win the backing of the more conservative Republicans and southern Democrats for the Eisenhower administration's proposed Taft-Hartley revisions.[52]

Rodgers was honest and spoke his mind, often in tough public speeches.[53] His political and philosophical conservatism matched Farmer's and in some ways went beyond it. Rodgers wanted the NLRB to assist the Eisenhower administration "in pulling back the outer reaches of the Federal bureaucracy" and restraining "the grasping hand of Government regimentation." Joining Farmer in expressing strong anticommunist feelings, Rodgers endorsed Eisenhower's program of internal security and promised to weed out any disloyal employees that the loyalty program might locate at the NLRB.[54]

With a subtle dig at the Herzog Board, Rodgers also promised to "carry out this law, not as it once was, not as some may wish it to be, but as it is."[55] In this regard he was more pointed than Farmer had been. Ironically, while describing the NLRB as a quasi-judicial agency concerned only with the interpretation and application of Taft-Hartley and "not with the accomplishment of social, economic, or political results," Rodgers, in the same speech, complained about the lack of active support for the Eisenhower administration among incumbent NLRB personnel. He deplored the lack of Republican appointees in NLRB policy-making and regional office positions:

> At the present time we are functioning with but four Board members, only two of whom were appointed by this administration. Moreover, at the present time virtually all of the policymaking and confidential positions on the Board's side of the agency, including the Solicitor and all division heads, are still held by persons appointed during or prior to the Truman administration.
>
> In addition, and even more important, the vast expanse of this agency's regional offices, whose personnel represents the only immediate and continuing contact between this agency and the public, remains under the supervision of a General Counsel appointed by the Truman administration. All regional directors long predate this administration, as indeed do virtually all of the regional personnel.[56]

Rodgers wanted a Republican NLRB in Washington and throughout the regions. In the meantime, he pledged to reverse the unsound interpretations of the labor-oriented Herzog Board.[57]

After Rodgers's appointment to the NLRB, Senator Hubert Humphrey accused the Eisenhower administration of packing the Board with members antagonistic toward unions. Republicans would not need to toughen Taft-Hartley legislatively, Humphrey asserted, when "they will achieve the same goal by packing the Board with anti-union members and interpreting out of existence whatever protections for unions Taft-Hartley carried over from the Wagner Act."[58] Conservative Republican senator Barry Goldwater saw the same possibility and, in part out of fear that the Eisenhower administration might be willing to soften Taft-Hartley in November 1953, urged the White House not to weaken the act, "especially in view of the fact that we now have a Board dedicated to its proper interpretation."[59]

Albert Beeson

Although there was little organized opposition to the appointment of Farmer and Rodgers to the Board, the next appointment, to finish out the term of Truman appointee Paul Styles, who resigned effective August 31, 1953,[60] was contested, because it would give Republicans a majority on the Board for the first time since the Wagner Act was passed in 1935. Although Truman's last appointee to the Board, Ivar Peterson, sometimes voted with Farmer and Rodgers on certain issues (while the other Truman appointee, Abe Murdock, either dissented or decided not to participate), by the winter of 1953 the two new Eisenhower members had deadlocked with the two holdover Democratic members in twenty to thirty cases involving vital issues such as jurisdiction and secondary boycotts. The third Republican appointment to the Board, therefore, would be a most important swing member with a deciding vote.[61]

Secretary of Commerce Sinclair Weeks urged the appointment of forty-seven-year-old Albert Beeson, who was highly recommended by some of the secretary's friends.[62] At the time of his nomination Beeson was director of industrial relations for the Food Machinery and Chemical Corporation in California, a diversified firm manufacturing food-processing and packaging machinery, industrial chemicals, and other items such as small tractors and armored personnel carriers for the army. Beeson, who said he was not a lawyer but had read labor law for many years,[63] had worked exclusively for management. Although Secretary of Labor James Mitchell preferred another person for the job, he later recommended Beeson as his second choice after receiving communications from Vice-President Nixon. Nixon called Beeson a "personal friend who had done a lot of work for the administration, both during the campaign and since we have been in Washington"; "he is also a friend of [Attorney General Herbert] Brownell's."[64]

Beeson was unsophisticatedly outspoken when he first appeared before the Senate Labor Committee on January 20, 1954. At the outset, he told the committee that as a part-time college lecturer he had frankly informed his students that he was teaching "an enlightened capitalism, and if they did not care to hear that they should take another course." Beeson said he was there "to explain the American enterprise system, from the businessman's viewpoint," a system he called "enlightened selfishness." Committee member Goldwater said that it was refreshing to find a businessman who had the courage to defend the free enterprise system. Beeson resented the suggestion that no businessman could be objective and free from prejudice: "To subscribe to this viewpoint . . . would inevitably support the Marxian theory of division of classes and separate the members of the productive team of American industry."[65]

Beeson charged the Herzog Board with stretching the law to read meanings into Taft-Hartley that were not intended to be there and agreed that it would be his obligation as a member of the Board to redress what he said was the pro-labor bias of the Herzog Board.[66] Beeson spoke carelessly, however, while criticizing the Truman Board's employer free-speech rulings under the Wagner Act. He told the committee how as director of industrial relations for the National Radio Corporation he had "free speeched" the "Pennsylvania Dutch people" in one of the company's plants and defeated the union. He added, "Now, you could say, if you like in that instance, that I was a union buster." Later in the hearings, when it appeared that his nomination was in jeopardy, Beeson admitted that it was foolish to have used the phrase "free speeched" and to have suggested that he was a union buster. He asserted he had always done his best "to see that our labor relations were such that perhaps the employees didn't need a union."[67] Beeson would be caught up in even more embarrassing equivocations and contradictions, raising serious doubts about his qualifications for the job.[68]

After five hours of heated debate and over the objections of the AFL and the CIO, the Senate confirmed Beeson by a narrow vote of forty-five to forty-two. Forty-two Republicans and three southern Democrats provided the margin of victory. The White House exerted heavy pressure to keep Republican senators in line, many of whom supported Beeson without enthusiasm.[69]

During the Beeson hearings Senator Herbert Lehman talked about the importance of an NLRB with the power to affect the daily lives and welfare of workers as well as the interests of industry and to reverse, within one year, the entire trend of labor policies in the country.[70] The new Eisenhower appointees were placed on the Board to make major changes in many important labor policies, and they accomplished their objective in slightly over one year. Overwhelmingly, those changes favored employers. The conservative and pro-employer philosophies of the new appointees, the stated outlines of doctrinal changes they decided to make even before confronting the facts and circumstances of specific cases, the political context in which they were appointed, and the magnitude of the changes in Board labor policy and the speed with which they were brought about led to the public perception that the NLRB would decide cases according to the philosophy or labor policy of whatever administration was in power.[71]

Doctrinal Changes

Farmer and his colleagues reduced the range of cases over which the NLRB would exercise its jurisdiction. Until Rodgers took office, however, the holdover members of the Board repeatedly out-voted Farmer. Over Farmer's objection, for example, Houston and Peterson voted to assert jurisdiction over a small garage operator in Wisconsin who had a franchise agreement with General Motors, because the garage was "an essential element in a Nation-wide system of automobile manufacturing and distribution." Farmer said that this small business, operated by the owner, his wife, and two mechanics, was "an essential part of the operations of General Motors in precisely the same respect and roughly to the same degree as a single drop of salt water is an essential ingredient of the Pacific Ocean."[72] It was not until Beeson arrived in March 1954, however, that the Republican-appointed majority on the Board was able to develop a new set of standards that would place many firms and their workers beyond the reach of Taft-Hartley.[73]

In in July 1954 the NLRB announced new and considerably higher dollar-volume standards that would have to be met before the Board would assert jurisdiction.[74] In comparison with the Herzog Board's 1950 standards, the yearly required direct and indirect outflow dollar volume of business for enterprises other than retail stores was doubled; the minimum required direct outflow for retail stores was quadrupled and the direct and indirect inflow doubled; and for service establishments, the required dollar volume of services furnished to interstate commerce was quadrupled. Businesses that the new Board regarded as fundamentally local, such as intrastate trucking, radio and television stations, newspapers, local utilities (gas, power, and water), and public transportation systems, which had no minimum dollar requirements under the 1950 standards, now had to meet annual dollar volumes of business ranging from $100,000 to $3,000,000.[75]

The Board applied its new jurisdictional standards for the first time in October 1954 (after the administration's bill failed in the Senate) in a series of eight cases, all involving petitions for representation elections. In these decisions Farmer, Rodgers, and Beeson declined to assert jurisdiction over an intrastate trucking company, a rice-drying cooperative, two supermarkets, an office building, a gas utility company, and a franchised automobile dealer.[76] The majority and the dissenters chose one of these cases, the *Breeding Transfer Co.,*[77] for an acrimonious exchange of views on the new standards.

The three Republican-appointed members emphasized that their new standards were based on the same criteria used by the Herzog Board in 1950: the need to bring the Board's caseload down to manageable size, partly so that the Board could give adequate attention to more important cases; recognition of the relative unimportance to the national economy of essentially local enterprises; and budgetary constraints.[78] Despite their many public speeches advocating less federal and more state authority over labor relations, Farmer and Rodgers denied, unconvincingly, that those statements had anything to do with the narrowing of the NLRB's jurisdiction.[79]

Murdock in his dissent said that he would speak bluntly because there was "reason for bluntness." He charged, without rebuttal by the majority, that there was not a "scintilla of evidence" to support the claim that the reduction in jurisdiction was due to limitations of funds or personnel. Quoting liberally from the speeches of Farmer and Rodgers, Murdock also charged that the slash in the NLRB's jurisdiction was simply the fulfillment of the new members' "avowed belief in the philosophy of returning a greater share of Federal authority to state and local governments." As a consequence of such states' rights predilections, Murdock warned, "hundreds of thousands of employers and millions of employees at work in these enterprises are now cut out from the Act, [in] the very area in which organization of employees is least advanced and most vigorously pressed at the present time."[80]

Paradoxically, it was the Republican-sponsored Taft-Hartley Act that had enlarged the scope of federal control and, unlike the Wagner Act, drastically restricted the conditions under which the board could cede jurisdiction to the states.[81] Probably because many of the states with labor relations statutes in 1947 had "little Wagner Acts," Taft-Hartley proponents in Congress added a provision to the act (Section 10[a]) prohibiting the Board from ceding jurisdiction where a state labor law was inconsistent with Taft-Hartley or had received an interpretation inconsistent with the corresponding provisions of Taft-Hartley. Congress thus established a uniform national labor policy unaffected by any inconsistent state law. The Board's new jurisdictional standards, therefore, substantially increased the number of employers and employees in an unregulated "no man's land."[82]

The new jurisdictional policy also had the effect of allowing an increasing number of employers and unions to engage in activities illegal under Taft-Hartley without fear of NLRB intervention. This was particularly true at the time in many of the areas eliminated from the new Board's consideration, such as substantial numbers of retail and department stores, where union organization was being pressed vigorously. It was in these small establishments that self-organization was most difficult and repressive tactics by employers most effective; employers, with immunity from federal action, could discharge employees for union activities, instigate company-dominated unions, refuse to bargain with union representatives, and in many other ways improperly interfere with workers' rights to organize and bargain collectively. On the other hand, small employers, often vulnerable to any illegal tactics of labor unions, had no recourse to the NLRB against secondary boycotts or picketing, jurisdictional strikes or picketing, forced closed shops, refusals to bargain, or picketing to force them to make workers join unions against their will. Whichever way the consequences of the new Board's jurisdictional policy cut, however, it was totally inconsistent for an agency that was responsible for applying a statute designed to promote industrial peace to adopt jurisdictional standards that facilitated industrial strife.[83]

Employer "Free Speech"

Captive Audience Speeches

Of all the new Board's rulings, the ones on employer speech, particularly the reversal of the Herzog Board's rules concerning employer captive audience speeches and interrogations of employees about union activities and attitudes, were the most publicized and the most criticized.[84] The first Wagner Act Board, under the chairmanship of J. Warren Madden, had required employers to remain strictly neutral in regard to their employees' organizational activities. In the opinion of Madden and his colleagues any anti-union statement by an employer to employees who depended on him for their livelihoods was bound to carry an implied threat of economic reprisals for disregarding the employer's wishes.

In 1941 Judge Learned Hand confirmed the Madden Board's approach in language that is still quoted: "Words are not pebbles in alien juxtaposition; they have only a communal existence; and not only does the meaning of each interpenetrate the other, but all in their aggregate take their purport from the setting in which they are used, of which the relation between the speaker and the hearer is perhaps the most important part."[85]

Not all the circuit courts of appeals, however, agreed with the Madden Board view.[86] Finally, in 1941 the Supreme Court, in *NLRB v. Virginia Electric & Power Co.*, said that the Constitution protected employer speech as long as it was not coercive, although the Court noted that speech could be coercive when examined in the totality of an employer's conduct.[87]

Because of the Supreme Court's decision the Board abandoned its strict neutrality approach to employer speech and ruled generally that anti-union statements, unless patently coercive, violated the Wagner Act only when found to be part of a coercive course of conduct. In one key area, however, the Board continued to apply its conception of an employer's superior economic position as an instrument of intimidation and coercion. Following an earlier decision in *American Tube Bending*,[88] the Board, shortly before the passage of Taft-Hartley, held in *Clark Brothers Co.* (Board member Gerard Reilly dissenting) that the act of requiring employees to listen to anti-union speeches on company property during worktime—a captive audience—was per se a violation of the act. Forcing employees to listen, in that Board's opinion, interfered with their right *not* to receive information concerning unions; it was the Board's obligation to protect "employees against that use of the employer's power which is inherent in his ability to control their action during working hours."[89]

Taft-Hartley's Section 8(c) provided that the "expressing of any views, argument, or opinion . . . shall not constitute . . . an unfair labor practice . . . if such expression contains no threat of reprisal or force or promise of benefit." As revealed by the legislative history of 8(c), Congress wanted, among other things, to eliminate the Board's *Clark Brothers* captive audience ruling.[90] Although in the face of Section 8(c) the Herzog Board abandoned *Clark Brothers,*[91] it did so without resolving the question whether an employer who delivered a captive audience speech was obliged, on union request, to provide a similar opportunity to a union. The Herzog Board was still determined to regulate captive audience speeches.

In *Bonwit Teller*[92] the employer, six days before a representation election, closed its department store, assembled its employees on the main selling floor, and delivered an anti-union speech. The employer, who had a rule (valid for department stores) forbidding solicitation by union organizers on the selling floor at all times,[93] denied a union request to address the employees under similar circumstances. Because the employer used company time and property to present its own anti-union views while barring similar presentations of pro-union views, the Board found it guilty of a discriminatory application of the special privilege given department stores to promulgate the broadest rules against union solicitation. The Board's decision was also based on the commission of other unfair labor practices by the company.

In what became the focus of great controversy, however, the Herzog Board also read Section 7 to guarantee employees the right "to hear both sides of the story under circumstances which reasonably approximate equality."[94] This interpretation was consistent with Section 8(c), the Board maintained, because it was not the employer's speech that was illegal but the employer's denial of an equal opportunity for the union to speak. The Board had shifted from finding captive audience speeches unlawful to requiring an employer to grant equalizing captive audience opportunities to unions, and from emphasizing the right of employees not to receive information they did not want to receive to emphasizing the employees' right to receive all available information.[95]

Soon, often over Chairman Herzog's dissents, a majority of the Board extended its principle of equal opportunity to hear well beyond the peculiar circumstances of *Bonwit Teller,* to situations in which there were no other unfair labor practices,[96] the no-solicitation rule applied only to working hours,[97] there was no rule against solicitation,[98] and the union had other media in which to discuss representation election issues.[99] Finally, in *Metropolitan Auto Parts*[100] the Board made explicit for the first time its conviction that under all circumstances in captive audience cases equal opportunity required union access to an employer's premises for a reply speech.

Management representatives had complained vigorously to the Senate and

House labor committees about the Herzog Board decisions in *Bonwit Teller* and *Metropolitan Auto Parts*. In December 1953, before Beeson joined the Board, Farmer and Rodgers (with the concurrence of Peterson on more limited grounds) in *Livingston Shirt Corp.* reversed all the expansions of the original *Bonwit Teller* decision in unfair labor practice cases. The majority stated the new rule:

> In the absence of either an unlawful broad no-solicitation rule (prohibiting union access to company premises on other than working time) or a privileged no-solicitation rule (broad, but not unlawful because of the character of the business) an employer does not commit an unfair labor practice if he makes a pre-election speech on company time and premises to his employees and denies the union's request for an opportunity to reply.[101]

Since the Livingston Shirt Corporation had a lawful rule prohibiting union solicitation only during working hours and the union had access to the employer's premises on nonworking time, the majority said that the employer was under no obligation to grant the union's reply request. The reasoning used by Farmer and Rodgers in the majority opinion and Murdock in his lengthy dissent reflected the still-unresolved conflict over the statutory purposes of Taft-Hartley. The majority talked of property rights, employer free speech, and the preeminence of the individual's right to choose after an open debate to join or not join a union.[102]

The majority also rejected the requirement of employer neutrality in union representation campaigns as well as the conception of implied threats of economic reprisals for union activity allegedly inherent in an employer's control over employees' livelihoods. According to Farmer and Rodgers, Congress wanted employers as well as unions to "be free to attempt by speech or otherwise to influence and persuade employees in their ultimate choice, so long as the persuasion is not violative of the express provisions of the Act."[103] Employers could now play a major role in influencing the employees' choice of union or no union. The majority found nothing in the statute or in legislative history that would restrict an employer "in the use of his own premises for the purpose of airing his views" or would impose "an affirmative obligation *to donate his premises and working time* to the union for the purpose of propagandizing the employees."[104] Representation elections were becoming open contests between employers and unions for the support of employees, an approach that until then the NLRB had always opposed.

Murdock based his dissent on a very different conception of the purpose of Taft-Hartley—the one carried over from the Wagner Act. He maintained that the declared congressional policy was one not of neutrality but of encouraging the practice and procedure of collective bargaining. In his view "practically every employer speech on company time and property is designed to perpetuate individual bargaining and to discourage collective bargaining." Murdock reviewed the history of the Board's long-held position "that one of the most potent and effective methods by which self-organization of employees could be stifled was through employer pressure transmitted at and to assemblies of employees at the place where they worked." To the extent legally possible, Murdock said, the Board should effectuate the congressional policy "by seeing that the parties who seek to implement that policy by bringing collective bargaining to the employees have an equality of opportunity to have their arguments reach the employees in the same effective forum used by those who would defeat collective bargaining."[105]

Interrogations of Employees

After Beeson joined the Board, he, Farmer, and Rodgers in *Blue Flash Express*[106] reversed another long-established Board rule that any systematic employer interrogation of employees about their protected union activities was per se an unfair labor practice.[107] Adopting instead an "under all the circumstances test," the Eisenhower majority decided that it was not an unfair labor practice for the general manager of the Blue Flash Company to "interview" all the company's employees individually in his office to find out if they had signed union cards, ostensibly so that he might know how to answer a union's claim of majority status. Although the general manager told the employees the alleged purpose of his questioning and assured them that their union status was immaterial to him, every employee denied signing a union card although each of them had done so only five days before being interrogated.[108]

Murdock and Peterson held that the majority's approach ignored the "realities of industrial life" and was contrary to the declared policy of the act to encourage collective bargaining.[109] They condemned direct questioning by an employer as well as espionage, surveillance, and polling as an invasion of the privacy in which employees were entitled to exercise their statutory rights, as a coercive isolation forcing an employee to "stand alone without the anonymity and support of group action," and as an implied threat of economic reprisal.[110] As evidence of such intimidation, the dissenters pointed to the interrogated employees' fear-inspired false denials of union adherence, which gave their employer grounds for refusing to bargain with a union that, in fact, represented all the employees in the bargaining unit.[111]

Murdock and Peterson, in response to the majority's assertion that the employer in *Blue Flash* was motivated only by a good-faith doubt about the union's majority status, maintained that there was no need for an employer to use interrogation with its coercive effect to reply to a union's request for recognition. Several approved methods were available, the dissenters noted: an employer could ask the labor organization for proof of its majority, request the union to petition for an NLRB representation election or file such a petition itself, agree to submit union authorization cards to a third party for verification, or refuse to bargain with the labor organization if the employer had a genuine doubt about its majority status.[112]

Farmer, not only in *Livingston Shirt* and *Blue Flash,* but also in his public comments, attempted to justify the reversal of established and important prior Board doctrines as merely conforming the Board's decisions to those of the circuit courts of appeals: "Once the courts have spoken on the construction of a particular provision of the statute, the Board has no choice, if it is to pay proper respect to our system of laws, but to conform its own decisional policies to the prevailing judicial view."[113] This argument was not persuasive. It was not unusual, and certainly not improper, for the Board to persist in a particular interpretation of the act in the face of conflicting interpretations in the circuit courts of appeals—until the Supreme Court decided the issue. Even by Farmer's standard, however, *Livingston Shirt* was a rush to reversal, since only one circuit court had considered the *Bonwit Teller* doctrine by the time the Farmer Board rejected it.[114] And in *Blue Flash,* in which the majority claimed that at least six circuits had explicitly or implicitly rejected prior Boards' per se approach to employee interrogations, most of decisions cited did not involve systematic interrogations.[115] The Board was under no compulsion to renounce the established interrogation doctrine since that issue remained unsettled in most circuits.

Fact Finding and Fact Interpretation: The Abandonment of *General Shoe*

The new Board redefined the law not only by reversing case doctrines but also through its control of the fact-finding process. The amount of evidence required to establish bad faith, interference, or discrimination is a matter of degree, not precise definition, and by choosing one degree of proof rather than another, a Board can change the outcome of many cases.[116] That was particularly evident in the Eisenhower Board's decision to analyze the content of an employer's statements in isolation from the circumstances in which the statements were made.

The question whether an employer's statement contains a threat of reprisal or promise of benefit is essentially a matter of fact interpretation. The new Board's interpretation of the facts of these cases, without explicitly changing any doctrines, so widened the area of permissible employer interference in representation election campaigns as to abandon the Herzog Board's laboratory conditions rule set forth in *General Shoe*.[117] What past boards had considered promises of benefits or threats of reprisals were now deemed only prophesies, predictions, privileged statements of legal positions, or harmless isolated incidents.

In *American Laundry Machinery Co.*, for example, the Eisenhower Board found no *General Shoe* situation because an employer's preelection announcement of progress on a formula that could result in substantial increases in employees' vacation and holiday pay was not a promise of benefit. In the opinion of the new Board "the announcement at most conveyed a vague suggestion of the possibility that at some indeterminate date the Employer might evolve a formula whereby these benefits could be increased."[118] Murdock saw the facts differently, especially since the union had made increased vacation and holiday benefits a representation campaign issue: the employer's announcement "furnished employees with a reasonable basis for believing that benefits suggested by the employer would be forthcoming without the aid of union representation [and] clearly implied a promise of economic benefit." In Murdock's opinion "sanctioning a clearly implied promise of gain by an employer who possessed the power to convert prophecy into reality" seriously restricted the employees' freedom of choice.[119] In another case, in which company officials told some employees that the company would have to move away if the union won the upcoming representation election, the new Board saw no reason to set aside the election (which the union lost), because it considered the employer's statements nothing more than predictions of the possible impact of wage demands on the employer's business.[120]

To prior Boards, a statement by an employer before a representation election that it would not bargain with a winning union, and if any bargaining did occur it would be only after protracted litigation, interfered with the employees' free choice of representatives and was grounds for setting aside the results of an election.[121] The new Board in *Esquire, Inc.*, however, saw these statements merely as expressions of the employer's legal position: "The Employer had the clear right to litigate this legal issue, and if he had the right to do it, he had the right to say he would." Company pledges that the union would get no more than the company was willing to give without a union were now seen as "at most" a statement of the employer's preference for dealing directly with its employees. To Murdock, the employer's conduct was calculated to create in the minds of the employees the impression that it would be futile to vote for the union.[122]

Employer speech came to be regarded as no more than preelection propaganda to which a union had the privilege to reply if it desired.[123] In late June 1954 the new Republican-appointed majority in *The Liberal Market, Inc.* put the finishing touches on *General Shoe:* "The Board must recognize that Board elections do not occur in a laboratory where controlled or artificial conditions may be established. We seek to establish ideal conditions insofar as possible, but we appraise actual facts in the light of realistic standards of human conduct."[124] There was now little chance that the Farmer Board would set aside representation election results on the basis of employer statements amounting to anything less than indisputable unfair labor practices.

The Eisenhower Board's Approach to Employer Speech

There was a certain degree of semantic fraud in referring to the captive audience, interrogation, and election campaigning cases as issues of employer free speech. The phrase concealed the real policy issue: the extent to which, if at all, an employer was to be permitted to exert economic power through speech in regard to employees' choice of and participation in unions.[125] The Eisenhower Board actively and purposely deregulated employer speech and involvement in the employees' choice whether to unionize. This policy choice clearly favored employers' resistance to unionization. The new Board went beyond the notion of protecting an individual employee's statutory right to chose or reject unionization and the collective bargaining process to the creation of an employer right to resist and obstruct unionization, a consequence definitely inconsistent with and contrary to the Wagner Act statutory policy, retained in Taft-Hartley, of promoting and encouraging collective bargaining. The NLRB's position had moved from absolute employer neutrality in the early years of the Wagner Act to one of sanctioning active employer resistance to unionization under Taft-Hartley. The deregulation of employer speech was not neutral and did not create equality between unions and management. It simply increased the ability of employers to use their economic power to defeat unionization efforts. Systematic interrogations and captive audience speeches are among the most effective methods employers have to resist unionization and collective bargaining.[126]

In regard to the content of employer free speech, Taft-Hartley was "becoming a law of how something is to be done rather than of whether it may be done"[127]—a matter primarily of form, focusing less on what could be said and more on how to say it. As one critic put it at the time, only the "most blatantly and stupidly phrased of promises and threats" would be prohibited.[128] The new Board's approach increased the need for the loophole lawyer, phrasing promises and threats to look like predictions and prophecies, personal opinions, possibilities, and statements of legal positions. If the Eisenhower Board's analysis of the content of employer speech in representation campaigns remained essentially unchanged for the "ill-advised and the contemptuous," it opened important new opportunities for the sophisticated to exercise economic power.[129]

Gerard Reilly, defending the new Board's decisions in the area of employer speech, rejected as "the sheerest kind of nonsense" contentions "that arguments of executives or supervisors subject workers to a 'brain washing.'" According to Reilly, everyone with practical experience in the field of labor relations knew that workers take both management and union attempts at persuasion "with a grain of salt" and, in fact, were likely to vote for union representation if they suspected their employer of improper pressure. He dismissed prior Board rulings because they were based on what he considered the mistaken notion that employees were intimidated by even the mildest anti-union expressions by supervisors because of the employer's economic power.[130]

Nevertheless, whatever policy was being advocated, no one knew just what the effect of an employer's anti-union statement on employees actually was or how that effect might differ according to various circumstances. Clyde Summers stated at the time: "What is seriously needed is a careful and objective study of the psychological impact of employer statements made under various conditions. Such a study might suggest wholly new and different rules to govern employer free speech."[131] Labor policy was being made without an empirical basis or evidence of its effect.

Other Decisions Affecting Union Power

At the same time that the Eisenhower Board was deregulating employer resistance to unionization, particularly during representation election campaigns, it was tightening its regulation of unions' use of economic weapons against employers. Collective bargaining had long been presumed the heart of the national labor policy. In essence, collective bargaining means the private adjustment of conflicts over wages, hours, and working conditions by the negotiation and administration of collective bargaining agreements between employers and unions. The legal framework that regulates and deregulates strikes, lockouts, picketing, and other economic weapons, as well as conduct during organization campaigns, influences not only the balance of power between employers and unions in the collective bargaining process (and, therefore, how the process works) but also whether there will be organization and collective bargaining at all.

Certainly, bargaining power is a consequence more of economic forces than of legal rules—the statutory right to strike does not mean that unions have the power to conduct successful strikes—but through regulation the law had nurtured and protected economically weaker parties in exercising their right to organize and had restrained the use of superior economic force, for the purpose of encouraging unionization and collective bargaining. The new members of the Eisenhower Board pursued a course that limited the power of unions in the industrial relations system. The Board, moreover, made no claim, as it had in the speech cases, that its new approaches to strikes, lockouts, picketing, boycotts, and other secondary pressures were dictated by an obligation to conform to the rulings of the circuit courts of appeals. In fact, many of its key decisions curtailing the economic power of labor organizations were contrary to consistent judicial approval of prior Board doctrines. The Eisenhower Board followed the circuit courts only when it desired to do so, that is, when the circuit courts' interpretations were in harmony with the new Board's policy choices.[132]

Hot Cargo Clauses

Although Section 8(b)(4) does not use the term "secondary boycott," a phrase as loaded with opprobrium as "employer free speech" is with approval, it did contain a general prohibition against union secondary pressures directed at "neutral" employers. The intent was to prohibit unions from pressuring these allegedly neutral or secondary employers to cease doing business with a primary employer with whom a union had a direct dispute, thereby increasing the pressure on the primary employer to concede to the union.[133] Long before Taft-Hartley, however, various unions, particularly the Teamsters, had obtained "hot cargo" provisions in their collective bargaining contracts. These provisions permitted unionized employees of secondary employers covered by these agreements to refuse to handle the products of "unfair" primary employers, such as struck or unorganized employers, or an employer whose working conditions did not meet union standards or whose goods did not carry a union label.

In 1949 the Herzog Board, in *Conway's Express,* found nothing in Section 8(b)(4)(A) of Taft-Hartley that prohibited a union and an employer from voluntarily including a hot cargo clause in their contract. In the opinion of the Herzog Board, since the secondary employers in *Conway* had consented in advance to permit their employees to refuse to handle the goods of an employer involved in a labor dispute with the union, "their employees' failure to deliver freight or accept freight from Conway trucks was not in the literal sense a 'strike' or 'refusal' to work" as those words were used in Section 8(b)(4)(A).[134] In sum, nothing in Taft-Hartley prohibited secondary employers from voluntarily refusing to deal with other employers.

Three years later the Second Circuit Court of Appeals affirmed the Board's decision in *Conway's Express*.[135] There were no Board or court decisions to the contrary when the hot cargo issue came before the Eisenhower Board. The matter arose when the McAllister Transfer Company refused to recognize the Teamsters as its employees' bargaining representative. The Teamsters then sought to enforce its hot cargo agreements with three shipping companies, to have those secondary employers stop doing business with McAllister. For different reasons, Farmer, Rodgers, and Beeson found that the Teamsters' conduct violated Section 8(b)(4)(A). Rodgers and Beeson said that it was their duty to reverse the *Conway* doctrine because they considered hot cargo clauses per se violations of the act. Rodgers and Beeson would not allow private parties to accomplish by agreement conduct that Congress intended to eliminate.[136]

In light of the Farmer Board's heavy reliance on one adverse circuit court of appeals decision as an explanation for rejecting the Herzog Board's *Bonwit Teller* doctrine, the majority's offhanded dismissal of the Second Circuit's support of *Conway's Express* undercut the new Board's contention that doctrinal changes were necessary to conform to circuit court rulings. Farmer, although concurring in the outcome in *McAllister,* chastised his colleagues in the majority for going too far. In a pointed comment he admonished, "Judges must resist the temptation to devise legal precepts to accommodate their moral judgments that this conduct or that is either laudable or indefensible."[137]

Picketing at a Secondary Situs

Since the object of Section 8(b)(4)(A) was to protect neutral third parties, picketing at the premises of a secondary employer was presumed to be a violation. In certain situations, however, such as the transportation industry, the situs of a primary dispute might not be fixed and the primary employer with whom the union had a dispute might be constantly moving from one location to another during a work day. In 1949 the Herzog Board, in *Schultz Refrigeration Service,*[138] allowed a union to follow the trucks of a primary employer and picket them while deliveries were being made at secondary customers' premises, on the theory that the trucks were extensions of the primary premises and there was no other effective way to picket under the circumstances.[139] The Farmer Board said, in *Washington Coca Cola Bottling Co.,*[140] however, that it would not permit roving situs picketing at secondary sites if the primary employer, such as the Washington Coca Cola Company, had permanent establishments in the vicinity where the union could and did picket.

The Herzog Board, in *Crowley's Milk*,[141] had also permitted picketing at secondary premises if the picketing union sought to persuade the secondary employer's customers not to buy the primary employer's products. In *Washington Coca Cola,* however, the Farmer Board limited that exception to situations in which the picketing occurred only at customer entrances and notices on picket signs were clearly limited to the primary employer's products. If an entrance being picketed was used by both the customers and the employees of the secondary employer, moreover, the new Board declared the picketing unlawful pressure against the employees of the secondary employer.[142] The Farmer Board placed other limitations on union picketing at common work sites where secondary employers shared the premises of a primary employer.[143]

Unprotected Strike Activity

In another series of decisions the Eisenhower Board, by reducing the scope of employee-protected concerted activity, increased the hazardousness of exercising the right to strike, the basic means by which employees demonstrate and apply their collective bargaining power. Apparently determined to discourage strike-related violence, the new Board, in *BVD Company, Inc.,* refused reinstatement and back pay to strikers who continued to picket peacefully during strike-related violence committed by other, unidentified persons. The Board found no evidence of a civil or criminal conspiracy by the strikers to commit violence and admitted that the strikers had no control over the unknown guilty parties and that there was no evidence the strikers had instigated or participated in the violent acts. The Board majority said, however, that it was not the responsibility of the strikers that was at issue but whether it would further the purposes of the act to require the company to reinstate and make back pay awards to the employees "as if no untoward conduct occurred." To ignore the "widespread physical violence, destruction of property, intimidation and threats" that had taken place, the majority said, would put a premium on force and violence in the conduct of strikes.[144] The Farmer majority denied that its decision impaired the right to strike or held blameless employees responsible for the lawlessness of strangers:

> But we do say that strikers have no right to protection when they, at the very least, welcomed the aid of criminal elements who took over their strike and desecrated it with violence and terrorism. We are forced to conclude that those strikers who continued to picket not only approved and ratified the violence but actually invited

it. We are compelled to this conclusion because there is no evidence in the record that the strikers took any action at all—by admonishment, denunciation, or public pronouncement—to discourage the commission of violence or to disassociate themselves from it.[145]

These strikers, innocent of wrongdoing, lost their jobs for failing to comply with previously nonexistent requirements. Murdock protested "this unprecedented and sweeping removal of innocent employees from the protection of the Act" and called it a "harsh policy of imputing the guilt of others to innocent strikers."[146]

Section 7 of Taft-Hartley guarantees employees the right to organize for the purpose of collective bargaining and to engage in other concerted activities, including strikes. When the Board or courts exclude certain strike activity from the coverage of Section 7, employees engaging in such excluded activity are left unprotected from employer retaliatory measures such as discharge. It would be an unfair labor practice for an employer to retaliate against an employee for engaging in protected concerted activity.

The new Board substantially narrowed the area of protected concerted activity by finding certain otherwise lawful strike activity indefensible on other grounds. In *Pacific Telephone and Telegraph Co.,* the union, instead of striking the entire company at once, picketed only one office at a time on an irregular basis during a nine-day period. The Board characterized this action as a "multiplicity of little 'hit and run' work stoppages" intended to "harass the company into a state of confusion." It was "a form of economic warfare entirely beyond the pale of proper strike activities" and, in the majority's opinion, was not entitled to the protection of the act.[147]

The Board also condemned a union's tactics against the Personal Products Company—organized refusals to work overtime, extension of rest periods from ten to fifteen minutes, slowdowns, and unannounced walkouts—as unprotected harassing tactics that prevented the employer from making any dependable production plans or delivery commitments. In the opinion of the majority the union's tactics were irreconcilable with the act's "requirement of reasoned discussion in a background of balanced bargaining relations."[148]

Beeson and Rodgers looked only at the nature of the union methods and offered no criteria by which to measure or define what constituted indefensible conduct. They made it clear, however, that if employees engaged in unprotected activity, there was no limit on the retaliatory measures an employer could take. In *Valley City Furniture,* for example, the employer, in violation of the act, had unilaterally increased the work day by one hour; the union refused to work the extra hour in protest of the company's failure to bargain about the longer workday. That was also an unprotected tactic, the Board concluded (even though it lasted only one day), because the union, by trying "to bring about a condition that would be neither strike nor work," was attempting to dictate the terms and conditions of employment. Rodgers and Beeson said that the employer's discharges of those employees who participated in the stoppage "were lawful self-protective actions against these unprotected strikes."[149] Rodgers and Beeson also found indefensible and unprotected the union's bargaining tactic in *Honolulu Rapid Transit Co.* of continuing to work five days each week but refusing to report for work on Saturdays and Sundays in a seven-day, around-the-clock work situation. They said that the "part-time weekend strike" could be described only as a usurpation of management's right to determine workers' schedules and hours of work.[150]

Although agreeing in each of these cases that the union's strike tactics were unprotected, Farmer noted that it was "unduly harsh and legalistic" to hold that every form of employee unprotected activity gave an employer license "to engage in every and all forms of retaliatory or unlawfully motivated discrimination."[151] He gave controlling influence to an employer's business needs in determining the extent to which an employer could properly interfere with employees' concerted activities and the extent of the employees' protection in such situations.[152]

The Farmer Board also rejected the Herzog Board's determination that unless a contract contained a no-strike clause, a union could strike to modify a contract anytime during the life of a contract, as long as it satisfied Taft-Hartley's sixty-day notice requirement.[153] The new Board in *Lion Oil* restricted the right to strike during the term of a collective bargaining agreement to those situations in which the parties had expressly agreed to reopen the contract during its life to consider modification of its terms; otherwise, a union could not lawfully strike until its contract had expired. The right to strike during the term of a contract was denied in the absence of a reopening provision even though the contract did not contain a no-strike provision.[154] According to Peterson and Murdock, the Farmer Board's interpretation in effect added a no-strike provision to every contract that did not contain a reopening clause.[155]

Despite a proviso to Section 8(b)(4)(A) safeguarding an employee's right to refuse to cross a picket line at the business location of an employer other than the employee's own, the Eisenhower Board, in *Auto Parts,* upheld the discharge of an employee who did not want to make deliveries where a union had a picket line but arranged for a fellow employee to do so. The employer said that the employee had to do his own assigned work or the company had no use for him. In the opinion of the new Board the statutory proviso meant only that such a refusal was not an unfair labor practice; it did not protect the employee from discharge for failing to perform the job he was hired to do.[156] The new Board, by ruling this conduct unprotected, rendered the statutory proviso meaningless.

In another case, *Terry Poultry Co.,* the Republican-appointed majority found no discrimination in an employer's discharge of two employees who, in violation of a plant rule, left their work without permission to present a grievance to a plant superintendent. Although acknowledging that the employees were involved in concerted activity, the majority said that this did not entitle them to ignore a reasonable plant rule.[157] Murdock and Peterson charged Farmer, Rodgers, and Beeson with severely restricting the scope of protected activity by giving greater weight to an employer's need to make plant rules than the statutory right of employees to engage in concerted activities concerning their wages, hours, and working conditions.[158]

Lockouts

Business representatives who appeared before the House Labor Committee in 1953 also objected to the Herzog Board's decisions in *Morand Bros. Beverage*[159] and *Davis Furniture*[160] that nonstruck members of an employer bargaining association would be guilty of unlawful discrimination if they locked out their employees when a union called a strike against another member of the association. The Truman Board and the courts, however, had permitted certain lockouts when there were special economic or business reasons making it impractical or impossible for the employer to continue operations under threat of an immediate strike.[161] In *Buffalo Linen Supply Co.,* however, the Eisenhower Board upheld a lockout by nonstruck members of a multiemployer association, undertaken not because of economic necessity but in anticipation of a union plan to strike, or "whipsaw," each employer member individually. A trial examiner had found the lockout unlawful retaliatory conduct because there was no evidence that the strike was likely to spread to nonstruck employers.[162] The majority, however, found an "implicit threat" of future strike action against other members of the association. In the face of what the new Board saw as an attempt by the union to exert economic pressure "to atomize the employers' solidarity" that was the fundamental aim of the multiemployer bargaining relationship, the majority considered the nonstruck members' lockouts "defensive and privileged in nature" rather than retaliatory and unlawful.[163]

"For the first time in the history of the National Labor Relations Act and its amendments," Murdock complained, "a majority of this Board is holding that the mere threat of a strike justifies discrimination against employees to discourage them from engaging in concerted activities for their mutual aid and protection."[164] According to Murdock, it was for Congress, not the Board, to decide if employers' right to use a lockout was the logical corollary of employees' lawful right to strike.[165] The Farmer Board's rejection of the Herzog Board's approach to lockouts in *Morand* and *Davis* greatly increased the economic weaponry available to employers in collective bargaining while reducing the unions' economic arsenal.

Refusals to Bargain and the Scope of Bargaining

Under Taft-Hartley, an employer is obliged to recognize and bargain with a labor organization that clearly represents a majority of the employees in an appropriate bargaining unit. Although usually the Board certified a labor organization as an exclusive bargaining agent as the result of a secret ballot, NLRB-conducted election, the old Board for many years also accepted union authorization cards as proof of a union's majority. The NLRB set aside representation elections that were lost because of employer unfair labor practices and ordered employers to bargain with a union on the basis of signed authorization cards. Farmer strongly objected to the use of authorization cards. He was unwilling to rely on them rather than on the results of secret ballot elections because he believed these cards were not reliable evidence of employees' true desires. Farmer said he would not substitute a doubtful test for the conclusive representation election.[166] His view became the Board's rule in *Walmac*.[167]

Later in *Aiello*,[168] the new majority held that when an employer refused to bargain with a union on the basis of authorization cards, the union had to choose either to go to a representation election *or* to file refusal-to-bargain charges with the Board. It was the Herzog Board's policy to permit a union, even after it had participated in a representation election with knowledge of an employer's unfair labor practices, to bring unfair labor practice charges.[169] As Peterson pointed out in his dissent in *Aiello,* moreover, the prior Board's approach met with approval in every court of appeals to which it was presented.[170] The Eisenhower majority, so concerned with the views of courts of appeals in other cases, in this case simply dismissed unanimous court approval of the Herzog Board's approach: prior court approval, they said, "does not render improper" the new Board's determination.[171]

The new Board said that it wanted only to protect the NLRB's procedural machinery from abuse by not wasting time and the public's money in useless and repetitive proceedings that gave unions two rather than one opportunity to demonstrate majority status.[172] But Peterson claimed that the new majority completely disregarded the Board's obligation to prevent unfair employer refusals to bargain designed to force a union to file an election petition: "This places an inequitable premium on an employer's unlawful conduct for, although the employer is the wrongdoer, the union is given the illusory choice of guessing correctly that it can win the election or withdrawing its petition and pursuing the longer and more time-consuming procedure of going through an unfair labor practice proceeding."[173] The *Aiello* decision increased the possibilities for an employer that wanted to escape its statutory responsibilities to bargain with a union chosen by its employees; the decision did nothing to foster the policy of collective bargaining.

The Eisenhower Board's decisions defining the scope of collective bargaining, however, reaffirmed and expanded the decisions of prior Boards and the courts. The Board ruled in *Whitin Machine Works,* for example, that, on request, an employer was obliged to provide a union with wage information essential to the intelligent representation of the employees. Farmer, wanting to conclude the "endless bickering and jockeying" that characterized the unusually large number of these cases coming to the Board, said, over Beeson's vigorous dissent, that employers had a continuing obligation to submit wage and related information to the bargaining agent of their employees without regard to the information's immediate relation to collective bargaining or the administration of a collective bargaining contract.[174]

In two other cases the new Board ordered a company to bargain with its union about the *effect* on its employees of moving its plant to a new location[175] and of a stock purchase plan already in effect.[176] Beeson dissented in both cases. He read the act's preamble to protect the legitimate rights of management and labor from interference by the other party: "Management cannot and should not be permitted to interfere with the internal affairs of unions. Conversely unions cannot and should not be permitted to interfere with matters solely within the province of management."[177]

The majority, however, did not advocate joint union-management determination through collective bargaining of what Beeson called "management prerogatives." The members of the majority reassured Beeson that bargaining about stock purchase plans had at most an "incidental effect" on management rights and that his fears of dire consequences were "more illusory than real."[178] In fact, in cases in which a union did negotiate a collective bargaining provision giving the union authority to resolve disputes over employee seniority, the Eisenhower Board held that the contractual clause itself was a per se violation of the act (Section 8[b][2]) despite a contractual provision forbidding the union from discriminating on the basis of union membership or nonmembership in the resolution of those disputes.[179] The new Board reversed prior Board policy[180] because seniority matters were "particularly within the knowledge" of an employer. Clearly, the Eisenhower Board was substituting its own conception of which substantive provisions of collective bargaining agreements were reasonable and acceptable.[181] Beeson did not have to worry that the new Board would approve union intrusion into areas of "management rights."

Concluding Observations

Within eighteen months the Eisenhower-appointed majority had reversed, drastically modified, or, through interpretation of facts, abandoned almost every Herzog Board doctrine to which employers had objected during the 1953 hearings before the House and Senate labor committees. The Republican administration Board's decisions deregulating employer representation campaign conduct facilitated and protected employer resistance to unionization, particularly by permitting employers to exert their economic power through speech. At the same time, the new Board tightened its regulation of the use of economic weapons by unions, thereby reducing unions' exercise of economic power at the workplace and making it more hazardous for employees to exercise their right to strike.

These important policy changes in the NLRB's interpretation of Taft-Hartley also reflected the value judgments of the new board members. Farmer, Rodgers, and Beeson, even before they decided a single case, advocated a reduction in federal control of labor relations and withdrawal of the NLRB from local disputes, promised reversal of "unsound" Wagner Act–oriented decisions of the Herzog Board, sympathized with employer complaints that the Herzog Board was on a mission to help unions organize and gain collective bargaining rights, and were convinced that unions had become "too powerful."

Despite Farmer's protestations, his Board was not neutral, nor could any Board be neutral. The Board must always make choices between competing values and policies, and that is exactly what the Farmer Board did. Its policy choices simply made it easier for employers to defeat employees' attempts to organize for collective bargaining and more difficult for unions to apply economic pressure on employers to achieve their goals. The value orientations of Board members, moreover, influence their fact finding and fact interpretation, as evidenced by the Eisenhower Board's approach to the *General Shoe* line of cases.

As one commentator assessed the first months of the Eisenhower Board, "seldom in the history of the Board has so much law been made so quickly by so few."[182] The new Board's decisions concerning jurisdiction, speech, and economic weapons involved more than correcting the "mistakes" of prior, Democratic administration NLRBs. Those decisions constituted major changes in national labor policy.

There clearly was a political factor in the new Board's making of labor policy. The nature and scope of the doctrinal changes and the speed with which they were made (especially the large number of decisions made in December 1954, the last month of Beeson's term) belied Farmer's assertion on becoming chairman that "politics play a proper part in the enactment of laws but politics have no place in their administration."[183] Many of the statutory changes that the Eisenhower administration and dissatisfied employers could not get Congress to enact in 1953 and 1954 were made part of the law by the NLRB through administrative interpretation. Among the most important were Taft's proposal to broaden the protection of employer speech, so that an employer's anti-union statements could not be grounds for setting aside an NLRB representation election that a union lost, and the move toward states' rights, reflected mainly in efforts to reduce the NLRB's jurisdiction.

Farmer had warned that the NLRB "should never be thought of . . . as a political organization."[184] Yet if the NLRB had been dominated by liberal Democrats for eighteen years, as employers and Republicans charged, the major changes in labor policy rapidly made by the new Republican-controlled Board substantiated perceptions that the meaning of the Taft-Hartley Act depended on which party had won the last election.[185]

8

Labor Law Reform, Employer Style

More Changes in the National Labor Policy

Control over appointments to the NLRB remained with the Republicans throughout the 1950s, since Eisenhower retained the presidency by defeating Adlai Stevenson again in 1956 by ten million votes, almost double his margin of victory in 1952.[1] During the same period, however, Democrats regained and strengthened their control of the House and Senate, increasing their margin over the Republicans in the House from 29 in 1954, to 33 in 1956, to 129 in 1958, and in the Senate from 1 in 1954, to 4 in 1956, to 20 in 1958.[2] (Eisenhower was the first president to have to deal with three successive opposition majorities in both houses.)[3] Particularly after the resounding Democratic victories in the 1958 congressional elections over a Republican Party beset with rising inflation, unemployment, and a falling gross national product, the recently merged AFL-CIO mistakenly believed it would be in command of the 86th Congress.

The relationship of organized labor to the Democratic Party, however, was changing. Both political parties were moving toward the political middle, seeking out independent voters who wanted a "politics of moderation."[4] Although the national Democratic Party's overall record on progressive social welfare issues (especially when compared to the Republicans') continued to retain the allegiance of organized labor, many Democrats in the House and Senate were anti–organized labor or uninterested in labor matters.[5] Thus organized labor had an uneasy relationship with the Democratic Party in the 1950s.[6] CIO president Walter Reuther maintained, for example, that "labor law reform would eventually come when the public realized and began to appreciate the role labor had played in pressing for progressive legislation."[7]

Ironically, in the late 1950s the press and the widely publicized McClellan committee hearings persuaded the public that unions were typically controlled by corrupt and arrogant leaders, such as Dave Beck and James Hoffa of the Teamsters; that few union officers were freely elected; that the views of these union leaders were contrary to the wishes of their membership; and that union treasuries were systematically looted by union bosses. The public demanded and got labor reform in 1959, but it was hardly what organized labor had in mind when it used the same phrase. Instead, it got a code for the regulation of internal union affairs, including disclosure of union records, elections of union officers, the use of trusteeships, the handling of union funds, and the conduct of intra-union disciplinary and expulsion proceedings. Although the original idea was to keep legislation concerning internal union reforms separate from amendments to Taft-Hartley, the political pressure for internal reform was converted into some amendments to the act designed to make unionization more difficult and weaken the bargaining power of unions—in part because of serious strategic blunders by the labor movement. Willard Wirtz summarized the results of this attempt at labor reform:

> The McClellan Committee's proper concern about "labor racketeering" was molded into a demand that "racket picketing" be prohibited, and this became the camouflage for a movement against all "recognition" or "organizational" picketing. The false impression was generated that the 1947 Act contained no restrictions on secondary boycotts, and the "hot cargo" clauses in the Teamsters' contracts were used to illustrate the need for additional prohibitions. What emerged as Title VII [of the Labor-Management Reporting and Disclosure Act of 1959] was a weird combination of responsible attempt at repair of a twelve-year-old statute which needed repair—and of irresponsible political opportunism.[8]

Although labor did not come away empty-handed—the noncommunist affidavit section was repealed, pre-hire contracts for the construction industry were approved, representation elections were expedited, and replaced economic strikers could vote in an NLRB election held within a year of the start of a strike—management obtained its key goals of closing "loopholes" in the act's picketing and boycott provisions and opening the way for greater state control of labor relations matters.

Once again, major changes were made in Taft-Hartley without empirical evidence about how the law was working in practice or about the particular labor problems the new legislation was supposed to resolve. In fact, no congressional hearings were held on the 1959 amendments, which were hammered out between House and Senate conferees. As with Taft-Hartley in 1947, many of these amendments were simply the products of compromises designed to remove obstacles to the passage of the Labor-Management Reporting and Disclosure Act of 1959. The Taft-Hartley Act labor policy was still being manipulated for political gain, ideological commitment, and economic power advantages.

After the Farmer Board's controversial reversals of the case doctrines of prior Democrat-appointed boards, the NLRB, under its new chairman, Boyd Leedom, operated at a less conspicuous and less intensive level. The Leedom Board, however, reaffirmed the Farmer Board's decisions and issued several important opinions of its own, particularly in the areas of picketing and secondary boycotts. The Republican-appointed NLRB, however, did not participate or contribute in any significant way to the development of the 1959 amendments to Taft-Hartley. Chairman Leedom testified in June 1959 before a Joint Subcommittee of the House Labor Committee and in February 1959 before a subcommittee of the Senate Labor Committee, both of which were considering labor-management reform legislation. On these occasions, however, his comments were limited to administrative and jurisdictional matters.[9]

Republican Appointments

The terms of member Albert Beeson and General Counsel George Bott both expired in December 1954. *Fortune* magazine acknowledged that during Beeson's brief tenure the Eisenhower Board had "tilted noticeably in the direction of management" in landmark cases by removing the employees of many small firms from the protection of the act, sharply narrowing the area of lawful union secondary activity, and expanding the "free speech" rights of employers.[10]

According to public reports, Beeson refused a full five-year term on the Board.[11] As talkative when he left as when he arrived, the "gung-ho" industrialist from California who "had a hard time believing the things that went on in Washington, D.C.,"[12] took some parting shots at the NLRB. He deplored the lack of practical experience among his colleagues on the Board and the agency's staff: "The NLRB operates under the handicap of having nobody on the Board or on its 1200 man staff who's ever worked in a plant or who knows the problems of industry." Beeson said that it was not until he began taking his legal assistants "through eastern factories" that any of them understood "the difference between a drill press and a lathe" or "why several unions under one roof make factory operation difficult." Courts uphold NLRB decisions because of the agency's expertise, Beeson added, but "as you may have gathered, I don't think it's very expert."[13]

Boyd Leedom

In regard to future Republican appointments to the Board, Beeson told reporters, Vice-President Nixon had said that the "row" in the Senate over Beeson's appointment would look like "a patty cake game" compared to the anticipated difficulty in getting a conservative Republican through the new Democratic Congress.[14] In a battle reminiscent of the ideological conflicts between Secretary of Labor Martin Durkin and Secretary of Commerce Sinclair Weeks, Durkin's successor, James Mitchell, considered a moderate-to-liberal Republican, vied with the conservative Weeks for control of appointments to the NLRB. Before the November 1954 congressional elections Weeks, Senator William Knowland of California, and other Republican conservatives urged the appointment of Michael Bernstein, former Taft aide on the Senate Labor Committee, as either a Board member or general counsel. Other White House staffers, aware that Bernstein was recognized as "management's man," warned that his nomination could create another "Beeson affair."[15] Mitchell resisted, and he and Weeks remained deadlocked until after the Democrats regained majorities in the House and Senate. Then the conservatives relented and Mitchell made the choice. He and the administration decided to pursue a noncontroversial figure who was not closely identified with either political party or with labor or management.[16]

Mitchell chose Boyd Leedom, a judge on the South Dakota Supreme Court.[17] The forty-eight-year-old Republican had received his undergraduate degree from Black Hills Teachers College in South Dakota and a law degree from the University of South Dakota. After several years in the general practice of law, Leedom served for ten years as city attorney in Rapid City. He served one term in the state senate (1949–51) and was an unsuccessful candidate for the Republican nomination for governor in the 1950 primary election. Leedom was appointed to fill a vacancy on the Supreme Court of South Dakota in 1951 and was elected to a full six-year term in 1954. His only labor experience was as a neutral member of a National Railroad Adjustment Board that handled approximately forty railway labor disputes in 1954. As Republican senator Karl Mundt of South Dakota put it when he introduced Leedom at his confirmation hearings before the Senate Labor Committee, "Judge Leedom comes from a State where the controversial problems which understandably sometimes develop between capital and labor are happily absent, because we have no large industrial institutions, and consequently we have no great labor organizations."[18]

A spokesman for organized labor described Leedom as a country lawyer with no record at all in labor relations—but "we know very well he's 100 percent against us."[19] Those who served on the Board with Leedom remembered him as a "gentle and kind man" who conducted prayer meetings each morning;[20] a "great humorist"[21] but not a strong leader or expert in labor law.[22] Despite his inexperience, no senator of either party on the Labor Committee asked Leedom about his views on the law he would have to interpret. It took the committee only ten minutes to approve Leedom's nomination and send it to the Senate floor. Within thirty minutes the committee had also approved, although not unanimously, the more controversial nomination of Theophil Kammholz for NLRB general counsel.[23]

Theophil Kammholz

For almost eleven months before Bott's term as general counsel expired, White House strategists had been concocting a plan to force his resignation before the November 1954 congressional elections, so that Senate confirmation of his Republican-named successor would be more likely.[24] They preferred to ask Bott for his resignation and, only if he refused, to proceed to have the attorney general prepare a letter for Eisenhower advising Bott that he was removed from office.[25] By early March, however, special counsel Bernard Shanley, presidential assistant Max Rabb, and others advised against further action on the plan to remove Bott until the administration had settled on a successor.[26] Some of this caution was probably due to Bott's determination to resist removal. According to Bott, Sherman Adams called him to the White House and asked him what his plans were: Bott said, "Mr. Adams, my plans are to finish out my term," and smiled. When Adams told Bott that the White House could oust him, the general counsel replied, "My lawyers tell me that there would be a lawsuit if you did."[27]

Although Board member Rodgers had been the early choice of conservatives such as Secretary of Commerce Weeks and Senator Knowland,[28] the administration nominated Theophil Kammholz for general counsel. Weeks supported the choice. Although Republicans were unable to have Kammholz confirmed before the November 1954 congressional elections, the administration renewed the nomination in January 1955.[29] Kammholz, forty-five years old when nominated, had received his undergraduate and law degrees from the University of Wisconsin. He worked for ten years with law firms in Wisconsin and was counsel of the National War Labor Board in Chicago. In November 1943 he joined the Chicago law firm of Pope & Ballard, where he represented employers in collective bargaining negotiations, grievance arbitration, and proceedings before the NLRB. From 1952 until his appointment as NLRB general counsel, Kammholz was a partner in another Chicago law firm: Vedder, Price, Kaufman & Kammholz.[30]

The anticipated heavy opposition to Kammholz's appointment from organized labor never materialized. Aside from Chicago printing trade unions that complained about Kammholz's conduct in a case more than twelve years old,[31] only Democratic senators Paul Douglas of Illinois and Pat McNamara of Michigan opposed the nomination. They objected to the Eisenhower administration's appointment to the Board of representatives of employers and others with a clearly "pro-employer orientation." Douglas and McNamara feared a further weakening of public confidence in the impartiality of the NLRB if the most powerful job at the agency was given to "another long-time advocate of employer interests."[32] Their objections had no apparent effect on anyone, and the Senate proceeded to confirm Kammholz's nomination on March 8, 1955.[33]

Although no senator on the Labor Committee questioned Kammholz closely about his beliefs concerning labor relations, he did say that he rejected the "philosophy of class conflict," which he maintained was "diametrically opposite to the concept of free enterprise, and free relations between organized labor on one hand and employers on the other."[34] In speeches delivered shortly after he assumed office the new general counsel identified protection of the rights of the individual employee as the central purpose of Taft-Hartley—in contrast to the Wagner Act, which he said emphasized collective groups and collective bargaining to the detriment of the individual worker's rights. Although Kammholz acknowledged the retention of an employee's right under the Wagner Act to join a labor organization without fear of employer retaliation, he emphasized that Taft-Hartley contained "the added provision that the employee is also free to refrain from any or all labor organization activities if he so desires." He also stressed that times had changed since the Wagner Act, and "big unionism"— particularly the newly merged AFL-CIO—was "coming abreast of the big businesses with which it deals." Echoing Guy Farmer, Kammholz said that the NLRB was the neutral, impartial, evenhanded protector of the "little guy," keeping the "individual worker from being completely engulfed in this day of big business and big unions."[35]

Kammholz deplored the lack of understanding between employers in the business community and the people in the Board's regional offices. In his opinion the Wagner Act did not promote rapport between employers and the regional offices because it "was aimed exclusively at employers as potential transgressors." Again, echoing Farmer and Rodgers's critical allusion to the Herzog Board and its predecessor Wagner Act NLRBs, Kammholz said that the regional boards' application of the statute did not call for a "crusade."[36] Relations between NLRB regional offices and employers were to be recast.

Kammholz named as associate general counsel Kenneth McGuiness, a former attorney for the Columbia-Geneva Steel Division of the U.S. Steel Corporation and field representative for the California Association of Employers in San Francisco who was invited by Beeson to join the Board as his associate chief counsel in 1954.[37] Kammholz and McGuiness were convinced that the NLRB's regional offices were "loaded with a bunch of New Deal liberals who could not be depended upon to do an honest job."[38] Kammholz put McGuiness in charge of the NLRB's twenty-one regional and seven subregional offices. McGuiness acknowledged that he and Kammholz were trying to make "a very pro-union agency more balanced." The associate general counsel told regional office personnel that it was their responsibility to protect individual employees, not employers or unions. He was concerned because the agency's staff, particularly people in responsible positions, had been brought in during Wagner Act days.[39]

Confronted with what he considered "philosophical zealots" who resisted "changing the direction of the agency," McGuiness appointed several assistant general counsels in charge of different sections of the country: "So they were our own people and they kept a very close eye on, and gave us a chance to get a closer look at, what was really happening in the regions." He realized that "a lot of people were nervous," but the objective was to rid the agency of philosophically union-oriented people.[40] Many career attorneys at the NLRB considered McGuiness a hatchet man who "wanted everything to be different from the way it had been and to be ultra-conservative." Inside the organization it was a period of turmoil as many resigned and new people were hired in what some at the NLRB saw as a deliberate attempt to move the agency far to the right.[41]

Gerald Brown, who was regional director in San Francisco when Kammholz became general counsel and who subsequently served as a Board member for ten years, said that, after Kammholz, Robert Denham did not seem so bad to the people in the field. In Brown's words, "I think they [Kammholz and McGuiness] felt we had a different view about things than they did. We felt the purpose of the act was to encourage collective bargaining . . . but I don't think Mr. Kammholz and Mr. McGuiness necessarily agreed with that."[42]

Kammholz accepted his appointment as general counsel with the understanding that it would be for only two years rather than the full four-year term, because he could not afford it financially.[43] He was general counsel from March 1955 to the end of December 1956; McGuiness subsequently served as acting general counsel for three months, from January to March 1957.

Political Compromise: Leedom as Chairman

Only two months after Kammholz began as general counsel, NLRB chairman Guy Farmer advised President Eisenhower and the president's assistant, Sherman Adams, that he did not want to be reappointed when his term expired on August 27, 1955. Farmer, who was making $45,000 a year before becoming chairman, said he could not exist on his NLRB salary.[44]

The need to replace Farmer and name a new chairman of the Board triggered another round of conflict between Weeks and Mitchell and conservative and liberal Republicans inside the administration. Mitchell tried to resolve the matter by asking Farmer to accept reappointment, but he declined.[45] Board member Philip Ray Rodgers became acting chairman when Farmer's term expired before a replacement was chosen.[46] When the deadlock continued into November 1955, Alexander Smith, chairman of the Senate Labor Committee, told Sherman Adams that without the fifth place being filled and without a permanent chairman, the Board was deadlocked two to two on several important issues. "From the Administration's standpoint," Smith said, "many of the policies of the Roosevelt and Truman Administrations are continuing in effect, and this cramps the style of the President's appointees."[47]

Finally, on November 18, 1955, Eisenhower designated Boyd Leedom chairman of the NLRB and nominated little-known sixty-three-year-old NLRB trial examiner Stephen Bean to the Farmer vacancy. Both moves were compromises between conservative and liberal factions in the administration. Bean, a surprise choice to both labor and management, had been Republican mayor of Woburn, Massachusetts, a suburb of Boston where Weeks resided. Congressional sources said that Bean had been sponsored by Weeks and accepted by Mitchell.[48] Mitchell's acquiescence may have been due partly to his strong preference for promoting career employees from within and his aversion to appointing people directly from labor or management to the NLRB.[49]

Kammholz and McGuiness: Personnel Changes to Control the Regional Offices

Kammholz described Bean as a gentleman not given to controversy. His legal assistant for two years, Warren Davison, recalled him as a "fine guy to work for," a "very laid-back fellow," "always the epitome of the Massachusetts gentleman." Another colleague, Frank Kleiler, remembered him as a competent trial examiner who, after he became a Board member, would "sit back and rely entirely upon his chief legal assistant and other staff" to handle the issues.[50]

For the first time in nearly a year the NLRB had a full complement of Board members and a general counsel. Almost immediately, however, Senator Joseph McCarthy, trying to rekindle his ill-fated search for communists in government after being censured by the Senate in December 1954,[51] charged, in November 1955, that the NLRB was "honeycombed" with security risks.[52] In December, Herbert Fuchs, former attorney and supervisor in the NLRB's pre–Taft-Hartley Act Review Division, told the House Un-American Activities Committee that he and sixteen other attorneys at the NLRB in the late 1930s and 1940s were communists. Fuchs's revelations were stale,[53] and as usual McCarthy never delivered on his charges.

Leedom and Kammholz responded quickly, however, and expanded by three hundred the number of jobs at the NLRB labeled "sensitive," meaning that those selected for the positions had to pass an investigation by the FBI. (This move increased the number of "sensitive" jobs to 500 of 1,630 positions in the agency.) Leedom admitted that the Board had acted in response to McCarthy's charges and the House Un-American Activities Committee hearings: "If we are honeycombed with communists—and I don't think we are—it would have to be in areas where the security program didn't reach."[54]

It is difficult to disentangle the reasons for the large number of personnel changes made at the NLRB in this early stage of the Kammholz-McGuiness period. Some employees were fired or forced out as a result of the NLRB's "security program." In March 1956 Senator Wayne Morse accused Kammholz of dismissing or demoting, for political reasons, long-time NLRB attorneys and administrators and replacing them with "politically approved" personnel who would make doctrinal changes that reduced the protection of labor and increased the rights of management.[55] Morse hit hard at Kammholz, charging him with instituting a new policy prohibiting regional directors from dismissing unfair labor practice charges against unions until those charges were brought to the attention of the new general counsel, even in circumstances in which the only union conduct alleged to be illegal was lawful under controlling Board and court decisions. Morse claimed, moreover, that when charges regarded as doubtful were filed against employers, those charges were dismissed. Morse also accused Kammholz of spending less than 50 percent of his time at his desk in Washington because he was making speeches before employer groups around the country: "Congress did not establish the office of General Counsel of the Board to serve as a propaganda arm of the Republican Party."[56]

Alexander Smith, former chairman of the Senate Labor Committee (Democrat Lister Hill of Alabama was the new chairman) and then ranking Republican member of the committee, and Senate minority leader William Knowland of California submitted a written defense of Kammholz to Morse on July 9, 1956.[57] Smith and Knowland had attached to their report replies to Morse's criticisms from NLRB chairman Leedom and General Counsel Kammholz, submitted at Senator Hill's request.[58] Kammholz defended his case handling, said that the estimate of his speech-making time was "grossly exaggerated," and claimed that some reassignment of personnel and "introduction of new blood" was necessary to make the agency more efficient.[59] Leedom dismissed Morse's charges as dealing with only "two-tenths of 1 percent" of the 4,615 decisions issued by the NLRB in fiscal years 1954, 1955, and the first half of 1956:

"Admittedly, two-tenths of 1 percent is a rather small area for purposeful distortion of the congressional intent."[60] Farmer and Rodgers had often made similar claims, emphasizing, for example, that about 95 percent of the Board's decisions were unanimous.[61] Despite a surface plausibility, these statistics were deceiving. Leedom's 4,615 decisions, for example, included all contested representation and unfair labor practice cases regardless of difficulty or problem. Representation cases, by far the most numerous, usually involved technical questions of when an election should be held or whether a particular occupation should be included in a bargaining unit. It was misleading to use agreement in cases of this sort as evidence of unanimity of opinion among Board members. Often such unanimity in a Board decision is the result not of agreement on the issues but of the practice whereby dissenters in private follow the majority's ruling in public until a new majority can be mustered to overturn it. A dissenter is often silenced, moreover, by the need to get along.

The most serious defect in the aggregate case statistics used by Leedom and his colleagues to indicate unanimity at the Board was, however, qualitative, not quantitative. A small number of rulings on matters of pivotal importance can change the direction and character of an agency's regulation even when most other doctrines remain the same. In his charges Morse cited what he considered "32 major precedent-setting" changes made by the Eisenhower Board in statutory interpretation or administrative policy.[62] The influence of rulings on key issues extends beyond just those matters. As one former NLRB litigation attorney put it: "they set a tone which subtly, but inevitably and significantly, guides the host of Board employees—in the everyday performance of the agency's work. Investigative zeal is dulled or whetted, or its direction changed, as the mood of the agency heads is gauged. These consequences may not be capable of statistical demonstration, but they nonetheless exist, as everyone familiar with institutional activity knows."[63] Major policy, administrative, and ideological changes had been made by Eisenhower's appointees to the NLRB; it was dissembling to pretend, through the manipulation of case statistics or otherwise, that nothing unusual or important had happened.

Doctrinal Changes: The Same Direction at a Slower Pace

The Eisenhower Board, under Leedom's chairmanship, continued to make important policy changes, many of which were long sought by management. They were implemented more slowly and with less fanfare than during Farmer's chairmanship, however.[64] In one of several important decisions made in Farmer's last weeks as chairman, the Board, in a case involving the Sand Door and Plywood Company, further diminished the significance of a hot cargo provision in a collective bargaining agreement as a defense to an unfair labor practice charge against a union. In the opinion of a new Board majority of Leedom, Farmer, and Rodgers, while it was permissible for an *employer* to agree voluntarily to boycott the goods of another employer, it was an unfair labor practice for a *union* to appeal to the employees of that employer to implement contractual hot cargo rights. According to the Board, such instruction from a union party to a contractual hot cargo provision constituted an inducement of employees to engage in a concerted refusal to handle goods no less than it would in the absence of such an agreement.[65]

Although the Republican-appointed members of the Board expanded the government's regulation of what economic weapons unions could use in support of their collective bargaining demands, Farmer (in one of his last decisions as chairman) and Leedom opposed an extension of government regulation of the subjects for collective bargaining. Roosevelt- and Truman-appointed Boards had since at least 1940 decided what were and were not obligatory subjects for compulsory bargaining.[66] In *Borg-Warner* the employer insisted as a condition of agreement that the collective bargaining contract include a clause requiring the employees to take a secret ballot vote on the employer's last offer before engaging in a strike, as well as a recognition clause that excluded as a party to the contract the Board-certified international union and substituted its uncertified local affiliate. Although neither of these clauses was unlawful in itself and both would have been permissible if mutually agreed on voluntarily, a majority (Truman appointees Murdock and Peterson joined by Rodgers) held that insistence on either of these clauses was a refusal to bargain because neither clause was an obligatory subject of collective bargaining. The majority saw the employer's recognition clause as an improper demand on the union to bargain away its Board-certified status and the ballot clause as an attempt by the employer to deal directly with its employees as individuals in derogation of the union's status as exclusive bargaining representative, causing a dilution of union authority, diffusion of its responsibility, and dissipation of its strength.[67]

Farmer, joined by Leedom in his dissent, said that the Board had no statutory authority to outlaw good-faith proposals of lawful contract clauses. The outgoing chairman said that it was "a meaningless play on words to say that some proposals are 'bargainable' but must be withdrawn the moment the other party indicates opposition to them."[68] Farmer cited the Supreme Court's 1952 decision in *American National Insurance* overruling the Herzog Board's opinion that it was a per se refusal to bargain for an employer to insist on a clause reserving to management exclusive authority to determine several conditions of employment, including promotions, discipline, and work scheduling. In that case the Supreme Court said that the "Board may not, either directly or indirectly, compel concessions or otherwise sit in judgment upon the substantive terms of collective bargaining agreements."[69] Farmer, citing *American National Insurance,* concluded that what a collective bargaining contract should contain was an issue for determination "across the bargaining table and not by the Board."[70] In a plea to let the parties protect their own interests and have more freedom to make their own bargains, Farmer claimed that the majority's approach "would bring about a premature and artificial crystallization of labor-management relations and, moreover, would inject the Government into the collective bargaining process to a degree which would be disruptive to labor-management relations."[71]

Whatever the merits of the majority's approach to *Borg-Warner,* it was at least inconsistent to maintain that the Board could regulate the choice of economic weapons to be used in the collective bargaining process but not the substantive terms on which the parties contract.[72] The process of collective bargaining requires that economic sanctions be available to both parties; otherwise, there will be only polite listening and terms of employment established by employer fiat. The availability and effectiveness of economic sanctions certainly affect the outcome of the bargain, including the substantive provisions of a contract. Thus it was disingenuous for Farmer and Leedom to advocate free, unregulated collective bargaining at the same time they were limiting the economic weapons unions could use to bring about favorable outcomes in collective bargaining.

After Farmer left, the Board continued to restrict union bargaining tactics, ruling in 1957 in *Insurance Agents' International Union* that a union's on-the-job "harassing tactics" during negotiations for a new contract were "plainly 'irreconcilable with the Act's requirement of reasoned discussion in a background of balanced bargaining relations upon which good-faith bargaining must rest.'"[73] The unionized insurance agents' "Work without Contract" program, which the agents argued was a concerted slowdown no different than a strike, included refusals to write new business, reporting late to work, remaining in the office in the mornings "doing what comes naturally," picketing and distributing leaflets in front of company offices, securing policyholders' signatures on petitions supporting the union, and refusing to submit certain reports or to work after 4:30 P.M., contrary to what they customarily did. The Board saw the union's "utter disregard" of assigned duties as the "antithesis of reasoned discussion it was duty-bound to follow." The union's willingness to continue bargaining did not fulfill its obligation to bargain in good faith, the Board said: "At most, it demonstrates that the Respondent was prepared to go through the motions of bargaining while relying upon a campaign of harassing tactics to disrupt the Company's business to achieve acceptance of its contractual demands."[74]

Although the Leedom Board issued other decisions reducing union rights from their extent under the Herzog Board,[75] its restrictions on peaceful picketing were the most important and controversial. The Leedom Board, like the Farmer Board, treated employer speech and union speech differently. These Eisenhower Boards essentially ignored the effect of the context of the employer's speech—the setting in which it was made and the entire course of employer conduct of which it was a part—while treating union picketing as inherently coercive, precisely because of its setting.

These approaches were contradictory: treating the act of union picketing itself rather than what was said on a picket's placard as evidence of coercion but, in assessing the lawfulness of employer speech, considering only the individual words uttered and disregarding the commonly accepted proposition (on which the Truman and Roosevelt Boards operated) that because of employees' economic dependence on employers, employer communications usually had an inherently coercive impact on employees. If a picket distributing leaflets outside a store was exercising coercion rather than persuasion, why was it different for a manager to pass out letters to employees inside the store? As one commentator asked, "Why, if picket line speech is *per se* subject to prohibition because of the inherently coercive aspects of its setting, [is] an employer's speech to employees on plant time and property not equally vulnerable to *per se* suspicion, if not *per se* prohibition?"[76]

Two important cases illustrate the Eisenhower Boards' conflicting approaches to employer and union speech. In one case, decided shortly before Farmer left the Board in the summer of 1955, a majority of the Board ignored the context of employer unfair labor practices, including unlawful interrogations and discharges of employees as well as unlawful support for an employee organization, and found literature distributed by the employer to be anti-union in nature but not coercive. The Board reasoned that expressions of opinion cannot be unfair labor practices if the expressed arguments on their face contain no threats or promises of benefits. The majority explicitly rejected the contention that the employer's violations of Taft-Hartley converted otherwise protected opinions into unfair labor practices.[77] As in *Livingston Shirt*,[78] the majority also said that it was not an unfair labor practice for the employer to enforce against its employees a plant rule prohibiting posting, solicitation, and the distribution of literature while breaking its own rules by engaging in anti-union solicitation in the plant. The majority, not even mentioning the possibly coercive effects of the employer's in-plant solicitation, put management, kinglike, above its own rules: "Management prerogative certainly extends far enough so as to permit an employer to make rules that do not bind himself. Otherwise, an employer can only enforce a rule he promulgates so long as he conducts himself according to the rule."[79]

On October 30, 1957, a new Republican-appointed majority[80] ruled in *Curtis Bros., Inc.* that any union picketing for exclusive recognition by an employer when representing less than a majority of the employees coerces employees in violation of the act. The Board reasoned that the union picket line itself was a signal to employees not to report for work, to customers not to buy the company's products, and to suppliers not to deliver; it was a device used to damage the employer economically "to the point where his financial losses force him to capitulate to the Union's demands." That, of course, involved direct pressure on the *employer*, however, and Section 8(b)(1)(A) prohibited a union from restraining or coercing *employees* in the exercise of their statutory rights. The Board found nothing that limited the meaning of restraint or coercion to *direct* application of pressure by the union on the employees; *indirect* pressure was enough: "Damage to the employer during such picketing is a like damage to his employees. . . . The diminution of their financial security is not the less damaging because it is achieved indirectly by a preceding curtailment of the employer's interests."[81]

Murdock accused the majority of adopting an interpretation of the act seriously detrimental to the rights of employees to engage in concerted activities.[82] He claimed that Congress never intended 8(b)(1)(A) to be used to bar peaceful picketing, whatever its object, but only to prohibit union coercion of employees involving actions such as threats of reprisals in the course of organizing campaigns, mass picketing, and violence.[83] Murdock pointedly charged the Republican-appointed majority with applying a double standard:

> Furthermore, no such extreme theory of coercion as that advanced in the majority decision has been applied to the acts of employers. Inherent in the employment relationship is the possibility of economic loss if an employee displeases his employer and the possibility of gain if an employee finds favor with the employer. Yet, an employer may urge upon employees his preference as to union representation, may disparage unions and their leaders and may predict that unfavorable economic consequences will result from self-organization without being found to coerce his employers in violation of Section 8(a)(1). In each of these situations, the possibility of economic loss is evident to employees if they do not support the employer's position, and in each situation the employer's conduct affects the exercise by employees of their rights under Section 7.[84]

In a companion case, *Alloy Mfg. Co.*, the majority extended its *Curtis Bros.* doctrine to equate placing an employer's name on a "We Do Not Patronize" list, in an attempt to gain exclusive recognition, with picketing for recognition, because both were intended to inflict financial loss on an employer and, if successful, employees' earnings were threatened and their jobs endangered. In sharp contrast to its views on employer speech, the Republican majority rejected the contention that "We Do Not Patronize" lists were merely expressions of views, arguments, or opinions protected by Section 8(c) of the act.[85] In its implementation of the national labor policy of collective bargaining carried over from the Wagner Act to Taft-Hartley—a policy based on the theory that economic pressure exercised by employers and unions on each other would result in mutually acceptable compromise—the Republican majority from Farmer's through Leedom's chairmanships, with its decisions about what constituted threats, coercion, or restraint, was seriously weakening unions' ability to bring economic pressure to bear on employers.[86]

Curtis Bros. is a good example. In that case the incumbent union went on strike in an attempt to obtain a contract with the employer. The employer, as it was legally entitled to do, replaced these economic strikers with permanent replacements.[87] According to the law at the time, the strikers were ineligible to vote in the subsequent election requested by the employer; only their replacements could vote. As expected, the union lost the election. Ironically, what was once a majority union engaged in a lawful economic strike became by operation of the statute a minority union. By application of the Board's *Curtis* doctrine, moreover, it could be enjoined from continued picketing. In sum, a labor organization representing a majority of an employer's employees could engage in a lawful economic strike only at the risk of having its membership permanently replaced, losing a subsequent election in which these members could not participate, and being deprived of the right to picket the employer,[88] or, under *Alloy,* denied even the right to put the employer on a "We Do Not Patronize" list. It was a result so extreme that it could be said justifiably that a law originally intended to encourage employees to join unions and to engage in collective bargaining was now being used to protect resistance to organization and prevent collective bargaining.

There were other indications that the Eisenhower Board had reversed the Truman Board's application of the act. During the terms of Truman appointees Denham and Bott, from 1948 to 1954, for example, an average of approximately 77 percent of all unfair labor practice complaints issued by the general counsel's office were against employers and 23 percent were against unions. That rate was consistent on a yearly basis, ranging from a low of 69 percent in 1948 to a high of 83 percent in 1952. During the tenure of the first Republican-appointed general counsel, Theophil Kammholz (March 1955–January 1957), however, unfair labor practice complaints issued against employers dropped to

57 percent of all such complaints in 1955 and 44 percent in 1956. In 1956, for the first time since the passage of Taft-Hartley, the general counsel's office issued more unfair labor practice complaints against unions than against employers. From 1955 through 1957 the percentage of complaints issued by Republican general counsels balanced out at 53.6 percent against employers and 46.4 percent against unions.

Complaints issued as a proportion of charges made against employers also dropped, from an average of 13 percent during the Denham-Bott period to approximately 8 percent when Kammholz was general counsel. At the same time, the ratio of complaints issued to charges made increased for unions, from an average of 13 percent under Truman-appointed general counsels to more than 17 percent under Kammholz. In 1956, Kammholz's only full year with the NLRB, his office issued complaints in only 9 percent of the charges made against employers but in more than 23 percent of the charges made against unions.[89]

Beginning in 1954, moreover, there was a sharp decline in the percentage of union victories in NLRB-conducted representation elections and in the percentage of voters in those elections supporting unionization. The proportion of union representation election wins dropped from slightly over 72 percent in the Truman Board period after Taft-Hartley to 63 percent from 1954 to 1958. The proportion of participants in those elections who voted for union representation decreased from an average of 75 percent from 1948 to 1953 to 66 percent from 1954 to 1958. In both categories the percentages decreased each year from 1954 to 1958.[90]

The Merged AFL-CIO

The decline in support for unions was due to many factors, not the least of which was the public humiliation and castigation of unions in the second half of the 1950s. At the same time that the newly united AFL-CIO proclaimed itself the greatest union force in United States history, it pledged to eliminate corruption and racketeering from its ranks.[91] When the AFL and CIO merged in late 1955, congressional investigations into the improper use of labor union pension and welfare funds had already begun. Conservative columnists, such as Arthur Krock of the *New York Times,* evoked a vision of a pressure group of unprecedented political power fully capable of gaining absolute control of the economy,[92] and the president of the National Association of Manufacturers warned of a "ghost government" in which union leaders would "pull strings behind the scenes and direct the destinies of the nation."[93]

Eisenhower, in a telephoned talk to the founding convention of the new AFL-CIO, praised labor for its unique contribution to the national welfare,[94] but privately he deplored stories of "ruffianly tactics" in unions and asked his cabinet about antitrust legislation to check such a "tremendously large organization unrivaled by others in the same field."[95] The AFL-CIO's decision in the mid-1950s to make repeal of Section 14(b) (the anti-union-security provision of Taft-Hartley) its first legislative priority, particularly when readily translated by its opponents as a demand for compulsory unionism, only reinforced the widely publicized charge that unions had become "too powerful."

In early 1956 an unidentified assailant threw a bottle of acid across the forehead, eyes, and nose of labor columnist Victor Riesel, well known for his unrelenting denunciations of what he called "a dangerous combine between 'big-time labor leaders and known criminals.' "[96] The Riesel story—his subsequent blindness and courageous return to work, the apprehension by the FBI of two exconvicts linked to labor rackets in the garment industry, and their conviction and sentencing—remained in the news throughout 1956 as a symbol of labor brutality and violence.[97] By mid-June 1956 Eisenhower, reportedly spurred by the blinding of Riesel, told AFL-CIO president George Meany that he planned to take action against "underworld infiltration" into unions. Meany said organized labor would cooperate as long as any investigation concentrated on ridding unions of corruption and not on weakening organized labor.[98] The investigation of corruption and the weakening of organized labor, however, could not be separated.

For two and a half years, beginning with its formation in January 1957, the McClellan Committee on Improper Activities in Labor-Management Affairs, commonly known as the Labor Rackets Committee, trumpeted report after report of corruption and the misuse of funds by labor unions, particularly the Teamsters.[99] Amplified by television and the press, the Labor Rackets Committee's hearings provided a sensational revelation every day concerning the iniquities of its main targets, Teamster union president Dave Beck and his successor, James Hoffa. To the public, although there was no evidence to support the breadth of its indictment, labor unions came to mean Teamsters, and union leaders to be synonymous with arrogance and bossism, hand-tailored silk suits, mansions, costly automobiles, violent suppression of workers' rights, and theft of members' money and pensions.[100]

The hearings dealt a heavy blow to union organizing, particularly in the South.[101] Republican senator Irving Ives, appearing on the popular television news show *Face the Nation,* said that unions were in a "most awful mess" that "could set labor back ten or twenty years."[102] That was a conservative estimate; unions have never shaken free of the images created in the McClellan committee hearings.

Organized labor drew false hope from the outcome of the 1958 congressional elections, in which the Republican Party suffered its worst defeat since the beginning of the depression.[103] The Democrats gained fourteen Senate seats, increasing their margin over the Republicans to thirty (64 to 34), and an additional forty-nine seats in the House, where their majority was 283 to 154. After November 1958 organized labor deluded itself into believing that it not only could control the content of any legislation dealing with improper practices by unions but also could demand "sweeteners"—changes in Taft-Hartley favorable to unions—as the price for its cooperation in passing any such bill.

The AFL-CIO (especially the former AFL leadership) underestimated the enormous pressure on Congress to pass union reform legislation; the public mood demanded it. Neither the Democratic Party nor any of its potential candidates for president in 1960 could ignore that pressure. Possibly because it came to believe the popular propaganda concerning unbridled union power, the AFL-CIO, moreover, still did not appreciate that it was more a captive of the Democratic Party than the party was a captive of the AFL-CIO. Organized labor simply had no reasonable alternatives to the Democratic Party, and although the Democrats wanted to minimize harm to labor, the party, particularly in a presidential election period, needed to respond to the public outcry.

As explained by Harvard law professor Archibald Cox, Senator John Kennedy's chief legislative adviser and a key participant in fashioning reform legislation, Kennedy and his supporters wanted to keep internal union reforms separate from Taft-Hartley amendments. If the two were confused, the need for internal reforms could easily be used to enact amendments intended to hamper unionization and weaken the bargaining power of existing unions.[104]

Union strategists, however, insisted on a "one package" deal, conditioning their support for the moderate Kennedy-Ervin reform bill on Taft-Hartley amendments long sought by organized labor.[105] This serious blunder by the AFL-CIO facilitated the passage of legislation that not only more severely regulated internal union affairs but also tightened rather than relaxed Taft-Hartley restrictions on union organizing and bargaining tactics.[106] According to one commentator, this tactic proved that union leaders were still apprentices in legislative package-handling.[107]

The Use of Labor Reform to Amend Taft-Hartley

The AFL-CIO's enemies were more astute, more clever, and better organized than the labor federation. Various management groups worked closely with White House staff people, such as Gerald Morgan, now deputy assistant to the president, to develop a unified legislative strategy.[108] Management wanted to close what it considered Taft-Hartley loopholes concerning picketing and secondary boycotts and increase the applicability of state laws to labor relations while retaining unchanged the other provisions of the act. Rather than pursue openly its goal of changing the power balance between management and labor, management organizations exploited the public's indignation at widely publicized evidence of corruption in some unions. Chambers of commerce and other business groups produced "just plain folks" who told Congress and the media how they had been hurt by coercion within their unions, secondary boycotts, or organizational picketing. An unidentified administration spokesman noted, "We wanted this to look like the people against the labor bosses and not Big Labor against Big Business or even against the Administration."[109]

While appearing to stay on the sidelines, business organized massive letter-writing campaigns, circulated an editorial from the *New York Herald Tribune* portraying Hoffa as Public Enemy No. 1 and Riesel as Public Victim No. 1, and sponsored the nationwide showing on the popular Armstrong Cork Company's "Circle Theater" of the television drama *The Sound of Violence,* an hour-long presentation about hoodlums in the jukebox industry that ended with an appeal from Senator John McClellan "to do something about the evils shown." Approximately twenty-five million people saw *The Sound of Violence* the first time it was shown.[110] Armstrong Cork, a member of the U.S. Chamber of Commerce's Secondary Boycott Committee,[111] decided to rerun the program as a summer repeat not long before the final vote on labor reform legislation.

While focus was kept on the public as the source of demand for a labor reform law, Gerald Morgan, Michael Bernstein (now counsel to the Republicans on the Senate Labor Committee), Gerard Reilly, Ted Iserman, Thomas Shroyer, and Kenneth McGuiness, all important influences on the development and administration of the Taft-Hartley Act labor policy, worked behind the scenes to draw up a more restrictive labor reform bill. The Taft-Hartley amendments they wrote further curbed the use of organizational picketing, secondary boycotts, and hot cargo agreements and increased the applicability of conservative state laws interpreted by conservative state courts. These proposed amendments had powerful appeal to southern Democrats in the House and Senate who wanted to keep the South union-free, ensuring an unorganized pool of low-cost labor to attract new industry.[112]

Reilly, now chairman of the U.S. Chamber of Commerce's Labor Relations Committee, drafted the original bill, which included changes in Taft-Hartley desired by management. These changes, introduced into the House by representatives Philip Landrum, Democrat from Georgia, and Robert Griffin, Republican from Michigan, became, with some important alterations, the Labor-Management Reporting and Disclosure Act of 1959. Shroyer, former adviser to Taft and counsel to the Senate Labor Committee during the passage of Taft-Hartley, assisted Reilly in drafting the Landrum-Griffin bill, and McGuiness, only a short time before associate general counsel and acting general counsel of the NLRB, acted as a legislative draftsman and labor consultant to the Republicans on the House Labor Committee. Iserman, a participant in the development of Taft-Hartley legislation and representative of the American Small Business Association, worked closely with the southern Democratic chairman of the Senate Labor Committee, Graham Barden, and with influential Republican congressman Charles Halleck.[113]

On August 7, 1959, over all the major television and radio networks, Eisenhower delivered a speech written by Gerald Morgan and Edward McCabe of the White House staff. Following the "people demand change" theme, the president portrayed himself as a man with no political motivations who spoke only on behalf of the interests of all the people. Eisenhower left no doubt that among the leading labor reform bills before Congress, he preferred Landrum-Griffin. He cited several examples of what he considered improper picketing and boycotting, emphasizing: "I want that sort of thing stopped. So does America."[114]

As Eisenhower said, Taft-Hartley matters, in the main, distinguished Landrum-Griffin from the other reform bills. Although picketing, boycotting, and state jurisdiction figured only marginally and indirectly in the McClellan committee investigation (and were certainly not the revelations that aroused the public), they were central to the labor-management power struggle and had been masqueraded successfully as reform measures.

A week after Eisenhower's speech the House adopted the Landrum-Griffin bill, 229 to 201. In late April 1959 the Senate had approved the Kennedy-Ervin bill, which contained a "bill of rights" for union members proposed by McClellan but also the Taft-Hartley "sweeteners" demanded by the AFL-CIO. The outcome of the subsequent bargaining in the House-Senate conference left no doubt about the success of those who used the popular outcry for reform of internal union practices to achieve additional Taft-Hartley restrictions on organized labor—thereby weakening unions in their attempts to organize the unorganized, particularly in the South.

Title VII of the Labor-Management Reporting and Disclosure Act of 1959 contained almost all the amendments to Taft-Hartley. One amendment, intended to eliminate the "no-man's land" in labor relations, prohibited the NLRB from declining jurisdiction over any dispute over which it would have asserted jurisdiction under the agency's dollar-volume standards in effect on August 1, 1959, but permitted state agencies or courts to assert jurisdiction over interstate commerce cases rejected by the Board because they did not meet those standards.[115]

Congress, pointing at the Teamsters and going further than either the Eisenhower Board or the Supreme Court, banned hot cargo agreements by adding a wholly new unfair labor practice (Section 8[e]) making it illegal for an employer and union to enter into such a contract and invalidating hot cargo agreements previously made.[116] Exceptions were made for the construction and garment industries.[117]

Congress made other changes in Section 8(b)(4) to close what the administration called loopholes in the secondary boycott prohibition. The Supreme Court had ruled in *Rice Milling*[118] that it was not an unfair labor practice for pickets at a primary site to prevail on a single truck not to pick up produce at the plant, because Section 8(b)(4) made it unlawful for a union to induce or encourage employees of a neutral employer to engage in "concerted," not individual, refusal to perform such services in the course of their employment. The amendments attempted to close this so-called loophole by deleting the word "concerted" from that provision of the act.

The Republican minority on the Senate Labor Committee described the limitation of the secondary boycott prohibition to inducement of "employees" of a neutral employer as "the biggest loophole in the present law."[119] The Truman and Eisenhower Boards had ruled lawful union pressure applied directly to a secondary employer rather than to the employees of the secondary employer.[120] The amended language made it unlawful for a union to threaten, coerce, or restrain any *person,* not only secondary employees, engaged in commerce for statutorily prohibited secondary objectives.[121]

The language of that amendment, standing alone, would appear to make unlawful all union attempts to persuade consumers to boycott an employer with whom a union had a labor dispute.[122] A clarification was inserted stating that nothing in Section 8(b)(4) was to be construed to prohibit a union from using publicity to advise the public and consumers that goods were produced by an employer with whom the union had a dispute and were being distributed by another employer. Two important conditions were added, however, that placed serious new restrictions on unions' attempts to promote consumer boycotts: There could be no picketing of neutral establishments, and the publicity (handbills, newspaper advertisements, radio announcements) must not induce employees of neutral employers to refuse to perform any services at the distributor's place of business. This ban on consumer picketing accomplished for business a long-sought reversal of the Truman Board's *Crowley's Milk Co.*[123] decision and other rulings upholding union picketing to induce or encourage customers (but not the employees of another employer) to refrain from buying the products of an employer with whom it had a dispute.[124]

Although the concept of the innocent third party permeates all considerations of the secondary boycott issue, an involved third-party employer cannot be neutral. When a union pickets a retailer who is selling a product produced by a primary employer with whom the union has a dispute, the retailer will be assisting the union if it refuses to handle the primary employer's product during the labor dispute. On the other hand, the retailer will surely help the primary employer (though somehow less obviously, to many people) if it does continue to sell the primary employer's product. In either case the retailer is an ally of one side or the other. Under those circumstances it was legitimate and justifiable for unions to attempt to enlist the consumer public on its side.[125]

These amendments denied unions a realistic opportunity to obtain consumer support, not only by banning consumer picketing but also by making the inherently weaker forms of publicity unlawful if they succeeded in persuading employees of anyone other than the primary employer "to refuse to pick up, deliver, or transport any goods, or not to perform any service at the establishment of the employer engaged in such distribution." As one scholar put it, "union pressure is maximized only if ingress and egress of goods is denied or other employees are induced to cease handling the goods in dispute. Publicity which is permitted only if it does not have this effect may be better than nothing, from the union's point of view, but not a great deal better."[126]

Congress also amended Taft-Hartley to tighten the restrictions on recognition and organizational picketing.[127] This amendment, among other things, prohibited picketing for recognition or organization purposes where a valid NLRB representation election had been conducted within the preceding twelve months (8[b][7][B]) or where such picketing had continued without a petition's being filed for a representation election within a reasonable period of time (not to exceed thirty days) (8[b][7][C]). In contrast to the ban on consumer picketing in the secondary boycott amendments, however, Congress, in Section 8(b)(7)(C), permitted informational and consumer picketing of primary employers even though no representation election was requested, as long as it did not induce "any individual employed by any other person in the course of his employment not to pick up, deliver or transport any goods or not to perform any services."[128]

Concluding Observations

By the end of the 1950s the Eisenhower Boards' interpretations of Taft-Hartley, furthered by the 1959 amendments to the act, had shifted emphasis from the encouragement of collective bargaining through unionization to the sanction of employer resistance to unionization, the employees' right to reject unionization and collective bargaining, and the protection of employers from "unfair" union economic weapons. That shift was portrayed as a legitimate effort to protect individual employee rights, particularly the right to choose no union; the freedom of speech, especially employer speech in opposition to unionization; and neutral ("innocent") employer third parties, even those handling the products of and providing services to primary employers.

The Eisenhower Board and Congress's limitation on recognition and organizational picketing illustrates a most important consequence of this change in philosophical and ideological approach to the labor law. Before the Wagner Act, unions often engaged in top-down organizing by applying concerted pressure on an employer to force its employees into a union. In many industries non-unionized employers and their employees were in perpetual competition with unionized employers and their employees, and unions sought to eliminate business competition based on differences in labor standards, arguing that no unorganized employer had a right to pay substandard wages (or unorganized employee to work at below-standard wages) without interference from those organized employees who were injured as a consequence.

In the pre-Wagner laissez-faire view of the Norris-LaGuardia Act that the federal government had no useful role to play in labor disputes, union concerted action became legitimate in what Justice Oliver Wendell Holmes called "the free struggle for life." In those circumstances it made no difference "whether the unorganized employees joined a union because they wished to join, because the employer forced them to join in order to save his business, or because the power of the union to deprive them of jobs by shutting down the business left no viable alternative. Any sacrifice of their desires or of the employer's interests was a cost of one form of competition."[129]

But top-down organizing, even union economic pressure on employees, was contrary to the Wagner Act's ideal of self-organization by employees without interference by employers. The justification for statutorily banning these traditional forms of union organizing, no matter how great a union's interest in protecting the wages and working conditions of its members from the economic consequences of substandard wages and working conditions of unorganized competitors, was that the Wagner and Taft-Hartley acts made such methods unnecessary and inappropriate because employers were now prevented from coercing or in any other way interfering with their employees' choice of bargaining representatives.[130]

The Wagner Act required unions to give up many of their traditional organizing weapons in return for certain statutory guarantees of protection to be enforced by the NLRB. Yet over the years, particularly after the passage of Taft-Hartley and during the Eisenhower Boards' administration of the act in the 1950s, many of those statutorily guaranteed protections were withdrawn as employer resistance to union organization was substantially deregulated and even protected while ever-increasing restrictions were placed on union organizing techniques, especially picketing. Although this trend struck directly at the very justification for banning many traditional union organizing methods, organized labor was locked into a law that in important ways was being used to defeat union organization for collective bargaining. This outcome was the very one feared by many in the AFL when the Wagner Act was being considered: placing regulatory power in an administrative agency of the federal government was dangerous, because the exercise of that power would not be limited to agencies friendly to union organization and collective bargaining.

The Leedom Board did not participate in drawing up the 1959 amendments to Taft-Hartley. Those amendments, not based on empirical evidence, were the result of cooperation between the Eisenhower White House and employers, political opportunism, and horse trading, as with Taft-Hartley, between the House and Senate in conference. Nevertheless, in two terms the Eisenhower administration and its appointees to the NLRB had substantially changed the direction of the national labor policy.

9

The New Frontier Labor Board
A Commitment to Industrial Democracy

The passage of the Landrum-Griffin amendments in 1959 once again demonstrated the limited extent of the Democratic Party's commitment to organized labor and Taft-Hartley Act reform. Many liberals, in and out of the party, moreover, no longer considered organized labor a force for social reform; from their perspective there was little to distinguish "big labor" from "big business."[1]

What historian Arthur Schlesinger called the "alarmingly narrow margin"[2] of John Kennedy's presidential election victory over Richard Nixon in 1960 only sharpened the differences between labor and the Democrats. Despite the popular impression that Kennedy was fighting for lofty ideals, he and Nixon differed little in doctrine, as both sought the votes of the broad political center. Kennedy succeeded, but barely, in appearing prudent and moderate without alienating the more liberal elements of the Roosevelt coalition. After two-thirds of the eligible voters went to the polls in one of the largest turnouts in U.S. history, Kennedy won the presidency by less than two-thirds of 1 percent of the popular vote: 34,221,349 to 34,108,546.

Although Kennedy won, the Republicans gained 20 seats in the House while the Democrats lost 19, reducing the Democratic majority from 128 to 99. The Democratic majority in the Senate (64–36) remained unchanged. The outcome of these elections made the Kennedy administration even more dependent on Democratic conservatives—particularly southern conservatives, referred to by Vice-President Lyndon Johnson as the "Confederates."[3]

By the time of Kennedy's election, moreover, union membership was declining, attempts to organize the unorganized were generally unsuccessful, and the AFL-CIO was torn by an internal jurisdictional battle between craft unions in the building trades and industrial unions in the mass production industries and by personal feuding between George Meany and Walter Reuther.[4] A merged federation that in 1955 envisioned doubling its membership was engaged, in 1960, in a holding action designed to keep the already organized organized. It was not a temporary setback, and organized labor's continued decline further weakened its influence in the Democratic Party.

In this dismal climate the AFL-CIO, with its unerring knack for pursuing futile and self-destructive political objectives, chose repeal of Section 14(b) (the anti-union-security provision of Taft-Hartley) as its primary legislative goal. Except for civil rights legislation, nothing could have been more divisive to the Democratic Party.[5] It certainly reinforced the image created by the McClellan committee of powerful and greedy labor bosses grabbing dues money from helpless workers forced to join labor unions.

Even though organized labor had worked hard to elect Kennedy,[6] repeal of Section 14(b) had no chance during his administration. What Kennedy did do for organized labor, however, was to appoint a new chairman and member to the NLRB, who along with an Eisenhower-appointed carryover member brought about widespread reversals of Eisenhower Board doctrine and interpreted Taft-Hartley in ways that encouraged unionization and collective bargaining, restricted employer interference with worker organization, and ultimately caused the most powerful employers in the country to join in a coordinated resistance to what they believed were threats to their "right to manage."

The "New Frontier" Labor Board

Kennedy chose Frank McCulloch, fifty-five-year-old administrative assistant to Democratic senator Paul Douglas of Illinois, to be the new chairman of the NLRB.[7] Boyd Leedom, NLRB chairman under Eisenhower, who still had four years of his term left, remained on the Board as a member. McCulloch replaced Arthur Kimball,[8] a short-term recess appointee whom Eisenhower had nominated to replace Stephen Bean, who had retired when his term expired in August 1960. McCulloch, who graduated from Williams College and Harvard Law School, worked for a Chicago law firm from 1930 to 1935 before becoming industrial relations secretary for the Council for Social Action of the Congregational-Christian Churches of America, a lawyer–social worker type of post that he held until 1946. From 1946 to 1949 McCulloch served as director of the Labor Education Division at Roosevelt University, where he set up a program for union members to study labor and social problems.

Former acting general counsel Kenneth McGuiness, a persistent critic of the Kennedy NLRB, observed caustically that, although McCulloch was associated with a large law firm early in his career, "his official resumé, which lists 'evening settlement work' during the same period, discloses his own recognition of more abiding interests in other activities."[9] McCulloch followed in the tradition of his parents, both of whom were lawyers who played prominent roles in civic affairs and Illinois Democratic politics. His mother, Catharine Waugh Mc-Culloch, a college classmate of Jane Addams, was a leader in the suffragette movement, and both his parents were active in settlement and social work.

In 1946 and until his appointment to the NLRB McCulloch helped Senator Douglas draft and handle labor legislation, particularly when Douglas served on the Senate Labor Committee, and acted as the senator's liaison with labor. During this period McCulloch was involved in efforts to repeal Taft-Hartley in 1949, the confirmation hearings for Eisenhower's nominees to the NLRB, and the Landrum-Griffin hearings in 1959. His duties put him in close contact with Senator Kennedy when the future president was dealing with the same issues as a member of the Senate Labor Committee.[10]

McCulloch's understanding of the purpose of the act differed fundamentally from that of Guy Farmer and the other Eisenhower appointees. McCulloch rejected the claim that Taft-Hartley had shifted the law's purpose away from encouraging collective bargaining. In his opinion Taft-Hartley was not neutral but promoted collective bargaining, and it was the Board's objective to achieve universal acceptance by labor and management of the collective bargaining policy originally set forth in the 1935 Wagner Act and incorporated intact into Taft-Hartley.[11] He echoed Wagner in asserting that collective bargaining was more than an effective method to settle disputes between labor and management; it was the way to bring about a democratic movement to correct industrial injustices and to replace industrial autocracy with industrial democracy.

McCulloch acknowledged that much of the country's business and industry and many communities rejected the national labor policy and actively prevented collective bargaining from even getting started. Consequently, he expected that the 1960s would see a continuing struggle for the full rights of self-organization and bargaining. The Board's major job would be "to persuade and impel" employers and unions to accept collective bargaining as the foundation of their labor-management relations.[12]

McCulloch, like Wagner, also envisioned collective bargaining as a means to the realization of social justice through the creation of a broader democracy in the society. In that sense McCulloch saw management opposition to collective bargaining as contrary "not only to the law but to social policy as a democratic nation."[13] The problems of labor union members and employers, McCulloch believed, went far beyond wages, hours, and working conditions to include "civil rights, equality of opportunity, full employment, low-cost housing, improved medical care, better education at all levels, enriched leisure opportunities, a safe and satisfying life between retirement and death, [and] a voice in one's own destiny."[14] Near the end of his chairmanship, in 1969, he spoke of shared responsibility in decision making as the foundation of democratic government and of the need to extend legitimate participation to all, particularly "those who live in poverty, who find the doors of opportunity closed because of their race, who send their children to inadequate schools, who are inadequately fed, who have inadequate medical and health care, and who otherwise do not enjoy the abundance which surrounds them."[15]

As one of his management critics saw it, McCulloch's parents had imbued their son with an "activist liberal," "New Deal, left of center philosophy" that was only strengthened by his years with Senator Douglas. In McCulloch's mind, according to this critic, collective bargaining had a value that transcended "property rights, individual rights [and] employer rights" and "was such a useful thing that every possibility for its exercise and application must be encouraged."[16] Former acting general counsel McGuiness summed up management's view: "Frank was philosophically very union oriented."[17]

McCulloch inspired strong feelings in those who worked with him and against him during his years at the NLRB. No one, however, questioned his integrity, dedication, ability, and intelligence. He was described as an "extraordinary man," a "wise" and "gentle" man,[18] "hard-working," "one of the finest persons I have ever known,"[19] "very, very bright,"[20] "outstanding in his personal relationships with his fellow Board members, his staff and the public, and his grasp of the law,"[21] a "scholar," a "man of absolutely overwhelming charm" and "good manners" even when being treated with hostility, and a "gracious southern gentleman."[22]

Friends and foes agreed that there was "a lot of steel beneath the surface."[23] McCulloch was a powerful chairman described by one colleague as "absolutely the best" in organizing and conducting Board agenda meetings to achieve the results he desired, "somewhat like a conductor with a symphony"[24]—and "he always had his way in the most diplomatic way."[25] At the Johnson White House in the mid-1960s McCulloch was considered the strongest of all the members in both personality and intellect, the most analytical, and the best at perceiving legal distinctions. The Johnson administration also recognized that McCulloch "added a social outlook to his generally pro-labor philosophy."[26] To McCulloch's critics, he was "dominant,"[27] "hard as nails,"[28] "a man of stern principle who would have resigned before he would hold that property rights are superior to collective bargaining or that employee rights are not superior to employer rights,"[29] and one who would "hold the Board in session for hours and hours trying to influence the vote."[30]

One week after McCulloch was sworn in, Kennedy appointed Gerald Brown, NLRB regional director in San Francisco, to replace Board member Joseph

Jenkins.[31] In 1957 Eisenhower had chosen Jenkins, a thirty-eight-year-old pro-Eisenhower Democrat, to replace Truman appointee Ivar Peterson.[32] Brown, who was not a lawyer, had an undergraduate degree in history from West Texas State College and a master's degree in economics from the University of Texas and was studying for a Ph.D. in economics at the University of North Carolina when he accepted a job as a field examiner in the NLRB's Atlanta office in 1942. He came up through the ranks of the NLRB staff before joining the Board. After leaving the Atlanta office he was a field examiner in the Chicago regional office and an examiner in charge of the NLRB's subregional office in Memphis from 1945 to 1947, and for fourteen years he served as regional director in San Francisco.[33]

Although Brown was the only nonlawyer on the Board, he knew as much about labor law as any lawyer.[34] He was also the most efficient of the Kennedy Board members, consistently turning out more caseload work than any of his colleagues.[35] Philosophically, as his former chief counsel, Ralph Winkler, recalled, Brown "felt the problems of labor with a deep, deep feeling, with great understanding and great intelligence."[36] At the White House he was described as "strong minded and the one who most generally follows the line of organized labor."[37]

Brown's commitment to unionization and collective bargaining came partly from his academic studies of labor and economic history and partly from his work in the field as an NLRB regional staff member. Brown brought to the Board a special expertise, what McCulloch called "an enormous experience," acquired in almost twenty years of investigating charges; conducting representation elections; going into union halls, factories, and offices; talking with union members and unorganized workers and foremen and managers; and otherwise dealing with the problems of labor and management in the field. Consequently, Brown's views were an interesting mixture of pragmatism and principle. He emphasized, for example, that collective bargaining is problem-centered and more effective when participants concentrate on day-to-day problems rather than on defining abstract principles.[38] Yet he also articulated what became a most controversial concept of the role of the NLRB in making labor policy. It was a foray into philosophy for which, as McCulloch said later, Brown "got a terrible bruising" from employers and certain members of Congress, particularly Philip Landrum and Robert Griffin.[39]

In his first speech after becoming a Board member Brown expounded his convictions concerning the purpose of the law and the responsibilities of the NLRB. In sum, he maintained that the NLRB was charged with promoting the public policy of encouraging collective bargaining as a democratic method of solving labor problems. He rejected Eisenhower NLRB chairman Farmer's notion of the government as a neutral party, indifferent to employees' choice between individual and collective action. Brown agreed with Farmer, however, that no case precedent is good if it is wrong. Just as Farmer's comment signaled reversals unfavorable to organized labor, management understood the meaning of Brown's pledge to change Board policies when there were better approaches or where established doctrines were outmoded or unsound.

Most alarming to employers, however, was Brown's characterization of the NLRB as a "policymaking tribunal," which contradicted Farmer's contention that it was not the Board's place to formulate labor policy. In Brown's opinion it was not possible simply to enforce the statute as written. In many areas, he said, the words of the statute were unclear or too general, yet the Board had to develop a substantive body of case law from such terms. Even when the statutory language was unambiguous, Brown said, the Board often had to choose among conflicting policies. Brown, also contradicting Farmer's public protestations that politics had no place in the administration of the law, talked frankly of the influence of personal values and political philosophy on Board decisions: "While denying politics an improper place in the decision making process, I do not deny that a Member's viewpoint may be influenced by his background or philosophy, nor do I suggest that Board membership would be identical under different administrations."[40]

McCulloch also invoked Farmer's statement "that he was not appointed to rubberstamp the decisions of Board members before him."[41] Only days after Brown's speech McCulloch reaffirmed his new colleague's view that the law was not crystal clear or the cases so uniform that the application of the law could be a purely mechanical function: "It would also be fatuous to assert that in this complex field, the personal orientation of a Board member plays no role in his interpretation of the Act."[42]

Although it was almost eighteen months after Eisenhower was elected before his appointees constituted a majority on the Board, the Kennedy administration had a majority within a few months, because McCulloch and Brown were joined by holdover John Fanning, a Democrat appointed by Eisenhower in December 1957. Fanning, a graduate of Providence College and Catholic University Law School, was forty-one when he joined the Board after working for fifteen years in the Labor Department and in the Department of Defense, where he was in charge of industrial relations.[43] During his years in the Defense Department, dealing primarily with labor relations problems in the construction of army installations, Fanning became friendly with Secretary of Labor Mitchell (then at the Pentagon) and with many craft union officials, particularly in the AFL's International Brotherhood of Electrical Workers (IBEW) and International Association of Machinists (IAM).

When Mitchell asked him to accept appointment to the Board, Fanning reminded him that he was a Democrat. Mitchell replied, "That's why I'm interested in you. It would be a good thing if this Board was bipartisan and I know enough about you and your labor philosophy to know that there would be no objection from management or labor unions to your appointment."[44] Fanning had the right credentials for the job, he was not in any way controversial, and he had the influential support of Al Hayes, president of the IAM, a union Eisenhower considered moderate.[45] Although Fanning prided himself on being nonpartisan, and cited as evidence his unprecedented appointment to five successive terms by five presidents of different political parties, he was seen by some as very friendly to craft unions and even "pro-AFL."[46]

Aside from public comments referring to collective bargaining as the keystone of the act,[47] Fanning did not philosophize about the purpose of the law or the NLRB. He was seen as cautious and always "sensitive to the climate," with "great survival capacity."[48] To the Johnson White House, Fanning was "generally pro-labor but more pragmatic and less academic than McCulloch."[49]

Fanning replaced Murdock, the Board's last Truman appointee, not only as a Democratic member but also as the Eisenhower Board's chief dissenter. Fanning estimated that in his first year on the Board he dissented one hundred times.[50] As he saw it, McCulloch and Brown adopted his dissents and joined with him to make a new majority.[51] (Farmer agreed: "Everybody says 'the McCulloch Board'—I think Fanning is probably more responsible than McCulloch for many of these decisions.")[52] McCulloch noted, "Fanning's dissents before I ever got there helped to advise me and the Board constituency about basic issues."[53]

The General Counsel: An Eisenhower Holdover

For the first two years of McCulloch's chairmanship, Stuart Rothman, an Eisenhower appointee, was general counsel. Kenneth McGuiness had served only two months as acting general counsel after Kammholtz resigned in January 1957. Eisenhower replaced him in March with forty-nine-year-old Jerome Fenton. A graduate of the University of Iowa and Harvard Law School, Fenton had practiced law in Detroit and was vice-president of industrial relations at Pan American World Airways from 1943 to 1954. He also served as assistant to the administrator of Veterans Affairs before becoming special assistant to William Brucker, who was then general counsel of the Defense Department. Brucker was Secretary of the Army when Fenton became NLRB general counsel.[54] Fenton resigned under pressure in March 1959 after a bitter personal feud with the Board (particularly Chairman Leedom) reminiscent of the Denham-Herzog battles, demonstrating once again the defects inherent in this separation of functions at the NLRB.[55]

Two days after Fenton resigned, Eisenhower nominated Stuart Rothman, forty-five-year-old solicitor of the Department of Labor, over the strenuous objection of Senator Barry Goldwater. The president's choice was seen as a victory for Secretary of Labor Mitchell over the conservatives in the Republican Party.[56] After graduating from the University of Minnesota Law School, where he was editor of the law review, Rothman received a master of laws degree from Harvard. At the time he became general counsel, his entire career had been in state and federal government.[57] Rothman, the consummate manager, routinely worked seven-day weeks. He was described as a "task-master" who dealt rigorously with himself, the "kind of man who always has as much to do as any man can handle but somehow manages to take on one more task."[58]

While the new Democratic majority of the Board was making major and extensive doctrinal changes based on its understanding of the purpose and meaning of the law and the role of the NLRB in formulating U.S. labor policy, the new general counsel, other than making the now routine pledge that he would be neither pro-union nor pro-management,[59] had a more limited emphasis. He talked of eliminating the large case backlogs at the general counsel's office through "plain hard work,"[60] and the inculcation of positive attitudes toward modern management techniques ("sometimes in the face of strongly entrenched cynical bureaucratic attitudes").[61] He also encouraged the voluntary settlement of charges filed in the regional offices instead of what he saw as the common practice of disposing of pending cases primarily by taking them to trial, and promoted improved communication and increased cooperation between the regional offices and private practitioners representing unions and employers.[62] In sum, Rothman wanted the NLRB to operate in the same way as large, successful private law firms.[63]

Rothman's admirers at the NLRB considered this "shy, desk-ridden" man[64] the "greatest administrator the Board ever had."[65] They described him as a tough "managerial genius" who "created management by objectives long before business schools even thought of the concept,"[66] and "a no-nonsense guy," "a man for his times" who came to an NLRB long plagued by case-handling delays and backlogs.[67]

The Pucinski Committee

Even before Kennedy's election in 1960 and his subsequent appointment of McCulloch and Brown to the Board, the Democrat-controlled House Labor Committee, after their party's impressive victory in the 1958 congressional elections, created a subcommittee on the NLRB for the purpose of publicly condemning the Eisenhower Board not only for case backlogs and delays but also for case decisions considered contrary to the purposes of Taft-Hartley.[68] Democratic congressman Roman Pucinski of Illinois, who chaired the subcommittee, said that the investigation of the NLRB was conducted in response to the complaints of labor leaders that the Board was biased and unfair.[69]

By the time the Pucinski hearings began in May 1961, however, the Democrats had a majority on the Board, and in view of the committee's understanding and conciliatory treatment of Chairman McCulloch[70] and witnesses critical of the previous Board's policies, it became obvious that the investigation's sole target was the Eisenhower Board. In the words of one journalist, "most of the time was spent belaboring a ghost—the old Eisenhower board which was due for exorcising by the new Kennedy appointments."[71] Just as the House Labor Committee in 1953 had set an agenda for the incoming Eisenhower appointees through its sympathetic hearing of the complaints of business against the Truman-appointed NLRB, the Pucinski committee, by criticizing the Eisenhower Board's interpretations of the act and recommending new policy choices, helped change the course of the NLRB and U.S. labor policy for almost the next ten years.

As the assistant general counsel who helped prepare General Counsel Rothman's presentation to the Pucinski committee put it, "it was all preordained." "Mr. Pucinski had 'made up his mind' before the hearings."[72] A Democratic Congress was responding to pressure from organized labor to conduct the investigation. Yet once again, the AFL-CIO missed an extraordinary opportunity to reorient labor policy to organized labor's advantage. Shortly before the Pucinski committee hearings began, for example, AFL-CIO Industrial Union Department attorney David Feller complained to Walter Reuther about the AFL-CIO's lack of interest in and "woeful" lack of preparation for the hearings. Only smaller unions such as the Textile Workers had a complete case for presentation, and that was not enough to sustain a full-scale investigation.[73]

Pucinski's committee began its public hearings on May 8, 1961, and over fifteen days in May and June heard fifty-eight witnesses. Industry witnesses were not featured.[74] Although testimony covered a wide range of topics, the most important subjects were substantive issues such as free speech, including the use of race hate speech in organizing campaigns; captive audience speeches; NLRB determination of an appropriate unit for collective bargaining; the overall problem of delay in representation and unfair labor practice cases; and the Board's policies and attitudes concerning the purposes of the act.

The unions that were prepared to testify before the Pucinski committee, particularly the Textile Workers, the Amalgamated Clothing Workers, and the International Union of Electrical Workers, complained primarily about how the

NLRB, by making a union-organizing campaign a deregulated contest between employers and unions, had enabled employers to prevent unionization of expanding southern industry. According to union officers and organizers, representation campaigns in southern mill towns were ordeals of brainwashing and intimidation. The employers who dominated those towns not only threatened union supporters with warnings of mill closings and discharge ("in the small mill towns where most textile plants are located, a discharge amounts almost to banishment from the community") but also mobilized other forces against them, including the press, radio, clergy, and police; had bankers and merchants call in the debts of pro-union workers; and exploited racial and religious hatred.[75]

Race hate speech was given special attention by union representatives, who told the committee of southern employers who warned their employees that "if the union won, colored people would get promotions instead of white people,"[76] vilified unions as run by "God damned Jews" and "nigger lovers,"[77] and in various other ways took advantage of racial prejudice to persuade workers to reject unionization, such as posting in their plants large-scale reproductions of newspaper photographs showing International Union of Electrical Workers president James Carey dancing with a black woman over the caption, "Race mixing an issue as workers vote."[78] Union witnesses pointed to an explosive situation in the South where, as the hearings were taking place, Freedom Ride buses were being burned in Alabama and their occupants brutally beaten: "When you draw upon this kind of passion . . . this kind of folk-custom and use that for the purpose of warping a person's mind and disturbing his ability to think clearly and objectively . . . you have indeed prevented the free and untrammeled choice of that person."[79] Union representatives condemned the Eisenhower Board for ignoring the use of race hate propaganda to defeat unions.[80]

Union witnesses explained how organizing campaigns had to withstand not only hostile employer speeches but also local community pressures from anti-union chambers of commerce, newspapers, ministers' associations, bankers, merchants, and police.[81] Many local chambers of commerce and community development organizations used the appeal of cheap labor and no unions, with assurances that the situation would stay that way, to attract industry and business to the South, particularly from highly unionized sections of the country where workers enjoyed better wages and working conditions.[82] (As a northerner from Chicago, Pucinski said that it made no difference to a working man in Chicago whether he lost his job because of imports produced by cheap labor in Japan or because of imports produced by cheap labor in Mississippi).[83] Where community leaders supported anti-union campaigns, union representatives wanted them recognized as agents of the employers.[84]

Union witnesses also severely criticized the Eisenhower Board's captive audience doctrine, its approach to bargaining unit determinations, and the inadequacies of its remedies. The Board's holding in *Livingston Shirt*[85] that a union hall as a forum for discussing union representation issues was equal to a captive audience speech on an employer's property was derided as "utter and complete nonsense, unworthy of an administrative agency supposedly possessed of some expert knowledge of the facts of labor life in America today."[86] The general counsel of the Textile Workers told the committee, for example, that unions were left with no effective access to workers when faced with plants in remote rural areas, the car-pooling of employees from widely scattered homes in many surrounding communities onto company property (where outside union organizers were prohibited), and resistance to permitting unions to rent meeting places in town or to buy radio time or newspaper space.[87]

The general counsel of the Retail Clerks charged that the Eisenhower Board had disregarded the interests of employees in determining appropriate bargaining units within which representation elections would be conducted, thereby routinely denying employees the opportunity to bargain collectively with their employers.[88] By holding that an employer's administrative division was the only appropriate bargaining unit, for example, the Eisenhower Board required the Retail Clerks union to win a majority of votes in a unit comprising not only retail employees but also porters, mechanics, laborers, truck drivers, warehousemen, office workers, and stock clerks, sometimes in a large geographical area including many stores.[89]

Union witnesses also emphasized the inadequacy of NLRB remedies to prevent deliberate and repeated violations of the act. They claimed that many employers knowingly committed unfair labor practices to defeat union organizing drives because the penalty for violating the law amounted to little more than routine expenses for operating the business ("a license fee for union busting"), a small price to pay for not having to bargain collectively with their employees.[90] Consequently, when an employer's unfair labor practices had made a fair representation election impossible, and a union had clearly represented a majority of the employees in an appropriate bargaining unit before commission of the unfair labor practices, union witnesses wanted the Board to order the employer to bargain with a union on the basis of signed union authorization cards.[91]

Kennedy's Reorganization Plan No. 5

The Pucinski committee hearings also became booster sessions for President Kennedy's Reorganization Plan No. 5, intended to speed up the Board's handling of unfair labor practice cases. The committee called delay in NLRB case processing the greatest impediment to carrying out the congressional policy of encouraging collective bargaining and blamed the ever-increasing caseload of Board members for much of that delay.[92] As the total number of representation and unfair labor practice cases filed with the NLRB increased from more than 13,000 in 1957 to more than 21,000 in 1960, the Board's backlog of undecided cases rose from 410 in 1958 to an unprecedented 1,151 one month after McCulloch became chairman in 1961. That was despite a constant increase in the Board's production from 2,100 formal decisions in 1958 to a projected 2,900 in 1961, equaling 55 decisions a week, or 11 per day.[93]

As soon as McCulloch became chairman, the Board, in an attempt to reduce this enormous case backlog, delegated to its regional directors the authority to decide whether a question of representation existed, to determine appropriate units for collective bargaining, to direct a representation election to ascertain whether employees wanted to be represented by a particular labor union for collective bargaining, to certify a union as bargaining agent if it won an election, and to rule on other matters involving elections such as objections and challenged ballots.[94] The Board also sharply limited the circumstances under which it would grant requests to review the regional directors' actions.[95]

The president's Reorganization Plan No. 5 proposed a comparable delegation to trial examiners of the Board's authority to decide unfair labor practice cases. At the time, the Board was required to grant automatically a full *de novo* review of the whole record made before the trial examiner as well as the examiner's findings of fact, conclusions of law, and recommendations in every case in which a party filed exceptions to a trial examiner's report—and exceptions were filed 75 percent of the time.[96] Unions, employers, and employees with unfair labor practice complaints had to wait approximately a year and a half on the average for a Board decision. In an effort to speed up the Board's case handling and reduce the backlog of undecided unfair labor practice cases, Plan No. 5 authorized the Board to exercise its discretion and to grant reviews of trial examiners' reports only when a party established the merit of an appeal according to standards to be formulated by the Board or when any two members of the Board decided in their discretion to grant review.[97]

Plan No. 5 was not a new idea. In 1946 Congress had enacted the Administrative Procedure Act, which created an independent corps of hearing examiners with civil service status and protection and, in most cases, gave their decisions greater finality.[98] In February 1960, moreover, a Senate Labor Committee advisory panel of twelve labor law experts, headed by Archibald Cox, unanimously recommended greater finality for trial examiners' reports in unfair labor practice cases, with only limited grounds for review by the Board.[99] Also, in 1959 McKinsey & Co., a management consulting firm hired by the NLRB to improve the organization and management of the agency's operations in Washington and in the field, identified delay in decision making at the Board level as a major problem requiring urgent attention.[100] The consultants said that the great deal of time that Board members and their staffs spent reading and analyzing hearing records, trial examiners' intermediate reports, and associated materials was not warranted, since 71 percent of the contested trial examiner reports were affirmed in full, 18 percent were affirmed in part, and only 7 percent were reversed in full.[101] (Stuart Rothman was more pointed, calling these extensive reviews a waste of time.)[102] Feuding between Leedom and General Counsel Fenton prevented implementation of the consulting firm's recommendations.[103]

Finally, shortly before President Kennedy took office, he appointed Harvard Law School dean James Landis to study and report on the federal government's regulatory agencies. Although Landis focused on the friction between the general counsel and the Board, he was also concerned about decision-making delays at the Board-member level, and he, too, recommended that more finality be given to trial examiners' reports. Landis's report generated a series of administrative agency reorganization plans, including Plan No. 5.[104]

Members of the Board, Republican and Democratic appointees alike, unanimously supported Plan No. 5, as did General Counsel Rothman. Support also came from unlikely sources such as former Eisenhower Board chairman Guy Farmer; Gerald Reilly, conservative former Board member now representing business interests; and Joseph Jenkins, former Eisenhower appointee to the Board.[105]

Strong opposition also developed, however. It was first articulated before the Pucinski committee by former general counsel Theophil Kammholz and longtime Democratic Board critic and former Taft aide Thomas Shroyer,[106] and then organized by the U.S. Chamber of Commerce and the National Association of Manufacturers. In debates before the Senate and House government operations committees, opponents led by the NAM and the Chamber of Commerce charged that Plan No. 5 would permit delegation of Board decision-making power to low-level employees; that litigants would be denied their right to review by presidentially appointed Board members; that the reorganization plan would make the Board chairman a "czar" with unlimited power; and that Congress should legislate grounds for review in unfair labor practice cases as it did in 1959 in representation cases.[107]

The opponents of Plan No. 5, therefore, professed a greater concern for the rights of litigants before the Board than about delays in Board decision making. As the associate general counsel of the NAM put it, "one man's delay is another man's due process."[108] Employer groups had more important but less discussed reasons to oppose the plan. The Chamber of Commerce, the NAM, and other employer associations suspected that Plan No. 5 would be used to aid union organization, especially in the South. As the vice-president and general counsel of the Hanes Knitting Company in North Carolina told North Carolina senator Sam Ervin, "the purported idea behind the reorganization is to expedite the business of the Board, but we are very fearful that the real plan behind it is to further the plan of Union reorganization, particularly in the South."[109] Employers, including many in the South, wanted to maintain delays in Board procedures because delay often favored them in their efforts to remain non-union.[110] There was also a long-held belief among employers, going back to Wagner Act days, that many NLRB trial examiners had "leftist sympathies."[111] Although the NAM, the Chamber of Commerce, and other employer groups had no confidence in the new Kennedy Board, they preferred to have decisions made by politically appointed Board members, who because of their visibility were more vulnerable to political and public pressure than trial examiners obscured from public view.[112]

McCulloch, who was lobbying contacts he had made during his years as legislative assistant to Senator Douglas,[113] approached Ervin but found that "the management community had gotten to Senator Ervin," who told McCulloch, "I'm sorry, Frank, I'm committed." (McCulloch noted later that he saw "this thread running through my whole Board service—the textile industry coming to seek [Ervin's] support and influence on NLRB matters.")[114]

Although the House and Senate government operations committees recommended approval of Plan No. 5,[115] a Republican–southern Democrat coalition killed the plan on July 20, 1961, by a 231–179 vote on the House floor.[116] The defeat of Plan No. 5 was a great disappointment to McCulloch and his colleagues on the Board.[117] Like the 1959 vote on Landrum-Griffin, the vote on the plan accurately revealed the congressional majority's true position on union-management issues. The Board and its supporters in Congress realized that favorable legislative changes were out of the question.

The Pucinski Committee Sets an Agenda

National labor policy would be changed in the 1960s, therefore, not by legislative enactment but by the new Kennedy Board's reinterpretation of the Taft-Hartley Act, just as the Eisenhower Board had done in the 1950s. In another striking historical parallel, the Democrat-controlled Pucinski committee help set an agenda for the McCulloch Board's doctrinal and policy changes just as the Republican-controlled House Labor Committee had done for the Farmer Board in 1953. This time, however, the connection between the House committee and the Board was more direct. Pucinski recalled that his committee issued a report "which changed the course of the NLRB for years to come."[118] The report was written by Daniel Pollitt, a professor of law at the University of North Carolina and special assistant to Chairman McCulloch.[119] As Pollitt and McCulloch remember it, the Pucinski committee, after three months of hearings, was having difficulty drafting a satisfactory report and asked the Board for help: "Mc-Culloch thought this was an opportunity for us," Pollitt recalled, "so we got together with Pucinski."[120] Pucinski adopted most of Pollitt's work and issued the majority report without revealing the Board's role in its authorship.[121]

Pollitt and the Republicans who attached their minority views to the Pucinski committee report agreed that the hearings were intended "to prepare the way for Frank McCulloch and the new Board."[122] With a political blind spot concerning the House Labor Committee's role in facilitating the Eisenhower Board's reinterpretation of the act in 1953, the Republican minority accused the Pucinski committee majority of giving the Board specific suggestions for change.[123]

The majority's specific recommendations for change centered on the problem of delay in NLRB decision making, employer speech during representation campaigns, the inadequacy of NLRB remedies, and the approach to ascertaining an appropriate unit for collective bargaining. Although Plan No. 5 had been defeated before the Pucinski committee issued its report, the majority advised the Board to adopt its own system of limited review of trial examiners' decisions in unfair labor practice cases.[124]

The committee majority considered race hate speech contemptible, but its uncertainty as to whether the Constitution protected such utterances led it to urge the Board to allow the Supreme Court to decide if it was an unfair labor practice.[125] The majority also advised the Board to set aside elections where pressures from groups in the community on employees created an atmosphere of fear and confusion and prevented the holding of free elections.[126] Most pointedly, the committee condemned the inequity of the Eisenhower Board's captive audience doctrine; asked the McCulloch Board to reexamine the *Livingston Shirt*[127] decision, in which the Farmer Board had first articulated that doctrine; and even proposed a return to the Truman Board's equal opportunity doctrine whereby unions were allowed equal time and equal access to employees.[128]

The committee was particularly concerned about the impotence of NLRB remedies, and it advised the Board to exercise its full remedy power to take the profit out of unfair labor practices.[129] In a specific recommendation that promised to be a boon to union organization, especially in the South, the committee pressed the McCulloch Board to revitalize the Truman Board's *Joy Silk Mills*[130] doctrine and order an employer to recognize and bargain with a union without a representation election when that union could demonstrate, on the basis of signed authorization cards, that it represented a majority of the employees in an appropriate unit before its majority status was undermined by employer unfair labor practices.[131]

The committee also said that consideration should be given to imposing criminal penalties for willful commission of unfair labor practices, allowing injured parties to sue in federal or state court for double or triple damages, and barring those who knowingly and repeatedly committed unfair labor practices from government contract awards. The committee also encouraged the Board to disbar from practice before the NLRB any attorney who willfully advised the commission of unfair labor practices.[132]

The Pucinski committee majority accused the Eisenhower Board of disregarding the interests of employees and deferring to employers in its determinations of appropriate bargaining units, thereby denying employees the opportunity to bargain collectively with their employers.[133] By recommending that the McCulloch Board apply "more realistic standards" in determining a bargaining unit,[134] the majority confirmed the fears of those who opposed unionization that, as the Republican minority put it, "everything possible would be done to help unions win elections and to insure that employees become and remain members of unions."[135] Even before the Pucinski committee had finished its hearings, McCulloch promised to give thorough consideration to its criticisms and proposals.[136]

Concluding Observations

The Pucinski committee hearings were only indirectly about employer speech, bargaining unit determinations, remedies, and delays. The underlying purpose of the hearings and the majority's final report was to reestablish as the national labor policy the federal government's encouragement of collective bargaining and the organization of employees into unions. Throughout the hearings Pucinski referred repeatedly to Congress's intent to encourage workers to organize for the purpose of collective bargaining.[137] The committee chairman and union witnesses accused the Eisenhower NLRB of being opposed to collective bargaining and of frustrating and obstructing the national labor policy through its "twisted" interpretations of the law.[138] The issue was joined, however, when former NLRB regional attorney and aide to Senator Taft, Thomas Shroyer, representing the American Retail Federation, and former Eisenhower-appointed general counsel, Theophil Kammholz, came before the committee to reaffirm the contrary labor policy that had guided the Eisenhower Boards: "Your Government doesn't give a darn whether you join a union or not" but "will protect your right to join or not to join."[139]

In its final report the Pucinski committee majority rejected the contention that the 1947 addition to Section 7 of the right to refrain from organization and collective bargaining had the effect of changing national labor policy "from one of governmental encouragement of self-organization and collective bargaining to one of governmental indifference."[140] The committee concluded with a powerful affirmation of a national labor policy of federal government encouragement of collective bargaining and unionization: "The preamble [of the Taft-Hartley Act] states explicitly that the Act is premised upon the philosophy that nonunionization—individual bargaining—is bad not only for the employee but for the United States; that self-organization and collective bargaining is good for the Nation."[141]

President Kennedy's new appointments, Chairman Frank McCulloch and Gerald Brown, were committed to that national labor policy. McCulloch knew that the dominant voices in the management community were critical of any Board that took the act's preamble seriously.[142] The new Kennedy Board not only would reverse quickly a host of Eisenhower Board case decisions but would apply its understanding of the national labor policy to areas that even prior Democrat-appointed Boards had not touched.

The McCulloch Board came as close to a full and effective implementation of a national labor policy encouraging unionization and collective bargaining as the Wagner Act Board chaired by J. Warren Madden did in the two years after the Supreme Court ruled that law constitutional. In response, the most powerful employers in the country organized themselves in massive and active resistance. The result was a showdown in the 1960s between the NLRB and U.S. employers over the direction of the national labor policy. It would be the last time that the NLRB was committed over any sustained period to encouraging unionization and collective bargaining.

10

A New Labor Policy
Taking Industrial Democracy Seriously

New Labor Policy Choices

For eight years, the Eisenhower Board had deregulated employer opposition to unionization and collective bargaining and intensified the regulation of unions' use of economic weapons, particularly organizational picketing. McCulloch, Brown, and Fanning quickly set about reversing Eisenhower Board policy, just as the Farmer Board had done to the Truman Board's doctrines in the early 1950s. Almost immediately, the new Board greatly increased restrictions on employer speech and lessened restrictions on union economic weapons, including organizational picketing. The new Board also issued early decisions changing existing rules governing the appropriateness of bargaining units in ways that increased the likelihood of unionization. Those and other Kennedy-Johnson Board decisions—placing limitations on management rights; applying new and extraordinary remedies; facilitating union organizing in various ways, including ordering employers to recognize and bargain with unions on the basis of signed authorization cards rather than secret ballot representation elections; and disallowing certain management bargaining strategies—became rallying points for employer opposition to the NLRB.

As one administrative law expert put it at the time, "policy-making is politics."[1] This axiom applied to both the Kennedy and Farmer Boards. Each chose among possible policy alternatives concerning unionization and collective bargaining. For the next eight years, the Board chose policies favorable to unionization and collective bargaining.

Organized labor was getting nowhere in its attempt to repeal Section 14(b), despite Kennedy's election, and had no hope of legislatively reforming Taft-Hartley or Landrum-Griffin. Consequently, organized labor counted on receiving substantial help from the new Board in strengthening its hand at the bargaining table, rebuilding unions' sagging membership, and particularly, opening the South to union organizers.[2] At the same time that organized labor was foundering on both organizing and legislative fronts, employer spokesmen were portraying unions publicly as mighty economic monopolies with powerful political influence on legislators.[3] Whether these public warnings about union power were employers' true perceptions or were exaggerated deliberately to persuade the public, the Kennedy Board majority considered them the railings of a marginal group of extremely conservative employers and not representative of the mainstream of major corporations, which the Board believed had accepted unions and collective bargaining. The new Board was seriously mistaken on both counts.

Reversals of Eisenhower Board Policy

Picketing and the Landrum-Griffin Amendments

In late February 1961, only a few weeks before Frank McCulloch and Gerald Brown joined the Board, the Eisenhower Board issued its first interpretations of the Landrum-Griffin organizational and recognitional picketing amendments to Taft-Hartley.[4] In a series of landmark decisions the Eisenhower Board interpreted the new amendments to prohibit a union from picketing for more than thirty days for recognition even though it was picketing to protest an employer's unfair labor practices,[5] to outlaw recognitional picketing after thirty days even when it caused no stoppage of deliveries and truthfully advised the public that an employer was non-union and did not have a union contract,[6] to define even small-scale interferences with deliveries as sufficient to make publicity picketing unlawful,[7] and to prohibit picketing to force bargaining as well as recognition.[8]

Only six weeks after the Eisenhower Board announced these decisions, McCulloch, Brown, and Fanning agreed to reconsider them at the requests of the unions involved and over the objections of Leedom and Rodgers. The new Board majority offered several reasons, some more persuasive than others, for the urgency with which it set out to revise Eisenhower Board doctrines: to meet the demands of a constantly changing industrial economy, "outside prompting" from the Pucinski hearings and report, and new guidelines resulting from the Supreme Court's reversal of many Eisenhower Board decisions.[9]

Put more accurately, the new majority would not accept and apply decisions with which they fundamentally disagreed. Ironically, they found ample support for their reversals of Eisenhower Board policies in the statements of Guy Farmer, the first chairman of an Eisenhower-appointed Board, who said pointedly:

My job is to interpret the law as I read it, not as somebody else who preceded me thought that it should read. I would not be so foolhardy as to blandly disregard the opinions of my predecessors, but I took an oath to administer the Statute, not someone else's view as to what the statute means. I would not have taken the job, and I certainly would not remain in it, if I thought that my sole function was to administer the Statute in a straight jacket fashioned by the interpretations made by my predecessors on the Board.[10]

Board member Brown later said that he had "some fun" quoting Guy Farmer to those criticizing the Kennedy Board for not respecting *stare decisis*.[11] McCulloch, Brown, and Fanning moved quickly to reconsider the Eisenhower Board's Landrum-Griffin decisions not only because they considered them wrongly decided but also because they were convinced that lame-duck Eisenhower appointees had rushed to get those decisions out before the incoming Kennedy appointees could get their hands on them.[12]

In a series of decisions the new majority reversed the direction the Eisenhower Board had taken in interpreting the new amendments' prohibitions against recognitional and organizational picketing. In *Blinne*[13] the Kennedy Board permitted organizational and recognitional picketing for more than thirty days, if a union filed a meritorious refusal-to-bargain charge against an employer. Picketing then could continue until the unfair labor practices ceased. The Kennedy Board also broadened considerably unions' opportunity to picket lawfully in other situations. The new majority in *Crown Cafeteria,* contrary to the Eisenhower Board's earlier ruling in that case,[14] read the information picketing proviso (Section 8[b][7][C]) to protect picketing for the purpose of truthfully advising the public, including customers, that an employer did not employ members of or have a contract with, a labor organization, even when recognition or organization was the objective of the picketing.[15] In *Barker Bros.* McCulloch, Fanning, and Brown further expanded the protection the publicity proviso afforded recognition and organizational picketing by permitting, as the Eisenhower Board had not, isolated instances of interference with deliveries and services. Informational picketing was now protected unless the general counsel could prove that it had interfered with, disrupted, or curtailed an employer's business in a substantial way.[16]

In *Calumet Contractors* the new majority permitted union picketing to publicize the fact that an already unionized employer was not paying the prevailing union wage rate in the area, because the union's objective could be achieved without the employer's either bargaining with or recognizing the picketing union.[17] The Board majority then made area-standards picketing immune from the 1959 Landrum-Griffin picketing prohibitions, even when such picketing interfered with deliveries and services to the employer.[18] Similarly, the majority rejected the Eisenhower Board's doctrine equating picketing to force an employer to reinstate discharged employees with unlawful picketing for recognitional or organizational purposes.[19] The Board also removed picketing to protest an employer's unfair labor practices from the statutory prohibition against picketing within twelve months of a valid representation election.[20]

McCulloch, Brown, and Fanning also increased unions' lawful opportunities to extend their disputes with primary employers to secondary sites. In 1962, for example, the Board eased restrictions on common situs picketing by substituting a case-by-case approach in which the place of the picketing would be only one circumstance among others in determining the lawfulness of the picketing.[21] Despite the widespread belief that many of the 1959 Landrum-Griffin amendments were intended to close certain "loopholes" in the Taft-Hartley secondary boycott provisions,[22] the Board's new majority, in another important series of cases, interpreted those provisions to expand the lawful limits of union secondary activity. For example, in *Lohman Sales Co.* McCulloch, Brown, Fanning, and this time Leedom ruled among other things that "mere handbilling" was not picketing.[23] Rodgers, the sole dissenter, accused his colleagues of having emasculated the intent of the Landrum-Griffin secondary boycott provisions by sanctioning the "indiscriminate handbilling of virtually any business."[24]

Lockouts

With an unusual combination of McCulloch, Brown, and Leedom in the majority (and an even more unusual pairing of Rodgers and Fanning in dissent), the Board, in *Brown Food Store,*[25] treated the Eisenhower Board's decision in *Buffalo Linen Supply*[26] as an isolated exception to the rule against employer lockouts for union activity. In *Buffalo Linen,* in which a union had struck one member of a multiemployer bargaining group, the Eisenhower Board had permitted the nonstruck employers to lock out their employees as a defensive measure to protect the solidarity of the multiemployer unit against whipsawing by the union. In *Brown Food Store* the nonstruck employer members of a multiemployer bargaining group also locked out their employees after a union had struck one employer in the group, but unlike the case in *Buffalo Linen,* all the employers, struck and nonstruck, continued to operate, with supervisors, relatives, and temporary employees. That was the critical difference, in the *Brown Food* majority's opinion.

The majority characterized a lockout as a "drastic form of discrimination" against employees for engaging in union activities and concluded that its use in *Brown* far exceeded the limited purpose endorsed in *Buffalo Linen.* The nonstruck employers who locked out their employees and operated with replacements in *Brown* did not do so to protect the integrity of the employer unit, the Board majority said, but rather to inhibit a lawful strike; it was a retaliatory, not a defensive, lockout.[27] One critic commented, "The Board again appears to have acted on the notion that the law condemns employer action merely because it blunts the effectiveness of a strike."[28]

Employer Speech

The McCulloch majority also treated employer speech and union speech differently[29] but, in contrast to the Eisenhower Board, was more likely to accept the wording of union picket signs at face value (as in its reversals of the Eisenhower Board's Landrum-Griffin picketing decisions) while sharply restricting the lawfulness of employer speech by assessing it in full context. Unlike the Eisenhower Board, the new majority also treated the representation election as fundamentally different from political elections and employee voters as vulnerable to coercion and manipulation.[30] Consequently, the Kennedy Board regulated employer campaign activities closely and sought to impose higher standards to ensure workers a reasoned and free choice. Board member Brown clearly articulated the new majority's assumptions in a speech exposing what he called the "mythical aspects" of employer speech:

> A myth is that equality necessarily exists between employers and unions, . . . and hence that equal rights and limitations are required as to both. . . . The employer is known to the employees, controls their jobs and income, and has the power effectively to express his displeasure. In contrast, the union is frequently an unknown quantity and is on the outside trying to "sell itself" to the employees. And even if the union is known, it usually has no *independent* power to affect the economic well-being of the employees.
>
> In addition, studies have revealed that deference patterns predispose people to respond automatically towards those to whom they have been in the custom of responding. Employees are accustomed to deferring to the employer in the plant and will tend to do so whether in performing a shop operation or carrying out some less objective course, such as voting against a union.[31]

It was a controversial approach, not only because of the increasing bitterness of representation campaigns[32] but also because there was often a fine, if not imperceptible, line between permissible and impermissible speech. The difficulties of regulating employer speech caused experts such as Derek Bok of Harvard to propose an alternative policy, which instead of restraining employer speech would guarantee union representatives equal opportunity to reply, an opportunity some union organizers told Bok they preferred to strict limitations on employer speech.[33] The Kennedy Board chose, however, to apply more stringent standards to employer representation election campaign speech by reviving the 1948 *General Shoe*[34] doctrine. In that case the Herzog Board had limited the reach of Taft-Hartley's employer speech protection to unfair labor practice proceedings so that conduct that made employee free choice improbable would sometimes warrant setting aside an election, even though the conduct did not constitute an unfair labor practice. The Herzog Board fashioned a strict standard of "laboratory conditions" in which to determine the uninhibited desires of the employees. The Eisenhower Board, while not entirely abandoning the *General Shoe* doctrine, applied the "free speech" protection of the act to both unfair labor practice and representation election proceedings. Consequently, the Eisenhower Board normally set aside elections and ordered new ones only when an employer's statements themselves constituted an unfair labor practice.[35]

In *Dal-Tex Optical Co.*[36] the Kennedy Board said that it would use the laboratory conditions of *General Shoe* and not Section 8(c) to determine if employer interference was sufficient to justify ordering a new representation election. In this and other cases the Kennedy Board overruled much of the Eisenhower Board's doctrine concerning employer speech by reading employer statements about the possibilities of going out of business, relocating, strikes, shutdowns, and other dire consequences of union demands and policies as threats, not predictions, of events beyond an employer's control. Other employer statements, about hiring permanent replacements for any employee who went on strike, bargaining "from scratch" so that employees might end up economically worse off than they were without a union, or refusing to bargain with any union until ordered by a court and then only after exhausting all available (and lengthy) judicial appeals, were now impermissible implied threats in the judgment of the Kennedy Board, instead of what the Eisenhower Board saw as protected declarations about an employer's legal position.[37] The new Board majority said that it would look to the economic realities of the employer-employee relationship and not to the form of an employer's statement in deciding whether employer speech substantially interfered with a representation election.[38] The McCulloch Board did not intend to be limited "to a mere textual analysis of documents."[39]

The Kennedy and Eisenhower Boards disagreed not only in their conceptions of what the employer-employee relationship ought to be but also in their assumptions about what the realities of the relationship actually were. Former chairman Farmer justified much of his Board's deregulation of employer speech on the theory that employees were more educated, more sophisticated, and better able to recognize representation election campaign propaganda than they were in the 1930s. Although the new Kennedy Board majority denied that its stricter regulation of employer campaign speech downgraded the intelligence of employees,[40] many of its decisions were protectionist and based on the presumption that workers were susceptible to propaganda, promises, misrepresentations, and other employer influences.[41]

In *Plochman and Harrison-Cherry Lane Foods, Inc.* and *Carl T. Mason Co.*,[42] for example, the employers in representation election campaigns used not only speeches and pamphlets but also a motion picture, *And Women Must Weep*, produced by the National Right to Work Committee, to dissuade their employees from voting for a union.[43] The unions in both cases lost their elections, and the Board, in a now customary three-to-two vote, set the results aside and ordered new elections. The movie, professionally produced in color with a dramatic musical soundtrack, claimed to be a documentary replay of an actual strike. In the film the strike, perpetrated by a ruthless union leader against the wishes of the members, destroys friendships, attracts outside goons who terrorize the good people who want to work, leaves wives with no food for their children and fearful for their husbands' safety, and results in extreme acts of violence, including the shooting of a baby, staged to impute guilt to the union.

McCulloch, concurring with Brown and Fanning's application of the total-context criterion in these cases, singled out the motion picture as much more powerful than the printed or spoken word in arousing emotions and influencing attitudes and in its lasting effects.[44] McCulloch said that the film, with its distortion of the facts, created an atmosphere of "emotional prejudice" inconsistent with a "sober and informed exercise of the franchise," although he admitted that a few "sophisticated" people might see *And Women Must Weep* for what it was, "propaganda intended to create anti-union feeling": "But such films are not meant for sophisticated audiences. I have no doubt that among audiences of working men and women as well as others, 'And Women Must Weep' is emotionally overpowering. It pictures a labor dispute as one in which Americanism, religion, family, motherhood, and innocent childhood are arranged on one side, and goons, brutes, and murderers on the other or prounion side."[45]

In contrast to the limited responsibilities of public officials conducting essentially unregulated political elections, the Kennedy Board said in *Sewell Mfg. Co.* that it had to *oversee* the propaganda activities of the participants in NLRB-conducted elections to guarantee voters reasoned, untrammeled choice.[46] Organized labor also wanted the Board to set aside all elections lost by unions in which employers used race hate propaganda. Unions argued that such communications made it impossible to establish laboratory conditions or a reasoned and untrammeled choice because of the emotion engendered by the race issue, particularly in the South.[47] In *Sewell Mfg. Co.*, however, the Board chose to treat such racial appeals no differently than other campaign speech and applied the same *General Shoe* laboratory-conditions standard it had reactivated only a few weeks before in *Dal-Tex.*

In *Sewell* the employer used a barrage of race hate literature to defeat attempts by the Amalgamated Clothing Workers to organize employees in rural towns in Georgia. Over a period of months the employer distributed to employees copies of *Militant Truth,* a privately issued monthly publication repeatedly linking labor leaders with communism and interracial marriage.[48] Applying the same principle as it did in *Plochman (And Women Must Weep)*, the Board said that it would not tolerate appeals or arguments that could have no purpose but to inflame the racial feelings of voters.[49] Yet the Board, citing Eisenhower Board case precedent,[50] said that it would keep hands off appeals to race and not set aside an election if the appeal to race was a "temperate, factually correct" statement of the union's position on integration.[51]

The Pucinski committee had condemned not only race hate speech but also the Eisenhower Board's *Livingston Shirt*[52] doctrine, which permitted employers to present their views on unionism to captive audiences of employees on company property while denying unions the same opportunity. The committee had recommended a return to the Truman Board's approach of granting unions equal time and access to employees during representation campaigns. In *May Company Department Stores,* a case mistakenly heralded as a complete return to the equal opportunity doctrine articulated by the Herzog Board in *Bonwit Teller,*[53] McCulloch, Fanning, and Brown ruled that, although a department store (because of the customer-oriented nature of its business) was privileged to prohibit union solicitation in the store's selling areas during both working and nonworking time, the employer committed an unfair labor practice when it made anti-union speeches to massed assemblies of employees on company property and then denied union requests for an equal opportunity to address the same employees.[54] The majority said that the employer created a glaring imbalance in opportunities for organization by seizing for itself the most advantageous circumstances to deliver its anti-union message to employees while relegating the union and its employee supporters "to relatively catch-as-catch-can methods of rebuttal such as home visits, advertised meetings on the employees' own time, telephone calls, letters, and the various mass media of communication."[55] If the May Company chose to use its premises for its anti-union campaign, it was obliged to grant a union request to address the employees under similar circumstances.

May Department Stores represented another phase of the recurring problem of striking a balance between an employer's right to maintain production and discipline in its establishment and employees' right to self-organization. Supreme Court decisions, in particular, had tipped the balance in favor of employers' property and management rights. In 1945, the Court, in *Republic Aviation*,[56] upheld an employer's ban on employee solicitation during working time. In *Babcock & Wilcox*[57] the Court said that an employer was not obliged to permit nonemployees to use its premises for organizational purposes, absent a showing that the employees could not be reached by other means. In *Nutone*[58] the Court held that when a company had a rule against employee solicitation during working hours, the employer did not have to grant employees any greater organizational rights on the premises even when the employer violated its own rules by engaging in anti-union conduct on the premises.

There was no way to compare the effectiveness or adequacy of alternative means of communication available to a union, however desirable such a comparison might be. As Harvard law professor Derek Bok put it in an important article on the regulation of campaign tactics, "in blunt language, then, to insist that these alternatives be considered is simply to invite a succession of unarticulated conclusions, which will be of little use in future cases."[59] In 1962 the conclusions that McCulloch, Fanning, and Brown drew were based on what they believed would encourage organization for the purpose of collective bargaining.

Bargaining Unit Determinations

The new majority also encouraged unionization and collective bargaining by redefining bargaining units in a way that increased the chances that labor organizations would win elections. As the NLRB's first chairman, J. Warren Madden, observed, "the Board's answer to the unit question is often decisive as to whether or not there is to be collective bargaining just as the definition of the boundaries of a political election district may determine which party will win such an election."[60] The Pucinski committee had accused the Eisenhower Board of denying employees an opportunity to bargain collectively by favoring employer interests in its determination of appropriate bargaining units. McCulloch, Fanning, and Brown decided, in *Quaker City Life Insurance Co.*,[61] therefore, to reverse long-standing NLRB precedent and permit the organization of insurance agents into units smaller than employerwide or statewide.

Similarly, in 1962 the Board overturned a long-standing rule that the appropriate unit for collective bargaining in retail chain store operations should include employees of all stores within an employer's administrative division or geographic area. In *Sav-On Drugs, Inc.*[62] the Board said that the old rule, by requiring very large units, had impeded employees' statutory right to self-organization. That had been a major complaint of representatives of the Retail

Clerks union when they appeared before the Pucinski committee. Under the new *Sav-On Drugs* policy single-store and other smaller units could be found appropriate for collective bargaining. "In those cases we did change the unit rules," McCulloch recalled later, "because we thought the old ones were not adapted to a reasonable growth in collective bargaining." He added, "Now it should be easy to say this made it easier for unions to organize and achieve recognition for bargaining. But that was the purpose of the law."[63]

The *Fibreboard* Decision: A Challenge to Management Rights

Shortly after McCulloch became chairman but before Brown became a member, the Eisenhower Board (with Fanning dissenting and McCulloch not participating) ruled that the Fibreboard Corporation had no statutory obligation to bargain with its employees' union about the company's decision to contract out all its bargaining unit maintenance work when the company's motivation was economic rather than discriminatory.[64] Granting that the statutory obligation on employers to bargain was unquestionably broad, Leedom, Rodgers, and Jenkins said that it was not broad enough to compel bargaining over "basic management decisions" such as to what extent to risk capital and managerial effort.

Fanning, relying on a contrary decision by the Herzog Board requiring an employer to bargain over its intent to subcontract,[65] said that the majority's decision would permit employers to abolish every job in a bargaining unit and thereby eliminate union representation. Even though the duty to bargain included no duty to yield, had Fibreboard bargained about its decision to contract out maintenance work, the company and union might have agreed on a solution short of subcontracting the entire maintenance operation. That possibility, Fanning maintained, was "the goal of sound collective bargaining, which the Act [was] designed to foster and encourage."[66]

Fanning's dissent became the new majority opinion after Brown joined the Board. In what management attorney Frank O'Connell later called a disgraceful act of "villainy," Eisenhower-appointed general counsel Stuart Rothman asked the new Board to reconsider the Eisenhower Board's *Fibreboard* decision.[67] McCulloch said that many employers never forgave Rothman for petitioning the Board for reconsideration of *Fibreboard,* which resulted in a Kennedy Board decision that "upset people for years."[68] When *Fibreboard* returned to the agenda, however, the Board faced a two-to-two deadlock because Brown, as regional director in San Francisco, had issued the complaint against Fibreboard and had participated in regional efforts to settle the case. Leedom volunteered to drop out so that Brown would not have to be involved. As a result, *Fibreboard* was decided by a panel of three: McCulloch, Fanning, and Rodgers.[69]

McCulloch and Fanning overruled the Eisenhower Board's *Fibreboard* decision for the same reasons Fanning had set forth in his dissent in that case. They ordered the company "to restore the *status quo ante* by reinstituting its maintenance operation and fulfilling its statutory obligation to bargain." Dissenter Rodgers warned that if the new Board's *Fibreboard* decision stood, all economic actions undertaken by management, "whether it be the discontinuance of an unprofitable line, the closing of an unnecessary facility, or the abandonment of an outmoded procedure," would be subjects of mandatory bargaining.[70]

With the McCulloch Board's *Fibreboard* decision the NLRB entered what an internal agency memorandum called "a new contentious phase of its existence."[71] Employers knew that this decision, if carried to its logical conclusion and extended to its full reach, could substantially restrict management power and flexibility. (As usual in these disputes over fundamentals, however, the issue was posed as one of management rights rather than management power.) As *Fibreboard* worked its way to the Supreme Court in the mid-1960s, conservative columnists, such as Arthur Krock of the *New York Times,* said that the Court's ruling on the rights of corporate management would determine the future of American free enterprise.[72] Management spokesmen predicted that the Board's *Fibreboard* rule would put U.S. industry at a serious competitive disadvantage and retard economic expansion by prohibiting the movement of capital to lower wage areas; prohibiting employers from obtaining the lowest cost of production; preventing the discontinuance of unprofitable lines or products; inhibiting automation, mergers, and consolidations; and removing a natural economic regulator on the abuse of union power—the elimination or movement away of bargaining-unit jobs whenever a union forced too costly a deal on an employer.[73] Other employer representatives spoke publicly of the Board's attempt to "committee-ize" the management of U.S. business or to "foist" the codetermination of fundamental business decisions, conjuring up un-American substitutes for the capitalistic system.[74]

Even employers who ostensibly had accepted unionization and collective bargaining resisted mightily any encroachment on what they considered the exclusive rights and privileges of management.[75] Former NLRB chairman Farmer articulated management's position on collective bargaining: Collective bargaining was simply a "mechanism" for giving employees a collective "voice" to express their own interests in wages, hours, and working conditions. When Congress imposed the duty to bargain, Farmer maintained, it did not intend to subject basic managerial decisions to joint decision through collective bargaining.[76]

The NLRB expressed a sharply different understanding of collective bargaining and management rights in its brief to the Supreme Court in *Fibreboard*. Contrary to management's claims about its rights, the NLRB argued that the national labor policy "does not undertake to assign prerogatives to management or labor, nor does it specify a list of subjects of joint concern." The Board defined a broad scope for collective bargaining, saying that the national labor policy was concerned with methods for resolving *"whatever"* conflicts of interest arose between labor and employers, "at least when they directly relate to tenure of employment."[77] The NLRB's statement of its position was widely quoted publicly and in management circles and was understood by employers to portend "codetermination":

> It may be objected that the literal reading [of the statute] would give labor unions a statutory right to bargain about a host of subjects heretofore regarded as "management prerogatives," including prices, types of product, volume of production, and even methods of financing. Such is doubtless the logical, theoretical consequence of giving effect to the literal sweep of words, although the Board has never gone so far. As a practical matter, however, the scope of collective bargaining is confined by the range of *employees' vital interests.*[78]

At the same time that the new Board majority was expanding government regulation of collective bargaining, a group of distinguished academic experts, in a study sponsored by the Committee on Economic Development, recommended deregulation of the duty to bargain: "The present national policy calling on the parties to bargain in good faith has developed into an unwarranted intrusion into the business of the parties and a source of voluminous and wasteful litigation. The subjects to be covered, the procedures to be followed, the nuances of strategy involved in bargaining are best left to the parties themselves."[79] NLRB staff members, who had seen subcontracting, plant removals, and shutdowns used to avoid collective bargaining and destroy newly organized unions, disagreed with that recommendation. As they put it, "we witness daily, in the cases we process, the efforts of respondents to avoid and evade their duty to bargain by a variety of devices and stratagems. Without the governmental interference complained of by the [CED group], we are convinced that good faith bargaining would be a rarity."[80]

Darlington Manufacturing: A Constitutional Management Right?

Another highly publicized and debated management rights dispute, involving the Darlington Manufacturing Company of South Carolina, raised the question of whether an employer could close an entire plant to avoid unionization. The issue was particularly important to employers who had moved south in search of non-union and low-wage labor as well as to employers threatening to close up if unionized. It was equally critical to the Textile Workers Union of America and other unions still trying to organize southern mill hands.[81] In the words of one TWUA representative, *Darlington* had been used "as a propaganda weapon against us in every election since the plant closed. We have lost elections because employees are fearful of mill closings, dismissals, and long periods of unemployment."[82]

In 1956 the TWUA began an organizing campaign among the employees of Darlington, one of twenty-seven mills and seventeen companies, all unorganized, comprising the family-owned Deering Milliken Company, headed by Roger Milliken, whose mills had long been a target of the union. The Darlington plant employed approximately six hundred people in a city of five thousand. Milliken stated openly that his anti-union feelings were a major reason for the shutdown of the Darlington mill, warning that management did not intend to share its prerogatives with labor union leaders.[83]

Despite the company's vigorous resistance, including threats to close the mill if the employees voted for the union, on September 6, 1956, the TWUA won a representation election, but by only eight votes, 256 to 248. As he threatened, Milliken decided to close the mill the same day the employees voted for the union. Company officials told the employees that the decision to liquidate was caused by the election and encouraged them to sign a petition disavowing the union. Eighty-three percent did, but Milliken was unmoved: "As long as there are 17 percent of the hard core crowd here, I refused to run the mill."[84] The plant ceased operations in November, and all mill machinery and equipment was sold at auction in December.[85]

Although the Eisenhower Board began proceedings against Darlington in 1956, the case would not be concluded until after almost thirty years of legal maneuvering and other shameful delays. The Kennedy Board issued the first decision in October 1962.[86] Darlington claimed the absolute right to go out of business for whatever reason, even if anti-union animus was one of the reasons. McCulloch, Brown, Fanning, and Leedom firmly rejected Darlington's contention: "A plant shutdown resulting in the discharge of employees that is partly due to employees' union activities constitutes an unfair labor practice, even assuming the genuineness of Darlington's economic reasons for closing the mill." They called Darlington's conduct contrary to the fundamental spirit and purpose of the statute. Darlington, the majority said, had destroyed the possibility of collective bargaining by shutting its plant after the employees had exercised their statutory right to choose a union representative.[87]

McCulloch, Brown, and Fanning found Darlington to be only one part of a single employer, Deering Milliken Company and its affiliated corporations. Acknowledging the futility of ordering discriminatorily discharged employees reinstated to a closed plant and emphasizing the suffering of more than five hundred discharged employees "thrown into the ranks of the unemployed in a very small city," the Board held Darlington and Deering Milliken liable for back pay until the discharged employees were able to obtain substantially equivalent employment.[88] The Board also ordered Darlington to reinstate the discriminatorily discharged employees if the plant resumed operations. In the event Darlington remained closed, however, the Board ordered Deering Milliken to offer employment to the discharged employees in its other mills in South Carolina and adjacent states and to put those for whom no work was currently available on a preferential hiring list to be the first hired when equivalent positions did become available.[89] The Textile Workers union was dissatisfied, however, because it wanted the Board to order Deering Milliken to reopen the Darlington Mill and offer reinstatement there.[90]

The Board's *Darlington* decision precipitated what one newspaper columnist called a "synchronized political drive" against the NLRB.[91] Roger Milliken, an influential force in the conservative wing of the Republican Party, was already unhappy with the "liberal" Nixon-Rockefeller labor plank adopted at the 1960 Republican convention. He worked closely with the National Right to Work Committee and was a member of the executive committee of the ultraconservative John Birch Society.[92]

Darlington hired what *Time* magazine called an unusual advocate to argue its case before the Supreme Court, North Carolina's Democratic senator, Sam J. Ervin, Jr. Although no law prevented members of the Senate or House from trying cases in court, *Time* reported, "purists looked askance at a U.S. Senator representing a private client against the U.S. Government—to say nothing of the fact that Ervin's constituents include thousands of North Carolina textile workers."[93] Ervin had helped prepare himself by attending the oral arguments before the Supreme Court in the *Fibreboard* case.[94]

Not only was there no conflict of interest in his representing Darlington, Ervin told the Supreme Court, it was actually "harmonious" with his obligations as a senator, since that office required him to uphold the Constitution and the right to go out of business at any time was a constitutional right. During his argument before the Supreme Court on behalf of Darlington, Ervin quoted from the Bible, claimed that free enterprise in the textile industry rode on the case, said he was "fighting for the economic freedom of all Americans," and concluded by thanking the Court for its patience in listening to "this country lawyer."[95]

J.P. Stevens: A Case for More Powerful Remedies

Employers feared not only NLRB-inspired incursion by unions into management rights but also NLRB-supported congressional efforts to increase the effectiveness of Board remedies. In the mid-to-late 1960s the J.P. Stevens textile company became the symbol not only of some employers' persistent and pervasive intimidation of employees to prevent unionization but also of the powerlessness of the NLRB to remedy the results of these unfair labor practices or to change the conduct of unreconstructed violators of the Taft-Hartley Act.

J.P. Stevens, a family-owned concern headed by Robert T. Stevens, secretary of the army in the Eisenhower administration, was the second largest textile manufacturer in the world. The company was headquartered in New York City's garment district but had approximately forty-two thousand employees at seventy plants concentrated in North and South Carolina.[96] Burlington Industries (the world's largest textile manufacturer), Deering Milliken, and Stevens constituted the big three textile operations in the South. The Textile Workers Union of America, which focused on the textile industry in the Carolinas as part of the AFL-CIO Industrial Union Department's all-out organizational drive in the South, abandoned its unsuccessful strategy of targeting small, single-plant operations. The union chose instead to concentrate on J.P. Stevens, because workers there seemed receptive to organization, at least initially, and the firm was financially sound and geographically centralized in the generally unorganized South. Most of all, a union breakthrough at Stevens, the most militantly anti-union company in the anti-union textile industry, would have great symbolic significance for the entire union organizing drive in the South.[97] As the Industrial Union Department (IUD) saw it, "once any large group of workers in Southern textiles proves [J.P. Stevens] can be beaten and conditions improved, it will sweep the South."[98]

After the TWUA lost its first four NLRB representation elections in Stevens plants amid numerous unfair labor practice charges, the IUD turned to its friends in Congress for support. At the IUD's urging, the Democratic chairman of the House Labor Committee, Adam Clayton Powell, sent the committee's chief investigator, Odell Clark, to several southern states to look into complaints of violations of workers' rights.[99] The TWUA took advantage of two days of exploratory hearings, held by the House Labor Committee in September 1961, to condemn J.P. Stevens's "sadistic, cruel, and inhuman" anti-union tactics as well as the NLRB's prolonged delays and ineffectual remedies.[100]

Chief Investigator Clark also castigated the South, particularly the Carolinas, as a place where company and company-prompted community action denied employees their statutory right to join unions by using race baiting as a method of dividing workers; linking unions with communism and civil rights protests; and interrogating, threatening, and increasing the work loads of known union supporters. Based on what he saw in the South, Clark identified excessive delay and ineffective remedies as the main weaknesses of labor law. He berated southern judges, so dominated by the "power structure in their communities" that they would issue injunctions against anyone but employers and the Ku Klux Klan.[101]

Robert Stevens accused the House Labor Committee of allowing the TWUA to use its open hearing for "unrestrained," "slanderous," and "libelous" attacks on his company. Contrary to union witnesses' accusations, he wrote the committee, J.P. Stevens "yielded to no one" in its efforts to have good relations with "our people" and to provide them with steady jobs, excellent working conditions, and constantly rising wages and benefits.[102]

In a series of decisions from 1965 through 1969, however, the NLRB and the Second, Fourth, and Fifth circuit courts of appeals found J.P. Stevens guilty of unlawful interrogation, threats, intimidation, and coercion of employees for engaging in union activity, as well as surveillance of union meetings and the harassment and discharge of union supporters on various pretextual grounds.[103] Former Eisenhower-appointed Board chairman Boyd Leedom, who became a trial examiner in 1964 when his second term on the Board expired and who heard one of the J.P. Stevens cases, saw clearly the immoral as well as the illegal nature of the company's actions. Offended by the systematic lying under oath of J.P. Stevens officials, in addition to the company's egregious unfair labor practices, Leedom wrote:

> If an employer will offend to the extent of unlawfully discharging an employee thereby depriving him of the means of livelihood under circumstances making other employment most difficult, and will in addition compound such wrong in a forum of law by misrepresenting the facts, then such an employer would hardly hesitate to commit the other wrongs of denying decent pay, suitable working conditions, and adequate fringe benefits that might reasonably be expected to sustain the employee in illness and in his unproductive years. Such additional wrongs, if heaped on the unlawful discharge, create a situation so aggravated and so out of tune with a humane, civilized approach to industrial relations, that in proper perspective, they should shock even those least sensitive to honor, justice and decent treatment.[104]

Despite these NLRB and court decisions, J.P. Stevens employees were realistically pessimistic: "Deep down, most of them feel J.P. Stevens is too big down here for the Federal Government—that the little NLRB isn't going to tell big J.P. what to do in South Carolina."[105] J.P. Stevens did continue its policy of breaking the union throughout this period, flouting eight separate unanimous NLRB decisions that found the company guilty of "flagrant," "massive and deliberate" unfair labor practices.[106] By the summer of 1967 the TWUA had proceeded to NLRB representation elections in four areas in North and South Carolina with groups of Stevens plants and lost all of them.[107] The company boasted, "The labor board steadily rules in favor of the union and just as steadily our employees vote against the union."[108]

The customary NLRB remedies were inadequate to rectify the wrongs committed by a persistent repeat offender such as J.P. Stevens.[109] The Board kept deciding against Stevens, the company persisted in its unlawful conduct, the TWUA continued to lose representation elections at Stevens plants—and the Board kept setting those elections aside and ordering reruns. J.P. Stevens was losing all its battles with the NLRB but was clearly winning its war against unionization.

Acknowledging that its conventional remedies could not undo the effect of the massive and deliberate unfair labor practices being committed, the Board devised some novel remedies for the J.P. Stevens violations. In addition to reinstatement with back pay plus interest, the Board ordered Stevens to post notices in all its plants in North and South Carolina (not just those involved in specific cases before the NLRB) promising to remedy its violation of the Taft-Hartley Act and to refrain from further unlawful activity; to mail a copy of the notice to each of its employees in those plants; to require company officials to read these notices during working-time meetings to all its employees in the Carolinas; to grant the TWUA, on request, access to plant bulletin boards for one year; and to give the TWUA a list of the names and addresses of all its employees in all its plants in North and South Carolina. The Board rejected, however, the TWUA's contention that in cases such as J.P. Stevens, in which a union had been prevented from obtaining a majority because of an employer's pervasive unfair labor practices, the NLRB should direct the employer to recognize and bargain with the union. Although the TWUA might have gained majority status except for the company's violations of the law, in the Board's opinion it was doubtful that the act required or permitted the issuance of a bargaining order where a union never attained support of a majority of the employees.[110]

The circuit courts of appeals sustained the Board's J.P. Stevens decisions, but the Second Circuit refused to enforce the Board's order requiring Stevens to grant bulletin board facilities to the union, limited reading of notices to only those plants where unfair labor practices had occurred, and gave Stevens the option of having the notices read by a Board representative rather than a management official. Later the Second Circuit found justification for granting the union access to company bulletin boards but no justification for requiring Stevens to give the union the names and addresses of company employees.[111]

TWUA president William Pollock called those remedies "innocuous."[112] Most of all, the TWUA, IUD, and AFL-CIO objected to the federal government's award of lucrative contracts to employers such as J.P. Stevens that repeatedly violated federal laws. It was a strange system, unions charged, that jailed textile workers when they were seeking only fair treatment for violating strike injunctions and at the same time rewarded lawbreaking employers such as J.P. Stevens with lush government contracts.[113] The Department of Defense, for example, increased its contracts with Stevens from $3.9 million in 1964, to $14.7 million in 1965, to $75.8 million in 1966, despite the company's continued unlawful conduct even after the issuance of NLRB complaints, decisions, and orders.[114]

In May 1966 the AFL-CIO Executive Council passed a resolution urging President Johnson to issue an executive order withholding government contracts from employers who discriminated against employees because of union activities, just as President Kennedy, by executive order, had denied government contracts to employers who discriminated against employees because of race.[115] There was strong opposition to the council's proposal. Senator Richard Russell of Georgia, chairman of the Senate Armed Services Committee, wrote Johnson praising Robert Stevens and maintaining "that even a violation of labor law should not restrict an agency of the government from accepting the lowest and best bid for critical services and material."[116] Russell's counterpart in the House, Mendel Rivers of South Carolina, told the president that the NLRB decision in *J.P. Stevens* was "one of the most classic travesties of justice that has ever come to my attention." Rivers also told Johnson that the AFL-CIO's proposal "would deny uniforms to servicemen and women in Vietnam."[117] Rivers accused the Board of acting punitively against both a great company that had benefited the nation and "the unselfish patriot" at its head who had served his country in two wars.[118] The Defense Department, whose procurement program for clothing and textiles had tripled in size, informed the White House that Robert Stevens had played "a strong and aggressive role in securing the support of other clothing and textile manufacturers in fulfilling military needs."[119]

Robert Stevens pressed the White House for a letter saying that the Johnson administration had no intention of denying government contracts to firms charged with violations of labor law. Stevens covered his appeal with patriotism, calling for the nation "to unite behind our Commander-in-Chief in the critical situation that faces us in South Vietnam" and promising not to tolerate anything adversely affecting the flow of military supplies to "our boys in Vietnam."[120] It was an effective argument, because organized labor did not want to be tarred with the brush of impeding the war effort, a concern McCulloch believed kept the AFL-CIO from pushing as hard as it might have on that issue.[121] The Defense Department subsequently decided that it did not have the authority to deny government contracts to J.P. Stevens or other employers merely because of repeated violations of the National Labor Relations Act.[122] Despite close consultation with McCulloch, Johnson's staff, although admitting that Stevens's labor practices were "Neanderthal," advised the president not to issue an executive order.[123]

Organized labor's goals, including enforcement of the labor law, were not a top priority in either the White House or Congress. Johnson's advisers feared that a proliferation of executive orders barring government contracts to law violators could burden the government's business with social policy requirements. Business was the first concern of the White House as well as of employers. Symbolic of organized labor's continued lack of influence in the White House, Clark Clifford, former Truman confidant and friend and close adviser to Johnson, had become special counsel to J.P. Stevens. George Meany sensed that Stevens now had a stronger "in" with the White House than did organized labor.[124]

Other New NLRB Remedies

The Johnson administration's unwillingness to move against even the most notorious violators of Taft-Hartley, along with the impossibility of getting pro-labor legislation through Congress, left it to the NLRB to fashion new remedies. In 1962 the McCulloch Board, in *Isis Plumbing & Heating Co.,*[125] ordered employers to add 6 percent interest to back pay awards to unlawfully discharged employees. Despite the publicity given to the novel remedies the agency did create and apply, however, the NLRB was actually very cautious in developing more effective remedies. Employer resistance to the law, moreover, was much more widespread than what many thought was unique to the J.P. Stevens fringe type. The Taft-Hartley Act was meeting a determined challenge, resulting in many deliberate violations.[126]

The NLRB caseload had more than doubled to an unprecedented total by 1967, including an all-time high of 17,040 unfair labor practice cases filed, almost triple the number filed in 1957. Two out of three of the unfair labor practice charges against employers, moreover, claimed violation of the most clearly understood provision of the law—discrimination against employees for engaging in union activity (Section 8[a][3])[127]—which, McCulloch told a House Subcommittee on Labor in 1966, evidenced an unwillingness to accept the basic tenets of the law beyond any increase in caseload caused by an expanding economy or persistent union organizing drives.[128] The first major empirical study of how the Board's remedies for violations of Section 8(a)(3) were working (conducted by future congressman and secretary of defense Les Aspin) revealed that, although 82 percent of discriminatorily discharged employees in the sample wanted to be reinstated, less than half accepted the opportunity to return to their jobs, and half of those who did not go back cited fear of company retaliation as a reason. Seventy percent of those who accepted reinstatement subsequently left the company, with two-thirds of them citing "bad company treatment" as the reason.[129] Not one of the employees placed on preferential hiring lists was ever asked to return to work. The Board's remedies in discrimination cases were ineffective, the study concluded, not only because employers had the power to dissuade discriminatees from accepting reinstatement and forcing them out if they did, but also because of delays, the weaknesses of the Board's posted-notice requirements, and the inadequacy of back pay orders.[130]

The Board's caution in applying innovative remedies was due in part to the unwillingness of many courts to enforce them, as in the J.P. Stevens cases. Behind the scenes the Board developed several more potent and innovative remedies and submitted them to Congressman Frank Thompson, chairman of a Special Subcommittee on Labor, to present as his own proposals. Thompson was being advised by Daniel Pollitt, former McCulloch special counsel.[131] These proposed remedies included awarding triple back pay where an unlawful discharge was intentional or repeated; eliminating the tax loophole whereby a discriminatory employer could deduct an NLRB back pay award as a business expense; denying government contracts to repeat offenders; giving nonemployee union organizers access to nonwork areas of a plant when an election was set aside because of employer misconduct; requiring employers whose unfair labor practices prevented a union from achieving majority status to recognize the union and bargain with it on a members-only basis; and making Taft-Hartley's Section 10(l) mandatory injunction provision applicable to cases involving discrimination for union activity.[132]

By early 1968 the Board contemplated strengthening its reinstatement remedy by having employers submit reports to regional directors for a period of one year concerning the treatment and status of workers reinstated after a discriminatory discharge. This proposal was intended to assure discriminated-against employees who had returned to work, those considering an offer of reinstatement, and other employees at the workplace that the Board would be able to protect them on the job.[133] Increasing employee confidence in the power of the Board to obtain compliance with the law was a most important objective of all these proposals, since a union was defeated in seven of ten cases in which employers committed unfair labor practices during organizing campaigns. Unions won elections or were recognized voluntarily in 68 percent of the cases in which employers complied with the law.[134] Another objective was to get unlawfully discharged employees back to their jobs as soon as possible, since the longer the time between discharge and final resolution of the case, the more likely it was that discriminated-against employees would accept compromise settlements, taking needed back pay in return for a promise not to accept reinstatement. To reduce the financial pressure on these discharged employees, Congressman Thompson proposed a bill creating a Board-administered "Subsistence Fund" to make loans to discharged employees equal to their weekly wages while their cases were pending.[135]

McCulloch called the Aspin study a devastating demonstration that the remedies of the Board were not sufficient to achieve the purposes of Taft-Hartley.[136] Thompson's bill and all the other proposals to strengthen NLRB remedies, however, died in Congress. There was no commitment in the Kennedy-Johnson White House, in Congress, or in the courts to the vigorous enforcement of the national labor policy even at the most basic level of preventing employers from unlawfully interfering with their employees' decision to unionize or not.

Authorization Cards

The Board, relying on the 1961 recommendation of the Pucinski subcommittee of the House Labor Committee[137] for permission and protection, moved on its own to revive the Herzog Board's *Joy Silk*[138] doctrine. That doctrine required employers to bargain with unions that no longer represented a majority of an employer's employees when an employer's unlawful conduct had dissipated the union's majority and made a fair representation election impossible. Although in the early days of the Wagner Act the Board had considered cards signed by a majority of the employees in an appropriate bargaining unit adequate proof of majority support for a union, it had been the Board's policy since 1939 to hold secret ballot elections whenever an employer questioned a union's majority claim.[139] The Board ordered an employer to recognize and bargain with a union without an election only when an employer's misconduct made a fair election impossible or when an employer demonstrably had no doubt about the union's majority but still withheld recognition.[140]

The McCulloch Board in its case decisions from 1961 to 1964 expanded the obligation of employers to bargain on the basis of nonelection showings of support for unions. The Eisenhower Board, in 1954, had ruled in *Aiello Dairy Farms*[141] that, if a union knew that an employer's preelection unfair labor practices might jeopardize its authorization card majority, it could either file refusal-to-bargain charges or petition the NLRB for an election but not both. In 1964 the McCulloch Board in *Bernel Foam Products Co.* eliminated *Aiello*'s "Hob-

son's choice." Now, despite knowledge of the employer's preelection misconduct, a union that participated in a representation election and lost could also
file refusal-to-bargain charges, provided that it could demonstrate majority status, usually by authorization cards it had obtained during its organizing campaign.[142]

The Board majority rejected dissenting member Leedom's advocacy of rerun
elections as an adequate remedy in such cases, because the vast majority of
rerun elections (one study showed 69 percent) were won by the party whose
misconduct unjustly interfered with the original election. This lingering effect
of electioneering misconduct, the majority said, required a remedy strong
enough to deny employers any benefit from their unlawful refusal to bargain,
and to discourage them from demanding unnecessary elections or interfering
with their employees' freedom of choice.[143]

One effect of *Bernel Foam* was to increase the influence of authorization
cards.[144] Although the number of cases in which the Board ordered employers to
bargain with a union on the basis of authorization cards or some other convinc-
ing evidence of majority support remained a very small percentage of Board
certifications of unions through its representation election process,[145] there was a
sharp increase in the number of these nonelection bargaining orders during the
Kennedy-Johnson Board years.[146] No matter how egregious an employer's preelection unfair labor practices, however, the Board limited these bargaining orders to situations in which a union had the support of a majority of employees
before the unlawful conduct occurred. As one critic of this approach commented, "the employer is thus encouraged to commit unfair labor practices at
the earliest observation of union activity within his plant."[147]

Critics of the bargaining order based on authorization cards rather than representation elections claimed that it denied employers their free-speech opportunity to influence employees, and employees their opportunity to receive information about the disadvantages of unionism and to change their minds during a
representation election campaign. The lack of secrecy surrounding card sign-
ings, moreover, did not guarantee free choice, critics said, because employees
were pressured to conform publicly to what fellow workers were doing.[148] When
employer unfair labor practices destroyed the validity of an NLRB representation election, however, even *Joy Silk* bargaining orders were not very effective
against employers that waged lengthy legal battles against unions and "dissipated the union's majority through multiple violations," particularly discharges
of union supporters.[149] Nevertheless, the McCulloch Board majority, consistent
with its understanding of the purpose of the act, chose the remedy with the
greatest chance of resulting in collective bargaining.

Equal Opportunity Access

The Board followed only part way the recommendations of the Pucinski committee to increase the access of union organizers to the employees they sought to organize. In the mid-1960s the Board held open oral argument on the questions whether a union was entitled to have access to an employer's premises during work-time to reply to an employer's captive audience speech and to procure the names and addresses of the employees eligible to vote in a representation election.[150] Senator Ervin, who was representing Darlington Mills in court, urged President Johnson "to do whatever he could to prevent any such regulations."[151] Ervin sent Johnson a letter from a "constituent" from which Ervin had removed both the letterhead and signature.[152] The unidentified constituent said that "such rules would be unabashed and outrageous efforts on the part of the Labor Board to assist the Unions" and called on Ervin to ask Johnson to take quick and determined action to block the new rules. Ervin had masked the identity of John P. Baum, vice-chairman of the board of J.P. Stevens.[153]

In *Excelsior Underwear, Inc.* the McCulloch Board gave unions an assist in organizing by requiring employers to furnish an NLRB regional director the names and addresses of all eligible employee voters within seven days after the parties entered into a consent election agreement or after the Board directed a representation election. The regional director, in turn, would give the list to the union. This higher standard of disclosure was necessary, the Board reasoned, because a lack of information about one of the options available was a major impediment to "a free and reasoned choice" by employees.[154] The Board decided, however, to defer any reconsideration of the Eisenhower Board's captive audience doctrine until there was sufficient experience with the "increased opportunity for employees' access to communications which should flow from *Excelsior.*"[155]

Unions now criticized the McCulloch Board for doing nothing to redress the powerful advantage employers held in convening employees in the plant to listen to anti-union messages. Some employers, meanwhile, promised to resist the *Excelsior* rule.[156]

In January 1967 the McCulloch Board also upset management by announcing a new leaflet and election notice program that in plain language explained the election process, informed employees of their right under federal law to vote for a union, and gave specific examples of improper conduct that could result in an election's being set aside.[157] Incongruously, the Board made posting of the notice to employees voluntary.[158] Even then, employers charged that the election notice program constituted government bias and prejudice against employers and amounted to direct encouragement of unionization.[159] Ironically, as McCulloch explained, the language to which employers objected was lifted almost verbatim from the National Labor Relations Act itself.[160] As one former Board attorney said, "the more you explained to people what the law was about, and what they were entitled to, the more they would become aware of this law and take advantage of it. Of course management didn't like that."[161]

The *Ex-Cell-O* Remedy

As the Pucinski committee noted, obtaining union recognition was only the first step to collective bargaining.[162] Employers' refusal to bargain with the chosen representatives of their employees was what Fanning called "a direct confrontation with the congressional mandate to encourage collective bargaining."[163] The McCulloch Board, as part of its attempt to find out how its own remedies were working, invited University of Pittsburgh professor Philip Ross to study the agency's effectiveness in getting employers to comply with their statutory duty to bargain. Although employers "by and large" accepted NLRB policies and procedures, Ross concluded, the Board's major shortcoming was its failure to adopt "adequate and realistic" remedies where an employer demonstrated a continuing intent to frustrate the act; employers could flagrantly violate the law and succeed in destroying collective bargaining.[164]

The wording of the Board's collective bargaining order had remained essentially unchanged since the earliest duty-to-bargain cases in 1935, when the Board ordered guilty employers to "cease and desist" from refusing to bargain collectively and to begin bargaining with the union in "good faith . . . with the object of making an agreement."[165] The Pucinski committee had expressed its dissatisfaction with this "slap on the wrist" type of remedy.[166] Those remedies certainly had not discouraged violations of Section 8(a)(5), the employer duty-to-bargain provision. In 1959 the number of refusal-to-bargain cases constituted less than 16 percent of all 8(a) violations charged; by 1967 they had increased to 35 percent of all such charges, exceeded only by anti-union discrimination cases. In the same period the number of employer refusal-to-bargain cases found to have merit increased from 26 to 37 percent.[167]

Since an order to bargain in good faith was the only remedy applied regardless of whether an employer delayed the process further by obtaining judicial review of the Board's decision, it cost many employers only attorneys' fees and court costs to avoid their bargaining responsibility. It was a small investment with a high payoff. Litigation took time, and since years often elapsed before a court finally ordered such an employer to bargain, a union's majority may have been lost, its supporters demoralized, and its bargaining power weakened to the point where any contract it might be able to secure would be no better than what the employer was prepared to give without a union.[168] Ross's study verified what employers and unions knew first hand: "The longer the litigation, the less likely . . . the prospect of signing a first contract." Eighty-six percent of all newly certified unions were successful in getting a first contract, but a first contract was obtained in only 50 percent of the cases closed after a Board order and in only 36 percent of the cases closed after circuit court enforcement.[169]

In *Ex-Cell-O Corp.* and three companion cases[170] the McCulloch Board took under consideration an important new remedy in refusal-to-bargain cases that would have ordered an employer to reimburse its employees for the loss of wages and fringe benefits they would have obtained through collective bargaining if the employer had not refused to bargain in good faith. The Board held oral arguments on the proposed remedy in July 1967 amid great controversy. Former NLRB acting general counsel Kenneth McGuiness and former NLRB attorney Stanley Strauss represented the Ex-Cell-O Corporation.[171] The important question, as Congressman Thompson put it, was whether Taft-Hartley's good-faith bargaining requirements were "to be given substance as well as sound."[172]

General Electric and Boulwarism

One Board decision, the *General Electric* "Boulwarism" case,[173] became a highly publicized symbol—to management of the extremes to which the McCulloch Board was willing to go to promote collective bargaining, and to unions of a hard-line management resistance to collective bargaining that could spread if successful. Although a comprehensive three-year contract was concluded in 1960 between General Electric and its principal union, the International Union of Electrical, Radio and Machine Workers (IUE), the NLRB's finding of bad-faith bargaining was based on the company's strategy and tactics in the negotiations. Developed in the late 1940s under the direction of Lemuel R. Boulware, a corporation vice-president with extensive marketing experience, GE's labor policies were best understood by the phrase "job marketing." The company attempted to market its jobs and policies to workers in the same general fashion in which it successfully marketed its products to consumers. It determined what the customer-worker wanted through attitude surveys, supervisors' reports, and studies of bargaining developments in other companies, as well as the union's formal demands. It then fashioned a product (contract offer) to meet these desires as far as possible, while also meeting the company's obligations to other groups, such as stockholders and consumers. Finally, it merchandised the result.

The merchandising step was the most controversial aspect of Boulwarism. General Electric believed that its first offer to a union should be what it considered as "full and fair" as possible, and all the company intended to provide in the final contract, not the niggardly opener of the typical bargaining ritual that made unions appear indispensable. It wanted to demonstrate management's willingness to "do right voluntarily" by its workers.[174] If the union could prove the company's offer erroneous in some factual respect, or if the bargaining environment, such as the general price level or settlements in other key industries, drastically changed during the course of negotiations, then the company professed its willingness to alter its offer. Occasionally, the company offered a series of options or otherwise indicated its willingness to change the mix of its bargaining package. But GE flatly refused to change the size of its first-offer package in order to play the haggling game, stave off a strike, or make the union negotiators look good to their constituents.[175]

The keystone of the merchandising strategy called for the company to present its bargaining position directly to employees, thus reducing the union's opportunity to distort management's offer and building support for the company's position so that employees, in turn, could influence the union to accept it. To those ends, NLRB trial examiner Arthur Leff found, General Electric had "fashioned an elaborate employee communications system, making use of plant newspapers, daily news digests, employee bulletins, letters to employees' homes, television and radio broadcasts, and other media of mass communication." Supervisors were expected to gain the confidence of employees and persuade them of the correctness of company decisions.[176]

A majority of the McCulloch Board, affirming Trial Examiner Leff's intermediate report without change, found GE guilty of bad-faith bargaining based on the company's entire course of conduct and not solely its approach to bargaining.[177] Other language in the majority opinion, however, strongly suggested that the Board would have found GE's bargaining strategy unlawful even if it had stood alone. In the majority's opinion neither of GE's principal tactics—the first and final offer or the communications program—was a violation of Section 8(a)(5), but when taken together in total context, they constituted evidence of management's refusal to bargain in good faith. In criticizing the first tactic, offering a "fair and firm" proposal at the outset, the Board insisted that it was not requiring all employers to start low and bargain upward as proof of their good faith. Nevertheless, the Board reserved the right to appraise a significant departure from "normal" negotiating tactics as circumstantial evidence of an employer's state of mind:

This "bargaining" approach [used by GE] undoubtedly eliminates the "ask-and-bid" or "auction" form of bargaining, but in the process devitalizes negotiations and collective bargaining and robs them of their commonly accepted meaning. "Collective bargaining" as thus practiced is tantamount to mere formality and serves to transform the role of the statutory representative from a joint participant in the bargaining process to that of an adviser. In practical effect, Respondent's "bargaining" position is akin to that of a party who enters into negotiations "with a predetermined resolve not to budge from an initial position," an attitude inconsistent with good-faith bargaining.[178]

In Leff's language, performance of an employer's duty to bargain in good faith "contemplates full acceptance by management of the representative status of the union, not as a bare adviser, but as a joint participant in the establishment of wages, hours, and working conditions." GE, however, treated the union as a "competitor for employee support rather than the voice and ears of the employees it represents."[179] In sum, the company entered negotiations with a "take-it-or-leave-it" attitude and tried to deal with the union through its employees rather than deal with its employees through their union.[180]

General Electric appealed the decision immediately,[181] accusing the Board, in dictating the bargaining process to be followed, of assuming powers denied it by the act and the Supreme Court, of limiting freedom of speech,[182] and of imposing new restrictions on the basic rights of management to operate a business responsibly, efficiently, and profitably and to stay competitive and provide jobs.[183] It was yet another example, one management critic said, of "the McCulloch disposition that anything that thwarts unionization is *per se* bad."[184]

Concluding Observations

The Kennedy-Johnson Board in the 1960s, convinced that it was the policy of the Taft-Hartley Act to encourage unionization and collective bargaining, did more than reverse important Eisenhower Board doctrines. McCulloch and his colleagues on the Board interpreted the act in ways intended to facilitate and protect employee organization and to require employers not only to bargain collectively but to accept the union as a joint participant in working out solutions to labor-related problems of mutual interest.

Although not going as far in some respects as the recommendations of the Pucinski committee, the McCulloch Board facilitated unionization in several important ways. It intensified regulation of employer representation election campaign speech and other actions, including the resurrection and use of the Herzog Board's *General Shoe* doctrine. It increased the use of bargaining orders based on authorization cards rather than representation elections. It also required all employers to give the NLRB and, in turn, a union the names and addresses of all eligible employee voters within a specific period of time and implemented a new leaflet and election notice program informing employees in plain and understandable language of their rights under federal law to vote for a union. While tightening its regulation of employer representation campaign activities to offset employers' great advantage in communicating with employees at the workplace, the Board lessened restrictions on unions' statutory right to engage in picketing intended to organize employees or obtain recognition from an employer. Other Board decisions loosening restrictions on union secondary boycott activity and limiting an employer's statutory right to lockout had the potential of increasing union bargaining power.

The McCulloch Board's rulings making fundamental management decisions subjects of mandatory bargaining were the most controversial and the most strongly opposed by employers because they threatened management power. Many employers accepted unionization and collective bargaining but intended to keep control over the scope and manner of collective bargaining. They vigorously resisted Board decisions requiring the surrender of their prerogatives and permitting union "encroachment" into matters previously determined unilaterally by management. These decisions drew the battle line between the Board and U.S. industry because they enforced the act's conception of joint union-management participation contemplated originally by Senator Wagner.

Management charged the NLRB with nullifying congressional intent, harassing free enterprise, and forcing codetermination on U.S. industry. Many employers supported legislation to transfer the NLRB jurisdiction over unfair labor practices to the federal district courts.[185] Employers also stressed the need to maintain management rights, prerogatives, power, and flexibility in the new worldwide economic competition, in which survival depended on unencumbered and creative management responses. Employers were particularly interested in becoming more efficient through technological change, ending inflationary contract settlements with unions, and in other ways seeking to overcome the labor cost advantage enjoyed by foreign competitors.[186]

Ironically, as the Kennedy-Johnson Board was vigorously implementing a public policy encouraging collective bargaining and facilitating unionization, the AFL-CIO was continuing to decline in political and economic influence. Even after Johnson's overwhelming victory in the 1964 presidential election, ballooning the narrow Democratic majority of 1960 and 1962 to 68–32 in the Senate and 295–140 in the House, organized labor's legislative agenda had a lower priority. The AFL-CIO was a victim of its own limited political options. Johnson, for example, chose to avoid a divisive and bitter fight in the Senate over the AFL-CIO's proposal to repeal the act's union security provision (Section 14[b]) because it would have hampered his conduct of the war in Vietnam and threatened the passage of key portions of his Great Society program. Nevertheless, although the Johnson administration did not strengthen the AFL-CIO or the NLRB by legislation or executive order, the White House did reappoint McCulloch, Brown, and Fanning to additional terms.

In addition, liberal-minded academic intellectuals, the labor movement's historic ally, were calling for basic reforms in union democracy and individual rights within unions, the end of union discrimination against black and other minority workers, and a reconsideration of the union role in wage and price instability and retarded economic growth. In an extraordinary twist in public perception, unions, seen by many as liberating forces in the 1930s, were widely viewed as instruments of oppression and exploitation in the 1960s.[187] Management, blamed and often condemned for the suffering of the Great Depression, was generally considered the progressive provider of economic development, jobs, and income, and was trusted to keep the United States first in international economic competition.

11

Irreconcilable Differences

Everyone but Congress Making Labor Policy

The events of the 1960s illustrated how national labor law had been made and the inadequacy of the process. The issue of management prerogatives raised in *Fibreboard,*[1] for example, was at the core of the national labor policy. The determination of what business decisions should be subject to collective bargaining with a labor organization was, as one scholar put it, "but a step removed from the determination of whether or not there shall be collective bargaining at all."[2] Yet Congress defaulted and resolved no basic labor policy issue. It settled for merely tinkering with Taft-Hartley and having various Senate and House labor committees prime one Board or another to change doctrines to represent the different attitudes or policies of a new administration in the White House. Even the Taft-Hartley Act was to a great extent an amalgamation of conflicting Wagner Act and Taft and Hartley labor policies, leaving congressional intent unclear.

As a consequence of this legislative vacuum and ambiguity, national labor policy was made by the Supreme Court, which applied its own notions of what that policy should be. The personal values and ideologies of judges and a politically vulnerable administrative agency under constant hostile fire, therefore, made labor policy in the 1960s.

The Supreme Court upheld the McCulloch Board's *Fibreboard* ruling, although the Court carefully limited its decision to the facts of the case. It emphasized that the company's decision to contract out maintenance work did not alter the company's basic operation, that no capital investment was involved, and that the company merely replaced existing employees with those of an independent contractor to do the same work under similar conditions of employment. Under those circumstances, the Supreme Court said, requiring the employer to bargain about its decision to subcontract would not significantly reduce its freedom to manage the business.[3]

Justice Potter Stewart's concurring opinion, however, with which Justices

William O. Douglas and John Marshall Harlan joined, became the controlling definition of labor policy in this matter. Stewart's opinion was based on nothing more than his own notions of what the extent of an employer's obligation to bargain should be. In still-quoted language, Stewart excluded from an employer's statutory obligation to bargain even management decisions that ended employment entirely if those decisions were "at the core of entrepreneurial control" or were "fundamental to the basic direction of the corporate enterprise." Here national labor policy was made according to Stewart's own visceral test and ideological commitment to a free enterprise economy: "Congress may eventually decide to give organized labor or government a far heavier hand in controlling what until now have been considered the prerogatives of private business management. That path would mark a sharp departure from the traditional principles of a free enterprise economy."[4]

The Supreme Court used value judgments in making fundamental labor policy choices not only in *Fibreboard* but also in remanding *Darlington Mills*[5] to the Board and overruling the Board in two lockout cases, *American Ship Building* and *Brown Foods.*[6] In *Darlington,* for example, the Court raised an employer's decision to go out of business to the level of an absolute right unaffected in any way by the statutory rights of employees, even if vindictiveness toward the union was the reason for the liquidation.[7] In *American Ship Building* and *Brown* the Board had denied employers the use of the bargaining lockout because it gave employers "too much power" and defeated the congressional purpose of placing employees on a par with employers at the bargaining table.[8] After accusing the McCulloch Board of exceeding its authority by trying to balance the competing interests of labor and management, the Supreme Court proceeded, in permitting these lockouts, to set forth its own notion of the proper balance of economic power between labor and management.[9] The role the Court assumed in making labor policy was due not only to legislative inaction by Congress but also to what some commentators on labor law saw as a loss of confidence in an NLRB whose judgments from the beginning always seemed to bend with the political winds.[10] But how much confidence could be placed in a Supreme Court that without empirical evidence made fundamental labor policy choices on the basis of ideological value judgments?

As much as Congress deserves to be faulted for not resolving basic issues of labor policy, it is unreasonable to expect it to anticipate and legislate on every possible labor policy issue or to write legislation that does not need interpretation or gap-filling by the NLRB. The NLRB must make labor policy through its interpretation and application of the statute. Constant attacks from one quarter or another, however, weakened the Board's ability to perform its role. But none of the attacks on the NLRB before 1960 were comparable in sophistication, intensity, or power to those unleashed in the 1960s by a united group of the most powerful employers in the country. Their carefully coordinated opposition to the McCulloch Board was intended not only to check that Board's limitations on management prerogatives and encouragements to unionization and collective bargaining but also, with the election of a Republican president in 1968, to reform the national labor law to suit U.S. employers.

The roles of Congress, the NLRB, and the Supreme Court in making national labor policy had become blurred. Even worse, the national labor policy itself as expressed in the Taft-Hartley Act was confused, still containing unresolved conflicting statements of legislative purpose that Congress wrote into the law in 1947 as the result of misguided compromises. Absent a clear and definite statement of legislative intent, the direction of the national labor policy was left, in great part, to the outcome of the conflict between the McCulloch Board and U.S. industry.

Labor Policy Conservatives Leave the Board

The McCulloch majority, so objectionable to employers, remained intact throughout the 1960s—an outcome almost guaranteed after Lyndon Johnson soundly defeated Barry Goldwater in the 1964 presidential election and the Democrats increased their majorities in the House and Senate. McCulloch, Fanning, and Brown's position had been strengthened, moreover, when President Kennedy, in May 1963, appointed Arnold Ordman to replace Eisenhower appointee Stuart Rothman as general counsel of the NLRB. Although Rothman had clashed less with the Board than some of his predecessors, and organized labor had no serious complaints against him,[11] the Kennedy administration wanted one of its own in the powerful general counsel job. The president could afford to be bipartisan with one or two Board members who could be outvoted, but as *Business Week* observed, there was only one "mighty important" general counsel.[12]

Ordman was described by one news magazine as "an owlish-looking" family man whose only hobby was working late.[13] To co-workers at the NLRB, he was a kind and gentle lawyers' lawyer who loved his law books and arguing cases in court. He was not "enamored of administration," as was Rothman, yet, co-workers recalled, he proved that it was possible to "accomplish all the things Stuart Rothman accomplished without a stick and without creating tremendous fear."[14] Although not inclined to discuss his beliefs publicly, Ordman was convinced that democracy and free collective bargaining had been good for the country and that if either was surrendered, both would be lost.[15]

Ordman, who had been chief counsel for McCulloch from the time he became chairman, was an ideal choice for McCulloch.[16] At his swearing-in ceremony Ordman expressed strong personal respect for the chairman:

> My closest association for the past two years has been, of course, with the Chairman of the Board, Frank W. McCulloch. Frank McCulloch couples poise and dignity with a deep feeling of humanity, vision and perspective with a sure pragmatic sense, integrity with a sensitive regard for the needs and wants of others, and a great respect for law and legal tradition with a passionate devotion to their utilization for the commonweal. It is not wholly without regret that I leave my enviable post with him.[17]

Opponents claimed that McCulloch and Ordman's close personal relationship would undermine the independence of the general counsel's office.

Only two months after Ordman became general counsel, Kennedy nominated Howard Jenkins, a forty-eight-year-old Republican, a former labor and administrative law professor at Howard University, and the first African American to serve on the Board, to replace Philip Ray Rodgers.[18] Although there was no statutory requirement that a bipartisan balance be maintained on the Board, a practice of giving both political parties representation was emerging. Since an Eisenhower appointee was being replaced, even some Democratic senators considered the vacancy a Republican seat on the Board.[19] Jenkins, although a Republican, was far less conservative than Rodgers in his interpretations of the act. McCulloch remembered Jenkins as an "independent soul" who did not follow management's dictates.[20] To others at the agency, Jenkins was a "middle of the roader" who made careful judgments and was not always predictable.[21] McCulloch, George Meany, and Secretary of Labor Willard Wirtz supported President Johnson's decision to reappoint Jenkins in 1968.[22] The Kennedy-Johnson NLRB, with McCulloch, Brown, Fanning, and Jenkins, as well as General Counsel Ordman, all reappointed in the 1960s, had an unequaled continuity of leadership and top-level policy-making personnel. (Ordman became the first general counsel in NLRB history to be reappointed.)

Boyd Leedom's second term expired in late 1964. Although Wirtz urged Johnson to end the "tradition" of a three–two political split and replace Leedom with a Democrat,[23] Johnson, after considering other candidates, nominated Sam Zagoria, administrative assistant to moderate Republican senator Clifford Case of New Jersey. For nine years Zagoria had also worked as a reporter for the

Washington Post, where he chaired the American Newspaper Guild unit.[24] With the departure of Leedom and Rodgers, the McCulloch Board had lost its only labor policy conservatives. There was, therefore, no change in its basic labor philosophy or approach to the interpretation and application of Taft-Hartley.[25]

Opposition to the McCulloch Board: The First Reactions

As had been the case for all other NLRBs, opposition to the McCulloch Board and the labor policy it developed through its interpretation of the act was led by former Board members, politicians, management representatives, and business and labor federations. Now, however, complaints came from conservative politicians such as Philip Landrum, Robert Griffin, Sam Ervin, Barry Goldwater, and Strom Thurmond rather than liberals Roman Pucinski and Frank Thompson, and from the National Association of Manufacturers and the U.S. Chamber of Commerce rather than the AFL-CIO. As one labor columnist wrote, it depended on "whose orthodoxy is being gored."[26] Management spokesmen kept up what *Newsweek* magazine called a "drumfire of discontent."[27] The Board was blamed for helping unions gain dominance over the economy through decisions that encroached on management's authority to operate efficiently and compete effectively in a free market economy.[28] Overall, the theme of management's protest was the McCulloch Board's destruction of management rights by the imposition of a system of codetermination through collective bargaining.

Congressmen Landrum and Griffin led the early political opposition to the McCulloch Board. They accused the Board of a contemptuous refusal to follow the statutory mandate of their own Landrum-Griffin Act by creating loopholes to legalize many of the boycott and picketing abuses that they said Congress intended to eliminate in 1959. They too condemned the McCulloch Board's decisions as serious threats to the free enterprise system.[29] In 1963 Landrum submitted a bill (H.R. 8246) that stripped the NLRB of its judicial function by transferring jurisdiction over unfair labor practice cases to federal district courts.[30] Landrum's real purpose was to generate anti-NLRB publicity, publicly to rebuke the McCulloch Board for its pro-labor decisions, and to warn the Board of possible future consequences if it persisted. Each year from 1965 through 1969, bills depriving the NLRB of jurisdiction over unfair labor practices were introduced in Congress.

Such anti-NLRB proposals were only part of employers' overall anti–union power theme. Union monopoly became a regular subject of management seminars and education programs in the 1960s.[31] In 1962 the NAM became the principal supporter of the Center for the Study of Union Power at the Graduate

School of Business of the University of California at Los Angeles.[32] It was headed by John R. Van de Water, who nineteen years later became chairman of the NLRB under Richard Nixon. Charles Kothe, in charge of the NAM's Industrial Relations Division, hoped that as a result of the association's legislation program, the public would be so filled with disgust at union abuses of power that it would descend on Congress clamoring for legislation.[33]

The NLRB Response

The McCulloch Board was sensitive to the steady barrage of charges accusing it of being anti-employer.[34] As all NLRBs had done when under attack, McCulloch Board members and General Counsel Ordman made speeches around the country to proclaim their impartiality, explain and defend their decisions, and characterize the charges as unsupported and their critics as a "small minority of diehards" generating a crisis atmosphere.[35]

In an article published in 1962 McCulloch estimated the number of employers who deliberately flouted the law as a "very small percentage."[36] By 1965, however, he had experienced a "continuing and determined resistance to the national labor policy." In the doubling of the NLRB's caseload in the next eight years McCulloch found employers engaging in "sophisticated testing and probing . . . to find every possible loophole in the statute."[37]

Even employers who accepted collective bargaining, Gerald Brown observed, were now trying to confine it within narrow limits.[38] NLRB Executive Secretary Ogden Fields reported in October 1963 that election contests were increasingly bitter. The percentage of election petitions resulting in union certification had declined steadily over the years, Ordman noted, as the "element of fear" had become an integral part of most elections, associating unionization with financial loss or even economic catastrophe for employees and their employers.[39] Eighty-five percent of the NLRB's rising caseload involved organizing or new bargaining situations.[40] Two year later the *Wall Street Journal,* in an article entitled "Companies Fight Harder against Labor Attempts to Organize Employees," described a growing management sophistication in preventing the unionization of employees, including the now well-known utilization of certain law firms, consultants, and others skilled in "union avoidance" who specialized in ways to keep unions out."[41]

As employer opposition to self-organization and collective bargaining intensified, the McCulloch Board remained determined to promote collective bargaining as the objective of the Taft-Hartley Act and as an essential element of economic democracy and to encourage as well as protect employees in the exercise of their statutory right to self-organization.[42] In response to management's accusation that the McCulloch Board, through decisions such as *Fibreboard,* was trying to bring about union-management codetermination in the business enterprise, Board member Brown replied that "since the Wagner Act, the national policy of the United States has been to promote collective bargaining"; the "purpose of collective bargaining in our democratic society is to achieve 'co-determination'" of "wages, hours, and other terms and conditions of employment as a means of avoiding economic warfare."[43]

The NLRB-NAM Conferences

A series of conferences of representatives of the NLRB and the NAM held in various cities around the country between 1964 and 1966 demonstrated the NLRB's concern with management's public attacks. It also illustrated the fundamental nature of the labor policy differences between the employer community and the Board and the futility of trying to reconcile those differences by applying Lyndon Johnson's famous "Let us reason together" approach.

In June 1963 Werner Gullander, former corporation executive who became the first full-time president of the NAM in its sixty-seven-year history, asked Boyd Leedom to relay to his colleagues on the Board the NAM's professed desire to promote constructive industrial relations and improve communications with the NLRB. McCulloch then proposed a joint informal conference, which the NAM accepted. The Board anticipated a frank exchange about NLRB procedures and remedies and the effect of Board decisions on labor-management relations.[44] The NAM had other motivations. Gullander had been hired by the association to help it shed its "hard core, far right, Neanderthal image," which had resulted in a dismal legislative record and loss of membership.[45] In the opinion of many, however, the NAM was merely becoming more sophisticated in pursuing the same goals it always had.[46]

Douglas Soutar, vice-president of industrial relations for the American Smelting and Refining Company and influential management figure in the upcoming organized employer opposition to the McCulloch Board, told Gullander, "You're working with a dedicated left winger [McCulloch]—you don't have much hope."[47] Gullander, who learned before he accepted McCulloch's invitation that NLRB general counsel Ordman and NLRB staff members had already held several meetings with AFL-CIO officials, now suspected that McCulloch's agreement to hold conferences with the NAM was merely a ploy to demonstrate the NLRB's willingness to meet with management as well.[48] Although McCulloch saw the meetings with the NAM as an opportunity to clarify misrepresentations of Board decisions and to rebut incorrect interpretations of the law, he had no doubt that the NAM thought it could soften up the Board. "As it developed," McCulloch recalled, "their motives to attack and change the Board became more ardent."[49] The NAM saw these meetings as a way to influence Board decisions, not only to limit the extension of certain established interpretations of the act but also to discourage the Board from issuing new interpretations unfavorable to employers. Soutar expressed this objective succinctly to Gullander: "Ordman and his crowd certainly needed to understand our reactions to their decisions—particularly before they made them, if possible."[50]

Regional meetings, attended on the NLRB side by various chief counsels to Board members and the general counsel as well as regional directors and staff, and by local and national business and industry leaders, were held from January through March 1964 in New York, Milwaukee, Atlanta, Houston, and San Francisco. This series of conferences culminated on April 9 in a Washington, D.C., summit meeting of Chairman McCulloch and all members of the Board and their chief counsels, General Counsel Ordman and his associate and assistant general counsels, thirty-eight vice-presidents and directors of labor and industrial relations, several nationally known management attorneys, and the NAM's staff. The candid discussions at all these meetings concentrated on employers' obligation to bargain about subcontracting, plant removals, and plant sales (employers were particularly concerned about the numerous situations to which the Board might apply the *Fibreboard* doctrine); the requirements of good-faith bargaining; lockouts; the lawful latitude for employer opposition to union organizing; the determination of appropriate bargaining units; employer speech (with special consideration to representation election campaigns); and secondary boycotts and organizational picketing.[51]

In March 1965 the NLRB and the NAM agreed to hold another series of conferences around the country, again concluding with a summit meeting in Washington, D.C., on July 8.[52] The NLRB held two additional high-level conferences with the NAM in May and June 1966 and with the AFL-CIO organizing staff and Executive Council representatives in the summer of 1965.[53] Although the Board was appropriately diplomatic in its public reports about the "frank interchange," resulting in "better understanding" and the blunting of the "sharp edges of antagonism,"[54] it realized that the NAM conferences made no important changes in management's fundamental opposition to the Board and its decisions.

The NAM likewise concluded that there was "little chance for achieving changes in Board policies through such meetings."[55] After the top-level conferences in May and June 1966 the NAM refused to meet again.[56] Soon the Board was accusing the NAM of returning to its earlier tactics of circulating extreme misrepresentations of NLRB decisions.[57]

The NLRB was most disturbed, however, by the NAM's public assertions that the association had "softened up" the Board.[58] In reporting on the April 1965 summit meeting, for example, the NAM claimed, "Many industry representatives left the meeting with the distinct impression that these new insights offered to the Board would result in *Fibreboard's* 'bark being worse than its bite.'" The same NAM report quoted management participants as saying that the NLRB would now be very reluctant to expand the *Fibreboard* doctrine since Board members knew "they were being carefully watched and their partisanship was not going unnoticed."[59] After these public claims of intimidation it did not matter how sound the Board's reasons were for limiting or reversing a doctrine favorable to unions; the appearance of vulnerability to employer pressure would be unavoidable. It was an unfortunate consequence of the decision to meet regularly over an extended period of time with an organization of employers hostile to the NLRB's labor policy.

McCulloch realized that the meetings with the NAM were a hopeless undertaking in which management lawyers and ardent anti-labor people drove out people engaged in good-faith collective bargaining.[60] For once, McCulloch and the employers' leading spokesman for management rights, Frank O'Connell, director of industrial relations at Olin Mathieson Chemical Corporation, were in agreement. In O'Connell's opinion the meetings were a failure because the NLRB and employers were proceeding from diametrically opposed premises concerning the objectives and scope of the act:[61] Management "saw the Wagner Act—or the Taft-Hartley Act in its turn—as invasions, but limited invasions. McCulloch saw it as a new dawn. As the beginning of true worker participation in the managerial process. Now you really cannot accommodate the two views. One is a property-rights oriented view, the other is kind of socialist with a little 's'."[62]

The NAM proceeded to join with the U.S. Chamber of Commerce and the country's most powerful employers to mount a massive and coordinated attack on the McCulloch Board and its understanding of U.S. labor policy. In studied understatement, Frank McCulloch called the assault "an unfortunate development in our labor-management relations."[63]

The Organization of Employer Resistance

In the mid-1960s several top-level corporate executives, dissatisfied with the disorganized and uncoordinated nature of their anti-NLRB protest, held a series of meetings intended "to unify hundreds of major employers around a common cause."[64] The absence of a united front had always been a weakness in U.S. employers' political and public relations endeavors. Business and industry usually relied on trade associations to present their diverse views, which tended to be competitive rather than cooperative.[65] Even at more inclusive organizational levels the NAM represented mainly larger manufacturing companies, whereas the Chamber of Commerce comprised primarily small businesses. Consequently, "they danced to a different drummer on some issues."[66]

In addition, most large employers, in Frank O'Connell's words, were obsessed with maintaining a low profile and avoiding battles that could adversely affect financial results.[67] There was also no unanimity in U.S. employers' reactions to unionism and collective bargaining, which ranged from acceptance of organization and "effects" bargaining, to preference for operating without a union and adoption of wage and personnel policies that made unions appear unnecessary, to resistance (lawful and unlawful), to unionization.[68] In the opinion of the corporate organizers of unity conferences too much energy had been expended either in "baying at the moon" by supporting unattainable political solutions or in piecemeal attempts by one industry or another to seek remedial action for itself. They needed not only a unified effort but also a major change in the "climate of public understanding" and the mobilization of public opinion necessary for legislative support.[69]

The unity promoters first needed to find a common cause around which otherwise differing and reticent employers could come together. According to Douglas Soutar, one of the corporate executives who led the unity effort, the "exorcism of the NLRB" provided the organizing principle.[70] More specifically, employers were unanimous in their opposition to Board rulings that threatened their decision-making prerogatives. The organizational phase began in 1965, when Soutar and his close friend, Virgil Day, vice-president of General Electric and chairman of the Chamber of Commerce's Labor Relations Committee, agreed to set up a committee of "thought leaders" from "very big blue chip" companies. Twelve men were chosen by Soutar, Day, and Fred Atkinson, senior vice-President of R.H. Macy & Co., who agreed to chair the group. They came from the highest echelons of corporate labor relations.[71]

These men were selected, according to Soutar, because they had "clout," belonged to "all the trade associations in every nook and cranny in the country," worked for corporations with "billions of dollars," and had expertise in labor-management relations. The chief executive officers of these companies gave their financial support, but the corporate heads of labor relations, positions that did not exist in most companies until the mid-1950s, did the work. Calling itself the "No-Name Committee" or "Nothing Committee" because it originally had no authority or portfolio, the twelve (known in inner management circles as "the Twelve Apostles") set about solidifying support from their own firms, bringing in many other companies and trade associations, getting funding, and establishing a supervisory relationship with Chamber of Commerce staffers responsible for drafting legislative proposals.[72]

Three familiar legislative draftsmen—Guy Farmer, Gerry Reilly, and Theodore Iserman—attended the first meeting of the "Nothing Committee."[73] Farmer, who chaired the NLRB during Eisenhower's first term, had become an influential management attorney in Washington, D.C. Reilly, a politically conservative member of the Roosevelt-Truman NLRB, had helped write the Taft-Hartley Act as a legislative adviser to Senator Taft, as well as the Landrum-Griffin amendments to Taft-Hartley. He was also legislative counsel to General Motors, Chrysler, and General Electric and had served as counsel to the Republican minority on the Senate Labor Committee. Iserman, somewhat of a mystery man often described as a "Wall Street lawyer," had also worked on Taft-Hartley and Landrum-Griffin and represented Chrysler and General Motors.[74] Reilly, Farmer, and Iserman all had strong policy connections in Washington, which increased the value of their influence in the legislative process.

The first meeting of the "Nothing Committee" was also attended by William Ingles, president of the Labor Policy Association (LPA), an informal group of employers that financed research and publication of studies critical of union power and the NLRB under the Democrats.[75] Ingles, a former lobbyist, had represented companies such as Allis Chalmers, Inland Steel, and B.F. Goodrich as well as the American Mining Congress. Beginning in 1962, the LPA shared offices with the Chicago law firm of Vedder, Price, Kaufman & Kammholz (Kammholz was NLRB general counsel in the Eisenhower administration). Kenneth McGuiness, associate general counsel for the Eisenhower NLRB from 1955 to 1958 and Vedder, Price, Kaufman & Kammholz's resident partner in Washington, provided Ingles with legal counsel.[76] In 1963 the LPA published McGuiness's book, *The New Frontier NLRB,* a scathing attack on the McCulloch Board for which Landrum and Griffin wrote a foreword.[77]

The Labor Law Reform Project

The "Nothing Committee" soon became the steering committee for a three-phase labor law reform project. Phase one was the work being done by the "Troika" of Farmer, Reilly, and Iserman with the financial support of the Chamber of Commerce and the NAM. The Troika was responsible for conducting a comprehensive analysis of the Taft-Hartley Act section by section and for developing proposals for statutory amendments as well as commentaries on the NLRB's administration of the law.[78] The steering committee, which eventually became known as the Labor Law Reform Group (or occasionally as the Labor

Law Study Group), was responsible, through the Troika, for creating specific legislative proposals.

Phases two and three of the project involved persuading the public of the need for labor law reform and mobilizing opinion in favor of remedial legislation. The strategy in the first instance was to reach society's "thought leaders."[79] The public education phase—"climate creation" through a sophisticated public relations campaign—was a most important part of the project. One high-ranking project official explained: "It must be remembered that we do not have a 1946–47 strike situation or a 1958–1959 situation such as developed when the Teamsters were on television practically every day with Senator McClellan and Bobby Kennedy. If this Labor Law Study Project is to be launched successfully we will have to create our own climate."[80]

The Blue Ribbon Committee

The Labor Law Reform Group grew in power and influence as a more formal organizational structure developed. The Troika's work, although ultimately subject to approval by the Reform Group, was reviewed by the Blue Ribbon Committee (BRC), more than one hundred management lawyers representing the country's most powerful corporations as well as other employer interests. The BRC's size and diversity was designed to solidify the united front approach. Committee members included many former NLRB "graduates," who played key roles in management's labor law reform project and constituted an "NLRB-in-Exile," representing employers and spearheading the anti–McCulloch Board opposition.[81] Meeting in secret, the BRC reviewed and critiqued several confidential draft memoranda prepared by the Troika.[82] Although the NAM and the Chamber of Commerce financed the initial stage of the Troika's work, approximately forty to fifty major corporations later became the principal source of funding.[83]

By mid-1967 two more committees, both located in Washington, were functioning under the direction of the New York–based Labor Law Reform Group. Robert Borth, General Electric's lobbyist in Washington, chaired the Legislative Committee for lobbying key members of Congress.[84] Lambert Miller, general counsel of the NAM, and William Van Meter, the Chamber's General Manager, co-chaired the Trade Association Coordinating Committee, which represented a group of approximately forty important trade associations.[85] In November 1967 the Labor Law Reform Group hired Edward McCabe as its special counsel. McCabe had been an administrative assistant to President Eisenhower on labor issues. He also had collaborated with Reilly and Iserman in writing and lobbying for the Landrum-Griffin Act's amendments to Taft-Hartley.[86] Soutar said that McCabe was chosen because "having been in the White House, he knew his way around the Hill as well or better than anybody in Washington" and could provide direct access to key congressmen such as the "absolute czar" of the Senate, Everett Dirksen. O'Connell called McCabe "our link to the climate in Washington."[87]

The Labor Law Reform Group now met regularly at the Union League Club in New York and made progress reports to the chief executive officers of the most important corporations in the country, who gave their blessings and their money to the project. The LLRG also met regularly with the Troika as well as with the chairmen of the newly formed committees. Group members had continual contact with the White House, the secretary of labor, the secretary of the treasury, and influential politicians such as Dirksen, Gerald Ford, Landrum, and Griffin.[88]

Labor Law Reform Study

On November 6, 1967, the Troika submitted the fifth and final draft of its proposed amendments to Taft-Hartley, a 165-page document entitled *Labor Law Reform Study*. The report, in essence, was a catalog of what employers believed the most repugnant McCulloch Board decisions, matched with a series of legislative amendments designed to reverse those decisions. Edward McCabe wrote an unattributed foreword to the publication in which he deliberately omitted any references to the "ground rules" for the study, the names of the organizations that sponsored it, and even the names of those who prepared it, because that information "might well detract from the study itself by offering critics targets to shoot at."[89] As a consequence, the Troika's document bears no author's or sponsor's name. According to McCabe, the *Labor Law Reform Study,* as the product of "the objective and expert judgment of the Nation's most eminent labor law specialists," provided a legislative guide. McCabe concluded that a legislative remedy was the only recourse for rectifying the NLRB's infringement on the most basic prerogatives of management.[90]

The Troika—Farmer, Reilly, and Iserman—started with the act's statement of purpose. They proposed to eliminate from the law the affirmation that it was the policy of the United States to encourage the practice and procedures of collective bargaining. The NLRB, they charged, had used this policy statement in the act's preamble as a mandate to foster unionism, often against the wishes of employees or without giving employees an opportunity to express their choice in a free election. Rooting out this statement of purpose, which had been carried over from the Wagner Act, the Troika emphasized, would make the protection of employee free choice to join or refrain from joining a union—not the encouragement of collective bargaining—the undisputable purpose of Taft-Hartley.[91]

The *Labor Law Reform Study,* from the revision of the act's preamble through the Troika's substitution of either a labor court or the district courts for the NLRB,[92] was designed to increase the ability of employers to resist unionization or, if already organized, to widen the scope of permissible bargaining tactics they could adopt, while prohibiting unions from using certain economic weapons that could strengthen their bargaining positions. Other proposed amendments were intended to prevent the Board from imposing more powerful remedies for employer violations of the law. In sum, the goal was to help employers keep free of unions or, if unionized, retain unilateral control over managerial decisions.[93]

Climate Creation: The Manipulation of Public Opinion

The employer groups involved in the labor law reform project knew that there was no chance of changing the law unless Republicans triumphed in the 1968 presidential and congressional elections. Until then the Troika's *Labor Law Reform Study* was used for defensive purposes, mainly to dissuade Congress from accepting the House Labor Committee's proposals to make NLRB remedies more effective and to legalize common situs picketing. The Democratic leadership was unwilling to risk opening the whole act for amendment, particularly when the employer community was ready with major and extensive legislative changes. In Farmer's opinion the *Labor Law Reform Study* deterred unions and a "very liberal" Congress from strengthening the NLRB's remedy power or making any other changes in the law favorable to unions.[94]

After the last draft of the Troika's amendments had been circulated and approved by the Blue Ribbon Committee and the trade association group, the Labor Law Reform Group decided to launch phases two and three of the reform project.[95] Phase two consisted of attitude surveys to determine the most effective way to develop public opinion favorable to management's proposed legislative reforms. The third and final phase involved the use of a sophisticated public relations campaign to mobilize opinion.[96]

The approximately forty trade associations involved in the project were "mobilized for greater public opinion efforts."[97] The LLRG appointed an executive director to coordinate a public information program for participating trade associations directed at the "right publics" through "columnists, TV and radio commentators, plus appropriate magazines and newspapers."[98] Public information activities were coordinated among the LLRG, the trade associations, the legislative task force, and the Blue Ribbon Committee. No reform information was released unless it was cleared through a labor law information center.[99]

In addition, the Labor Law Reform Group hired the world's largest public relations firm, Hill & Knowlton, to spearhead its campaign to develop public acceptance of its proposals for labor reform. Hill & Knowlton, in the words of *Fortune* magazine, was well known "as a conservative organization favoring big business and opposing labor."[100] The firm had promoted and supported the legislative objectives of business for more than twenty-five years and had particularly close financial ties to the steel industry, particularly the Iron and Steel Institute. It was the steel industry's voice during the big strikes of 1937, 1952, and 1959, when it was most effective in persuading the public (and many steelworkers) that higher wages would lead to a price increase detrimental to all Americans.[101] Hill & Knowlton's business clientele also included the aircraft industry (obtaining federal government procurement programs); the oil and gas industry (seeking legislation to exempt natural gas producers from price regulation); pharmaceutical manufacturers (public relations counsel to the drug industry during a Senate investigation); the tobacco industry (helping cigarette companies defend against evidence that smoking was a danger to health); and the Remington and Winchester companies (fighting curbs on gun sales by defending the right of Americans to bear arms).[102] The firm also represented foreign countries, such as Saudi Arabia, which asked Hill & Knowlton to improve its image, to dispel the idea that its people were all burnoosed tribesmen, and to portray the government as working hard for the people.[103]

Hill & Knowlton was in the business of "image-shaping," designing campaigns "to make unknowns into public figures, to make playboys look like statesmen, to make weak companies look strong, or to switch the conversation to the strong points about strong companies that may be having weak moments," and to associate businesses with "progressiveness, financial stability, and good management."[104] The agency urged the Labor Law Reform Group, for example, to pick a "righteous-sounding name" such as the "Council for Fair Labor Laws," because the "right title can smooth a bill's path in Congress."[105]

Senior management of Hill & Knowlton assumed responsibility for developing and supervising the communications in support of the Labor Law Reform Project, particularly two vice-presidents, Malcolm Johnson and Stanley Sauerhaft. Johnson wrote the book that became the basis of the Marlon Brando movie *On the Waterfront,* concerning union racketeering on the New York docks, and Sauerhaft specialized in legislative matters.[106] At the outset Hill &

Knowlton developed case-history materials into a series of NLRB "horror stories," personalized with a human interest touch to make the injustices depicted relevant to everyone's way of life. The agency portrayed these stories as "an outrage against America's traditional sense of fair play," subtly showing management in the underdog position, unions preventing social and economic progress, and every person the loser as a consequence.[107]

From the beginning of its efforts Hill & Knowlton feared that its work would be undermined if the existence and identity of the Labor Law Reform Group was discovered and made public by unfriendly forces that could portray the reform project as the instrument of a reactionary employer group.[108] The LLRG, however, decided against revealing its identity or discussing publicly the work of those participating in the project. In part, the steering committee was heeding the wisdom of its adviser, Senator Everett Dirksen, who urged the group to "keep a very low profile." "Keep out of sight," Dirksen warned, "because, if anybody learns you're doing this drafting, you're going to be smeared and reviled and the labor guys will take care of you in a hurry."[109] As Soutar recalled, "we were always behind the scenes; we didn't want to get too prominent."[110]

There was a more important reason for not going public. By early October 1967 employers knew that the Senate Subcommittee on Separation of Powers, chaired by Sam Ervin, was scheduled to begin hearings the following February, with the NLRB a prime target. Employers saw these hearings as an excellent forum for management to present its labor law reform proposals.[111] Participants in the Labor Law Reform Project believed that employer testimony would carry more weight if offered by witnesses identified only as representatives of their own companies rather than as members of an organized management effort to rewrite the labor law and de-fang the NLRB and who could be pressed about the project's "origin, sponsors, and/or financiers."[112]

The media and methods to be used to convey the LLRG's message were evidence not only of the power of the public relations industry and the pervasiveness of its message delivery system but also of the cunning (some might say insidious) ways of getting the message into people's minds. Hill & Knowlton told the LLRG, for example, that the agency would provide story outlines and data to authors who were regular contributors to "Think" publications such as *Harper's, The Atlantic, Commonweal, Commentary,* and *Atlas,* because these journals had "influence entirely disproportionate to their circulation" and were "well read by people who are themselves idea disseminators—teachers, librarians, college students." The agency would also make an effort to exploit what Hill & Knowlton perceived as a disenchantment with unions among some liberal academics and commentators. The agency said that it would meet privately with "leading liberals" such as John Kenneth Galbraith, David Reisman, Seymour Harris, Robert Heilbroner, and C. Wright Mills to test their reaction to the need for labor law reform. It would then arrange to have those who were "most flexible and amenable" interviewed publicly. Liberals who criticized unions, the LLRG was advised, "could become our most effective advocates because they have acceptance within the liberal spectrum."[113]

The preparation of specialized scripts for radio commentators was important to Hill & Knowlton's program because there were "over 5,000 radio stations across the country" and American families "on the average own two radios." The agency also promised to try to interest one of the commercial television networks or the new educational network in producing a show tracing the development of the labor movement and labor law in the U.S." and emphasizing the great power unions now had in great part due to the NLRB."[114]

Other parts of the campaign of public persuasion that Hill & Knowlton presented to the Labor Law Reform Group involved attempts at subtle, to some extent subliminal, thought manipulation threatening to a democratic society. Hill & Knowlton said that it would work with television drama writers to get them to put illustrations of unfair labor laws into their continuing series. Television comedy series were also to be used "to focus gentle derision" on the NLRB and organized labor, because "sometimes scorn can be more effective than entreaty in shaking up somnolent thought patterns." The agency also planned to get union abuse worked into the story line of nationally syndicated comic strips, such as "Gasoline Alley," "Blondie," "Pogo," or "Peanuts."[115]

Finally, Hill & Knowlton alerted the Labor Law Reform Group to the great but "longer range payoff" of influencing junior high and high school textbooks and courses. The agency noted: "Even in union households, classroom work in civics, American history or economics at the junior high school and high school levels can be a nucleus opinion-molder on labor-management relations. Furthermore, the student who brings his new learning home is often an influencer of his parents and his brothers and sisters." The agency promised to work with the publishers and authors of civics, history, and economics textbooks to persuade them to use the case materials Hill & Knowlton had prepared.[116]

Vice-President Sauerhaft and other top Hill & Knowlton executives met with key magazine and newspaper editorial boards to promote the campaign for labor law reform.[117] The agency prepared a series of press release–style vignettes as a sourcebook for editorials, each dealing with specific Board decisions, in what Senator Wayne Morse later called "a homey prose style with the NLRB cast as the villain and individual workers and small employers as its victims."[118] The titles of these editorial vignettes reveal how the agency used the case histories: "Employer Damned If He Does or Doesn't under NLRB," "Court Rejects Fraudulent Union Card Majority," "NLRB and Courts Have Rewarded Strikers

for Flagrant Misconduct," "NLRB Ruling May Force Employer into Bank-
ruptcy," "Small Businessman Tells of Eight-Year 'Ordeal' under NLRB."[119]
Meanwhile, Hill & Knowlton vice-president Johnson, without revealing his employer's connection to the Labor Law Reform Project, gave speeches around
the country using these anti-NLRB stories to warn of a crisis threatening the
future of collective bargaining and to explain the reasons for his transformation
from a "starry-eyed" and "militantly pro-labor" reporter, to a "disillusioned"
member of the Newspaper Guild, to an investigator of union corruption.[120]

Hill & Knowlton also prepared a forty-five-page "Background Memorandum" on the need for labor law reform, essentially a summary in layman's
language of the Troika's final report. The memorandum hit hard at the excessive powers of labor unions ("Unions have the power to starve America, freeze
America, immobilize America, render America weak and defenseless") and of
the McCulloch Board, which "leaned over backward to favor unions and punish
employers." Readers of the memorandum were reassured, however, that the
"Labor Law Study Committee" identified as author sought no special favors for
business but only "equality of treatment and justice under the law for all."[121]

In February 1968, shortly before the Ervin committee hearings began, Victor
Riesel wrote of a "truly vast and unreported 'management movement,'" the
"broadest united front of large and small businesses in history" ready "for the
fight" to change what they considered a pro-union NLRB.[122] Legislative Committee chairman Borth alerted his colleagues to this "first public exposure of
our overall effort."[123] On August 2, 1968, Senator Morse, in a speech on the
Senate floor, gave the details of what he described as an "ominous development
concerning certain anti-labor forces" that were planning to revise the labor law
in 1969. After revealing what information he had about the work of Farmer,
Reilly, and Iserman, the Blue Ribbon Committee, and Hill & Knowlton, Morse
warned:

> This campaign which I have described is both serious and dangerous. It is serious
> because those who are leading it have carefully laid their plans to arouse public
> opinion with distorted slogans and misleading arguments. It is dangerous because
> its purpose is to unstabilize a scheme of labor law administration which has
> largely succeeded in bringing labor peace to the Nation while at the same time
> promoting free collective bargaining.[124]

The Ervin Committee

On March 26, 1968, only seven months before the presidential election, Sam
Ervin, chairing a special subcommittee of the Senate Judiciary Committee,

opened hearings, ostensibly to study the division of powers among the legislative, executive, and judicial branches of the federal government.[125] As William Gullander, president of the NAM, informed a constituent in May 1967, the desirability of a congressional investigation of the NLRB had been discussed in many management meetings. Gullander had been pessimistic about the idea because the House and Senate labor committees had been "so stacked on the wrong side of the fence over the years." Serious consideration was given, however, to the creation of a select committee "to do a job of this kind," such as the Smith committee investigation of 1939–40.[126]

Although Ervin claimed that his committee would focus on the major role in governance played by all administrative agencies, the NLRB was the only one scrutinized.[127] The composition of the five-member subcommittee, moreover, guaranteed hostile treatment of the NLRB, as southern Democrats Ervin and John McClellan of Arkansas, whose investigation of union corruption in the late 1950s forever stained organized labor, teamed with Republicans Everett Dirksen, adviser to the Labor Law Reform Group, and Roman Hruska of Nebraska. The only member friendly to the NLRB was Senator Quentin Burdick of North Dakota. According to unsubstantiated rumors, a member of the Ervin subcommittee staff "admitted in a private conversation that he heard 'some talk' about whether the Subcommittee's hearings should be utilized as part of the campaign to abolish the Board."[128] Although the scheduling of the Ervin committee hearings cannot be conclusively linked to the Labor Law Reform Project, the timing of the hearings and the committee's well-publicized criticisms of the McCulloch Board's decisions were, at the very least, fortuitous for the project's managers. There is persuasive evidence, however, that the Ervin committee cooperated with project participants, including Hill & Knowlton.

Edward McCabe, counsel to the LLRG, publicly denied any responsibility for arranging the hearings, saying that the Ervin committee "just came along."[129] When asked if the LLRG was involved in initiating the Ervin hearings, Soutar replied, "I'd say we fanned the flames; sure we were involved."[130] According to Soutar, the LLRG cooperated as much as it could. He explained: McCabe, for example, used his influence "on the Hill" to arrange for witnesses to testify, and the "ammunition" for these witnesses came from the Troika, the Blue Ribbon Committee, and Hill & Knowlton, with all these sources coordinated by committees in the Labor Law Reform Project.[131]

Ten of the fourteen management attorneys who testified before the Ervin committee represented a trade association affiliated with the Labor Law Reform Group or were members of the Blue Ribbon Committee or of firms represented on the it. Joseph Alton Jenkins, Board member during the Eisenhower years and a member of the BRC, represented an independent union critical of the

NLRB. Former congressman Fred Hartley of Taft-Hartley was ill, so his anti-NLRB statement was read by his legal adviser, John Kilcullen, who was also a BRC member. In addition to the NAM, the Chamber of Commerce, and the American Retail Federation, representatives of four other trade associations from the Labor Law Reform Project's Trade Association Coordinating Committee testified or submitted statements.[132] None of these witnesses revealed for the record their participation in or association with the Labor Law Reform Project.

McCabe also provided the staff of Ervin's subcommittee with information for use during the hearings.[133] The committee's staff gave *Reader's Digest* access to its files to gather material for a widely read August 1968 article berating a biased NLRB for "sanctioning union abuses, but restricting management rights." Later it was discovered that Hill & Knowlton had helped the *Digest* prepare the article, including doing research.[134]

Senator Morse had warned McCulloch in 1967 that because of employer-inspired opposition to the Board and pressure from the textile industry on Senator Ervin, "they were going to get after us," not through the House or Senate labor committees but through a subcommittee of the Judiciary Committee on separation of powers. McCulloch later called Ervin's approach "a fraud." In McCulloch's opinion Ervin performed nobly as a member of the full Judiciary Committee when he stood up to President Nixon in the Watergate case, because then the senator's constituency was the nation; as chairman of his special subcommittee, however, when his constituency "was the textile industry and other management groups," he wanted only "to haze the Board." The Ervin hearings, McCulloch concluded, simply gave the Blue Ribbon Committee and others in the labor law reform movement another opportunity to discredit the Board and make a public record on which to try to amend the law later.[135] Soutar claimed that Ervin was "nobody's tool" but acknowledged that the senator, coming from "his part of the country," had "strong views about what labor unions should and should not do" and had "a lot of constituents that felt strongly about such things."[136]

Use of congressional hearings as a partisan device to help bring about predetermined objectives was neither new nor unusual. It had been the standard congressional approach to questions of national labor policy from at least pre–Wagner Act days. As NLRB general counsel Arnold Ordman put it, Ervin represented "the interests of his clients and supporters, principally the textile industry down South," just as Congressman Pucinski "was really representing the views of the labor people that supported him." Neither set of hearings, he observed, should be regarded "as a dispassionate investigation by an unbiased authority."[137] The Ervin committee's choices of witnesses to appear and subjects to be discussed were determined by the conclusions it embraced long before a single witness testified. In choosing NLRB decisions most suitable for subcommittee examination, for example, Ervin committee staff selected (in the staff's words) those that "victimized employees," "suppressed" the right of free speech, "evaded" the congressional ban on secondary boycotts, "radically altered" the statutory duty to bargain, allowed unions to impose "heavy and arbitrary fines on employees," and denied employees "the statutory right to secret ballot elections in union representation matters."[138]

The Labor Law Reform Group's decision to mask its involvement was vindicated. Immediately after the close of the Ervin hearings, for example, conservative columnist John Chamberlain wrote approvingly of the extremely competent witnesses who charged the NLRB with rewriting the law to favor unions. "If it were merely a matter of professional right-wingers and chronic labor baiters saying this," Chamberlain noted with probably unintended irony, "the Ervin hearings would be quickly forgotten." Instead, Chamberlain told his readers, the roster of witnesses "included men who had held important places on the National Labor Relations Board itself, such as former chairman Guy Farmer, former NLRB member and Labor Department Solicitor Gerard Reilly, and former General Counsel of the NLRB, Theodore C. Kammholz."[139]

Witnesses associated with the LLRG hit hard at the McCulloch Board's *Fibreboard* doctrine. Frank O'Connell, for example, accused the Board of a calculated imposition by "administrative fiat" of a policy of "codetermination." Codetermination, O'Connell told the committee, was an "alien" doctrine, fundamentally contrary to the structure of U.S. industry because it involved the worker in the management of the enterprise. It had its deepest roots, O'Connell said, in socialism, particularly in Germany where it was a matter of national policy legislatively imposed on industry.[140] "In a capitalistic free-enterprise economy," O'Connell testified, "critical decisions on the use of capital and on the sound management of the business must be made by the owners and managers of that capital and by them alone."[141]

Although the committee's headlines were stolen by the assassinations of Robert Kennedy and Martin Luther King, uprisings on college campuses in opposition to the Vietnam war, general strikes in Europe, and the scramble for office triggered by President Johnson's decision not to run again, employer groups were satisfied that the Ervin hearings had served the useful purpose of focusing attention on the need for employer-approved labor law reform, which Congress had to confront sooner or later.[142] McCulloch (and Mozart Ratner, former NLRB attorney who testified before the committee) saw the hearings as part of an attempt to use intimidation to stop the Board, and possibly future NLRBs, from encouraging collective bargaining and fashioning stronger remedies to enforce that policy, as the McCulloch Board did.[143]

Although it would have been ideal, from the perspective of Hill & Knowlton and the Labor Law Reform Group, to have the Ervin committee report issued before the presidential election in November 1968, it was not possible to have a report prepared, published, and distributed in the brief period remaining between the end of the hearings and the election. In late August, Ervin, in a most unusual maneuver that indicated his close cooperation with the Labor Law Reform Project, issued his own "Tentative Subcommittee Findings," which were published by the National Small Business Association, a member of the Reform Project's Trade Association Coordinating Committee. Ervin's report echoed the Troika's charges and recommended that the Senate conduct a thorough review of the NLRB's administration of the law. That jibed perfectly with the LLRG's plan to press for legislative changes in Taft-Hartley after the November elections.[144] In a speech to the NAM in September 1968 Ervin accused the McCulloch Board of wanting a statute "which requires unionization wherever possible."[145] Hill & Knowlton was quick to circulate Ervin's "Tentative Subcommittee Findings" with its own editorial conclusion attached: "The weight of the evidence before the Subcommittee definitely was on the side of critics of the Board—[a] conclusion supported by Senator Ervin himself."[146]

Leaks about various aspects of the Labor Law Reform Group's plan appeared in newspapers and other publications as early as February 1968.[147] In a speech in the Senate on August 2, for example, Wayne Morse, emphasizing the unprecedented quantity of newspaper articles and editorials written about the NLRB since the beginning of 1968, was particularly disturbed by the number of virtually identical editorials sharply critical of the NLRB which had appeared at approximately the same time in newspapers in different parts of the country. As Morse suspected, "where there is smoke there is often a speech machine," and "Hill & Knowlton seems to be one of the main smoke machines in this effort to becloud public understanding."[148] Complete secrecy surrounding the origin, nature, and scope of the LLRG's anti–McCulloch Board activities, however, was not lifted until two days before election day. One week before the election the labor editor of the *Los Angeles Times,* Harry Bernstein, reported NLRB general counsel Ordman's charge that a large-scale campaign had been launched "to emasculate the nation's labor laws and the National Labor Relations Board." Ordman cited the *Reader's Digest* article but said that the campaign was far more widespread than one publication, because "papers and magazines are just picking up this campaign literature and running it as if it were their own." (A reporter for the *Washington Evening Star* had brought large amounts of Hill & Knowlton material to the NLRB.)[149] Bernstein's article also included the comments of Hill & Knowlton vice-president Stanley Sauerhaft, who admitted that his company had been hired "by 35 trade associations and about 100 large and small industrial companies" for an "educational campaign about the imbalance of labor laws." He also acknowledged that Hill & Knowlton had helped *Reader's Digest* prepare its article but denied that there had been mass mailings or an advertising campaign and dismissed Ordman's concerns about the campaign as "all out of proportion to its true size."[150]

On November 3, 1968, in an interview with Bernstein, Peter Pestillo, labor relations director for the U.S. Chamber of Commerce, openly confirmed for the first time from within the management coalition "that the nation's major corporations and almost every employer association [had] joined forces in a . . . concerted effort to limit the strength of labor unions." Pestillo declined to estimate the cost of Hill & Knowlton's public relations campaign. Other sources said that at least one million dollars had been made available for publicity. In a most incisive comment Bernstein noted that all the changes being sought by the employer coalition could be summarized best by its desire to strike the word "encourage" from the provision of Taft-Hartley that made it the policy of the United States to encourage the practice and procedure of collective bargaining. According to Pestillo, the government should be "neutral" in labor relations.[151]

Although Pestillo told Bernstein that Republican presidential candidate Richard Nixon had made no promise to support the employer coalition, he added that the coalition knew it would be finished if Hubert Humphrey was elected because Humphrey was "the closest we have ever come in this country to having a labor candidate for President."[152] On Monday, November 4, the day before the presidential election, AFL-CIO president George Meany made a previously unscheduled nationwide radio broadcast to tell listeners that the "U.S. Chamber of Commerce openly revealed the details of a big-business plot to destroy the labor movement in the next session of Congress." Meany acknowledged that these were strong words but quoted Pestillo's comments to prove he was not exaggerating. Meany went on to say that it was "no longer a matter of theory or report or rumor," since the "whole center of corporate power in America has been organized into a single force." He called on AFL-CIO affiliates to notify their local unions of the "plot" and to work to elect Humphrey and defeat the attack on labor.[153]

Concluding Observations

During the Ervin committee hearings, Harvard law professor Derek Bok identified as a hallmark of the industrial system in the United States the "very high degree of hostility that permeates our labor relations."[154] For many years, particularly during the McCulloch Board period, the NLRB and its supporters presumed that employer hostility to the Board and resistance to the Taft-Hartley Act came from ideologues at the margin of business and industry, especially family-owned corporations such as J.P. Stevens. The membership, objectives, and methods of the Labor Law Reform Project demonstrated conclusively, however, that employer opposition to the Board and resistance to certain provisions of the law were broadly based and included not only the most powerful corporations in the country but also most of the major employers in industries long considered models of the collective bargaining process.

Although many of these unionized employers wanted to get rid of their unions and unorganized employers wanted to stay union-free, other large employers did accept collective bargaining and did not want costly confrontations with their unions. But the collective bargaining these employers accepted, and often used advantageously to provide stability, predictability, and control within their plants, was confined to negotiating with unions about the effects of management's business decisions on wages, hours, and working conditions. It definitely did not include bargaining with unions over the employer decision-making process itself. Employers saw the McCulloch Board's *Fibreboard* decision—as limited as it was, particularly after Supreme Court Justice Potter Stewart applied his own pro-management values to it—as only the beginning of a radical change in the hierarchical, authoritarian labor relations structure that organized labor had accepted. These employers moved quickly and powerfully, therefore, to preserve their type of collective bargaining.

Employer power and control, or what employers preferred to call traditional collective bargaining, was doubly threatened by the combination of the Kennedy-Johnson Board's decision-bargaining concept of collective bargaining and the Board's commitment to the encouragement of the practice and procedure of collective bargaining. For those reasons alone, the employer coalition was bent on the elimination from Taft-Hartley of the language making it the policy of the federal government to encourage collective bargaining. If Congress left in the act only those provisions stressing the rights of employees to refrain from collective bargaining, the employer coalition knew it would be conclusive evidence that lawmakers intended the federal government to be a neutral guarantor of employee rights, indifferent to employees' choice between individual and collective action. With the government acting as a "neutral umpire" over employer and union efforts to influence employee choice, employers as the providers and deprivers of jobs would have a decided advantage.

The confrontation between the employer coalition and the McCulloch Board reflected in great part the conflict between these two opposing statements of purpose in Taft-Hartley, statements so fundamentally antithetical that they contemplated radically opposite national labor policies and roles for the federal government in labor relations. This dispute over congressional intent in Taft-Hartley, although never secret, was widely publicized in the 1960s. The McCulloch Board used Congress's policy statement encouraging collective bargaining to justify its decisions, whereas opponents of the Board used the policy statement in support of employee freedom of choice to condemn the Board for ignoring congressional intent. Although Congress was fully aware of the existence and great importance of this dispute over the fundamental purpose of the act, it failed to deal directly with the issue.

Congress had once again ignored its responsibility, missing, as McCulloch lamented, another "important opportunity for thoughtful, constructive appraisals of the operations of the rule of law in American labor relations."[155] Consequently, the Ervin committee produced only a large volume of quotable material for future employer legislative and public relations efforts, lent credence to the alleged need for labor law reform by holding the hearings and concentrating criticism on the NLRB, helped create an environment conducive to such changes in the next Congress, and provided a testing ground for the arguments and strategies to be used in the employers' campaign to reform the act and the NLRB. It was, as McCulloch described it, "a monument to what a special interest group can create" and "to the way it can use one government agency to try to dismantle or block or intimidate another."[156]

There was one final overriding development, fearsome in nature. While Senator Ervin, "country lawyer," defender of the Constitution, and acclaimed expert in constitutional law, was lamenting the decline of representative government, the most powerful corporations and trade associations in the country had entered into a secret alliance to change the labor laws to suit their own interests, in great part by manipulating, controlling, and even misleading public opinion by use of sophisticated public relations techniques. At the same time that Ervin was decrying how little "say" people had in the management of their own affairs,[157] this secret employer alliance was determined to abolish an NLRB whose decisions were intended to promote organization and collective bargaining to enable employees to participate in the management of their own affairs at their workplaces.

12

Making the Law Favor Employers Again

Corporate Labor Law Reform on Hold

The Labor Law Reform Group hoped the 1968 elections would provide two keys to the success of its Labor Law Reform Project: a favorably disposed Republican president, Richard Nixon, and a Congress at least not actively opposed to the group's legislative proposals. It got neither. Nixon won the presidential election but with barely a plurality of the popular vote. Moreover, he was also saddled with a Democratic Congress, at least until 1970. The Republicans still needed twenty-six seats in the House and nine in the Senate to gain a majority. As the LLRG saw it, Nixon would "tread softly on any major controversial legislation, including labor issues, during the 91st Congress."[1]

The LLRG considered Nixon more of a politician than Eisenhower and, therefore, more likely under the circumstances to act like a politician, trying to bring together the executive and legislative branches of government while wooing labor union officials and civil rights groups. There were other reasons for the LLRG to doubt that its reform project would be among Nixon's legislative priorities: the Vietnam war, inflation, civil disturbances, and law and order were the American public's top priorities.[2]

The LLRG also perceived congressional obstacles to the achievement of its legislative program. It feared that the Republican–conservative southern Democrat coalition was a thing of the past, because many southern Democrats, who voted conservatively on practically everything, were being replaced by a new breed interested in getting for the South its fair share of congessional appropriations. The House and Senate labor committees, moreover, were controlled by pro-labor Democrats. In fact, within its own councils the LLRG feared that either the House or Senate Labor Committee might conduct an investigation of the group's entire Labor Law Reform Project, revealing who was behind it, both individually and financially, and Hill & Knowlton's role in the "educational" phase of the program.[3]

There was no investigation of the LLRG, but the group's assessment of the

Nixon administration's response to its labor law reform proposals was accurate. Although they disagreed over the causes and remedies for inflation and unemployment in the 1970s, Nixon and AFL-CIO president George Meany were united in their passionate anticommunism, and Meany and his cohorts in the Federation delivered needed political support for the administration's pro-war policies in Vietnam. This commitment to the prosecution of the Vietnam war and Meany's intense dislike of the Democrats' liberal anti-war presidential candidate, George McGovern, caused the Federation in 1972 to break a forty-year tradition of supporting Democratic candidates for president. The AFL-CIO's policy of neutrality in the 1972 presidential campaign contributed to Nixon's landslide reelection victory. As columnist Stewart Alsop had predicted a year earlier, "to defeat the Democratic Presidential candidate, all that labor has to do is support him pallidly or not at all."[4]

The Meany-Nixon alliance on Vietnam was so tight that Nixon called Meany to the White House in April 1970 for a secret briefing by Henry Kissinger to get Meany's support for Nixon's decision to bomb enemy sanctuaries in Cambodia. After Nixon announced the bombing of Cambodia, Meany issued a statement pledging the Federation's full support.[5] There was no reason, therefore, for employers to expect the Nixon administration to jeopardize its good relationship with organized labor by advocating pro-business amendments to Taft-Hartley that most likely would be killed in Congress anyway.

Nevertheless, in late 1969, when the Nixon administration asked what relief business wanted, the twelve members of the LLRG's Steering Committee (the original "Twelve Apostles") unanimously responded that they wanted to change the law to eliminate decision bargaining and narrow the scope of mandatory collective bargaining.[6] The Labor Law Reform Group decided in 1969 to persist in its campaign but warned its colleagues to be prepared for a long haul of three or four years.[7]

Controlling Labor Policy by Controlling Appointments

By 1971 the LLRG had reassessed its program and approach. Its major problem, the group concluded, was that even if its labor law reform package were passed and implemented in 1971, it would be only a partial answer to the larger problems plaguing business. With a new, broader perspective, the group realized that employers were dealing not only with costs imposed by unions at the bargaining table but also with legislated costs on employers such as welfare, food stamps, unemployment insurance, minimum wages, health insurance, pensions, social security, and the pending occupational safety and health bill. The

LLRG anticipated that these costs would continue to rise and that greater responsibility would be placed on business for the safety and health of workers, the quality of products, and the quality of the environment.[8]

The LLRG took organized labor as its model. Labor's success in achieving its economic objectives, the group believed, was due "more to its near complete control of the appointive process" than to successful legislative ventures. As the LLRG saw it, organized labor had "gained control of the machinery of government to shape old laws to serve its interests." In the opinion of the LLRG, for example, organized labor had been able to retain most of its Wagner Act gains over more than thirty years and despite two major legislative reforms favorable to employers because of appointments resulting in a "pro-union" and "imaginative" NLRB.[9] Political appointments, therefore, became the most pressing goal of the LLRG. The Steering Committee designated one of its own, Douglas Soutar, to coordinate efforts to secure appropriate candidates for key government posts.[10]

Even earlier, just after Nixon's November 1968 election victory, Soutar and Frank O'Connell had moved promptly to organize an informal group of management lawyers to advise the new Republican administration on appointments to positions involving management-labor affairs, such as the NLRB, the Labor Department, and the Equal Employment Opportunity Commission. These management lawyers, predominantly members of the LLRG's Blue Ribbon Committee, functioned as a reliable source of business community opinion concerning the merits of proposed nominees.[11] The lawyers' group told the White House that the new NLRB chairman had to be "a person of wisdom who espouses a Republican philosophy."[12] In anticipation of the expiration of Sam Zagoria's term in December 1969, the LLRG Steering Committee met with Nixon's secretary of commerce, Maurice Stans, and several members of his staff. In pointed language they derided Zagoria as a "George Meany–Lyndon Johnson 'Republican'" whose reappointment would be a harsh slap in the face to employers.[13] When it became certain, however, that the Democrat-controlled Senate Labor Committee, under pressure from organized labor, would block the appointment of the LLRG's favorite candidates, the group decided not to jeopardize its relations with the Nixon administration by pressing hard-line demands on NLRB appointments.[14] Although the Nixon administration intended to give preference to the employer interests of the LLRG, it wanted to do so in ways not threatening to the broad political cooperation it needed to achieve its domestic and foreign programs. Consequently, Secretary of Labor George Schultz asked Soutar to find an acceptable candidate from neither the conservative nor liberal wing of the Republican Party.[15]

The final choice was what *Business Week* called "the ultimate in a compromise candidate": forty-eight-year-old management attorney and Blue Ribbon Committee member Edward Miller of the Chicago law firm of Pope & Ballard.[16] Nixon named Miller chairman, a move many employers hoped would cause McCulloch to "quit in a huff."[17] It did not; McCulloch remained on the Board as a member.

Miller grew up in Wisconsin and received his undergraduate and law school degrees from the University of Wisconsin separated by two years of service in the navy in World War II. He had been with Pope & Ballard from his graduation from law school in 1947 to his nomination hearings in May 1970. A "dark horse," Miller, as the *New York Times* stated, "has never argued what the legal world considers a definitive case, and until his nomination . . . he was virtually unknown outside the Chicago bar." The same article quoted Chicago union lawyers who described Miller as "soft-spoken," "dispassionate," "not a gung-ho type," and "no union buster."[18]

George Meany opposed the appointment solely because Miller had been a corporation lawyer throughout his professional career. No Democratic administration had ever nominated anyone who represented unions or employers in labor matters, Meany told the Senate Labor Committee during Miller's nomination hearings. Republican administrations had named management attorneys Guy Farmer and Joseph Jenkins to the Board as well as business executive Albert Beeson and employer attorney Theophil Kammholz as general counsel. Meany said that no one should be appointed to the NLRB from the ranks of labor or management, especially someone like Miller, who was likely to return to private practice representing employers.[19] According to Miller, the Board had a weakness he could remedy, since no present member "had direct practical experience in the field."[20]

Meany objected, but as Frank McCulloch noted, "you didn't hear any votes against his confirmation. If labor had really opposed him, you would have."[21] Compared with other employer-backed candidates for the Zagoria vacancy on the Board, Miller was the least objectionable choice for organized labor. Yet Miller's basic philosophy of the proper role of the federal government in labor relations and his understanding of the basic purpose of the Taft-Hartley Act were indistinguishable from those of Guy Farmer, the first chairman of the Eisenhower NLRB.

Both Farmer and Miller advocated minimum government involvement in labor-management relations. Farmer wrote in 1954 that "Uncle Sam's long arm has reached out to assert itself over too many labor-management situations which ought to be resolved closer to their origin."[22] When asked in 1970 about the federal government's role in labor relations, Miller answered, "My basic philosophy is: The less the better."[23] Miller, like Farmer, also emphasized the individual free choice and individual rights purposes of the Taft-Hartley Act. Miller's understanding of the basic purpose of the act was fundamentally contrary to McCulloch's:

> Frank [McCulloch] says the purpose of the Act is to encourage collective bargaining. I say, "But Frank, you didn't read the revision of the preface to the Act at the time of Taft-Hartley, which now clearly sets forth two objectives. The first one is freedom of choice of employees in deciding whether or not they want to join a union and be represented by a union, and, if so, by which union." And that freedom of choice is to my mind the keystone of the Act.[24]

In Miller's view, if employees choose collective bargaining, they have the statutory right to engage in collective bargaining. "But," Miller acknowledged, "the freedom of the employees to decide in the first instance interests me more than it interests Frank McCulloch."[25] The Board under Miller's chairmanship would reverse the major thrust of the McCulloch Board: the encouragement of collective bargaining and the facilitation of union organization. Miller, for example, aware of employers' dissatisfaction with a "very pro-labor" NLRB, echoed his predecessors on the Eisenhower Board, wanting his Board "to administer the law as written, with as little bias or sense of social mission as is humanly possible." When he went to the Board as chairman, Miller said he "was not going there on any crusade."[26]

Miller's impact on the doctrinal direction of the five-member Board was limited to dissenting opinions until McCulloch's term expired in August 1970. The Nixon administration, however, would not have a majority of its own appointees on the Board until Gerald Brown's term ran out in August 1971 or have its own choice for NLRB general counsel in place until Arnold Ordman left the agency in June 1971. In the spring of 1970 Nixon chose Ralph Kennedy, regional director of the NLRB's Twenty-first Regional Office, the only remaining regional director appointed by former general counsel Kammholz during the Eisenhower administration.[27] Kennedy, fifty-one, a career NLRB attorney, joined the agency in 1948 after four years in private practice, and worked in St. Louis, Buffalo, Fort Worth, Atlanta, and Washington before being promoted to regional director in St. Louis in 1955. He became regional director in Los Angeles in 1958. Kennedy's supporters included not only Kammholz but also influential Blue Ribbon Committee corporation lawyers. No one appeared at Kennedy's nomination hearing to oppose his appointment to the Board.[28] McCulloch was predictably disappointed with the Miller and Kennedy appointments. In his opinion too many candidates came from management law firms or from among the most conservative of the regional directors available.[29]

Employers had been eager for the term of McCulloch's colleague Arnold Ordman as general counsel to expire. Nixon's staff, working closely with Soutar, Kammholz, and the LLRG's Virgil Day,[30] nominated Peter Nash. (After completing his four-year term as general counsel in August 1975, Nash joined Kammholz & Day as a partner in their management law firm.)[31] Nash, the youngest NLRB general counsel since Taft-Hartley, when the position became one of presidential appointment, graduated in 1962 from the New York University Law School, where he was editor of the law review. He was in private practice for six years before becoming associate solicitor and then solicitor in the Department of Labor after Nixon became president.[32] At his nomination hearing Nash, consistent with his Republican-appointed predecessors on the Board and in the general counsel's office, told the Senate Labor Committee that the protection of individual rights was the paramount purpose of the act.[33] He thought that McCulloch and Ordman were "more pro-labor than I would have liked to have seen."[34]

In February 22, 1972, the last year of Nixon's first term, the president named John A. Penello, a Democrat and career NLRB attorney, to replace Gerald Brown, whose term had expired in August 1971. Penello had joined the NLRB in 1937 and worked as a field examiner, chief examiner, regional director in Minneapolis and Baltimore from 1948 to 1958, associate general counsel in Washington, D.C., from 1958 to 1959, and regional director in Baltimore from 1959 to his appointment as Board member.[35] Because of the Nixon administration's reluctance to name anyone, particularly another management attorney, who would generate strong opposition from organized labor, the LLRG settled for Penello, although he was a "middle of the roader, not very far to the right."[36]

The Nixon White House, moreover, told Soutar a month before the 1972 presidential election that John Fanning would be reappointed to an unprecedented fourth term because Nixon considered the political support of the building trades unions, always strong backers of Fanning, vital to his reelection plans. Once the Democrats passed over Humphrey and Muskie at their nominating convention, Nixon correctly anticipated picking up substantial support from organized labor in his campaign against George McGovern. The White House, however, wanting to avoid a short-sighted clash between the administration and management over Fanning, proposed a strategy to Soutar. In return for letting Fanning pass, employers were promised a "good deal" later, that is, a more acceptable pro-management appointment, to replace Howard Jenkins in 1973.[37] The elimination of Jenkins would change the balance of power on the Board significantly.

Many LLRG members supported a plan to put Nixon on the spot by backing a woman to replace Fanning, in this way embarrassing an administration publicly pledged to bringing more women into government. Nevertheless, the LLRG chose not to challenge Fanning's reappointment.[38] When Jenkins's term expired in August 1973, however, the White House did not deliver on its debt to management. The LLRG and other employer groups campaigned for the appointment of Betty Southard Murphy, a former NLRB attorney then in private practice.[39] Murphy appeared to have the inside track to the Board, particularly in light of efforts within administration and management circles to move Jenkins to the chairmanship of the Equal Employment Opportunity Commission. Murphy was shaken when a Nixon staff member called to say that Jenkins would be reappointed. According to Murphy, the caller was "extremely apologetic and embarrassed and apparently quite surprised by the decision himself."[40] Employers consulted by the LLRG realized that "if Jenkins wanted to be reappointed, Nixon would reappoint him because he was Republican, Black and experienced."[41]

The Miller Board's Reinterpretation of National Labor Policy

Senator Sam Ervin decided, almost two years after the close of his 1968 hearings on the NLRB, to publish a final majority report shortly before Nixon made Miller chairman of the NLRB. The Ervin committee majority criticized the McCulloch Board for emphasizing the establishment and maintenance of collective bargaining and giving "excessive weight" to the development of unionism, to the detriment of the individual rights of employees to reject collective bargaining and unionization.[42]

The Miller Board did not rush to make wholesale changes in McCulloch Board doctrine, in part because Nixon did not get three of his appointees on the Board until the last year of his first term. That and the tone of Chairman Miller's speeches helped create an aura of moderation and stability about the new Republican-appointed majority. Miller spoke constantly of the need for predictability and certainty in the application of the labor law and his belief that stability in Board doctrine was more important than reversing McCulloch Board precedent.[43] The perception of the Miller Board as moderate can be found even in former chairman McCulloch's cautiously worded assessment: the Miller "Board has undoubtedly moved in a generally more conservative direction" but in a way "contrary to labor's worst fears and management's highest hopes."[44] In contrast to popular impressions, however, the Miller Board had a major impact on the national labor policy, rejecting many McCulloch Board decisions and applying its own very different understanding of the purpose of the act. The Miller Board made important labor policy in the vital areas of NLRB remedies, management rights, bargaining, employer speech, permissible resistance to unionization and collective bargaining, appropriate bargaining unit determinations, lockouts, and deferral of statutory rights to the private labor arbitration process. Its decisions would increase employers' ability to resist unionization and reduce their obligation to bargain collectively if organized.

No Innovative Remedies

The McCulloch Board and its supporters had long advocated the development and use of more effective remedies to prevent lawbreakers from benefiting from their illegal activity. Miller was opposed to the imposition by the Board of what he considered overly broad and novel remedies. In reply to criticisms that Board remedies were too little and too late, he said that his Board would concentrate on resolving the "too late" rather than the "too little" by speeding up Board procedures to make existing remedies more effective.[45]

On August 29, 1970, in *Ex-Cell-O Corporation,*[46] a three-to-two majority of the Board decided that it did not have the authority to order the company, which had illegally refused to bargain, to compensate employees for monetary losses they incurred as a consequence of the employer's failure to agree to a contract that it would have agreed to if it had bargained in good faith. The Miller majority admitted the impotence of the Board's standard order to bargain in good faith and acknowledged the destructive effects of an unlawful delay on union bargaining strength and employee support for the union. The majority also recognized the Board's broad statutory authority to fashion remedies. Nevertheless, according to the majority, the proposed remedy was "close" to being punitive to employers and, therefore, went beyond the make-whole limits of the Board's remedy power,[47] was unduly speculative, and was contrary to a recent Supreme Court decision (*H.K. Porter Co., Inc.*)[48] holding that the Board did not have the authority to compel an employer or a union to agree to a substantive contractual provision. Consistent with Miller's view, the majority said that the solution in such cases was not more powerful remedies but procedural reform to give the highest priority to refusal-to-bargain cases.

McCulloch and Brown in dissent maintained that their compensatory remedy would not be punitive because it would do no more than reimburse employees for the loss caused by the unlawful denial of their opportunity for collective bargaining.[49] McCulloch and Brown also rejected the speculative nature of the remedy as a defense, arguing that an employer "must bear the risk of the uncertainty which was created by his own wrong."[50]

NLRB trial examiner Owsley Vose had found Ex-Cell-O Corporation guilty of a refusal to bargain and recommended the adoption of the unprecedented compensatory remedy in 1967. That same year, the McCulloch Board heard oral argument on the proposed remedy, in which management groups, individual employers, the AFL-CIO and several national unions, and other interested parties participated. But the final decision in the case was not made until August 1970, when Miller was chairman and McCulloch had only a few days remaining in his last term. During McCulloch's chairmanship the Board had discussed the issue extensively. After the exchange of several draft opinions McCulloch believed that he had "four and one-half votes" in favor of the remedy. He recalled that there were paragraphs in his and Brown's dissent that came from the original opinions of Fanning and Jenkins when they advocated the new remedy.[51]

The decision was delayed, in part because Fanning and Jenkins wanted to wait for the Supreme Court's decision in another case[52] to see whether the new remedy would apply to Ex-Cell-O or only prospectively to other employers who unlawfully refused to bargain. McCulloch believed that there were other reasons for the delay. Jenkins, whose term expired in August 1968, was not, in McCulloch's opinion, anxious to decide such a controversial case before he was reappointed. Jenkins and Fanning were aware, McCulloch commented later, "that there had been an election and Mr. Nixon had won."[53]

McCulloch would still have had a three-to-two decision sustaining the remedy if Zagoria had joined him and Brown. Zagoria knew that Nixon would not reappoint him, however, and he told McCulloch that he did not want to be the "swing man" in such an important and controversial decision, which generated strong feelings among the members of the McCulloch Board.[54] Years later Fanning remembered, "Frank [McCulloch] and Jerry [Brown] didn't talk to me for three weeks when I voted the other way. They thought I was a regular turncoat."[55] McCulloch always regretted his inability to persuade his colleagues to move ahead on *Ex-Cell-O* in 1967. He considered it one of his most important cases and one of his failures.[56]

The End of Decision Bargaining

The most decisive change in the Board's doctrine under Miller's chairmanship came after fellow Nixon appointees Kennedy and Penello joined the Board. Over Fanning and Jenkins's dissent the new Republican-appointed majority, without explicitly reversing the McCulloch Board's *Fibreboard*[57] decision, which the Supreme Court had upheld in 1964,[58] redefined the scope of the statutory obligation to bargain to exclude matters of fundamental managerial or entrepreneurial decisionmaking. In *General Motors,* the watershed case, the company had shifted part of its operation, a truck dealership, to another em-

ployer who held a franchise for the sale of GM trucks and leased its premises
from GM. Miller, Kennedy, and Penello, calling the transaction a sale, concluded that although General Motors was obliged to bargain about the effects of
the decision to sell part of its business, the underlying decision itself was not a
mandatory subject of bargaining because it was "financial and entrepreneurial
in nature."[59]

The McCulloch Board had given an expansive reading to the Supreme
Court's ruling in *Fibreboard* that the subcontracting in that case was a mandatory subject of bargaining. Miller and his colleagues followed instead the dicta
in Justice Stewart's concurring opinion immunizing employers from the obligation to bargain about prerogatives "at the core of entrepreneurial control." The
emphasis on Justice Stewart's opinion in *Fibreboard,* particularly by management lawyers, has often concealed the Supreme Court's firm endorsement in
that case of the national labor policy favoring the submission of such management decisions to collective bargaining. Fibreboard had contended that when an
employer could reduce costs by such devices as contracting out bargaining unit
work, there was no need to provide employees an opportunity to negotiate
similar economies or even a mutually acceptable alternative. Chief Justice Earl
Warren, who wrote the Court's opinion, was explicit in the Court's response:
"The short answer is that, although it is not possible to say whether a satisfactory solution could be reached, national labor policy is founded upon the congressional determination that the chances are good enough to warrant subjecting
such issues to the process of collective negotiation."[60] Ignoring that aspect of
the Court's decision, the Miller majority in *General Motors* simply asserted the
futility of bargaining over "core" managerial decisions: "Such managerial decisions ofttimes require secrecy as well as freedom to act quickly and decisively.
They also involve subject areas as to which the determinative financial and
operational considerations are likely to be unfamiliar to the employees and their
representatives."[61]

The McCulloch Board had consistently found a duty to bargain about employers' *decisions* involving subcontracting, plant removal, and plant closures
as well as the *effects* of those decisions.[62] According to Kennedy-Johnson Board
holdovers Fanning and Jenkins, the effects of such important business decisions
were so inextricably interwoven with the decisions themselves that "meaningful
bargaining over effects can only occur prior to the employer's making and
acting upon its decision."[63] The dissenters dismissed Stewart's concurring opinion and dicta concerning entrepreneurial decisions as "not the law of the case."
They also rejected the Miller majority's one-dimensional concern for the interests of General Motors. Instead, they emphasized the mutuality of interests
inherent in the collective bargaining process: "Such a change as a termination

of a portion of an employer's business is also of great significance for the employee who has 'invested years of his working life accumulating seniority, accruing pension rights, and developing skills that may or may not be salable to another employer' in the same way the employer has invested capital."[64]

In *General Motors* and similar decisions such as *Triplex Oil Refining* in 1971, *Summit Tooling Co.* in 1972, and *Kingwood Mining Co.* in 1974,[65] the Miller Board held that the duty to bargain must not significantly abridge the employer's freedom to manage his business.[66] The enormous potential of *Fibreboard* to become the basis for expanding the statutory duty to bargain to include managerial or entrepreneurial decision making was the driving force that had brought employers together to form their organized opposition to the McCulloch Board and to seek changes in the labor law. It was the Miller Board, however, using the dicta of Justice Stewart, that effectively defused the Mc-Culloch Board's and Supreme Court's *Fibreboard* decisions.

Deregulated Employer Speech in Representation Election Campaigns

The Ervin committee's final report accused the McCulloch Board of going "to the limit and beyond in finding a coercive impact in isolated and relatively innocuous remarks by employers." The committee majority also condemned the McCulloch Board's resurrection of the *General Shoe* doctrine (which held that the speech protections of Section 8[c] did not apply to representation elections) to invalidate elections lost by unions because noncoercive employer speech had disturbed "laboratory conditions."[67]

Under Miller's chairmanship, as had been the case with the Republican-appointed Boards in the 1950s, the NLRB became much more tolerant of employer expressions of opposition to attempted unionization. Rather than explicitly overrule *General Shoe,* the Miller Board simply drew different inferences concerning the probable effect of representation campaign speech on employee voters than did the McCulloch Board from essentially the same sets of facts. Consequently, employer anti-union campaign statements, assumed by the Mc-Culloch Board to have sufficiently adverse effects on employees to justify over-turning elections, drew no sanctions from the Republican-appointed Farmer and Miller Boards. Under the Nixon Board an employer statement to employees that signing union authorization cards would be "fatal" and cause "turmoil" became, in Miller, Kennedy, and Penello's view, a permissible expression of employer opinion protected by the free-speech provision of Taft-Hartley.[68] In another case, employer assertions that, if unionized, all bargaining "starts from scratch" and "everything is up for negotiation" were considered by the Miller majority not to be threatening the loss of current benefits in the event of a union victory but merely permissible expressions of the possible results of bargaining.[69] Another employer statement to employees that unionization would lead to plant removal, was seen by the Miller majority as merely an objective statement of the financial problems employers have when they become organized and a prediction that such problems could require relocation.[70] Miller's Board, like the Eisenhower Boards chaired by Farmer and Leedom, used its asserted perception of employees as more sophisticated and better educated than before and, therefore, better able to recognize and evaluate campaign propaganda as an additional justification for deregulating employer electioneering. In *LithoPress,* for example, Miller, Kennedy, and Penello reversed the McCulloch Board, concluding that the showing by an employer of the anti-union film *And Women Must Weep* during a representation election campaign neither violated the act nor constituted a sufficient basis for setting aside an election, even in the context of other employer violations of the act.[71]

The Miller Board's deregulation of employer speech enabled employers to wage aggressive anti-union campaigns and to develop and implement sophisticated representation campaign tactics in the 1970s and 1980s. Two years after he left the NLRB, Miller wrote of how business managers, their labor relations staffs, and their labor counsel had acquired extensive "knowhow" and experience in conducting campaigns to counteract union organizational efforts.[72] The deregulation of employer speech during Miller's chairmanship increased the ability of employers to resist the unionization of their employees by legal means.

Larger Bargaining Unit Determinations

The Ervin committee also accused the McCulloch Board of a single-minded intent to aid unionization through its determination of appropriate election units. By permitting smaller units for election purposes, the Ervin majority charged, the McCulloch Board enabled unions to establish footholds by organizing only small groups of employees before spreading through the employer's business. The committee was particularly critical of the McCulloch Board's unit determinations in the insurance and retail chain and department store industries.[73] The Eisenhower Boards had consistently approved much larger bargaining units in those businesses, usually including all employees in all stores or offices in an employer's administrative division or geographical area. The McCulloch Board rejected the Eisenhower Board policy because it often made organizing difficult, if not impossible.

In *Twenty-First Century Restaurant,*[74] which concerned a restaurant that was part of the McDonald's chain, the Nixon Board abandoned the McCulloch Board's presumption in favor of smaller units. A panel of Miller and Kennedy, with Fanning dissenting, overturned a regional director's decision finding a single restaurant unit appropriate, because all employer policies, including labor relations, were established at corporate headquarters and in administrative divisions. The majority made the employer's internal organization the controlling factor in determining an appropriate unit. In *Gray Drug Stores*[75] Miller, Kennedy, and Penello used the employer's administrative division and geographical area in approving a bargaining unit larger than requested by the union. In other illustrative cases the Miller majority chose a unit based on the extent of the employer's regional sales division[76] and a storewide unit of all employees when the union petitioned for a unit comprised only of salespersons.[77] The Nixon Board's reinstitution of the Eisenhower Boards' preferences for larger election units made it more difficult for unions to organize.

The Demise of Bargaining Orders and Authorization Cards

The Supreme Court, in its *Gissel Packing Co.* decision near the end of the McCulloch Board period in 1969, clearly approved of the Board's practice of issuing bargaining orders as a remedy for employer violations of the duty to bargain where a union had proven its majority status with signed authorization cards. The acknowledged superiority of the NLRB secret ballot election over union-solicited authorization cards as indicators of employee sentiment, the Supreme Court decided, did not render authorization cards totally invalid, because cards could be the most effective or the only way of ensuring employee choice when unlawful employer conduct disrupted the election process.[78] The Court required the Board to issue a bargaining order without the need of inquiring into a union's majority status based on cards or otherwise in "exceptional" cases marked by "outrageous" and "pervasive" unfair labor practices where the coercive consequences prevented a fair and reliable election. The Court also approved the Board's exercise of its discretion to issue a bargaining order "in less extraordinary cases marked by less pervasive practices which nonetheless still have the tendency to undermine majority strength and impede the election process." The appropriateness of bargaining orders based on lesser forms of employer misconduct, however, required a showing through authorization cards or otherwise that at one point the union was the choice of a majority of the employees.[79]

Even after *Gissel* the Ervin committee majority condemned the McCulloch Board's use of card checks instead of representation elections as a violation of congressional intent.[80] The Miller Board rarely exercised this Supreme Court–

approved authority. Chairman Miller wanted to limit severely the use of bargaining orders based on authorization cards.[81] In *Claremont Polychemical Corp.,*[82] even though the corporation president unlawfully threatened to close any unionized plant and offered benefits for withdrawal of support for the union, Miller and Kennedy found that the employer's violations did not prevent a free and fair election. The employer in *Green Briar Nursing Home*[83] physically assaulted, in the presence of employees, two union organizers who were trying to present him with authorization cards proving the union's majority status. In the opinion of the Miller majority the employer's conduct was not the type to produce a "lingering impact" on a subsequent representation election. Fanning remarked sarcastically that he did not read *Gissel* as requiring an employer's unfair labor practices to be "the direct cause of death or bloodshed in order to preclude the holding of a fair election and thereby merit a bargaining order."[84] In *Linden Lumber*[85] the Miller Board said that it was not unlawful for employers to refuse to extend recognition on the basis of a majority authorization card showing regardless of whether their reasons for refusal were good or bad.

Deferral of Statutory Matters to Private Labor Arbitration

Consistent with Chairman Miller's ideological preference for less government involvement in labor relations, the Nixon Board pursued a policy of deferral to private labor arbitration that many, not only organized labor, considered an abdication of the NLRB's statutory role.[86] Miller was outspoken in his belief "that the Board should stand aside with the onset of collective bargaining and allow the parties to govern themselves through contractual self-regulation, with the Board largely concentrating its efforts on organizational controversies."[87] At the same time, it was doubtful whether labor arbitrators had the expertise or even the inclination to enforce the act.[88]

The Eisenhower Board in *Spielberg Manufacturing Co.* established the principal of deferral to existing arbitral awards that met the guidelines set forth in that decision, including a requirement that the decision of the arbitrator not be repugnant to the purposes and policies of the act.[89] The McCulloch Board observed the *Spielberg* standard. Following its decision in *C & C Plywood Corp.,* however, the McCulloch Board refused to dismiss unfair labor practice charges of unlawful unilateral action by an employer during the term of a collective bargaining agreement simply because of the availability of contractual arbitration procedures and an employer's claim that its action was governed by a collective bargaining contract.[90] Nixon appointees Miller and Kennedy, with the concurrence of Gerald Brown, who had long favored deferral to arbitration, established a new and contrary policy.

In *Collyer Insulated Wire* an employer unilaterally changed wage rates, contending that this was permissible under the terms of its collective bargaining agreement with the union. When the union filed refusal-to-bargain charges with the NLRB, the employer asked that the case be held in abeyance pending resort to the parties' grievance-arbitration procedure. Miller and his colleagues dismissed the union's unfair labor practice charge and directed the union to resort first to the contractual grievance-arbitration procedure.[91] The *Collyer* doctrine, Fanning said in his dissent, would strip a party of statutory rights merely because of the *availability* of a grievance-arbitration procedure.[92]

Collyer, moreover, proved to be only a first step in the Nixon Board's expansion of the deferral-to-arbitration doctrine. As one commentary put it at the time, "the more than sixty related cases issued since *Collyer* show a determination on the part of the Board to take deferral to its outer limits."[93] General Counsel Nash advised NLRB regional offices, where all unfair labor practice charges were filed, that he favored Board deferral to the arbitration process "to the broadest extent consonant with the objectives of the Statute."[94]

A year after *Collyer* the Nixon Board, in *National Radio Co.,*[95] extended the deferral doctrine to discriminatory discharges for union activity. Fanning and Jenkins accused the Board majority of "subcontracting to a private tribunal the determination of rights conferred and guaranteed solely by the statute."[96] Deregulation of statutory issues through deferral to arbitration had a profound effect on labor law, not only because it was doubtful whether arbitrators could or would apply the statutory standards of a public law to the parties' private contractual "law" but also because arbitrators, mutually chosen and paid by employers and unions, could be reading statutory standards to fit the desires of these same parties. In effect, the Nixon Board gave employers and unions the power to alter their legal relationships by contract.[97]

The Murphy Board

After the Watergate scandal led to Nixon's abrupt departure from the White House in August 1974, his successor, former vice-president Gerald Ford, made three important appointments to the NLRB. In February 1975 he named Republican Betty Southard Murphy as chairman to replace Edward Miller, who had resigned on December 6, 1974. In November 1975 Ford chose management attorney Peter Walther to replace Ralph Kennedy, who had resigned on June 30, 1975, and John Irving to replace General Counsel Peter Nash, whose term had expired on August 1975.

Soutar and the Blue Ribbon Committee wanted another management attorney to replace former management attorney Miller, and they wanted a strong chairman who could control what they saw as the "delicate balance" on the Board.[98] After the Republicans suffered a post-Watergate drubbing in the 1974 congressional elections, however, White House adviser Bryce Harlow told Soutar that the air in the White House had a "smell of compromise"; to Soutar, compromise meant that no management lawyer would be nominated.[99] Betty Southard Murphy then indicated that she was available but only for the chairmanship.[100] (Murphy had been the LLRG's unsuccessful choice in 1973 to replace Howard Jenkins.) Management considered Murphy an acceptable solution to industry's problem. She was a conservative who had substantial union support, in part because she and her law firm represented labor as well as management.[101]

The Ford administration had two more opportunities to fill key NLRB vacancies when member Kennedy resigned and General Counsel Nash's term expired. Both appointments were of great importance to employers. Secretary of Labor John Dunlop and newly appointed chairman Murphy wanted a practicing management attorney from outside the Board who was not "so far to the right" as Kennedy. To fit that bill, Soutar proposed, after a nationwide search "with much in-fighting," management attorney Peter Walther of the Philadelphia law firm Morgan, Lewis & Brockius to replace Kennedy. Walther, forty-seven, had been an NLRB attorney for seven years in Philadelphia and Detroit before joining this law firm. As Soutar saw it, with Kennedy gone, Murphy and Penello needed a strong management attorney "to lean upon" in order to get three-to-two votes for management.[102] Although many employers backed candidates more conservative than Walther, political realism dictated that business could not expect to get "as strong a management type as Kennedy."[103]

Walther and the new NLRB general counsel, John Irving, took office in November 1975. Many employers had supported more conservative management attorneys for general counsel, including former Board member Kennedy. Outgoing general counsel Peter Nash, however, backed Irving, his deputy general counsel, as the best solution. Irving was generally acceptable to organized labor, and Soutar had determined that management was very comfortable with Irving as general counsel.[104]

As the November 1976 presidential election approached and the term of member Penello was about to expire, Ford, not looking for controversy on Capitol Hill, decided to renominate him. Although management attorneys were displeased with some of his decisions and employers had candidates they preferred, management was generally satisfied that Penello was the best it could get under the circumstances.[105]

Murphy's tour as chairman lasted only two years. After Jimmy Carter defeated Gerald Ford in the 1976 presidential election, he designated John Fanning chairman on April 14, 1977, although the composition of the Board, including Murphy, remained the same until near the end of 1977. During Murphy's chairmanship the Board, with some notable exceptions, continued Miller Board policies and issued only a few important policy-making decisions. In one of those major decisions, *Shopping Kart Food Market*,[106] the Murphy Board's Republican-appointed majority overturned the McCulloch Board's *Hollywood Ceramics*[107] rule by deciding that it would no longer set aside representation elections because of campaign misrepresentations. The decision expanded the Miller Board's deregulation of representation campaigning. It was also a return to the Eisenhower Board's position on deceptive campaign practices.[108] The language of the Murphy Board's decision echoed Guy Farmer's condemnation of the view of employees as naive and unworldly and reaffirmed his perception of them as "mature individuals who are capable of recognizing campaign propaganda for what it is and discounting it."[109]

In the main, however, the Board during Murphy's brief stint as chairman was generally moderate to mixed in its treatment of established doctrine and its formulation of new doctrines. During Murphy's chairmanship, for example, the Board made it more difficult for unions to organize, not only by further deregulating important aspects of representation election campaigning but also by choosing larger bargaining units in multiple-location health care operations over single-location or smaller units.[110] Nevertheless, the Murphy Board treated as protected concerted activity an individual employee's filing of a claim under a statute governing workplace safety because enforcement of the health and safety law benefited all employees.[111]

Murphy also provided the swing vote that reversed the Miller Board's expansion of *Collyer*[112] to include deferral to arbitration of discriminatory discharges for union activity. Although Fanning and Jenkins wanted to repeal *Collyer* completely, Murphy joined them, over the dissents of Republican appointees Walther and Penello, in deciding that the Board would no longer defer to labor arbitration those disputes involving individual employees' statutory rights guaranteed by the act.[113] Disagreeing with Fanning and Jenkins, who claimed that the *Collyer* policy had resulted in a substantial sacrifice of statutory protection for employees and only a slight decrease in the Board's work load, Murphy stated that the Board would continue to defer to arbitrators those disputes she described as being between an employer and a union, such as refusal-to-bargain situations, in which the principal issue, she said, was whether the complained-of conduct was permitted by the parties' contract.[114] Murphy's overall performance as chairman, though not even approximating a return to the McCulloch era, was disappointing to many employers and hardly what they expected when she was appointed.

The Business Roundtable

By 1972 things were better for the corporate members of the LLRG (by then known as the Labor Law Study Group, or LLSG), particularly because favorable changes in NLRB personnel had "eased their pain."[115] Business and industry realized, however, that the steady increase in the cost of doing business was due only partially to unionization and collective bargaining. More significant, in the view of LLSG members, was the increase in government intervention and regulation in all areas of business, proliferating even under a Republican administration. Regulations involving occupational health and safety, environmental pollution, consumer protection, energy use, and employment discrimination, they believed, were hamstringing the free enterprise system and went far beyond any restrictions placed on their foreign competitors.[116] They blamed government regulation and intervention for slow economic growth, diminished productivity increases, unemployment, inadequate savings and investment, and international trade problems.[117]

The situation was aggravated, LLSG executives were convinced, by a lack of public support and understanding for business. They believed that the public had exaggerated impressions of their profit margins and ability to control prices and of the division of income between employees and stockholders. These mistaken notions led to what the LLSG considered "unwise" laws and regulations involving tax, trade, and tariff policy as well as environment, energy, and labor. It was a "new crisis for capitalism" that required the direct involvement of corporate chief executive officers to resolve.[118]

The situation spurred efforts to build a broader coalition with higher-ranking executives than those in charge of labor relations and a broader agenda than that of the LLSG. Consequently, in 1972 the LLSG and the Construction Users Anti-Inflation Roundtable (CUAR) merged. The CUAR, headed by Roger Blough, former chairman of U.S. Steel, was an alliance of anti-union construction users and contractors formed to check the rising cost of labor in the building trades. The merger made good sense because both groups were committed to diminishing the power of organized labor and there was a great deal of overlap in their membership.[119] The merged organization became the Business Roundtable (BRT).[120]

In 1973 a third organization, the March Group, composed of more than forty chief executive officers of the country's most powerful corporations, joined the Business Roundtable.[121] The March Group had historical roots in the Business Council, which had served as a link between business and the federal government since the administration of Franklin Roosevelt. The March Group's merger with the BRT was logical since approximately two-thirds of the corporate members of the March Group had been associated with the LLSG and the CUAR.[122]

The Business Roundtable became an exclusive fraternity of the nation's most powerful and prestigious business leaders. These CEOs represented approximately two hundred of the largest corporations in the country from each sector of the economy, including the top ten of the 1978 Fortune 500. The Roundtable was the voice of business in Washington.[123] The BRT had great political power, wealth, organization, and influence with the mass media, with its strength centered in and exercised by the CEOs who were personally and actively involved in the organization's lobbying efforts.[124] As columnist Victor Riesel put it, "there has been nothing like this inside the worlds of commerce and industry."[125]

Now part of the Roundtable, the LLSG became the Labor-Management Committee (LMC), chaired by Douglas Soutar.[126] The LMC and the new Construction Committee, under the chairmanship of General Electric's Virgil Day, operated under the overall direction of the Policy Committee, made up of forty-six CEOs.[127] The now broader interests of the LMC were reflected in the creation of subcommittees or task forces on energy, pensions, national health insurance, workers compensation, and multinational corporations, as well as an editorial board for the Troika study.[128] The LMC, however, retained hopes of someday implementing the labor law reform study program.[129] Soutar remained in charge of the LMC's efforts to influence appointments to various governmental posts.

In the opinion of Roundtable member corporations the issues facing business were going to be decided in great part by public opinion.[130] The BRT formed the Public Information Committee to develop a "mature public understanding of how the business system operates" rather than simply react after business was "hit" by its critics. The PIC worked closely, for example, with the editor of *Reader's Digest* on a series of three articles on abuses of union power in the construction industry.[131] Since the Roundtable did not disclose its overall membership list, few knew at the time that *Reader's Digest* was a member.[132] In addition, the Roundtable and the LMC commissioned, for $1.2 million, a *Reader's Digest* series of monthly "advertisements" from 1975 to early 1976 describing how business works, proclaiming its great value to society, and refuting criticisms of the free market system.[133] The format was deliberately designed to make the published material look to readers "like any other article in the magazine."[134]

By the mid-1970s the LMC's range of interests had gone far beyond the original LLRG's aims of amending Taft-Hartley, blocking the McCulloch Board, and changing the membership of the NLRB. Within the Business Roundtable, moreover, labor law reform had become submerged in the host of other matters demanding attention.[135] As one Roundtable spokesman put it, labor relations legislation "is just another topic on the agenda, not a centerpiece the way it used to be."[136]

There had also been a significant mood change. Although the anti-union attitude remained, the Roundtable CEOs preferred a nonideological, noncombative approach. They practiced the politics of persuasion at the highest levels of government with parties of all types in order to achieve the best outcome for business on a broad range of national issues.[137] In the words of one lobbyist, "on the Hill today, there are no permanent friends and no permanent enemies. There are only permanent interests."[138] Francis O'Connell, one of the founders of the LLRG, condemned the Business Roundtable for avoiding "open engagement in the battles against organized labor power" and for having its courage "sapped by the arguments of image-conscious experts."[139] Several other Roundtable executives from the old LLRG agreed with O'Connell and wanted to "crank up the old mechanisms," but as Soutar observed, it was a "new ballgame."[140]

Over the years employers had been skillful at helping create the American public's impression of unions as a threat to the national economy, oppressors of the rights of individual workers, and enemies of the free enterprise system. That explains, at least partially, why after the Wagner Act business won every major labor law reform battle involving union power and the collective rights of workers but routinely lost legislative contests over programs designed to benefit workers as individuals.[141] In addition, government leaders at all levels collaborated with employers and often favored their interests because business and industry controlled jobs, prices, economic growth, the standard of living, and the economic security of everyone.[142]

Labor Law Reform, Union Style

After Watergate the Democrats won by a landslide in the 1974 congressional elections. The AFL-CIO counted 61 Senators and 279 House members (of 435) friendly to organized labor and its legislative agenda.[143] The House and Senate labor committees were even more dominated by friends of organized labor than before. Although the Republicans lost forty-three seats in the House and four in the Senate, labor's friends did not constitute the two-thirds majority necessary to override presidential vetoes. As former Nixon adviser Bryce Harlow told the Chamber of Commerce shortly after the election, business was "in for the most abusive, most disruptive, most disheartening season since the earliest New Deal days of 40 years ago" unless it could deliver enough votes to sustain presidential vetoes.[144]

After the 94th Congress took office, the Democratic majority and organized labor were soundly thrashed by President Ford's vetoes,[145] including his veto of labor's common situs bill, which would have reversed a twenty-five-year Supreme Court ban on picketing an entire construction site when a union had a dispute with a single subcontractor at the site.[146] Although it passed the House and Senate (after a lengthy filibuster), Ford vetoed the bill under heavy pressure from a massive lobbying effort by business, including the Business Roundtable, and his rival for the 1976 Republican presidential nomination, Ronald Reagan.[147]

Even after Democrat Jimmy Carter was elected president in 1976 and the Democratic Party retained its majority in Congress, organized labor's resubmitted common situs picketing bill was defeated in the House by a 217–205 vote. The bill's sponsor, Frank Thompson, attributed the bill's rejection in April 1977 to "a remarkably orchestrated and sophisticated alliance" of the Business Roundtable, the Chamber of Commerce, the National Association of Manufacturers, and the Associated General Contractors.[148] The business lobbyists' campaign concentrated on public portrayals of the bill as the creation of power-grabbing union bosses.[149]

The 1977 defeat of the common situs bill was a stunning rebuff to the AFL-CIO and reaffirmed organized labor's declining political clout. Carter's secretary of labor, Ray Marshall, who supported the bill, warned the AFL-CIO to "face the hard reality" that the nation's anti-union forces were growing in strength and influence.[150] Nevertheless, in mid-1977, after some negotiation and compromise with the president, the AFL-CIO launched a major legislative campaign for labor law reform.

Although Carter's sponsorship of this legislation helped improve his strained relations with George Meany and the AFL-CIO, the price of White House support included the abandonment of two important proposals backed by labor. One would have repealed Taft-Hartley's Section 14(b) (permitting states to ban compulsory union membership), and the other would have required the NLRB to certify unions as collective bargaining agents automatically, without representation elections, whenever 55 percent of an employer's workers signed union authorization cards. What remained in the AFL-CIO labor reform bill was significant enough to be characterized by one leading news magazine as "the most comprehensive reshaping of labor laws since Taft-Hartley's enactment 32 years ago."[151] It was a controversial bundle of procedural and substantive changes aimed in great part at reviving unions' sagging organizing efforts, particularly in the South. Except for a brief period during the McCulloch Board years, for example, the proportion of NLRB-conducted representation elections won by unions had declined from almost 80 percent in 1946 to slightly under 50 percent in 1976.[152] In the main, organized labor's 1977 reform bill reached back to the Pucinski committee's 1961 recommendations. The bill proposed to expedite NLRB case handling so employers could not use delays to deprive employees of their statutory rights, to strengthen the Board's remedy power in order to discourage violations of the act, and to give unions equal access to employers' property for representation election campaigning.

The more potent remedies in the bill included double back pay, with no deductions for interim income earned, for employees unlawfully discharged during a union organizational campaign or before the negotiation of a first collective bargaining contract. The bill also *required* the Board to seek reinstatement of such unlawfully discharged employees through the mandatory preliminary injunction provisions of Section 10(l) of the act, in the same way as 10(l) was applied to secondary boycotts and hot cargo agreements. This provision was intended not only to relieve discharged employees of the burdens of unemployment but also to demonstrate to other employees that the law could protect them swiftly and effectively. In addition, any employer found to be in repeated or willful noncompliance with an existing Board order or court decree enforcing a Board order could be barred from receiving federal government contracts for three years.[153] Finally, the bill revived the *Ex-Cell-O* remedy, recently rejected by the Board under Miller's chairmanship, by permitting the Board to order an employer that was guilty of bad-faith bargaining for a first contract to pay employees the wages they would have received had their employer bargained in good faith. The bill's equal access provision would have required the Board to guarantee labor organizations, during representation election campaigns, equal access to employers' premises to campaign in an "equivalent manner" whenever an employer communicated with employees on company time and property concerning representation issues.

In the meantime, the Business Roundtable's lawyers and the Republican minority on the House and Senate labor committees produced an "Employee Bill of Rights" based on the last Troika report.[154] The business coalition wanted employers to "be for something, and not always against something" and to make it appear that employers, not organized labor, had the best interest of employees at heart.[155] The employers' bill increased regulation of unions' internal affairs and thoroughly deregulated election campaign speech.[156]

On October 16, 1977, the House passed an amended version of the Carter administration's AFL-CIO labor law reform bill by a surprisingly wide margin of 257 to 163.[157] The Senate was not scheduled to vote on the bill until 1978. Business lobbyists conceded that they had been overconfident and out-maneuvered by labor in the House. They pledged to redouble their efforts to defeat the bill.[158]

Initially, the Business Roundtable was divided over whether to join the battle against the labor reform bill. Since the bill was aimed at employers that had resisted or otherwise avoided unionization, many already organized companies, such as General Motors, did not want to stir up conflict with their unions during difficult economic times over legislation that did not directly threaten them. Another bloc of employers in the Roundtable, however, such as Sears, Roebuck, which used unskilled labor; Firestone, Goodyear, and the steel industry, which were under heavy pressure from foreign competition; most of the large chemical companies, which depended on unorganized industries such as textiles; and many of the country's largest employers that were only partially unionized wanted to join the NAM and the Chamber of Commerce in opposing the bill. After vigorous internal debate the Roundtable's Policy Committee voted nineteen to eleven to close ranks with the other employer associations in forming a National Action Committee to lobby against the bill. Kenneth McGuiness, former NLRB general counsel whose Labor Policy Association represented the Roundtable in labor matters, was retained as NAC counsel.[159]

The labor law reform bill was among the most heavily lobbied in history.[160] The struggle became what Meany's executive assistant, Tom Donahue, called a "holy war."[161] Although large corporations such as those in the Roundtable provided most of the funding and Roundtable CEOs walked the halls of Congress, owners of small businesses, coordinated by their small business associations, did most of the "legwork."[162]

In the Senate, opposition to the bill was led by Utah Republican Orrin Hatch, who had introduced the "Employee Bill of Rights." Hatch led an effective filibuster, and his colleagues controlled the forty-one votes needed to prevent the shutoff of what they preferred to call "extended debate."[163] As a fallback strategy to delay indefinitely passage of the reform legislation and, consequently, all other pressing Senate business, Hatch and Senator Richard Lugar of Indiana gathered five hundred to one thousand amendments for Senate consideration.[164] After nineteen days of filibuster and a record six unsuccessful votes for cloture, the Senate voted on June 22, 1978, to send the Carter–AFL-CIO bill back to committee, where it died when the 95th Congress adjourned on October 15. Neither side had the votes to change the legislation governing the conduct of industrial relations.[165]

Concluding Observations

Two major events with long-lasting effects on union-management relations in the United States occurred in the 1970s. First, the Miller-Murphy Boards' Republican majorities quietly but effectively blocked or reversed the major thrusts of the McCulloch Board decisions that encouraged collective bargaining and facilitated union organization. These Boards pointedly interpreted the law to increase employers' unilateral decision-making power in matters affecting their employees, allow employers to exercise greater resistance to unionization and collective bargaining, and in other ways make it more difficult for unions to organize. These Boards also refused to approve or develop remedies sufficient to compel compliance with the law.

This time it was no short-term reversal. Although under John Fanning's chairmanship, from 1976 to 1980, the Board reversed some Miller-Murphy Board doctrines, the NLRB from 1968 to the present never again exhibited the commitment to the Taft-Hartley Act's purpose of encouraging unionization and collective bargaining that it demonstrated under McCulloch's leadership. For McCulloch, the act committed the federal government to be a promoter of industrial democracy through collective bargaining. With the exception of Carter's one term as president, however, interpretation and application of the act have been in the hands of Republican-appointed administrators for more than twenty years since the McCulloch Board. The themes of those Republican-appointed Boards have been employer rights, individual rights, and the federal government at best as neutral, indifferent to employees' choices concerning organization and collective bargaining. There was no encouragement of unionization and collective bargaining.

The defeat of the Carter administration's AFL-CIO labor reform bill in 1978 marked the beginning of a far more open employer resistance to unionization and collective bargaining. Organized labor felt betrayed and angry that the most active and powerful opponents of its reform bill included many already unionized corporations with whom the union hierarchy had cooperated and collaborated for decades. But the bitter labor-management confrontation over the proposed legislation was simply the latest, although most highly publicized, manifestation of a growing conviction among employers that being competitive in domestic and international markets required getting or remaining free of unions.

Appearing before a House Labor Committee five years after he left the NLRB, Frank McCulloch deplored the widespread, continuing defiance of the act, forty years after the Wagner Act and twenty-eight years after Taft-Hartley. He called for the creation of a "campaign mood" to confront employer resistance and noncompliance through public reaffirmation of "the individual's right to protect himself through self-organization and collective bargaining."[166] Instead, he saw only employer campaigns for "union avoidance," as it was euphemistically called.

As veteran labor reporter Abe Raskin put it, management "smelled blood" and was "on the attack in labor relations." An entire new industry of labor relations consultants had grown up in the 1970s specializing in what Raskin called "union busting sugarcoated as industrial psychology and behavioral science."[167] Even large firms that were already unionized were using these consultants to keep their newly opened plants non-union and to operate non-union wherever they could. It was rare to find an employer that recognized a union voluntarily.[168] The objective was to liberate management from union-imposed limits on its freedom to manage.

In the midst of management's campaign for a union-free environment, unions continued to decline in numbers and political influence. The public ranked union leaders only slightly above used-car dealers in opinion polls. Organized labor, moreover, seemed to be floundering without a cause that could revitalize the union movement, attract enthusiastic members, and rally supporters. As Raskin saw so perceptively, the demise of organized labor and collective bargaining would have serious repercussions for U.S. democracy: "It will be no blessing for the country much less for American workers, if the revulsion against the imperial Presidency leads to imperial status for corporate management operating on a global scale without any semblance of countervailing power in either government or labor."[169]

13

Management Interests over Workers' Statutory Rights
The Final Irrelevance of National Labor Policy?

Accommodation and Conflict: Democratic Appointments to the NLRB

Although Congress rejected union-sponsored labor law reform during Carter's one-term administration, the Carter White House was able to have a short-lived effect on the national labor policy through the appointment process. Democrats regained control of the Board when Carter named John Fanning chairman in April 1977 and, six months later, appointed NLRB executive secretary John Truesdale to replace Peter Walther, who had resigned. After that, Fanning, Jenkins, and Truesdale produced many rulings popularly associated with the Fanning Board. Betty Southard Murphy, who remained on the Board after being removed as chairman, and John Penello generally constituted a Board minority.

The Fanning Board was in control for only a few years but long enough to be accused by the conservative Heritage Foundation and a future Board member of violating management's right to manage by adopting "an activist stance manifested by an anti-business pro-labor bias."[1] Although the Fanning Board majority issued some important decisions, particularly in the areas of employer interference with representation election campaigns, protected concerted activity, the scope of collective bargaining, and deferral to labor arbitration, they amounted to no more than a blip on a long-term policy trend from the Miller Board through the Reagan-Bush years of removing restraints on employer resistance to unionization while sharply curtailing the scope of collective bargaining and diminishing its importance.

Carter got an earlier-than-expected chance to appoint a Board member when Peter Walther resigned in April 1977. Walther objected to what he called the "politicization" of the Board by certain of his Republican-appointed colleagues. At least one Board member other than Walther believed that after Carter's election Murphy's opinions had been "pro union," apparently part of an attempt by Murphy to retain her chairmanship. Another former high-ranking Nixon appointee to the NLRB accused Murphy of being "too political" and of "brown nosing labor heavily" after the presidential election.[2]

Organized labor's leading candidate to replace Walter was Daniel Pollitt, University of North Carolina law professor and former special counsel to Frank McCulloch. Management was "scared to death of Pollitt," and the Business Roundtable, Chamber of Commerce, National Association of Manufacturers, and textile industry (with special memories of *Darlington* and *J.P. Stevens*) lobbied key senators to discourage his selection. In Douglas Soutar's words, "it would have been too bad to turn the clock back to the first few years of the NLRB and those types."[3]

Employers realized they would not get one of their own. They also knew that Secretary of Labor Ray Marshall wanted to avoid a public confrontation over the appointment, which meant the Carter administration would push Pollitt only so far.[4] Walther and Fanning strongly supported nominating John Truesdale, then NLRB executive secretary. Truesdale, fifty-six, was a long-term career professional who had joined the NLRB as a field examiner.[5] For employers, Truesdale was not as management oriented as Walther but was certainly acceptable, particularly when compared to Pollitt. Although Truesdale, management believed, could "end up a little liberal," he was conservative enough to "help move Fanning to the middle."[6] Truesdale's appointment in August 1977 was in the tradition of many appointments to the NLRB, where as one scholar put it, "the President's incentive is to accommodate the interests of both sides, giving greater weight to the interests of the in group, and to arrive at solutions that divert neither attention nor resources from all other things the White House must do."[7]

As a result of the bitter fight over labor law reform in 1978, however, mutual accommodation between business and organized labor on NLRB appointments gave way to mutual mistrust and hostility. Organized labor, frustrated and angered not only by the defeat of its legislative program but also by what it considered employers' unfair tactics in working against the bill, retaliated by adopting a confrontational approach to three other NLRB appointments at the very end of the Carter administration.[8] The first controversy centered on the selection of a replacement for General Counsel John Irving, who left office in October 1979, one month before his term expired.[9] Carter nominated William Lubbers for the job. Lubbers, fifty-five, a University of Wisconsin Law School graduate, had been with the Board for twenty-seven years, twenty years of which he had served on Fanning's staff as an attorney-adviser, supervising attorney, and deputy chief counsel. In 1977 Chairman Fanning appointed Lubbers solicitor and, in 1978, executive secretary to replace Truesdale. Fanning called Lubbers "one of the finest lawyers the NLRB ever produced; the essence of judgment, ability, and application."[10]

Business representatives and some of Lubbers's Republican-appointed colleagues at the NLRB, however, considered the nominee "way to the left" and a "throw back to 1936" Wagner Act Board types.[11] More precisely, they intensely disliked Lubbers because he was the "high-priest's [Fanning's] creature," indoctrinated in Fanning's liberal philosophy and beholden to Fanning rather than independent as the statute required.[12] It would be, in the words of one management representative, "a return to the dark days of McCulloch-Ordman."[13] Many feared that an NLRB led by Fanning and Lubbers would implement at least some of the union labor law reform program just killed in Congress.[14]

In mid-October 1979 Senator Orrin Hatch and his aide, Robert Hunter, told Secretary Marshall that the nomination of "so biased a candidate" could be construed only as a case of "shoving it to business" on the part of organized labor and the White House, probably in response to the defeat of the labor law reform bill. Hatch promised a "real donnybrook" if Lubbers were nominated, saying that he would "do everything in his power to fight it."[15] At the same time, the status of Board member Murphy, whose term expired in a few months, was being discussed. Marshall said that Murphy was not his choice for reappointment. Hatch believed, however, that Marshall was "angling," using Murphy as part of a deal on Lubbers whereby "Marshall was willing to eat it by taking Murphy if [Hatch and business] were willing to eat it by taking Lubbers."[16] A Murphy-for-Lubbers trade never appealed to key employer representatives involved in the appointments process because they considered the job of general counsel much more important than the position of Board member.[17] The trade rumor persisted, however, and when her reappointment remained in doubt into December 1979, Murphy concluded that she was being held hostage to Lubbers's appointment and found that "disrespectful." When the White House was willing to offer her only an interim appointment, she resigned.[18]

In another maneuver designed to underscore the depth of employer opposition to Lubbers, former NLRB chairman Edward Miller, former general counsel Peter Nash, and former Board member Peter Walther appeared at Lubbers's nomination hearing and testified openly against his appointment. Although Miller described Lubbers as conscientious and able and Fanning as honorable and able, he caustically compared Lubbers's nomination to "running the judge's brother for District Attorney" and said that there were hundreds of capable lawyers qualified to be general counsel "who did not spend most of their legal career as an amanuensis for the present Chairman of the National Labor Relations Board."[19] Senator Hatch, using information provided by the Business

Roundtable, Chamber of Commerce, and Labor Policy Association, questioned Lubbers about his rumored assistance to the AFL-CIO in drafting the labor law reform bill. Although Lubbers denied helping write that legislation, he admitted that he and Fanning had met with AFL-CIO attorney Larry Gold and top Meany aide Thomas Donahue in July 1977 and subsequently with Gold "two or three" times to provide "technical assistance." When asked by Hatch if he had prepared any of Fanning's testimony on the labor law reform bill, Lubbers responded that his status at the time as "confidential advisor" to Fanning made it improper for him to reply to the question.[20]

The AFL-CIO persisted, however, and made Lubbers a test of Carter's commitment to unionized labor, particularly after the president's lukewarm efforts on behalf of the labor law reform bill.[21] When the Senate failed to act on the nomination before recessing, Carter gave Lubbers a recess appointment that permitted him to serve as general counsel until confirmed or rejected by the Senate or, if the Senate took no action, until the end of 1980.[22] Despite a filibuster supported by the Business Roundtable and organized by Hatch (or what Hatch preferred to call an "extended educational dialogue"), in April 1980 the Senate voted to confirm Lubbers for a full term as general counsel.[23]

The fight over Lubbers's nomination had taken months. Still, the organized labor–organized management confrontation over NLRB appointments continued. The Carter White House had decided not to announce Murphy's replacement, thirty-nine-year-old Donald Zimmerman, until after Lubbers's appointment was finally settled. In addition, John Truesdale's first term as Board member expired in August 1980. Organized business's strategy was to delay both appointments in this election year so that a Republican president could make the choices. Employers were convinced that Democratic presidents appointed "nominal Republicans with basic pro-labor sympathies."[24] Management's strategy of delay worked in Truesdale's situation but not in Zimmerman's.

Many employers were suspicious of Zimmerman, believing that he had been immersed too long in the liberal approach of his long-time mentor, Republican senator Jacob Javits of New York. In 1974 Javits had appointed Zimmerman minority counsel to the Labor Subcommittee of the Senate Labor and Human Resources Committee. He became minority counsel to the full committee in 1977.[25] In that capacity his cooperation with organized labor during the debate over the labor law reform bill convinced employers that Zimmerman "would be swept up in the Fanning majority."[26] The administration, however, would not withdraw its nomination. The Senate confirmed Zimmerman, but it took three cloture votes to end the anti-Zimmerman debate organized by Republicans and conservatives.[27] Zimmerman filled what at that time was the longest standing vacancy in the NLRB's history; it had been nine months since Murphy re-signed.[28]

In normal times organized business probably would not have tried to block Zimmerman or Truesdale.[29] Although some employers believed that Truesdale was basically a liberal who had "drifted to Fanning's side against employers" and "veered off like Betty Murphy did," many others considered him a moderate.[30] Nevertheless, Truesdale's reappointment was inextricably connected to the nominations of Lubbers and Zimmerman, whose appointments caused employers to unite in opposition to Truesdale. The strategy was to stall the reappointment decision until after the November presidential election and, in the meantime, to use the Truesdale renomination hearings as a platform for claiming that organized labor had gained control of the NLRB and for portraying Truesdale as one who favored employers only in the six months before his renomination hearing, when, Hatch charged, he was "running for this position."[31] The strategy worked. Truesdale's nomination was still pending when the Senate adjourned, and Carter had to make another recess appointment in order to return Truesdale to the Board.[32] Truesdale resigned on January 26, 1981, when the newly elected Republican administration of Ronald Reagan withdrew his nomination. The Board, still chaired by John Fanning, immediately named Truesdale executive secretary, the position he had held for five years before his appointment as Board member in 1977.[33]

The Reagan NLRB: An Ideological Pursuit of Conservative Goals

Truesdale's resignation left the Board with three members: Fanning, Jenkins, and Zimmerman. Penello had resigned on January 7, 1981, seven months before the expiration of his second term. Although a Democrat, Penello said that he stayed on the Board until after the November presidential election, at a substantial personal financial sacrifice, because he feared that the Carter administration would replace him with someone whose views were "philosophically incompatible" with his own.[34] At the very outset of his administration, therefore, President Reagan had the opportunity to make two appointments to the Board, including the designation of a new chairman.

The Business Roundtable Labor-Management Committee was prepared to move quickly to exploit the great opportunity the 1980 elections provided. Not only was a Republican conservative in the White House, but Republicans were a majority in the Senate. Although the House majority was nominally Democratic, organized labor estimated that it had only 130 reliable votes left in a total of 435.[35] The Reagan administration's transition team told the Business Roundtable that it planned to achieve more "balance" in the Board by selecting new members from the management community. The transition team also made a list of several important policy issues the new Board would need to confront. All of them involved controversial decisions of the Fanning Board, including whether an employer should be obliged to bargain about a decision to close part of its business, whether a union should be given greater access to private employer property for organizational purposes, and whether the NLRB had the authority to issue a bargaining order without a representation election when a union had never attained an authorization-card majority.[36]

The Business Roundtable designated Douglas Soutar to work closely with the Reagan transition team. Soutar was to be a source of nominations for positions below the level of cabinet secretary, primarily agencies in the labor-management area such as the NLRB, Equal Employment Opportunity Commission, National Mediation Board, and Occupational Safety and Health Administration. Employers wanted a strong Board chairman to "chill" general counsel Lubbers[37] and strong conservative candidates who could turn around a Board "gone so far to the left."[38] Still, management's nominees were not conservative enough for Reagan's White House advisers,[39] who judged candidates on the basis of ideology and involvement in the Reagan campaign without regard for accommodating the interests of labor and business.[40] The White House delayed its selection of anyone for the Board for almost six months. The delay suggested that the Reagan administration either was uninterested in labor-management matters or was trying to sabotage the Board, which for more than eight months was forced to function with only three members.[41]

By mid-April 1981 management groups had united behind Senator Orrin Hatch, now chairman of the Senate Labor Committee, to urge Reagan to appoint the committee's chief counsel, Robert Hunter, as chairman or member of the Board. Before becoming chief counsel when Hatch assumed the chairmanship of the Senate Labor Committee after the 1980 election, Hunter had been Hatch's legislative director and legislative adviser on the committee. In that capacity he had organized the successful anti-labor reform bill filibuster that Hatch had led in 1977–78. He had also served as Senate Labor Committee counsel for Republican senator Robert Taft, Jr., from 1974 to 1977. Hunter had NLRB experience as an attorney in the Buffalo and Cincinnati regional offices from 1969 to 1974.[42]

His supporters portrayed Hunter as evenhanded and fair and not an ideologue, although "generally conservative." They also described him as one who accepted collective bargaining and would promote "harmony between labor and management."[43] His views on labor relations as set forth in a chapter he wrote for the conservative Heritage Foundation's 1981 book *Mandate for Leadership:*

Policy Management in a Conservative Administration contradicted his supporters' claims. The Heritage Foundation was known as President Reagan's favorite "think tank," and its conclusions and recommendations reflected the opinions of the political right on the public policy issues of the day.[44]

Hunter's 48-page chapter, in a 1,093-page tome on restructuring the federal bureaucracy, was devoted primarily to the Department of Labor but included specific recommendations for changes in the Taft-Hartley Act and the NLRB. Most revealing was Hunter's call for repeal of those Taft-Hartley provisions "which establish collective rights as paramount to individual rights."[45] That had been a goal of employer groups since the Wagner Act was passed in 1935. To Hunter, the purpose of the act was not to encourage unionization and collective bargaining but "to balance the rights of employees to organize and select a union or to freely reject such representation."[46] This "personal free choice" to reject as well as choose collective bargaining, Hunter said at his nomination hearing, was the "heart" of the Taft-Hartley statutory scheme.[47] In his Heritage Foundation chapter Hunter criticized the NLRB for adopting an "'activist' stance manifested by an anti-business, pro-labor bias" and for straying from the "neutral role between labor and management" assigned the agency by Congress. In Hunter's opinion "the Board's bias had permeated the attitude of enforcement field officials throughout the NLRB's Regional Offices," justifiably causing employers to perceive the NLRB as anti-business.[48]

When questioned during his nomination hearing, however, Hunter was evasive, if not disingenuous, about the views he had expressed for the Heritage Foundation. He claimed that he did not consider himself the author of the chapter but was rather a project coordinator or team leader who simply "honchoed" a collective enterprise involving several individuals. The Heritage Foundation was actually the author of his chapter, Hunter said, since the foundation retained ultimate editing and publication rights and did not give him a chance to review the final product before it went to press.[49]

A footnote on the first page of the chapter identified Hunter as the person solely responsible for the chapter's contents and as the single source to which all views expressed in the chapter were to be attributed. When asked about the note, Hunter said that it was the foundation's note, not his, and that he knew nothing about it until it appeared in the final volume published for sale. Asked why he did not disclaim the document if it contained views alien to his own, Hunter evaded the question by thanking the committee for the opportunity to clarify the situation. Nevertheless, Hunter faced an affable panel of Democratic and well as Republican senators who voted unanimously to support his appointment.[50] The full Senate, by voice vote on September 15, 1981, confirmed Hunter as Board member to replace John Truesdale.[51]

Reagan's choice for the chairmanship and the seat vacated by the retiring John Penello was John Van de Water, a sixty-four-year-old professor and management consultant from southern California who advised employers on how to resist unionization.[52] In a surprise move Reagan granted recess appointments to Van de Water and Hunter in August 1981.[53] *Business Week* believed that Reagan was tilting the NLRB with a pro-management majority that would make it harder for unions to organize and easier for companies to avoid unionization or decertify existing unions.[54] At Van de Water's nomination hearing on September 30, 1981, the AFL-CIO, whose views on the nominee had not been sought by the White House, objected to the appointment of "a man who has devoted a substantial part of his professional career to putting together anti-union campaigns and anti-union materials."[55] AFL-CIO secretary-treasurer Thomas Donahue cited, among other things, an excerpt from a lecture given by Van de Water in which he boasted:

> In the last 130 union elections I've been involved in, where we had to go to an election—I couldn't even begin to count those situations where we got the union to withdraw after they had enough signups to have an election but they found that they couldn't win it—the unions have lost the election in 125 of the cases. The only cases where they've won the election was where there was no more than two weeks or less to plan management's campaign.[56]

In that same lecture, Donahue told the Senate Labor Committee, Van de Water advised employers that they could "almost always" tell employees whatever they wanted to; it was simply a matter of finding the right way to say it. Van de Water gave an example of what "almost nobody knew" employers could say to employees considering unionization: "Fellows and Ladies, I want you to know as a matter of company policy that even though we would bargain in good faith with the union, if it were voted in, if after good-faith bargaining we could not reach an agreement and the union called you out on strike, we would immediately hire replacements for strikers. And you people would be out of a job."[57]

On October 8, 1981, Van de Water claimed that the original tape of his lecture no longer existed and said that a magazine editor had prepared an edited version of his remarks, which he had not seen or authorized before its circulation. He was also unable to provide any useful information concerning the alleged success rate of his consulting operation in representation elections because neither his records nor his memory went back that far.[58] On November 19 the sixteen-member Senate Labor Committee by a tie vote failed to approve Reagan's nomination of Van de Water to be NLRB chairman.[59]

The Reagan administration resubmitted the Van de Water nomination to the

Senate on February 4, 1992. Under his recess appointment Van de Water was eligible to remain in office until the adjournment of the second session of the Senate in December 1982.[60] The decisive blow to Van de Water's nomination came from a most unexpected source. The National Right to Work Committee asked President Reagan to withdraw the nomination because Van de Water had publicly advocated the agency shop as a preferable alternative to right-to-work laws. He had also publicly approved a Fifth Circuit Court of Appeals ruling permitting union shop agreements on federal government enclaves in states where right-to-work laws prohibited such forms of union security.[61]

Van de Water failed to obtain Senate confirmation and resigned from the Board when his recess appointment expired in December 1982.[62] As objectionable as Van de Water was to organized labor, Reagan's next choice for the chairmanship, Donald Dotson, showed labor that it had won a battle but lost a war. One day before Van de Water's resignation John Fanning left the NLRB, where he had completed an unprecedented fifth term and spent twenty-five years.[63] John C. Miller, who had been chief counsel to Van de Water at the Board, served temporarily as chairman until the new Senate could confirm Dotson in 1983.[64] At the same time, Reagan announced his intention to nominate Patricia Diaz Dennis, a management attorney, as the Board's fifth member, to complete the remaining portion of Van de Water's term, which ran to August 27, 1986.[65]

Dotson, who filled the vacancy left by Fanning, was described by one analyst of appointments to the NLRB as "staunchly antiunion, a crusader for the Reagan cause, and a protégé of Jesse Helms," well-known conservative senator from North Carolina.[66] Dotson, forty-two, graduated from the University of North Carolina in 1960 and received a law degree from Wake Forest University in North Carolina after serving five years in the navy. After law school Dotson worked as an attorney in the NLRB's regional office in Winston-Salem, North Carolina. He left the NLRB in 1973 to be labor counsel for Westinghouse Electric Corporation before becoming chief labor counsel at Wheeling-Pittsburgh Steel Corporation in 1976. In 1981 President Reagan named Dotson assistant secretary of labor for labor-management relations.[67]

Conservative groups such as the National Right to Work Committee were delighted at the prospect of the appointment of Dotson to the Board because he would administer the act "with the view that worker rights and free choice predominate over parochial union or employer interests."[68] Nevertheless, although Dotson was expected to lean heavily toward management in Board cases and although he had practical agency and corporate experience in labor relations, many business leaders and organizations, including some of the most prominent former Republican appointees to the NLRB, were either opposed to or apprehensive about his appointment.[69] Business leaders, particularly members of the Business Roundtable, wanted someone who would move the Board in a pro-employer direction, but they preferred the nonconfrontational, quiet approach of former chairman Miller. Dotson was not the type they would have chosen: "He was too extreme and uncompromising—and, as insiders well knew, he had an abrasive personality that promoted administrative conflict, bad feelings, and instability." Yet it was Dotson as ideologue and loyalist who appealed to a Reagan White House seen as "interested in destroying established traditions, not in following them."[70]

The Senate posed little opposition this time, in part because it had already routinely confirmed Dotson as assistant secretary of labor. The AFL-CIO, which had used up too much political capital in blocking Van de Water, abandoned its plan to testify and lobby against Dotson.[71] The Senate confirmed Dotson without objection in February 1983, and he took the oath of office as NLRB chairman on March 21.[72]

The Dotson Board

Internal Dissension

Dotson plunged the NLRB into controversy almost immediately. On April 22 Hugh Reilly, who had worked closely with Dotson as his executive assistant at the Labor Department, became the Board's solicitor.[73] Before joining Dotson at the Department of Labor, Reilly had been a staff attorney for eight years with the conservative National Right to Work Legal Defense Fund.[74] Organized labor saw Reilly's appointment as turning "an agency whose purpose is to promote collective bargaining over to someone whose career has been devoted to destroying unionism."[75]

Within two weeks of Reilly's appointment, Dotson sought to reclaim the authority the Herzog Board had delegated to the general counsel to conduct enforcement of Board decisions in court. He proposed to give that authority to Solicitor Reilly.[76] Dotson told his Board colleagues that he would "make no bones about it": this was a "substantial change," not a "cosmetic change."[77] Because the general counsel to be stripped of this important authority was liberal William Lubbers, with a year remaining in his term, and the solicitor to be given the authority was conservative Hugh Reilly, Dotson's proposal portended a major political shift at the Board. The consequent public furor culminated in hearings in June 1983 before joint subcommittees of the House Labor Committee and Government Operations Committee.

Dotson told the joint committees that he wanted the solicitor to supervise the Board's enforcement activities because he had witnessed attorneys under the general counsel engage in "some of the sleaziest tactics" he had ever seen.[78] His proposed reorganization, Dotson claimed, was also intended to respond to the complaints of "sitting members" of the Board who believed the general counsel's Enforcement Division did not always accurately represent the Board's view to the courts. Under persistent and unfriendly questioning by the Democratic members of the subcommittees, however, Dotson could give no specific example of sleazy tactics and withdrew his characterization as "a little too strong."[79] Board members Jenkins, Zimmerman, and Hunter, moreover, when questioned directly, denied knowing of any case in which the general counsel had substantially misrepresented the Board's position in court. They also denied ever complaining to Dotson about any alleged misrepresentation by the general counsel.[80]

Dotson admitted that he had not consulted with Lubbers about the proposal or his concerns about alleged sleazy tactics or misrepresentations of the Board's positions in court. "Frankly," he said, "I didn't care what Mr. Lubber's opinion was."[81] One committee member accused Dotson of using his proposal to diminish Lubber's independence and authority, since it would be a year before President Reagan could appoint a new general counsel.[82]

The House committee unearthed two letters that anti-Dotson forces would certainly have used in any effort to block his nomination. In one, a letter to the *American Bar Association Journal* in August 1980, Dotson pilloried the Fanning Board for "its tendency to act as a legal aid society and organizing arm for unions." In the same letter he said that the strike had become a "concerted effort employing violence, intimidation, and political intervention" and that collective bargaining was often "labor monopoly, the destruction of individual freedom, and the destruction of the marketplace as the mechanism for determining the value of labor." In the other letter, written in January 1978 to another law journal, Dotson wrote that "unionized labor relations, shortsighted demands, greed, and debilitating work rules" were major reasons for the decline of once healthy industries. He also rose to the defense of J.P. Stevens, claiming that the union-organized boycott of the company was undertaken without the consent of Stevens employees, who, Dotson said, were trying to decertify their unions. At the end of this letter Dotson provided the address of the "J.P. Stevens Employees' Educational Committee," where more information would be made available.[83] William Clay, Democratic chairman of the Labor-Management Subcommittee, said that he "did not see how anyone holding these views could render an impartial and unbiased opinion."[84]

In the course of his exchanges with the joint committee Dotson set forth his understanding of the purpose of Taft-Hartley: "This law . . . gives people the right to refrain from union membership. There are people who seem to think that it is unlawful for an employer not to want a union in his business, and there are people who seem to think that there is something wrong with somebody who doesn't want to be a union member, but our law protects these people as well."[85] Dotson later charged that he was being subjected to a press-created drama of "good guys and bad guys" and that he had been cast in the role of Darth Vader leading the "forces of darkness." He denied that he was a union buster but coupled his denial to criticism of past NLRBs whose ignorance of the "laws of economics" had resulted in decisions rendering U.S. industry less able to withstand foreign competition.[86]

Although Dotson portrayed himself as the innocent victim of unfounded personal attacks, the Board itself was soon deep in internal feuding sparked by Dotson's personality and management style. Public reports of infighting at the agency focused on Dotson's abrasive and combative style and authoritarian behavior, which had caused dissension and mistrust even among the Board's conservative majority. Ironically, the interpersonal conflict was especially sharp between Dotson and fellow Reagan appointee Patricia Diaz Dennis, who consistently voted with Dotson in Board decisions and approved of the Reagan Board's policy of deregulating labor relations by reducing federal government involvement. Dennis, thirty-six, a labor relations attorney with the American Broadcasting Company for five years before joining the Board,[87] disapproved of Dotson's attempt to reduce the authority of general counsel Lubbers and believed that Reilly gave the agency an inappropriate "political flavor." In a shouting match with Dotson, Dennis argued that a quasi-judicial independent agency such as the NLRB "should be above brawling with editorial writers and commentators." Dennis, the only woman on the Board and one of the highest-ranking Hispanics in the Reagan administration, was particularly angered by a rumor that Dotson had made a racial slur by referring to her as a "breeder" when he learned that she was pregnant. (Dotson denied the rumor and called it "an outrageous thing.") Board member Hunter reportedly tried to duck the crossfire by keeping his office television set turned to daytime television shows.[88]

The Board was being wrecked not only by poor morale but by what some saw as a deliberate attempt to have the agency wither under the weight of an unprecedented and ever-growing backlog. The backlog of undecided unfair labor practice cases at the Board rose from 623 at the beginning of fiscal year 1983 to 1,095 at the beginning of 1984, the largest in the agency's history. The number of unfair labor practice cases decided by the Board dropped to 602 in 1983 from 1,051 in 1982. Even as a House subcommittee of the Government Operations Committee was pressing the Board to increase its monthly total of decided unfair labor practice cases, a goal set by Dotson of 125 each month dropped to 62 in May and 70 in June 1984.[89]

In 1984 two House subcommittees called the delays caused by the Dotson Board's policy of conscious inaction another manifestation of the Board's partisan bias, because delays almost always favored employers, adversely affected union organizing drives, and weakened the protection of workers' rights under the act. The Government Operations Subcommittee also condemned the Dotson Board's "icing" of more than six hundred unfair labor practice cases involving issues it wanted to decide contrary to precedent until the arrival of a case with a fact pattern providing the most suitable basis for a reversal of Board doctrine.[90] As these undecided cases piled up at the Board, the Reagan White House showed its satisfaction with or at least disinterest in the situation by not re-nominating Howard Jenkins in August 1983 and then allowing his vacancy on the Board to go unfilled for more than a year without even suggesting a possible replacement to the Senate.[91]

An Ideological Agenda

At the same time that the Dotson Board was hindering implementation of the act by allowing its case backlog to grow at unprecedented rates, its Reagan-appointed majority was delivering serious blows to unionization and collective bargaining in the cases it was deciding. A Dotson-led majority, unsympathetic to the Wagner Act–rooted purposes of Taft-Hartley, weakened the obligation to bargain collectively, once central to the purpose and policies of the act, by excluding management decisions it considered too important to an employer's business to be negotiated with a union. The Dotson Board's speedy and extensive overturning of precedents that conservatives considered pro-union brought about a shift in national labor policy that freed employers in many important ways from the constraints of workers and unions.

The intensity of this drive to overturn liberal precedents was controversial but not new. The Eisenhower Board had overruled Truman Board precedents in the same expeditious way, and the Kennedy Board, in turn, quickly overturned many key Eisenhower Board decisions. The Nixon and Ford Boards and the Carter Board continued the practice of reversing major doctrines of their philosophically incompatible predecessors. What was different during the Reagan presidency, however, was the economic context in which these changes in national labor policy occurred. The deindustrialization of the United States was under way. Particularly during the severe economic recession of the early 1980s, plant closings were commonplace, devastating whole communities. Businesses routinely relocated to non-union areas of the country. The rapid growth of the "union-busting" labor relations consultant industry, moreover, demonstrated many employers' determination to stay or become unorganized.[92] Writing in 1985, former Nixon Board member and management attorney Peter Walther admitted that strikes had become a more effective employer weapon than union weapon in the economic situation of the 1980s,[93] because employers were more likely to take advantage of their lawful authority to fill the jobs of economic strikers with permanent replacements.

The proportion of the nonagricultural workforce that was unionized had declined from approximately 35 percent in the 1950s to about 18 percent in 1987. This drop was due in great part to intensified employer resistance to unionization and collective bargaining as well as high unemployment levels and the harsh effects of foreign competition, especially on the formerly highly unionized but now deteriorating basic industries, such as steel and automobiles. Unions were on the defensive, fighting rear guard actions with "concession bargaining." At a time when the national labor policy favoring unionization and collective bargaining was in greatest jeopardy and in need of the strictest enforcement of those purposes in the act, however, the Dotson Board accelerated the decline of unionism and collective bargaining with rulings that made it more difficult for unions to organize and severely weakened collective bargaining. As Dotson saw it, the country's economic problems, including the difficulty in meeting foreign competition, were the best reasons for deregulating labor-management relations because the costs of federal regulation reduced management's ability to compete. The deregulation of business was a major goal of the Reagan administration.[94]

In October 1983 former NLRB general counsel John Irving predicted with what one observer called "chilling accuracy" precisely how the Dotson Board's decisions would respond to the frustration of employers with what Irving termed the liberal decisions of prior Boards, which he said intruded on the bargaining process, emphasized the promotion of unionization, and preferred employee rights over business necessity.[95] Former chairman John Fanning criticized the new Board for having an "agenda" for revoking long-standing doctrines, but that was not unprecedented, since friendly congressional labor committees had used the congressional hearing format in the past to provide "agendas" to newly appointed NLRBs.[96]

Irving predicted a series of reversals of prior NLRB doctrines in which the Dotson Board would permit employers, without bargaining, to make mid-contract plant relocations, absent specific contractual language forbidding such moves; choose private labor arbitration rather than NLRB procedures as the method of dispute resolution preferred by national labor policy; establish an employer's right to hire temporary replacements during a lockout; rarely if ever issue bargaining orders, regardless of the nature of employer unfair labor practices, where a union never obtained the support of a majority of the employees; and broaden the scope of the secondary boycott and picketing prohibitions. According to Irving, the Dotson Board would also set aside representation elections only because of "significant" unfair labor practices; permit employers to ban union solicitation on working time without requiring management to spell out specific examples of what constituted nonworking time; narrow the rights of union and nonunion employees to representation at investigatory interviews with management; and prohibit unions from fining strikers who resigned union membership and crossed picket lines to retain their jobs.[97] The Dotson Board did all that and more.

Board member Diaz Dennis attempted to portray the Dotson Board's decisions as merely a "return to normalcy" rather than a curtailment of the rights of individual employees and unions.[98] Irving characterized the Dotson reversals as a counter to the years when the "Board was on an extremely liberal, pro-union jag."[99] Former Board member Peter Walther, admitting that twenty-nine reversals of major Board doctrines in two years seemed "like a large number," tried to pass off the changes in labor policy with a quip: "To get from left field back to center field, one must move to the right."[100] Former Nixon Board chairman Edward Miller said that the Dotson Board decisions had "not effectuated any dramatic or key changes in any long-standing central concepts."[101]

On the contrary, the Dotson Board's rulings ended employers' statutory obligation to bargain about many major management decisions, substantially deregulated representation election campaigns, increased management's authority to discipline employees for engaging in activity previously protected by the act, and in many other ways elevated management's authority to manage over statutory obligations. The Dotson Board decisions also weakened unions at a time when the economic situation made them most vulnerable.

Facilitating Employer Resistance to Unionization

Like the Eisenhower and Nixon Boards, the Dotson Board rejected what it called the protectionism of Democrat-appointed Boards as unnecessary because employees were presumably mature adults capable of understanding and evaluating the campaign tactics and propaganda of employers and unions. The deregulation of representation campaigns began even before Dotson became chairman. In 1982 a majority of Van de Water, Hunter, and Zimmerman, in *Midland National Life Insurance*,[102] returned to the "sound principles" of the Murphy Board's *Shopping Kart Food Market*[103] doctrine of not inquiring into

the truth or falsity of campaign statements and not setting represent.
tions aside on the basis of misleading campaign statements.

After she joined the Board, Diaz Dennis embraced the *Midland* appro
is folly to profess belief in democracy—to believe that American workin_ men
and women are capable of choosing their mayors, congressional representatives
and presidents—then say that NLRB election campaigns must be closely regulated to protect the voters from their own possible misjudgments."[104] By equating political elections and representation elections, Diaz Dennis was resurrect-
ing an old justification for deregulating representation election campaigning that
was always at odds with the understanding that the relationship of politician to
citizen was fundamentally different from the relationship of employer to employee. As Judge Learned Hand stated more than fifty years before Diaz Dennis's assertion, words took on meaning only in the setting in which they were
used, and the "relation between the speaker and the hearer" was probably the
most important factor: "What to an outsider will be no more than the vigorous
presentation of a conviction, to an employee may be the manifestation of a
determination which it is not safe to thwart."[105] Circuit court judge Paul Hays,
commenting on a decision by his colleagues, put it another way: "The majority
opinion demonstrates once more the inescapable truth that United States Circuit
Judges safely ensconced in their chambers do not feel threatened by what employers tell their employees. An employer can dress up his threats in the language of prediction ('You will lose your job' rather than 'I will fire you') and
fool judges. He doesn't fool his employees; they know perfectly clearly what he
means."[106] In *Rossmore House*[107] Dotson, Hunter, and Diaz Dennis said that it
would no longer be per se an unfair labor practice for employers to interrogate
known union supporters during a representation campaign. In returning to the
Eisenhower Board's *Blue Flash* decision,[108] the Dotson Board rejected the Fanning Board's conclusion that questioning any employees about their union preferences, including known union advocates, was inherently coercive even in the
absence of threats or promises of benefits.[109] *Rossmore House* demonstrated the
Dotson Board's rejection of any possibility that such questioning of employees
by employers who controlled their jobs (unlike innocent political discussions)
could coerce those employees questioned as well as other employees aware of
the employer's interrogations.[110]

At the same time, the Dotson majority relaxed restrictions on what an employer could tell employees during a representation election campaign, particularly about the purportedly adverse economic consequences of unionization.
To the Dotson Board, employer statements to employees associating unionization with plant closings, strikes, unprofitability, and layoffs were merely accu-

rate communications of the "economic realities" of unionization and collective bargaining, understandably stressing the drawbacks rather than the advantages of union representation.[111] In the Reagan Board's opinion it was once again permissible for an employer to tell employees that collective bargaining began "from scratch" or from "ground zero," implying that employees could lose their existing pay and benefits if they unionized. One employer showed employees a blank sheet of paper to dramatize how they could lose with a union.[112]

The Reagan Board also found no violation when a supervisor told a worker that wearing a union button "may be hazardous to your health,"[113] or when a foreman asked a union supporter why he was wearing that "chicken shit badge,"[114] or when an employer emphasized to employees its legal right to relocate the plant despite the absence of any evidence suggesting it would do so.[115] The co-chairman of the American Bar Association's Committee on the Development of Law under the NLRA concluded: "The cumulative effect of the Board's permissive attitude toward interrogation of employees as to their union sympathies, and its failure to find threats inherent in language that unmistakably carries such connotations, is unmistakably damaging to union representation campaigns and encourages management to fight organizational efforts 'to the hilt.' "[116]

In another serious setback to union organizing efforts the Dotson Board ruled in *Gourmet Foods*[117] that under no circumstances—no matter how outrageous or pervasive an employer's unfair labor practices—would it issue a bargaining order when the organizing union was unable to demonstrate that it ever had majority support among the employees in an appropriate bargaining unit. In 1982, in *Conair Corp.,* the Carter Board majority of Fanning, Jenkins, and Zimmerman had issued the first nonmajority bargaining order. In *Conair* the majority accused the minority of Hunter and Van de Water of attempting to cloak their tolerance of the company's pervasive unfair labor practices during a representation campaign "in a defense of majoritarian principle" and said that they rejected "this masquerade."[118] By the time of *Gourmet Foods,* however, Fanning and Jenkins had departed and Zimmerman had become the dissenter. He still maintained that the nonmajority bargaining order was the only remedy sufficient to protect employees against employers whose unlawful acts were "so coercive as to prevent majority support from ever developing."[119]

Limiting Management's Obligation to Bargain

While the Dotson Board was facilitating employers' resistance to unionization, the Board and the Supreme Court were curtailing the statutory rights of those who did organize by characterizing certain management decisions as too important to be subject to collective bargaining with a union. The right to bargain collectively for higher wages, shorter hours, and better working conditions, including job security, is at the center of the Taft-Hartley Act's purposes and policies. In addition, many entrepreneurial decisions, such as contracting out or relocating bargaining unit work, total or partial closings of business operations, mergers, and replacing bargaining unit employees with computerized machinery, bear on all aspects of workers' jobs, possibly even determining if their jobs will exist.

Even before *Fibreboard,*[120] one of the most hotly contested issues in U.S. labor law was whether the act entitled workers and their representatives to participate in the making of major business and investment decisions. The worth of the act depends in great part on the importance of collective bargaining, which in turn depends in great part on where the line, if any, is drawn between exclusive management functions on one side and the subjects of joint union-management responsibilities on the other. Decisions that expanded employers' unilateral control over the most important entrepreneurial decisions undercut collective bargaining and, therefore, the purposes and policies of the act.

The greatest curtailment of employers' statutory obligation to bargain came in three cases: the Dotson Board's decisions in *Milwaukee Spring* and *Otis Elevator* and the Supreme Court's ruling in *First National Maintenance Corp.*[121] In 1981 the Supreme Court in *First National Maintenance,* a dicta-filled decision riddled with value judgments unsubstantiated by legislative history or any other evidence, removed employers' decisions to close part of their businesses from the list of mandatory subjects of bargaining.[122] The Court admitted that Congress had not indicated what issues of mutual concern to unions and management it intended to exclude from mandatory bargaining, if any. Nevertheless, the Court was not deterred from asserting, on the basis apparently of only the majority's notions of what the management-labor relationship ought to be, that "Congress had no expectation that the elected union representative would become an equal partner in the running of the business enterprise." The dominant influence of the personal value judgments of the majority of justices in this case is evidenced by their heavy reliance on Justice Potter Stewart's dicta concerning management rights in his concurring opinion in *Fibreboard.*[123]

Among other unsupported pronouncements, the Court said, "Management must be free from the constraints of the bargaining process to the extent essential for the running of a profitable business." It proceeded to fashion a cost-benefit test to determine if there was an obligation to bargain: "In view of an employer's need for unencumbered decision making, bargaining over management decisions that have a substantial impact on the continued availability of

employment should be required only if the benefit, for labor-management relations and the collective bargaining process, outweighs the burden placed on the
conduct of the business."[124] After applying this test abstractly to the issue of
partial closings, the Court simply asserted that "the harm likely to be done to
[First National Maintenance's] need to operate freely" in these matters "outweighs the incremental benefit that might be gained through the union's participation in making the decision."[125]

Justices William Brennan and Thurgood Marshall, in dissent, criticized the
majority for deciding an important question of industrial relations "on the basis
of pure speculation." Brennan and Marshall also rejected the majority's cost-
benefit test, not only because it too was based "solely on speculation" but also
because it was a one-sided approach that took into account "only the interests
of management" and failed "to consider the legitimate employment interests of
the workers and their union."[126] The message was clear: the more important the
entrepreneurial decision, the more excluded and protected it would be from the
reach of the statutory duty to bargain. Despite the Court's cautionary words
about the limited applicability of its decision,[127] the Reagan Board majority not
only adopted but extended the Supreme Court's value judgments favoring management prerogatives.

In August 1983 the Seventh Circuit Court of Appeals granted the Dotson
Board's motion to remand the *Milwaukee Spring* case to the new Reagan majority.[128] In *Milwaukee Spring* I the employer, after trying unsuccessfully to get the
union to agree to wage reductions during the term of a collective bargaining
agreement, transferred bargaining unit work, without the union's consent, from
its unionized plant to one of its non-union plants, where wage rates were much
lower. In 1982 Van de Water, Fanning, and Jenkins had agreed that the company's midcontract decision to cut labor costs by relocating bargaining unit
work without the union's consent was an unfair labor practice. They said that
the work was moved to avoid compliance with the wage provisions of the
parties' contract in repudiation of a collective bargaining agreement that
contained no explicit language permitting the company to transfer a part of
its unionized operations during the term of the contract without union consent.[129]

On remand from the court of appeals, *Milwaukee Spring* I was reversed by
Dotson, Hunter, and Diaz Dennis. They affirmed the company's transfer of
bargaining unit work to nonbargaining unit employees as a management right
that could be limited only by a contractual provision explicitly prohibiting such
transfers of work. Some sophistry lurked in the Dotson Board's contention that
the wage provisions of the parties' collective bargaining contract were not vio-

lated because there were no bargaining unit employees left, since their jobs were being performed elsewhere by non-union workers not covered by the contract. According to the majority, moreover, it was "not for the Board to create an implied work-preservation clause in every American labor agreement based on wage and benefits or recognition provisions," and it expressly declined to do so.[130] Because it would be an undisputed unfair labor practice for the employer to have reduced the contractually set wages paid to bargaining unit employees while continuing to have them perform the work, Zimmerman, in a lengthy dissent, argued that the majority's decision permitted the employer to accomplish indirectly what it would not have been permitted to do directly.[131]

Member Diaz Dennis claimed that the *Milwaukee Spring* II decision would encourage frank collective bargaining between a company with economic problems and a union now aware that its bargaining unit work could be sent elsewhere.[132] More likely, *Milwaukee Spring* II increased management's ability to oust unions or at least put them in a more vulnerable concessionary and compromising position at the bargaining table. Given the Reagan Board's subsequent decision in *Otis Elevator*,[133] moreover, Diaz Dennis's comment could be seen as cynical if not naive.

In 1981 Fanning, Jenkins, and Zimmerman had found the Otis Elevator Company guilty of a refusal to bargain when it bypassed its employees' union representative and dealt directly with bargaining unit employees about transferring them from their work site in New Jersey to Connecticut as part of the employer's decision to consolidate its research and development operations.[134] Once again, a court of appeals granted the Dotson Board's request for a remand to reconsider the decision in light of the Supreme Court's opinion in *First National Maintenance*. The Reagan Board unanimously reversed *Otis Elevator* I but on the basis of three different readings of *First National Maintenance*.[135]

A plurality of Dotson and Hunter fashioned a no-bargaining requirement that went far beyond not only the specific circumstances of the *Otis Elevator* case but also the limited reach of *First National Maintenance*. Dotson and Hunter excluded from mandatory bargaining any management decision that affected the "scope, direction, or nature of the business." The critical factor in determining whether an employer's decision was subject to mandatory bargaining, therefore, was the nature of the management decision, "*not* its effect on employees or a union's ability to offer alternatives." Bargaining could be required, Dotson and Hunter allowed, if an employer's decision "turns on direct modification of labor costs" and not a change in the basic direction or nature of the enterprise, but bargaining was not required if labor costs were only one factor among others in the decision.[136] Under the Dotson-Hunter approach, therefore, an almost impossible burden of proof was placed on a union to show that an employer's decision was based *solely* on labor costs before collective bargaining would be required.

Influenced most by "management's need for predictability, flexibility, speed, secrecy, and to operate profitably," Dotson and Hunter ignored the Supreme Court's case-by-case cost-benefit analysis approach (whatever its merits) and simply labeled in advance certain management decisions as not subject to mandatory bargaining: "Such decisions include, *inter alia,* decisions to sell a business or a part thereof, to dispose of its assets, to restructure or to consolidate operations, to subcontract, to invest in labor-saving machinery, to change the methods of finance or of sales, advertising, product design, and all other decisions akin to the foregoing."[137]

Diaz Dennis, in her concurring opinion, generally followed the *First National Maintenance* format requiring the general counsel to prove "that the benefit for the collective bargaining process outweighs the burden on business" before a management decision that focused on the profitability of the employer's operation could become a mandatory subject of bargaining.[138] Zimmerman said that a management decision may be amenable to resolution through collective bargaining where the decision was based on "overall enterprise costs," not just labor costs, but excluded from employers' bargaining obligation decisions "showing . . . the employer's urgent need for the kind of speed, flexibility, or secrecy as referred to by the Supreme Court in *First National Maintenance.* "[139]

Dotson, Hunter, and Diaz Dennis subsequently restricted unions' ability to negotiate the preservation of jobs by relieving employers of the obligation to bargain about even the type of subcontracting the McCulloch Board and the Supreme Court found to be a mandatory subject of bargaining in *Fibreboard*— holding that subcontracting decisions involved a "significant change in the nature and direction" of the business.[140] In an ironic twist on their exclusion of important management decisions from the statutory obligation to bargain, the Reagan Board also relieved employers of their obligation to bargain about certain other decisions because they were not important enough.[141]

Justice Stewart's concurring opinion dicta in *Fibreboard* about employers' prerogatives to make decisions that go to the "core of entrepreneurial control" had become, in the words of one writer, "an incantation" by the Dotson Board and the federal courts to allow employers to avoid bargaining—even their already collectively bargained contracts—when making important decisions about business operations.[142] The more important the management decision, the more the Board and the federal courts subordinated union and employee interests.

Diminished Protected Concerted Activity

The Dotson Board diminished the right to strike guaranteed by Taft-Hartley by prohibiting what previously had been statutorily protected strike and picket line conduct. Its decision in *Clear Pine Mouldings*,[143] for example, was a major departure from Board precedent and policy concerning strike conduct and subsequent reinstatement. Even Republican-appointed Boards had long held that strikers' oral threats against nonstrikers when unaccompanied by serious physical harm to persons or property would not justify an employer's refusal to reinstate those strikers. Strikes were understood to be emotional and heated events that usually involved intemperate and abusive language, extreme charges, and personal insults.[144]

The Reagan Board reversed this long-standing precedent in *Clear Pine Mouldings* by finding oral threats alone sufficient justification for discharging employees if the threat "reasonably tended" to coerce or intimidate employees in the exercise of their rights under the act. According to Dotson and Hunter, with Zimmerman and Diaz Dennis concurring, only "nonthreatening expressions of opinion" were statutorily protected.[145] One commentator called the Dotson-Hunter opinion "a pious pronouncement that employees must deport themselves as ladies and gentlemen or risk the loss of the job that created the emotion in the first place."[146]

Dotson and Hunter rejected another long-established doctrine in which the Board, in determining if reinstatement should be ordered, balanced the severity of an employer's unfair labor practices that provoked a strike against the gravity of a striker's misconduct. There were several reasons underlying this policy: the employer's unlawful conduct may have provoked the employee's misconduct, reinstatement in these situations prevented employers from benefiting from their unfair labor practices by discharging employees and weakening or destroying their unions, and other penalties such as criminal prosecution existed to deter or remedy employee misconduct.[147] Dotson and Hunter, however, said that the statute did not authorize employees to engage in misconduct "in proportion to their individual estimates of the degree of seriousness of an employer's unfair labor practices."[148] Now freed of the balancing test, which Dotson and Hunter said encouraged employee strike and picket line violence, employers, no matter what their unfair labor practices, were entitled to deny reinstatement to any employee whose behavior "exceeded the bounds of peaceful and reasoned conduct."[149] Given its deregulation of employer speech, the Dotson Board majority seemed more concerned with protecting employees from their fellow workers than from employers. The Board's intensified regulation of the speech of union strikers and picketers because other employees were

presumed to be intimidated by it did not jibe with the same Board's deregulation of employer speech in representation campaigns because employees in
those situations were presumed, on the contrary, to be mature, intelligent adults
immune to their employer's anti-union rhetoric, veiled threats, or misrepresentations.

Like other Republican-appointed Boards, the Reagan Board, while deregulating employer speech and other conduct, tightened its regulation of union
and employee conduct undertaken in support of collective goals, even when
these activities involved no violence or other misconduct. The Reagan Board,
for example, broadened its application of the act's secondary boycott provisions,[150] prohibited unions from fining members who resigned their union membership and returned to work during a strike,[151] and permitted employers to
refuse reinstatement to "sympathy" strikers who honored a lawful primary
picket line despite contractual clauses protecting them from discipline for doing
so on the theory that permanently replacing a striker was not the same as discipline.[152] The Dotson majority also read contracts with broad no-strike clauses
that did not specifically mention "sympathy" strikes to include their prohibition.[153] In *Harter Equipment, Inc.* the Reagan Board expanded an employer's
statutory immunity to lock out employees and operate with temporary replacements, because there was "no more fundamental employer interest than continuation of business operations."[154] As one scholar put it, however, it seemed
clearly a discriminatory reprisal for Section 7 activities to deny employees work
solely because of their collective bargaining efforts and then offer that work to
non-union replacements.[155] Former Republican-appointed NLRB chairman Edward Miller always considered that policy the unfair use of an economic
weapon[156]—a judgment underscored by the fact that five years after the lockout
the "temporary" replacements hired by Harter were still performing the jobs of
the employees they had replaced.[157]

Although even Republican-appointed Boards, including the Murphy Board,
had given an expansive reading to employees' Section 7 rights to engage in
concerted activity for the purposes of collective bargaining or other mutual aid
or protection, the Reagan Board considerably narrowed the circumstances under
which an individual employee's actions would be considered concerted activity
protected by the act. The Board's decision in *Meyers Industries,*[158] for example,
reversed a long line of Board decisions that had expanded the definition of
concerted activity to include not only a unionized individual's assertion of
rights under a collective bargaining agreement[159] and a federal or state statute[160]
but also all workers, organized or unorganized, who filed individual claims
under a statute governing workplace safety.[161] The prior Boards presumed that
fellow workers shared the individual's concern with the protested conditions

and supported the individual employee's complaint. In *Meyers Industries* the Reagan majority said that an individual employee would not be considered engaged in concerted activity unless it could be shown that the employee was acting with or on the authority of fellow employees, the employer knew the employee was not acting solely on his or her own behalf, and the activity was protected by the act.[162]

The Reagan Board also reversed a prior decision that had allowed unorganized as well as organized employees to be represented by co-workers in employer-conducted investigatory interviews.[163] In *Sears, Roebuck & Co.*[164] the Board denied unorganized employees a right to representation in a disciplinary interview or at any other time. Even in situations in which organized employees were unlawfully denied their rights to representation, moreover, the Reagan Board said that it would require an employer only to post a notice promising to cease and desist from further unlawful activity and would order an employee's reinstatement only when a discharge was based solely on the employee's refusal to participate in an unlawful interview.[165] As one critic charged, these decisions ignored the effect that disciplining individual employees would have on the collective interests and activities of other employees and allowed the employer to interfere with the development of a collective organization.[166]

Greater Deferral of Statutory Responsibility to Arbitration

Despite its purported concern for individual rights, critics charged the Dotson Board, in another controversial pair of decisions, with abandoning its statutory responsibility to protect the rights of individual employees. The charges focused on the Board's decision to defer certain statutory matters to private contractual grievance-arbitration procedures, not only by staying NLRB processes pending arbitration but also by substantially narrowing the circumstances under which the Board would hear a case after it had been arbitrated. In *United Technologies Corp.*[167] the Reagan majority overruled the Murphy Board's *General American Transportation Corp.*[168] decision and said that when a contractual grievance procedure was available, it would defer to arbitration not only in refusal-to-bargain cases but also in cases involving the alleged restraint or coercion of employees in the exercise of their statutory rights.

This new standard did not constitute a waiver of employees' statutory rights or relegate statutory rights to a private forum, the Dotson majority maintained, but was merely "a postponement of the use of the Board's processes to give the parties' own dispute resolution machinery a chance to succeed."[169] The majority's rationale presumed that the Board would not defer to an arbitration decision unless the arbitrator considered the unfair labor practice aspect of the case and issued a decision that was at least "not clearly repugnant to the purposes and policies of the Act." Those standards for deferral had been in place for more than thirty years, going back to the Eisenhower and Kennedy-Johnson Boards.[170] In *Olin Corp.,* however, the Dotson majority said that adequate arbitral consideration would be presumed if the contractual issue was "factually parallel" to the unfair labor practice issue and the arbitrator was presented "generally" with the facts relevant to the unfair labor practice.[171]

The Board also shifted the burden of proof to the party opposing deferral to demonstrate that the new standard for defining "considered" had not been met. In reconsidering what "clearly repugnant" meant, the Board said that an arbitral award did not have to be "totally consistent with Board precedent" and announced that it would defer "unless the award is 'palpably wrong,' i.e., unless the arbitrator's decision is not susceptible to an interpretation consistent with the act."[172]

According to the Dotson Board, its new deferral-to-arbitration policy was intended to give practical effect to the federal policy favoring labor arbitration. Although the Supreme Court had encouraged the use of labor arbitration to resolve contractual disputes and instructed lower courts to give great deference to arbitral awards, the Court had been unwilling to entrust the enforcement of statutory matters to private labor arbitrators.[173] More accurately, the Dotson deferral decisions were part of its intent to deregulate certain aspects of labor-management relations and to remove or weaken Board restraints on a wide range of employer conduct and decision making. Statutory rights had been subordinated to private interests.

After Dotson: Policing and Refining

Dotson left the NLRB in December 1987, when his term expired. Reagan named an already sitting Board member, James Stephens, chairman in January 1988. Stephens, a Republican and thirty-nine when appointed to the Board in 1985, had been labor counsel to the Senate Labor Committee immediately before his appointment and assistant minority labor counsel to the House Labor Committee from 1977 to 1981. He pledged "hard work, a commitment to fairness, and a belief in our system of peaceful industrial relations through law."[174]

Other than the doctrinal controversies surrounding the Dotson Board, the most striking feature of the Reagan-Bush period was the failure of both Republican presidents to make timely appointments to the Board, a failure compounded by an exceptionally high rate of turnover among Board members, particularly in comparison with the Kennedy-Johnson era.[175] The best evidence of the disregard with which the Reagan and Bush administrations treated the NLRB is that the Board was left with only four members for approximately half the 144 months between January 1981 and December 1992 and only three members for 13 percent of that time. The Board had a full complement of five members for only 38 percent of the twelve-year Reagan-Bush era.[176] In part because of this neglect, President Bill Clinton had an unprecedented opportunity to nominate four Board members in his first year in office.[177]

Among its more important case decisions, the Stephens Board, in *Pierce Corp.,*[178] reaffirmed the Dotson Board's *Midland*[179] ruling holding that representation election results would not be disturbed because of misstatements made during the campaign. Conforming to another Dotson Board precedent,[180] the Stephens Board, in *Herbert F. Darling, Inc.,*[181] exonerated an employer who discharged an employee on the mistaken belief that the employee had complained to the Occupational Safety and Health Administration, thereby triggering an OSHA investigation. According to the Stephens Board, the employee was not engaged in protected concerted activity because a single employee's attempts to enforce statutory rights were not presumed to be on behalf of other employees.

The Stephens Board reaffirmed another Dotson Board decision when in *E.I. duPont de Nemours*[182] it held that non-unionized employees are not entitled to representation in an employer's investigatory interview. The Stephens Board did substantially modify a Dotson Board ruling concerning union access to employer private property, only to have its decision reversed by the Supreme Court. In *Jean Country*[183] the Stephens Board said that in all access cases it would consider not only the strength of an employer's private property right and employees' rights under the National Labor Relations Act but also the availability of reasonable alternative means of communication with employees. (The Dotson Board considered the question of alternative means of communication relevant only when claims of property rights and of Section 7 rights were "relatively equal.")[184]

The quasi-public nature of the mall in which the Jean County store was located, the Board said, weakened the employer's private property claim. The Board found the employees' Section 7 rights worthy of protection because the union's picketing was lawful under the publicity proviso of Section 8(b)(7)(C), was confined to the front of the Jean Country store, and was peaceful and unobstructive. The alternative means of communication were inadequate, according to the Board, because the union's message to Jean Country customers would be substantially diluted, given the distance between the nearest public property and the mall entrances, the large number of stores in the mall, the large number of customers entering the mall, and the likelihood that picketing on remote public property would cause confusion among customers as to which store was being targeted, thereby involving neutral stores in the labor dispute.[185]

The Supreme Court, in an opinion delivered by Justice Clarence Thomas in *Lechmere, Inc.,*[186] struck down the Board's three-factor approach. Although as the dissent emphasized, the right of self-organization depends "in some measure on the ability of employees to learn the advantages of self-organization from others,"[187] the majority read the Court's 1954 decision in *Babcock & Wilcox*[188] narrowly and denied union access to employer private property except when the location of a plant and employee living quarters causes employees to be "isolated from the ordinary flow of information that characterizes our society."[189]

The Supreme Court majority, by allowing union access in only that single rare circumstance, gave overwhelming precedence to employer property rights over the statutory right of employees to organize. The *Lechmere* decision came after Justices William Brennan and Thurgood Marshall had left the Court. Brennan and Marshall, as one observer put it, were attuned to the needs "of minorities, of the disabled, of unionized workers, of the individual worker" and "more than any of the recent justices, understood the history and dynamics of collective bargaining." After their departure and replacement by Justices Clarence Thomas and David Souter, it was unclear who on the Supreme Court, if anyone, would articulate doctrines that would protect these groups.[190]

Marshall and Brennan had dissented vigorously from the Supreme Court's decision in *First National Maintenance.*[191] Since that decision and the Dotson Board's subsequent *Otis Elevator* II[192] ruling, which was actually three disparate interpretations of *First National Maintenance,* there was great confusion (or "chaos," as one former Reagan-appointed general counsel termed it)[193] about management's obligation to bargain about partial closures, relocations, mergers, and similar decisions seriously affecting employment. Among other cases in which the Board applied its *Otis* II tests, it decided in 1987 in *Dubuque Packing Co.*[194] that under any of the three tests the employer was not obliged to bargain with the union over its decision to relocate work from one of its plants to another. In 1989 the District of Columbia Circuit Court of Appeals, saying that the case raised "some of the most polarizing questions in contemporary labor law," remanded *Dubuque Packing* and urged the Board "to articulate a majority-supported" single rule to be used in determining if a particular management decision was a mandatory subject of bargaining.[195]

The Stephens Board subsequently reversed its original decision and found that the company did have a duty to bargain.[196] Overruling *Otis Elevator* II to the extent that it was inconsistent with the new ruling, the Board adopted a new standard as the D.C. Circuit had requested but limited its application to decisions to relocate work. Under the new test the general counsel had the burden of establishing that a relocation of bargaining unit work was "unaccompanied by a basic change in the nature of the employer's operation." If successful, the general counsel would then have made a case sufficient on its face to consider the relocation of work a mandatory subject of bargaining. An employer could rebut that case by establishing that there was a basic change in the scope and direction of the enterprise, that the work performed at the new location varied significantly from the work performed at the former plant, or that the work at the former plant was discontinued entirely. Alternatively, an employer could prove that labor costs were not a factor in the decision or that, even if they were, "the union could not have offered labor cost concessions that could have changed the employer's decision to relocate."[197]

Although the Board in *Dubuque Packing* II seems to have softened the *Otis* II tests (its meaning will depend on its application) the decision at its core still elevates profitability and unfettered management prerogatives over what the *Fibreboard* Supreme Court praised as the promotion of the "fundamental purpose of the Act by bringing a problem of vital concern to labor and management within the framework established by Congress as most conducive to industrial peace."[198] The fundamental purpose of the Taft-Hartley Act as then understood by the Supreme Court would require that the relocation of bargaining unit work as well as other management decisions seriously affecting employment be mandatory subjects of collective bargaining. It was no longer that way, even under the new *Dubuque Packing* approach.

Concluding Observations

The Reagan Board's decisions were neither objective nor balanced, nor were they merely reversals of the recent "radical" decisions of the Carter Board. Although the Dotson Board overturned many Carter Board doctrines, it also reversed many major policy decisions covering at least two decades of NLRB history.[199] Despite the rhetoric of individual rights and deregulation, the Dotson Board pursued a policy of freeing employers from many of the most important constraints of unionization and collective bargaining. Contrary to the claims of some Reagan Board defenders, moreover, the Dotson Board's decisions directly and significantly affected the conduct of labor-management relations.

Although some regarded the Dotson Board "as having the most activist, anti-union, and anti-employee orientation in [NLRB] history,"[200] the Reagan Board was not the first Board to be guided by a conservative philosophy in interpreting and applying the act or the first Board to reverse case precedents quickly and extensively. The Eisenhower and Kennedy-Johnson Boards also engaged in rapid reversals of many of their predecessor Boards' major policy decisions. But in part because of Dotson's missionary zeal and abrasive personality as well as the Reagan White House's ideological anti-unionism, the Reagan Board's decision making was far more intently and overtly politicized than any of its predecessors. As *Business Week* put it in 1987 as Dotson was preparing to leave the Board, "perhaps no appointment so symbolized the Reagan Administration's simple-minded pursuit of conservative goals as the choice of Donald L. Dotson."[201]

The Board's conservative decisions, moreover, gave employers what the same issue of *Business Week* called a "green light to at least try to bash unions."[202] It was an ideal time for even unionized employers to reconsider the value and inevitability of unionization, since organized labor was in serious decline and many of the country's major industries were in economic trouble. Employers in the United States had always resisted unionization of their employees, but this opposition had become much more sophisticated, intense, and widespread since the 1960s, as evidenced in part by the growth of the anti-union consultant industry. In the economic climate of the 1980s, marked by this heightened resistance to union activity, the Reagan Board's decisions, which weakened the influence of unions where workers were organized and made it more difficult for unions to organize where workers were unorganized, contributed to the decline of unionism and diminished the importance of the act.

Near the end of 1984, as the NLRA approached its fiftieth birthday, the House Labor Committee's Subcommittee on Labor-Management Relations reported its "unmistakable conclusion" that "labor law has failed." By failure, the committee meant that the Taft-Hartley Act had not achieved its purpose of encouraging collective bargaining and protecting employees from discrimination because of their views on unionization. On the contrary, the subcommittee said that the act was being used "as a weapon to obstruct collective bargaining" and to create only the illusion of protecting workers against discrimination. After fifty years of Wagner and Taft-Hartley, workers and unions were "being badly betrayed."[203]

The Republican minority on that committee accused the majority of "hyperbolic" election-year rhetoric. The minority's statement of the purposes of the act emphasized the preeminence of commerce as the statutory objective and relegated collective bargaining to a subordinate means of facilitating commerce. Congressional intent was not being served, the Republican minority concluded, whenever collective bargaining "unacceptably obstructed" the free flow of commerce.[204] Yet the more collective bargaining was subordinated to the economic interests of employers, whether by the NLRB, the Supreme Court, or Congress, the more irrelevant and fraudulent the act became.

The Stephens Board, sometimes referred to as Reagan Board II or the Bush Board, concentrated in the main on refining the decisions of the Dotson Board and other predecessor Boards and avoided the highly controversial doctrinal changes and internal squabbling of the Dotson period. In the words of Clifford Oviatt, who served on the Board from January 1990 through August 1993, "it cannot be persuasively argued that the Bush Board's decisions created giant deviations in the law under the Act. Although it obviously made interpretive refinements, it deferred . . . any major changes or corrections in the direction of the law to the Congress."[205]

Because of its low-keyed, noncontroversial approach, the Bush Board has been characterized as middle-of-the-road, even though it did not reverse or seriously modify most of the Dotson Board's major decisions. Collective bargaining was still being subordinated to the economic interests of employers.

14

Conclusion

Conflicting Statutory Purposes

U.S. labor policy has been at cross-purposes with itself ever since Congress incorporated into the Taft-Hartley Act in 1947 not only the Wagner Act statement that it is the policy of the federal government to encourage collective bargaining but also a new Declaration of Policy saying that the purpose of the act is to protect the rights of individual employees. Although there is no necessary conflict between the encouragement of collective bargaining and the protection of individual rights, experts at the time Taft-Hartley became law predicted correctly that the written affirmation of the protection of individual rights, particularly the right to refrain from engaging in collective bargaining, would be read as statutory justification for both the promotion of a policy of individual bargaining and employer resistance to unionization and collective bargaining. Since many of the most important employment decisions cannot be individually negotiated, the choice is not simply between individual and collective bargaining but rather between participation in and exclusion from that decision-making process.[1] The concept added to Taft-Hartley, of the federal government as a *neutral guarantor* of employee free choice between individual and collective bargaining, and indifferent to the choice made, is clearly inconsistent with the Wagner Act's concept, retained in Taft-Hartley, of the federal government as a promoter of collective bargaining. The Taft-Hartley Act contains both conceptions of the government's role.

NLRBs applying quite different policies, therefore, can choose between these contradictory statutory purposes and still claim that they are conforming to congressional intent. For that reason, there have been not merely revisions in NLRB case law (as would be expected and even necessary over the years) but radical changes that swing labor policy from one purpose to its direct opposite. These swings directly affect the ability of unions to organize and of managements to resist organization as well as the relative bargaining power of the parties. In sum, a Board's interpretation of the act determines the extent to

272

which there will be mutuality of decision making at the workplace. As a consequence, after more that forty-seven years of Taft-Hartley (and fifty-nine years since the Wagner Act) the United States has no coherent or consistent national labor policy.

Under the Wagner Act the right of workers to participate in decisions affecting their workplace lives was considered a fundamental compontent of social justice, and collective bargaining was deemed critical for a free and democratic society. The Wagner Act statement of purpose was carried over into Taft-Hartley, and Senator Robert Taft claimed that his and Congressman Fred Hartley's amendments did not change the essential collective bargaining theme of the Wagner Act labor policy. Yet Taft-Hartley's emphasis on the right to reject collective bargaining, the protection of employee and employer rights in their relations with unions, the inclusion of union unfair labor practices, and the federal government's new statutory image as neutral between individual and collective bargaining encouraged employers to resist unionization and collective bargaining. The same law, therefore, has been read as promoting collective bargaining and as promoting resistance to it.

The current state of U.S. labor policy cannot be fully understood without knowledge of the existence and influence of these conflicting interpretations of statutory purposes on the development of that policy. Any reconstruction of national labor policy must begin with a resolution of this fundamental disagreement about what the purpose of the law should be. In the meantime, the act is being interpreted to promote individual bargaining and undermine collective bargaining; at the same time, the claim is made that collective bargaining is still favored by government policy.

The NLRB's Role in Making Labor Policy

The existence of these potentially conflicting statements of purpose in the act has given the NLRB, and the political officials who appoint its members, a de facto power far beyond that ordinarily necessary for the interpretation and application of any statute. Lawmaking by the NLRB or by any other administrative agency is inevitable under any circumstances. The NLRB, in applying the act, must give specific meaning to broad statutory language, interpret where neither congressional intent nor statutory language is clear and unambiguous, and even fill gaps in the legislation. The Board, therefore, is never neutral. In carrying out its statutory mandate, the Board must choose among competing alternatives. Those alternatives represent the vital interests of opposed constituencies and conflicting views of what the national labor policy is or should be. Because of the contradictory statutory purposes in Taft-Hartley, however, successive NLRBs, over time and political administrations, are in the uniquely powerful position of choosing between fundamentally different national labor policies.

NLRB chairmen with strong personalities and convictions have exercised their power dramatically. For example, Frank McCulloch, chairman during the Kennedy-Johnson era, was influential in fashioning a labor policy that promoted collective bargaining. McCulloch and a majority of his colleagues relied on the collective bargaining policy in the Wagner Act that had been incorporated into Taft-Hartley to justify their encouragement of collective bargaining and the facilitation of unionization.

To McCulloch and his colleagues, particularly Gerald Brown, collective bargaining required employers not only to bargain about many traditional management prerogatives but also to accept unions as joint participants in the resolution of labor-related problems affecting wages, hours, and working conditions. To the McCulloch Board, the statutory collective bargaining policy was more than an effective way of settling labor-management disputes. It was a form of employer-union joint decision making. McCulloch, like Senator Robert Wagner, saw collective bargaining as a means to the realization of social justice through the development of democratic institutions to correct industrial injustices. Unionization and collective bargaining would replace industrial autocracy with industrial democracy.

The decisions of the Republican-appointed Boards chaired by Guy Farmer, Edward Miller, and Donald Dotson, by contrast, freed employers from many of the most important constraints of unionism and collective bargaining. Rather than encourage collective bargaining, these Boards preserved and increased employers' *unilateral* decision-making power in matters affecting their employees. Their focus was on not the collective bargaining policy in the Wagner Act that was incorporated into Taft-Hartley but on the newer provisions concerning individual free choice and the right to reject collective bargaining. As Chairman Miller put it, individual employee freedom of choice, not the encouragement of collective bargaining, is the "keystone of the act." He pointedly renounced, as did Farmer, any sense of "social mission" or "crusade" to help unions organize and gain collective bargaining rights.[2]

The Farmer, Miller, and Dotson Boards, however, were not neutral or indifferent protectors of employee choice between individual and collective bargaining. Their decisions deregulating employer conduct while tightening regulation of the use of economic weapons by unions increased employers' ability to apply their economic power to resist unionization and avoid collective bargaining. The Miller Board effectively blocked or reversed the major thrusts of the decisions of the McCulloch Board. This time, however, those decisions were not short-term reversals of U.S. labor policy.

With the exception of Jimmy Carter's one term in 1977–81, Republican administrations controlled appointments to the NLRB for more than twenty years after the McCulloch Board. During that time these Republican-appointed Boards, especially the Dotson Board, elevated management's authority to manage above employers' statutory obligation to bargain. During the Reagan presidency in particular, the Dotson Board seriously diminished the statutory obligation to bargain, once considered central to the act, by excluding management decisions considered too important to an employer's business to be negotiated with a union. Many of these decisions have a direct and significant impact on jobs.

The national labor policy became one of maximizing employers' ability to compete in domestic and foreign markets by deregulating the management end of labor-management relations. Dotson's NLRB subordinated collective bargaining to the economic interests of employers. Pursuit of that policy was particularly devastating to union organization and collective bargaining because it came at a time when the nation's major industries were in economic trouble and organized labor was already in a marked decline.

A historical perspective discloses how the NLRB, which in its early years contributed greatly to the growth of the strongest labor movement in the world, has hastened its decline, especially since 1970. It also reveals how a presidential administration can make or change labor policy without legislative action through appointments to the NLRB.

The national labor policy is in a shambles in part because its meaning seems to depend primarily on which political party won the last election. (The outgoing Republican-appointed chairman has already outlined those case doctrines most likely to be changed by the incoming Clinton administration Board members.)[3] That is an unacceptable way to make labor policy. These shifts cause not only instability in labor policy but also loss of respect for the NLRB, confusion and cynicism among practitioners, and fear among workers that they will not be consistently protected in the exercise of their statutory rights. Labor law reform, therefore, must not consist merely of changes in NLRB case doctrines, because it is only a matter of time before the appointees of another political party reverse those doctrines once again.

Congress, the Supreme Court, and the White House

Since 1947 Congress has defaulted on its responsibility to make and change labor policy. Lawmakers have not been able to get past short-term maneuverings for political advantage, political horse-trading, ideologically inspired emotion, unfounded and unsubstantiated beliefs about unions and labor relations, and the cavalier manipulation of labor policy to achieve other political objectives. The beauty of the Wagner Act was that almost every one of its provisions was rooted in the experience of two pre–Wagner Act labor boards whose personnel played major roles in writing the law. Since then, empirical evidence has had little or no place in the making of labor policy. Legislation is neither formulated on the basis of what actually happens at workplaces nor evaluated in light of its effects on the workings of labor-management relations. The same is true of NLRB decisions. Politics and speculation, not evidence, control.

Senate and House labor committees have failed to conduct the thoughtful, dispassionate, and expert investigations needed to inform lawmakers of how the country's labor relations are actually working and what needs to be done as a consequence. Congressional committees are often used, for example, to prepare an agenda of doctrinal changes for a new Board of the same political party rather than to inform Congress about needed legislative reforms.

As a result, the roles of Congress, the NLRB, and the Supreme Court in making national labor policy have been blurred and confused. When Congress abdicates its legislative function, the NLRB assumes a far greater than normal role in making labor policy. Because of the legislative vacuum and ambiguity, moreover, the making of national labor policy has also passed by default from Congress to the Supreme Court.

Early in the Reagan administration, for example, the Supreme Court, also without empirical evidence, made fundamental labor policy choices solely on the basis of the ideological value judgments of a majority of the justices. In many ways the Supreme Court took the lead in freeing management from the constraints of the law on the basis of pure speculation and value-laden dicta about the inviolability of management rights. (A good illustration is the Court's majority opinion in *First National Maintenance Corp. v. NLRB*.)[4] This trend has major significance for U.S. labor policy and those who propose to change it. Congressional pressure and White House appointments can reorient an NLRB, but normally legislation is needed to reverse the Supreme Court.

In the White House, no matter who the occupant, courageous leadership has been lacking. No president has been willing to risk pursuing a clear statement of the rights of workers or delineating statutory solutions to serious labor relations problems. Instead, administrations have done the minimum necessary to respond, or at least appear to be responding, to political pressure, to gain political backing, or to reward business or organized labor for its support in election campaigns. They then go through the motions of seeking reform while manipulating the situation for maximum political gain. As a result, any effort to reform the labor law must calculate carefully the strength of the incumbent administration's commitment. The Clinton administration's unwillingness in 1994 to provide the same intense political support that it gave to the North American Free Trade Agreement to a bill that would have made it illegal for an employer to hire permanent replacements for economic strikers raises doubts about the administration's commitment to significant labor law reform.[5]

Employer Resistance

Labor law reformers, moreover, must be aware of the extent to which the most powerful employers in the country will resist any threat to their management prerogatives. For many years, it was presumed that employer hostility and resistance to unionization and collective bargaining came from ideologues at the margin of business and industry. On the contrary, the determined opposition of U.S. employers taken as a whole has been the biggest obstacle to the acceptance of the congressionally sanctioned national labor policy of collective bargaining. This pervasive opposition is a primary reason the United States stands almost alone among democratic nations in leaving the great majority of its statutorily covered workers without any organization and representation at the workplace. Widespread employer defiance of the law has continued to the present time, almost sixty years after the Wagner Act and forty-eight years after Taft-Hartley.

The secret and coorrdinated effort undertaken by the country's major employers, including those already organized and considered models of corporate propriety, to combat the McCulloch Board on a series of fronts demonstrates the depth and breadth of this employer opposition. Their hidden campaign included the manipulation of both the media and public opinion and used means threatening to a democratic society. As the leaders of this resistance put it, they would never accept an industrial society in which a worker's voice was equal to management's or in which all management decisions were bargainable. For them, industrial democracy and free enterprise were fundamentally incompatible.

Employers who accepted collective bargaining used it advantageously as a way to provide stability, predictability, and control within their plants. Moreover, bargaining was limited to negotiating with unions about the effects of management's business decisions on wages, hours, and working conditions. Employers definitely did not bargain with unions as part of the management decision-making process itself. The Kennedy-Johnson Board's joint-participation concept of collective bargaining and its commitment to spreading the prac-

tice of collective bargaining caused even these employers to push for the elimination from Taft-Hartley of the language making it the policy of the federal
government to encourage collective bargaining.

The defeat of organized labor's reform bill in 1978 marked the beginning of
a far more open employer opposition to unionization and collective bargaining.
The bitter labor-management confrontation over the bill manifested a growing
conviction among employers that successful competition in domestic and international markets required either evading or resisting unions. It has become a
virtual article of faith that survival (and jobs) in this new era of economic
competition depends on strategies that are hostile to organized labor: unencumbered and creative management responses to change; the end of costly contracts
with unions; the retention or regaining of management prerogatives, power, and
flexibility; and the freedom to overcome other labor cost advantages enjoyed by
competitors. Business leaders continue to argue that these responses enable the
country to run economically, the wheels of the free enterprise system to turn,
and workers' pay envelopes to be filled.

Employers went on the attack with what one national news magazine called
a "green light" from the Dotson Board to bash unions.[6] There has been an all-
out push by employers since then to escape or evade union-imposed limitations
on their managerial authority. Euphemistically named "union-avoidance" programs have flourished. Unorganized employees understand the consequences of
employer hostility to unions and the likelihood of retaliation against union supporters. The anti-union circle is complete when employees' fear of retaliation
contributes to a public perception of unionization as unwanted because it is job-
threatening and when declining public support for unions in turn encourages
more employers to try to thwart unionization and collective bargaining.[7] At the
same time, because employers control jobs, economic recovery and development depend on their ability to compete successfully. Consequently, organized
employers have powerful political influence that could block any serious labor
law reform.

Unions and the National Labor Policy

Because Wagner–Taft-Hartley is a collective bargaining law, the fate of organized labor in the United States and the fate of the national labor policy and the
NLRB are intimately interrelated. Organized labor is in decline. Unions lose
more representation elections than they win. In 1992 union density sank to a
record low of 15.9 percent of all employed wage and salaried workers in the
country. Between the early 1960s and 1979 the drop in union density masked

an increase in union membership that simply was growing at a slower rate than overall employment. Since 1979, however, union membership has fallen while employment continues to rise.

Much of this decline can be attributed to widespread employer opposition to unionization and to NLRB decisions permitting and even facilitating that opposition. It is clearly shortsighted, however, to put all the blame on the Reagan administration, because union membership has been on a downward trend since the mid-1950s. Organized labor, for example, has not been able to shake the unsavory image created by the McClellan hearings in the late 1950s. Those dramatic televised hearings fixed in the public mind the still-powerful picture of exploited union members controlled by corrupt and dictatorial leaders whose only interest was personal enrichment. In an extraordinary reversal of public perception, unions, seen by many as liberating forces of social and economic justice in the 1930s, have come to be commonly regarded as instruments of oppression and exploitation.

Organized labor's political influence also declined after the late 1950s as both political parties began moving toward an ideological consensus that espoused a politics of moderation. Many liberals in the Democratic Party, moreover, no longer considered organized labor a force for social reform and saw little difference between "big labor" and "big business." Organized labor's legislative agenda was consistently given low priority. The AFL-CIO became a captive of the Democratic Party because it had no reasonable political alternative. Nevertheless, the party appointed and reappointed to the NLRB such people as Frank McCulloch, Gerry Brown, and John Fanning, who greatly advanced the national labor policy of collective bargaining.

In addition, organized labor has been guilty over the years of following an unwise legislative strategy that produced several costly blunders. Among the most damaging was the uncompromising demand for total repeal of Taft-Hartley after Harry Truman's upset election victory in 1948. Labor at that time rejected proposed changes in Taft-Hartley that the AFL-CIO would plead for thirty years later in its reform bill.

Unions must also bear some of the blame for restricting the scope of bargaining, which has fallen far short of the potential envisioned by Senator Wagner. In general, unions defined for themselves too narrow a role in the operation of the enterprise. Most unions' views on management prerogatives, for example, have been indistinguishable from those of most corporation chief executive officers. The McCulloch Board, in effect, pushed more for power sharing through collective bargaining than did organized labor. One commentator has called labor's renunciation of power sharing the "longest running mistake in the history of labor."[8] The "social compact" between organized labor and management, in which labor was junior partner—bargaining only in limited areas while allowing management unrestricted authority to manage—was the product of limited vision.

Among the volumes of advice given organized labor about how to revive itself, the best echoed Senator Wagner: "The brightest hope may lie in a return to appealing to that fundamental interest that unions have advanced so effectively in the past: the dignity of the individual working person and his [or her] full, genuine participation in the life of the workplace and of the broader community. That, at any rate, would be a reflection without distortion of the principles of social justice informing our national labor policy."[9]

Thoughts on National Labor Policy

Given the conflict and confusion over the central purpose of the Taft-Hartley Act, the United States needs a definite, coherent, and consistent statement of the intent of its national labor policy. That requires more than changing NLRB case doctrines or amending Taft-Hartley to tighten or loosen government regulation of the labor-management relationship. The recrafting of a national labor policy must begin with a precise and certain statement of its purpose and objectives. Fundamental questions must be confronted and answered.

These questions are moral and ethical more than they are legal, economic, or political. In the U.S. economic system employers, particularly corporations, are the dominant agents in producing and distributing most of the means by which people live and earn their living. The control these employers have over jobs, the use of scarce resources, and the distribution of products and services give them the power to affect people's lives, to harm or benefit them, to violate or protect their rights, to favor some over others for various reasons, to make or break their communities, and to make many of the rules that govern who gets what in the economy and what they have to do to get it.

Consequently, the overwhelming number of working people, even when prospering, are subject to the arbitrary will of others or to the allegedly impersonal forces of economic markets. Although the impact of employer decisions on human life is much more direct than the impact of most political decisions, the nation has been preoccupied with issues of political democracy while most people are subjugated to economic forces over which they are allowed to have little or no control. That is contrary to the promise this nation made to itself that it would be a democracy, and to the fundamental democratic purpose of the Wagner Act, which Senator Taft claimed remained the central objective of his new law. Its dedication to the idea that principles of democracy should apply at the workplace was the underlying strength of U.S. national labor policy and still is—at least when the act is read by Democrat-appointed NLRBs.

In a democracy private power is a public trust. The very purpose of the United States, although too rarely realized, was to enable the powerless to restrain the powerful. Neither private nor government power would be permitted to control human lives, because both would be subject to the public will. Democracy is working only when it meets this test—and the right of people to participate in the decisions that affect their lives is one of the most fundamental principles of democracy. The right of workers to participate in decisions affecting their workplace lives, on which the Wagner Act was based, is the policy most consistent with democratic principles. Independent labor organization and collective bargaining, therefore, are essential to democracy, not merely the consequences of management mistakes.

It is not possible to be morally neutral about these issues. It is also not possible to separate moral and ethical questions from economic and legal ones in fashioning a labor policy. At its most basic, for example, a national labor policy must determine the extent to which employers should be allowed to make decisions in isolation from the people, particularly employees, affected by those decisions and whether that decision-making power should be shared in some manner under some circumstances. The current national labor policy is muddled and ambiguous because the interpreters of the Taft-Hartley Act have answered this basic question in contradictory ways.

Many possible labor policy alternatives have been proposed. Some advocate managerial decision-making autonomy in an unregulated market. Others propose a strengthening of the collective bargaining, industrial democracy approach, making it eser for employees to become organized, increasing restrictions on employers' ability to resist unionization, providing more effective enforcement mechanisms and "swift, sure and sufficient" remedies for violations of employees' statutory rights,[10] and expanding employee participation in the decisions of the enterprise. Still others favor a mandatory system of elected employee-participation committees modeled after the German works councils; new forms of cooperative workplace arrangements, such as quality circles, joint labor-management committees, and various employer-created worker-participation schemes; or some blend of all these proposals. There has also been support for increasing the legal protection for individual employees, by replacing, for example, the current common law rule of employment at will with a law to protect some or all employees against unjust discharge.

It does not follow, however, that one national labor policy is just as morally good as another. We need to ask by what standards and for whose benefit government shall act in developing a national policy. For example, in March

1993, when Secretary of Labor Robert Reich announced the formation of a commission to reexamine the assumptions underlying the national labor policy, he emphasized evidence showing that when workers have a voice, the "yield is higher productivity." He did not define "voice." Earlier the secretary had discussed with the AFL-CIO Executive Council the role organized labor could have "in advancing the administration's agenda of giving all workers greater participation in their companies to improve productivity." The commission was asked to recommend changes in the law and practice of collective bargaining that would increase workplace productivity through labor-management cooperation.[11]

Increased efficiency and labor peace are appealing practical objectives, particularly in hard economic times. Labor-management cooperation, if based in genuine power sharing at the workplace (Senator Wagner called it industrial democracy), can enhance the dignity of employees and improve employers' ability to compete. The kind of excellence envisioned by Secretary Reich, however, cannot be compelled; it must be motivated. High-performance enterprises need employees who have an independent source of power that protects them from the adverse consequences of cooperating fully with management. Many researchers agree that "a positive labor/management relationship can be achieved more effectively if the workers protect and promote their interests through an organization which they control." If joint programs are unilaterally initiated and controlled by employers only as devices to achieve management's objectives, to be discarded when they no longer work or some other arrangement works better, employees remain powerless, suspicious, defensive, and less willing to cooperate fully.[12] Moreover, the decisions of the Supreme Court and the Reagan-appointed Dotson Board freeing employers from any statutory obligation to bargain about some of their most important decisions affecting jobs are "directly contrary to the language, philosophy and approach taken by industry and labor in developing truly cooperative ventures."[13] As Dunlop Commission member Douglas Fraser put it, "because I am deeply committed to the principle of workplace democracy, I cannot join in any statement that proclaims that you can have fully effective worker-management cooperation programs without having a truly equal partnership based upon workers having an independent voice."[14]

The sole or even primary purpose of a national labor policy should not be to increase worker productivity and employer competitiveness, although these effects may be by-products. The primary purpose of a national labor policy should be to find a moral basis for achieving human dignity, solidarity, and justice for all parties at the workplace and in the larger communities affected by what goes on at the workplace.

There are costs, even inefficiencies, in having an ethical society. The compelling argument for a national labor policy, however, is not that it increases employer competitiveness but that it embodies moral values. Senator Wagner's primary concern, to which he always subordinated the Wagner Act's other important legislative goals of economic recovery and industrial peace, remained the achievement of social justice through collective bargaining at the workplace.

Collective bargaining, though far from perfect, has given many employees an opportunity to participate in the determination of their wages, hours, and working conditions and other aspects of their lives on the job. Possibly the greatest single contribution of unions and collective bargaining is the grievance and arbitration process. These systems of industrial justice substituted more humane rules for arbitrary treatment and unilateral dictation and developed formal procedures to resolve claims of unfair treatment during the term of a collective bargaining agreement, by either voluntary settlement or recourse to an impartial third party. Unions also provide many working people with otherwise unavailable access to political forums. As the national labor policy is used to discourage unionization and collective bargaining, the protection and opportunities for legitimate participation that unions brought to even a minority of workplaces are lost.

Since about 1970 Taft-Hartley has primarily been interpreted and applied in ways that put federal government power in private employer hands by strengthening the managerial authority of employers who already had great power over their employees. That development, together with the decline of unionism, leaves unprotected the great majority of employees who do not have sufficient individual economic and political power to protect themselves. Almost sixty years after the Wagner Act the overwhelming majority of employees are unorganized and unrepresented and work unprotected by grievance and arbitration systems in situations where they may be fired at will for almost any reason. A truly democratic government would not be indifferent to the lack of democracy at the workplace.

Although a law embodying this national labor policy would itself influence community attitudes, a national climate also must be created that emphasizes democratic values and the importance of carrying those values over into the workplace. The organization of employees certainly would be facilitated, as it was during the early days of the Wagner Act, by a truthful claim by the national administration that unionism and collective bargaining are in the public interest. The federal government could demonstrate its commitment to organization and collective bargaining and its desire to have employees choose to participate by guaranteeing those who voted for representation a grievance procedure and arbitration even when a chosen representative failed to negotiate a first contract with an employer. Such a guarantee would discourage employers from deliberately rendering fruitless the employees' choice of collective bargaining. It would also provide the protection against arbitrary action to which every employee is entitled.

It is foolish and deceitful to make a commitment to a national labor policy of encouraging collective bargaining and then allow employers to block the implementation of that policy by legitimizing their opposition to collective bargaining and increasing their ability to resist unionization. A national labor policy favoring collective bargaining should minimize employer involvement in the process of employee choice.[15] Recommendations by experts such as Paul Weiler to shorten the period of preelection campaigning by holding an election within a matter of days on the basis of signed authorization cards would help reduce the opportunity for employer interference.[16] It would also enable the Board to avoid the bottomless pit of litigation over the meaning and intent of speech and its effect on employee choice.

Automatically certifying labor organizations that were victims of unfair labor practices that interfere with employee choice, even when there was no evidence that the labor organization seeking representation rights ever had support of a majority of the employees, would also discourage employers from committing such practices. This severe remedy would be justified not only because it would prevent employers from benefiting from their violations of the law but also because the unlawful behavior violates human dignity and the democratic process. In other words, legislation expressing a labor policy favoring worker organization and participation through collective bargaining and prohibiting discrimination for union activities should be and would be treated as a civil rights law, and violations would be treated as violations of civil rights.

The national labor policy should commit the NLRB to vigorous enforcement of Taft-Hartley. It should also encourage the Board to develop and use the full extent of its broad remedy power to promote voluntary compliance with the law. At the least, violators must no longer be able to profit from their violations. The vigor with which the law is enforced is an excellent test of the federal government's support of a national labor policy.

The national labor policy should continue to permit employees to form and select labor organizations as their representatives for collective bargaining, as long as those organizations are free of employer control. The federal government's support of and deference to labor organizations and collective bargaining, however, would not automatically result in democratic participation. These labor organizations must themselves be democratic and operate on the basis of workers' genuine consent and participation.

Finally, the national labor policy should encourage employers and labor organizations to bargain about all issues and decisions directly or indirectly affecting employees' working lives and, consequently, their families and communities. The current approach leaves it to the preordained and unsubstantiated value judgments of Supreme Court justices and Board members to assert what should or should not be an inviolate management prerogative. Opponents of codetermination have portrayed it as a foreign and un-American concept. Codetermination through worker participation, however, is consistent with the United States' concept of democracy. Workers whose livelihoods depend on the decisions of others should not be treated as outsiders.

There should be no doubt that a fundamental moral objective of the national labor policy is to help the powerless restrain the powerful. That objective can be met by eliminating the vulnerability that leaves workers at the mercy of other people or supposedly impersonal economic forces—either of which can transform them from self-reliant participants into helpless victims. The national labor policy, therefore, not only must protect the powerless from the arbitrary will of others but also must give them the opportunity to be actively engaged in securing their own rights and interests through participation in workplace decision making. Government encouragement and protection are essential to the exercise of democratic rights at the workplace.

That was the underlying philosophy and purpose of the Wagner Act. Many reject it today because it allegedly espoused a now supposedly archaic and unproductive confrontational approach. That is simply incorrect. Although the labor-management relationship is both adversarial and cooperative and the pursuit of justice and fairness often requires confrontation, the Wagner Act's ultimate objective was the establishment, through collective bargaining, of a system of labor-management cooperation based on mutual interest in the success of the enterprise. It was Taft-Hartley that was confrontational, because it enabled and encouraged employers to contest and resist organization and collective bargaining.

The collective bargaining policy carried over from the Wagner Act to Taft-Hartley has been diminished by some NLRBs, Congress, the Supreme Court, presidential administrations, employer resistance, and even organized labor. As a result, the current national labor policy favors and protects the powerful at the expense of the powerless. In the essential moral sense, therefore, to the extent that it incorporates the moral imperative within a genuinely democratic society, U.S. national labor policy must be judged a failure.

For years, many of those who have the power to be heard have called for minimum and inactive government. But inactive government is abusive and unjust when the weak and vulnerable are left to their fate. Freeing property from state control does not free ordinary people from the tyranny of property or the tyranny of being left alone when in need of help. It also tolerates, if not encourages, gross inequalities of social status and wealth so that life, liberty, and the pursuit of happiness become matters not of justice and rights but of economic fortune. Today most unjust acts and their consequences are simply redefined as misfortunes or the fault of the victims themselves.

Government encouragement and protection are absolutely essential to the exercise of democratic rights at the workplace. The real task is to get the government back on the side of the powerless at workplaces all around the United States so that the economy can exist for people. Now people exist for the economy. That is tyranny, not democracy.

Notes

Preface

1. "Fact Finding Report Issued by the Commission on the Future of Worker-Management Relations," *Daily Labor Report*, special supplement, no. 105, June 3, 1993, p. xi.
2. U.S. Department of Labor and U.S. Department of Commerce, Commission on the Future of Worker-Management Relations, *Report and Recommendations*, December 1994, Washington, D.C.
3. Ibid., p. xvii.
4. Ibid., pp. xviii, 4, 7.
5. Ibid., pp. xvii, 8.
6. Ibid., dissenting opinion of Douglas A. Fraser, following p. 12. Emphasis in original.
7. Ibid., pp. 18–24.
8. For a useful discussion of these subjects, see Sheldon Friedman et al., eds., *Restoring the Promise of American Labor Law* (Ithaca, N.Y.: ILR Press, 1994).

Chapter 1

1. James A. Gross, "Conflicting Statutory Purposes: Another Look at Fifty Years of NLRB Law Making," *Industrial and Labor Relations Review*, 39, no. 1 (October 1985): 10. See also Leon Keyserling, "The Wagner Act: Its Origin and Current Significance," *George Washington Law Review* 29 (December 1960): 215.
2. Gross, "Conflicting Statutory Purposes," p. 10. See also Leon Keyserling, "Why the Wagner Act?" in *The Wagner Act: After Ten Years*, ed. Louis Silverberg (Washington, D.C.: Bureau of National Affairs, 1945), p. 13.
3. James A. Gross, *The Reshaping of the National Labor Relations Board: National Labor Policy in Transition, 1937–1947* (Albany: State University of New York Press, 1981), p. 253. See also Gross, "Conflicting Statutory Purposes," p. 12.
4. Gross, "Conflicting Statutory Purposes," p. 12.
5. Congress, *Legislative History of the Labor Management Relations Act*, 93d Cong., 2d sess., 1947, 2:1535–44. (Hereinafter *Legislative History of the Taft-Hartley Act.*)
6. Ibid., p. 1536.
7. Ibid., p. 1653.

8. Although legislative intent should not be inferred from the comments of the opponents of the legislation, the remarks of Congressman Emanuel Celler and the observations of the House Minority Report to the Hartley bill (H.R. 3020) are historically accurate in identifying Smith and Hartley's objectives. Celler pointed out on the floor of the House that the Hartley bill eliminated the words "collective bargaining": "They do not appear in the purposes of the bill." He observed further: "You do away with that language by this bill and . . . anybody reading this pending bill will rightfully come to the conclusion that you not only do not put an imprimatur of approval on collective bargaining but intend to abolish collective bargaining. When you read the balance of the bill you can readily see that what you want to do is to do away with collective bargaining and have individual bargaining." Ibid., p. 776.

   What resulted from the conference committee negotiations was a compromise that retained with some amendment the Wagner Act's endorsement of collective bargaining and added the Hartley bill's Declaration of Policy, which made no mention of collective bargaining.

9. For an excellent description and analysis of the origins and content of the Taft-Hartley Act, see Harry A. Millis and Emily Clark Brown, *From the Wagner Act to Taft-Hartley* (Chicago: University of Chicago Press, 1950).

10. For a useful analytical summary of events in this period, see John Patrick Diggins, *The Proud Decades: America in War and Peace, 1941–1960* (New York: W. W. Norton, 1988), pp. 3–121; and R. Alton Lee, *Truman and Taft-Hartley* (Lexington: University of Kentucky Press, 1966), pp. 34, 37.

11. Lloyd Ulman, "Unionism and Collective Bargaining in the Modern Period," in *American Economic History,* ed. Seymour E. Harris (New York: McGraw-Hill, 1961), pp. 426–28.

12. Ibid., p. 427.

13. Millis and Brown deplored the imprecision of the phrase "too powerful." They asked if it meant the power to question management rules or to negotiate standardized wages, hours, and working conditions or the power to close down a huge corporation or an industry crucial to a locality or the nation. They pointed out that situations varied: "There may be powerful unions and associations of employers, as in Pacific Coast shipping; strong unions facing great corporations in mass production; division among unions as they face nation-wide operations such as those of Western Union; unions in many areas in the early stages of dealing or trying to deal with large chain-store companies; strong unions like the Teamsters, in highly strategic positions as they deal with thousands of employers, many of them small; a great union and associations of small employers organized in order to meet the union on a more equal footing; great textile mill chains in many of whose mills unions have never achieved even a precarious hold; and many other combinations and permutations of power relationships. In spite of the impressive over-all figures indicating union strength, the disparities are very great, with the balance on this side here, and the other side there. No indiscriminate weakening of the power of

unions could be expected to do justice or promote equality." *From the Wagner Act to Taft-Hartley,* pp. 272–73.

14. "The Veto Question," *New York Times,* May 7, 1947, p. 26, col. 2; "An Extreme Measure," *New York Times,* June 10, 1947, p. 26, col. 1.

15. Millis and Brown, *From the Wagner Act to Taft-Hartley,* p. 361.

16. Louis Stark, "All Senate Bills Denounced by AFL and CIO Aides at Hearing," *New York Times,* February 26, 1947, p. 19; Louis Stark, "Green at Senate Hearing Rejects All Labor Curbs," *New York Times,* February 19, 1947, p. 1.

17. Memorandum from W. C. Hushing to William Green, April 21, 1947, Folder 30, Box 47, Department of Legislation (1906–1978), George Meany Memorial Archives, Washington, D.C.: "I do not think it advisable for us to attempt to better the Senate bill by amendments . . . because our only hope of defeating this legislation is a veto, which we may be able to sustain in the Senate, which positively cannot be done in the House. . . . The roll call votes on passage of this legislation should be forwarded to all our affiliates . . . in order that they may take those who voted for the bill to task."

See also statement by President Green concerning a cross-country motorcade to Washington, D.C., June 17, 1947, Folder 7, Box 6; and M. S. Novik to George Meany regarding final financial statement for the AFL radio campaign, September 3, 1947, Folder 6, Box 6, Office of the Secretary Treasurer, Meany Archives.

18. "An Extreme Measure," *New York Times,* June 10, 1947, p. 26, col. 1; Arthur Krock, "Labor Leaders Offer a Blank Page as Alternative," *New York Times,* June 6, 1947; "AFL Fight on Ives Is Urged by Green," *New York Times,* July 15, 1947, p. 14, col. 1.

19. Transcript of AFL conference on the provisions of the Taft-Hartley Act, July 9, 1947, pp. 6 (quotation), 14–15, Folder 3, Box 6, Office of the Secretary Treasurer, Meany Archives.

20. Ibid., pp. 129–30.

21. George Meany speech, November 14, 1947, pp. 10–15, Folder 8, Box 7, Office of the Secretary Treasurer, Meany Archives. Meany identified the origin of the AFL's "slave labor law" characterization as the statement by Justices Oliver Wendell Holmes and Louis D. Brandeis in their dissent in the Supreme Court's *Bedford Cut Stone* decision (274 U.S. 37 [1927]): "If, on the undisputed facts of this case, refusal to work can be enjoined, Congress created by the Sherman law and the Clayton Act an instrument for imposing restraints upon labor which reminds one of involuntary servitude." Ibid., p. 11. Meany was referring to Taft-Hartley's provision for back-to-work injunctions in national emergency strikes.

22. Memorandum from Hushing to Green, April 21, 1947; Congressman William Lemke to William Green, March 7, 1947, Folder 28, Box 47, Department of Legislation, Meany Archives: "I will state that I feel that labor lost an opportunity by not bringing in a pro-labor bill around which its friends could have rallied. . . . If this had been done in time, I am sure this anti-labor legislation could have been defeated."

23. Joseph A. Loftus, "Labor Looks to Truman to Block Stiff Curbs," *New York Times,* April 20, 1947.

24. Letter from Truman to Senator Joseph Ball, January 8, 1947, PSF, Box 281, Harry S Truman Papers, Harry S Truman Library, Independence, Mo.

25. Press release, State of the Union address, January 6, 1947, pp. 4–6, O.F. 419-F, Box 1261, Truman Papers.

26. William S. White, "Congress Would Override Labor Veto, Truman Is Told," *New York Times,* June 4, 1947, p. 1; "Poll of Key Senate Democrats," *New York Times,* June 8, 1947.

27. "Excerpts from Comments of Political Leaders Regarding Tax and Labor Bills," undated, pp. 3, 6, Taft-Hartly Bill Correspondence File, Box 7, Clark Clifford Papers, Truman Library. As Alabama state vice-chairman W. J. Price put it, however, "I cannot conceive of labor leaving the Democratic Party, they have nowhere else to go." Ibid., p. 5.

28. Joseph Alsop and Stewart Alsop, "Labor Bill Veto?" *Washington Post,* June 2, 1947; Marquis Childs, "Politics and the Labor Bill Veto," *Washington Post,* June 23, 1947.

29. Gross, *Reshaping of the National Labor Relations Board,* pp. 258–59.

30. Secretary of the Interior Julius Krug to James Webb, June 16, 1947, "President's Correspondence, H.R. 3020," Box 7, Clifford Papers.

31. Joseph Alsop and Stewart Alsop, "Labor Bill: Next Round," *Washington Post,* June 23, 1947.

32. House, *Message from the President of the United States Returning without His Approval the Bill (H.R. 3020) Entitled the "Labor-Management Relations Act, 1947,"* 80th Cong., 1st sess., 1947, Doc. 334, pp. 1–2; press release of President Truman's radio address concerning his veto of the Taft-Hartley bill, June 20, 1947, "General: Taft-Hartley Act," Box 158, Eben Ayers Papers, Truman Library.

33. Sumner Slichter to John Steelman, June 10, 1947, "Taft-Hartley Bill 1947–48," O.F. 407, Box 1114, Truman Papers.

34. J. Douglas Brown to Clark Clifford, June 13, 1947, "Taft Hartley Veto Message," Box 5, David Stowe Papers, Truman Library; Douglas Brown to James Forrestal, June 9, 1947, "Taft-Hartley Bill Correspondence #1," Box 7, Clifford Papers.

35. Brown to Clifford, June 13, 1947.

36. William Leiserson to Clark Clifford, June 14, 1947, p. 2, "Taft-Hartley Bill Correspondence #2," Box 7, Clifford Papers. Leiserson wrote: "The main trouble with the Taft-Hartley Bill is that it hits at strikes, and hitting at strikes misses the point. Men do not stop work because they like to lose time and wages. It is because something vitally important to them is involved that they vote to go on strike. Unless those vital things are satisfactorily adjusted, prohibiting or enjoining the strikes is bound to be a futile gesture, as was made plain many years ago when all strikes were treated as criminal conspiracies."

37. Memorandum from George Taylor to Clark Clifford, June 14, 1947, p. 1, "Taft-Hartley Veto Message," Box 5, Stowe Papers.

38. Brown to Forrestal, June 9, 1947, p. 2.
39. Slichter to Steelman, June 10, 1947.
40. Leiserson to Clifford, June 14, 1947, p. 2.
41. Memorandum from Taylor to Clifford, June 14, 1947, pp. 6, 3. Emphasis added.
42. Millis and Brown, *From the Wagner Act to Taft-Hartley,* p. 273.
43. Ibid., p. 655.
44. Ibid., p. 665. One otherwise favorable review called this assessment an "emotional outburst" that was "more sweeping in its condemnation and less temperate in its language than appears to be justified by the substantive analysis of Dr. Millis." Harold Davey, review of *From the Wagner Act to Taft-Hartley, Industrial and Labor Relations Review* 4, no. 4 (July 1951): 604.
45. Ibid., p. 274.
46. For a related discussion, see Leon Keyserling to Clark Clifford, June 3, 1947, "Taft-Hartley Bill Correspondence #1," Box 7, Clifford Papers. See also Keyserling, "Why the Wagner Act?" pp. 5–33.
47. The nature and consequences of the NLRB's involvement with the Taft-Hartley bill are discussed in Chapter 2.
48. Memorandum from Paul Herzog to Truman, December 11, 1946, "Labor 80th Congress Domestic Affairs," Box 7, Clifford Papers. Herzog told Truman that the "public interest requires that the Administration make the first move to propose legislation that would protect both employers and employees from the use of economic pressure by labor organizations to compel an employer to violate or ignore a certification or order of the National Labor Relations Board." Among other possible modifications, in Herzog's opinion, was the inclusion in the Wagner Act of a "declaration of the sacred constitutional right" of free speech. Herzog warned, "Such a declaration could not, however, go far beyond present Board practice without opening the door to certain employers to embark on a campaign to interfere with their employees' right to chose their own bargaining representative."
49. Memorandum from Paul Herzog to Truman, June 11, 1947, p. 1, "Taft-Hartley Bill Analysis," Box 8, Clifford Papers.
50. *Legislative History of the Taft-Hartley Act,* 2:1575–86.
51. Herzog wrote in his diary, "Reynolds thinks [Taft-Hartley] bill is OK and should be signed, but is being loyal to Board majority view of Houston and myself." Paul Herzog Diary, week of June 9, 1947, Labor-Management Documentation Center, ILR, Cornell University.
52. *Legislative History of the Taft-Hartley Act,* 2:1577.
53. Leiserson to Clifford, June 14, 1947, pp. 3–4.
54. *Legislative History of the Taft-Hartley Act,* 2:1577.
55. Memorandum from Paul Herzog to Clark Clifford, June 6, 1947, p. 5, "President's Correspondence H.R. 3020," Box 7, Clifford Papers.
56. Memorandum from Taylor to Clifford, June 14, 1947, p. 6. Taylor noted an important connection between the elimination of experts and the Taft-Hartley bill require-

ment that, to survive judicial review, the findings of the board had to be supported by *substantial* evidence on the record considered as a whole.

57. *Legislative History of the Taft-Hartley Act,* 2:1578.

58. Ibid., p. 1579.

59. Memorandum from Herzog to Truman, June 11, 1947, p. 6.

60. Ibid., pp. 4, 6–7; memorandum from Herzog to Clifford, June 6, 1947, p. 4; Leiserson to Clifford, June 14, 1947, p. 5.

61. *Legislative History of the Taft-Hartley Act,* 2:1580.

62. Ibid., p. 1583.

63. Memorandum from Herzog to Truman, June 11, 1947, p. 5; memorandum from Herzog to Truman, December 11, 1946, p. 5.

64. Paul Weiler, "Promises to Keep: Security Workers' Rights to Self-Organization under the NLRA," *Harvard Law Review* 96 (June 1983): 1913.

65. W. Willard Wirtz, "The New National Labor Relations Board; Herein of 'Employer Persuasion,'" *Northwestern University Law Review* 49 (November–December 1954): 614.

66. Millis and Brown, *From the Wagner Act to Taft-Hartley,* p. 250.

67. Clyde Summers, "Politics, Policy Making, and the NLRB," *Syracuse Law Review* 6 (Fall 1954): 95.

Chapter 2

1. Joseph Loftus, "Wider Labor Rift Seen in Taft Law," *New York Times,* August 10, 1947, p. 7. Many city, state, and private agencies, such as the American Arbitration Association, were being asked to conduct employee elections. A. H. Raskin, "Labor, Employers, By-passing NLRB," *New York Times,* October 5, 1947, p. 58; Louis Stark, "Unions Weigh Plan to Sidestep NLRB," *New York Times,* July 2, 1947, p. 14. For unions' overall strategy, see Joseph Loftus, "Labor Is Bracing against New Law," *New York Times,* August 3, 1947. Not all unions chose to boycott the NLRB: "Union, Protesting, Obeys Labor Law," *New York Times,* July 30, 1947, p. 9; "Utilities to Get No-Strike Pacts," *New York Times,* August 19, 1947, p. 38; "How Groups Differ on NLRB 'Boycott,'" *U.S. News & World Report,* August 8, 1947, pp. 27–29.

2. Transcript of radio interview, September 2, 1947, Folder 8, Box 7, Office of the Secretary Treasurer, George Meany Memorial Archives, Washington, D.C.

3. Transcript of AFL conference on the provisions of the Taft-Hartley Act, July 9, 1947, pp. 20–21, Folder 3, Box 6, Office of the Secretary Treasurer, Meany Archives; Louis Stark, "200 AFL Chiefs Map Fight on Labor Act," *New York Times,* July 10, 1947, p. 1.

4. Joseph Loftus, "AFL Calls Illegal Two Points in Law," *New York Times,* June 29, 1947, p. 1.

5. "Counterattack by the Unions," *U.S. News & World Report,* July 11, 1947, pp. 25–26. President Green was not short of rhetoric: "Run Taft-Hartley, Green Dares

GOP," *New York Times,* August 20, 1947, p. 13; "Green Defies GOP to Nominate Taft," *New York Times,* August 12, 1947, p. 1; "National Stoppage on '48 Election Day Scheduled by AFL," *New York Times,* August 19, 1947, p. 1.

6. The Joint Committee, established pursuant to Sections 401 and 402 of the Taft-Hartley Act, was composed of seven members of the Senate Labor Committee and seven members of the House Labor Committee, including senators Robert Taft, Irving Ives, James E. Murray, and Claude E. Pepper and congressmen Clare E. Hoffman, John Lesinski, Graham Barden, and Augustus B. Kelley. Thomas Shroyer was chief counsel.

7. *Legislative History of the Taft-Hartley Act,* 2:1575–86.

8. Memorandum to the file, June 16, 1947, "Taft-Hartley and Labor Legislation," Box 6, Paul Herzog Papers, Harry S Truman Library, Independence, Mo.

9. Ball to Truman, June 16, 1947, "Taft Hartley Bill," O.F. 407, Box 1114, Harry S Truman Papers, Truman Library.

10. Paul Herzog Diary, week of June 16, 1947, Labor-Management Documentation Center (LMDC), ILR, Cornell University. Herzog noted in his diary, "Reynolds has always disapproved issuance of 'analysis.'"

11. Ibid., weeks of January 13, February 10, April 28, and May 5, 1947.

12. Ibid., weeks of March 3 and 10, 1947.

13. Oral History interview with Gerhard Van Arkel, July 24, 1975, pp. 8–16, LMDC.

14. Herzog Diary, week of January 13, 1947.

15. Oral History interview with Van Arkel, p. 17.

16. For more details concerning the work of this committee, see James A. Gross, *The Reshaping of the National Labor Relations Board: National Labor Policy in Transition, 1937–1947* (Albany: State University of New York Press, 1981), pp. 256–57.

17. Herzog Diary, weeks of February 24 and June 9, 1947; Oral History interview with Paul Herzog, January 6, 1972, p. 77, LMDC.

18. Herzog Diary, weeks of January 20 and February 3, 1947.

19. Ibid., week of January 27, 1947.

20. Arthur Krock, "The Chief Damage Done by the President," *New York Times,* June 24, 1947, p. 22; "The Labor Bill Becomes Law," *New York Times,* June 24, 1947, p. 22; *Cong. Rec.,* 80th Cong., 1st sess. (June 26, 1947), 93, pt. 6:7688.

21. Herzog Diary, weeks of May 26 and June 2, 1947.

22. Van Arkel to Truman, June 23, 1947, PPF File 5686, Box 1292, Truman Papers; "NLRB Counsel Resigns," *New York Times,* June 24, 1947, p. 2; "Ex-NLRB Counsel Assails Labor Act," *New York Times,* July 17, 1947, p. 11; "Glushien Quits NLRB," *New York Times,* July 1, 1947, p. 15 (Glushien was associate general counsel); "Two More NLRB Aides Quit," *New York Times,* August 5, 1947.

23. Van Arkel to Herzog, Houston, and Reynolds, June 23, 1947, PPF File 5686, Box 1292, Truman Papers. See also Oral History interview with Van Arkel, pp. 20–21.

24. Herzog Diary, week of June 9, 1947.

25. Oral History interview with Herzog, pp. 77–79.

26. Oral History interview with Herzog, pp. 79, 81.

27. Herzog Diary, week of June 9, 1947.

28. For a series of "Dear Paul" notes from Truman to Herzog and personal notes and gifts of classical music records from Herzog to Truman, see PPF File 1681, Box 1291, Truman Papers.

29. Herzog Diary, week of May 12, 1947.

30. Ibid., week of June 16, 1947.

31. Oral History interview with Herzog, pp. 80–81.

32. Herzog Diary, week of June 23, 1947; Louis Stark, "Truman Sees NLRB; Fairness Pledged," *New York Times,* June 25, 1947, p. 1.

33. Transcript of nationwide CBS broadcast by Paul Herzog, June 24, 1947, p. 1, "1947," O.F. 145, Box 623, Truman Papers; "Labor Board's Three Seasoned Men Determined to Carry out Law," *U.S. News & World Report,* July 11, 1947, pp. 52–55.

34. "Statement by the President at His News Conference," June 26, 1947, "General File, Taft-Hartley Act," Box 158, Eben Ayers Papers, Truman Library.

35. Section 3(d).

36. Ida Klaus, "The Taft-Hartley Experiment in Separation of NLRB Functions," *Industrial and Labor Relations Review* 11, no. 3 (April 1958): 378–79, 381–82, 385–86.

37. "How Counsel Chosen for Labor Board Would Use Board Powers: Defense for Employers' Rights and a 'Square Break' to Unions," *U.S. News & World Report,* August 1, 1947, pp. 50–51.

38. Louis Stark, "Truman Fills New NLRB, Denham Is General Counsel," *New York Times,* July 18, 1947, p. 1; Oral History interview with Mozart Ratner, July 25, 1988, pp. 31–33, LMDC.

39. Oral History interview with James Reynolds, July 25, 1975, pp. 18–19, LMDC.

40. Oral History interview with Herzog, p. 84. For Houston's background, see Gross, *Reshaping of the National Labor Relations Board,* pp. 245–46; for Reynolds's background, see Oral History interview with Herzog, pp. 31–33, and Oral History interview with Reynolds, pp. 4–5, 8, 13.

41. Bill Davidson, "Labor's Biggest Boss," *Collier's,* November 1, 1947, pp. 12–13, 84–87; "How Counsel Chosen for Labor Board," pp. 50–51; "Fair Target," *Time,* August 4, 1947, p. 11.

42. Oral History interview with Frank Kleiler, August 3, 1988, p. 7, LMDC.

43. Davidson, "Labor's Biggest Boss," pp. 13, 84.

44. Ibid., p. 84.

45. Ibid., p. 85.

46. Senate Committee on Labor and Public Welfare, *Confirmation of Nominees for National Labor Relations Board,* 80th Cong., 1st sess., 1947, pp. 5, 1 (hereinafter *Confirmation Hearings*); Davidson, "Labor's Biggest Boss," p. 84.

47. *Confirmation Hearings,* p. 10 (quotation); Davidson, "Labor's Biggest Boss," pp. 85–86.

48. Oral History interview with George Bott, August 10, 1988, p. 31, LMDC; Oral History interview with A. Norman Somers, August 1, 1988, p. 11, LMDC.

49. Oral History interview with Norton Come, July 29, 1988, p. 2, LMDC; Oral History interview with Bott, p. 32.

50. Oral History interviews with Paul Herzog, January 6, 1972, pp. 82–86, and July 15, 1975, p. 63, LMDC.

51. Oral History interview with Meta Barghausen, July 24, 1975, pp. 15–16, LMDC.

52. Oral History interview with Marcel Mallet-Prevost, August 4, 1988, p. 7, LMDC.

53. Oral History interview with Bott, p. 28; Oral History interview with William Feldesman, July 28, 1988, p. 9, LMDC.

54. "Denham v. NLRB," *Newsweek,* January 23, 1950, p. 67; "Labor Board's Three Seasoned Men," p. 54; Oral History interview with Van Arkel, pp. 21–22; Oral History interview with Herzog, January 6, 1972, pp. 82–83.

55. Section 3(a) provided that the NLRB's membership would be increased from three to five.

56. "Ball Is Made Chairman of New Labor Act Study," *New York Times,* July 22, 1947, p. 16.

57. *Confirmation Hearings,* pp. 2, 10–11.

58. Ibid., pp. 12, 14–15.

59. Ibid., pp. 17, 21.

60. Ibid., p. 17.

61. Louis Stark, "NLRB His Domain, President Asserts," *New York Times,* August 12, 1947, p. 16. See also "Truman Hits GOP on Labor Policy," *New York Times,* August 15, 1947, p. 9.

62. *Confirmation Hearings,* pp. 23–26, 30, 37–41.

63. Ibid., pp. 24, 39.

64. Ibid., pp. 24–25.

65. Ibid., pp. 35, 49, 90.

66. Ibid., pp. 54–64. See also Gross, *Reshaping of the National Labor Relations Board,* pp. 152–225, for a discussion of the Smith committee and Murdock's role.

67. *Confirmation Hearings,* p. 57. Even Denham's friend Senator Donnell believed Ball was asking for too much; he asked Ball what he meant by "sympathetic administration" and commented, "It seems to me we have a law here and it seems to me Senator Murdock is going to enforce it. I cannot see the 'sympathy' part." Ibid., pp. 58–59.

68. Ibid., pp. 59, 62.

69. Joseph Loftus, "Senate Unit Backs Nominees to NLRB," *New York Times,* July 26, 1947, p. 26; "Senate Fight Due on NLRB Counsel," *New York Times,* August 10, 1947, p. 1.

70. Loftus, "Senate Unit Backs Nominees," p. 26.

71. "New NLRB Team," *Business Week,* July 26, 1947, p. 88.

72. David Lawrence, "Labor Law Majority Held Outmaneuvered by Board Choices,"

Washington Star, July 25, 1947, in *Cong. Rec.,* 80th Cong., 1st sess. (December 16, 1947), 93, pt. 9:11447.

73. "NLRB Appointees Left Unconfirmed," *New York Times,* July 28, 1947, p. 8; Senator James Murray to Truman, July 28, 1947, O.F. 145, Box 623, Truman Papers. Murray told Truman, "If the matter had come to a vote in the Senate, I am sure that they all would have been confirmed."

74. C. P. Trussell, "Truman Makes Recess Appointees of Three Nominees to Expanded NLRB," *New York Times,* August 1, 1947; Harold B. Hinton, "Truman Flies Back to Washington; Faces Decision on NLRB Nominees," *New York Times,* July 30, 1947, p. 1.

75. "Two New on NLRB, Cite Public's Right," *New York Times,* August 2, 1947, p. 26. In what would become a most ironic comment, Denham said, "If we all play together on this team, keeping the objective in mind at all times, we can't go wrong." Ibid.

76. Lawrence, "Labor Law Majority"; Loftus, "Senate Unit Backs Nominees," p. 26.

77. "Truman 'Warning' Quoted," *New York Times,* August 17, 1947, p. 6; "Throttling of NLRB Is Alleged by Union," *New York Times,* August 14, 1947, p. 27.

Chapter 3

1. NLRB, *Thirteenth Annual Report,* for the fiscal year ended June 30, 1948 (Washington, D.C.: GPO, 1949), pp. iii, 1, 3–9, 13–15.

2. Ida Klaus, "The Taft-Hartley Experiment in Separation of NLRB Functions," *Industrial and Labor Relations Review* 11, 3 (April 1958): 378.

3. Ibid., pp. 378–79.

4. Robert Denham, "The Taft-Hartley Act," *Tennessee Law Review* 20 (February 1948): 170–71.

5. Oral History interview with Paul Herzog, January 6, 1972, p. 91, Labor-Management Documentation Center (LMDC), ILR, Cornell University.

6. Senate Committee on Labor and Public Welfare, *Confirmation of Nominees for National Labor Relations Board,* 80th Cong., 1st sess., 1947, p. 3 (Hereinafter *Confirmation Hearings.*)

7. Oral History interview with Frank Kleiler, August 3, 1988, p. 3, LMDC.

8. Ibid. Kleiler helped "construct" the memorandum of understanding.

9. Oral History interview with Herzog, p. 84.

10. Louis Stark, "Herzog Speech Indicates How Denham Role Grew," *New York Times,* October 3, 1947, p. 3.

11. For the full text of the *Memorandum Describing Statutory and Delegated Functions of the General Counsel,* see *Federal Register* 13 (February 13, 1948): 654. For a summary, see NLRB, *Thirteenth Annual Report,* pp. 9–10. See also Denham, "Taft-Hartley Act," pp. 169–71, and Klaus, "Taft-Hartley Experiment," pp. 379–80.

12. Klaus, "Taft-Hartley Experiment," pp. 379–80.

13. Section 9(h). Emphasis added.
14. Louis Stark, "Denham Is Reported Determined to Keep Anti-Red Affidavit Rule," *New York Times,* August 30, 1947, p. 28.
15. "Unions Are Warned on a Red Disclaimer," *New York Times,* August 18, 1947, p. 19; Louis Stark, "Loyalty Test Form Issued by Denham," *New York Times,* August 20, 1947, p. 13. Later Denham narrowed his definition of "officer" to the president and secretary-treasurer of both organizations plus the nine vice-presidents of the CIO and the thirteen vice-presidents of the AFL. John Cort, "The Labor Movement: Lewis Does It Again," *The Commonweal,* October 10, 1947, pp. 625–26; "CIO Risks in Boycott of NLRB," *U.S. News & World Report,* August 29, 1947, p. 25.
16. Stark, "Loyalty Test Form," p. 13; Louis Stark, "Denham Disputed on Anti-Red Rule," *New York Times,* August 19, 1947, p. 20: "The Joint Congressional Committee would have been satisfied if Mr. Denham had stated that all local and national officers of a single national labor organization would have to sign the anti-Communist affidavit if their locals were to be eligible for appearance before the NLRB"; Louis Stark, "Hartley 'Red View' Weighed by NLRB," *New York Times,* September 5, 1947, p. 9; Louis Stark, "Officials Disagree on Filing by Unions," *New York Times,* September 9, 1947, p. 22.
17. "AFL Stand Will Not Affect NLRB Rule, Denham Says," *New York Times,* September 14, 1947, p. 2; "NLRB Firm in Call for Union Pledges," *New York Times,* September 22, 1947, p. 10.
18. Cort, "Labor Movement," p. 626.
19. Ibid., pp. 625–26; Joseph Loftus, "Lewis Forces AFL to Boycott NLRB for Affidavit Rule," *New York Times,* September 13, 1947, p. 1; Joseph Loftus, "Lewis Wants War on New Labor Act," *New York Times,* September 14, 1947, p. 1.
20. Louis Stark, "AFL Fights NLRB on Anti-Red Rule," *New York Times,* September 17, 1947, p. 22.
21. Ibid.; Louis Stark, "AFL Slated to Back Lewis on Affidavit," *New York Times,* September 26, 1947, p. 19.
22. "NLRB Rules on Compliance with Registration and Affidavit Requirements," press release, (R-7), October 7, 1947, NN 3-25-86-1, Record Group (RG) 25, National Archives (NA); Louis Stark, "Affidavit Test Is Planned by CIO," *New York Times,* September 16, 1947, p. 17; Louis Stark, "First Test Today of NLRB Affidavit," *New York Times,* October 1, 1947, p. 25.
23. Lawrence Davies, "AFL Waits on NLRB in Affidavit Issue," *New York Times,* October 6, 1947, p. 1; "Green Hails Labor for Barring Slump," *New York Times,* October 7, 1947, p. 22.
24. At first it was rumored that Herzog was "leaning in the direction of reversal," with Reynolds and Gray supporting Denham, and Houston and Murdock opposing Denham. Stark, "AFL Slated," p. 19. Later it was rumored that Gray might join the other four members in opposing Denham. Louis Stark, "NLRB Is Expected to Overrule, 4–1, Denham Red Stand," *New York Times,* October 2, 1947, p. 1; Louis

Stark, "Reversal Hinted of Denham Stand," *New York Times,* October 4, 1947, p. 8. See also: Louis Stark, "AFL, CIO Yielding on Oath Predicted," *New York Times,* August 28, 1947, p. 26.

25. Louis Stark, "Expect Overriding of Denham Today," *New York Times,* October 6, 1947, p. 17.

26. Louis Stark, "NLRB Overruling of Denham Put Off," *New York Times,* October 7, 1947, p. 22.

27. Ibid.; Stark, "Expect Overriding," p. 17.

28. Stark, "NLRB Overruling," p. 22.

29. Memorandum from Denham to Herzog, October 14, 1947, NN 3-25-86-1, RG 25, NA. The agreement concerned the financial reporting requirements of Section 9(f).

30. 75 NLRB 11 (1947).

31. Ibid., pp. 12–14.

32. Ibid., p. 16.

33. Louis Stark, "NLRB Cancels, 4–1, Denham Red Order for AFL-CIO Chiefs," *New York Times,* October 8, 1947, p. 1.

34. Ball added that the question of requiring AFL and CIO officers to sign the affidavits was never discussed when the bill was under consideration, "so actually there was no departure from intent." Ibid.

35. "Not in Conflict Says Taft," *New York Times,* October 8, 1947, p. 6.

36. "Now the Trouble Starts," *The Nation,* October 18, 1947, p. 398.

37. "NLRB Ruling Averts Split," *Business Week,* October 11, 1947, p. 88.

38. Congress, *Report of the Joint Committee on Labor-Management Relations* (March 15, 1948), 80th Cong., 2d sess., Rept. 986, Majority Report, pp. 10–11 (hereinafter *Joint Committee Intermediate Report—Majority Views*); "Breakdown of NLRB Boycott," *U.S. News & World Report,* October 17, 1947, pp. 22–26; "Textile Union to File Non-Communist Oath," *New York Times,* October 7, 1947, p. 22; Lawrence Davies, "Committee Weighs AFL Charter Shift," *New York Times,* October 9, 1947; Lawrence Davies, "AFL Rebuffs Lewis, Overwhelms Plea to Defy Labor Law," *New York Times,* October 15, 1947, p. 1; Louis Stark, "UAW Capitulates in Taft Act Fight, to Sign Affidavits," *New York Times,* November 1, 1947, p. 1; "Green Files with NLRB Non-Communist Affidavit," *New York Times,* November 6, 1947, p. 31.

39. "The First Hundred Days," speech before the Institute on Labor Law of the University of Minnesota, December 6, 1947, p. 7, Paul Herzog Papers.

40. "The Labor Management Relations Act: The First Two Hundred Days," speech by Herzog to the Industrial Relations Conference of the Chamber of Commerce, March 18, 1948, p. 2, "1948," O.F. 145, Box 624, Harry S Truman Papers, Harry S Truman Library, Independence, Mo. The Board had scheduled oral argument in the first case arising under Section 8(b) of the act for March 30. At the time of Herzog's speech 420 such cases had been filed. Ibid., p. 6.

41. "Decisions of the NLRB under the Labor Management Relations Act," speech before the Pacific Coast Management Conference, April 21, 1948, p. 1, and "The

National Labor Relations Board Today," speech before the Commonwealth Club of California, April 23, 1948, pp. 2–3, Herzog Papers.

42. Section 403 read, "The committee shall report to the Senate and the House of Representatives not later than March 15, 1948, the results of its study and investigation, together with such recommendations as to necessary legislation and such other recommendations as it may deem advisable and shall make its final report not later than January 2, 1949."

43. *Joint Committee Intermediate Report—Majority Views,* pp. 3, 32, 43, 44–46. The committee had studied Botany Mills, Passaic, N.J.; B.F. Goodrich Co., Akron, Ohio; Murray Corp., Detroit; R.J. Reynolds Co., Winston-Salem, N.C.; George A. Hormel Co., Austin, Minn.; International Harvester Corp., Chicago; and Lincoln Electric Co., Cleveland.

44. Congress, *Report of the Joint Committee on Labor-Management Relations* (April 1, 1948), 80th Cong., 2d sess., Rept. 986, Part 2, Minority Report, pp. 2–4, 23. (Hereinafter *Joint Committee Intermediate Report—Minority Views.*) The minority also charged that the majority, "using the same outrageous methods that they have used in passing the Taft-Hartley Act," deliberately "kept their report a secret from the minority until the day before we were required to vote for or against" it. *Cong. Rec.* 80th Cong., 2d sess. (March 15, 1948), 94, pt. 2:2847.

45. *Joint Committee Intermediate Report—Majority Views,* p. 4.

46. *Joint Committee Intermediate Report—Minority Views,* p. 16.

47. Ibid., p. 16.

48. Ibid.

49. *Joint Committee Intermediate Report—Majority Views,* p. 8.

50. NLRB, *Thirteenth Annual Report,* pp. 47–48.

51. *NLRB v. Fainblatt,* 306 U.S. 601 (1948).

52. Philip Feldblum, "Jurisdictional 'Tidelands' in Labor Relations," *Virginia Law Review* 38 (February 1952): 187–99; Archibald Cox and Marshall J. Seidman, "Federalism and Labor Relations," *Harvard Law Review* 64 (December 1950): 211–45; Bernard Goodman and Robert Griggs, "Jurisdiction of NLRB under Self-Imposed Limitations," *Michigan Law Review* 50 (April 1952): 899–915.

53. Louis Stark, "NRB Challenged by Its Legal Head," *New York Times,* March 18, 1949, p. 28.

54. House Committee on Expenditures in the Executive Departments, *Investigation to Ascertain Scope of Interpretation by General Counsel of NLRB of the Term "Affecting Commerce" as Used in the Labor Management Relations Act, 1947,* 80th Cong., 2d sess., 1948, H. Rept. 2050, p. 1. (Hereinafter *Expenditures Committee Report.*)

55. James A. Gross, *The Reshaping of the National Labor Relations Board: National Labor Policy in Transition, 1937–1947,* (Albany: State University of New York Press, 1981), pp. 75, 79, 182, 252.

56. *Expenditures Committee Report,* p. 2.

57. House, *Hearings before the Subcommittees of the Committee on Education and*

Labor and of the Committee on Expenditures in the Executive Departments, Investigation to Ascertain Scope of Interpretation by General Counsel of NLRB of the Term "Affecting Commerce" as Used in the Labor Management Relations Act, 1947, 80th Cong., 2d sess., 1948, p. 10. (Hereinafter *Expenditures Committee Hearings.*)

58. Oral History interview with George Bott, August 10, 1988, p. 19, LMDC.

59. For a biography of Brownell, see Marjorie Dent Candee, editor, *Current Biography* (New York: H.W. Wilson, 1954), pp. 120–23; *Who's Who in America,* vol. 28 (Chicago: Marquis—Who's Who, 1954), p. 347.

60. *Expenditures Committee Hearings,* p. 16.

61. *Expenditures Committee Report,* p. 5.

62. Ibid., pp. 5–6.

63. 83 NLRB 564 (1949); 83 NLRB 587 (1949).

64. 83 NLRB at 565–66.

65. Ibid., p. 566.

66. Congress, *Hearings before the Joint Committee on Labor-Management Relations on the Operation of the Labor-Management Relations Act, 1947,* 80th Cong., 2d sess., 1948. (Hereinafter *Joint Committee Hearings.*)

67. Ibid., pp. 51, 76; Joseph Loftus, "Union Shop Voting Opposed by NLRB in a Taft Act Report," *New York Times,* May 25, 1948, p. 1.

68. *Joint Committee Hearings,* p. 54. Eighty-nine percent of the eligible voters voted in favor of union shop authorization (actually, over 94 percent of those voting, since those not voting were, in effect, casting "no" votes). Ibid., pp. 54, 79.

69. Ibid., p. 61.

70. *Inland Steel Company,* 77 NLRB 1 (1948).

71. Ibid., pp. 4, 7, 11–13. Gray dissented: "I strongly believe that neither employers nor unions should be *required* by this Board to bargain collectively on a subject matter which has *not* become an industry or general business practice. . . . That neither employers nor unions have regarded retirement programs as a *compulsory* subject for collective bargaining generally, is readily understandable from the complexities and confusions which would inevitably result from such a step. . . . I can only conclude that the Congress used the words 'wages, hours, and working conditions' in the then existing normally accepted common usage of the terms. That did not include retirement programs." Ibid., pp. 17–19. Emphasis in original.

72. Joseph Loftus, "Ball Group Maps Taft Act Inquiry," *New York Times,* April 16, 1948, p. 19. The agenda for the Joint Committee's hearing included the following statement: "What is a sound, permanent solution to the problem of union welfare funds? . . . Is a jointly administered welfare fund desirable or workable, particularly where a large employer may deal with a dozen or more different unions?" *Cong. Rec.,* 80th Cong., 2d sess. (May 4, 1948), 94, pt. 4:5241.

73. For calls to amend the act to relieve employers of the *obligation* to bargain about employee benefit programs but still permit them to do so if they wished, see *Joint Committee Hearings,* pp. 141, 455, 825.

74. "Industry Attacks NLRB Pension Rule," *New York Times,* June 3, 1948, p. 18.
75. *Joint Committee Hearings,* pp. 1128–29.
76. 70 NLRB 802 (1946).
77. Such violations are known as "per se" violations.
78. 77 NLRB 577, 578 (1948). One law note commented: "Section 8(c) was enacted merely to broaden the employer's area of free speech by precluding the use of such statements as a basis for, or evidence of, a finding of unfair practices. In order to give appropriate effect to this Section, it is not necessary that compulsory audiences now be sanctioned." "'Compulsory Audience' No Longer an Unfair Labor Practice Per Se," *Columbia Law Review* 48 (November 1948): 1100. See also "Employer Who Addresses Captive Audience Must Give Union Equal Opportunity," *Harvard Law Review* 65 (February 1952): 695–97.
79. 77 NLRB 124 (1948).
80. Ibid., p. 127 fn. 10.
81. Ibid., pp. 126, 127.
82. Ibid., p. 126. Reynolds and Gray dissented: "It is paradoxical, to say the least, that now, after Congress has so strongly rejected the Board's prior construction of the Act in relation to the Constitutional guarantee of free speech, that this Board should construe privileged expressions of opinion as creating an atmosphere which prevents employees from freely expressing their choice of representatives in a Board-conducted election. If the expression or dissemination of views, arguments, or opinion by an employer is to be afforded the full freedom which the amended Act envisages, it follows that the Board cannot justify setting aside elections merely because the employer avails himself of the protection which the statute specifically provides." Ibid., p. 131.
83. *Joint Committee Hearings,* p. 1151.
84. Ibid., p. 1152. Herzog told the Joint Committee: "I might say for the record, although it is not customary to do this, that a decision will be issued within a week, a copy of which will be sent to the Committee if it desires to have it. It is a case which will point out the limitations on the General Shoe doctrine. I do not think I ought to mention the name of the case at this time." Ibid.
85. Senate, *Senate Hearings before the Committee on Labor and Public Welfare on S. 249, a Bill to Diminish the Causes of Labor Disputes Burdening or Obstructing Interstate and Foreign Commerce and for Other Purposes,* 81st Cong., 1st sess., 1949, pp. 1270–71. (Hereinafter *Senate Repeal Hearings.*)
86. Ibid., p. 1557. Shroyer's speech, given at French Lick, Indiana, is reprinted in full on pp. 1552–57.
87. Louis Stark, "NLRB Counsel Sues Two Unions on Charge New Law Is Defied," *New York Times,* September 24, 1947, p. 1. See also *Senate Repeal Hearings,* pp. 1273–74; House, *House Hearings before a Special Subcommittee of the Committee on Education and Labor on H.R. 2032, a Bill to Repeal the Labor-Management Relations Act of 1947, to Reenact the National Labor Relations Act of 1935, and*

for Other Purposes, 81st Cong., 1st sess., 1949, p. 1080. (Hereinafter *House Repeal Hearings.*)

88. *Senate Repeal Hearings,* p. 1649, citing Joseph Loftus, "Ball Calls Proposals of ITU in Baltimore, 'Thinly Veiled Closed Shop Camouflage,'" *New York Times,* October 8, 1948, and "Hartley Says ITU Policy Violates Law," *Editor and Publisher Magazine,* August 30, 1947, p. 5.

89. *Cong. Rec.,* 80th Cong., 2d sess. (March 25, 1948), 94, pt. 3:3489–90. The number of suits against the ITU depended in part on how case consolidations were counted. See *Senate Repeal Hearings,* p. 1278, for ITU counsel Van Arkel's calculation, and p. 1300, for General Counsel Denham's.

90. *Senate Repeal Hearings,* p. 1271.

91. For ITU president Woodruff Randolph's opinions, see *House Repeal Hearings,* pp. 1077–92. Denham attacked the ITU in a speech to the National Association of Manufacturers: "Industry Warned on Closed Shop," *New York Times,* December 5, 1947, p. 21. See also "House Unit Hears Three Dispute Issues in Inquiry on Chicago ITU Strike," *New York Times,* December 23, 1947, p. 18.

92. "Ban on ITU Strikes Drafted for Court," *New York Times,* March 23, 1948, p. 19; *House Repeal Hearings,* pp. 1081–82: "The ITU was enjoined from refusing to bargain collectively, from asking for 'conditions of employment' . . . from asking that agreements be canceled on 60 days notice, from seeking to cause employers to discriminate against non-union men, from attempting to maintain closed shop conditions, or from supporting strikes for any of those purposes." Joseph Loftus, "ITU Counsel Defies Subpoena of NLRB," *New York Times,* December 23, 1947, p. 18.

93. David Findling, associate general counsel, to Truman, August 19, 1948, O.F. 1684, Box 1190, Truman Papers; reproduced in *Senate Repeal Hearings,* pp. 1109–10. Unless otherwise indicated, the description of the meeting with Taft is based on Findling's account.

94. "Denham Disputes Charge of ITU that Taft Interfered in NLRB," *New York Times,* August 24, 1948, p. 16; *Senate Repeal Hearings,* p. 1180.

95. See *Senate Repeal Hearings,* p. 1634, for a reproduction of Joseph Loftus, "Taft Would Hold ITU for Contempt—Senator Calls for Action on an Injunction Requiring Union to Conform to Labor Law," *New York Times,* August 14, 1948.

96. Findling added, "We questioned the practicality of any such suggestion, but said we would consider it further."

97. Truman to Findling, August 20, 1948, O.F. 1684, Box 1190, Truman Papers.

98. "Denham Disputes Charge," p. 16.

99. "Putting on the Heat," *Washington Post,* September 16, 1948, reproduced in *Senate Repeal Hearings,* pp. 1635–36.

100. *Senate Repeal Hearings,* pp. 1100–1101, 1106.

101. "Denham Disputes Charge," p. 16.

102. *Senate Repeal Hearings,* p. 1633.

103. "Legislative Pressure," *Washington Post,* August 25, 1948, reproduced in *Senate Repeal Hearings,* p. 1635.

Chapter 4

1. Harry S Truman, *Memoirs*, vol. 2, *Years of Trial and Hope* (Garden City, N.Y.: Doubleday, 1956), p. 177.
2. John Patrick Diggins, *The Proud Decades: America in War and Peace, 1941–1960* (New York: W. W. Norton, 1988), p. 102.
3. Truman, *Years of Trial and Hope*, pp. 180, 183.
4. Ibid., pp. 184–85.
5. Ibid., pp. 185–86.
6. Diggins, *Proud Decades*, p. 104.
7. Truman, *Years of Trial and Hope*, pp. 207–8.
8. Felix Belair, "Truman Sees Era of Fear in a Republican Victory: Says Labor Is Threatened," *New York Times*, September 7, 1948, p. 1; "Truman Declares Taft Act Is Unfair in Curbs on Labor," *New York Times*, September 2, 1948, p. 1.
9. Truman, *Years of Trial and Hope*, pp. 209–11, 219.
10. Ibid., p. 222 (quotation); "Planks in the Major Party Platforms Compared," *New York Times*, July 15, 1948, p. 10.
11. Louis Stark, "Labor Chiefs Hail Vote as 'Mandate,'" *New York Times*, November 4, 1948.
12. Louis Stark, "Repeal of Taft Act Predicted by Tobin," *New York Times*, November 16, 1948, p. 1 (quotation); "Tobin to Ask End of Closed Shop Ban," *New York Times*, November 9, 1948, p. 18. Maurice Tobin, former governor of Massachusetts (1945–46) and mayor of Boston (1938–44), replaced Secretary of Labor L. B. Schwellenbach, who had died on June 10, 1948.
13. Louis Stark, "Quick Return to Wagner Act Pressed on Congress by AFL," *New York Times*, November 15, 1948, p. 1; Louis Stark, "AFL Would Curb Perilous Strikes," *New York Times*, November 23, 1948, p. 1; Louis Stark, "Wagner Act Urged for Stop-Gap Role," *New York Times*, November 10, 1948, p. 18; "Experts Discuss Labor Law Change," *New York Times*, November 13, 1948, p. 17.
14. Stark, "Quick Return to Wagner Act," p. 1.
15. Diggins, *Proud Decades*, p. 110.
16. Memorandum from William L. Batt to Clark Clifford, September 14, 1948, "L-M Relations Act No. 2," Box 2, Charles Murphy Papers, Harry S Truman Library, Independence, Mo. (quotation); Stark, "Labor Chiefs Hail Vote," p. 9.
17. "Labor Bills Face a Fight," *New York Times*, November 6, 1948, p. 7.
18. Joseph Loftus, "Truman Advisors Divided on Labor," *New York Times*, December 25, 1948, p. 20.
19. John Morris, "Taft Set to Fight for Leading Role," *New York Times*, December 19, 1948, p. 54; William White, "GOP Hinted Willing to Ease Taft Law," *New York Times*, November 18, 1948, p. 1; Louis Stark, "Industry Indicates It Will Cooperate on New Labor Law," *New York Times*, November 6, 1948, p. 1.
20. "President to Keep Domestic Program Based on New Deal," *New York Times*, November 17, 1948.

21. Joseph Loftus, "AFL-CIO Coalition on Taft Act Urged," *New York Times,* December 17, 1948, p. 33; Joseph Loftus, "Truman Hears CIO on New Labor Law," *New York Times,* December 30, 1948, p. 12.

22. "'Business as Usual' Is Program of NLRB, Says Denham, while Present Law Stands," *New York Times,* November 12, 1948, p. 2.

23. Congress, *Report of the Joint Committee on Labor-Management Relations* (December 31, 1948), 80th Cong., 2d sess., Rept. 986, part 3, p. 2. (Hereinafter *Joint Committee Final Report—Majority Views.*)

24. "Text of President Truman's Message to Congress on the State of the Union," *New York Times,* January 6, 1949, p. 4; Louis Stark, "Labor Chiefs Hail Truman Proposals," *New York Times,* January 6, 1949, p. 1.

25. William White, "Labor Law Repeal Put into Senate: Long Fight Likely," *New York Times,* January 7, 1949, p. 1; Louis Stark, "'Packet' Labor Bill Linked to Truman," *New York Times,* January 11, 1949, p. 32.

26. Louis Stark, "Unions Fear a 'Run-Around' in Labor Plans of Congress," *New York Times,* January 7, 1949, p. 1; Louis Stark, "Flexibility Is Aim in Labor Law Plan," *New York Times,* January 4, 1949, p. 7.

27. Stark, "'Packet' Labor Bill," p. 32.

28. Louis Stark, "AFL Presses Plan on New Labor Act," *New York Times,* January 13, 1949, p. 16.

29. Louis Stark, "Stern Fight Is Likely over New Labor Law," *New York Times,* January 9, 1949, sec. 4, p. 4e.

30. William White, "Democrats Speed End of Taft Law," *New York Times,* January 25, 1949, p. 1; Senate, *Senate Hearings before the Committee on Labor and Public Welfare on S. 249, a Bill to Diminish the Causes of Labor Disputes Burdening or Obstructing Interstate and Foreign Commerce and for Other Purposes,* 81st Cong., 1st sess., 1949, p. 19 (hereinafter *Senate Repeal Hearings*); Herzog to Truman, November 24, 1948, NN 3-25-86-1, Record Group (RG) 25, National Archives (NA).

31. The full text of the Thomas bill appears in *Senate Repeal Hearings,* pp. 9–15.

32. Ibid., pp. 10–11. See also "Text of Administration's Bill to Repeal the Taft-Hartley Law and Re-enact the Wagner Act," *New York Times,* January 30, 1949, p. 48.

33. "Administration Argument," *New York Times,* February 13, 1949, sec. 4., p. 2e.

34. See *Senate Repeal Hearings,* pp. 445–46, for CIO general counsel Arthur Goldberg's written comments concerning the need to compromise.

35. Joseph Loftus, "AFL Seen Friendly to New Labor Bill," *New York Times,* February 4, 1949, p. 20; Joseph Loftus, "AFL Council Votes to Back Labor Bill," *New York Times,* February 5, 1949, p. 6; Memorandum, "The Sell-out on Taft Hartley," May 6, 1949, p. 6, Folder 21, Box 48, Department of Legislation (1906–1978), George Meany Memorial Archives, Washington, D.C. Hereinafter "Sell-out on Taft-Hartley." This memorandum is unsigned. It appears to have been prepared by supporters of the United Mine Workers and various left-wing unions within the CIO.

When checked against newspaper accounts and other documents cited here, it proved accurate in every respect.

36. Loftus, "AFL Seen Friendly," p. 20.
37. *Senate Repeal Hearings,* p. 118.
38. Ibid., p. 145. For additional case-handling statistics for the period August 22, 1947–December 1948, see ibid., pp. 1039–60.
39. Ibid., pp. 432, 683–85, 690.
40. Ibid., pp. 1890, 1902–8, 2336–38; James A. Gross, *The Reshaping of the National Labor Relations Board: National Labor Policy in Transition, 1937–1947* (Albany: State University of New York Press, 1981), pp. 61–84, 200–225.
41. *Senate Repeal Hearings,* pp. 2369, 2559–60. Pepper drew the anger of the NAM's representative when he charged that "it was the poor people whose sons went to the battlefields and a lot of the manufacturers' sons who stayed at home and got rich." Ibid., p. 2370. Pepper later apologized for his remark. Ibid., pp. 2728–29.
42. Ibid., pp. 2061, 2063. Neely said he meant nothing "personal" by his accusations.
43. Ibid., p. 857. For Taft's protest and Murray's reply, see pp. 857–58, 1800–1802.
44. Ibid., pp. 2359–61.
45. Ibid., pp. 3181–82.
46. Ibid., pp. 3196–97, 3200, 3202, 3443–45, 3466–67.
47. Ibid., pp. 201–2. Morse reproached Herzog for jesting about the Board's relationship with the Joint Committee on Labor-Management Relations.
48. Ibid., pp. 154, 1034. The Thomas bill retained the Board's authority to seek an injunction to enforce a Board decision.
49. Ibid., p. 212. A district court in New York had earlier issued a decision involving this exact arrangement, a decision that became widely known as the "allied doctrine." *Douds v. Metropolitan Federation of Architects,* 75 F. Supp. 672 (S.D.N.Y. 1948); see *Senate Repeal Hearings,* p. 1312.
50. *Senate Repeal Hearings,* pp. 45, 245.
51. Ibid., p. 147. In Section 9(b)(3) Taft-Hartley stated flatly, "Employees on strike who are not entitled to reinstatement shall not be eligible to vote." Since, pursuant to the Supreme Court's decision in *NLRB v. Mackay Radio & Telegraph Co.,* 304 U.S. 333 (1938), economic strikers (striking over wages, hours, or working conditions) could be permanently replaced, Taft's agreement to repeal this provision was very important.
52. *Senate Repeal Hearings,* p. 147.
53. Ibid., p. 164.
54. Morse wanted the elimination of injunctions, the protection of the voting rights of economic strikers, the "rewording" of the secondary boycott provision, and the abolition of the independent office of general counsel. Louis Stark, "Morse Outlines Labor Bill 'Truce,'" *New York Times,* February 17, 1949, p. 20; Louis Stark, "Morse, Ives Work on New Labor Bill," *New York Times,* February 25, 1949, p. 20.
55. "Taft Bars Retreat on Labor Bill Stand," *New York Times,* February 27, 1949, p. 45.

56. Louis Stark, "Labor Bill Hearing Is Ended in Senate," *New York Times,* February 24, 1949, p. 15.

57. W. H. Lawrence, "President Threatens Tour to Fight for His Program," *New York Times,* February 25, 1949, p. 1; Stanley Levey, "Green Is Doubtful of Taft Act Repeal," *New York Times,* February 26, 1949, p. 3. Green termed the situation "touch and go" and believed that "only a few votes will mean the difference between repeal and no repeal."

58. Louis Stark, "Tobin Fails to Stir Labor Bill Action," *New York Times,* March 3, 1949, p. 28; Louis Stark, "Senate Unit Votes Truman Labor Bill; GOP Assails Action," *New York Times,* March 5, 1949, p. 1; Louis Stark, "Taft Act Assailed in Senate Report," *New York Times,* March 22, 1949, p. 10. For the majority Senate Committee Report, see Senate, *Report to Accompany S. 249,* 81st Cong., 1st sess., 1949, S. Rept. 99, pp. 1–79. (Hereinafter *Senate Repeal Committee Majority Report.*) For minority views, see Congress, *Report to Accompany S. 249,* 81st Cong., 1st sess., 1949, Rept. 99, Part 2, pp. 1–92. (Hereinafter *Senate Repeal Committee Minority Report.*)

59. Louis Stark, "President Claims Powers to Enjoin National Strikes," *New York Times,* February 4, 1949, p. 1.

60. Memorandum from Tobin to Truman, February 21, 1949, "Taft-Hartley Bill 1949–1953," Box 114, O.F. 407, Harry S Truman Papers, Truman Library.

61. Stark, "Labor Bill Is Seen without Changes," p. 8. The majority included John Lesinski and John Kennedy.

62. House, *House Hearings before a Special Subcommittee of the Committee on Education and Labor on H.R. 2032, a Bill to Repeal the Labor-Management Relations Act of 1947 to Reenact the National Labor Relations Act of 1935, and for Other Purposes,* 81st Cong., 1st sess., 1949, p. 1160. (Hereinafter *House Repeal Hearings.*) Morgan testified that he was present at all the meetings of the House-Senate conference committee on Taft-Hartley in the capacity of counsel to the House managers. The drafting of the final bill to carry out the policies decided by the conference committee was done jointly by Gerard Reilly, special counsel for the Senate committee; Thomas Shroyer, general counsel for the Senate committee; Dwyer Shugrue, counsel for Senator Irving Ives; and Morgan. Ibid., pp. 1161, 1163.

Morgan admitted that he was paid $7,500 by the Republican National Committee. Ibid., pp. 1163, 1168. He acknowledged working with Reilly and Iserman and remembered meeting "once" with "Mr. Smethurst, who is counsel for the National Association of Manufacturers." Ibid., pp. 1162, 1171–72, 1178.

63. Ibid., p. 805.

64. Louis Stark, "House Group Votes Truman Labor Bill," *New York Times,* March 25, 1949, p. 15.

65. "House Group Maps Strong Labor Bill," *New York Times,* April 2, 1949, p. 2.

66. Joseph Loftus, "Labor Bill Backed by House Coalition Tightens Taft Law," *New York Times,* April 6, 1949, p. 1.

67. *Cong. Rec.,* 81st Cong., 1st sess. (April 28, 1949), 95, pt. 4:5281. The chairman of

the Republican Policy Committee, Joe Martin of Massachusetts, admitted that his committee "sought advice and assistance from both Republicans and Democrats in Congress and we had very helpful suggestions from our associates in another branch of the Congress." Ibid., May 3, 1949, p. 5505.

68. For the text of the Wood bill as introduced, see ibid., pp. 5257–65. Louis Stark, "Repeal Bill Keeps Most of Taft Act," *New York Times,* April 15, 1949, p. 1.

69. Louis Stark, "AFL Demands Taft Act Test Vote; Receptive to Revision of Old Law," *New York Times,* January 5, 1949, p. 7.

70. Louis Stark, "Rival Sides Rally in Labor Bill Fight," *New York Times,* April 26, 1949, p. 20; Harry Acreman, Executive Secretary, Texas Labor League for Political Education, to the secretaries of all central councils, April 14, 1949, Folder 44, Box 30, Department of Legislation, Meany Archives; Joseph Loftus, "Labor Bill Debate Opens in the House; Outcome in Doubt," *New York Times,* April 27, 1949, p. 1.

71. Joseph Loftus, "Yielding Is Shown on New Labor Bill," *New York Times,* April 28, 1949, p. 1.

72. Memorandum from Hushing to Green (regarding Rayburn), April 26, 1949, Folder 44, Box 30, Department of Legislation, Meany Archives.

73. Memorandum from Hushing to Green (regarding McCormack), April 26, 1949, Folder 44, Box 30, Department of Legislation, Meany Archives.

74. *Cong. Rec.,* 81st Cong., 1st sess. (April 29, 1949), 95, pt. 4:5360.

75. Louis Stark, "Six Key Concessions Made in Labor Bill by House Leaders," *New York Times,* May 3, 1949, p. 1.

76. For the text of the Sims bill as introduced, see *Cong. Rec.,* 81st Cong., 1st sess. (May 3, 1949), 95, pt. 4:5506–9.

77. "Truman-Rayburn Rift Brings Sabath, 83, to White House to 'Smooth' Things Over," *New York Times,* May 17, 1949, p. 21.

78. *Cong. Rec.,* 81st Cong., 1st sess. (May 3, 1949), 95, pt. 4:5531.

79. "Sell-out on Taft-Hartley," p. 4.

80. Ibid.

81. Louis Stark, "Thomas Sees Base for a Compromise in Taft Labor Bill," *New York Times,* May 11, 1949, p. 1; Joseph Loftus, "Wood's Draft of Labor Bill Dies in House," *New York Times,* May 5, 1949, p. 1; Joseph Loftus, "House Approves Labor Bill Keeping Taft Features; Truman Forces Lose, 217–203," *New York Times,* May 4, 1949, p. 1. It was reported that "representatives of the AFL and CIO at the Capitol, also in desperation, quietly passed the word to their friends to go along with the substitute, although the top leadership of these organizations remain unreconciled to the injunction feature." Loftus, "House Approves," p. 1.

82. *Cong. Rec.,* 81st Cong., 1st sess. (May 3, 1949), 95, pt. 4:5522.

83. Ibid., pp. 5535–43; Loftus, "House Approves Labor Bill," p. 1.

84. *Cong. Rec.,* 81st Cong., 1st sess. (May 3, 1949), 95, pt. 4:5519.

85. Ibid., p. 5543. For a concise comparison of the Taft, Wagner, Wood, and Sims bills, see "Here's a Comparison of Labor Bills: Taft, Wagner, Wood, and Sims," *New York Times,* May 4, 1949, p. 33.

86. *Cong. Rec.*, 81st Cong., 1st sess. (May 4, 1949), 95, pt. 4:5597. Marcantonio requested an engrossed copy of the Wood bill.
87. For an explanation of the switch in votes, see Loftus, "Wood's Draft," p. 1; Arthur Krock, "Red Riding Hood Reprieves the Wolf," *New York Times,* May 5, 1949, p. 26; "Members Defend Wood Bill Switch," *New York Times,* May 5, 1949, p. 30.
88. *Cong. Rec.,* 81st Cong., 1st sess. (May 4, 1949), 95, pt. 4:5589–90; Louis Stark, "Taft Group Offers Its Own Labor Bill," *New York Times,* May 5, 1949, p. 31.
89. *Cong. Rec.,* 81st Cong., 1st sess. (June 29, 1949), 95, pt. 7:8590–94. Thomas told the Senate: "I agree with the Senator from Ohio that his amendment is a great improvement over the Taft-Hartley law as it stands. I accept his own thesis that it is an improvement in 28 different particulars. Some of those particulars are very major, and some are very minor, but, at any rate, there is the honest and straightforward admission that the law should be changed." Ibid., p. 8590.
90. *Cong. Rec.,* 81st Cong., 1st sess. (June 8, 1949), 95, pt. 5:7402; *Senate Repeal Committee Minority Report,* p. 5. For a discussion of the Hartley-Taft compromises, see Gross, *Reshaping of the National Labor Relations Board,* pp. 251–55.
91. For a complete list of Taft's proposed amendments, see *Cong. Rec.,* 81st Cong., 1st sess. (May 4, 1949), 95, pt. 4:5589–90.
92. *Cong. Rec.,* 81st Cong., 1st sess. (June 6, 1949), 95, pt. 6:7247; (June 14, 1949), 95, pt. 6:7641; *Senate Repeal Committee Minority Report,* p. 70. See also Chapter 1.
93. *Cong. Rec.,* 81st Cong., 1st sess. (June 6, 1949), 95, pt. 6:7244.
94. For a list of Taft-Hartley provisions retained by Taft, see *Cong. Rec.,* 81st Cong., 1st sess. (May 4, 1949), 95, pt. 4:5589–90.
95. "CIO and AFL Assail Taft Amendments," *New York Times,* May 8, 1949, p. 53.
96. "Text of Letter Concerning CIO Attitude on Taft-Hartley Act Repeal, Written by Arthur Goldberg, CIO General Counsel, to Senator Elbert Thomas of Utah, Chairman of the Senate Labor Committee, and Representative John Lesinski of Michigan, Chairman of the House Labor Committee," May 12, 1949, pp. 1–2, 4, press release, "Labor-Management Relations Act No. 1," Box 2, Murphy Papers.
97. Louis Stark, "Senate Narrows Injunction Issue," *New York Times,* June 24, 1949, p. 18.
98. Louis Stark, "Injunction Voted into Labor Bill by Senate, 50–40," *New York Times,* June 29, 1949, p. 1.
99. Arthur Krock, "Very Narrow Victories and Defeats," *New York Times,* July 5, 1949, p. 22.
100. Stark, "Injunction Voted into Labor Bill," p. 1.
101. Louis Stark, "Labor Drops Fight to Alter Taft Law," *New York Times,* June 30, 1949, p. 1.
102. *Cong. Rec.,* 81st Cong., 1st sess. (June 29, 1949), 95, pt. 7:8578. For Taft's analysis of his own proposals, see pp. 8586–90.
103. William White, "Lucas Doubts 81st Will Kill Taft Act," *New York Times,* December 13, 1949, p. 40.
104. "President Says He Will Fight Taft Law until It Is Repealed," *New York Times,*

September 6, 1949, p. 1; Anthony Leviero, "Truman Bids Farmers, Labor Unite to Assure Fair Deal; Assails 'Selfish Interests,'" *New York Times,* September 6, 1949, p. 1; "Green Won't Speak at Lehman's Rally," *New York Times,* October 3, 1949, p. 10; Joseph Loftus, "Labor Needs Unity, Tobin Warns AFL," *New York Times,* October 5, 1949, p. 23; "Ex-Senator Listed in Taft Act Lobby," *New York Times,* August 22, 1949, p. 10.

105. For a detailed and critical section by section analysis of Taft's amendments, see *Cong. Rec.,* 81st Cong., 1st sess. (June 14, 1949), 95, pt. 6:7640–46. A list of union attorneys who participated in the preparation of this analysis appears on p. 7646.

106. *Senate Repeal Hearings,* p. 2577.

Chapter 5

1. Oral History interview with Stephan Gordon, August 1, 1988, p. 8, Labor-Management Documentation Center (LMDC), ILR, Cornell University.

2. Oral History interview with Paul Herzog, January 6, 1972, pp. 88–90, LMDC. Herzog recalled that Denham insisted on having the private bathroom. Herzog concluded that at some point "it would have to be understood the Chairman of the Board was still the top fellow." His strategy included deliberately leaking the story to columnist Drew Pearson ("I was capable of a newspaper leak"). Ibid., p. 89. See also *Cong. Rec.,* 81st Cong., 1st sess. (April 27, 1949), 95, pt. 4:5139.

Denham had a different version: "What happened was this: When the agency was preparing to move into new offices in January, 1949, and we were discussing assignment of space, someone asked who was to get the corner office, which had a private shower. J. Copeland Gray, then a board member, remarked innocently to Herzog, 'Paul, why don't you and Bob toss up a coin and see who gets it?' Without a word, Herzog stalked out of the room. I learned later that he was furious that anybody but the chairman would be considered for it, and gave Gray a dressing down for even suggesting the possibility. As it turned out, I was assigned offices at the other end of the hall, and without my requesting it a shower was also installed for me." Robert Denham, as told to Stacy V. Jones, "And So I Was Purged," *Saturday Evening Post,* December 30, 1950, p. 73. See also *Cong. Rec.,* 81st Cong., 1st sess. (April 27, 1949), 95, pt. 4:5139; according to newspaper reports, Denham made the opening move when he demanded the principal suite in the NLRB's new headquarters in the Federal Security Building at Third and C Streets S.W. in Washington. When Herzog insisted that the chairman, not the general counsel, was entitled to that choice location, Denham went to the Public Building Administration and asked for duplicate facilities in the suite he was finally assigned at the other end of the corridor. PBA officials confirmed that Denham had made such a request and that they did as he asked. One paper commented: "A shower bath battle between two top officials of the National Labor Relations Board generated lots of steam but the affair was cleared up when each contestant got a private stall." "Two Office Suites with Baths Solve Herzog-Denham Dispute," *Washington Star,* February 17, 1949.

3. Senate, *Hearings before the Committee on Expenditures in the Executive Departments, United States Senate, on S. Res. 248, Reorganization Plan No. 12 of 1950,* 81st Cong., 2d sess., 1950. (Hereinafter *Senate Reorganization Plan No. 12 Hearings.*) See, for example, p. 96.

4. Ida Klaus, "The Taft-Hartley Experiment in Separation of NLRB Functions," *Industrial and Labor Relations Review* 11, 3 (April 1958): 381.

5. Anthony Leviero, "Truman Confident," *New York Times,* January 5, 1950, p. 1. For the text of Truman's address, see "Text of President Truman's Message to Congress on the State of the Union," *New York Times,* January 5, 1950, p. 10.

6. Memorandum from H. C. Hushing to William Green, December 2, 1949, Folder 45, Box 30, Department of Legislation (1906–1978), George Meany Memorial Archives, Washington, D.C.

7. Clayton Knowles, "Green Delays Taft Act Fight until after Elections in Fall," *New York Times,* January 2, 1950, p. 1.

8. *Cong. Rec.,* 81st Cong., 1st sess. (June 29, 1949), 95, pt. 7:8586.

9. 82 NLRB 1264 (1949).

10. 86 NLRB 1166, 1170 (1949); "NLRB Upholds Dismissal of Unfair Practice Complaint Involving Drug Store, on the Basis of Earlier Decision Declining Jurisdiction in Election Case," press release (R-254), November 4, 1949, NN 3-25-86-1, Record Group (RG) 25, National Archives (NA).

11. *Cong. Rec.,* 81st Cong., 2d sess. (May 10, 1950), 96, pt. 5:6858–60.

12. *Senate Reorganization Plan No. 12 Hearings,* p. 124.

13. *Cong. Rec.,* 81st Cong., 2d sess. (May 10, 1950), 96, pt. 5:6859.

14. "The Present Political Climate," *New York Tribune,* January 13, 1950 (quotation); "Open Fight Developing in Denham Feud with Members of NLRB," *Washington Star,* January 14, 1950; "Counsel Denham Criticizes Board," *U.S. News & World Report,* January 20, 1950, pp. 48–49; "Denham vs. the NLRB," *Newsweek,* January 23, 1950, p. 66.

15. A. H. Raskin, "Counsel to NLRB Bluntly Assails It," *New York Times,* January 13, 1950, p. 1 (quotation); David Lawrence, "Respect for Law Seen as Matter of Whim inside Government," *Washington Star,* January 13, 1950.

16. "Appeal NLRB Cases, Denham Tells Bosses," *Washington Post,* January 13, 1950.

17. "NLRB Schism," *Washington Post,* January 18, 1950. This article also appears in *Cong. Rec.,* 81st Cong., 2d sess. (January 18, 1950), 96, pt. 13:A396.

18. "Remarks of NLRB General Counsel Robert N. Denham before New York Personnel Management Association," November 24, 1947, O.F. 145 (1947), Box 623, Harry S Truman Papers, Harry S Truman Library, Independence, Mo.

19. Senate, *Senate Hearings before the Committee on Labor and Public Welfare on S. 249, a Bill to Diminish the Causes of Labor Disputes Burdening or Obstructing Interstate and Foreign Commerce and for Other Purposes,* 81st Cong., 1st sess., 1949, pp. 1725, 1285–86. (Hereinafter *Senate Repeal Hearings.*)

20. Ibid., pp. 1264–68.

21. Ibid., p. 1265; Denham, "And So I Was Purged," p. 73. See also Louis Stark,

"Employees of NLRB Appeal on Denham," *New York Times,* November 29, 1947, p. 30; Paul Klein, "Mr. Denham Plays God," *The Nation,* December 13, 1947, pp. 640–41.

22. Memorandum from Paul Herzog to Matthew J. Connelly, March 1, 1950, and "NLRB Revises Delegation of Functions to General Counsel," press release (R-293), February 25, 1950, O.F. 145 (1950), Box 624, Truman Papers; "Board Memorandum Describing the Authority and Assigned Responsibilities of the General Counsel of the NLRB" (effective October 10, 1950), Box 9, NN 3-25-86-1, RG 25, NA.

23. Memorandum from Herzog to Connelly, March 1, 1950.

24. Memorandum from Spingarn to Clifford, "Robert N. Denham, General Counsel of the NLRB," November 17, 1949, "NLRB," Box 24, Charles Murphy Papers, Truman Library.

25. Clayton Knowles, "Twenty-one Agency Shifts Asked by Truman; Denham Would Go," *New York Times,* March 14, 1950, p. 1.

26. See *Senate Reorganization Plan No. 12 Hearings,* pp. 1–2, for the full text of Reorganization Plan No. 12.

27. *Cong. Rec.,* 81st Cong., 2d sess. (March 20, 1950), 96, pt. 3:3693–95.

28. Ibid., pp. 3694, 3695.

29. Ibid., p. 3694. According to the task force, "if the general counsel refused to issue a complaint on the ground that the employer or trade union is within its legal rights in refusing to bargain, the complainant has no appeal to the Board or the courts. Thus the general counsel possesses a species of rule-making power: His interpretation of that particular section may very well be conclusive." Ibid.

30. Ibid., p. 3695.

31. Ibid.

32. *Senate Reorganization Plan No. 12 Hearings* (which contains on pp. 7–13 a summary of the testimony before the House Committee on Expenditures concerning Reorganization Plan No. 12); Senate, *Reorganization Plan No. 12 of 1950 Providing for Reorganization of the National Labor Relations Board* (April 24, 1950), 81st Cong., 2d sess., S. Rept. 1516 (hereinafter *Senate Reorganization Plan No. 12 Report*); House, *Reorganization Plan No. 12* (March 28, 1950), 81st Cong., 2d sess., H. Rept. 1852.

For Herzog's testimony, see *Senate Reorganization Plan No. 12 Hearings,* pp. 10–12, 112–47. For Denham's testimony, see pp. 174–213. See also "The Proper Separation of Functions for Administering Our National Labor Relations Program," *Illinois Law Review* 46 (July–August, 1951): 465–78.

33. *Senate Reorganization Plan No. 12 Hearings,* pp. 17–18, 22 (quotations); *Cong. Rec.,* 81st Cong., 2d sess. (May 11, 1950), 96, pt. 5:6873.

34. *Cong. Rec.,* 81st Cong., 2d sess. (May 11, 1950), 96, pt. 5:6873.

35. Ibid. (quotation), *Senate Reorganization Plan No. 12 Hearings,* p. 16.

36. *Senate Reorganization Plan No. 12 Hearings,* pp. 104, 115.

37. *Cong. Rec.,* 81st Cong., 2d sess. (May 11, 1950), 96, pt. 5:6883.

38. *Senate Reorganization Plan No. 12 Hearings,* p. 151.

39. Ibid., pp. 12–13, 239.

40. Ibid., pp. 32, 34–35 (quotations); Louis Stark, "Taft Sees Politics in NLRB Reform," *New York Times,* April 5, 1950, p. 38; *Cong. Rec.,* 81st Cong., 2d sess. (May 10, 1950), 96, pt. 5:6874.

41. Memorandum from Ralph Burton to Charles Stauffacher, "NLRB Vacancy," January 4, 1950, "NLRB," Box 24, Murphy Papers.

42. Styles, forty-two years old in 1950, was appointed on February 2 and took office on February 27, 1950. He had begun work at age eleven as a printer's apprentice and came to the NLRB in 1937 as a field examiner in the Atlanta office. He left in 1943 to become assistant director of disputes for the Regional War Labor Board in Atlanta and eventually became director of disputes and a public member and vice-chairman of the regional board. He returned to the NLRB in 1945 as director of the Tenth Region in Atlanta.

    Styles had also worked as a weaver and loom fixer in an Alabama cotton mill and as an editor, reporter, printer, and pressman for a weekly newspaper in Huntsville, Alabama. He served as co-chairman of the Industrial Committee of the Huntsville Chamber of Commerce from 1935 to 1937 and, from 1933 to 1937, as president of the Huntsville Trades and Labor Council (AFL). NLRB Information Division, "Paul L. Styles Named to Board" (L-29), February 2, 1950, NN 3-25-86-1, RG 25, NA.

43. "Styles in Top Spot for Opening on NLRB," *Business Week,* January 28, 1950, p. 99.

44. *Senate Reorganization Plan No. 12 Hearings,* p. 32.

45. Oral History interviews with Herzog, January 6, 1972, p. 95, and July 15, 1975, p. 37; "NLRB Moderate Unlikely to Stay," *New York Times,* December 21, 1949.

46. In reply to an inquiry from Taft, former president Hoover sent a telegram saying that he could not recollect any discussion by his commission of a plan to abolish the NLRB general counsel's office. See Stark, "Taft Sees Politics," p. 38; *Cong. Rec.,* 81st Cong., 2d sess. (May 11, 1950), 96, pt. 5:6865, for the Herbert Hoover telegram; *Cong. Rec.* (May 10, 1950), 96, pt. 5:6808, for a contrary view from a member of the commission; and *Cong. Rec.* (May 11, 1950), 96, pt. 5:6867, for the comments of Senator Irving Ives. Two senators who served on the Hoover Commission, John McClellan of Arkansas and George Aiken of Vermont, confirmed that the commission made no specific recommendation concerning the general counsel's office, but they agreed that the "situation had been discussed, but had been put aside because a matter of policy on which Congress had recently acted was involved." Clayton Knowles, "Two Reform Plans Killed in Senate; Truman Rebuffed," *New York Times,* May 12, 1950, p. 1; see also "Did Hoover Undercut T-H?" *Business Week,* April 15, 1950, p. 122. The Citizens Committee for the Hoover Report also refused to take a position on the NLRB separation-of-functions issue. "Hoover Unit Fails to Back Two Plans," *New York Times,* April 14, 1950, p. 15.

47. *Senate Reorganization Plan No. 12 Hearings,* p. 19 (quotations); *Cong. Rec.,* 81st Cong., 2d sess. (May 10, 1950), 96, pt. 5:6881.

48. Louis Stark, "Political Aim Laid to NLRB Reform," *New York Times,* March 22, 1950, p. 10; "Ralph Church Dies at House Hearing," *New York Times,* March 22, 1950, p. 27.

49. Press release of Truman's telegram to Vice-President Barkley, May 11, 1950, O.F. 145 (1950), Box 624, Truman Papers.

50. Knowles, "Two Reform Plans," p. 1; "Roll-Calls on Reorganization," *New York Times,* May 12, 1950, p. 18.

51. *NLRB v. Postex Cotton Mills,* 181 F.2d 919 (5th Cir., May 5, 1950). In that case the officers of the Textile Workers Union had signed the noncommunist affidavits but the officers of their parent CIO had not. The court said that it was the "amply justified and validly sustained view of substantially the entire membership of Congress (as is likewise true of all loyal Americans generally) that since Communist ideology has been shown so flagrantly incompatible with the principles of American democracy that both cannot exist in any one system of government, its destructive influence in all phases of government should properly be removed if lawful means are available." It concluded: "We think the language of the statute, considered in the light of Congressional purpose, the evil to be remedied, and the means provided to effectuate that purpose, evidences Congressional intent to wholly eradicate and bar from leadership in the American labor movement, at each and every level, adherents of the Communist party and believers in the unconstitutional overthrow of our government." Ibid. p. 920.

52. Denham-NLRB Split Widens," *Business Week,* May 20, 1950, pp. 126–27.

53. Memorandum from Harold Enarson, special assistant in the White House office, to David Stowe, White House administrative assistant and speech writer, "The First Hundred Days (or 'In Bed with Denham')," undated, "T-H Veto Message," Box 5, David Stowe Papers, Truman Library. The memorandum critiques Herzog's "First Hundred Days" speech, delivered on December 6, 1947, before the Institute on Labor Law of the University of Minnesota, on file in the LMDC.

54. Denham had met with presidential adviser John Steelman about what Denham called the "administrative problems within the Board which have been so highly publicized." He told Steelman, "Probably nothing is to be gained by dwelling on the relations between the Board and General Counsel other than to comment that on several occasions, I have urged the Board to join me in trying to find a smooth working arrangement. The last such occasion was following the rejection of Plan 12. My memo to the Board on that occasion and the Board's reply, are attached for your information. I think they reflect what I am trying to describe." Denham to Steelman, May 19, 1950, O.F. 145 (1950), Box 624, Truman Papers.

55. Memorandum from Herzog to Denham, May 22, 1950, NN 3-25-86-1, RG 25, NA.

56. "Denham NLRB Meet First Time in Months," *New York Times,* May 24, 1950, p. 3.

57. Memorandum from Herzog to the file, May 29, 1950, NN 3-25-86-1, RG 25, NA.

58. Ibid.

59. Robert Denham, "Don't Let NLRB Repeal Taft-Hartley," *Factory Management and Maintenance* 108 (May 1950): 86, 89–90.

60. Memorandum from Herzog to the file, May 29, 1950.

61. Herzog to Truman, July 19, 1950, O.F. 145 (1950), Box 624, Truman Papers. Herzog first informed Truman of his desire to resign in February. Herzog to Truman, February 27, 1950, ibid.

62. Herzog to Senator Howard McGrath, July 14, 1949; Herzog to Truman, August 2, 1949; Herzog to Peyton Ford, assistant to the attorney general, August 19, 1949, "Federal Judgeships," Box 5, Paul Herzog Papers, Truman Library.

63. Oral History interview with Herzog, January 6, 1972, p. 87.

64. White House press release, July 24, 1950, NN 3-25-86-1, Box 2, RG 25, NA; Truman to Herzog, July 24, 1950; Herzog to Truman, July 24, 1950, O.F. 145 (1950), Box 624, Truman Papers. Herzog's term covered the period August 27, 1950, to August 27, 1955.

65. "Truman Asks NLRB Term for Herzog," *Chicago Journal of Commerce,* July 25, 1950.

66. 85 NLRB 621 (1949).

67. Memorandum from Herzog to the file, "*Vulcan Forging* Brief," July 13, 1950, NN 3-25-86-1, Box 2, RG 25, NA.

68. Memorandum from Denham to the Board, July 18, 1950, NN 3-25-86-1, Box 2, RG 25, NA.

69. Memorandum from Herzog to Murphy, July 21, 1950, NN 3-25-86-1, Box 2, RG 25, NA.

70. Memorandum from Klaus to Herzog, August 1, 1950, NN 3-25-86-1, Box 2, RG 25, NA.

71. "Motion for Enlargement of Time to File Brief in Behalf of the National Labor Relations Board," in the U.S. Court of Appeals for the Sixth Circuit, July 31, 1950, NN 3-25-86-1, Box 2, *NLRB v. Vulcan Forging Company,* No. 11,131, RG 25, NA. See also Joseph Loftus, "Labor Board Irked by Denham's Brief," *New York Times,* August 3, 1950, p. 24.

72. Denham to Steelman, August 8, 1950, NN 3-25-86-1, Box 2, RG 25, NA.

73. Denham to Steelman, August 12, 1950, "NLRB," Box 24, Murphy Papers.

74. Confidential memorandum from Russell P. Andrews, of Steelman's staff, to Steelman, August 17, 1950, "NLRB," Box 24, Murphy Papers.

75. Memorandum from Andrews to Steelman, "Mr. Denham's Peace Plan—A New Munich?" August 16, 1950, "NLRB," Box 24, Murphy Papers.

76. Confidential memorandum from Andrews to Steelman, August 17, 1950.

77. Memorandum from Andrews to Steelman, "Mr. Denham's Peace Plan—A New Munich?"

78. Herzog to Murphy, August 17, 1950, "NLRB," Box 24, Murphy Papers.

79. Copy of Joseph Ball, *Washington Letter,* August 12, 1950, "NLRB," Box 24, Murphy Papers.

80. Board to Truman, September 15, 1950, NN 3-25-86-1, Box 2, RG 25, NA.

81. Denham, "And So I Was Purged," p. 22 (quotations); Louis Stark, "Denham Is Ousted as NLRB Counsel," *New York Times,* September 16, 1950, p. 1; Joseph Loftus, "Denham Quits Job with Reluctance," *New York Times,* September 17, 1950; "Texts of Denham and Truman Letters," *New York Times,* September 17, 1950, p. 85.

82. Transcript of Bert Andrews's interview with Denham on ABC radio, September 23, 1950, NN 3-25-86-1, Box 2, RG 25, NA.

83. *Cong. Rec.,* 81st Cong., 2d sess. (September 19, 1950), 96, pt. 17:A6648; "Partial Pay-off," *Washington Post,* September 18, 1950.

84. Denham, "And So I Was Purged," pp. 22–23, 73–74. For Congressman Clare Hoffman's concurrence, see *Cong. Rec.,* 81st Cong., 2d sess. (September 19, 1950), 96, pt. 11:15141.

85. Denham, "And So I Was Purged," p. 74 (quotations); Edwin A. Lahey, "Denham Tells Ouster Story," *Chicago Daily News,* September 18, 1950.

86. Klaus, "Taft-Hartley Experiment," p. 376. Klaus concluded: "Little, if anything, was said by the conferees as to the reasons which prompted agreement to the scheme of separation adopted in conference, nor was any clear picture given of just what the conference measure sought to accomplish in principle or in practice." Ironically, Taft "sought to demonstrate that the proposals would really make little change in the procedures and regulations already developed by the Board"; he "gave no reason, however, as to why a scheme of separation beyond that called for the Administrative Procedure Act was necessary for the National Labor Relations Board." Ibid., pp. 377–78.

87. Ibid., p. 389.

Chapter 6

1. Oral History interviews with Mozart Ratner, July 25, 1988, p. 19; William Feldesman, July 28, 1988, p. 27; and Howard Kleeb, July 23, 1975, p. 28, Labor-Management Documentation Center (LMDC), ILR, Cornell University; "It Could Have Been Worse," *Business Week,* October 7, 1950, pp. 118–19; "Confirmed as NLRB Counsel," *New York Times,* December 14, 1950, p. 72. See also "NLRB Clarifies," *U.S. News & World Report,* October 13, 1950, p. 46.

2. Joseph Loftus, "Career Man Named to Denham's Post," *New York Times,* September 29, 1950, p. 21; "Bott Is Sworn in as NLRB Counsel, Succeeding Denham," *Baltimore Sun,* September 30, 1950; "Bott Named NLRB Counsel," *Baltimore Sun,* September 29, 1950; Oral History interviews with Norton Come, July 29, 1988, p. 18; and Frank Kleiler, August 3, 1988, p. 5, LMDC.

3. "Will New Counsel End NLRB Feud?" *U.S. News and World Report,* October 6, 1950, p. 41 (quotations); "It Could Have Been Worse," pp. 118–19.

4. Woodruff Randolph, president of the ITU, to Truman, September 22, 1950, "General Counsel Endorsements," O.F. 145 (1950), Box 625, Harry S Truman Papers,

Harry S Truman Library, Independence, Mo.; "It Could Have Been Worse," p. 119.

5. David McConnell, "George J. Bott Gets Denham's NLRB Post," *New York Herald Tribune,* September 29, 1950.

6. Bott also withdrew the appellate brief Denham had filed with the Sixth Circuit Court of Appeals over the Board's objection. Bott's application to the Sixth Circuit Court of Appeals, "For Leave to Withdraw Brief on File and to File New Brief," October 2, 1950, NN 3-25-86-1, Box 2, Record Group (RG) 25, National Archives (NA); "Peace in NLRB," *Business Week,* October 14, 1950, p. 121.

7. For details, see NLRB, *Fifteenth Annual Report,* for the fiscal year ended June 30, 1950 (Washington, D.C.: GPO, 1951), pp. 5–6.

8. Joseph Loftus, "Area of Authority Defined by NLRB," *New York Times,* October 6, 1950, p. 18; Raymond Blair, "NLRB Tune: Hearts and Flowers," *New York Herald Tribune,* October 8, 1950.

9. "Peace in NLRB," p. 121.

10. William Weart, "CIO Soon to Talk Fusion, Green Says," *New York Times,* May 10, 1950, p. 35; Louis Stark, "Green Denounces Taft, Dixiecrats," *New York Times,* June 1, 1950, p. 18.

11. "82d: Critical Congress," *New York Times,* January 7, 1951, sec. 4, p. E2. In the Senate the number of Democrats decreased from 54 to 49 while Republicans grew from 42 to 47; in the House, Democrats dropped from 263 to 235 and Republicans increased from 171 to 199.

12. A. H. Raskin, "Taft Wins in Ohio by a Wide Margin," *New York Times,* November 8, 1950, p. 1; A. H. Raskin, "Taft Leader for 1952 Nomination by Big Ohio Sweep, Say Backers," *New York Times,* November 9, 1950, p. 1.

13. Memorandum from W. C. Hushing to William Green, February 16, 1951, Folder 48, Box 30, Department of Legislation (1906–1978), George Meany Memorial Archives, Washington, D.C.

14. NLRB, *Fifteenth Annual Report,* pp. 11–12, 16–17; "Labor Settles for Change of the Taft-Hartley Law," *New York Times,* October 21, 1951, sec. 4, p. 10.

15. John Patrick Diggins, *The Proud Decades: America in War and Peace, 1941–1960* (New York: W. W. Norton, 1988), p. 115.

16. W. H. Lawrence, "Truman Items Lag as Congress Trails 'Do-Nothing' 80th," *New York Times,* May 14, 1951, p. 1. Lawrence commented: "In baseball terms, it could be said that the President's batting average, so far as Congress is concerned, is a meager .081."

17. Stephen E. Ambrose, *Eisenhower,* vol. 1, *Soldier, General of the Army, President-Elect, 1890–1952* (New York: Simon and Schuster, 1983), pp. 500–501, 515.

18. Ibid., p. 515.

19. Diggins, *Proud Decades,* p. 125.

20. Ambrose, *Eisenhower,* 1:476–77, 542. The required criteria for a running mate were that he be "a card-carrying member of the Old Guard who nonetheless was

acceptable to the moderates, especially the Dewey people; a prominent leader of the anti-Communist cause; an energetic and vigorous campaigner; a relatively young man, to offset Eisenhower's age; a man from the West to offset Eisenhower's association with Dewey and New York; a man who had made a contribution to Eisenhower's winning the nomination." Ibid., pp. 542–43.

21. Ibid., pp. 569, 571.

22. Diggins, *Proud Decades,* p. 126.

23. Ibid., p. 127.

24. "Eisenhower Makes Pennsylvania Bid," *New York Times,* June 14, 1952, p. 1.

25. A. H. Raskin, "AFL Men Hear Him," *New York Times,* September 18, 1952, p. 1. According to Raskin, "icy silence greeted [Eisenhower's] statement that he favored amendment as opposed to repeal."

26. Taft to Sherman Adams, September 19, 1952, Dwight D. Eisenhower Library, Abilene, Kan.

27. Ibid. Taft wrote: "Certainly the section was not intended to permit union busting, and I don't think it does."

28. A. H. Raskin, "Union Backing Set," *New York Times,* September 23, 1952, p. 1.

29. Memorandum for President Truman from David H. Stowe, March 6, 1952, "Taft-Hartley 1952," Box 5, David H. Stowe Papers, Harry S Truman Library, Independence, Mo.

30. "Democrats Scored on Labor Policies," *New York Times,* October 26, 1951, p. 13.

31. Gilbert Gall, *The Politics of Right to Work: The Labor Federations as Special Interests, 1943–1979* (New York: Greenwood Press, 1988), p. 63.

32. Ibid., p. 62.

33. Quoted in Stephen E. Ambrose, *Eisenhower,* vol. 2, *The President* (New York: Simon and Schuster, 1984), p. 24. Durkin was a registered Democrat who supported Stevenson. He had been president of the Plumbers and Steamfitters union since 1943. Born in Chicago in 1894, he became an apprentice steamfitter at age seventeen. He served in World War II. "Durkin Supported Stevenson in Race," *New York Times,* December 2, 1952, p. 34; William Conklin, "AFL Man Is Named Labor Secretary; Weeks Gets a Post," *New York Times,* December 2, 1952, p. 1.

34. Elie Abel, "Meany Held Sure of AFL Election Today; Schnitzler May Be Secretary-Treasurer," *New York Times,* November 25, 1952, p. 22.

35. Durkin told reporters, "An appointment like mine could only happen in America." "Durkin Bids Unions Stress Labor Peace," *New York Times,* December 16, 1952, p. 21; "Durkin Supported Stevenson in Race," *New York Times,* p. 34.

36. "Taft Breaks Truce by Calling Durkin 'Incredible' Choice," *New York Times,* December 3, 1952, p. 1. Later Taft said that his statement was no hasty action: "I took great care in writing it and I think it speaks for itself." "Durkin Rules out Politics in New Job," *New York Times,* December 4, 1952, p. 45.

37. "Durkin Rules out Politics," p. 45; Leo Egan, "Dewey Sees Amity Assured in Capital," *New York Times,* December 5, 1952, p. 5; "Durkin Plans Talks to Change Labor Pact," *New York Times,* December 10, 1952, p. 31.

38. "Taft Joins in the Vote to Approve Durkin," *New York Times,* January 17, 1952, p. 1.

39. "Durkin Rules out Politics," p. 45.

40. Gall, *Politics of Right to Work,* pp. 61–62.

41. Members of the committee were Matthew Woll of the International Photoengravers Union, George M. Harrison of the Brotherhood of Railway Clerks, Dan Tracy of the International Brotherhood of Electrical Workers, Richard Walsh of the International Alliance of Theatrical Stage Employees, and Richard Gray of the Federation's Building Trades Department. A. H. Raskin, "AFL Draws Taft Law Charges on Injunction and Closed Shop Ban," *New York Times,* February 10, 1953, p. 1.

42. Gall, *Politics of Right to Work,* pp. 61–62.

43. Memorandum from Wilton B. Persons to Sherman Adams, February 12, 1953, "Taft-Hartley Act," O.F. 124-G, Box 641, Eisenhower Library.

44. Minutes of cabinet meeting of February 20, 1953, "February 20, 1953," Box 1, Papers as President/Cabinet, p. 4, Eisenhower Library.

45. Memorandum for the president "Various Efforts to Secure Agreement on Taft-Hartley Act Amendments," from Bernard Shanley and Gerard Morgan, September 30, 1953, p. 2, "Taft-Hartley," Box 37, Papers as President/Administration. (Hereinafter Shanley-Morgan memorandum.)

46. "Legislative Leadership Meeting—Supplementary Notes," May 25, 1953, "Legislative Meetings, April to May 1953," Box 1, Papers as President, Eisenhower Library; "Legislative Leadership Meeting—Supplementary Notes," June 24, 1953, "Legislative Meetings, June–July 1953," Box 1, Papers as President.

47. Memorandum from Stephen Dunn to Bernard Shanley, May 6, 1953, "Working Papers—8," Box 83, Records as President/Confidential Subject Series, Eisenhower Library.

48. Shanley-Morgan memorandum, pp. 2–3.

49. Ibid, p. 3.

50. Ibid., pp. 3–4.

51. Bernard Shanley Diary, June 6, 1953, pp. 911–12, "White House Days 5," Box 2, Eisenhower Library. According to Shanley, Eisenhower then smiled and said, "I realize this but I wanted to get the story straight because one is just as bad as the other. It seems to be a complete impossibility to get them to agree on any basis." Eisenhower wrote in his diary: "Weeks seems so completely conservative in his views that at times he seems to be illogical. I hope . . . that he will soon become a little bit more aware of the world as it is today." Ambrose, *Eisenhower,* 2:23.

52. Memorandum for the president from Bernard Shanley, September 30, 1953, p. 1, "Taft-Hartley," Box 37, Papers as President/Administration.

53. Shanley Diary, May 7 and June 4, 1953, pp. 818 (quotation), 891, "White House Days 4," Box 2.

54. Ibid., June 23, 1953, p. 958.

55. Shanley-Morgan memorandum, pp. 3–4; "Eisenhower Joins Talks on Taft Law," *New York Times,* June 20, 1953, p. 32.

56. Shanley-Morgan memorandum, p. 5; Senator Paul Douglas told the press he was

unable to discover the "parentage" of this staff committee print. Chairman Smith had made the lawyers' draft public without revealing its authorship. "Senators Put off Study of Taft Act," *New York Times,* May 26, 1953, p. 19.

57. "Eisenhower Joins Talks."

58. Shanley-Morgan memorandum, p. 5.

59. Ibid.

60. Shanley Diary, June 25, 1953, p. 966, "White House Days 5," Box 2.

61. Shanley-Morgan memorandum, p. 6.

62. Shanley Diary, September 1953, pp. 1188A, 1188B, "White House Years 1," Box 2. See also ibid., no date, p. 624A, "White House Days 1," Box 1.

63. Shanley Diary, July 6, 1953, p. 996, "White House Years 1," Box 2; Joseph Loftus, "Message on Labor Blocked by Nixon," *New York Times,* August 6, 1953, p. 14.

64. "Text of 19-Point Revision of Taft-Hartley Act Proposed in Undelivered Presidential Message, as published in the *Wall Street Journal,* August 3, 1953," Folder 6, Box 31, Department of Legislation (1906–1978), George Meany Memorial Archives, Washington, D.C. (Hereinafter "Text of 19-Point Draft Message.") The draft message also appears in Albert Clark, "Eisenhower Circulates His Ideas for Revising Taft-Hartley Law," *Wall Street Journal,* August 3, 1953, p. 1 (the full text appears on p. 4); "Here's New Labor Law If—" *U.S. News & World Report,* August 14, 1953, p. 69.

65. "Text of 19-Point Draft Message," recommendation 17.

66. Ibid., recommendations 8, 9, 16.

67. Ibid., recommendations 11, 15.

68. Ibid., recommendations 4, 13.

69. Shanley Diary, July 28, 1953, p. 1103, "White House Years 2," Box 2.

70. Edwin Lahey, "Senator Taft—'He Was Not a Common Man,'" *Chicago Daily News,* July 31, 1953; "Robert A. Taft," *New York Herald Tribune,* August 1, 1953.

71. Shanley Diary, July 31, 1953, pp. 1115–16, "White House Years 2," Box 2.

72. Memorandum from Dunn to Shanley, July 31, 1953, "Taft-Hartley Working Papers 5," Box 83, Records as President/Confidential Subject Series. (Hereinafter Dunn's Memorandum on the 19 Points.)

73. Memorandum from Smith to Shanley, "Proposed Presidential Message Dealing with Amendments to the Taft-Hartley Act," April 1, 1953, "Taft-Hartley Working Papers 5," Box 83, Records as President/Confidential Subject Series. Smith wrote: "The proposal to modify the secondary boycott provisions with regard to construction projects could greatly weaken the support we have received from small construction firms all over the country. The existing provisions of the law have received great support from small business generally." Ibid., pp. 1–2.

74. Ibid., p. 2.

75. Smith to Shanley, August 1, 1953, "Taft-Hartley Working Papers 5," Box 83, Records as President/Confidential Subject Series.

76. Shroyer wrote: "I shall confine my comments on the proposed message to what I sincerely believe would have been Senator Taft's views with respect to it. As you

know, during recent weeks I have several times gone over the labor legislation picture with Senator Taft and spent some time with him the day before he went to New York discussing his views with respect to Taft-Hartley amendments." Memorandum from Tom Shroyer to Senator Smith, July 31, 1953, p. 1, "Taft-Hartley Working Papers 5," Box 83, Records as President/Confidential Subject Series.

77. Ibid.

78. Ibid., pp. 1–2.

79. Ibid.

80. Shanley said, "That was not the fact." Shanley Diary, August 1, 1953, p. 1117, "White House Years 2," Box 2.

81. Smith to Shanley, August 1, 1953, and Dunn to Shanley, July 31, 1953, "Taft-Hartley Working Papers 5," Box 83, Records as President/Confidential Subject Series.

82. Shanley Diary, August 1, 1953, p. 1118.

83. "Draft of Message Eisenhower Proposes on Taft-Hartley Law Changes," *Wall Street Journal,* August 3, 1953, p. 4.

84. Clark, "Eisenhower Circulates His Ideas."

85. Shanley Diary, August 3, 1953, p. 1120, "White House Years 3," Box 2.

86. Ibid. Durkin did, however, give an interview to Edwin Lahey of the *Chicago Daily News,* outlining some of the administration's "major concessions to organized labor."

87. Shanley Diary, August 3, 1953, pp. 1120, 1121. Shanley noted in his diary, "This certainly did not jibe with the information we had." Ibid., p. 1121.

88. Joseph Loftus, "Labor Policies and Politics Collide at the White House," *New York Times,* September 28, 1953, p. 17. Loftus considered this view a "hangover" from the 1952 presidential campaign, when Dewey supported Eisenhower against Taft.

89. Joseph Ball, "How to Save Taft-Hartley," *The Freeman,* September 21, 1953. Ball dismissed the explanation that the message was merely a "working draft."

90. Goldwater to Eisenhower, September 1, 1953, "Taft-Hartley Working Papers 5," Box 83, Records as President/Confidential Subject Series.

91. Shanley Diary, August 4, 1953, p. 1123, "White House Years 3," Box 2. One White House "spokesman" said the draft had not reached even the "semi-final stage." Joseph Loftus, "President Defers Taft Act Message, *New York Times,* August 4, 1953, p. 18.

92. Shanley Diary, August 12 and 24, 1953, pp. 1149, 1170, "White House Years 3," Box 2.

93. Ibid., August 12, 1953, p. 1149.

94. Memorandum from Shanley to Morgan, August 28, 1953, "Taft-Hartley Working Papers 5," Box 83, Records as President/Confidential Subject Series.

95. Arthur Sylvester, "Business Is Victor as Durkin Resigns," *Newark Evening News,* September 11, 1953.

96. "Eisenhower and Durkin Letters," *New York Times,* September 11, 1953, p. 12; "Mr. Durkin's Story," *Washington Post,* September 24, 1953, p. 10.

97. The press reported: "Then with a thrust of his jaw, [Eisenhower] added that to his knowledge he had never broken an agreement with any associate in his life; that if he had ever broken an agreement it was something that he did not understand was made." Joseph Loftus, "President Denies Breaking Pledge," *New York Times,* October 1, 1953, p. 1.

98. "AFL Chief Asserts Eisenhower Yields," *New York Times,* September 18, 1953, p. 14; "Nixon to Go to AFL as Harmony Envoy," *New York Times,* September 20, 1953, p. 1.

99. According to press reports, "two-thirds of the audience joined in derisive laughter. The laughter started at the rear of the hall and quickly gained volume as a majority of the delegates seized the opportunity to show how they felt about Mr. Nixon's speech." After the laughter "Nixon raced" through the president's letter "at such speed that few of the delegates could follow it." A. H. Raskin, "AFL Mocks Nixon as He Minimizes Durkin's Charge," *New York Times,* September 24, 1953, p. 1.

100. A. H. Raskin, "AFL Backs Durkin against President by Unanimous Vote," *New York Times,* September 26, 1953, p. 1.

101. "Durkin Walks Out," *New York Times,* September 13, 1953, sec. 4, p. 1.

102. Joseph Loftus, "Secretary Durkin Quits Cabinet Post," *New York Times,* September 11, 1953, p. 1; Joseph Loftus, "Adjustments in Labor Field Delayed by Administration," *New York Times,* May 14, 1953, p. 22.

103. Shanley Diary, September 1953, pp. 1188A, 1188B, "White House Years 1," Box 2; Eisenhower Library, Shanley Oral History interview, May 16, 1975, p. 50.

104. "Copies of DDE Personal 1953–1954," p. 2, Box 9, Papers as President/Dwight David Eisenhower Diary, Eisenhower Library.

105. Albert Clark, "Cabinet Conservatives Move to Balk Durkin's Rewrite of Labor Law," *Wall Street Journal,* September 4, 1953, p. 1.

106. James Reston, "President Discusses Driscoll as the Successor to Durkin," *New York Times,* September 13, 1953, p. 1.

107. "Mitchell Is Called 'Capable and Fair,'" *New York Times,* October 9, 1953, p. 14. Mitchell was serving as an assistant secretary for manpower and reserve affairs for the army and was on leave from his position as vice-president of personnel and labor relations at Bloomingdale Brothers, Inc. He attended New York University and began his business career with the Western Electric Company. He became director of the Emergency Relief Administration in Union County, New Jersey, serving until 1936, when he returned to Western Electric as personnel and training director. Later Mitchell served as special labor relations adviser to General Brehon Somervell, then director of the Works Progress Administration in New York. From 1942 to 1945 Mitchell was director of the Industrial Personnel Division at the headquarters of the Army Services Forces in Washington, and in 1945 he became director of personnel and labor relations for R.H. Macy & Co. in New York. He held that post until 1947, when he joined Bloomingdale's. Ibid.; Joseph Loftus, "President Names Store Executive Labor Secretary," *New York Times,* October 9, 1953, p. 1.

108. Joseph Loftus, "White House Silences Weeks on Labor Law," *New York Times,* November 6, 1953, p. 1.

109. Joseph Loftus, "President Acts to Enhance Labor Secretary's Prestige," *New York Times,* October 12, 1953, p. 20; Loftus, "President Names Store Executive."

110. A. H. Raskin, "Mitchell Predicts Taft Act Revision," *New York Times,* November 19, 1953, p. 1. Described as a "tall shaggy man, wearing a navy blue suit and a blue polka dot tie," Mitchell said he was opposed to outright repeal but that Eisenhower would fight to have provisions unfair to labor removed from the law. According to press reports, the CIO delegates "listened politely but unenthusiastically" and gave him "a spattering of applause" when he finished. Ibid.

111. Shanley Diary, November 1953, p. 1244, "White House Years 2," Box 2.

112. Michael Bernstein to I. Jack Martin (administrative assistant to the president) with memorandum "Senator Taft's Last Views on Revision of the Taft-Hartley Act" attached, November 3, 1953, "Taft-Hartley Working Papers 2," Box 82, Records as President/Confidential Subject Series. (Hereinafter Bernstein memorandum.)

113. Shanley Diary, November 21, 1953, p. 1296, "White House Years 2," Box 2.

114. Ibid., p. 1295.

115. Senate Committee on Labor and Public Welfare, *Proposed Revisions of the Labor-Management Relations Act of 1947,* 83d Cong., 2d sess., 1954, p. 2988. (Hereinafter *Senate Labor Committee on Taft-Hartley Revisions.*)

116. "Text of Eisenhower's Message Seeking Amendments in Taft Labor Bill," *New York Times,* January 12, 1954, p. 9; Eisenhower's message to Congress on Taft-Hartley, January 11, 1954, Folder 7, Box 31, Department of Legislation, Meany Archives. (Hereinafter Eisenhower's 1954 Taft-Hartley Message.)

117. Joseph Loftus, "Labor Message Asks U.S. Poll Employees in Walkouts," *New York Times,* January 12, 1953, p. 1.

118. Joseph Loftus, "Labor Embattled on U.S. Strike Poll," *New York Times,* January 13, 1953, p. 1.

119. Ibid.

120. Ibid.; Meany press release, January 13, 1954, Folder 7, Box 31, Department of Legislation, Meany Archives.

121. Loftus, "Labor Message," p. 1.

122. *Senate Labor Committee on Taft-Hartley Revisions,* pp. 2974, 2979–90.

123. Halleck had played a major role in earlier NLRB history, particularly as a member of the special House Committee to investigate the NLRB. See James A. Gross, *The Reshaping of the National Labor Relations Board: National Labor Policy in Transition, 1937–1947* (Albany: State University of New York Press, 1981), pp. 151–225. For Eisenhower's assessment of Halleck, see "Copies of DDE Personal 1953–1954," January 1, 1954, p. 7, Box 9, Records as President/Dwight David Eisenhower Diary. For Halleck's recommendation, see memoranda to Joseph Dodge, January 25, 1954, p. 2, and February 8, 1954, p. 2, "Legislative Meetings 1954," Box 1, Papers as President.

124. Joseph Loftus, "House Unit Votes Labor Board Curb," *New York Times*, March 4, 1954, p. 36; "NLRB Curb Survives," *New York Times*, March 5, 1954, p. 8.
125. "Lock-out Right Pushed," *New York Times*, March 13, 1954, p. 31.
126. "Labor Boycotts Curbed in House," *New York Times*, March 24, 1954, p. 20.
127. "House Unit Votes End of 'Cool-Off,'" *New York Times*, April 2, 1954, p. 14.
128. Joseph Loftus, "House Unit Backs Pre-Strike Poll," *New York Times*, April 3, 1954, p. 32. The House Labor Committee rejected motions to ban industry-wide strikes and lockouts and a proposal to ban all union security. "Change in Labor Law Rejected," *New York Times*, March 11, 1954, p. 19. For a complete statement of the Senate Labor Committee's actions on the president's recommendations, see *Cong. Rec.*, 83d Cong., 2d sess. (May 3, 1954), 100, pt. 5:5834–36.
129. *Cong. Rec.*, 83d Cong., 2d sess. (May 3, 1954), 100, pt. 5:5846.
130. Ibid., p. 5850.
131. Ibid., pp. 5846–47.
132. Senator Robert Upton to Sherman Adams, May 19, 1954, "Taft-Hartley Act 6," O.F. 124-6, Box 641, Eisenhower Library.
133. "Eisenhower Backs State Labor Role," *New York Times*, May 6, 1954, p. 18.
134. Memorandum from Walter J. Maston to W. C. Hushing, "Taft-Hartley Amendments," March 29, 1954, Folder 9, Box 31, Department of Legislation, Meany Archives.
135. *Cong. Rec.*, 83d Cong., 2d sess. (May 5, 1954), 100, pt. 5:5947; Joseph Loftus, "Broad State Rule over Labor Urged in Senate Battle," *New York Times*, May 4, 1954, p. 1.
136. *Cong. Rec.*, 83d Cong., 2d sess. (May 7, 1954), 100, pt. 5:6202–3; "Taft Act Changes Killed by Senate; Democrats Solid," *New York Times*, May 8, 1954, p. 1.
137. "Taft Act Changes Killed," p. 1.
138. "Copies of DDE Personal 1953–1954," p. 5, Box 9, Papers as President/Dwight David Eisenhower Diary.
139. Ibid., p. 6. Eisenhower noted: "I found [Taft] to be far less reactionary than I had judged him to be from a reading of his speeches and public statements. In some things, I found him extraordinarily 'leftish.' This applied specifically to his attitude toward old-age pensions. He told me that he believed every individual in the United States, upon reaching the age of 65, should automatically go on a minimum pension basis, paid by the Federal Government."
140. Ibid., p. 7.

Chapter 7

1. Gerard Reilly, "A Return to Legislative Intent," *Georgetown Law Journal* 43 (March 1955): 373–74.
2. For examples of union criticism, see Thomas Harris, "A CIO View," *Georgetown Law Journal* 43 (March 1955): 345–46.

3. Reilly, "Return to Legislative Intent," p. 374. See also statement of Joseph C. Wells before the House Labor Committee: House Committee on Education and Labor, *Matters Relating to the Labor-Management Relations Act of 1947, and for Other Purposes,* 83d Cong., 1st sess., 1953, Pursuant to H. Res. 115, pp. 3793–99. (Hereinafter *House Labor Committee on Taft-Hartley Revisions.*)

4. See *Digest of the Record of 1953 Hearings on Taft-Hartley Act Revision* (Washington, D.C.: Bureau of National Affairs, 1953). (Hereinafter *Digest of Hearings.*)

5. *Digest of Hearings,* pp. 193–96. Specific cases are discussed later. For the comments of union witnesses, see ibid., pp. 196–98.

6. 77 NLRB 124 (1948). Labor leaders opposed extending Section 8(c) to representation cases. See *Digest of Hearings,* pp. 203–4.

7. 96 NLRB 608 (1951).

8. *Digest of Hearings,* pp. 205–9. Union witnesses complained that even *Bonwit Teller* did not give unions equal opportunity to reach employees because it could not match the employer's authority and economic power. Meany asked that captive audience speeches be prohibited. Ibid., p. 209.

9. 87 NLRB 972 (1949), *enforced,* 195 F.2d 906 (2d Cir. 1952). A "hot cargo" clause is a contractual agreement between a union and management that the employer will not require employees to handle any goods shipped or made by other employees on strike or unorganized or in some other way "unfair."

10. 87 NLRB 502 (1949).

11. 87 NLRB 755 (1949).

12. 92 NLRB 255 (1951).

13. 102 NLRB 996 (1953); 99 NLRB 1391 (1952).

14. 84 NLRB 360 (1949).

15. *Digest of Hearings,* pp. 144–58. For union witnesses' comments, see pp. 158–61. See also House Committee on Education and Labor, *Report Pursuant to H. Res. 115 on Matters Relating to the Labor-Management Relations Act of 1947,* 83d Cong., 2d sess., 1954, pp. 8–12. (Hereinafter *House Report on H. Res. 115.*)

16. 91 NLRB 409 (1950); 94 NLRB 279 (1951). See also *Digest of Hearings,* pp. 175–78. For union witnesses' views, see *Digest of Hearings,* p. 178; and *House Report on H. Res. 115,* p. 17.

17. 94 NLRB 142 (1951); see also *Allied Mills,* 82 NLRB 854 (1949).

18. *Digest of Hearings,* pp. 77–79.

19. Ibid., pp. 69–72. For union witnesses' comments, see p. 72.

20. 102 NLRB 656 (1953).

21. 90 NLRB 1205 (1950); *House Report on H. Res. 115,* p. 8.

22. See *Digest of Hearings,* pp. 20–22, 292–97, 307–8, for the criticisms by management witnesses. For the views of union witnesses, see pp. 22–25, 297–98, 308–9.

23. There was some criticism of the Board before the Senate Labor Committee, but few NLRB case decisions were discussed. As noted previously, the House Labor

Committee's approach to Taft-Hartley amendments was much more severe than that of the Senate Labor Committee.

24. "Three of Five NLRB Seats Open," *New York Times,* June 30, 1953, p. 43.

25. Len Hall, chairman, Republican National Committee, memorandum to the file, July 7, 1953, "Appointments," Box 4, Records as President/Confidential Subject Series, Eisenhower Library, Abilene, Kan. After "studying Presidential appointments," Hall concluded that they were economically, geographically, and politically out of balance; were too heavily on the side of people with big industrial backgrounds; had not recognized "our so-called ethnic or minority groups"; and had demonstrated "the natural tendency of all of us to pick people or seek people who we personally know, or who are known to friends of ours."

26. "Suggested Memorandum from the President to Members of His Cabinet," July 7, 1953, "Appointments," Box 4, Records as President/Confidential Subject Series.

27. Michael Bernstein to Bernard Shanley, August 25, 1953, "Taft-Hartley Working Papers 5," Box 83, Records as President/Confidential Subject Series.

28. Paul Herzog to Truman, April 28, 1953, "Resignation File," Box 6, Paul Herzog Papers, Harry S Truman Library, Independence, Mo.; *Cong. Rec.,* 83d Cong., 1st sess. (1953), pt. 9:8481.

29. *Cong. Rec.,* 83d Cong., 1st sess. (1953), pt. 9:10437.

30. *Cong. Rec.,* 83d Cong., 2d sess. (1954), pt. 2:2005.

31. See James A. Gross, *The Reshaping of the National Labor Relations Board: National Labor Policy in Transition, 1937–1947* (Albany: State University of New York Press, 1981), pp. 230–31, for a discussion of the work of the Review Division.

32. Senate Committee on Labor and Public Welfare, *Nomination of Guy Farmer to be a Member of the National Labor Relations Board,* 83d Cong., 1st sess., 1953, pp. 1–4; "Guy Farmer Gets Labor Board Post," *New York Times,* July 8, 1953, p. 21; "Change Begun in Labor Board," *U.S. News & World Report,* July 17, 1953, pp. 88–89.

33. Memorandum from Staff Secretary Minnich to the file, April 28, 1953, "Miscellaneous—F January 1953—July 1958," Box 1, Papers of Staff Secretary Minnich, Eisenhower Library.

34. Guy Farmer, "The National Labor Relations Board," *West Virginia Law Review* 56 (June 1954): 82; Guy Farmer, "The NLRB: Its Past, Present, and Future," *Tennessee Law Review* 23 (February 1954): 117; Mozart G. Ratner, "Policy-Making by the New 'Quasi-Judicial' NLRB," *University of Chicago Law Review* 23 (Autumn 1955): 20–21 (quoting from Farmer's speeches); Joseph Loftus, "States' Role Urged in U.S. Labor Cases," *New York Times,* July 13, 1953, p. 15. For an excellent review of the decisions of the Eisenhower Board, see "The NLRB under Republican Administration: Recent Trends and Their Political Implications," *Columbia Law Review* 55 (June 1955): 852–906.

35. Farmer, "National Labor Relations Board," p. 85.

36. "NLRB's Head Calls for New Curbs against Reds in Labor," *New York Herald Tribune,* October 22, 1953.

37. Oral History interview with Guy Farmer, December 12, 1984, pp. 11–12, 50–54, Labor-Management Documentation Center (LMDC), ILR, Cornell University. Farmer said that he did not know how this infiltration affected Board decisions, if at all. Ibid., pp. 13, 50–54. See Chapter 3 for a discussion of loyalty boards at the NLRB.

38. Oral History interview with Farmer, pp. 14–17, 19–20; Farmer, "National Labor Relations Board," p. 81; Farmer, "The NLRB," p. 116.

39. Edward L. Kimball, "The 'Eisenhower' Board: Taft-Hartley under a Republican Administration," *Utah Law Review* (Spring 1955): 404 n. 175.

40. Farmer, "NLRB," pp. 12 (quotation), 15.

41. Guy Farmer, "The NLRB: A Standard of Criticism," *Georgetown Law Journal* 43 (March 1955): 343. Farmer also wrote: "Some of our critics operate on the unspoken premise that those parts of the written law which they regard as morally wrong should be given a quiet, administrative interment, while those parts which they approve should be enforced with a crusading vigor. Those who are imbued with this attitude are prone to vent their spleen against the law by criticizing its administration. It is a strange paradox that the charge of bias is most frequently made by those who do not seek impartiality so much as special dispensation." Ibid., p. 337.

42. Farmer, "The NLRB: A Standard of Criticism," p. 342; Farmer, "National Labor Relations Board," pp. 83–84.

43. Farmer, "National Labor Relations Board," pp. 83–84.

44. Farmer to Eisenhower, November 23, 1953, "NLRB (1)," Box 217, Records as President/O.F. 37, Eisenhower Library.

45. Transcript of the NLRB 50th Anniversary Conference, October 22–23, 1984, p. 16, LMDC.

46. Ibid., p. 89; Oral History interview with Farmer, p. 31 (quotation).

47. Memorandum from Charles Willis to the file, October 17, 1953, "NLRB (1)," Box 217, Records as President/O.F. 37.

48. H. J. Porter to Sherman Adams, December 1, 1953; Farmer to Willis, April 21, 1954 (in response to pressure to fire Dr. Edwin Elliott, regional director in Fort Worth, Texas), "NLRB (1)," Box 217, Records as President/O.F. 37; Farmer to Willis, July 7, 1954, "NLRB (2)," Box 217, Records as President/O.F. 37.

 Those who worked with Farmer referred to him as "very able and friendly" (Oral History interview with Marcel Mallet-Prevost, August 4, 1988, p. 13); "a wonderful man to deal with" (Oral History interview with Stephan Gordon, August 1, 1988, p. 42); "an able chairman, a fine lawyer, tough-minded, easy to work with" (Oral History interview with Theophil Kammholz, October 13, 1988, p. 13); "a very gracious man, a very intellectual man, very fair" (Oral History interview with Stanley Strauss, August 12, 1988, p. 13); "a very good technician [with] a practical grasp of legal problems" (Oral History interview with William Feldesman, July 28,

1988, p. 20); and an "excellent lawyer [and] very scholarly guy" (Oral History interview with Francis A. O'Connell, May 23, 1987, p. 27; all on file in LMDC).

49. Transcript of the NLRB 50th Anniversary Conference, p. 28. Farmer added: "I just don't see how you can justify saying that this is really not important because this is what goes on; and there's nothing particularly wrong with it. Well, everything is wrong with it! Everything is wrong with it! Because . . . it's becoming worse and worse." Ibid., p. 87.

50. "Eisenhower Gaining Control of NLRB," *New York Times,* August 29, 1953, p. 20; "Eisenhower Names Two Defense Aides," *New York Times,* July 29, 1953, p. 10.

51. Oral History interviews with Strauss (p. 12), Berton Subrin (August 5, 1988, p. 6, LMDC), Gordon (p. 42), and O'Connell (p. 55). Strauss also remembered: "I used to call him in private, Father Rodgers. Whenever anybody had a personal problem . . . they were apt to find unsympathetic views by other Board members but Rodgers was always on their side, was always in effect taking the viewpoint of the individual employee and was very generous toward them." Oral History interview, p. 12. Subrin recalled that shortly after he was hired, he nervously asked Rodgers for time off to spend with his wife and firstborn child: "He proceeded to tell me the story about his one child, who I think was retarded, and how he built a house for him up in the attic, and he said, 'That's more important to me than any of these cases. . . . You take all the time you want off.'" Oral History interview, pp. 6–7.

52. Seymour Scher, "Regulatory Agency Control through Appointment: The Case of the Eisenhower Administration and the NLRB," *Journal of Politics* 23 (November 1961): 678–79.

53. Oral History interview with Strauss, p. 12; Oral History interview with Subrin, pp. 7–8. Subrin remembered: "Stanley [Strauss] always tried to out-conservative Rodgers. In a private discussion before this Board meeting, Stanley was taking this very conservative position and was trying to persuade Rodgers of the merits of the position, and Rodgers just looked at him. He says, 'Stanley, cut the shit.' That was typical Rodgers. [Rodgers] said, 'Let's face it, I am going to vote the conservative line, but don't give me all of the bologna about why it's right and why the legislative history supports it; that's a bunch of garbage.'" Oral History interview with Subrin, pp. 7–8.

54. Senate Committee on Labor and Public Welfare, *Nomination of Albert Cummins Beeson to be a Member of the National Labor Relations Board,* 83d Cong., 2d sess., 1954, pp. 70–71. (Hereinafter *Beeson Confirmation Hearings.*)

55. Ibid., p. 68. See also "More Rights for Employers?" *U.S. News & World Report,* September 11, 1953, p. 85; "Eisenhower Gaining Control," p. 20.

56. *Beeson Confirmation Hearings,* p. 71.

57. Ibid., p. 70.

58. "Humphrey Charges 'Packing' of NLRB," *New York Times,* October 6, 1953, p. 25.

59. Goldwater to Wilton Persons, special assistant to the president, November 23, 1953, "Taft-Hartley Act (5)," O.F. 124-G, Eisenhower Library.

60. Paul Styles to Eisenhower, August 3, 1953, "NLRB (1)," Box 217, Records as President/O.F. 37.

61. "NLRB: Key to Coming T-H Debate," *Business Week,* January 16, 1954, p. 162.

62. B. Allen Rowland, special assistant to Secretary Weeks, to Willis, December 14, 1953, "NLRB (1)," Box 217, Records as President/O.F. 37.

63. *Beeson Confirmation Hearings,* p. 11. See pp. 1–3 for Beeson's biographical sketch.

64. Memorandum from Mitchell to Sherman Adams, November 27, 1953; memorandum from "Lo" to "CF," November 26, 1953, "NLRB (1)," Box 217, Records as President/O.F. 37.

65. *Beeson Confirmation Hearings,* pp. 3–4, 57, 90.

66. Ibid., pp. 5, 8, 9, 22.

67. Ibid., pp. 22, 92.

68. Before these admissions, however, the Senate Labor Committee, on January 26, 1954, despite a table-pounding protest by the CIO's James Carey, voted seven to six to report Beeson's nomination favorably to the full Senate. "Senate Group Backs NLRB Nominee," *New York Times,* January 27, 1954, p. 1. During confirmation hearings on January 20 and 22 Beeson told the committee that he had severed his relationship with his employer, thus losing his pension rights. *Beeson Confirmation Hearings,* pp. 4, 25; "Senators Call Beeson," *New York Times,* January 30, 1954, p. 29. Democratic Senator Herbert Lehman challenged Beeson, however, with a January 7 California newspaper report of an interview in which Beeson had said he expected to return to the company after serving on the Board. Beeson denied making that statement and said that the reporter who wrote the article had apologized to him. *Beeson Confirmation Hearings,* p. 25. Later Beeson admitted that he had made the statement as reported in the paper but said he was guilty of only an honest mistake because he had become confused. The newspaper denied that it had misquoted Beeson or that any of its reporters had apologized to him.

According to the company's official press release, Beeson would be on a leave of absence coinciding with his term at the NLRB. Beeson then told the committee that he had given an "oral resignation" to his employer's board of directors. When Lehman asked the company's president if Beeson had "orally resigned," the president answered, "No sir; he has not." "NLRB Nominee Gets 2d Hearing," *New York Times,* January 31, 1954, p. 44.

While Beeson was reduced to making self-deprecating and irrelevant appeals to the committee—"I suggest it is pretty difficult for a country boy to come before some trained Senators and never make a misstatement"—Eisenhower tried to pull him from the fire by saying publicly that he and others in his administration still thought Beeson "was a good man." Privately, the White House was lobbying some southern Democrats to support Beeson's confirmation when the issue came to the Senate floor. Clayton Knowles, "Eisenhower Backs Beeson's Fitness," *New York Times,* February 4, 1954, p. 11.

In a final effort to salvage the nomination committee chairman Smith asked Beeson if he was willing, on confirmation as a Board member, to send a resignation to his company "without any if's, but's, and and's." Beeson replied, "Yes, Sir." He added: "I think this is setting a very unfortunate precedent for businessmen who have perhaps much larger pensions at stake, but my wife and I are glad to make the sacrifice. If that will make the Democratic side happier and more content in their minds I am glad to do that." *Beeson Confirmation Hearings,* p. 202. See also Senator Kennedy's remarks in ibid., p. 164; "Beeson Declares He'd Quit Concern," *New York Times,* February 6, 1954, p. 9.

69. *Cong. Rec.,* 83d Cong., 2d sess. (1954), 100, pt. 2:1999, 2005; Clayton Knowles, "Beeson Wins NLRB Post, 45–42, after Senate Fight," *New York Times,* February 19, 1954, p. 1.

70. *Beeson Confirmation Hearings,* p. 121.

71. "NLRB: A Wrong Concept," *New York Times,* January 23, 1954, p. 12.

72. *Klinka's Garage,* 106 NLRB 969, 970, 974 (1953) (Styles and Murdock not participating). See also "Eisenhower Gaining Control," p. 20.

73. Farmer and Rodgers agreed on that objective but not on the method to be used. Farmer favored not asserting jurisdiction over employers with small numbers of employees, approximately twenty-five or fewer, whereas Rodgers wanted to increase the dollar amount of business needed to have the Board consider a case. Although willing to go along with his Republican-appointed colleagues on the Board, Beeson was skeptical of the plan to cut the Board's jurisdiction, because most state laws could not give small employers the same protection they could get from Taft-Hartley. "Trimming T-H's Scope," *Business Week,* April 24, 1954, p. 152.

74. "NLRB Announces Changes in Standards for Its Exercise of Jurisdiction," press release (R-445), July 1, 1954, NLRB Files, Washington, D.C.

75. "NLRB Jurisdictional Standards and State Jurisdiction," *Northwestern University Law Review* 50 (May–June 1955): 192–93; "Comparison of 1954 Jurisdictional Standards with 1950 Jurisdictional Standards" (no date), pp. 1–4, NN 3-25-86-2, Box 2, Record Group (RG) 25, National Archives (NA); "NLRB Shakes Off Minor Local Cases," *Business Week,* July 10, 1954, p. 144; Farmer, "National Labor Relations Board," p. 86; "NLRB Narrows Its Powers Again," *New York Times,* July 15, 1954, p. 33; "NLRB to Accept Fewer Small Cases," *New York Times,* July 1, 1954, p. 23. "Direct outflow into interstate commerce covers goods produced or handled for out-of-state shipment or services performed outside of the state. Indirect outflow into interstate commerce connotes goods or services furnished to instrumentalities or channels of commerce, public utilities or transit systems, or enterprises shipping goods or performing services out of state. Direct inflow from interstate commerce connotes purchases which have come directly from outside the state to the concern involved. Indirect inflow from interstate commerce describes purchases of goods which originated outside the state but come to the business concerned from a dealer within the same state." "NLRB Jurisdictional Standards," p. 192.

76. "NLRB Applies New Jurisdictional Standards," press release (R-467), October 28, 1954, NLRB Files.

77. 110 NLRB 493 (1954).

78. Ibid., p. 497.

79. The majority stated, however, "If one of the inevitable consequences of our action is to leave a somewhat larger area for local regulation of disputes, we do not share our colleagues' apparent view that this is a sinister development." Ibid.

80. Ibid., p. 502. Murdock estimated that 25 to 33 percent of the Board's jurisdiction had been eliminated. The majority called it a 10 percent reduction in caseload and a 1 percent reduction in the number of employees affected. Ibid., pp. 498–500. See also Murdock's comments, pp. 504, 506–8.

81. For an interesting presentation of the evolution of the NLRB's approach to its jurisdiction, see Margaret B. Schulman, "Does the NLRB Have the Power to Decline to Exercise Its Jurisdiction?" *George Washington Law Review* 26 (March 1958): 448–57. See also Dexter Hanley, "'No-Man's Land' in Labor Relations—A Survey," *Georgetown Law Journal* 43 (November 1954): 67–71.

82. Farmer to Sherman Adams, October 12, 1953, "NLRB—S.O.U.," Box 12, Bryce Harlow Papers, Eisenhower Library.

83. Fred Whitney, "NLRB Jurisdictional Policies and the Federal-State Relationship," *Labor Law Journal* (January 1955): 5–6; "The Discretionary Jurisdiction of the NLRB," *Harvard Law Review* 71 (January 1958): 538; Harris, "CIO View," p. 356; Reilly, "Return to Legislative Intent," pp. 394–96; Clyde Summers, "Politics, Policy Making, and the NLRB," *Syracuse Law Review* 6 (Fall 1954): 104–5.

84. See, for example, Robert Koretz, "Employer Free Speech under the Taft-Hartley Act," *Syracuse Law Review* 6 (Fall 1954): 82–92; Donald Wollett and James Rowen, "Employer Speech and Related Issues," *Ohio State Law Journal* 1 (Summer 1955): 380–402; Richard Mittenthal, "Employer Speech—A Life Cycle," *Labor Law Journal* (February 1954): 101–10; "Limitations upon an Employer's Right of Noncoercive Free Speech," *Virginia Law Review* 38 (December 1952): 1037–57; Walter Daykin, "The Employers' Right of Free Speech under the Taft-Hartley Act," *Iowa Law Review* 37 (Winter 1952): 212–41; "Employer's Free Speech during Working Hours as Unfair Labor Practice," *University of Chicago Law Review* 14 (December 1946): 104–12; W. Willard Wirtz, "The New National Labor Relations Board; Herein of 'Employer Persuasion,'" *Northwestern University Law Review* 49 (November–December 1954): 594–618; "Unions Turn on Labor Board," *U.S. News & World Report,* September 3, 1954, p. 93.

85. *NLRB v. Federbush Co.,* 121 F.2d 954, 957 (2d Cir. 1941). The Seventh Circuit Court of Appeals, in *NLRB v. Falk Corp.,* 102 F.2d 383, 389 (1939), had found that "the voice of authority may . . . provoke fear and awe quite as readily as it may bespeak fatherly advice. The position of the employer . . . carries such weight and influence that his words may be coercive when they would not be so if the relation of master and servant did not exist."

86. "Limitations upon an Employer's Right," pp. 1038–40.

87. 314 U.S. 469, 477 (1941).

88. 44 NLRB 121 (1942).

89. 70 NLRB 802 (1946).

90. Koretz, "Employer Free Speech," p. 85. See also Senate, 80th Cong., 1st sess., 1947, S. Rept. 105, pp. 23–24.
91. *Babcock and Wilcox Co.,* 77 NLRB 577 (1948).
92. 96 NLRB 608 (1951).
93. Mittenthal, "Employer Speech," p. 102 n. 13. This rule was valid because of the presence of customers on the selling floors of department stores. The Board had approved rules prohibiting union solicitation in those areas at all times. *May Department Stores,* 59 NLRB 976 (1944), *enforced,* 154 F.2d 533 (8th Cir. 1946).
94. Mittenthal, "Employer Speech," p. 102.
95. Ibid., p. 105.
96. *Biltmore Mfg. Co.,* 97 NLRB 905 (1951).
97. *Higgins, Inc.,* 100 NLRB 829 (1952).
98. *Biltmore Mfg. Co.,* 97 NLRB 905 (1951).
99. *National Screw Mfg. Co. of California,* 101 NLRB 1360 (1952) (Herzog dissenting).
100. 102 NLRB 1643 (1953) (Herzog dissenting).
101. 107 NLRB 400, 409 (1953).
102. Ibid., p. 406.
103. Ibid.
104. Ibid., pp. 406–7. Emphasis added.
105. Ibid., p. 411. In a companion case, *Peerless Plywood Co.,* 107 NLRB 427 (1953), which involved union objections to a representation election because of an employer captive audience speech that occurred less than twenty-four hours before the election was held, Farmer, Rodgers, and Peterson decided "that last-minute speeches by either employers or unions delivered to massed assemblies of employees on company time have an unwholesome and unsettling effect and tendency to interfere with that sober and thoughtful choice which a free election is designed to reflect." Ibid., p. 429. Accordingly, the majority established a rule to be applied in all election cases, prohibiting employers and unions from making election speeches on company time to massed assemblies of employees within twenty-four hours of the scheduled time for an election. Violation would cause an election to be set aside.

    Murdock saw this rule, supposedly based on "undocumented and nebulous experience," as a contradiction of the majority's contention that free speech was unqualified and that there was nothing in the statute or congressional intent "to restrict an employer in the use of his own premises for the purpose of airing his views." He believed that the new rule constituted an admission "that an employer's speech on company time and property may interfere with a free choice of a bargaining representative" and pointed to what he considered the absurdity of permitting such speeches if given twenty-four and a half but not twenty-four hours before a scheduled election. Ibid., pp. 416, 432.
106. 109 NLRB 591 (1954).
107. *Standard-Coosa-Thatcher,* 85 NLRB 1358 (1949). The new Eisenhower majority

and the dissent agreed that isolated and casual questioning was not a violation of the act, 109 NLRB at 597.

108. 109 NLRB at 592.

109. Ibid., p. 595.

110. Ibid., pp. 596–97.

111. Ibid., p. 598.

112. Ibid., p. 600.

113. Farmer, "The NLRB: A Standard of Criticism," p. 338.

114. *Bonwit Teller Inc. v. NLRB,* 197 F.2d 640 (2d Cir. 1952), appeared to reject the Board's equal opportunity approach by observing, "If Bonwit Teller were to abandon that [no-solicitation] rule, we do not think it would then be required to accord the Union a similar opportunity to address the employees *each* time [the employer] . . . made an antiunion speech." Ibid., p. 646. The Second Circuit left no doubt about its position in *NLRB v. American Tube Bending,* 205 F.2d 45 (2d Cir. 1953), when it upheld the Board on a discriminatory application of a no-solicitation rule but added, "If . . . the Board's order in the case at bar had depended upon the [employer's] refusal or failure to allow [the union] to address the employees on the property during working hours it could not stand." Ibid., p. 46.

115. See Wollett and Rowen, "Employer Speech," p. 398 n. 66, citing *Sax v. NLRB,* 171 F.2d 769 (7th Cir. 1948); *NLRB v. Winer,* 194 F.2d 370 (7th Cir. 1952); *NLRB v. England Bros.,* 201 F.2d 395 (1st Cir. 1953); *NLRB v. Tennessee Coach,* 191 F.2d 546 (6th Cir. 1951); *NLRB v. Montgomery Ward,* 192 F.2d 160 (2d Cir. 1951); *NLRB v. Associated Dry Goods Corp.,* 209 F.2d 593 (2d Cir. 1954); *NLRB v. Reynolds & Manley Lumber Co.,* 212 F.2d 1555 (5th Cir. 1954).

116. Summers, "Politics, Policy Making, and the NLRB," p. 97.

117. 77 NLRB 124 (1948).

118. 107 NLRB 511, 512–13 (1953).

119. Ibid., p. 514.

120. *Chicopee Mfg. Corp.,* 107 NLRB 106, 107 (1953). See also *Sparkletts Drinking Water Co.,* 107 NLRB 1462 (1954).

121. *Metropolitan Life Insurance Co.,* 90 NLRB 935 (1950). In *National Furniture Manufacturing Co.,* 106 NLRB 1300, 1302 (1953), the Farmer Board said, "To the extent that *Metropolitan Life Insurance* is inconsistent that case is hereby overruled."

122. 107 NLRB 1238, 1239 (1954). See also *National Furniture Mfg. Co.,* 106 NLRB 1300 (1953) (Murdock not participating).

123. *United Mfg. Co.,* 107 NLRB 21, 22 (1953).

124. 108 NLRB 1481, 1482 (1954).

125. See, for example, Wirtz, "New National Labor Relations Board," p. 596.

126. Summers, "Politics, Policy Making, and the NLRB," p. 103. One commentator concluded: "It is harder to understand the Board's being willing to fall back on the argument that 'equality' dictates an employer's being free to speak against the union on company property inasmuch as the union may speak freely against the employer

on union property. Beneath the saddle of this logic there rest the cockle burr facts that in the typical pre-election organizational setting the union frequently has no conveniently located property and cannot, in any event, assemble anything like the audience the employer can if he calls the meeting on company time and premises. It is wholly legitimate to conclude that this is a socially and economically desirable advantage for employers to have. It is only dishonest, though, to conceal this conclusion in the cloak of 'equality'—unless, indeed, the argument is simply that no governmental restraint on anybody amounts to equality of freedom from governmental restraint, which seems hardly worth talking about." Wirtz, "New National Labor Relations Board," p. 614.

127. Wirtz, "New National Labor Relations Board," p. 609.
128. Ratner, "Policy-Making," p. 33.
129. Wollett and Rowen, "Employer Speech," p. 386.
130. Reilly, "Return to Legislative Intent," p. 383 n. 40.
131. Summers, "Politics, Policy Making, and the NLRB," p. 107.
132. Kimball, "'Eisenhower' Board," p. 404.
133. Bernard Cushman, "Secondary Boycotts and the Taft-Hartley Law," *Syracuse Law Review* 6 (Fall 1954): 113.
134. 87 NLRB 972, 983 (1949) (Reynolds dissenting).
135. *Rabouin d/b/a Conway's Express v. NLRB,* 195 F.2d 906 (2d Cir. 1952).
136. *McAllister Transfer Co.,* 110 NLRB 1769, 1774, 1784 (1954). Even if one can assume that a hot cargo clause constitutes a waiver of an employer's statutory protection, however, Murdock and Peterson pointed out: "Despite the fact that under Sections 7 and 13 of the Act the employees' right to strike is protected, it is well settled that their bargaining representative can enter into a contract with their employer containing a no-strike clause and if the employees breach the provision the employer does not violate the Act if he discharges them. It can hardly be gainsaid that by executing such an agreement the employees' right to strike, in effect, has been waived. Yet, as with respect to the secondary employer's right under Section 8(b)(4)(A), we know of nothing in Sections 7 and 13 which proscribe this kind of waiver." Ibid., pp. 1794–95.
137. Ibid., p. 1788. In *McAllister,* unlike *Conway's Express,* the secondary employers, even though parties to hot cargo agreements with the union, directed their employees to handle all freight. Farmer, without reversing *Conway's Express* or finding hot cargo provisions contrary to public policy, concluded that if a secondary employer chose not to comply with its "hot cargo" agreement, it would be an unfair labor practice for the union party to that agreement to attempt to compel compliance through pressure on their members who were employees of the secondary employer. Although Farmer did not rule hot cargo clauses per se violations of the act, as did Rodgers and Beeson, the practical effect of his interpretation was to render hot cargo agreements meaningless by permitting employers to renege on them and making it an unfair labor practice for a union in such a situation to attempt to rely on its contractual agreement. Ibid., pp. 1788–90.

138. 87 NLRB 502 (1949).
139. Later, in *Moore Dry Dock*, 92 NLRB 547 (1950), the Herzog Board detailed the prerequisites for such ambulatory or roving situs picketing: "(1) Picketing may only be carried on when the truck is at the premises of the secondary employer, (2) the truck must be engaged in its normal course of business, (3) the picketing must clearly show that the dispute is with the trucking company, (4) the picketing must be reasonably close to the truck locations." See "Section 8(b)(4)(A)— Changes in Board Interpretation," *Northwestern University Law Review* 50 (May–June 1955): 254.
140. 107 NLRB 299 (1953).
141. 102 NLRB 996 (1953).
142. 107 NLRB at 303–4.
143. For example, the new Board required union picket signs to state clearly that the dispute was with the primary employer and was not directed beyond the primary employer; a sign saying "working conditions on this job are unfair to the Carpenters District Council" was not precise enough. *Local Union No. 55 (Professional and Businessmen's Life Insurance Co.)*, 108 NLRB 363, 365 (1954).

   In a similar case a union picketed at the entrance to a construction project employing a non-union painting contractor. The picket signs read, "This job unfair to Painters Local No. 1730, AFL." Later, after seeking the advice of an attorney, the union substituted the name of the non-union subcontractor for the phrase "this job" on their picket signs. The Eisenhower Board found this change "insufficient to apprise employees that the picketing was no longer extended to neutrals in aid of the union's dispute with the primary employer." *Brotherhood of Painters, Decorators and Paperhangers of America, Local Union No. 1730*, 109 NLRB 1163 (1954); quotation, p. 1168.
144. 110 NLRB 1412, 1415–16 (1954).
145. Ibid., p. 1417.
146. Ibid., pp. 1421, 1426.
147. 107 NLRB 1547, 1547–50 (1954).
148. *Textile Workers Union of America, CIO (Personal Products Co.)*, 108 NLRB 743, 745–47 (1954).
149. 110 NLRB 1589, 1595–96 (1954).
150. 110 NLRB 1806, 1809 (1954).
151. *Valley City Furniture*, 110 NLRB 1589, 1599 (1954).
152. *Honolulu Rapid Transit Co.*, 110 NLRB 1806, 1812–13 (1954).
153. *Wilson & Co., Inc.*, 105 NLRB 823 (1954).
154. 109 NLRB 680, 684 (1954).
155. Ibid., pp. 689–90. The interpretation given that section of the act by the chairman, Beeson, and Rodgers, Murdock charged, was "based essentially upon what they individually believe would be good policy rather than upon the language of the statute or legislative history." Ibid., pp. 696–97.
156. 107 NLRB 242, 243 (1953).
157. 109 NLRB 1097, 1098 (1954).
158. Ibid., pp. 1101–2.

159. 91 NLRB 409 (1950), on remand 99 NLRB 1448 (1950).

160. 94 NLRB 279 (1951), on remand 100 NLRB 1016 (1952).

161. For example, *Betts Cadillac Olds, Inc.*, 96 NLRB 268 (1951). For other cases, see "NLRB under Republican Administration," p. 884 n. 166.

162. 109 NLRB 447, 448 (1954). The nonstruck members advised the union that the locked-out employees would be recalled when the union ended its strike.

163. 109 NLRB at 448.

164. Ibid., p. 449.

165. Ibid., p. 451.

166. *Southeastern Rubber Manufacturing Co.*, 106 NLRB 989, 994 (1953).

167. 106 NLRB 1355 (1953).

168. *Aiello Dairy Farms*, 110 NLRB 1365 (1954).

169. *M. H. Davidson*, 94 NLRB 142 (1951). The majority in *Aiello* said that it was overruling *Davidson*. See 110 NLRB at 1368 n. 6.

170. 110 NLRB at 1369, 1372.

171. Ibid., p. 1370.

172. Ibid., p. 1369. Peterson said that there was only an "insignificant" difference in expense and energy between processing a representation proceeding after an election had been set aside and completion of an unfair labor practice proceeding. Ibid., p. 1376.

173. Ibid., p. 1375.

174. 108 NLRB 1537, 1541 (1954).

175. *Bickford Shoes, Inc.*, 109 NLRB 1346 (1954).

176. *Richfield Oil Corp.*, 110 NLRB 356 (1954).

177. Ibid., pp. 362–63, 366–68 (quotation, p. 368).

178. Ibid., p. 363.

179. *Pacific Intermountain Express*, 107 NLRB 837 (1954).

180. *Firestone Tire and Rubber Co.*, 93 NLRB 981 (1951).

181. One commentator noted: "In *NLRB v. American National Insurance Co.* [343 U.S. 395 (1952)] the Supreme Court held that Section 8(d) permitted each party to bargain for unilateral control of subjects in the field of wages, hours, and conditions of employment. Seniority rights are, of course, such a subject. Indisputably, the employer is free to bargain for unilateral control over resolution of seniority disputes. Yet the Board precludes the union from doing likewise." Ratner, "Policy-Making," p. 30.

182. Summers, "Politics, Policy Making, and the NLRB," p. 98.

183. Farmer, "National Labor Relations Board," p. 83.

184. Ibid.

185. Wirtz, "New National Labor Relations Board," p. 322.

Chapter 8

1. Stephen E. Ambrose, *Eisenhower*, vol. 2, *The President* (New York: Simon and Schuster, 1984), p. 370. Eisenhower received 35,581,003 votes; Stevenson, 25,738,765. In 1956 the Democrats won no state outside the South.

2. *Party Line-Up: Congress and the Presidency, 1854–1964* (Washington, D.C.: Congressional Quarterly Service, 1965), p. 63.

3. John Patrick Diggins, *The Proud Decades: America in War and Peace, 1941–1960* (New York: W. W. Norton, 1988), p. 325.

4. Ibid., p. 306.

5. Gilbert Gall, *The Politics of Right to Work: The Labor Federations as Special Interests, 1943–1979* (New York: Greenwood Press, 1988), p. 77.

6. Diggins, *Proud Decades*, p. 32.

7. Gall, *Politics of Right to Work*, p. 78.

8. Willard Wirtz, "The Labor-Management Reporting and Disclosure Act of 1959: A Symposium," *Northwestern University Law Review* 54, no. 6 (January–February 1960): 662–63.

9. House Joint Subcommittee of the Committee on Education and Labor, *Hearings on H.R. 3540, H.R. 330, H.R. 4473, and H.R. 4474 and Related Bills Regarding Labor-Management Reform Legislation*, 86th Cong., 1st sess., 1959, part 5, pp. 2287–324; Senate, *Hearing before the Subcommittee on Labor of the Committee on Labor and Public Welfare on S. 505, S. 748, S. 76, S. 1002, S. 1137, and S. 1311*, 86th Cong., 1st sess., 1959, pp. 603–13.

10. "Labor: Politics and the NLRB," *Fortune*, October 1956, p. 238.

11. "Behind the Headlines: Labor Legislation: Erosion by Appointment," *New Republic*, 132 (November 12, 1954): 3; "Fight for Posts on Labor Board," *U.S. News & World Report*, November 19, 1954, p. 114.

12. Oral History interview with Frank Kleiler, August 3, 1988, pp. 11–12, Labor-Management Documentation Center (LMDC), ILR, Cornell University.

13. Copy of Beeson's December 30, 1954, interview with the *San Jose Mercury*, Folder 48, Box 36, Department of Legislation (1906–1978), George Meany Memorial Archives, Washington, D.C.

14. Ibid.

15. Memorandum from Charles F. Willis to Sherman Adams, June 7, 1954, "NLRB (2)," Box 217, Records as President/O.F. 37, Eisenhower Library, Abilene, Kan.

16. "Teaming up to Attack the GOP," *Business Week*, February 26, 1955, p. 105; "NLRB—The Mitchell Way," *Fortune*, February 1958, p. 214.

17. "Finucane Named as High Army Aide," *New York Times*, January 25, 1955, p. 16; "Nominated for NLRB," *Business Week*, February 19, 1955, p. 170.

18. Senate Committee on Labor and Public Welfare, *Nomination of Boyd Leedom to Be a Member of the National Labor Relations Board*, 84th Cong., 1st sess., 1955, pp. 1–2 (quotation), 5. (Hereinafter *Leedom Confirmation Hearings*.)

19. "Senate Labor Group O.K.'s Leedom for Key NLRB Post," *Baltimore Sun*, February 26, 1955.

20. Oral History interviews with Stephan Gordon, August 1, 1988, p. 42; and Berton Subrin, August 5, 1988, pp. 9–10 (quotation), LMDC. Subrin also remembered that Leedom "got a number of us interested in being Big Brother to some car thieves in northeast Washington." Oral History interview, p. 9.

21. Oral History interview with Kleiler, pp. 12–13.
22. Oral History interviews with William Feldesman, July 28, 1988, p. 21; Stanley Strauss, August 12, 1988, p. 14; and Warren Davison, August 8, 1988, p. 16, LMDC.
23. "Senate Labor Group O.K.'s Leedom."
24. Unsigned memorandum, "NLRB General Counsel," July 26, 1954, attached to memorandum from Bernard Shanley to Charles F. Willis, April 6, 1954, "General Counsel—NLRB," Box 219, Records as President/O.F. 37.
25. Memorandum from Willis to Herbert Brownell, February 9, 1954; memorandum from Willis to Sherman Adams, February 9, 1954; memorandum, "George Bott—General Counsel NLRB—Removal," from "S" [Sherman Adams] to Willis, undated, "NLRB (2)," Box 45, Records as President/Confidential Subject Series, Eisenhower Library.
26. Memorandum from Shanley to Willis, March 2, 1954; memorandum from Rabb to Willis, March 3, 1954, "NLRB (2)," Box 45, Records as President/Confidential Subject Series.
27. Oral History interview with George Bott, August 10, 1988, p. 51, LMDC.
28. Memorandum from Willis to Adams, June 7, 1954, "General Counsel—NLRB," Box 218, Records as President/O.F. 37.
29. "New Congress Eyes NLRB," *Business Week,* January 8, 1955, p. 50; "NLRB Is Facing Lag in Operation," *New York Times,* December 19, 1954, p. 49; "NLRB in Predicament as Counsel's Term Ends," *New York Times,* December 21, 1954, p. 23.
30. Senate Committee on Labor and Public Welfare, *Nomination of Theophil Carl Kammholz to Be General Counsel of the National Labor Relations Board,* 84th Cong., 1st sess., 1955, pp. 1–3 (hereinafter *Kammholz's Confirmation Hearings*); "Taft-Hartley's Key Man," *Business Week,* May 21, 1955, pp. 166–67.
31. *Kammholz's Confirmation Hearings,* pp. 16–37, 48–52.
32. *Cong. Rec.,* 84th Cong., 1st sess. (March 8, 1955), 101, pt. 2:2117–18.
33. Ibid., p. 2122; "NLRB Aide Approved," *New York Times,* March 9, 1955, p. 30.
34. *Kammholz's Confirmation Hearings,* p. 39.
35. Copy of Kammholz's speech to the Illinois State Chamber of Commerce, October 14, 1955, pp. 1–6; address before the National Affairs Forum sponsored by the Pittsburgh Chamber of Commerce, December 6, 1955, pp. 5–11, 19–20, Folder 49, Box 36, Kammholz Papers, Department of Legislation, Meany Archives.
36. "Effecting Better Understanding between Employers and NLRB Regional Offices," address by Kammholz, *Daily Labor Report,* no. 12, January 18, 1956, p. D-1, Kammholz Papers. See also Theophil Kammholz, "NLRB Regional Offices and the Employer," *Labor Law Journal* 7 (March 1956): 137–38.
37. "General Counsel Appoints Special Assistants," press release (R-479), May 1, 1955; "Kenneth McGuiness Appointed Associate General Counsel" (R-487), August 4, 1955, NLRB Files, Washington, D.C.
38. Oral History interview with Norton Come, July 29, 1988, p. 20, LMDC.
39. Oral History interview with Kenneth McGuiness, August 1, 1988, pp. 5–6, LMDC.

40. Ibid., pp. 8–11.
41. Oral History interviews with Come, p. 20; Marcel Mallet-Prevost, August 4, 1988, pp. 18–19, LMDC; Gordon, p. 24.
42. Oral History interview with Gerald Brown, May 26, 1987, pp. 62–64, LMDC.
43. Oral History interview with Theophil Kammholz, October 13, 1988, pp. 5, 24, LMDC.
44. Memorandum from Farmer to Adams, May 20, 1955, "NLRB (2)," Box 217, Records as President/O.F. 37; Oral History interview with Guy Farmer, December 12, 1984, pp. 31–32, LMDC.
45. Joseph Loftus, "Labor Post Splits President's Aides," *New York Times,* August 6, 1955, p. 31; "NLRB Post May Go to Aide of Mitchell," *New York Times,* July 11, 1955, p. 44; "Labor Jobs Test GOP Strategy," *Business Week,* August 6, 1955, pp. 130–31.
46. "NLRB Head Resigns," *New York Times,* August 20, 1955, p. 34; "NLRB Rulings," *Business Week,* September 3, 1955, p. 90.
47. Memorandum from Senator Smith to Adams, November 14, 1955, "Taft-Hartley," Box 82, Records as President/Confidential Subject Series.
48. Allen Drury, "Eisenhower Picks NLRB Chairman," *New York Times,* November 19, 1955, p. 1; "December Vote," *Business Week,* November 26, 1955, p. 168.
49. "NLRB Loses Last Trace of Truman Regime," *Business Week,* January 4, 1958, p. 39; "NLRB—The Mitchell Way," p. 214.
50. Oral History interviews with Kammholz, p. 14; Davison, pp. 1–2, 16; Kleiler, pp. 13–14.
51. Ambrose, *Eisenhower,* 2:220.
52. Drury, "Eisenhower Picks NLRB Chairman," p. 1; *Cong. Rec.,* 84th Cong., 2d sess. (1956), 102, pt. 1:493 [a letter from Senator Joseph McCarthy to Senator John McClellan, November 2, 1955] (quotation).
53. Murrey Marder, "All Called Reds Long off Payroll," *Washington Post and Times Herald,* December 14, 1955, p. 18; John Herling, "Tales of Old NLRB," *Washington Post and Times Herald,* December 14, 1955, p. 2; Frank Hughes, "Former Professor at American U. Makes Charge at Chicago Hearing," *Washington Post and Times Herald,* December 14, 1955, p. 2. For a discussion of communism at the NLRB in the 1930s and 1940s and Fuchs's role, see James A. Gross, *The Reshaping of the National Labor Relations Board: National Labor Policy in Transition, 1937–1949* (Albany: State University of New York Press, 1981), pp. 145–50.
54. Joseph Loftus, "NLRB Widens 'Sensitive' Jobs," *New York Times,* December 30, 1955.
55. *Cong. Rec.,* 84th Cong., 2d sess. (1956), 102, pt. 4:5466. Morse acknowledged the "assistance" of former NLRB attorney Mozart Ratner. Ibid., p. 5469.
56. Ibid., pp. 5463, 5466 (quotation).
57. Ibid., pp. 12070–83; Morse's response appears on pp. 15560–62.
58. For the full text of these letters, see ibid., pp. 12076–78.
59. Ibid., p. 12078. For Morse's reply, see pp. 15552, 15555.

60. Ibid., p. 12076. For Leedom's comments on Mozart Ratner, see ibid.

61. Ibid., p. 15556.

62. Ibid., p. 15555.

63. Ibid., p. 15556. See also Bernard Dunau, "The Role of Criticism in the Work of the National Labor Relations Board," *Proceedings of the Sixteenth Annual New York University Conference on Labor* 16 (1963): 211–13.

64. "NLRB Seeks Broader Powers," *Business Week,* October 19, 1957, pp. 157–60; "Labor: Politics and the NLRB," p. 238.

65. *Local 1976, United Brotherhood of Carpenters and Joiners of America,* 113 NLRB 1210, 1215–17 (1955).

66. Archibald Cox and John T. Dunlop, "Regulation of Collective Bargaining by the National Labor Relations Board," *Harvard Law Review* 63 (January 1950): 397–98. Since 1940 the NLRB had declared that Section 9(a) covered, in addition to wages and hours, such subjects as holiday and vacation pay, discharges, pensions, bonuses, profit sharing, work loads and work standards, insurance benefits, the closed or union shop, subcontracting, shop rules, work schedules, rest periods, and merit increases. Ibid.

67. *Wooster Division of Borg-Warner Corp.,* 113 NLRB 1288, 1294–95 (1955).

68. Ibid., pp. 1299–1300.

69. 343 U.S. 395, 408 (1952).

70. Ibid.

71. 113 NLRB at 1306.

72. This inconsistency was continued by the Supreme Court when it upheld the majority's decision in *Borg-Warner* (*NLRB v. Wooster Division of Borg-Warner Corp.,* 356 U.S. 342 [1958]) and the Eisenhower Board's decision in *Insurance Agents'* (*NLRB v. Insurance Agents' International Union,* 361 U.S. 477 [1960]).

73. 119 NLRB 768, 771–72 (1957), quoting from *Textile Workers Union of America, CIO, and Local 1172* (*Personal Products Co.*), 108 NLRB 743, 747 (1954).

74. 119 NLRB at 769–72.

75. See, for example, *Mountain Pacific Chapter of the Associated General Contractors,* 119 NLRB 883 (1957); "Administrative Law Making through Adjudication: The National Labor Relations Board," *Minnesota Law Review* 45 (March 1961): 623–24; *Pine Industrial Relations Committee, Inc.,* 118 NLRB 1055 (1957).

76. Thomas G. S. Christensen, "Free Speech, Propaganda, and the National Labor Relations Act," *New York University Law Review* 38 (April 1963): 271–73.

77. *Nutone, Inc.,* 112 NLRB 1153, 1154–55 (1955).

78. 107 NLRB 400 (1953).

79. See Murdock's dissent in *Nutone, Inc.,* 112 NLRB at 1157–58.

80. On March 28, 1957, Joseph Alton Jenkins replaced Ivar Peterson, whose term had expired on August 27, 1956. Jenkins's appointment is discussed in Chapter 9.

81. *Drivers, Chauffeurs, and Helpers Local 639* (*Curtis Bros., Inc.*), 119 NLRB 232, 236 (1957).

82. Ibid., p. 256. Murdock argued: "Inherent in any picketing is the possibility of eco-

nomic loss due to curtailment of the employer's business. Inherent in any picketing is an effect upon Section 7 rights since picketing necessarily affects the right of employees to refrain from supporting the concerted activity of picketing and any purpose to which it may be directed." Ibid.

83. Ibid., pp. 258–59.

84. Ibid., p. 263.

85. *International Association of Machinists, Lodge 942, and Alloy Mfg. Co.,* 119 NLRB 307, 309–10 (1957).

86. For other cases, see *Amalgamated Meat Cutters and Butcher Workmen of North America, Local No. 88. (Swift and Co.),* 113 NLRB 275 (1955); *Retail Fruit & Vegetable Clerks' Union Local 1017 (Crystal Palace Market),* 116 NLRB 856 (1956) (this case overruled *Ryan Construction Co.,* 85 NLRB 417 [1949]); and *The Patterson-Sargent Co.,* 115 NLRB 1627 (1956).

87. *NLRB v. Mackay Radio & Telegraph Co.,* 304 U.S. 333 (1938).

88. This analysis is based on a dissent by Board member John Fanning in *Paint, Varnish & Lacquer Makers Union, Local 1232 (Andrew Brown Co.),* 120 NLRB 1425, 1431 (1958). Fanning's appointment is discussed in Chapter 9.

89. Figures compiled from NLRB annual reports, 1948–58. See also memorandum from Millard Cass to Mitchell (with attached charts), January 3, 1957, "1957—NLRB," Box 137, James Mitchell Papers, Eisenhower Library.

90. Ibid.

91. C. P. Trussell, "Union Heads Say Merger Creates Political Strength," *New York Times,* September 6, 1955, p. 18; A. H. Raskin, "Clean-up Begun by Unified Labor," *New York Times,* December 8, 1955, p. 1; Stanley Levey, "Meany Vows Fight on Bias When Labor's Ranks Unite," *New York Times,* February 27, 1955.

92. Arthur Krock, "Blocs in the Path toward Electoral Reform," *New York Times,* February 24, 1955, p. 26.

93. Homer Bigart, "Meany Says NAM Attempts to Curb Union Labor Vote," *New York Times,* December 10, 1955, p. 1.

94. A. H. Raskin, "Merger Official," *New York Times,* December 6, 1955, p. 1.

95. Eisenhower to Henry Cabot Lodge, February 21, 1955, "February, 1955 (1)," Box 9, Papers as President/Eisenhower Diary, Eisenhower Library; minutes of cabinet meeting, February 18, 1955, p. 3, "February 18, 1955," Box 4, Papers as President/Cabinet, Eisenhower Library.

96. A. H. Raskin, "Thug Hurls Acid on Labor Writer; Sight Imperiled," *New York Times,* April 6, 1956, p. 1; "The Riesel Affair," *New York Times,* April 8, 1956, sec. 4, p. 2.

97. "Riesel Loses Sight from Burns of Acid," *New York Times,* May 5, 1956, p. 1; Will Lissner, "Riesel to Resume Work Next Week," *New York Times,* May 18, 1956, p. 2; "Riesel Carries On," *New York Times,* May 6, 1956, sec. 4, p. 2; Stanley Levey, "FBI Solves Riesel Case; Reports Acid-Hurler Slain," *New York Times,* August 18, 1956, p. 1; Edith Evans Asbury, "Three in Riesel Blinding Sentenced to Prison," *New York Times,* December 8, 1956, p. 1.

98. "Eisenhower to Act on Union Rackets," *New York Times,* June 6, 1956, p. 1.

99. For a discussion of the composition of this committee, see Alan K. McAdams, *Power and Politics in Labor Legislation* (New York: Columbia University Press, 1964), pp. 36–40; "Senate Votes Inquiry on Labor Rackets; McClellan May Head Eight-Member Panel," *New York Times,* January 31, 1957, p. 17.

100. McAdams, *Power and Politics,* pp. 11–12, 39–40; Willard Wirtz, "The Labor-Management Reporting and Disclosure Act of 1959: A Symposium," *Northwestern University Law Review* 54 (January–February 1960): 660. Abe Raskin of the *New York Times* commented: "They came to tell Andrew Furuseth, the tall, gaunt Norseman who founded the Sailors Union of the Pacific, that he might have to go to jail for violating a no-strike injunction; he looked around the roach-ridden hall bedroom that was his home. 'You can put me in jail,' he said, 'But you cannot give me narrower quarters than as a seaman I have always had. You cannot give me coarser food than I have always eaten. You cannot make me lonelier than I have always been.' Now the Lincoln of the sea is nineteen-years dead, and the headlines reek with the exploits of a new generation of labor leaders to whom austerity is a long-discarded companion." "The Moral Issue that Confronts Labor," *New York Times Magazine,* March 31, 1957, sec. 6, p. 17.

101. Joseph Loftus, "Union Organizing Hurt by Hearings," *New York Times,* April 7, 1957, p. 1.

102. Allen Drury, "Inquiry Expects New Data on Beck," *New York Times,* April 1, 1957, p. 17.

103. Ambrose, *Eisenhower,* 2:488.

104. Archibald Cox, "The Landrum-Griffin Amendments to the National Labor Relations Act," *Minnesota Law Review* 44 (December 1959): 258.

105. For an excellent analysis of how Landrum-Griffin became law, see McAdams, *Power and Politics;* the Kennedy-Ervin bill is discussed on pp. 56–112. (When first introduced, the bill was designated S. 505 but later became S. 1555.)

106. Cox, "Landrum-Griffin Amendments," p. 259.

107. Benjamin Aaron, "The New Labor Bill," *The Nation,* November 21, 1959, p. 373.

108. McAdams, *Power and Politics,* pp. 71–73, 272.

109. Ibid., p. 133.

110. Memorandum from John A. Stuart to Sybyl Patterson, National Association of Manufacturers interoffice memorandum, October 15, 1957; memorandum from Patterson to Charles R. Sligh, Jr., "Recommendations of Subcommittee on Labor Disputes and Collective Bargaining," September 12, 1957; memorandum by Patterson, "Promotional Ideas on Labor-Management Problems," October 4, 1957, Box 14, National Association of Manufacturers Archives, Hagley Museum and Library, Wilmington, Del.; McAdams, *Power and Politics,* p. 159.

111. McAdams, *Power and Politics,* p. 177.

112. Ibid., pp. 192–93, 215–16.

113. Ibid., pp. 62, 79–80, 128, 180–83, 216–17, 253.

114. Joseph A. Loftus, "President Urges Bipartisan Bill on Labor Reform," *New York Times,* August 7, 1959, p. 1.

115. In 1957 the Supreme Court ruled in *Guss v. Utah Board,* 353 U.S. 1, that a state

tribunal may act in a case within the NLRB's Taft-Hartley jurisdiction only when the NLRB had ceded jurisdiction to the state under Section 10(a) of the act. A refusal by the NLRB to exercise jurisdiction over a case did not vest a state tribunal with jurisdiction. At the time of the *Guss* decision no such agreements existed.

In response to *Guss,* the NLRB in 1958 reduced the extent of the no-man's land when it revised its dollar-volume jurisdictional standards downward in order to increase the number of cases it would accept. Chairman Leedom estimated that the new standards would increase the NLRB's workload by 20 percent. For the new standards, see NLRB, *Twenty-third Annual Report,* for the fiscal year ended June 30, 1958 (Washington, D.C.: GPO, 1959), pp. 7–8.

116. *Local 1976, United Brotherhood of Carpenters and Joiners of America* (*Sand Door*), 357 U.S. 93 (1958). In *Sand Door* the Supreme Court held, as had the NLRB, that hot cargo clauses were unenforceable though not illegal.

117. For a brief discussion of those exceptions, see *The Labor Reform Law* (Washington, D.C.: Bureau of National Affairs, 1959), pp. 93–94.

118. *NLRB v. International Rice Milling Co.,* 341 U.S. 665 (1951).

119. *Labor Reform Law,* pp. 86, 228. The minority report appears in full on pp. 219–65.

120. *International Brotherhood of Electrical Workers,* 82 NLRB 1028 (1949); *International Brotherhood of Teamsters,* 112 NLRB 923 (1955).

121. Section 8(b)(4)(A).

122. Cox, "Landrum-Griffin Amendments," p. 274.

123. 102 NLRB 996 (1953).

124. Under those decisions picketing was unlawful only when it induced or encouraged employees of a neutral employer to refuse to work or perform services.

125. R. W. Fleming, "Title VII: The Taft-Hartley Amendments," *Northwestern University Law Review* 54 (January–February 1960): 692–93.

126. Ibid., p. 692.

127. Organizational picketing was directed at employees, whereas recognition picketing was directed at an employer.

128. One commentator noted, "Here there is a square conflict between the historic union organizing technique and the election process." Fleming, "Title VII," p. 698.

129. Cox, "Landrum-Griffin Amendments," p. 263.

130. Ibid., pp. 269–70; Fleming, "Title VII," pp. 698–99.

Chapter 9

1. For an interesting discussion of the political relationship between organized labor and the Democratic Party at this time, see Gilbert Gall, *The Politics of Right to Work: The Labor Federations as Special Interests, 1943–1979* (New York: Greenwood Press, 1988), pp. 136–39; John Patrick Diggins, *The Proud Decades: America in War and Peace, 1941–1960* (New York: W. W. Norton, 1988), pp. 338–40.

2. Arthur Schlesinger, *One Thousand Days: John F. Kennedy in the White House* (Cambridge, Mass.: Houghton Mifflin, 1965), p. 76.

3. Ibid., p. 10.

4. A. H. Raskin, "Lag in Unionizing Worrying Labor," *New York Times*, February 10, 1960, p. 16; Arthur Krock, "Three Houses Divided against Themselves," *New York Times*, July 7, 1960, p. 30.

5. Gall, *Politics of Right to Work*, p. 138.

6. See, for example, A. H. Raskin, "Labor Drive Aids Kennedy's Hopes," *New York Times*, November 6, 1960, p. 44.

7. "Kennedy Selects NLRB Chairman," *New York Times*, February 5, 1961, p. 38.

8. Kimball, a sixty-one-year-old Republican at the time of his appointment, was staff director of Eisenhower's Advisory Committee on Government Organization. He had served six years in the State Department and had also worked for the Veterans Administration and the Bureau of Employment Security. "Committee Staff Chief Appointed to NLRB," *New York Times*, April 5, 1960, p. 5; "Kimball Gets Post," *New York Times*, September 14, 1960, p. 26.

9. Kenneth McGuiness, *The New Frontier NLRB* (Washington, D.C.: Labor Policy Association, 1963), p. 3.

10. "Kennedy Selects NLRB Chairman," p. 38; "New NLRB Chief once Union Member," *Washington Star*, February 5, 1961; "McCulloch Picked to Be NLRB Chief," *Washington Post*, February 5, 1961, p. A2; "Sen. Douglas Aide Named NLRB Chief," *Cleveland Plain Dealer*, February 5, 1961.

11. Frank McCulloch, "The How and Why of Recent NLRB Decisions," address before the American Management Association, February 15, 1962. Reprinted in *Daily Labor Report*, no. 33, February 15, 1962, p. D-9; James A. Gross, "Conflicting Statutory Purposes: Another Look at Fifty Years of NLRB Law Making," *Industrial and Labor Relations Review* 39, no. 1 (October 1985): 16–17.

12. Frank McCulloch speech, "Developing Issues in Collective Bargaining," press release (R-809), October 19, 1961, pp. 3–4, NLRB Files, Washington, D.C.

13. Oral History interview with Frank McCulloch, September 5, 1989, Labor-Management Documentation Center (LMDC), ILR, Cornell University, pp. 34, 139.

14. McCulloch, "Developing Issues," p. 20.

15. Frank W. McCulloch, "Development and Contribution of the National Labor Relations Act," *Alabama Lawyer* 30 (April 1969): 162.

16. Oral History interview with Frank O'Connell, May 23, 1987, pp. 40–41, LMDC.

17. Oral History interview with Kenneth McGuiness, August 1, 1988, p. 20, LMDC.

18. Oral History interview with Stephan Gordon, August 1, 1988, pp. 45–46, LMDC. Gordon added, "I did not have many heroes in my life, but Frank McCulloch was one of them."

19. Oral History interview with John Truesdale, August 2, 1988, pp. 28–29, LMDC.

20. Oral History interview with Warren Davison, August 8, 1988, pp. 17–18, LMDC. Davison recalled that McCulloch was a poor joke-teller but "when he got into the speech itself, he burnt with a fire that was just like an old-time preacher. . . . You didn't have to agree with it, but, man, you could really understand that guy really felt for the Labor Act." Ibid., p. 18.

21. Oral History interview with Thomas Miller, September 8, 1989, p. 14, LMDC.
22. Oral History interview with O'Connell, pp. 50, 73–74.
23. Oral History interview with Sam Zagoria, August 9, 1988, p. 39, LMDC.
24. Oral History interview with Berton Subrin, August 5, 1988, p. 12, LMDC.
25. Oral History interview with Gordon, p. 46.
26. Memorandum for the record by Ed Sherman, December 15, 1964 (information based on a conversation with William Lubbers of the NLRB), "NLRB," Container No. 804, Files of John Macy (Chairman, Civil Service Commission), Lyndon Baines Johnson Library, Austin, Tex.
27. Oral History interview with McGuiness, p. 20.
28. Oral History interview with Stanley Strauss, August 12, 1988, p. 13, LMDC.
29. Oral History interview with O'Connell, p. 169.
30. Oral History interview with Guy Farmer, December 12, 1984, p. 27, LMDC.
31. Brown was appointed to complete Jenkins's unexpired term (five months) and for a new five-year term beginning August 27, 1961. "Board Nominee Brown Gets Senate Committee Approval," *Daily Labor Report,* no. 69, April 11, 1961, p. A-10; "President Names Gerald A. Brown to Second Five-Year Term on Labor Board," *Daily Labor Report,* no. 163, August 22, 1966, p. A-3.
32. Jenkins, a management attorney in a Fort Worth, Texas, law firm at the time of his appointment to the Board, reflected, as did Stephen Bean and Philip Ray Rodgers before him, Secretary of Labor Mitchell's strong desire to appoint federal career employees to the NLRB. Jenkins had been a trial attorney in the NLRB's Fort Worth office from 1948 to 1951 before serving as chief of the Enforcement and Litigation Branch of the Wage Stabilization Board from 1951 to 1953 and entering private practice. After graduating from the University of Utah, Jenkins, while attending Georgetown University Law School, worked as an assistant to Senator Abe Murdock, whom he joined as a member of the Board in 1957. "Former NLRB Trial Attorney Is Named to Fill Board Vacancy," *Business Week,* February 9, 1957, p. 169.

Jenkins was flamboyant, a "courtly figure, very large and rotund," who talked in "stentorian tones" and "blew hard on everything." He was a Texan by choice and "used to wear a big western hat" around the NLRB. Oral History interviews with Subrin, p. 12, and Frank Kleiler, August 3, 1988, p. 14, LMDC.
33. Senate Committee on Labor and Public Welfare, *Hearings on the Nomination of Gerald A. Brown to be a Member of the National Labor Relations Board,* 89th Cong., 2d sess., 1966, p. 2.
34. Conclusion based on Oral History interviews with Ralph Winkler, August 4, 1988, p. 11, LMDC; Subrin, p. 13; Strauss, p. 14; and Melvin Wells, July 27, 1988, p. 13, LMDC.
35. Oral History interview with Edward Miller, October 23, 1984, p. 11, LMDC.
36. Oral History interview with Winkler, p. 11.
37. Memorandum for the record by Sherman, December 15, 1964.
38. Oral History interview with Gerald Brown, May 26, 1987, p. 130, LMDC.
39. Oral History interview with Frank McCulloch, December 7, 1984, p. 27, LMDC.

40. Gerald Brown, "The NLRB on the New Frontiers," press release (R-838), speech delivered at Duke University on February 9, 1962, NLRB Files. For a summary, see "Member Brown Views Labor Board as Policy Making Tribunal," press release (R-841), February 10, 1962, NLRB Files.

41. Senate Committee on Labor and Public Welfare, *Hearings on the Nomination of Frank W. McCulloch to be a Member of the National Labor Relations Board,* 89th Cong., 1st sess., 1965, p. 18.

42. McCulloch, "How and Why," p. D-2.

43. "John H. Fanning Reappointed to NLRB," press release (R-903), December 12, 1962, NLRB Files; "Treasury Aide Sworn," *New York Times,* December 21, 1957, p. 8; "Rankin Is Named Belgrade Envoy," *New York Times,* December 14, 1957, p. 10.

44. Oral History interview with John Fanning, October 6, 1984, p. 11, LMDC.

45. Oral History interview with O'Connell, p. 33.

46. Oral History interviews with Zagoria, p. 41; Farmer, p. 45; O'Connell, p. 33 (quotation); Subrin, p. 4; and McCulloch (1984), p. 24.

47. John Fanning, "The Changing Pattern of Issues in Labor Relations Cases before the Board," *George Washington Law Review* 29 (December 1960): 272. As he put it in his oral history interview, Fanning believed that the purpose of the act was "to encourage collective bargaining, to stabilize labor-management relations; and to encourage collective bargaining, you have to have a union in a plant to represent the employees so they can bargain with the employer on some kind of an equal basis." Oral History interview with Fanning, p. 68.

48. Oral History interviews with McCulloch (1984), pp. 23–24; and Daniel Pollitt, September 7, 1989, p. 18, LMDC.

49. Memorandum for the record by Sherman, December 15, 1964.

50. Transcript of the NLRB 50th Anniversary Conference, October 23–24, 1984, p. 76, LMDC; "NLRB Loses Last Trace of Truman Regime," *Business Week,* January 4, 1958, p. 38.

51. Oral History interview with Fanning, p. 29.

52. Oral History interview with Farmer, p. 67.

53. Oral History interview with McCulloch (1984), p. 36.

54. "Fenton Reported Choice as Labor Board Counsel," *New York Times,* January 30, 1957, p. 16; "U.S. Aides Nominated," *New York Times,* February 8, 1957.

55. Fenton said he was quitting because he needed to earn more than the general counsel's $20,000 annual salary. "NLRB Aide May Quit," *New York Times,* March 14, 1959, p. 9; "NLRB Counsel Quits; Calls Pay Inadequate," *New York Times,* March 15, 1959, p. 58.

56. "Rothman Given Coveted Post of NLRB Counsel," *Philadelphia Inquirer,* March 27, 1959; "Victory Seen for Mitchell on Rothman," *Baltimore Sun,* March 27, 1959; "Rothman Opposed," *New York Times,* March 28, 1959, p. 36; "Nomination Attacked," *New York Times,* March 31, 1959, p. 21; "Rothman Confirmed," *New York Times,* May 15, 1959, p. 25.

57. For a chronology of Rothman's government service, see Senate Committee on La-

bor and Public Welfare, *Hearings on the Nomination of Stuart Rothman to Be General Counsel, NLRB,* 86th Cong., 1st sess., 1959, p. 3.

58. "Laboring Labor Expert," *New York Times,* March 27, 1959, p. 15.

59. "Interpreter of Labor Reform," *Business Week,* September 5, 1959, p. 96.

60. Stuart Rothman, "Four Ways to Reduce Administrative Delay," *Tennessee Law Review* 28 (Spring 1961): 334.

61. Stuart Rothman, "Office of the General Counsel of the NLRB," *Labor Law Journal* 12 (August 1961): 701.

62. Rothman, "Four Ways," p. 341; Rothman, "Office of the General Counsel of the NLRB," pp. 701–2.

63. Memorandum from Rothman to all regional directors and officers-in-charge, "Let My Professional Pride Be My Guide" (SR-226), February 1, 1961, NLRB Files.

64. "Laboring Labor Expert," p. 15.

65. Oral History interview with Norton Come, July 29, 1988, p. 23, LMDC.

66. Oral History interview with John Higgins, July 26, 1988, p. 22, LMDC.

67. Oral History interview with Joseph De Sio, August 2, 1988, pp. 4, 9, LMDC.

68. House, *Hearings before the Subcommittee on National Labor Relations Board of the Committee on Education and Labor,* 87th Cong., 1st sess., 1961. (Hereinafter *Pucinski Committee Hearings.*)

69. Oral History interview with Roman Pucinski, October 13, 1988, pp. 1–2, LMDC; Oral History interview with Pollitt, p. 8.

70. Oral History interview with McCulloch (1989), p. 57.

71. Thomas R. Brooks, "Time for a Labor Court?" *The Commonweal,* January 5, 1962, p. 388.

72. Oral History interview with Gordon, p. 67.

73. Gall, *Politics of Right to Work,* p. 139.

74. In its final report the majority said that despite its invitation and "repeated public requests, industry representatives did not respond to the extent spokesmen for labor groups [did]." House, *Report of the Subcommittee on National Labor Relations Board of the Committee on Education and Labor, Administration of the Labor-Management Relations Act by the NLRB,* 87th Cong., 1st sess., 1961, p. 5. (Hereinafter *Pucinski Committee Report.*) See also *Pucinski Committee Hearings,* part 1, p. 590.

75. *Pucinski Committee Hearings,* part 1, pp. 150–51.

76. Ibid., part 1, pp. 558, 566.

77. Ibid., part 2, p. 973.

78. Ibid., part 1, pp. 560, 573. For other examples of race hate literature, see ibid., part 1, pp. 299–309. Benjamin Wyle, general counsel of the Textile Workers Union of America, noted that this material often came from an unidentified "central source": "I pointed out the coincidence of the same literature, the same letters, sent by employers to employees, the same posters appearing in various parts of the country, sometimes 500, 400, 700 miles apart." Ibid., part 1, p. 272.

79. Ibid., parts 1 and 2, pp. 568, 741, 980.

80. Ibid., part 2, pp. 903–4. Union representatives also denounced appeals to racial bias when used by unions. Ibid., part 1, p. 591.
81. *Pucinski Committee Report,* pp. 59–60.
82. *Pucinski Committee Hearings,* part 1, pp. 152, 607–8.
83. Ibid., part 1, p. 577.
84. *Pucinski Committee Report,* p. 60. For the details of a specific case, see *Pucinski Committee Hearings,* part 1, pp. 179–80, as well as pp. 252, 606.
85. 107 NLRB 400 (1953).
86. *Pucinski Committee Hearings,* part 1, p. 720.
87. *Pucinski Committee Report,* pp. 56–57.
88. Ibid., p. 61.
89. *Pucinski Committee Hearings,* part 1, pp. 497, 726; *Pucinski Committee Report,* pp. 61–62.
90. *Pucinski Committee Hearings,* part 1, pp. 156–57, 500–501, 534; *Pucinski Committee Report,* p. 21.
91. *Pucinski Committee Hearings,* part 1, pp. 429–30, 503–5. Other remedies union witnesses asked for included self-enforcing Board orders (p. 594), granting a contract as a matter of right if one is not achieved after an election has been won (p. 633), and making all injunctions mandatory "if there is a showing that irreparable injury would be sustained by the person injured unless the injunction were issued" (p. 840).
92. *Pucinski Committee Report,* pp. 8, 10.
93. "Statement of National Labor Relations Board in Support of Reorganization Plan No. 5," June 5, 1961, p. 11, NN 3-25-86-2, Box 6, Record Group (RG) 25, National Archives (NA).
94. Such delegation was permitted by the Landrum-Griffin amendments to Taft-Hartley, specifically Section 3(b).
95. "Statement of National Labor Relations Board," p. 11.
96. *Pucinski Committee Hearings,* part 2, p. 1319.
97. For the full text of Reorganization Plan No. 5 of 1961, see House, *Message from the President of the United States Transmitting Reorganization Plan No. 5, Prepared in Accordance with the Reorganization Act of 1949, as Amended, and Providing for Reorganization in the National Labor Relations Board,* H. Doc. 172, 87th Cong., 1st sess., 1961, pp. 17–18.
98. The Administrative Procedure Act of 1946 took the authority to hire, promote, or fire trial examiners away from the NLRB. See "Trial Examiners," *Business Week,* January 24, 1948, p. 75.
99. Senate, *Organization and Procedure of the National Labor Relations Board,* Report to the Senate Committee on Labor and Public Welfare Pursuant to S. Res. 66 and S. Res. 141, 86th Cong., 2d sess., 1960, pp. 13–14.
100. For the complete report of McKinsey & Co., see *Pucinski Committee Hearings,* part 3, pp. 1619–1710.
101. "Statement of National Labor Relations Board," p. 5.

102. House, *Hearings before a Subcommittee of the House Committee on Government Operations on Reorganization Plan No. 5 of 1961,* 87th Cong., 1st sess., 1961, p. 4. (Hereinafter *House Committee on Government Operations.*)

103. *Pucinski Committee Hearings,* part 3 (McKinsey Report), pp. 1620–28, 1672–76; memorandum from L-W (Barton & Carr) and OMO (Guffey) to the director, "Interim Report on NLRB Management Survey," January 7, 1959, "NLRB," Box 20, Gerald Morgan Papers, Eisenhower Library, Abilene, Kan.; memorandum (with attached staff report) from the director of the Bureau of the Budget to Mitchell, March 1, 1960, p. 8, "1960—National Legislation Department of Labor & Budget," Box 183, James Mitchell Papers, Eisenhower Library; memorandum from Leedom to the file, "Management Survey," October 16, 1958, NN 3-25-86-1, Box 2, RG 25, NA.

104. "Landis Report to Kennedy on Federal Agencies Would Reorganize Labor Board," *Daily Labor Report,* no. 250, December 27, 1960, pp. A-1–A-2.

105. *Pucinski Committee Hearings,* part 1, pp. 830–32, 763–65; part 2, pp. 1021–22.

106. Ibid., part 2, pp. 939–48; part 1, pp. 744, 758. Shroyer represented the American Retail Federation.

107. For a summary of the major arguments for and against Plan No. 5, see Senate, *Hearings before the Committee on Government Operations, United States Senate, on Reorganization Plan No. 5 of 1961, NLRB,* S. Res. 158, 87th Cong., 1st sess., 1961, pp. 7–8. (Hereinafter *Senate Committee on Government Operations.*)

108. *House Committee on Government Operations,* p. 37.

109. T. O. Moore, vice-president and general counsel, P. H. Hanes Knitting Co. (Winston-Salem, N.C.), to Senator Ervin, June 16, 1961, Series IV, no. 119, National Association of Manufacurers Archives, Hagley Museum and Library, Wilmington, Del.

110. *Pucinski Committee Hearings,* part 2, p. 1039; Leedom to Congressman E. Y. Berry, July 14, 1961, NN 3-25-86-2, Box 7, RG 25, NA.

111. "Trial Examiners," p. 78. Former Board member Joseph Alton Jenkins told the Pucinski committee that employers "by and large" did "not have much confidence in the trial examiners. I think their attitude . . . is probably a carryover from the days of the Wagner Act." *Pucinski Committee Hearings,* part 2, p. 1034.

112. Oral History interview with O'Connell, p. 47.

113. See, for example, McCulloch to Senator Edmund Muskie, member of the Senate Government Operations Committee, June 30, 1961; McCulloch to Congressman William Dawson, chairman of the House Government Operations Committee, June 30, 1961, NN 3-25-86-2, Box 6, RG 25, NA. McCulloch also sent a series of letters to editors of numerous newspapers around the country, including the *Raleigh News and Observer,* the *Milwaukee Journal,* the *St. Louis Post Dispatch,* the *Des Moines Register,* the *Atlanta Constitution,* the *New York Times,* and the *Louisville Courier Journal.*

114. Oral History interviews with McCulloch (1984), pp. 51–52; (1989), p. 71.

115. House, *Report [to Accompany H. Res. 328] Approving Reorganization Plan No. 5*

of 1961 (National Labor Relations Board), 87th Cong., 1st sess., 1961, H. Rept. 576. For the views of nine Republicans who voted to disapprove Reorganization Plan No. 5, see, pp. 15–19. See also "Reports on NLRB Reorganization Plan Are Filed by Committee," *Daily Labor Report,* no. 122, June 26, 1961, p. A-16; "Senate Committee Approves Reorganization Plan for NLRB," *Daily Labor Report,* no. 136, July 17, 1961, p. A-6 (Senator Ervin voted against the plan, along with Republican senators Karl Mundt and Carl Curtis); "Kennedy Wins Test on NLRB Changes," *New York Times,* July 18, 1961, p. 14.

116. *Cong. Rec.* 87th Cong., 1st sess. (1961), 107, pt. 10:13078. Twenty-five did not vote. For the debate in the House, see pp. 12905–32, 13069–78.

117. McCulloch to Senator Hubert Humphrey, July 27, 1961, NN 3-25-86-2, Box 6, RG 25, NA; Oral History interview with McCulloch (1989), p. 11.

118. Oral History interview with Pucinski, p. 3.

119. Ibid., p. 23.

120. Oral History interviews with Pollitt, p. 12, and McCulloch (1984), p. 42, 112–13; (1989), p. 58.

121. Oral History interview with Pollitt, p. 13. Pollitt recalled: "We were concerned about the propriety of all this, but we figured it was a proposal and it was a review of the evidence and the testimony, and that any party was entitled to submit proposed findings of fact for consideration, which is what we did. And so, in a sense, Pucinski adopted most of our work. But it's the Pucinski Report, not our report." Ibid. See also Oral History interview with McCulloch (1984), p. 42.

122. Oral History interview with Pollitt, p. 14.

123. *Pucinski Committee Report,* Minority Views, pp. 76–78. See also separate views of Congressmen Pucinski, pp. 79–80, and Griffin, pp. 81–84.

124. *Pucinski Committee Report,* p. 20. For the committee's recommendations to expedite representation cases, see pp. 9–16. For the committee's recommendation to reduce delays in the enforcement of Board orders, see p. 31.

125. Ibid., pp. 3–4, 55.

126. Ibid., p. 61.

127. 107 NLRB 400 (1953).

128. *Pucinski Committee Report,* pp. 4, 58–59.

129. Ibid., pp. 2, 22.

130. 85 NLRB 1263 (1949), 185 F.2d 732 (D.C. Cir., 1950), *cert. denied,* 341 U.S. 914 (1951).

131. *Pucinski Committee Report,* pp. 23–24.

132. Ibid., pp. 27–28. The committee considered but did not adopt recommendations to make "knowing" commission of an unfair labor practice "penal, punishable like any other Federal crime." Ibid.

133. Ibid., pp. 61, 63.

134. Ibid., p. 63.

135. Ibid., Minority Views, p. 77.

136. *Pucinski Committee Hearings,* part 2, p. 1317.

137. Ibid., part 1, pp. 266–67, 514, 661.
138. Ibid., pp. 148, 365, 374, 614.
139. Ibid., part 1, p. 742; part 2, pp. 937, 966.
140. *Pucinski Committee Report,* p. 67. Section 7 of the Wagner Act, the committee majority argued, even without the right-to-refrain language, protected the right of employees not to join a union. Under the Wagner Act the right to join or not join, however, was protected only against employer coercion, domination, and discrimination. The subsequent addition to Taft-Hartley's restrictions on unions (the unfair labor practices set forth in Section 8[b]), therefore, required an "explicit mention in Section 7 of that aspect of self-organizational freedom against which union violations are generally aimed; namely, the right to refrain." The majority held, "Since much mention, however, did not alter the substance of Section 7, reference to the right to refrain did not warrant expansion of the new restrictions upon unions beyond the bounds marked by the prohibitions themselves and their legislative history." Ibid.
141. Ibid., p. 67.
142. Oral History interview with McCulloch (1984), p. 54.

Chapter 10

1. Cornelius J. Peck, "The National Labor Relations Board, 1965–1966: A Change in the Mood of the Judiciary?" *Proceedings of the Nineteenth Annual New York University Conference on Labor* 19 (1966): 4.
2. Roscoe Born, "Unions Ask Bargaining Aid, 'Friendly' NLRB, Voice in the Cabinet," *Wall Street Journal,* November 22, 1960, p. 1; John Grimes, "Some Employers Fear 'Kennedy's NLRB' Is Favoring Union Side," *Wall Street Journal,* November 28, 1961, p. 1; "NLRB Shifts Its Course with Democrats in Driver's Seat," *Business Week,* October 28, 1961, p. 83; "AFL-CIO Vows to Organize; Some Think NLRB Changes Are Helpful," *Daily Labor Report,* no. 238, December 11, 1961, p. A-2.
3. Kenneth McGuiness, *The New Frontier NLRB* (Washington, D.C.: Labor Policy Association, 1962), p. 16.
4. See, for example, Thomas Christensen, "The 'New' NLRB: An Analysis of Current Policy," *Proceedings of the Fifteenth Annual New York University Conference on Labor* 15 (1962): 220–21.
5. *Charles A. Blinne d/b/a C.A. Blinne Construction Co.,* 130 NLRB 587 (1961); *Stork Restaurant,* 130 NLRB 543 (1961); *Charlton Press,* 130 NLRB 727 (1961).
6. *Crown Cafeteria,* 130 NLRB 570 (1961) (Fanning and Jenkins dissenting).
7. *Stork Restaurant,* 130 NLRB 543 (1961).
8. *Teamsters Union Local 705 and Cartage and Terminal Management Corp.,* 130 NLRB 558 (1961) (Kimball dissenting). See also "NLRB Decides Four Leading Cases under New Legal Limitations of Recognition Picketing," press release (R-769), February 22, 1961, NLRB Files, Washington, D.C.

9. John Fanning, "The NLRB in Transition," *Catholic University Law Review* 12 (1963): 17–18. Among the more notable cases, none of which set any new guidelines for the Kennedy Board to follow in Landrum-Griffin picketing cases, the Supreme Court reversed the Eisenhower Board's *Curtis,* 362 U.S. 274 (1960), and *O'Sullivan,* 362 U.S. 329 (1960), cases; the Court concluded that neither the language nor the legislative history of Section 8(b)(1)(A) was intended to prevent peaceful picketing or organizational activity even though it had an unlawful objective. Other Eisenhower Board decisions reversed by the Supreme Court were *Insurance Agents,* 361 U.S. 477 (1960); *Mountain Pacific,* 365 U.S. 667 (1961); and *Brown-Olds,* 365 U.S. 651 (1961). The Supreme Court also upheld the International Typographical Union in disputes going back to 1947, when that union led the challenge to Taft-Hartley and Senator Taft: *News Syndicate,* 365 U.S. 695 (1961), and *Haverhill Gazette,* 365 U.S. 705 (1961).

The NLRB's associate solicitor maintained that no new procedure was involved in the withdrawal of certain cases from the courts: "Thus, the Board has taken this action whenever, in its view, the issue presented in a court proceeding is significantly affected by a Supreme Court or Board decision or, on obviously less frequent occasions, when the Act under which it operates has been amended." Saul J. Jaffe to William Barton, February 28, 1962, NN 3-25-86-2, Box 10, Record Group (RG) 25, National Archives (NA). See also: "The NLRB in Action," address by Frank McCulloch, *Daily Labor Report,* no. 77, April 19, 1962, p. D-2.

10. Guy Farmer, speech before the Joint Conference of the Industrial Relations Committees of the Edison Electric Institute, the Southeastern Electric Exchange, and the Southwestern Personnel Group, press release (R-437), January 21, 1954, p. 4, NLRB Files. See also Oral History interview with Frank McCulloch, December 7, 1984, p. 192, Labor-Management Documentation Center (LMDC), ILR, Cornell University.

11. Oral History interview with Gerald Brown, May 26, 1987, p. 98, LMDC. *Stare decisis* is a rule by which common law courts are slow to interfere with principles announced in former decisions and often uphold them even though they would decide otherwise if the question were a new one.

12. Oral History interview with Brown, pp. 85, 92, 121; "Union Picketing to Get Bargaining Rights Sharply Restricted by NLRB in Four Decisions," *Wall Street Journal,* February 23, 1961.

13. 135 NLRB 1153 (1962); Fred Whitney, "NLRB Membership Cleavage: Recognition and Organizational Picketing," *Labor Law Journal* 14 (May 1963): 452–56.

14. 130 NLRB 570 (1961).

15. 135 NLRB 1183, 1184–85 (1962). In a related decision, also reversing prior Eisenhower Board doctrine, the Kennedy Board decided that informational picketing completely divorced from any object of recognition, organization, or bargaining was completely outside the scope of Section 8(b)(7). *Stork Restaurant,* 135 NLRB 1173 (1962), reversing the earlier Eisenhower Board decision in the same case: 130 NLRB 543 (1961).

16. 138 NLRB 478, 488–89 (1962). Leedom and Rodgers charged the majority with making this Landrum-Griffin amendment "mean what it does not say, and say what it does not mean." 138 NLRB at 496–97.

17. 133 NLRB 512, 512–13 (1962). According to the Eisenhower Board, a picketing union's "disclaimer of interest in the bargaining unit, indeed its affirmative statement that it would never bargain in such a unit is, therefore, in the circumstances here present, an inadequate defense; for despite [the union's] disclaimer, the picketing necessarily had as its ultimate end the substitution of the [union] for the certified bargaining agent." The Eisenhower majority added, "It is immaterial, moreover, that the [union] may have had other objects since recognition or bargaining need not be the sole object of the picketing to be violative of Section 8(b)(4)(C). It is sufficient if an object of the picketing be one proscribed by Section 8(b)(4) of the Act." 130 NLRB 78, 82 (1961).

Section 8(b)(4)(C) prohibited "forcing or requiring any employer to recognize or bargain with a particular labor organization as the representative of his employees if another labor organization has been certified as the representative of such employees under the provisions of section 9."

18. *Claude Everett Construction Co.,* 135 NLRB 321 (1962).

19. *Fanelli Ford,* 133 NLRB 1468 (1961).

20. *Bachman Furniture,* 134 NLRB 670 (1961).

21. *Plauche Electric,* 135 NLRB 250 (1962).

22. Archibald Cox, Derek Bok, and Robert Gorman, *Cases and Materials on Labor Law,* 10th ed., (Mineola, N.Y.: Foundation Press, 1986), p. 642.

23. 132 NLRB 901, 905–6 (1961).

24. Ibid., p. 914. That is exactly what happened. See, for example, *Middle South Broadcasting,* 133 NLRB 1698 (1961), and *Houston Armored Car Co.,* 136 NLRB 110 (1962).

25. 137 NLRB 73 (1962).

26. 109 NLRB 447 (1954).

27. 137 NLRB at 75–76. Rodgers and Fanning called the *Brown* decision "illogical." They saw no reason to accept the majority's conclusion that the use of temporary replacements unlawfully discouraged union membership, "particularly since the employees in the case were expressly told by [the employers] they would have their jobs at the end of the strike." Ibid., p. 77.

28. Bernard Meltzer, "Lockouts: Licit and Illicit," *Proceedings of the Sixteenth Annual New York University Conference on Labor* 16 (1963): 28. See also Bernard Meltzer, "Lockouts under the LMRA: New Shadows on an Old Terrain," *University of Chicago Law Review* 28 (Summer 1961): 614–28.

29. For an excellent discussion of this issue, see Thomas G. S. Christensen, "Free Speech, Propaganda, and the National Labor Relations Act," *New York University Law Review* 38 (April 1963): 243–79.

30. See, for example, *Sewell Mfg. Co.,* 138 NLRB 66, 69 (1962). For a useful discussion of the differences between an NLRB election and a political election, see Lester Asher, "NLRB Representation Elections—Some of the Problems Confront-

ing Unions," *Proceedings of the Seventeenth Annual New York University Conference on Labor* 17 (1964): 214–16. For a contrary view, see Bernard Samoff, "NLRB Elections: Certainty and Uncertainty," *University of Pennsylvania Law Review* 117 (December 1968): 232–33.

31. Gerald Brown, "Freedom of Choice and the National Labor Policy," speech before the Labor Law Section, State Bar of Texas, San Antonio, July 5, 1962, pp. 6–7, "Free Speech, etc.," Box 13, McCulloch Papers, LMDC.

32. "Speech by NLRB Executive Secretary Ogden Fields," October 31, 1963, p. 3. "Free Speech, etc.," Box 13, McCulloch Papers.

33. Derek Bok, "The Regulation of Campaign Tactics in Representation Elections under the National Labor Relations Act," *Harvard Law Review* 78 (November 1964): 91–92. Others recommended: "Joint employer-union debates in the plant and at union meetings; radio and television question-and-answer sessions with a panel of correspondents; posting of union campaign literature on plant bulletin boards; and joint employer-union leaflets." Samoff, "NLRB Elections," p. 250.

34. 77 NLRB 124 (1948).

35. *National Furniture Co.,* 119 NLRB 328 (1957).

36. 137 NLRB 1782 (1962).

37. For other early McCulloch Board speech cases, see *Oak Manufacturing Co.,* 141 NLRB 1323 (1963); *Haynes Stellite Co.,* 136 NLRB 95 (1962); *Trane Co.,* 137 NLRB 1506 (1962); *R.D. Cole Mfg. Co.,* 133 NLRB 1455 (1961); *Somismo, Inc.,* 133 NLRB 1310 (1961); and *Myrna Mills,* 133 NLRB 767 (1961).

38. *Dal-Tex Optical Co.,* 137 NLRB 1782, 1787 (1962). In *Oak Manufacturing Co.,* 141 NLRB at 1325, the Board quoted Justice Oliver Wendell Holmes: "A word is not a crystal, transparent and unchanged; it is the skin of a living thought and may vary greatly in color and context according to the circumstances and the time in which it is used."

39. *Carl T. Mason, Co.,* 142 NLRB 480, 483 (1963).

40. In *Oak Manufacturing Co.,* 141 NLRB at 1355, for example, the Board said that it was precisely because employees understood the import of the employer's message that the integrity and purpose of a representation election were destroyed.

41. This debate is still going strong more than thirty years later. See, for example, *Midland National Life Insurance Co.,* 263 NLRB 127 (1982).

42. 140 NLRB 11 (1962); 142 NLRB 480 (1963).

43. For details about the making of this movie and the International Association of Machinists film, *Anatomy of a Lie,* made in response, see Robert A. Bedolis, "The NLRB Reviews 'And Women Must Weep,'" *Business Management Record,* July 1963, pp. 51–56, NN 3-25-86-1, Box 4, RG 25, NA.

44. McCulloch relied on several cases cited in *Carl T. Mason,* 142 NLRB at 485 n. 7.

45. Ibid., p. 486.

46. 138 NLRB 66, 69 (1962).

47. Daniel H. Pollitt, "The National Labor Relations Board and Race Hate Propaganda in Union Organizing Drives," *Stanford Law Review* 17 (March 1965): 376, 395.

48. Daniel Pollitt, memorandum, "Race-Hate Propaganda in NLRB Representation

Elections," undated, NN 3-25-86-1, Box 4, RG 25, NA. The masthead of *Militant Truth* read, "A National Publication Interpreting Current Events from a Fundamental Christian and Constitutional American Viewpoint." Pollitt, "National Labor Relations Board," pp. 397–98.

49. *Sewell Mfg. Co.,* 138 NLRB at 71. The Board set aside a second election in the same case for the same reason. See *Sewell Mfg. Co.,* 140 NLRB 220 (1962).

50. *Sharnay Hosiery Mills,* 120 NLRB 750 (1958). See Robert Fuchs and David Ellis, "Title VII: Relationship and Effect on the National Labor Relations Board," *Boston College Industrial and Commercial Law Review* 7 (Spring 1966): 577.

51. 138 NLRB at 71. For a union's appeal to race in a representation election campaign, see *Allen Morrison Sign Co.,* 138 NLRB 73 (1962).

52. 107 NLRB 400 (1953). For an interesting discussion of this issue, see Benjamin Aaron, *Employer Free Speech: The Search for a Policy,* University of California Institute of Industrial Relations, reprint no. 115 (1962), p. 51. Reprinted in Joseph Shister, Benjamin Aaron, and Clyde Summers, eds., *Public Policy and Collective Bargaining* (New York: Harper and Brothers, 1962).

53. 96 NLRB 608 (1951).

54. 136 NLRB 797, 802 (1962); Fanning, "NLRB in Transition," pp. 23–26.

55. 136 NLRB at 801–2.

56. 324 U.S. 793 (1945).

57. 351 U.S. 105 (1956).

58. 357 U.S. 357 (1958). The circumstances of *May Department Stores* were similar to those in *Nutone,* but the Board majority attempted to distinguish the *Nutone* decision because the situation there did not involve a department store and the no-solicitation rule in effect applied only to working time. 136 NLRB at 801.

59. Bok, "Regulation of Campaign Tactics," p. 98.

60. Quoted in *Metropolitan Life Insurance Co.,* 156 NLRB 1408, 1411 (1966).

61. 134 NLRB 960 (1961). The old rule was established in *Metropolitan Life Insurance Co.,* 56 NLRB 1635, 1640 (1944).

62. 138 NLRB 1032 (1962).

63. Oral History interview with McCulloch (1984), pp. 86–87. In addition to the Pucinski committee, a group of academics in a study sponsored by the Committee for Economic Development said that the Board ought to consider this "building block" approach: *The Public Interest in National Labor Policy* (New York: Committee for Economic Development, 1961), pp. 72–74.

64. *Fibreboard Paper Products Corp.,* 130 NLRB 1558, 1559 (1961). The company estimated that it would save $225,000 each year by contracting out all its maintenance work.

65. *Timkin Roller Bearing Co.,* 70 NLRB 500, 518 (1946).

66. 130 NLRB at 1562, 1565.

67. Oral History interview with Francis O'Connell, May 23, 1987, pp. 35, 57–58, LMDC. O'Connell said that he did not know why Rothman "chose to do that thing which was so desirable to McCulloch and Fanning, except that I think he entertained the implausible hope that he would be reappointed General Counsel."

68. Oral History interviews with Frank McCulloch, September 5, 1989, pp. 98–99, LMDC; 1984, p. 95.

69. Oral History interview with Brown, pp. 101–2.

70. 138 NLRB 550, 555, 558–60 (1962).

71. Harry Brickman, NLRB Operations Analysis Section, "Preliminary Report; Remedies in NLRB Cases Involving Subcontracting, Shutdown, Etc.," January 1965, p. 1, Box 5, RG 25, NA.

72. Arthur Krock, "Free Enterprise at Stake before the Court," *New York Times,* October 23, 1964; Raymond Moley, "NLRB's Thrust for Power," *Newsweek,* April 8, 1963, p. 100.

73. Owen Fairweather, "Fibreboard," *Arbitration Journal* 19 (1964): 80–81.

74. "Smethurst Sees NLRB Decision Reviving Union Plans to 'Committeeize' Business," *Daily Labor Report,* no. 194, October 5, 1964, p. A-14.

75. Oral History interview with McCulloch (1984), p. 115.

76. Guy Farmer, "Good Faith Bargaining over Subcontracting," *Georgetown Law Journal* 51 (1963): 578; Guy Farmer, "Bargaining Requirements in Connection with Subcontracting, Plan Removal, Sale of Business, Merger, and Consolidation," *Labor Law Journal* (December 1963): 960.

77. Brief for the National Labor Relations Board, *Fibreboard Paper Products Corp. Petitioner v. NLRB,* in the Supreme Court of the United States, October Term, 1964, no. 14, p. 63, McCulloch Papers.

78. Ibid., pp. 22–23. Emphasis added. Employers realized that if the "range of employees' vital interests" determined the scope of bargaining, the result would be "co-determination of business decisions." Tracy Ferguson, speech, "The Changes ahead in Management's Attitude toward Labor Legislation," November 10, 1964, p. 3, Series I, no. 26, National Association of Manufacturers Archives, Hagley Museum and Library, Wilmington, Del.

79. Committee for Economic Development, *Public Interest,* p. 85.

80. Brickman, "Preliminary Report," pp. 8–10.

81. "Limits on Labor and Management," *Time,* April 9, 1965, p. 66.

82. Richard Gorrell, "Roger Milliken and the Textile Union," *The Reporter,* December 1962, p. 32.

83. "Olin Johnston and Roger Milliken," *John Herling's Labor Letter,* July 25, 1964, p. 3.

84. "Decision of National Labor Relations Board in Case of Darlington Manufacturing Company, et al.," *Daily Labor Report,* no. 204, October 18, 1962, p. D-2.

85. Memorandum from Reed Johnson, regional director, Eleventh Region, to Kenneth McGuiness, associate general counsel, December 28, 1956, Box 80, RG 25, NA.

86. *Darlington Mfg. Co.,* 139 NLRB 241 (1962). For a chronology of the delays leading up to the Board's decision, see *Daily Labor Report,* no. 204, October 18, 1962, p. D-1. Frank McCulloch called it "a shameful case, the way it dragged out. There were outrageous delays." Oral History interview with McCulloch (1984), pp. 70–71.

87. *Daily Labor Report,* no. 204, October 18, 1962, pp. D-3 (quotation), D-6.

88. Ibid., pp. D-6–D-10. For Leedom's dissent, see pp. D-10–D-11. For Rodgers's dissent, see pp. D-11–D-12.

89. Ibid., p. D-9.

90. "Court to Review Both Union and NLRB Questions in Textile Mill Closing Case," *Daily Labor Report,* no. 77, April 20, 1964, pp. A-12–A-13.

91. "Olin Johnston and Roger Milliken," pp. 3–4.

92. "Meany and Pollock Comment after Court Denies Review of NLRB Darlington Case," *Daily Labor Report,* no. 9, January 14, 1969, p. A-4. In 1969 Milliken became an economic adviser to President Nixon.

93. "Limits on Labor and Management," p. 66.

94. "Senator Ervin to Argue for Company in Darlington Mills Case in Supreme Court," *Daily Labor Report,* no. 213, October 30, 1964, p. A-10.

95. "Ervin Tells Court Darlington Mills Close for Economic Reasons, not to Avoid Union," *Daily Labor Report,* no. 239, December 9, 1964, p. AA-5; "Court Urged to Affirm Fourth Circuit that Employer Can Quit for Any Reason," *Daily Labor Report,* no. 240, December 10, 1964, pp. A-5–A-8.

96. Vera Rony, "Labor Drives to Close the South's Open Shop," *The Reporter,* November 18, 1965, p. 31.

97. Kenneth G. Slocum, "A Campaign to Organize Southern Plants Meets Formidable Opposition," *Wall Street Journal,* May 11, 1966, p. 1.

98. Walter Rugaber, "Attempt by Union to Organize J.P. Stevens & Co. Workers Has Wide Effect in the South," *New York Times,* August 16, 1967, p. 7.

99. House Committee on Education and Labor, *Hearings on Investigation of the Administration of the National Labor Relations Act, as Amended, by the National Labor Relations Board,* 89th Cong., 1st sess., 1965, p. 5.

100. Ibid., p. 41.

101. Ibid., pp. 5–7.

102. See Robert Stevens's letter to the Powell committee in ibid., pp. 325–26.

103. 157 NLRB 869 (1966), *enf. as modif'd.,* 380 F.2d (2d Cir. 1967); 163 NLRB 217 (1967), *enf. as modif'd.,* 388 F.2d 896 (2d Cir. 1967); 167 NLRB 266 (1967) and 167 NLRB 258 (1967), *enf. as modif'd.,* 406 F.2d (4th Cir. 1968); 171 NLRB 163, *enf.,* 417 F.2d 533 (5th Cir. 1969). See also 179 NLRB 254 (1969).

104. Trial examiner's decision, TXD-12-67, in *J.P. Stevens & Co., Inc.,* p. 40, NLRB Files.

105. Slocum, "Campaign to Organize," p. 1.

106. Quotations are from the Board's first decision in the *J.P. Stevens* series, 157 NLRB 869 (1966), but the language characterizes all the cases.

107. The Board set aside three of these four elections and ordered then rerun.

108. "NLRB Says Stevens Was Unfair to Labor, Orders Rehiring of 71 Pro-Union Workers," *Wall Street Journal,* March 23, 1966, p. 4.

109. Trial examiner's decision, TXD-12-67, in *J.P. Stevens, Inc.,* p. 57.

110. "Excerpt from Decision of NLRB in Case of J.P. Stevens and Co., Inc. (Official Text)," *Daily Labor Report,* no. 47, March 9, 1967, p. D-3. In regard to the notices

that the company was ordered to post, mail to employees, and read aloud at employee meetings, the *Wall Street Journal* editorialized that the NLRB was requiring J.P. Stevens to make "a public confession" in violation of "deeply imbedded . . . Anglo-Saxon law." "The Public Confessional," *Wall Street Journal,* September 15, 1967, p. 18.

111. Charles Morris, ed., *The Developing Labor Law* (Washington, D.C.: BNA, 1971), pp. 870–72.

112. Pollock to McCulloch, April 5, 1966, with attached letter from Pollock to every member of the House and Senate, dated April 1, 1966, McCulloch Papers.

113. "Award of Contracts to J.P. Stevens & Co. Is Bone of Contention to Textile Union," *Daily Labor Report,* no. 108, June 3, 1968, p. A-7.

114. Memorandum to the file, "Defense Prime Contract Awards," undated, McCulloch Papers. The NLRB listed J.P. Stevens among its "flagrant and/or repeated violators of Section 8(a) of the Act." Memorandum from Harry Brickman, chief, Operations Analysis Section, to McCulloch, April 7, 1967, McCulloch Papers.

115. "Unions to Demand Contract Ban for Violators of U.S. Labor Act," *New York Times,* May 19, 1966.

116. Richard Russell to Lyndon Johnson, May 23, 1966, "NLRB Violators," McCulloch Papers.

117. Telegram from Mendel Rivers to Lyndon Johnson, May 23, 1966, "NLRB Violators," McCulloch Papers.

118. *Cong. Rec.,* 89th Cong., 2d sess. (1966), 112, pt. 29:A3297.

119. Memorandum from John Steadman, Department of Defense, to Joseph Califano, assistant to Lyndon Johnson, May 21, 1966, p. 2, Collection WHCF [PQ], Container no. 1, Lyndon Baines Johnson Library, Austin, Tex.

120. Robert Stevens to Lyndon Johnson, July 11, 1966, Collection WHCF [PQ], Container no. 1, LBJ Library.

121. Oral History interview with McCulloch (1989), pp. 124–25.

122. Cyrus Vance, deputy secretary of defense, to George Meany, August 25, 1966, "NLRA Violators," McCulloch Papers; James A. Gross, *The Reshaping of the National Labor Relations Board: National Labor Policy in Transition, 1937–1947* (Albany: State University of New York Press, 1981), p. 193. For an interesting discussion of the president's power to debar through an executive order, see Meghan H. Engelhardt, "Coping with Persistent NLRA Violators: The Potential for Debarment through Executive Order," *Iowa Law Review* 66 (January 1981): 425–37.

123. Oral History interview with McCulloch (1989), pp. 122–24; memorandum from Harry McPherson to Lyndon Johnson, April 19, 1967, pp. 1–3, Collection "Aides—McPherson," Folder "Labor," Box 24, LBJ Library.

124. John Herling, "A Non-Happening," *Washington Daily News,* October 19, 1967, p. 3.

125. 138 NLRB 716 (1962). For an excellent discussion of the legislative history of Section 10(c), the NLRB's remedy power, see memorandum from Saul J. Jaffe, acting solicitor to the Board, August 10, 1967, NN 3-25-82-2, Box 7, RG 25, NA.

126. Memorandum from Harry Brickman, chief of the Operations Analysis Section, to McCulloch, "An Analysis of Proposals for Novel NLRB Remedies," August 1968, p. 2, "Remedies—Aspin EBM—Brickman," McCulloch Papers.

127. NLRB, *Thirty-second Annual Report,* for the fiscal year ended June 30, 1967 (Washington, D.C.: GPO, 1968), pp. 1, 3, 5.

128. House Special Subcommitte on Labor of the Committee on Education and Labor, *Hearings on Bills to Amend the National Labor Relations Act,* 89th Cong., 2d sess., 1966, pp. 47–48. (Hereinafter *Thompson Committee Hearings* [1966].)

129. House Special Subcommittee on Labor of the Committee on Education and Labor, *Hearings on a Bill to Amend the National Labor Relations Act in Order to Increase the Effectiveness of the Remedies,* 90th Cong., 1st sess., 1968, pp. 4–6. (Hereinafter *Thompson Committee Hearings* [1967].) The fact that this was the first study of the effectiveness of NLRB remedies is a sad commentary on the empirical basis for Board policy and decisions.

For a broader discussion of the availability of empirical evidence on which to base Board decisions, see James A. Gross, "Economics, Politics, and the Law: The NLRB's Division of Economic Research, 1935–1940," *Cornell Law Review* 55 (February 1970): 321–47.

130. *Thompson Committee Hearings* (1967), pp. 4, 5–12. The author of the study found that "the legalistic language of the notices cannot be understood by the employees. Company violations, which the notice is designed to offset, are in almost every case committed in person (as when a company official delivers a threatening speech). To offset such violations by a posted notice is very difficult." The study also found "that the backpay check does not fully compensate for the loss of steady earnings. The Discriminatee may need the money immediately to pay his bills, and he may have no money at all. A sum of money some months in the future . . . will not help him in his present situation." Ibid., pp. 9–10.

131. Oral History interview with McCulloch (1989), pp. 4–5.

132. *Thompson Committee Hearings* (1966), pp. 70–75.

133. Memorandum from Harry Brickman to McCulloch, April 3, 1968, pp. 4–7, "Remedy—Aspin Study," McCulloch Papers.

134. Memorandum from Harry Brickman, to McCulloch, March 3, 1967, pp. 1–3, "Remedy—Aspin Study," McCulloch Papers.

135. *Thompson Committee Hearings* (1967), pp. 1–2.

136. Oral History interview with McCulloch, (1989), pp. 120–21.

137. *Pucinski Committee Report,* pp. 23–24.

138. 85 NLRB 1263 (1949), *enf.,* 187 F.2d 732 (D.C. Cir. 1950).

139. *Cudhay Packing Co.,* 13 NLRB 526 (1939). See also "Memorandum of Labor Secretary W. W. Wirtz to Senator Javits of New York," *Daily Labor Report,* no. 148, August 3, 1965, p. D-2.

140. "Memorandum of Labor Secretary Wirtz," p. D-3.

141. 110 NLRB 1365 (1954).

142. 146 NLRB 1277, 1279–80 (1964).

143. Ibid. pp. 1279–81, 1282–83. See also Daniel H. Pollitt, "NLRB Re-Run Elections: A Study," *North Carolina Law Review* 41 (Winter 1963): 212; McCulloch to Paul Shaw, director, Industrial Relations Department, Commerce and Industry Association of New York, November 2, 1965, p. 1, "Re-Run Elections," Box 5, RG 25, NA.

144. Frederic T. Spindel, "Union Authorization Cards: A Reliable Basis for an NLRB Order to Bargain?" *Texas Law Review* 47 (December 1968): 96.

145. Memorandum from Robert Volger, associate executive secretary, to Ogden Fields, executive secretary, September 5, 1969, "Gissell," Box 3, McCulloch Papers. According to this memorandum, certifications based on card majorities rather than representation elections rose from 1.1 percent in 1962 to 3.6 percent in 1968.

146. Memorandum from Robert Volger to McCulloch, "Card Statistics," May 3, 1968, "Gissell," Box 3, McCulloch Papers. The number of bargaining orders based on card majorities increased from 35 in 1963 to 107 in 1967.

147. Michael H. Stephens, "Recent Developments in the Creation of Effective Remedies under the National Labor Relations Act," *Buffalo Law Review* 17 (Spring 1968): 842. See *H.W. Elson Bottling Co.,* 155 NLRB 714, 715–16 (1965).

148. Spindel, "Union Authorization Cards," pp. 89–90; Frederic T. Spindel, "Refusal-to-Recognize Charges under Section 8(a)(5) of the NLRA: Card Checks and Employee Free Choice," *University of Chicago Law Review* 33 (Winter 1966): 389–90.

149. Benjamin Wolkinson, "The Remedial Efficacy of NLRB Remedies in *Joy Silk* Cases," *Cornell Law Review* 55 (November 1969): 21–22.

150. Participants included not only the representatives of the parties involved in four cases before the Board but also the AFL-CIO, the International Brotherhood of Teamsters, the U.S. Chamber of Commerce, and the National Association of Manufacturers. "Unions Tell NLRB They Want Total Access to Employers' Plants in Election Drives," *Daily Labor Report,* no. 97, May 20, 1965, pp. A-8–A-10; "Labor Board to Hear Oral Argument May 20 on Equal Time Controversy," *Daily Labor Report,* no. 94, May 17, 1965, pp. A-4–A-5; "Will Organizing Be Made Easier?" *Business Week,* May 29, 1965, p. 111.

151. Sam Ervin to the president, December 1, 1965, NN 3-25-86-2, Box 8, RG 25, NA.

152. Oral History interview with McCulloch (1984), p. 43. The altered document is found in NN 3-25-86-2, Box 8, RG 25, NA.

153. The content of the "constituent's letter" matches a letter sent by John P. Baum, vice-chairman of the board of J.P. Stevens, to Mills B. Lane, Jr., president of Citizens & Southern National Bank, November 15, 1965, which is also found in NN 3-25-86-2, Box 8, RG 25, NA.

154. 156 NLRB 1236, 1239–40 (1966).

155. Ibid., pp. 1240–41.

156. Sam Zagoria, speech before the New Jersey Chamber of Commerce and American Association of Industrial Management, press release (R-1092), October 20, 1967, pp. 4–5, NLRB Files.

157. "NLRB Announces Leaflet and Notice Program to Inform Workers of Rights in Voting for Collective Bargaining Representation," press release (R-1064), January 20, 1967, NLRB Files. McCulloch credited Board member Sam Zagoria with initiating and implementing the program. Ibid., p. 3.

158. McCulloch to Michael Manatos, April 7, 1967, Collection WHCF, FG, Container no. 296, LBJ Library; Oral History interview with McCulloch (1984), p. 76.

159. Telegram from Burton A. Zorn, chairman, Industrial Relations Committee, Commerce and Industry Association of New York, to McCulloch, January 31, 1967, NN 3-25-86-1, Box 4, RG 25, NA; *Right to Work News,* news release no. 352, March 8, 1967, NN 3-25-86-1, Box 11, RG 25, NA.

160. Ogden Fields, executive secretary, to Woodrow J. Sandler, Esq., February 13, 1967, NN 3-25-86-1, Box 4, RG 25, NA.

161. Oral History interview with Gordon, pp. 74–75.

162. House, *Report of the Subcommittee on National Labor Relations Board of the Committee on Education and Labor, Administration of the Labor-Management Relations Act by the NLRB,* 87th Cong., 1st sess., 1961, p. 24. (Hereinafter *Pucinski Committee Report.*)

163. "New and Novel Remedies for Unfair Labor Practices," address by John H. Fanning, *Daily Labor Report,* no. 228, November 21, 1968, p. D-3.

164. Philip Ross, *The Labor Law in Action: An Analysis of the Administrative Process under the Taft-Hartley Act* (Washington, D.C., September 1966), pp. 1–2, 17.

165. *Delaware New Jersey Ferry Co.,* 1 NLRB 85, 96 (1935); *Baer Co., Inc.,* 1 NLRB 159, 163 (1935).

166. *Pucinski Committee Report,* p. 2.

167. Memorandum from Harry Brickman, "The Need for Strengthening NLRB Remedies in Cases Involving Refusal to Bargain," April 1967, pp. 3–4, "Remedies—Ex-Cell-O—Zinke," McCulloch Papers.

168. Ibid., pp. 5–7, 8–9; George P. Parker, "Employee Reimbursement for an Employer's Refusal to Bargain: The Ex-Cell-O Doctrine," *Texas Law Review* 46 (April 1968): 770, 774.

169. Ross, *Labor Law in Action,* pp. 6, 12, 16.

170. *Ex-Cell-O Corp.,* No. 25-CA-2377 (NLRB trial examiner's decision, March 2, 1967); *Zinke's Foods, Inc.,* No. 30-CA-372 (NLRB trial examiner's decision, December 18, 1967); *Herman Wilson Lumber Co.,* No. 26-CA-2536 (NLRB trial examiner's decision, January 4, 1967); *Rasco Olympia, Inc.,* No. 19-CA-3189 (NLRB trial examiner's decision, December 5, 1966).

171. "NLRB Schedules Two-Day Oral Argument on Proposals for Employee Reimbursement Remedies in Cases Involving Unlawful Refusal to Bargain," press release (R-1083), July 10, 1967, NLRB Files. For an interesting discussion of the pros and cons of the *Ex-Cell-O* remedy, see Theodore St. Antoine, "A Touchstone for Labor Board Remedies," *Wayne Law Review* 14 (Fall 1968): 1039–58; Stephen Schlossberg and John Silard, "The Need for a Compensatory Remedy in Refusal-to-Bargain Cases," *Wayne Law Review* 14 (Fall 1968): 1059–85; Kenneth McGui-

ness, "Section 8(a)(3) of the Labor Act: Problems and Legislative Proposals," *Wayne Law Review* 14 (Fall 1968): 1086–1103.

172. "Monthly Summary of the Activities of the NLRB as Submitted to the President of the United States—July, 1967," p. 1, RG 25, NA.

173. 150 NLRB 192 (1964).

174. Ibid., p. 207; James A. Gross, Donald E. Cullen, and Kurt L. Hanslowe, "Good Faith in Labor Negotiations: Tests and Remedies," *Cornell Law Review* 53 (July 1968): 1025–26. See also Morris D. Forkosch, "'Take It or Leave It' as a Bargaining Technique," *California Western Law Review* 3 (Spring 1967): 46–50; "'Boulwarism': Legality and Effect," *Harvard Law Review* 76 (Fall 1963): 807–10, 817–18; Herbert Northrup, *Boulwarism* (Ann Arbor: University of Michigan Bureau of Industrial Relations, Graduate School of Business, 1964).

175. Gross et al., "Good Faith," pp. 1025–26.

176. 150 NLRB at 208–9.

177. Ibid., pp. 193, 196. Other violations included a failure to provide information requested by the union during negotiations and the company's attempt to deal separately with locals on matters properly the subject of national negotiations and to persuade locals separately to abandon the strike.

178. Ibid., pp. 195–96.

179. Ibid., pp. 268, 273.

180. Ibid., pp. 194–95, 274.

181. For the story of the "race to the courthouse," see *NLRB v. General Electric,* 418 F.2d 736, 736–38 (2d Cir. 1969). See also Oral History interviews with McCulloch (1984), pp. 62–63, and Strauss, pp. 37–40.

182. GE sought American Civil Liberties Union participation on its behalf in briefs before the Second Circuit Court of Appeals, but the ACLU's Labor Committee declined by a vote of seven to three. John de J. Pemberton, executive director, ACLU, to Joseph Rauh, Jr., Esq., May 11, 1965, "GE—CA2," McCulloch Papers; Oral History interview with McCulloch (1984), p. 68; (1989), pp. 31–32.

183. General Electric press release, December 16, 1964, p. 1, "GE—CA2," McCulloch Papers; Virgil Day, "Management Freedom and Responsibilities: Some Industrial Relations Issues," speech before the Kansas City Personnel Management Association, January 26, 1966, p. 1, "GE—CA2," McCulloch Papers; Virgil Day, "Bad Faith Bargaining: NLRB's Finding against GE Raises Some Serious Questions," *Wall Street Journal,* June 28, 1965, p. 10.

184. Oral History interview with O'Connell, p. 89.

185. "Business Group Sees President's Remarks on T-H Changes as Chance to Reform NLRB," *Daily Labor Report,* no. 10, January 15, 1965, pp. A-5–A-7.

186. Herbert Northrup, "Management's 'New Look' in Labor Relations," *Industrial Relations* 1 (October 1961): 9–24.

187. Jack Barbash, "Federal Regulation and the Unions—Discussion," *Proceedings of the Twenty-first Annual Winter Meeting,* Industrial Relations Research Association, December 29–30, 1968, p. 303.

Chapter 11

1. 138 NLRB 550 (1962).
2. Clyde Summers, "Labor Law in the Supreme Court, 1964 Term," *Yale Law Journal*, 75 (November 1965): 82.
3. 379 U.S. 203, 209 (1964).
4. Ibid., pp. 223, 225–26. See also Summers, "Labor Law," p. 62.
5. 380 U.S. 263 (1965).
6. 380 U.S. 300 (1965); 380 U.S. 278 (1965).
7. 380 U.S. at 272. Summers, "Labor Law," pp. 64–67.
8. 380 U.S. 300, 315; 142 NLRB 1362 (1963).
9. 380 U.S. 300, 318.
10. Summers, "Labor Law," p. 86; Howard Lesnick, "The Labor Board and the Courts of Appeals: A Crisis of Confidence," in *Proceedings of the Twenty-first Annual New York University Conference on Labor* (New York: Matthew Bender, 1968), pp. 35–51; Cornelius J. Peck, "The National Labor Relations Board, 1965–1966: A Change in the Mood of the Judiciary?" in *Proceedings of New York University Nineteenth Annual Conference on Labor* (New York: BNA, 1967), pp. 3–33.
11. "Stuart Rothman Leaves NLRB," press release (R-934), October 1, 1963, NLRB Files, Washington, D.C.; "Rothman's Successor," Press Associates, Inc., April 8, 1963, Box 13, Record Group (RG) 25, National Archives (NA). Rothman joined the Washington, D.C., office of the law firm of Royall, Koegel & Rodgers.
12. "NLRB Job up for Grabs," *Business Week*, April 6, 1963, p. 74.
13. "'New' Man at NLRB," *Newsweek*, May 6, 1963, p. 67.
14. Oral History interviews with John Higgins, July 26, 1988, p. 3; Stephan Gordon, August 1, 1988, pp. 33–34; Norton Come, July 29, 1988, pp. 27–28; Joseph De Sio, August 2, 1988, p. 25, Labor-Management Documentation Center (LMDC), ILR, Cornell University.
15. "NLRB General Counsel Ordman Sworn in for New Term on Anniversary of NLRA," *Daily Labor Report*, no. 129, July 5, 1967, p. A-7.
16. "NLRB Chairman Appoints Trial Examiner Arnold Ordman to Be His Chief Counsel," press release (R-776), March 29, 1961, p. 1, NLRB Files. For Ordman's biographical sketch, see Senate Committee on Labor and Public Welfare, *Hearings on Arnold Ordman to Be Reappointed as General Counsel of the NLRB*, 90th Cong., 1st sess., 1967, p. 3.
17. "Arnold Ordman Sworn in as NLRB General Counsel," press release (R-920), May 14, 1963, p. 4, NLRB Files.
18. "Howard Jenkins Sworn in as Member of NLRB," *Daily Labor Report*, no. 169, August 29, 1963, p. A-11; "Howard Jenkins Sworn in as Member of NLRB," press release (R-930), August 29, 1963, NLRB Files. For Jenkins's biographical sketch, see Senate Committee on Labor and Public Welfare, *Hearings on Howard Jenkins, Jr., to Be a Member of the NLRB*, 88th Cong., 1st sess., 1963, pp. 6–7.
19. Senate Committee on Labor and Public Welfare, *Hearings on Howard Jenkins*, p. 7.

20. Oral History interview with Frank McCulloch, September 5, 1989, p. 20, LMDC.

21. Oral History interviews with William Feldesman, July 28, 1988, p. 25; Warren Davison, August 8, 1988, p. 18; Stephan Gordon, who remembered Jenkins as a man of "tremendous integrity," p. 47; Stanley Strauss, August 12, 1988, pp. 17–18; and Berton Subrin, August 5, 1988, pp. 14–15, LMDC.

22. Memorandum from John Macy to Johnson, May 10, 1968, Folder "NLRB," Collection "John Macy Files," Container no. 804; memorandum from Ernest Goldstein to Johnson, May 24, 1968, Collection "Aides–Goldstein," Container no. 5; memorandum from Macy to Johnson, April 26, 1968, Collection "Name Series—Jenkins," Container no. 64, Lyndon Baines Johnson Library, Austin, Tex.

23. Memorandum from Macy to Johnson, December 16, 1964, Folder "NLRB," Collection "John Macy," Container no. 804, LBJ Library.

24. "Zagoria Takes Oath as New NLRB Member," *Daily Labor Report,* no. 75, April 20, 1965, p. A-1; "Zagoria, Assistant to Senator Case, Is Appointed to Fill Labor Board Vacancy," *Daily Labor Report,* no. 54, March 27, 1965, p. A-1; "Sam Zagoria Sworn in as Member of NLRB," press release (R-1006), April 20, 1965, NLRB Files. Zagoria was remembered by his co-workers as "one of Washington's colorful figures" but, like Jenkins, "middle of the road." Oral History interview with Subrin, pp. 17–19.

25. McCulloch to Johnson, November 30, 1964, "Program Suggestions," Box 8, McCulloch Papers, LMDC.

26. John Herling, "Blast against the NLRB," *Washington News,* January 23, 1962.

27. "NLRB or JFKLB?" *Newsweek,* February 25, 1963, p. 78.

28. "Emergency Disputes Position Paper," report to NAM Task Force by Douglas Soutar, July 7, 1967, pp. 1–16, Series IV, Box 125, National Association of Manufacturers Archives, Hagley Museum and Library, Wilmington, Del.

29. "The Attack on Management Rights," *Iron Age,* January 21, 1965, p. 42; Phil Landrum, "The National Labor Relations Board's Repeated Record of Deliberate Distortion," *Journal of Public Law* 12 (1963): 240–42; "Remarks of Congressman Landrum of Georgia and Griffin of Michigan on Decisions of NLRB," *Daily Labor Report,* no. 119, June 19, 1963, p. E-6.

30. "Landrum Revives Bill to Divest NLRB of Unfair Labor Practice Jurisdiction," *Daily Labor Report,* no. 167, August 27, 1963, p. A-1. For the full text of the bill, see "Landrum Bill to Transfer Unfair Labor Practice Cases from NLRB to Federal District Courts," *Daily Labor Report,* no. 167, August 27, 1963, pp. D-1–D-4.

31. "Emergency Disputes Position Paper," p. 3; see ibid. for copies of seminar programs and listings of speakers; "Union Objectives and Methods," speech by Harry Lambeth, labor attorney, Chamber of Commerce, *Daily Labor Report,* no. 199, October 12, 1960, pp. D-1–D-3.

32. "Minutes, NAM Industrial Relations Committee," April 18, 1963, p. 9, Series I, Box 26, NAM Archives. See also "NAM Head Suggests Labor Monopoly Laws; Study Project Draws Fire from Unions," *Daily Labor Report,* no. 196, October 8, 1962, pp. A-7–A-9.

33. "NAM Opens Fight on Unions' Power," *New York Times,* October 7, 1962.

34. David Benetar, "The Sensitive NLRB," *Wall Street Journal,* September 21, 1965.

35. "Brown Raps Charges against Board and Idea that Law Contains Clearly Fixed Guidelines," *Daily Labor Report,* no. 83, April 27, 1962, p. A-9; "Recent Trends in NLRB Decisions," address by Gerald Brown, *Daily Labor Report,* no. 23, February 1, 1963, p. E-3; "Compulsion and Freedom in Collective Bargaining," address by Frank McCulloch, *Daily Labor Report,* no. 47, March 8, 1963, p. D-1; "Beneath the Tumult and the Shouting," address by Arnold Ordman, *Daily Labor Report,* no. 213, October 31, 1963, p. D-1; "Collective Bargaining Today—As Seen at the NLRB," address by Gerald Brown, *Daily Labor Report,* no. 52, March 18, 1965, p. D-1.

36. Frank McCulloch, "A Tale of Two Cities: Or Law in Action," *American Bar Association Section on Labor Relations Law* 14 (1962): 24.

37. "Remarks of Labor Board Chairman Frank McCulloch before Texas Manufacturers Association," *Daily Labor Report,* no. 209, October 28, 1965, p. E-2.

38. "Collective Bargaining Today," p. D-2.

39. "NLRB Spokesman Rebuts Criticism of Board Policies in Area of Employer Free Speech," *Daily Labor Report,* no. 213, October 31, 1963, p. A-2.

40. "Remarks of Labor Board Chairman," p. E-5.

41. Neil Ulman, "Companies Fight Harder against Labor Attempts to Organize Employees," *Wall Street Journal,* January 19, 1966, p. 1. Conferences discussing ways to "combat union organizing drives" were drawing "upward of 1,000 executives," compared to an average of "barely 400" as recently as 1963. Ibid.

42. "Recent Trends in NLRB Decisions," p. E-1.

43. "Collective Bargaining Today," pp. D-2–D-3.

44. Oral History interview with McCulloch (1989), pp. 24–26; McCulloch to W. P Gullander, president, NAM, September 17, 1963, "NLRB Business," Box 1, McCulloch Papers.

45. Oral History interview with Francis O'Connell, May 23, 1987, p. 75, LMDC.

46. Frank Prial, "Business Group Edges from Far Right, Pushes Its Own Social Plans," *Wall Street Journal,* May 31, 1966, p. 1.

47. Transcript of telephone conversation with Gullander concerning meetings with McCulloch, October 30, 1963, pp. 1–2, Douglas Soutar Papers, LMDC.

48. Ibid., p. 1; memorandum from Howard W. Kleeb, acting executive secretary, to Fanning, October 3, 1963, Box 9, RG 25, NA. Kleeb acknowledged that the Board had met approximately eight times "around the country" with AFL-CIO representatives and once in Washington, D.C. Ibid.

49. Oral History interview with McCulloch (1989), pp. 25–26.

50. Oral History interview with Douglas Soutar, September 7, 1989, pp. 97–98, LMDC.

51. NAM Industrial Relations Division, *"Let Us Reason Together": Report on NAM-NLRB Conference and Five Previous Regional Meetings* (New York: National Association of Manufacturers, 1964), pp. 4–8, Soutar Papers; "Monthly Summary of

the Activities of the NLRB as Submitted to the President of the United States—February, 1964," p. 1, RG 25, NA.

52. NAM Industrial Relations Division, *Perspective on Industrial Relations,* March 31, 1965, p. 4, Soutar Papers.

53. "Monthly Summary of the Activities of the NLRB as Submitted to the President of the United States" for August 1965 and March, April, July, and August 1966, RG 25, NA.

54. "Monthly Summary of the Activities of the NLRB as Submitted to the President of the United States—March, 1964," p. 2, RG 25, NA; "Remarks of Labor Board Chairman," p. D-1; "Monthly Summary of the Activities of the NLRB as Submitted to the President of the United States—December, 1964," pp. 2–3, RG 25, NA.

55. Minutes, NAM National Labor Policy Subcommittee, May 9, 1967, p. 3, and December 1, 1966, p. 3, Series I, Box 26, NAM Archives.

56. "The National Labor Relations Board during the Administration of President Lyndon B. Johnson, November, 1963—January, 1969," p. 104, Collection "History—NLRB," Container no. 1, LBJ Library.

57. McCulloch to Gullander, March 18, 1968, Series IV, Box 119, NAM Archives.

58. Oral History interview with McCulloch (1989), pp. 30–31.

59. NAM Industrial Relations Division, *"Let Us Reason Together,"* pp. 11, 14.

60. Oral History interview with McCulloch (1989), pp. 26–28.

61. Oral History interview with O'Connell, p. 73.

62. Ibid., p. 74.

63. Oral History interview with McCulloch (1989), p. 33.

64. Oral History interview with Soutar, p. 25.

65. Ibid., p. 32.

66. Ibid., p. 27.

67. Oral History interview with O'Connell, pp. 15–16. O'Connell remarked, "There are not many Congressional medals that I would dish out to American big business when it comes to battling . . . standing up for principles." Ibid., p. 143.

68. Oral History interview with Soutar, pp. 134–35.

69. "Summary of Objectives and Activities of the Labor Law Study Committee," October 4, 1971, p. 4, Francis O'Connell Papers, LMDC.

70. Oral History interview with Soutar, pp. 26, 126.

71. Letter dated November 10, 1967 (a draft news release that the group decided not to use), Series IV, Box 125, NAM Archives. The following companies were represented: American Telephone & Telegraph, Ford Motor Company, U.S. Steel, Union Carbide, General Dynamics, B.F. Goodrich, Humble Oil and Refining, Columbia Gas System Service, and Sears, Roebuck.

72. Oral History interview with Soutar, pp. 63–65.

73. Ibid., p. 63.

74. Shelley Coppock, "Management Opposition to the NLRB during the 1960s" (M.S. thesis, Cornell University, 1987, pp. 150–51. Coppock's thesis is a first-rate discussion and excellent source on this subject. For Reilly's time with the Board in

the 1940s and his role in drafting the Taft bill, see James A. Gross, *The Reshaping of the National Labor Relations Board: National Labor Policy in Transition, 1937–1947* (Albany: State University of New York Press, 1981), pp. 240–42, 253–54.

75. Self-description by William Ingles, president, LPA, October 23, 1964, "'A' File NLRB Attacks," Labor Policy Association, Inc., McCulloch Papers. Ingles wrote, "We offer each year substantial awards to graduate students and faculty members in the colleges and universities for papers on the problems of union power." Ibid., p. 3.

76. Memorandum, "Labor Policy Association and William Ingles," December 4, 1964, "Labor Policy Association," Box 6, McCulloch Papers. See also Oral History interview with Soutar, p. 64.

77. Kenneth McGuiness, *The New Frontier NLRB* (Washington, D.C.: Labor Policy Association, 1963). McGuiness accused the Board, among other things, of ignoring what he saw as Congress's intent "to subordinate the encouragement of collective bargaining to employees' right to choose not to be unionized or engage in collective bargaining." Ibid., pp. 14–15. See also ibid., p. xi; "Decisions of NLRB Majority Undermine Intent of Congress and Favor Unions, Author Claims," *Daily Labor Report*, no. 118, June 18, 1963, pp. A-3–A-5; "Is 'Kennedy Board' Rewriting Labor Law?" *U.S. News & World Report*, July 8, 1963, pp. 91–92.

78. "Summary of Objectives and Activities of the Labor Law Study Committee," pp. 2–3, O'Connell Papers.

79. "Minutes, NAM National Labor Policy Subcommittee," December 1, 1966, p. 3.

80. Memorandum from R. T. Borth, "Responsibilities of Executive Director—Labor Law Study Project," April 5, 1967, p. 4, Series IV, Box 125, NAM Archives.

81. "Remarks of Chairman Frank McCulloch at University of Oklahoma," *Daily Labor Report*, no. 99, August 22, 1969, p. E-1. NLRB "graduates" on the BRC included Farmer, Reilly, Jenkins, Kammholz, McGuiness, Rothman, Shroyer, William Barton (general counsel of the Chamber of Commerce and former trial examiner), and Eugene Keeney (former attorney in the general counsel's office, 1952–58, who initiated the Blue Ribbon Committee while heading the Chamber's Labor Relations Department). Edward Miller, who would be appointed NLRB chairman after Nixon became president, was also a BRC member.

82. "The New Campaign to Abolish the NLRB and Rewrite the Labor Act," undated, no author specified, p. 2, "Materials: Domestic Labor," Box 113, Collection "Willard Wirtz," John Fitzgerald Kennedy Library, Boston.

83. "Summary of Objectives and Activities," p. 6; "NAM Executive Committee Report," submitted by H. C. Lumb, T. C. Allen, and Lambert Miller, February 15, 1971, pp. 2–3, Soutar Papers.

84. Memorandum from R. T. Borth, "Responsibilities of Executive Director—Labor Law Study Project," April 5, 1967; William Van Meter, general manager, U.S. Chamber of Commerce, to Lambert Miller, general counsel, NAM, March 23, 1967, Series IV, Box 125, NAM Archives.

85. Memorandum from Frederick G. Atkinson to Labor Law Study Group and support-

ing committees, "Release of Information in Response to Outside Inquiries," p. 2, Series IV, Box 125, NAM Archives.

86. Coppock, "Management Opposition," p. 160.

87. Oral History interviews with Soutar, pp. 78–79, and O'Connell, p. 163.

88. Oral History interview with Soutar, pp. 68–69.

89. McCabe to R. W. Markley, vice-president, Washington Staff Ford Motor Company, August 4, 1967, Series IV, Box 125, NAM Archives.

90. *Labor Law Reform Study: Amendments to the Labor Management Relations Act,* November 6, 1967, pp. iv–vi, "BR-LLSG-Hill & Knowlton," Box 6, Soutar Papers.

91. Ibid., pp. A-1–A-3.

92. The Troika took a deliberately ambivalent position on this potentially divisive issue. Ibid., pp. S-4–S-5.

93. Management resisted encroachments on its prerogatives not only by the NLRB but also by labor arbitrators. For the Troika's response to the Supreme Court's *Trilogy,* which greatly expanded the powers of labor arbitrators, (see *United Steelworkers v. Warrior & Gulf Navigation Co.,* 363 U.S. 574 [1960]; *United Steelworkers v. American Mfg. Co.,* 363 U.S. 564 [1960]; *United Steelworkers v. Enterprise Wheel & Car Corp.,* 363 U.S. 593 [1960], see ibid., pp. R-2, R-7, R-11.

94. Coppock, "Management Opposition," pp. 156–58, 179 n. 52.

95. "Summary of Objectives and Activities," p. 7.

96. "Minutes, NAM Labor Policy Subcommittee," December 1, 1966, pp. 2–3.

97. "Minutes, NAM Subcommittee on Collective Bargaining," October 10, 1967, p. 1, Series I, Box 26, NAM Archives.

98. Memorandum from Borth, "Responsibilities of Executive Director," pp. 2–3.

99. "Supplementary Material—Agenda," January 6, 1967, pp. 2–3, Series IV, Box 125, NAM Archives.

100. T. A. Wise, "Hill & Knowlton's World of Images," *Fortune,* September 1, 1967, p. 140.

101. Ibid.

102. Ibid., pp. 98–99, 140–42; "Communication Plan in Support of Labor Law Revision," submitted by Hill & Knowlton at the request of the Labor Law Reform Group, May 1967, pp. 2–4, Series IV, Box 125, NAM Archives. (Hereinafter "Communication Plan, May 1967.")

103. Wise, "Hill & Knowlton's World of Images," p. 99.

104. Ibid., p. 101.

105. "Communication Plan, May 1967," p. 5; "A Communication Program to Help Obtain Fair Labor Laws," Hill & Knowlton, August 1967, p. 1, Series IV, Box 125, NAM Archives. (Hereinafter "Communication Program, August 1967.")

106. "Communication Plan, May 1967," pp. 8–9.

107. "Communications Program, August 1967," pp. 2–3.

108. Ibid., p. 2.

109. Oral History interview with O'Connell, pp. 127–28.

110. Oral History interview with Soutar, p. 73.

111. "Minutes, NAM Subcommittee on Collective Bargaining," October 10, 1967, pp. 1–2.

112. Unsigned memorandum, November 10, 1967, author not identified, considering a series of questions, including whether the "prime movers" should be identified to Congress, the public, and the press, Series IV, Box 125, NAM Archives.

113. "Communication Program, August 1967," pp. 5–6.

114. Ibid., p. 7.

115. Ibid., pp. 7–8. There is no evidence to indicate whether or not this phase of the program was ever implemented, but the plan was acceptable to the Labor Law Reform Group.

116. Ibid., pp. 8–9.

117. Harry Bernstein, "U.S. Official Charges Massive Attack on NLRB Is Under Way," *Los Angeles Times,* October 29, 1968.

118. *Cong. Rec.,* 90th Cong., 2d sess. (August 2, 1968), 114, pt. 19: 24992.

119. Series of NLRB "horror stories," prepared by Hill & Knowlton, no date, Series IV, Box 125, NAM Archives.

120. Malcolm M. Johnson, "Crisis in Labor Relations," speech before the American Society for Training and Development, October 20, 1967, pp. 2–5, Series IV, Box 125, NAM Archives.

121. "Background Memorandum: The Need for Labor Law Reform," December 14, 1967, pp. 1–4, Series IV, Box 125, NAM Archives; Johnson, "Crisis in Labor Relations," p. 5.

122. Victor Riesel, "Top Industrialists Organize to Challenge Pro-Labor Laws," *Human Events,* February 17, 1968.

123. Memorandum from R. T. Borth, February 15, 1968, Series IV, Box 128, NAM Archives.

124. *Cong. Rec.,* 90th Cong., 2d sess. (August 2, 1968), 114, pt. 19: 24991, 24993.

125. "Ervin Committee to Hold Public Hearing on How Well Labor Board Administers Law," *Daily Labor Report,* no. 39, February 26, 1968, pp. AA-3–AA-4; "Ripe for Review," *Wall Street Journal,* March 14, 1968, p. 16.

126. Gullander to William Ruffin, chairman of the board, Erwin Mills, Inc., May 12, 1967, Series IV, Box 96, NAM Archives. For a discussion of the Smith committee and its historic consequences, see Gross, *Reshaping of the National Labor Relations Board,* pp. 151–225.

127. Senate Subcommittee on Separation of Powers of the Committee on the Judiciary, *Hearings on Congressional Oversight of Administrative Agencies,* 90th Cong., 2d sess., 1968, p. 1. (Hereinafter *Ervin Committee Hearings.*)

128. "The New Campaign to Abolish the NLRB and Rewrite the Labor Act," undated and unsigned, p. 8 n. 3, "Materials: Domestic Labor," Box 113, Kennedy Library.

129. "NAM-Chamber Inspired Labor Law Study Group to Continue Despite Election," *Daily Labor Report,* no. 224, November 15, 1968, p. A-11.

130. Oral History interview with Soutar, p. 144.

131. Ibid., p. 145.

132. Coppock, "Management Opposition," pp. 166–67, 183 nn. 89, 90, 91. For the statement of former congressman Hartley, see *Ervin Committee Hearings,* pp. 44–49.

133. McCabe to William C. Treanor (Hamel, Morgan, Park & Saunders), February 26, 1968, Series IV, Box 128, NAM Archives.

134. "NAM-Chamber Inspired Labor Law Study Group," p. A-11; George Denison and William Schulz, "Let's Enforce Our Labor Laws Fairly," *Reader's Digest,* August 1968, pp. 119–25. At the conclusion of the article, readers are invited to send other examples of "unjust" NLRB decisions to the *Digest.* Ibid., p. 125.

135. Oral History interviews with McCulloch (1984), pp. 69–70; (1989), pp. 45–47.

136. Oral History interview with Soutar, pp. 144–45.

137. Oral History interview with Arnold Ordman, August 10, 1988, p. 32, LMDC.

138. "Unfair Labor Practice Cases, as Decided by the NLRB and Reviewed by United States Courts of Appeals and the Supreme Court. Proposed Examination of this Subject by Separation of Powers Subcommittee," and "The Range of Decisions by the NLRB . . . The Extent to Which These Decisions Have Circumvented the Intent of Congress and Encroached upon the Policy-Making Functions of the Legislative Branch," memoranda prepared for the Ervin subcommittee, undated and unsigned, Series IV, Box 128, NAM Archives.

139. John Chamberlain, "We've Had Some Important Hearings on Our Perverted Labor Law," for release, June 13, 1968, Series IV, Box 128, NAM Archives. Chamberlain mentioned no one who testified in favor of the NLRB.

140. *Ervin Committee Hearings,* pp. 683–85.

141. Ibid., pp. 688, 692.

142. U.S. Chamber of Commerce, "The Need for Labor Law Reform," *Here's the Issue* 7 (June 28, 1968): 1. See also "NLRB Imposes 'Co-Decision,' NAM Testifies," *NAM Reports,* May 6, 1968, p. 1; "NAM Details NLRB's Departures from Law," *NAM Reports,* June 17, 1968, p. 12; "Does NLRB Follow the Law?" *NAM Reports,* September 16, 1968, p. 4; "NLRB Rulings Curb Rights," *NAM Reports,* October 21, 1968, p. 10; "Labor Law Loopholes—Roadblocks to Progress," *NAM Reports,* November 18, 1968, p. 10.

143. *Ervin Committee Hearings,* pp. 213–14; Oral History interview with McCulloch (1989), p. 48.

144. "Ervin Issues His 'Tentative Findings' on Subcommittee Investigation of NLRB," *Daily Labor Report,* no. 168, August 27, 1968, pp. A-2–A-3. For the full text of Ervin's "tentative" conclusions, see *Cong. Rec.,* 90th Cong., 2d sess. (September 5, 1968), 114, pt. 19:S10288.

145. "Excerpt from Remarks of Senator Sam J. Ervin of North Carolina to Meeting of Board of Directors of National Association of Manufacturers," *Daily Labor Report,* no. 186, September 23, 1968, p. D-1.

146. "The Case against the NLRB: Highlights of Testimony before the Senate Subcommittee on Separation of Powers," March–June 1968, pp. 65–68, Series IV, Box 125, NAM Archives.

147. Riesel, "Top Industrialists Organize"; Stanley Levey, "Ax Honed for NLRB on

GOP Hopes," *Washington Daily News,* September 23, 1968, p. 9; "Statement by Congressman Thompson (Dem., N.J.) on 'The Attack on the NLRB,'" *Daily Labor Report,* no. 198, October 9, 1968, pp. D-1–D-2; *Cong. Rec.,* 90th Cong., 2d sess. (August 2, 1968), 114, pt. 19:24991–96.

148. *Cong. Rec.* (August 2, 1968), 114, pt. 19:24992.

149. Bernstein, "U.S. Official," p. 1; memorandum from Tim Bornstein to McCulloch, "Conversation with Dick Critchfield, *Washington Evening Star,*" June 28, 1968, "NLRB—File AA New Submission 1990," Box 5, McCulloch Papers.

150. Bernstein, "U.S. Official." Vice-President Sauerhaft of Hill & Knowlton is quoted as saying that his company "was called by the *Reader's Digest* and we helped them get material for the article." Ibid.

151. Harry Bernstein, "Major Firms Unite to Limit Unions' Strength," *Los Angeles Times,* November 3, 1968, p. 1.

152. Ibid.

153. "For Immediate Release, November 4, 1968," Folder 48, Box 36, Department of Legislation, 1906–1978, George Meany Memorial Archives, Washington, D.C.

154. *Ervin Committee Hearings,* p. 129.

155. McCulloch, "Development and Contribution of the National Labor Relations Act," *Alabama Lawyer* 30 (April 1969): 159.

156. Oral History interview with McCulloch, (1989), p. 56.

157. *Ervin Committee Hearings,* p. 3.

Chapter 12

1. Virgil Day to "The Fair Labor Law Study Group," with attachment, "Some Thoughts on the 1968 Elections and the Impact on the Labor Law Study Project," p. 2, "LLRS-LLSG," Box 7, Douglas Soutar Papers, Labor-Management Documentation Center (LMDC), ILR, Cornell University.

2. Ibid., p. 4.

3. Ibid., pp. 2–3, 6–7, 9.

4. Stewart Alsop, "Labor and the Liberals," *Newsweek,* November 22, 1971, p. 140; "Meaning of the '72 Vote to Labor Unions," *U.S. News & World Report,* November 20, 1972, p. 100; "Nixon's Freeze and the Mood of Labor," *Time,* September 6, 1971, p. 9; B. J. Widick, "Unusually Chilly for Labor Day, 1971: Labor's Rough Year," *The Nation,* September 6, 1971, p. 166.

5. Memorandum from Francis O'Connell to Soutar, June 1, 1970, with attached copy of Victor Riesel, "Meany Throws Labor Support behind U.S. Invasion of Cambodia," dispatched May 5, 1970, Box 7, "LLSC—General," Soutar Papers.

6. Peter J. Pestillo, of General Electric, to Carl H. Hageman, vice-president, Union Carbide Corporation, September 25, 1969, with attachment concerning labor law priorities survey, p. 1, "LLRS-LLSG," Box 7, Soutar Papers.

7. Soutar to Fred Atkinson, November 12, 1969, p. 4, "BR Old," Box 7, Soutar Papers.

8. "Summary of Objectives and Activities of the Labor Law Study Committee," pp. 10–13, Francis O'Connell Papers, LMDC.

9. *Labor Law Reform Progress,* confidential report to members of the "Fair Labor Law Study Group," vol. 1, no. 1, (July 1971), "Special Report" insert, "LLSC— Progress Reports," Box 6, Soutar Papers.

10. Ibid., p. 2.

11. O'Connell to John N. Mitchell, Office of the President-Elect, December 11, 1968, "Blue Ribbon Panel (Lawyers)," Box 6, Soutar Papers.

12. Owen Fairweather to Soutar, September 29, 1969, with attached memorandum, "Appointments to the NLRB," September 25, 1969, "Blue Ribbon Panel (Lawyers)," Box 6, Soutar Papers.

13. Memorandum from Pestillo to Virgil Day, November 7, 1969, "LLRS-LLSG Labor Law Reform Study," Box 7; Soutar to Atkinson, November 12, 1969, "BR Old," Box 7, Soutar Papers.

14. Pestillo to Soutar, November 12, 1969, "BR Old," Box 7, Soutar Papers.

15. Oral History interview with Douglas Soutar, September 7, 1989, p. 103, LMDC.

16. "A Dark Horse for the NLRB," *Business Week,* February 21, 1970, p. 35.

17. "Business Sees a Way to Change NLRB," *Business Week,* November 29, 1969, p. 102.

18. "Labor Board Nominee—Edward Boone Miller," *New York Times,* February 21, 1970, cited in Senate Committee on Labor and Public Welfare, *Hearings on Nomination of Edward B. Miller to Be a Member of the National Labor Relations Board,* 91st Cong., 2d sess. 1970, pp. 2–4. (hereinafter *Miller Nomination Hearings*); "Edward Miller Sworn in as Chairman of NLRB," press release (R-1161), June 3, 1970, pp. 3–4, NLRB Files, Washington, D.C.; "Dark Horse," p. 35.

19. *Miller Nomination Hearings,* pp. 34–36.

20. Ibid., p. 25.

21. Charles Culhane, "Labor Report—NLRB Busy Defusing Disputes, Draws Little Notice until Appointment Time," *National Journal* 2 (December 19, 1970): 2759.

22. Guy Farmer, "The NLRB: Its Past, Present, and Future," *Tennessee Law Review* 23 (February 1954): 112; James A. Gross, "Conflicting Statutory Purposes: Another Look at Fifty Years of NLRB Law Making," *Industrial and Labor Relations Review* 39, no. 1 (October 1985): 14.

23. "Changes ahead in Washington's Labor Policies?" *Nation's Business,* September 1970, p. 70.

24. Oral History interview with Edward Miller, September 8, 1989, p. 38, LMDC.

25. Ibid.

26. Edward B. Miller, "Ruminations on the Board," *Journal of the Missouri Bar* (August 1975): 402 (quotations); Oral History interview with Miller, p. 13.

27. "Critics Slice at NLRB Power," *Business Week,* August 8, 1970, p. 61.

28. Senate Committee on Labor and Public Welfare, *Hearings on Nomination of Ralph E. Kennedy to Be a Member of the National Labor Relations Board,* 91st Cong., 2d sess., 1970, pp. 15–17.

29. Oral History interview with Frank McCulloch, September 5, 1989, p. 15, LMDC.

30. Nomination notebooks, April 23–August 17, 1971, Soutar Papers.

31. "Former NLRB General Counsel Peter G. Nash Becomes Partner in Chicago-Based Law Firm," *Daily Labor Report*, no. 173, September 5, 1975, p. A-6. The firm was Vedder, Price, Kaufman, Kammholz & Day.

32. "Peter G. Nash Sworn in as NLRB General Counsel," press release (R-1201), August 24, 1971, NLRB Files. Eugene E. Goslee had been named acting general counsel in June 1971 after Ordman's term expired. See "Eugene E. Goslee Designated Acting NLRB General Counsel by President," *Daily Labor Report*, no. 123, June 25, 1971, p. A-11.

33. Senate Committee on Labor and Public Welfare, *Hearings on Nomination of Peter G. Nash to Be General Counsel of the National Labor Relations Board*, 92d Cong., 1st sess., 1971, p. 3.

34. Oral History interview with Peter Nash, July 27, 1988, p. 30, LMDC.

35. Senate Committee on Labor and Public Welfare, *Hearings on Nomination of John A. Penello to be a Member of the National Labor Relations Board*, 92d Cong., 2d sess., 1972.

36. Nomination notebooks, August 17–November 6, 1971, Soutar Papers. By prior agreement with Mr. Soutar, I do not identify those making personal assessments of nominees or potential nominees when such assessments are recorded in his notebooks.

37. Soutar's handwritten notes, October 27, 1972, "1972 Fanning Reappointment No. 2," Box 11, Soutar Papers.

38. Ibid.

39. Soutar to Kendrick, July 23, 1973, "Appointments-Assorted," Box 13, Soutar Papers.

40. William Spalding to Soutar, August 27, 1973, and April 1, 1974, "Loose Material," Box 12, Soutar Papers.

41. Collection of personal comments concerning Jenkins's possible reappointment, June 26, 1973, blank file, Box 11, Soutar Papers.

42. Senate, *Report of the Committee on the Judiciary: Congressional Oversight of Administrative Agencies (NLRB)*, 91st Cong., 1st sess., 1970, pp. 3–4, 21, 24. (Hereinafter *Ervin Committee Report*.)

43. Oral History interview with Miller, pp. 46–47; William Isaacson, "Discernible Trends in the 'Miller' Board—Practical Considerations for the Labor Counsel," *Labor Law Journal* 23 (September 1972): 531.

44. Frank W. McCulloch and Tim Bornstein, *The National Labor Relations Board* (New York: Praeger, 1974), p. 76.

45. Isaacson, "Discernible Trends," pp. 533–34.

46. 185 NLRB 107 (1970).

47. 185 NLRB at 108–9. The majority also believed that it was inappropriate to impose "a large financial obligation" on an employer that had not flagrantly defied the statutory policy but had "merely sought judicial affirmance" of the Board's decision that a representation election should not be set aside. Ibid.

48. 397 U.S. 99 (1970).
49. 185 NLRB at 116–17.
50. Ibid., p. 117.
51. Oral History interview with Frank McCulloch, December 7, 1984, pp. 106–7, LMDC.
52. *NLRB v. Wyman-Gordon Co.*, 394 U.S. 759 (1969).
53. Oral History interview with McCulloch (1984), p. 107.
54. Ibid., p. 108.
55. John Fanning's comments, transcript of the NLRB 50th Anniversary Conference, October 22–23, 1984, pp. 78–79, LMDC.
56. Oral History interviews with McCulloch (1984), p. 110; (1989), p. 112.
57. 138 NLRB 550 (1962).
58. *Fibreboard Paper Products Corp. v. NLRB*, 379 U.S. 203 (1964).
59. 191 NLRB 951, 951–52 (1971). The trial examiner had said that the transaction was not a sale but a transfer to a franchiser.
60. 379 U.S. 203, 214 (1964).
61. 191 NLRB at 952.
62. Ibid., p. 953.
63. Ibid., p. 954.
64. Ibid., p. 953. Jenkins and Brown, took this quotation from *Ozark Trailers,* 161 NLRB 561, 566 (1966).
65. 194 NLRB 500 (1971); 195 NLRB 479 (1972); 210 NLRB 844 (1974).
66. J. Ralph Beaird and Mack A. Player, "Whither the Nixon Board," *Georgia Law Review* 7 (Summer 1973): 622.
67. *Ervin Committee Report*, pp. 7–8.
68. *Airporter Inn Hotel,* 215 NLRB 824, 826–27 (1974).
69. *Stumpf Motor Co.,* 208 NLRB 431, 432 (1974); William A. Krupman, "Election Campaign Strategy: NLRB Expands Employer Rights," *Employee Relations Law Journal* 1 (Spring 1976): 607–8.
70. *Birdsall Construction Co.,* 198 NLRB 163, 163 (1972).
71. 211 NLRB 1014 (1974).
72. Edward Miller, "The Getman, Goldberg, and Herman Questions," *Stanford Law Review* 28 (July 1976): 1163.
73. *Ervin Committee Report*, pp. 14–15.
74. 192 NLRB 881 (1971); NLRB, *Thirty-seventh Annual Report*, for the fiscal year ended June 30, 1972 (Washington, D.C.: GPO, 1972), pp. 56–57.
75. 197 NLRB 924 (1972) (Fanning and Jenkins dissenting); NLRB, *Thirty-seventh Annual Report*, pp. 57–58.
76. *Frito-Lay,* 202 NLRB 1011 (1973) (Fanning and Jenkins dissenting).
77. *Wickes Furniture,* 201 NLRB 606 (1973) (Fanning and Jenkins dissenting).
78. 395 U.S. 575, 602 (1969).
79. Ibid., pp. 613–15.
80. *Ervin Committee Report,* pp. 9, 24.

81. Isaacson, "Discernible Trends," p. 540.

82. 196 NLRB 613 (1972).

83. 201 NLRB 503 (1973).

84. Ibid., p. 505.

85. 190 NLRB 718 (1971).

86. William J. Isaacson and William C. Zifchak, "Agency Deferral to Private Arbitration of Employment Disputes," *Columbia Law Review* 73 (November 1973): 1406–8; Isaacson, "Discernible Trends," p. 533.

87. Isaacson and Zifchak, "Agency Deferral," p. 1391.

88. Beaird and Player, "Whither the Nixon Board," p. 623.

89. 112 NLRB 1080 (1955); Isaacson and Zifchak, "Agency Deferral," pp. 1388–89. Under the *Spielberg* guidelines the arbitration hearing had to be fair, the arbitration decision had to be final and binding, and the decision of the arbitrator could not be repugnant to the act. A fourth criterion was added in *Raytheon Co.,* 140 NLRB 883 (1963): The arbitrator had to consider the unfair labor practice aspect of the case.

90. 148 NLRB 414 (1964); Beaird and Player, "Whither the Nixon Board," p. 625.

91. 192 NLRB 837 (1971).

92. Ibid., pp. 849–50.

93. Isaacson and Zifchak, "Agency Deferral," p. 1392.

94. Ibid., p. 1393.

95. 198 NLRB 527 (1972); Reginald Alleyne, "Arbitrators and the NLRB: The Nature of the Deferral Beast," *Industrial Relations Law Journal* 4 (1981): 594 n. 32.

96. 198 NLRB at 533.

97. For an interesting discussion of this matter, see Isaacson and Zifchak, "Agency Deferral," pp. 1396–98.

98. Soutar's handwritten notes, August 27, 1974, "Appointments—Assorted," Box 13, Soutar Papers.

99. Ibid., November 20, 1974.

100. Ibid., December 6, 1974.

101. Nancy Hicks, "A Woman for NLRB," *New York Times,* January 9, 1975. Before attending law school, Murphy worked as a freelance reporter in Europe, the Middle East, and Asia and then as a Washington correspondent for United Press International. Soutar and his colleagues made certain that she was not openly identified as management's candidate. Soutar's handwritten notes, December 6, 1974.

102. Soutar Report for the Labor-Management Committee to the Business Roundtable Policy Committee, September 3, 1975, pp. 3–4, "LMC—More Recent General," Box 8, Soutar Papers; "Peter D. Walther Sworn in as NLRB Member," press release (R-1419), November 26, 1975, NLRB Files.

103. Nomination notebooks, June–August 1975, Soutar Papers. In Soutar's opinion "we were lucky to get a totally management oriented candidate of Walther's abilities." Soutar memorandum to the file, March 11, 1976, "Appointments—Assorted," Box 13, Soutar Papers.

104. Soutar Report for the Labor-Management Committee, pp. 3–4.

105. Soutar memorandum to the file, June 22, 1976, "Appointments—Assorted," Box 13, Soutar Papers; "Senate Labor Committee Holds Hearing on Penello Renomination to Board," *Daily Labor Report,* no. 141, July 21, 1976, p. A-10.
106. 228 NLRB 1311 (1977).
107. 140 NLRB 221 (1962).
108. *United Aircraft Corp.,* 103 NLRB 102 (1953).
109. Lee Modjeska, "Commentaries on the National Labor Relations Board: 1977," *Ohio State Law Journal* 39 (1978): 8.
110. NLRB, *Forty-first Annual Report,* for the fiscal year ended June 30, 1976, (Washington, D.C.: GPO, 1976), pp. 53–55. For a discussion of cases, see pp. 52–55.
111. *Alleluia Cushion Co.,* 221 NLRB 999 (1975).
112. *General American Transportation,* 228 NLRB 808 (1977).
113. That is, violations involving Sections 8(a)(1) and (3) and 8(b)(1)(A) and (2).
114. Cases, for example, involving alleged violations of Section 8(a)(5)'s obligation to bargain.
115. "Douglas Soutar 'talk,'" June 16, 1975, p. 1, "BRT Annual Meeting," Box 6, Soutar Papers.
116. "LMC Report at BRT Annual Meeting," June 17, 1974, p. 4, "BRT and LMC," Box 11, Soutar Papers.
117. Sar A. Levitan and Martha R. Cooper, *Business Lobbies: The Public Good and the Bottom Line* (Baltimore: Johns Hopkins University Press, 1984), p. 8.
118. Business Roundtable *Report,* No. 73-6, June 15, 1973, p. 2, "BR Post-Murphy," Box 6, Soutar Papers.
119. Levitan and Cooper, *Business Lobbies,* pp. 35–36; Mark Green and Andrew Buchsbaum, *The Corporate Lobbies: Political Profiles of the Business Roundtable and the Chamber of Commerce* (New York: Public Citizens, 1980), pp. 79–83.
120. Minutes of meeting at the Links Club, New York City, October 16, 1972, p. 3, "BR Post-Murphy," Box 6, Soutar Papers.
121. Business Roundtable *Report,* No. 73-5, May 23, 1973, pp. 1–2, "BR Post-Murphy," Box 6, Soutar Papers.
122. Levitan and Cooper, *Business Lobbies,* p. 37. For a discussion of the March Group and the Business Council, see pp. 30–31, 35–38.
123. Green and Buchsbaum, *Corporate Lobbies,* pp. 68–69; Levitan and Cooper, *Business Lobbies,* p. 35.
124. Green and Buchsbaum, *Corporate Lobbies,* pp. 66, 160.
125. Tracy Ferguson to Soutar, November 16, 1972, including Victor Riesel, "The Business Roundtable," *Syracuse Post Standard,* November 16, 1972, "Public Information Committee," Box 8, Soutar Papers.
126. Soutar became chairman as of January 1, 1973, succeeding Frederick Atkinson of R.H. Macy.
127. "Labor-Management Committee Minutes," October 26, 1972, "BR-LMC Meetings, 1972–1974," Box 9, Soutar Papers. An organizational chart is attached to these minutes.

128. List of committees and each one's membership, January 22, 1974, "BR—Member Structure Committees," Box 6, Soutar Papers.

129. Minutes of the Business Roundtable Labor-Management Committee meeting, February 18, 1974, pp. 2–3; and December 6, 1973, pp. 3–4, "BR-LMC Meetings, 1972–1974," Box 9, Soutar Papers.

130. Minutes of the Business Roundtable Labor-Management Committee meeting, February 18, 1974, p. 3; "Spokesmanship," presentation by J. D. deButts to the Business Roundtable, June 16, 1975, p. 3, "Public Information Committee, 1970–1977," Box 8, Soutar Papers.

131. Memorandum from Paul M. Lund, chairman, Public Information Committee, to members of the Policy, Construction, Labor-Management, and Public Information committees, June 4, 1973, "BR Post-Murphy," Box 6, Soutar Papers.

132. Green and Buchsbaum, *Corporate Lobbies,* p. 68.

133. Edward Thompson, managing editor, *Reader's Digest,* to James Freeman, of the Business Roundtable, May 27, 1975, "Public Information Committee, 1970–1977," Box 8, Soutar Papers. The letter lists the articles published in *Reader's Digest*'s "Roundtable series."

134. Memorandum from John D. Harper, chairman, Business Roundtable, to BRT members, April 16, 1974, "Public Information Committee, 1970–1977," Box 8; minutes of the Business Roundtable Policy Committee meeting, January 10, 1974, pp. 3–4, "BR Policy Committee Meetings, 1973–1976, Box 10, Soutar Papers.

135. W. B. Murphy, outgoing chairman, Business Roundtable, to Virgil Day, September 21, 1973, "BR Post-Murphy," Box 6, Soutar Papers.

136. "Revamped Business Stance toward Washington Noted on Labor Issues," *Daily Labor Report,* no. 28, February 10, 1975, p. C-2, (quotation); minutes of the Business Roundtable Labor-Management Committee meeting, March 18, 1982, "LMC More Recent," Box 8, Soutar Papers. By 1982 the Labor-Management Committee was considering adopting a "more descriptive" name, since about 90 percent of its agenda items concerned "nonunion related subjects." The two most mentioned names were Human Resources Committee and Employee Relations Committee. Minutes, March 18, 1982, pp. 7–8.

137. "Revamped Business Stance," pp. C-1–C-3.

138. Walter Guzzardi, Jr., "Business Is Learning How to Win in Washington," *Fortune,* March 27, 1978, p. 54.

139. Francis A. O'Connell, "Too Cozy with Labor?" letter to *Fortune,* May 22, 1978, p. 124.

140. Soutar's handwritten notes on a copy of O'Connell's letter to *Fortune.*

141. Levitan and Cooper, *Business Lobbies,* pp. 115, 140.

142. Green and Buchsbaum, *Corporate Lobbies,* p. 5.

143. "Labor's Biggest Victory Ever: Will It Bring Results?" *U.S. News & World Report,* November 18, 1974, p. 96.

144. Remarks by Bryce N. Harlow at the U.S. Chamber of Commerce, Washington, D.C., January 22, 1975, "LMC General 1975," Box 10, Soutar Papers.

145. "Labor's Losing Battle on Capitol Hill," *Business Week,* July 14, 1975, p. 56.

146. *NLRB v. Denver Building and Construction Trades Council,* 341 U.S. 675 (1951).

147. Levitan and Cooper, *Business Lobbies,* pp. 120–21.

148. "Big Labor's Big Defeat," *Newsweek,* April 4, 1977, p. 54.

149. For a fuller account, see Levitan and Cooper, *Business Lobbies,* pp. 121–22.

150. "Labor Reform Faces Potent Opposition," *Business Week,* May 2, 1977, p. 36.

151. "The Battle That's Brewing over Changes in Labor Laws," *U.S. News & World Report,* July 25, 1977, p. 77.

152. Ibid.

153. AFL-CIO, "Brief Synopsis of Labor Law Reform," special report on labor law reform, H.R. 8410 and S. 1883.

154. Soutar memorandum to the file, "Labor Law Reform—Business Roundtable," April 2, 1979, "BR-LMC," Box 9, Soutar Papers.

155. Green and Buchsbaum, *Corporate Lobbies,* p. 124; Levitan and Cooper, *Business Lobbies,* pp. 131–32.

156. "Labor Law Reform: The Regulation of Free Speech and Equal Access in NLRB Representation Elections," *University of Pennsylvania Law Review* 127 (January 1979): 792–97.

157. Ibid., p. 794. Before final action the House limited the equal access provision to captive audience situations, gave employers a right to reply to union speeches given at union halls, and made the equal access provision applicable to decertification and de-authorization elections as well as representation elections. Ibid. See also Peter Nash, "The Labor Reform Act of 1977: A Detailed Analysis," *Employee Relations Law Journal* 4 (Summer 1978): 64–65, 69.

158. "Unions Hit the Comeback Trail in Congress," *U.S. News & World Report,* October 17, 1977, pp. 112–13; Soutar to Senator Lowell Weicker, May 30, 1978, "Labor Law Reform," Box 6, Soutar Papers.

159. Thomas Ferguson and Joel Rogers, "Labor Law Reform and Its Enemies," *The Nation,* January 6–14, 1979, pp. 19–20; Levitan and Cooper, *Business Lobbies,* p. 130; Green and Buchsbaum, *Corporate Lobbies,* p. 77; "The New Chill in Labor Relations," *Business Week,* October 24, 1977, p. 33.

160. Green and Buchsbaum, *Corporate Lobbies,* p. 118.

161. "The Big Guns Aim at Labor Law Reform," *Business Week,* February 13, 1978, p. 31.

162. Levitan and Cooper, *Business Lobbies,* pp. 130–31.

163. "A Filibuster Ahead," *Time,* May 29, 1978, p. 20.

164. "Battle Heats up over a New Labor Law," *U.S. News & World Report,* June 5, 1978, p. 90; "Labor Law Reform May Drown," *Business Week,* June 5, 1978, p. 49; "The Unions Needed One More Vote," *Time,* July 3, 1978, p. 17.

165. For a full account of the Senate treatment of the bill, see Levitan and Cooper, *Business Lobbies,* pp. 128–36; Green and Buchsbaum, *Corporate Lobbies,* pp. 118–27; and "Labor Law Reform: The Regulation of Free Speech and Equal Access," pp. 792–97.

166. "Statement of Frank W. McCulloch to the Special Subcommittee on Education and Labor, House of Representatives," November 18, 1975, p. 28, "Delegation—Reform BB," Box 5, McCulloch Papers, LMDC.

167. A. H. Raskin, "It Isn't Labor's Day," *The Nation,* September 9, 1978, p. 197. See also "Embattled Unions Strike Back at Management," *Business Week,* December 4, 1978, pp. 56–57. "To keep nonunion workers relatively satisfied, companies are using a variety of techniques, including periodic surveys of employee attitudes, training programs to upgrade skills, complaint-airing sessions, worker 'participation' in decision-making and formal systems of step-by-step hearings modeled on union grievance procedures." "Embattled Unions," p. 56. "Taking Aim at 'Union-Busters,'" *Business Week,* November 12, 1979, p. 98; "The Union-Busters," *Newsweek,* January 28, 1980, p. 68. As one management attorney put it, "a company would rather pay the lawyers $100,000 a year because management is saving four or five times that in salary hikes." "Union-Busters," p. 68.

168. "Embattled Unions," p. 56.

169. A. H. Raskin, "Management's Hard Line: 'Class War' or Labor's Chance to Reform?" *Monthly Labor Review,* February 1979, p. 36.

Chapter 13

1. Robert P. Hunter, "The Department of Labor," in *Mandate for Leadership: Policy Management in a Conservative Administration,* ed. Charles L. Heatherly (Washington, D.C.: Heritage Foundation, 1981), p. 493. (Hereinafter Hunter, *Mandate for Leadership.*)

2. Nomination notebooks, April 6–July 19, 1977, pp. 4–5, 55, Douglas Soutar Papers, Labor-Management Documentation Center (LMDC), ILR, Cornell University.

3. Ibid., p. 63.

4. Ibid., pp. 14–15.

5. Truesdale came to the NLRB after receiving a master's degree from Cornell University. After leaving the agency for six years, he returned as associate executive secretary from 1963 to 1968 before becoming executive secretary in 1972, the same year he received a J.D. from the Georgetown University Law Center.

6. Nomination notebooks, April 6–July 19, 1977, pp. 4–5.

7. Terry Moe, "Interests, Institutions, and Positive Theory: The Politics of the NLRB," in *Studies in American Political Development* (New Haven: Yale University Press, 1987), 2:250.

8. Ibid., pp. 263–64.

9. "NLRB General Counsel Irving to Resign One Month before Expiration of Term," *Daily Labor Report,* no. 133, July 10, 1979, p. A-3.

10. "Lubbers Succeeds Truesdale as NLRB Executive Secretary," *Daily Labor Report,* no. 94, May 15, 1978, p. A-1.

11. Nomination notebooks, July 27, 1979–March 24, 1980, p. 4, Soutar Papers.

12. Ibid., pp. 1 (quotation), 22–23.

13. Ibid., pp. 4–5, 16, 57.

14. Mailgram from the Industrial Relations Representatives of the Members of the Business Roundtable to Soutar, December 5, 1979,"Appointments—Assorted," Box 13, Soutar Papers.

15. Memorandum, October 10, 1979, p. 1, "Appointments—Assorted," Box 13, Soutar Papers.

16. Memorandum, October 17, 1979, Nomination notebooks, July 27, 1979–March 24, 1980.

17. Second memorandum, October 17, 1979, nomination notebooks, July 27, 1979–March 24, 1980.

18. "Murphy Resigns from NLRB Rather than Accept White House Offer of Interim Term," *Daily Labor Report,* no. 238, December 10, 1979, pp. A-13–A-14; "Betty Southard Murphy Resigns from NLRB," press release (R-1598), December 10, 1979, NLRB Files, Washington, D.C.; "Betty Southard Murphy to Enter Private Practice in Washington," Division of Information, NLRB Bulletin, December 31, 1979, NLRB Files.

19. "Statements before Senate Labor and Human Resources Committee on Nomination of William Lubbers as NLRB General Counsel," *Daily Labor Report,* no. 242, December 14, 1979, p. F-3.

20. Senate Committee on Labor and Human Resources, *Hearings on William A. Lubbers of Maryland to be General Counsel of the NLRB,* 96th Cong., 1st sess., 1980, pp. 27–29, 61, 65–68.

21. Moe, "Interests, Institutions, and Positive Theory," p. 264.

22. "Carter Administration Announces 'Recess Appointment' of Lubbers as General Counsel," *Daily Labor Report,* no. 249, December 27, 1979, p. A-13; "Lubbers Takes Oath of Office Pending Confirmation by Senate," *Daily Labor Report,* no. 1, January 2, 1980, p. A-12.

23. Philip Shabecoff, "Conservatives Filibuster to Prevent Carter Nomination to Labor Board," *New York Times,* April 17, 1980; "Lubbers Confirmed as NLRB General Counsel by 57–39 Vote after Filibuster Is Ended," *Daily Labor Report,* no. 80, April 23, 1980, pp. A-8–A-10.

24. Stanley Strauss and Peter Nash to Soutar, March 25, 1980, "Appointments—Assorted," Box 13, Soutar Papers.

25. "Don Zimmerman Is Front Runner for NLRB Member," *Employment Relations Report,* January 16, 1980, "Appointments—Assorted," Box 13, Soutar Papers.

26. Nomination notebooks, July 27, 1979–March 24, 1980, p. 128.

27. "Debate Begins on Nomination of Zimmerman to NLRB," *Daily Labor Report,* no. 147, July 29, 1980, p. A-7; "Senate Confirms Don A. Zimmerman for NLRB after Approving Motion to Cut off Debate," *Daily Labor Report,* no. 152, August 5, 1980, pp. A-9–A-11.

28. "Senate Confirms Zimmerman," p. A-10.

29. Moe, "Interests, Institutions, and Positive Theory," p. 265.

30. Soutar's handwritten notes of conversations with various management representatives, August 15 and 19, 1980, "Appointments—Assorted," Box 13, Soutar Papers.

31. Senate Committee on Labor and Human Resources, *Hearings on John C. Truesdale of Maryland to Be a Member of the NLRB,* 96th Cong., 2d sess., 1980, pp. 3, 43, 88.

32. "President Makes Recess Appointment to Return John Truesdale to NLRB," *Daily Labor Report,* no. 207, October 23, 1980, pp. A-8–A-9.

33. "Truesdale Resigns as NLRB Member, but Returns to Post of Executive Secretary," *Daily Labor Report,* no. 17, January 27, 1981, p. A-7.

34. "Resignation of NLRB Member John Penello," *Labor Relations Reporter* 106 (January 19, 1981): 41.

35. Minutes of the Business Roundtable Labor-Management Committee meeting, November 18, 1980, p. 1, "LMC—More Recent General," Box 8, Soutar Papers; "Dark Days ahead for Labor in Washington," *U.S. News & World Report,* November 17, 1980, p. 106.

36. R. T. McNamar, Office of the President-Elect, to Peter Pestillo, vice-president for labor relations, Ford Motor Co., December 11, 1980, with attached analysis of NLRB "Mission" and "Major Policy Issues and Recommended Positions," Box 10, "Schub 772," Soutar Papers.

37. Nomination notebooks, November 6, 1980–May 19, 1981, p. 7, Soutar Papers.

38. Soutar's handwritten notes of telephone conversations, April 27, 1981, "Appointments—Assorted," Box 13, Soutar Papers.

39. Nomination Notebooks, November 6, 1980–May 19, 1981, p. 152; Bernard Weinraub, "Reagan's Brain Trust: Font of Varied Ideas," *New York Times,* December 1, 1980, p. A-1.

40. Moe, "Interests, Institutions, and Positive Theory," pp. 266–67.

41. "A Peril to NLRB Peacemaking," *Business Week,* October 12, 1981, p. 102.

42. "New Candidate Emerges for NLRB Chairman; Business Groups Meet to Coordinate Strategy," *Daily Labor Report,* no. 67, April 8, 1981, p. A-6–A-8. Hunter received a degree in business administration from the University of Connecticut in 1962, a law degree from Vanderbilt University in 1965, and a master's degree in labor law from New York University in 1966.

43. "Political Analysis," memorandum from Richard F. Kibben, of the Business Roundtable, to Soutar, April 13, 1981, loose papers, Soutar Papers.

44. Levitan and Cooper, *Business Lobbies,* p. 49.

45. Hunter, *Mandate for Leadership,* p. 469. Hunter also recommended elimination of the "judicial anti-trust exemption for union anticompetitive monopoly power"; the "judicially-created exemption from punitive damages against union officials," the prohibition of strikes, and compulsory arbitration in the public sector. Ibid., pp. 469–70.

46. Ibid., p. 493; "The Hatch Strategy for Reining in Labor," *Business Week,* December 1, 1980, p. 46.

47. Senate Committee on Labor and Human Resources, *Hearings on the Nomination of Robert P. Hunter of Virginia to Be a Member of the NLRB*, 97th Cong., 1st sess., 1981, p. 4. (Hereinafter *Hunter Nomination Hearings.*)

48. Hunter, *Mandate for Leadership*, pp. 493–97 (quotations, pp. 493–94).

49. *Hunter Nomination Hearings*, pp. 6–7, 9. The NLRB press release announcing Hunter's departure from the Board in 1985 lists his chapter in *Mandate for Leadership* among his authored publications. "NLRB Member Hunter to Enter Private Practice of Law," press release (R-1746), July 18, 1985, NLRB Files.

50. *Hunter Nomination Hearings*, pp. 9–10.

51. "NLRB Member Hunter Is Confirmed by Senate; Committee Hearing on Van de Water Postponed," *Daily Labor Report*, no. 179, September 16, 1981, pp. A-2–A-3.

52. "White House Names Management Consultant from California as Next Chairman of NLRB," *Daily Labor Report*, no. 117, June 18, 1981, pp. A-7–A-9.

53. "Recess Appointments to NLRB," *Labor Relations Reporter*, 107 (August 24, 1981): 319.

54. "Reagan NLRB Tips toward Management," *Business Week*, July 6, 1981, p. 27.

55. Senate Committee on Labor and Human Resources, *Hearings on the Nomination of John R. Van de Water of California to Be Chairman of the NLRB*, 97th Cong., 1st sess., 1981, p. 38. (Hereinafter *Van de Water Nomination Hearings.*)

56. Ibid., p. 56. The full text appears on pp. 55–62. Donahue's comments appear on pp. 65, 79, 81, 87.)

57. Ibid., p. 64.

58. Van de Water to Hatch, October 8, 1981, *Van de Water Nomination Hearings*, p. 139.

59. "Committee Refuses to Confirm Van de Water, Blocks Bid to Send Nomination to Senate Floor," *Daily Labor Report*, no. 223, November 19, 1981, pp. AA-1–AA-2; Senate Action on NLRB Chairman," *Labor Relations Reporter*, 108 (November 30, 1981): 249.

60. "AFL-CIO Renews Opposition to Van de Water's NLRB Appointment," *Daily Labor Report*, no. 31, February 16, 1982, p. A-12.

61. "Right to Work Issue Threatens to Hurt Van de Water Nomination," *Daily Labor Report*, no. 38, February 25, 1982, p. A-7; "Right to Work Committee Asks President to Withdraw Van de Water Nomination to NLRB," *Daily Labor Report*, no. 170, September 1, 1982, pp. A-3–A-5; "National Right to Work Committee Calls on President to Block Van de Water Nomination to NLRB," *Right to Work News*, August 26, 1982, "Appointments—Assorted," Box 13, Soutar Papers.

62. "Van de Water Leaves NLRB Chairmanship; Board Reduced to Only Three Members," *Daily Labor Report*, no. 243, December 17, 1982, p. A-14; Moe, "Interests, Institutions, and Positive Theory," p. 266.

63. "Van de Water Leaves," p. A-14.

64. "John C. Miller Sworn in as NLRB Chairman on Recess Appointment," press release (R-1679), December 27, 1982, NLRB Files. Miller, a Republican, had

served as the NLRB's acting general counsel for three months in 1975, the agency's solicitor, an administrative law judge, and chief counsel to Chairman Van de Water. Miller also served as Republican counsel for the House Labor Committee. He is the only person to have been both NLRB chairman and acting general counsel.

65. Office of White House Press Secretary, press release, November 22, 1982, "NLRB 2," Box 11, Soutar Papers. Dennis graduated from the University of California at Los Angeles in 1970 and the Loyola University of Los Angeles School of Law in 1973.

66. Moe, "Interests, Institutions, and Positive Theory," p. 268.

67. "Reagan Administration Names Dotson to Be Assistant Secretary of Labor," *Daily Labor Report,* no. 74, April 17, 1981, p. A-4; "Donald L. Dotson Assumes Duties as NLRB Chairman," press release (R-1683), March 9, 1983, NLRB Files; "Dotson Confirmed by Senate to Head Labor-Management Services Administration," *Daily Labor Report,* no. 134, July 14, 1981, p. A-2.

68. "White House Plans Quick Action to Fill Two Vacancies at NLRB," *Daily Labor Report,* no. 222, November 17, 1982, p. A-9.

69. Soutar's handwritten notes of conversations concerning Dotson, October 22, 1982, "White House 12-82," Box 11, Soutar Papers.

70. Moe, "Interests, Institutions, and Positive Theory," p. 268 (quotations); nomination notebooks, October 14, 1982–March 14, 1984, pp. 1–4, Soutar Papers.

71. "AFL-CIO Challenges Qualifications of Reagan Administration's NLRB Choice," *Daily Labor Report,* no. 227, November 24, 1982, p. A-11; "AFL-CIO Opposition to Dotson Fizzles; Senator Hatch Seeks Early Confirmation," *Daily Labor Report,* no. 22, February 1, 1983, p. A-6.

72. "Dotson Nomination to NLRB Gains Approval of Senate Labor Committee," *Daily Labor Report,* no. 33, February 16, 1983, p. A-8; "Senate Confirms Nomination of Donald Dotson to Head NLRB," *Daily Labor Report,* no. 34, February 17, 1983, p. A-5; "Labor Ends Bid to Block Dotson as NLRB Chief," *Wall Street Journal,* February 2, 1983, p. 3.

73. "Hugh L. Reilly Appointed NLRB Solicitor," press release (R-1685), April 24, 1983, NLRB Files; "Former Right-to-Work Foundation Attorney Named Legal Advisor to Five-Member NLRB," *Daily Labor Report,* no. 79, April 22, 1983, pp. A-3–A-4.

74. House Subcommittee on Labor-Management Relations of the Committee on Education and Labor, and House Manpower and Housing Subcommittee of the Committee on Government Operations, *Joint Hearings: Oversight on the NLRB,* 98th Cong., 1st sess., 1984, p. 80. (Hereinafter *Dotson-Reilly Hearings.*)

75. Patrick Owens, "Unionbuster at the NLRB," *The Nation,* July 23–30, 1983, p. 71.

76. For a memorandum from Berton Subrin, acting solicitor, to Dotson, "Taking Back Enforcement," April 21, 1983, see Transcript of Board meeting, May 4, 1983, *Dotson-Reilly Hearings,* pp. 382–99.

77. *Dotson-Reilly Hearings,* p. 391.

78. Ibid., pp. 10, 388.

79. Ibid., pp. 2, 54, 61.

80. Ibid., pp. 58–61.

81. Ibid, pp. 8–10, 13, 39.

82. Ibid., p. 52.

83. Ibid., pp. 45–47.

84. Ibid., p. 47.

85. Ibid., p. 43.

86. "Remarks by NLRB Chairman Donald Dotson before Maryland Chapter of Industrial Relations Research Association," *Daily Labor Report,* no. 189, September 28, 1983, pp. D-1–D-2.

87. Senate Committee on Labor and Human Resources, *Hearings on Nomination of Patricia Diaz Dennis of California to Be a Member, NLRB,* 98th Cong., 1st sess., 1983, pp. 29–36; "Hatch and Kennedy Agree to Poll Committee on Nomination of Patricia Dennis to NLRB," *Daily Labor Report,* no. 72, April 13, 1983, pp. A-9–A-10; "Dennis Discusses NLRB Backlog, Pending Issues," *Daily Labor Report,* no. 212, November 1, 1983, pp. A-11–A-12.

88. Bill Keller, "Infighting at Labor Board Is Reported," *New York Times,* July 11, 1984, p. A21; Pete Early, "'Infighting' Cited among NLRB Staff," *Washington Post,* July 12, 1984.

89. House Subcommittee on Labor-Management Relations of the Committee on Education and Labor, *The Failure of Labor Law—A Betrayal of American Workers,* 98th Cong., 2d sess., 1984, H. Rept. 98, pp. 11–14 (hereinafter *House Report on the Failure of Labor Law*); Steven Greenhouse, "Recent Rulings and Long Delays Anger Unions. But NLRB Says It's Neutral," *New York Times,* February 5, 1984.

90. Robert Douglas Brownstone, "The National Labor Relations Board at 50: Politicization Creates Crisis," *Brooklyn Law Review* 52 (Winter 1986): 229 n.2, 271 n. 203. See also pp. 264–65 nn. 163–64, 168–71. For Dotson's explanations, see p. 268 nn. 181–86.

91. "Howard Jenkins, Jr., Informs President Reagan He Does Not Desire a Fifth Term as NLRB Member," press release (R-1690), August 9, 1983, NLRB Files; "White House Narrows Search for Replacement for Republican NLRB Member Howard Jenkins," *Daily Labor Report,* no. 145, July 27, 1983, p. A-5.

92. See, for example, Barry Bluestone and Bennett Harrison, *The De-Industrialization of America* (New York: Basic Books, 1982); Jules Bernstein, "Union-Busting: From Benign Neglect to Malignant Growth," *University of California, Davis Law Review* 14 (Fall 1980): 77.

93. Peter Walther, "The NLRB Today," *Labor Law Journal* 36 (November 1985): 808.

94. Douglas E. Ray, "The 1986–1987 Labor Board: Has the Pendulum Slowed?" *Boston College Law Review* 29 (December 1987): 1–3; Paul Alan Levy, "The Unidimensional Perspective of the Reagan Labor Board," *Rutgers Law Journal* 16 (Winter 1985): 269, 270–71, 275–79, 276 n. 44, 337–38; Patricia Diaz Dennis, "Principles That Guide My Decisionmaking," *Stetson Law Review* 15 (Fall 1985): 5.

95. "Remarks on Changes at NLRB before Annual Institute on Labor Law," *Daily Labor Report,* no. 202, October 18, 1983, pp. F-1–F-3.

96. John Fanning's comments, transcript of the NLRB 50th Anniversary Conference, October 22–23, 1984, pp. 79–81, LMDC.

97. "Remarks on Changes at NLRB, pp. F-3–F-6.

98. "NLRB Member Dennis Defends Decisions as Swing Back to Normalcy at Board," *Daily Labor Report,* no. 82, April 27, 1984, p. A-7.

99. "NLRB Rulings That Are Inflaming Labor Relations," *Business Week,* June 11, 1984, p. 123.

100. Walther, "NLRB Today," p. 803.

101. Lee Modjeska, "The Reagan NLRB, Phase I," *Ohio State Law Journal* 46 (1985): 130.

102. 263 NLRB 127 (1982).

103. 228 NLRB 1311 (1977).

104. Diaz Dennis, "Principles," p. 10.

105. *NLRB v. Federbush,* 121 F.2d 954, 957 (2d Cir. 1941).

106. *NLRB v. Golub Corp.,* 388 F.2d 921, 929 (2d Cir. 1967).

107. 269 NLRB 1176 (1984).

108. 109 NLRB 591 (1954).

109. *PPG Industries, Inc.,* 251 NLRB 1146 (1980).

110. See, for example, Sorrell Logothetis, "An Analysis of Significant Recent Decisions of the National Labor Relations Board: An Organized Labor Perspective," *Capitol University Law Review* 14 (Spring 1985): 332–33.

111. Bruce Feldacker, *Labor Guide to Labor Law,* 3d ed. (Englewood Cliffs, N.J.: Prentice Hall, 1990), p. 83. See p. 100 n. 13 for case citations.

112. Francis T. Coleman, "The New 'New' Reagan National Labor Relations Board and the Outlook for the Future," *Federal Bar News & Journal* 34 (July–August 1987): 257; Thomas F. Phalen, Jr., "The Destabilization of Federal Labor Policy under the Reagan Board," *Labor Lawyer* 2 (Winter 1986): 8–9; *Riley-Beaird, Inc.,* 271 NLRB 155 (1984).

113. Logothetis, "Analysis of Significant Recent Decisions," p. 334; *Yeargin Construction Co.,* 271 NLRB 725 (1984).

114. *Premier Rubber Co.,* 272 NLRB 466 (1984).

115. Levy, "Unidimensional Perspective," p. 305 n. 191; *National Micronetics,* 277 NLRB 993 (1985).

116. Logothetis, "Analysis of Significant Recent Decisions," p. 334. For another controversial ruling concerning solicitation and distribution on an employer's premises, see *Our Way, Inc.,* 268 NLRB 394 (1983).

117. 270 NLRB 578 (1984).

118. 261 NLRB 1189, 1194 (1982).

119. Archibald Cox, Derek Curtis Bok, and Robert A. Gorman, *Cases and Materials on Labor Law,* 10th ed. (Mineola, N.Y.: Foundation Press, 1986), p. 345.

120. 379 U.S. 203 (1964).

121. 268 NLRB 601 (1984); 269 NLRB 891 (1984); 452 U.S. 666 (1981).
122. Employers were still obliged to bargain about the effects of their decisions.
123. 452 U.S. at 676–79.
124. Ibid., pp. 678–79.
125. Ibid., p. 686. For the majority's application of the test, see pp. 680–86.
126. Ibid., pp. 689–90.
127. Ibid., pp. 685 n. 22, 687.
128. "NLRB to Rule on Legality of Moving Work to Non-Union Plants to Cut Costs," press release (R-1693), September 16, 1983, NLRB Files.
129. *Milwaukee Spring Division of Illinois Coil Spring Co.,* 265 NLRB 206 (1982).
130. *Milwaukee Spring Division of Illinois Coil Spring Co.,* 268 NLRB 601 (1984).
131. Ibid., p. 610.
132. "Dennis Defends Decisions," p. A-8.
133. 269 NLRB 891 (1984).
134. *Otis Elevator Co.,* 225 NLRB 235 (1981).
135. *Otis Elevator Co.,* 269 NLRB 891 (1984).
136. Ibid., p. 892.
137. Ibid., p. 893 n. 5.
138. Ibid., p. 897.
139. Ibid., p. 901.
140. *Ausable Communications, Inc.,* 273 NLRB 1410 (1985); *Garwood-Detroit Truck Equipment,* 274 NLRB 113 (1985).
141. Laurence J. Cohen and Victoria L. Bor, "The National Labor Relations Act under Seige: A Labor View of the Reagan Board," in *Labor Law Developments 1985, Thirty-first Annual Institute, Southwestern Legal Foundation* (New York: Matthew Bender, 1985), pp. 4-11–4-12. See *Benchmark Industries,* 270 NLRB 22 (1984).
142. Logothetis, "Analysis of Significant Recent Decisions," p. 359.
143. 268 NLRB 1044 (1984).
144. For cases, see Modjeska, "Reagan NLRB," pp. 124–26.
145. 268 NLRB at 1047.
146. Terry A. Bethel, "Recent Decisions of the NLRB—The Reagan Influence," *Indiana Law Journal* 60 (Spring 1985): 283.
147. Modjeska, "Reagan NLRB," p. 125.
148. Bethel, "Recent Decisions," p. 282.
149. *Clear Pine Mouldings,* 268 NLRB at 1047. Zimmerman and Diaz Dennis did not comment on this point.
150. See, for example, *United Scenic Artists, Local 829,* 267 NLRB 858 (1983); Levy, "Unidimensional Perspective," pp. 365–69.
151. *Local Lodge 1414 (Neufeld Porsche-Audi),* 270 NLRB 1330 (1984), overruling *Machinists Local 1327 (Dalmo-Victor),* 263 NLRB 984 (1982).
152. *Butterworth-Manning-Ashmore Mortuary,* 270 NLRB 1014 (1984).
153. *Indianapolis Power and Light,* 273 NLRB 1715 (1985).
154. 280 NLRB 1597, 1599 (1986).

155. Walter Oberer, "Lockouts and the Law: The Impact of *American Shipbuilding* and *Brown Food," Cornell Law Quarterly* 51 (Winter 1966): 198.

156. Edward B. Miller, "The National Labor Relations Act—Which Way Is the Pendulum Swinging Now?" in *Labor Law Developments 1987, Thirty-third Annual Institute, Southwestern Legal Foundation* (New York: Matthew Bender, 1987), p. 2-14.

157. Rosemary Collyer, "Recent NLRB and Court of Appeals Decisions and Developments in the Office of the General Counsel," in *Labor Law Developments 1990, Thirty-sixth Annual Institute, Southwestern Legal Foundation* (New York: Matthew Bender, 1990), p. 2-9.

158. 268 NLRB 493 (1984).

159. *Interboro Contractors,* 157 NLRB 1295 (1966).

160. *Allelulia Cushion,* 221 NLRB 999 (1975).

161. Ibid.

162. 268 NLRB at 497.

163. *Materials Research,* 262 NLRB 1010 (1982).

164. 274 NLRB 230 (1985).

165. *Taracorp. Industries,* 273 NLRB 221 (1984), reversing *Kraft Foods,* 251 NLRB 598 (1980).

166. Levy, "Unidimensional Perspective," p. 285.

167. 268 NLRB 557 (1984).

168. 228 NLRB 808 (1977).

169. "NLRB Revised Policy of Deferring to Arbitration," press release (R-1713), January 24, 1984, p. 2, NLRB Files.

170. *Spielberg Mfg. Co.,* 112 NLRB 1080 (1955); *Raytheon Co.,* 140 NLRB 883 (1963).

171. 268 NLRB 573, 576–77 (1984).

172. Ibid. p. 574.

173. See Levy, "Unidimensional Perspective," p. 375 n. 544 for case citations.

174. "President Reagan Names James M. Stephens Chairman, NLRB," press release (R-1805), January 7, 1988, NLRB Files; "White House Names Member Stephens to Succeed Dotson as Board Chairman," *Daily Labor Report,* no. 5, January 8, 1988, p. A-8.

175. See, for example, Charles J. Morris, "Renaissance at the NLRB—Opportunity and Prospect for Non-Legislative Procedural Reform at the Labor Board," *Stetson Law Review* 23 (Fall 1993): 104.

176. In the twelve years of Reagan-Bush administrations there were fifteen Board members: John Truesdale (1977–81); Donald Zimmerman (1980–84); Robert Hunter (1981–85); John Van de Water (August 1981–December 1982); John Miller (December 1982–March 1983); Donald Dotson (1983–87); Patricia Diaz Dennis (1983–86); Wilford W. Johansen, NLRB career lawyer and regional director in Los Angeles (1985–89); Marshall Babson, management attorney specializing in labor and employment law (1985–88); James Stephens (1985–); Mary Cracroft, former NLRB attorney in private practice when appointed to the Board (1986–91); John

Higgins, NLRB career lawyer and deputy general counsel (1988–89); Dennis De-
vaney, general counsel for the Federal Labor Relations Authority (1988–94); Clifford Oviatt, attorney in private practice specializing in labor and employment law
(1990–93); and John Raudabaugh, attorney in private practice specializing in labor
and employment law (1990–93). Years of service are based on data provided by
NLRB executive secretary John Truesdale on March 4, 1993.

177. The Board (as of March 1994) was composed of Chairman Stephens, Dennis De-
vaney, and John Truesdale. On January 26, 1994, Clinton named NLRB executive
secretary and former Board member John Truesdale to a recess appointment on the
Board. The Board had been down to two members since November 1993; the
interim appointment allowed the Board to have a quorum. Other Clinton nominations languished in the Senate. "Recess NLRB Appointment Brings a Quorum to
Board," *Daily Labor Report,* no. 16, January 26, 1994, p. A-1.

In June 1993 Clinton nominated William B. Gould IV, Stanford Law School
professor since 1972, as chairman. The senate did not confirm Gould until March 2,
1994, and he was sworn into office on March 7. Gould was a 1961 graduate of the
Cornell Law School and a 1958 graduate of the University of Rhode Island. Before
joining the Stanford faculty, he was assistant general counsel of the United Automobile Workers and an NLRB attorney in Washington, D.C. Gould was also a
prolific author of books and law journal articles.

Although Clinton nominated Margaret Anne Browning on August 17, 1993, to
become a member of the NLRB, the Senate did not confirm her appointment until
March 2, 1994. Browning, a union attorney, was a founding partner in the Philadelphia labor law firm now known as Spear, Wilderman, Borish, Endy, Spear &
Runckel. She received her law degree in 1978 from the University of Pennsylvania
after graduating from Swarthmore College in 1972. Browning also served as an
adjunct professor of labor law at the Rutgers School of Law in Camden, New
Jersey.

In order to break the logjam on the Gould and Browning appointments, in February 1994, Clinton nominated management attorney Charles I. Cohen, a partner in
the Washington, D.C., law firm of Ogletree, Deakins, Nash, Smoak & Stewart.
Cohen, who was also confirmed on March 2, 1994, had spent more than ten years
(1979 to 1990) with another prominent management law firm in Washington, D.C.,
Vedder, Price, Kaufman, Kammholz & Day. From 1971 to July 1979 he was a
deputy regional attorney, supervisory attorney, and senior attorney in the NLRB's
Philadelphia regional office and attorney with the general counsel's office in Washington. He was an adjunct professor at Catholic University's Columbus School of
Law from 1982 to 1985. Cohen graduated from Tulane University in 1967 and
from the University of Pittsburgh Law School in 1970.

Clinton also appointed Fred Feinstein general counsel. He was confirmed by the
Senate on March 2, 1994. From 1977 to 1994 Feinstein was employed by the
House Education and Labor Subcommittee on Labor-Management Relations. He
was chief counsel to the subcommittee from 1990 to 1994, after serving as its staff

director and counsel from 1980 to 1990. From 1975 to 1977 Feinstein was a field attorney with the NLRB's Eleventh Region, comprising North and South Carolina. He was an elementary school teacher in East Harlem from 1969 to 1971 and an adjunct professor at the Georgetown University Law School from 1990 to 1992. Feinstein graduated from the Rutgers University Law School (at Newark, New Jersey) in 1974 after graduating from Swarthmore College in 1969.

178. 288 NLRB 97 (1988).
179. *Midland National Life Insurance Co.*, 263 NLRB 127 (1982).
180. *Meyers Industries*, 268 NLRB 493 (1984); 281 NLRB 882 (1986), *enforced, Prill v. NLRB*, 835 F.2d 1481 (D.C. Cir. 1987).
181. 287 NLRB 1356 (1988).
182. 289 NLRB 627 (1988).
183. 291 NLRB 11, 14 (1988).
184. *Fairmont Hotel Co.*, 282 NLRB 139, 141 (1986).
185. For an interesting discussion of this case and its implications, as well as a review of other Stephens Board decisions favorable to union access to employer private property, see Catherine Waelder, "Union Access to Private Property: *Jean Country*," in *Proceedings of the Forty-fourth Annual New York University Conference on Labor* (New York: Matthew Bender, 1991), pp. 101–27.
186. 112 S.Ct. 841 (1992).
187. Ibid., p. 850.
188. 76 S.Ct. 679 (1954).
189. 112 S.Ct. at 849.
190. Robert Rabin, "Labor and Employment Law Decisions of the United States Supreme Court, 1990 Term," in *Labor Law Developments 1992, Thirty-eighth Annual Institute, Southwestern Legal Foundation* (New York: Matthew Bender, 1992, pp. 1-2–1-3.
191. 452 U.S. 666 (1981).
192. *Otis Elevator Co.*, 269 NLRB 891 (1984).
193. Collyer, "Recent NLRB and Court of Appeals Decisions," p. 2-1.
194. 287 NLRB 499 (1987). For a discussion of these decisions as well as an excellent analysis of the *Dubuque Packing Co.* issues, see Eugene Cotton, "The Duty to Bargain over Decisions to Relocate or Subcontract Work: The *Dubuque Packing* Case," in *Proceedings of the Forty-fourth Annual New York University Conference on Labor* (Boston: Little, Brown, 1991), pp. 23–81.
195. *Dubuque Packing Co.*, 880 F.2d 1422, 1435–36 (D.C. Cir. 1989).
196. *Dubuque Packing Co.*, 303 NLRB 386 (1991).
197. Ibid, p. 391.
198. *Fibreboard Paper Products Corp. v. NLRB*, 379 U.S. 203, 210–11 (1964).
199. Cohen and Bor, "National Labor Relations Act under Siege," p. 4-41. See n. 164 for case citations.
200. Logothetis, "Analysis of Significant Recent Decisions," p. 327.
201. "Dotson's Exit: A Lot More than Politics," *Business Week,* November 9, 1987, p. 114.

202. Ibid.
203. House Committee on Education and Labor, *The Failure of Labor Law—A Betrayal of American Workers,* 98th Cong., 2d sess., 1984, pp. 1, 24.
204. Ibid., p. 28.
205. Clifford Oviatt, Jr., "The Bush NLRB in Perspective: Does the Playing Field Need Leveling?" *Hofstra Law Journal* 11 (Fall 1993): 93.

Chapter 14

1. Roy J. Adams, "The Right to Participate," *Employee Responsibilities and Rights Journal* 5 (1992): 97.
2. Oral History interview with Edward Miller, September 8, 1989, pp. 13, 38, Labor-Management Documentation Center (LMDC), ILR, Cornell University.
3. "NLRB May Chart New Course during Clinton Administration," *Daily Labor Report,* no. 84, May 4, 1993, p. D-27. The first Democrat-appointed members of the NLRB arrived in the spring of 1994. President Clinton named as chairman William Gould, Stanford University Law School professor, and, as members, Margaret Browning, a founding partner of the Philadelphia law firm of Spear, Wilderman, Borish, Endy, Spear & Runckel, and Charles I. Cohen, a former NLRB attorney who was with the Washington law firm of Ogletree, Deakins, Nash, Smoak & Stewart at the time of his appointment. Clinton also appointed Fred Feinstein general counsel. Feinstein had been counsel to the Subcommittee on Labor-Management Relations of the House Education and Labor Committee.
4. 452 U.S. 666 (1981).
5. Catherine S. Manegold, "Senate Republicans Deal a Major Defeat to Labor," *New York Times,* July 13, 1994, p. D18.
6. "Dotson's Exit: A Lot More than Politics," *Business Week,* November 9, 1987, p. 114.
7. See, for example, Julius Getman and F. Ray Marshall, "Industrial Relations in Transition: The Paper Industry Example," *Yale Law Journal* 102 (June 1993): 1812.
8. Thomas Geoghegan, *Which Side Are You On? Trying to Be for Labor When It's Flat on Its Back* (New York: Farrar, Straus, and Giroux, 1991), p. 246.
9. Theodore St. Antoine, "National Labor Policy: Reflections and Distortions of Social Justice," *Catholic University Law Review* 29 (Spring 1980): 556.
10. "Recommendations of Professor Charles J. Morris to the Commission on the Future of Worker-Management Relations," *Daily Labor Report,* no. 6, January 10, 1994, p. E-6.
11. "Reich to Establish Commission to Examine Nation's Labor Laws," *Daily Labor Report,* no. 30, February 17, 1993, p. AA-1. Despite persistent claims that the Bush Board's decision in *Electromation, Inc.,* 309 NLRB 990 (1992), would stifle worker-participation plans and prevent labor-management cooperation, Charles Morris was correct when he wrote that "*Electromation* was a garden-variety Section 8(a)(2) case; it was not about worker-participation or labor-management coop-

eration. It is pure myth to view it as such." "Labor Law Scholar Sees Unionization as Key to Greater Workplace Cooperation," *Daily Labor Report,* no. 6, January 10, 1994, p. E-4.

Both *Electromation* and a subsequent Board decision, *E. I. du Pont de Nemours & Co.,* 311 NLRB 893 (1983), involved employers who committed clear violations of Section 8(a)(2) of the act, which prohibits employer interference with or domination of a labor organization. Morris also cites former NLRB chairman Miller's comment that employee-involvement programs are possible in both union and non-union companies "without the necessity of any change in current law." Ibid.

12. Getman and Marshall, "Industrial Relations in Transition," pp. 1813–14, 1878–79; Theodore St. Antoine, "The Legal and Economic Implications of Union-Management Cooperation: The Case of GM and the UAW," in *Proceedings of the Forty-first Annual New York University Conference on Labor* (New York: Matthew Bender, 1988), pp. 8-1–8-23.

13. Getman and Marshall, "Industrial Relations in Transition," p. 1885.

14. Department of Labor and Department of Commerce, Commission on the Future of Worker-Management Relations, *Report and Recommendations,* December 1994, Washington, D.C.

15. Some recommend that worker participation through organization and collective bargaining be universal and not left to employee choice. See, for example, Adams, "Right to Participate," pp. 95–96.

16. See, for example, Paul Weiler, "Promises to Keep: Securing Workers' Rights to Self-Organize under the NLRA," *Harvard Law Review* 96 (June 1983): 1769.

Index